THE UKRAINE

A History

THE UKRAINE

A History

by

W. E. D. ALLEN

Author of
A History of the Georgian People

NEW YORK

RUSSELL & RUSSELL · INC

1963

FIRST PUBLISHED, 1940

REISSUED, 1963, BY RUSSELL & RUSSELL, INC.

BY ARRANGEMENT WITH CAMBRIDGE UNIVERSITY PRESS

L. C. CATALOG CARD NO: 63-8355

947. 71
AL 5 u
69067
march, 1970

PRINTED IN THE UNITED STATES OF AMERICA

To N. M.

Half Ukrainian
Half Angel

Strength and honour are her clothing;
She laugheth at the time to come;
She openeth her mouth with wisdom,
And the law of kindness is on her tongue.
Give her of the fruit of her hands,
And let her own works praise her.

PROVERBS, 31

PREFACE

UNDERTAKEN in more leisured days, this book was unfinished on the outbreak of war.

Three or four scholars, Russian and Ukrainian, have collaborated in the preparation of the material—and in the completion of the maps and index which service abroad compelled me to leave undone. In the circumstances of today these friends wish to remain anonymous. I can only say that it would not have been possible to cover the researches involved without their constant and generous help.

I am deeply indebted to Professor Ellis H. Minns for his kindly and painstaking interest in the revision of the proofs and in the proper transliteration of Ukrainian, Russian and Polish names.

It is a difficult moment at which to produce a book which is intended as a serious contribution to an English understanding of the history of Eastern Europe and which it is hoped may help to clarify the details of the difficult Ukrainian problem. But for the encouragement and friendship of Professor Minns and the enterprising policy of the Syndics of the Press the book could not have appeared in print.

W. E. D. ALLEN

1940

CONTENTS

MAPS

THE UKRAINIAN LANGUAGE

The Russian or Eastern branch of Slavonic falls into three divisions, Great Russian, Little Russian or Ukrainian, and White Russian. The last, spoken in the former governments of Vitebsk, Minsk and Mohilev, has only claimed to be a written language since the Revolution: it is very close to Great Russian save for certain points in which it makes a transition to Polish, its Western neighbour, South Great Russian and Ukrainian. The other two branches have always called themselves simply "Russian", the Great Russians calling the South-Western language "Little Russian", which was resented by its speakers. These latter, unable in practice to establish their claim to be called "Russians", have adopted the words "Ukraina" and "Ukrainian" from the part of their country most distinguished in history (v. p. 64). The name "Ruthenian" is simply a foreigner's mishandling of *Rusin* = "one Russian man". It is applied mostly to the Western Ukrainians, but in older usage (e.g. in Latin books) to any Russian.

The Ukrainians claim that their language is the true representative of the speech current in Kievan Russia before the Mongol invasion: it has certainly kept certain points, e.g. the use of the vocative case and the distinction between *e* and *ye*, now lost in Great Russian: on the other hand it has changed original *g* into *h* (which does not exist in Great Russian), *o* in certain cases into *i*, *ê* into *i*, "hard *l*" often into *v* or *w*, etc., and has borrowed many words from Polish and even from German.

The Ukrainian language varies greatly in different parts of its wide area, the speech of the Kiev region and, curiously enough, the archaic dialects of "Carpathian Rus" differing less from Great Russian than does that of Galicia. The train of circumstances by which Galician became the foundation of the modern literary language is set forth in Chapter v (pp. 247 sqq.).

The shaded band on Map I shows the extreme limits of Ukrainian speech, but the borders are very vague and within them much Great Russian is spoken: along the sea in "New Russia" and to the East Great Russian is really dominant. In the extreme West the towns mostly speak Polish and the countryside Ukrainian.

NAMES AND TRANSLITERATION

The personal names that occur in this book are mostly Ukrainian, Great Russian and Polish: in the authorities used, written in some ten languages, they are spelt in all sorts of ways and it is impossible to arrive at strict consistency in orthography. Christian names in universal use have mostly been given their English form, Slavonic names in the form most common in English. Polish surnames are written as Polish, Hungarian and Rumanian in their correct forms, Turkish a little haphazard.

For Great Russian and Ukrainian surnames the systems of transliteration recommended by the British Academy have been adopted. The reasons for the details of these systems are set out in *Proc. Brit. Acad.* VIII (1917).

Note that Ukrainian i corresponds to Russian и, и to Russian ы (but not so thick in sound), ï to *yi* which Russian can hardly express: *i* is used for Russian and Ukr. ий at the end of names, and *y* for Ukr. ий.

Certain families began by being Ukrainian or Lithuanian and became Polish (v. p. 52): they have been written as Ukrainian save when the Polish form seemed too familiar to change (but Polish has been rather avoided for typographical reasons), e.g. Ukr. Ostroz'ky, Polish Ostrożski, is better known in the Russian form Ostrozhski; Ukr. Chartoryys'ky as Polish Czartoryski; Ukr. Vyshnevets'ky, Polish, Wiśniowecki; Ukr. Chetvertyns'ky, Polish, Czetwertyński. It seemed right that the great national hero Khmelnyts'ky should keep his Ukrainian form as against the Polish Chmielnicki.

The variations in place names are even greater: the Ukrainian forms are mostly unfamiliar and have only been used for the more obscure places: the Great Russian forms are simpler to render and have mostly been preferred. The case of Lvov is a good example, Old and Great Russian, L'vov; Polish, Lwów (pronounced Lvuv); Ukr. L'viv; German, Lemberg; French, Léopol: or Russian, Chigirin; Ukr. Chyhyryn; Polish, Czehryń.

E. H. M.

1940

TABLE OF ALPHABETS

Transliteration	Great Russian	Ukrainian	Polish	Transliteration	Great Russian	Ukrainian	Polish
a	а	а	a	p	п	п	p
			ą (*nasal*)	r	р	р	r
b	б	б	b				rz (*sounds zh*)
ch	ч	ч	cz	s	с	с	s
d	д	д	d	s′ *or* sy	с (*soft*)	с (*soft*)	ś
dz	дз	дз	dz	sh	ш	ш	sz
dz′ *or* dzy (*soft*)		дз (*soft*)	dź	shch	щ	щ	szcz
dzh	дж	дж	dż	t	т	т	t
e	э (e)	е	e	ts	ц	ц	c
ë	ё (*sounds yo*)	йо	io	ts′ *or* tsy		ц (*soft*)	ć
			ę (*nasal*)	u	у	у	u
f	ф	ф	f	v	в	в	w
g	г	ґ	g	y *consonant*	й	й	j (i)
h	(г)	г	h	y *vowel*	ы	и	y
i	и	і	i	ya	я	я	ia, ja
k	к	к	k	ye (*Gt. R.* e)	e	є	ie, je
l	л (*hard*)	л (*hard*)	ł	yi		ї	ji
l′ *or* ly	л (*soft*)	л (*soft*)	l	yu	ю	ю	iu, ju
m	м	м	m	z	з	з	z
n	н	н	n	z′ *or* zy	з (*soft*)	з (*soft*)	ź
n′ *or* ny	н (*soft*)	н (*soft*)	ń	zh	ж	ж	ż
o	о	о	o	(′) *represents* ь		ь	(′)
			ó (*sounds u*)				

but has mostly been omitted.

In Ukrainian soft дз, с, ц, з (Polish dź, ś, ć, ź) sound almost dzh, sh, ch, and zh.

CHRONOLOGICAL TABLE

VII c. B.C. Scythian invasion. Greek colonization.
I c. B.C. Roman power.
III c. A.D. Goths.
IV c. Huns.
V c. Slavs' expansion.
VI c. Avars.
VII c. Khazars. Bulgars.
VIII c. Magyars.
IX c. Varangians. 862 Rurik. Kiev.
911 Oleg and Byzantium.
945 Igor and Byzantium.
972 Svyatoslav. Pechenegs.
980–1015 Vladimir the Great, baptized 987.
992–1025 Boleslaw of Poland.
1019–54 Yaroslav the Wise.
1054 Cuman–Polovtsy.
1113–25 Vladimir Monomakh.
1147 Novgorod prosperous. Moscow first mentioned.
1169 Rise of Vladimir-Suzdal. Andrew of Bogolynbovo takes Kiev.
Shift of population to N.E. and N.W. Foundation of Halych.
1204 Latins take Constantinople.
1224 Battle of Kalka. Mongols.
1240 Batu sacks Kiev. Mongol-Tartar domination.
Rise of Teutonic Orders.
Lithuania begins to rise.
Daniel of Galicia.
1261 Greeks recover Constantinople.
Moscow begins to rise.
1316–42 Gedymin of Lithuania. Metropolitan of Kiev moves to Moscow.
1333–70 Casimir of Poland.
1345–77 Olgerd.
1349 Galicia absorbed by Poland.
1353 Moscow chief agent of Tartars.
1380 Dmitri Donskoy. Kulikovo Field.
1385 Treaty of Krevo. Jagiello marries Jadwiga.
1398 Invasion of Tamerlane.
1399 Vitovt defeated on Vorskla.
1410 Teutonic Order defeated at Tannenberg.
1413 Union of Horodlo. Crimean Khanate. First Cossacks.
1453 Fall of Constantinople.
1471 Novgorod falls to Moscow.
1475 Fall of Caffa. Turks in Crimea.
1484 Kiev sacked by Crim Tartars.

1505 Peasants fixed to land in Poland.
1526 Battle of Mohács.
1529 Lithuanian Statute; revised 1566.
1540 Revival of Kiev.
1552 Fall of Kazan.
1557 Foundation of *Sech*.
1569 Union of Lublin between Poland and Lithuania.
      Turks defeated before Astrakhan.
1578 First Cossack Regiments in Polish service.
1590 Kosiński's revolt.
1594–6 Nalivayko's revolt.
1596 Church Union of Brest. Cossacks raid Turks.
1603–12 Muscovy. Time of Troubles.
1614 Sahaydachny Hetman.
1617 J. Boretsky Metropolitan of Kiev.
1621 First defeat of Turks at Khotin.
1625 Cossacks in touch with Moscow.
1632 Peter Mohila Metropolitan of Kiev.
1636–8 Pavluk's risings; defeat at Kumeyki.
1648 Great rising of Cossacks under Bohdan Khmelnytsky.
      Zborov Agreement.
1654 Pereyaslav Agreement between Cossacks and Moscow.
1657 Death of Khmelnytsky.
1658 Vyhovsky Hetman: Hadyach Agreement with Poles.
1663 John Casimir crosses Dniepr.
1665 Bryukhovetsky's Agreement with Moscow.
1667 Peace of Andrusovo: Moscow stronger than Poland. Doroshenko.
1672–81 Turkish invasions ending in Treaty of Baghchi-Saray.
1683 Sobieski relieves Vienna.
1687 Mazeppa Hetman.
1689 Peter the Great.
1699 Treaty of Karlowitz. W. Ukraine under Poland.
1700 Charles XII defeats Peter at Narva.
1704 Mazeppa rules all Ukraine.
1708 Mazeppa joins Charles. Skoropadsky Hetman.
1709 Peter destroys *Sech*. Battle of Poltava. Death of Mazeppa.
1711 Peter defeated by Turks on R. Pruth.
1722 Little Russian Collegium.
1730 New *Sech*. *Haydamak* revolt.
1750 Razumovski Hetman. New Russia being settled.
1762 Catherine II. Hetman abolished.
1768 Confederation of Bar. *Haydamaks* at Uman.
1770 Zaporogians fight Crimea.
1775 *Sech* finally destroyed.
1783 Crimea annexed. New Russia organized.
1792 Cossacks moved to R. Kuban.
1793 Second Partition of Poland. Ukraine all united with Russia.
1803–23 Adam Czartoryski spreads Polish influence.

1812 Napoleon's invasion. Ukraine not affected.
1830 Ukrainian movement begins in Galicia.
1831 Polish insurrection. Reaction against Poles.
1848 Peasant risings in Galicia. Ukrainian movement in Kiev. Shevchenko.
1861 Emancipation of the Serfs. Kiev *Hromada*. Antonovich.
1868–72 *Prosvita* and Shevchenko Societies in Lvov.
1878 Laws against Ukrainian books in Russia.
1890 Austria encourages Ukrainians. Hrushevsky. Emigration from
   Russian Ukraine to Siberia and Far East.
1900 Donets coal-basin being developed.
1905 Russian revolution failed. Ukrainian books allowed.
1905–14 Swift industrial development.
1914 War. Russians invade Galicia.
1915 Retreat from Galicia. Refugees in Kiev.
1917 February, Revolution.
   March, Hrushevsky and Vinnichenko set up *Rada* at Kiev.
   June, Autonomous Ukrainian Republic proclaimed.
   August, Bolshevik agitation in S. Russia.
   October, Revolution. December, Armistice.
1918 January, Brest–Litovsk negotiations.
   February, German and Austrian armies occupy Ukraine.
   April, *Rada* gives way to Hetman as Skoropadsky.
   November, Armistice in West.
   December, Directoria takes Kiev. German evacuation proceeding.
   Anarchy in S. Russia. Ukrainian S.S.R. proclaimed.
1919 January, Directoria leaves Kiev. Petlyura.
   September, Volunteer Army takes Kiev.
   December, end of Directoria. Repulse of Volunteer Army.
   Kiev taken by Soviets.
   Carpathian Rus assigned to Czecho-Slovakia.
1920 April, Poles take Kiev.
   June, they retreat. Bolsheviks invade Poland.
   October, Armistice. Poland obtains not only Galicia but Kholm
   and Volkynia with Ukrainian population.
1921 Great Famine and typhus.
   Return of Hrushevsky. Period of Ukrainization.
1929 Agriculture collectivized.
1930–1 Ukrainian 'plots' suppressed: persecution of 'kulaks'.
1932 Second Famine: oppression of peasants.
1936 New constitution of U.S.S.R. as a unified state.
1939 March, Hungary recovers Carpathian Rus.
   September, U.S.S.R. seizes Ukrainian districts hitherto in
   Poland.
1940 June, U.S.S.R. seizes N. Bukovina and Bessarabia.

GENERAL MAP OF SOUTH RUSSIA

Scale 1 = 5,000,000

About 80 m. to the inch,   50 km. to the centimetre

0 10 20 30 40 50   100m. 0   50   100   150   200km.

Approximate Boundary of Ukrainian Speech

CHAPTER I

THE RIVER WORLD AND THE KIEVAN
STATE (UP TO 1240)

§ 1. THE GEOGRAPHICAL FACTOR IN
RUSSIAN HISTORY

RUSSIA is a land of rivers. The element of frustration in Russian history comes from the fact that all the rivers of the Great Eurasian Plain debouch into land-locked or ice-packed seas. The fine rivers of Siberia spend themselves in Arctic waters. The Dvina, north-westward artery from the Central Russian river system, flows to the Baltic. Southward the Dniestr, the Dniepr and the Don descend to the warm waters of the Black Sea to find the single outlet to the Mediterranean through the narrow straits which separate Europe from Asia. Eastward the Volga, greatest of Russian rivers, casts its waters into the Caspian, the largest of Asiatic lakes.

The rivers offer to the whole Eurasian Plain the possibility of a close-knit unity. Rapids are rare—those of the Dniepr are famous; the rivers are broad and slow flowing over the vast level plain. Only the enterprise of man was necessary to convert the primeval streams into a system of communications. Geographically, a north-south development of historical life would seem inevitable; and from early times the river routes from the Black Sea to the Baltic were known to the trading communities of the Mediterranean. Yet the very network of rivers which gives promise of a unified and ordered development of life over the Eurasian Plain offers at the same time opportunity for the intrusions of alien elements. So the early history of the Eurasian Plain is the history of the penetration of the region by successive invasions from east, west and north, and of the percolation of the most diverse influences. Regional cultures were created by exterior action, and, so far as there is evidence in historical times, by the fusion of invaders, generally not very numerous, with the conquered inhabitants. This was certainly the case with the medieval states of Novgorod and Kiev, where a Scandinavian warrior and trader class imposed themselves on a primitive Slav population.

The third and youngest cultural growth in medieval Russia was that which radiated from Moscow. Here, owing to the proximity of the Volga and the close relation between the Grand Duchy of Muscovy and the Golden Horde, Mongol and Islamic influences imparted a peculiarly sombre and conservative tone to the reviving Russian state. The 'Asiatic' character of this third Russian culture may be contrasted with the enterprising 'western' complexion of 'Baltic' Novgorod and with the 'Mediterranean' brilliance of southern Kiev.

The Volga had always been a channel through which Oriental influences penetrated towards the north. In the days of the Khazar kingdom in the eighth century Persian, Arab and Jewish elements were strong. Klyuchevski, moreover, has emphasized the significance of the Finno-Ugrian substratum in the primitive population of the Volga basin. Here Voguls, Cheremises, Votyaks and other primordial Finnic tribes were enserfed by the Suzdal princes in the twelfth century. The new Russia which emerged in the Grand Duchy of Muscovy, and which for the first time conquered the river network of the Eurasian Plain from *within*, was a different Russia (less Slav and less European) from the Russias of Kiev and Novgorod.

The north-south trend in Russian history, which should found a unity upon the river network, is countered by a pull east-west. The Great Eurasian Plain has no limit north-westward till it reaches the Baltic and the North Sea; none westward till the Carpathians; while south-eastward it is lost in the Aralo-Caspian desert zone which stretches to the T'ien-Shan and beyond to the Khingan. Thus in comparatively recent times temporarily great powers like Poland and Sweden have exercised a formidable pressure upon the undefined borderlands. In earlier times the Germanic peoples in migration swept through to the Black Sea; the Goths ruled the South Russian land for two centuries. From the east successive waves of the Altaian peoples rode in from the desert zone of Inner Asia. The Hunnish and Avarian invasions of the southern steppelands on the way to Central Europe are very comparable to the later Mongol invasions of the thirteenth century. The Mongols were in fact merely the final wave of the Altaian peoples, who established themselves rather more effectively and for a longer period of time because their ruthless military qualities had been refined by the competence of Chinese and Persian statecraft.

The exposure of the Russian land both towards the west and towards the south-east made chronic the factors of instability and uncertainty which have affected all phases of Russian history. The fluidity of frontiers and the repetition of invasions have introduced complicated racial issues. The Russian state of the Muscovite Tsars was founded upon a real geographical unity, and it was a natural response to the slackening of pressures from the east. But the state which the first Ivans compounded out of Slav, Finnic and Tatar material was never a racial unity, and when the Russian Empire expanded *outward* without limit, as its enemies had formerly pressed *inward* without limit, it absorbed into its sphere peoples, Slav and non-Slav, who were historically attached to other regions and who felt the attraction of other cultural worlds.

§2. SOUTH RUSSIA BEFORE THE SLAVS

Many peoples occupied South Russia before the Slavs. Numerous cultures flourished there before the beginnings of written history. The fan of rivers round the Black Sea (from east to west, Kuban, Don, Dniepr, Bug, Dniestr, Pruth, Danube) nourished a vast area which linked the Asiatic with the Trans-Danubian and Mediterranean worlds. At periods in archaeological time a common culture appears to have covered the whole area between the Caucasus and the upper valley of the Danube. This common cultural background of forms and designs does not, of course, necessarily imply a racial uniformity. In fact the remains of different physical types and differing burial practices indicate the movements and settlements of a diversity of peoples.

The first historical period in South Russia began with the Greek colonization, the origins of which go back to the eighth century B.C. The Greeks themselves were undoubtedly the heirs of older thalassocracies in the Pontus—Minoan and Mycenaean. The Xth, XIth and XIIth Books of the *Odyssey* and the legend of the Argonauts suggest the existence of more ancient cultural epochs, which the archaeological wealth of the Kuban affirms.

The Greek colonial civilization in the Pontus has been well described by Minns and Rostovtsev. The Greek colonists round the northern shores found the Scythians in possession of the South Russian steppelands. The Scythians were probably an Altaian nomad aristocracy with an Iranian language and culture ruling over a variety of subject peoples, many of whom were cultivators. The influence not only of Greece but also of Iran and Upper Asia is to be discovered in the remarkable art which flowered under the patronage of the Scythian princes. The economy of the Scythians, based on stock-raising and agriculture, was complementary to that of the Greek states, and for several centuries both the Greek colonial cities and the Scythian rulers of the Pontic hinterland grew rich on the enormous trade which developed between the steppelands and the Mediterranean. Athens became dependent on Scythian wheat, particularly during the Peloponnesian War, and the Pontus was often an issue in the politics of the Hellenic world. Peisker thinks that the demand for grain in Greece caused the nomad Scythians to utilize whole-sale the agricultural populations who were under their subjection. He recalls that Herodotus includes various peoples, nomads and husbandmen, evidently not of the same origin, under the name Scythian; the latter sowed grain 'not for food, but for sale', and he considers that there can be no doubt that Slav tribes were included among these transplanted agriculturalists.

The fourth century B.C. was the heyday of the Pontic cities, when the Greco-Scythian kingdom of Bosporus, dominating the Straits of Kerch (Cimmerian Bosporus), tapped the rich wheatlands of the Don and the Kuban and controlled the transit trade which passed between the Black Sea littoral and the peoples of interior Asia. Other cities attained great wealth and sheltered varied populations— Tyras by the Dniestr, Olbia at the mouth of the Bug, Chersonesus Taurica in the Crimea, Tanais in the delta of the Don.

The peculiar world around the Pontus, steppeland chieftains, Greek city-states and Anatolian potentates, attained a passing unity under the genius of Mithradates Eupator. Reinach has illuminated the grand mind of Mithradates, who aspired to win in the east when Hannibal had already lost in the west. Mithradates failed, and the Romans became the heirs of the Greek foundations round the Black Sea. But the days of the Helleno-Scythian synthesis were over. In the second century B.C. the relatively long peace of the steppe had been disturbed by the Sarmatians, another nomad people, probably of Iranian speech, living to the east of the Don, descendants of whom are still perhaps to be identified in the Ossetes of the central Caucasus. Dislodging and absorbing the Scythians, the wilder Sarmatians moved over the steppe towards the west. The old economic unity of the south of Russia was disturbed. Chersonesus, Olbia and Tyras could only enjoy security behind strong walls and under the protection of Roman garrisons. In the first and second centuries A.D. the Roman Empire became involved in a difficult struggle with the Sarmatians along the line of the Danube; Trajan's victory over them brought images of these distant barbarians to adorn the reliefs on the column dedicated to him in Rome.

During the second and third centuries A.D. the Sarmatians were mastered by the Germanic Goths and Herules. The kingdom of Bosporus was conquered; Chersonesus Taurica was hemmed in; Tyras and Olbia were destroyed. The Gothic kingdom lasted two centuries and 'was the only non-nomadic episode in the history of the steppe'. The hordes of Asia were in movement. Before the end of the fourth century the Goths had been broken by the Huns—the first of the known Altaian peoples who were to ride against the ancient world.

After them were to come Bulgars, Avars, Khazars, Magyars, Peche-negs, Kipchaks, Mongols. 'Like the *buran*, the furious tempest of the steppe, each of these hordes drove its predecessor in wild flight over the civilized lands of Europe, extirpated the Slav peasantry which had settled in the grass steppe, and passed over the tree steppe plundering and murdering so that the Slavs were forced to leave this zone too and to withdraw into the marshes of Polesia'.(1)

§ 3. THE ORIGIN OF THE SLAVS

The nomads played a dominating part in the history of the South Russian steppeland from prehistoric times until the fifteenth century A.D., and in Central Europe their sinister and destructive intervention was to affect the course of European history at intermittent periods between the fifth and thirteenth centuries. In fact not a few of the problems of modern Europe are traceable to the impact of the Asiatic nomads upon the homelands of the Slav and Germanic peoples.

Peisker, in brilliant chapters in the *Cambridge Medieval History*, con-trasts the character of the two racial stocks whose compound was to form the basis of the population of Russia and of the greater part of Central and South-Eastern Europe.

'The nomads of the Asiatic background', in the opinion of Peisker, 'all belong to the Altaian branch of the Ural-Altaic race.... Everything speaks for one single place of origin for the mounted nomads, and that is the Turanian-Mongol steppes and deserts. These alone, by their enormous extent, their unparalleled severity of climate, their uselessness in summer, their salt vegetation nourishing countless herds, and above all by their indivisible economic connec-tion with the distant grass-abounding north—these alone gave rise to a people with the ineradicable habits of mounted nomads.'

In contrast to the Altaian nomad the Slav has always been the peaceful tiller of the soil—the natural victim of the rading Asiatic horseman and of the Scandinavian river pirate and trader. In the view of Procopius the Slavs were not malignant and villainous, but harmless and naïve; according to Maurice: 'They are hardened to heat, frost, wet, nakedness and hunger, and are well-disposed to strangers.' Adam of Bremen found that there were no more hospitable people than the Slavs of Pomerania.

The Slavs form with the Balts (the Lithuanians, Latvians and original Prussians) the Balto-Slavonic group of the Indo-European family. Their languages have much in common with German on the one hand and with Iranian on the other. 'The differentiation of Balto-Slavonic into Old Baltic and Old Slavonic, and then of Old

Slavonic into the separate Slavonic languages, was caused partly by
the isolation of various tribes from one another, and partly by mutual
assimilation and the influence of related dialects and unrelated languages. Thus it is not a matter of genealogy only, but partly due to
historical and political developments.'

A vast literature exists on the subject of the original homeland of
the Slavs. Peisker accepts the view of the Polish botanist Rostafinski,
based on evidence from botanical geography, that the differentiation
of the Slavs from the Balts took place in prehistoric times in the
region of Polesia—the great region of marshes which forms a rough
triangle between the modern towns of Brest-Litovsk, Mohilev and
Kiev.

Originally the Slavs, like the Germans, had no collective name; in
Peisker's view the name of the Slavs is correctly *Slovêne* (sing.
Slovênin); it is probably a *nomen topicum* meaning roughly 'inhabi-
tants of the *slovy*'. Another view is that Slovêne means the people
with the 'word' *Slovo*, as opposed to the Nêmtsy, the Slav word for
German, i.e. the 'dumb' people who cannot 'take in' what you say.
The name applied originally only to one populous tribe. The East
Romans came into contact at first with a part of this tribe and thus
named all other Slav tribes north of the Danube *Sklavenoi, Sthlavoi*.

Peisker emphasizes how the salt-desert zone of the Asiatic background developed the wild mounted nomad. Just as the mounted
nomad was the son and product of the arid salt deserts, so the Slav
fisher and husbandman was the son and product of the marsh. 'The
Slav and the mounted nomad, like the lands of their origin, are
diametrical extremes, and the murderous irony of fate made them
neighbours. The one was a soft anvil, the other a hammer hard as
steel. A second not less weighty hammer (the Germans) came into
play, and the anvil was beaten flat.'(2) Perhaps his metaphor would
have fitted better if he had spoken of a steel hammer, a hard anvil and
soft iron between them.

Peisker has analysed the fundamental difference in character between the expansion of the Germans and the expansion of the Slavs:
'Dry and tolerably fertile forest land contains so much cultivable soil
that it cannot easily be over-peopled: so here men form societies and
states arise. But primitive man cannot wrest a foot of land from the
marsh; on the contrary, he extends it by making dams, transforming
small streams into great fish-ponds. Thus as the cultivable oases become smaller, the population huddles closer together. Dry forest
land makes its inhabitants stronger, but the marsh has a degenerating
influence. Forest land, however, is not inexhaustible; when what has
been reaped from it is not made up by dunging, or by allowing it to

lie fallow—in short, when the soil is merely worked out—it can no longer support the growing population, and compels migration or expansion at the cost of the neighbourhood. But the unwarlike inhabitants of the marshland can conquer nothing, and can only spread gradually where they meet with no resistance. This is upon the whole the difference between the expansion of the Germans and that of the Slavs. The Germanic migration was eruptive as a volcano, the Slavonic a gradual percolation, like that of a flood rolling slowly forward. Some Germanic people or other leaves its home: in the search for a new home they rouse their neighbours, and they in turn rouse theirs, and so it goes on until a hemisphere is thrown into commotion, strong states fall to pieces, mighty peoples perish, and even the Roman Empire quakes. And the Slavs? They have occupied and thickly populated immeasurable regions unnoticed by the annalists, and even now we ask in vain how this could have taken place so noiselessly, and whence have come the countless millions of Slavs.'

The Slavs thus enter into history during the period of the great migrations—harried and conquered by the Germans, and ravaged and driven by the Altaian nomad peoples. And long before the ninth century the inhabitants of the marshy forests along the great rivers were already suffering from the depredations of Scandinavian pirates. Germano-Slavic and Altaio-Slavic states began to form. The third century A.D. had seen a Germanic state on the Dniepr. But it was the Altaians who formed the great Empires and who swept the uprooted Slav agriculturalists with them into Central and South-Eastern Europe. In the fifth century the Hunnic Empire stretched from the Don to the lower Rhine; in the seventh century the Avars ruled from the Baltic to the Peloponnesus; and the Bulgars and the Magyars successively dominated Central Europe between the Adriatic, the Aegean and the Carpathians. But there remained of the great Altaian Empires, after they had disappeared from history, only the numerous Slav peoples whom they had forced along with them, and who formed peasant states in the lands which the nomads had conquered from the Romans and the Germans. In the Avar Empire, Peisker shows that 'the dominating Avar nomad class was absorbed as a nation and language by the subjugated Slavs, but even after the destruction of the Avar Empire it survived socially with Slav names'. The same social phenomenon is to be observed later in the Varangian-Scandinavian Empire which arose in South Russia.

After the collapse of the Avar Empire in the first decade of the seventh century, following the revolt of the Slav peasant masses against the nomad overlords, the first Slav states emerged in Central Europe, in each case under peasant princes, for the line in Slovenian

Carinthia, the Bohemian Přemyslids, and the Polish Piasts were all of peasant origin. In widely differing geographical environments, subject to a variety of cultural influences, and undergoing processes of racial admixture with neighbouring peoples, the Western Slavs became a part of Europe and grew into distinct nations. Meanwhile those groups which had escaped the great Altaian tempests, and which had remained in the marshes and the forests along the primeval rivers, were multiplying and spreading into the vast untouched lands which held the destiny of Russia. In the seventh century, following the overthrow of the Avar Empire in Central Europe, Slav tribes were settling along the Dniepr. In the following century they are found scattered along its affluents as far as the upper reaches of the western Dvina. At the beginning of the ninth century they had already occupied the lake district which was to form the future territory of Novgorod. (3)

§ 4. THE RIVER WORLD: KHAZARS AND VARANGIANS

The great industrial and commercial revival of the Mediterranean and Middle Eastern lands following the social and moral revolution effected through the successful propagation of Islam was undoubtedly an important factor in the opening up of the river world of the Great Eurasian Plain. The establishment of the Khazar kingdom on the Volga was almost contemporaneous with the conquest of Persia and eastern Caucasia by the Arabs. The Khazar kingdom was similar in character to the earlier Scythian and Sarmatian kingdoms, in that a nomad ruling class—in the case of the Khazars certainly of Altaian stock—controlled an area inhabited by a variety of populations, both sedentary and nomadic. And the Arabs had to the Khazars something of the relation which the Greeks had had to the Scythians. In the eighth century the Khazar walled camp, placed where the angle of the Volga approaches closest to that of the Don, had already become transformed into the cosmopolitan metropolis of Itil. Here a varied population lived and traded in peace under the protection of the Khazar Khaqan. People had settled there from the four quarters of Asia—pagan Finns and Slavs, Christian Greeks, Armenians and Georgians, Jews and Muslims from Iran and the Arabian countries. There is a story, based on the second-hand accounts of one or two Muslim travellers, to the effect that the Khazar Khaqans had adopted the Hebrew faith, which has passed into history. Recently Grégoire's researches have challenged interested exaggerations of this tradition. It is clear, however, that the influence of the Jews, who had become the most active agents of the commerce of the Caliphate, was substantial in the Khazar kingdom, and it is probable that the commonly observed mongoloid type among East European Jews, particularly in the Ukraine, Poland and Roumania, derives from the conversions and intermarriages which were no doubt frequent in the swarming trading camps of the Khaqans.

In the eighth century the Khazar kingdom assumed formidable political pretensions; the Khaqans had a preponderating influence in Black Sea politics and negotiated on equal terms with the Byzantine Emperors; marriages were arranged between the courts of Itil and Byzantium. At the same time, in spite of their partial dependence on the traffic with the Muslim cities of Iran, Shirvan and Iraq, the Khaqans did not hesitate to challenge the Caliphs for the control of Derbend and the eastern Caucasus.

The Khazars had established themselves along the river ways which led down to the shores of the Caspian and the Black Sea. The great Volga route apparently was already used in the seventh century. Along the Kama, where the Bulgars had settled, was carried a trade with the Urals and Siberia. By the affluents of the Volga access could be had to the streams which flow north-west into Lake Ladoga. From there down the Neva was the way to the Baltic Sea.(4)

The Scandinavians were aware of this route to the south and east. Scandinavian settlements arose among the Finnish tribes living on the shores of Lakes Ilmen and Ladoga and on the White Lake, and along the upper Volga. Their posts were at the same time of a trading and of a military character. The Scandinavians, the fearless Varangians, afforded protection to the merchant flotillas which went down along the waterways in the direction of the Khazars, or which were proceeding up to the Baltic Sea. The Khazar kingdom, in the days of its prosperity, offered an open market to all trading 'guests'.

The almost simultaneous spread of the Slavs round the shores of Lake Ilmen and along the banks of the Dniepr favoured the search of the Scandinavians for another and more westerly route towards the south which might enable them to trade direct with the Byzantine world without their having to depend upon the Khazar rivers.

During the ninth century the famous way 'from the Varangians to the Greeks' was opened up. From the Baltic the trading flotillas travelled up the Neva to Lake Ladoga, whence they navigated the Volkhov to Lake Ilmen; from Ilmen they went along the Lovat to the region of the affluents of the western Dvina. After conquering all the obstacles of a difficult portage, they proceeded up the western Dvina to the point where it nears the Dniepr. Thence they made use of the smaller rivers to shorten the new short cut, and the way down the Dniepr led into the Black Sea. Immense hardships and difficulties must have been overcome before the Vikings looked at last upon the sea which could carry them to the capital of the ancient world. But the 'golden Tsargrad' of the Slavs lay beyond the endless rivers, and drew on the avid seamen, as in another age the legend of Eldorado drove their descendants across the oceans to the conquest of new continents.

The Slav settlements along the rivers had made it possible to penetrate into lands which had been uninhabited before. And the great waterway which the Varangians travelled served as a link between the Slav tribes scattered over the wide spaces of the Great Russian Plain. Along that water road Russia was born.

The system of the Khazar market towns along the rivers served as a ground plan for the Varangians. Cities were built: Kiev on the Dniepr, Novgorod on Lake Ilmen, and others later. And these were Russian towns—the towns of 'Rus'. No one ever called Kiev the town of the Polyane, nor Novgorod the town of the Slavs, nor Smolensk that of the Krivichi. The Finns called the people who crossed the Baltic Sea 'Ruotsi'. The Varangians were called 'Rus' by the Slavs, who had borrowed the name from the Finns. The name was also used by the Khazars and Arabs and by the Byzantines, and penetrated with the same meaning into Western Europe. (5)

Soon after the middle of the ninth century, Varangian rulers appear almost simultaneously in Novgorod, in Polotsk on the western Dvina and in Kiev. Oleg (Helgi), generally recognized as the founder of the peculiar 'Varangian-Russian' state in Kiev, was a typical Viking 'konung' who alternately traded and waged war. He pushed back towards the Don the Khazars who had reached the Dniepr and who were levying tribute on the local Slav population. He continued, however, to trade with the Khazar kingdom, making use of the 'Khazar way'—which followed the Desná, an affluent of the east bank of the Dniepr, then its tributary the Seym, and further the smaller affluents of the Donets, which in its turn falls into the Don.

In the same way Oleg made war on and traded with the Greeks. The campaign which brought him to the walls of Constantinople in 911 was successful not so much on account of the booty secured as in the agreement which he exacted defining the trading rights and privileges of 'Rus'.

After Oleg, Igor (Ingvar), and his talented and energetic wife Olga (Helga), pursued the Varangian undertaking in the south of Russia. In his military activities against Byzantium, Igor was not very fortunate, but he succeeded, in the year 945, in concluding another trading agreement with the Greeks. Among the signatures on this agreement are those of the envoys of Igor and Olga, of

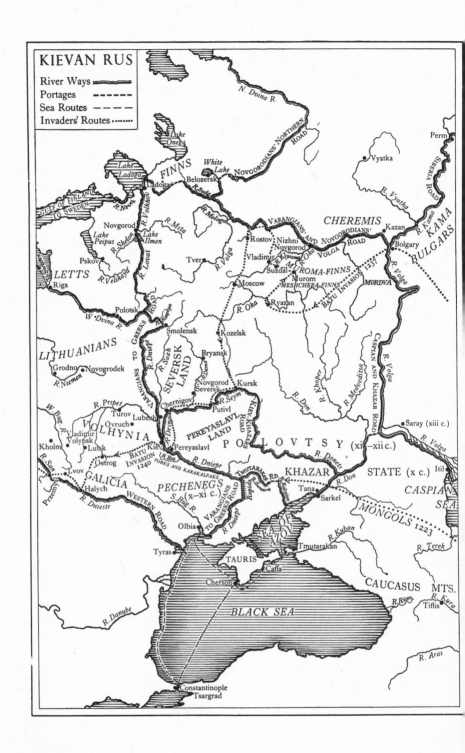

KIEVAN RUS

River Ways
Portages
Sea Routes
Invaders' Routes

Svyatoslav their son and of other local chiefs, and also those of Russian merchants. Scandinavian names still prevail over names of Slav origin. But the son of Igor and Olga, Svyatoslav, already bears a Slav name. Svyatoslav was in fact the last Scandinavian 'konung'.

Incessant wars occupied the reign of Svyatoslav. He undertook campaigns against the Kama Bulgarians and against the Khazar kingdom, which he ruined. He thereby rendered a poor service to the nascent Kievan state, for the weakened Khazars ceased henceforth to act as a barrier against the Altaian nomads. A new horde, the wild and plundering Pechenegs (Greek, Patzinakitai), probably a mingling of Altaian and North Caucasian elements, appeared in the steppes to the north of the Black Sea. They penetrated as far as the Dniepr and threatened Kiev, while Svyatoslav was away waging war on the Danube, first against the Bulgarians, and then against the Greeks. Having suffered defeat at the hands of the Greeks, who imposed a treaty whereby he undertook the obligation to supply Byzantium with grain, Svyatoslav was making his way back to Kiev when he perished in a Pecheneg ambush.

Such was the Varangian prologue to the Kievan state which was to grow to florescence with an almost incredible rapidity in the course of the eleventh century. (6)

§5. THE KIEVAN STATE

Under Vladimir the Saint (980–1015) and Yaroslav the Wise (1019–54), the Kievan state—a historical phenomenon in the highest degree peculiar and even strange—reached the stage of its full expression in less than a hundred years. Rostovtsev, the historian of the Greek and Iranian synthesis in South Russia, could not resist the temptation of concluding his work with an outline of Kievan Russia. 'The extraordinary difference which existed between Kievan Russia and Western Europe to this day appears inexplicable. In the West— agriculture and feudalism; in Russia—trade and the city-state.'

The study of the Greco-Scythian trading system led its historian to a true comprehension of the state which had arisen, with the help of the Scandinavians, among the Eastern Slavs. Kievan Russia certainly cannot be explained by Greco-Iranian tradition. But it can be explained through the geographical and natural conditions, which had not altered since the Greco-Iranian period. The trade which had called forth to life the Greco-Iranian colonization later created Kievan Russia and determined its peculiar forms of state. The historian Klyuchevski describes Kiev as 'the Russia of city and trade' in contrast to 'the Russia of principalities and agriculture', which, in the fourteenth and the first part of the fifteenth centuries, took form in the north between the upper Volga and the Oká.

Vladimir the Saint and Yaroslav the Wise were Kievan princes of the tenth–eleventh centuries, and were still, to a certain extent, Varangians. And the Varangians, in the opinion of Klyuchevski, were naught else but 'armed merchants'. The city looked upon the prince as on 'a hired retainer' whose duty it was 'to look after the welfare of the Russian land and to fight the pagans'. Already, under Svyatoslav, the citizens of Kiev were displeased with their prince because he did not fulfil his duties. He went off on distant campaigns and left Kiev to defend itself as best it could against Pecheneg raids. 'Prince, thou goest away for foreign lands and neglectest thine own' —these were the words addressed to him. The city, therefore, could approve one prince, and disapprove of another. After Svyatoslav's death, the Kievan people did not wish to have Yaropolk as their prince, but preferred Vladimir to him. At the time of the struggle for Kiev after Vladimir's death, Svyatopolk, fearing that he would be driven away by the Kievans, 'called the people together and began to distribute furs to some and money—of which he distributed great quantities—to others'. The people of Novgorod, on one occasion, asked for a certain prince, saying: 'We have nurtured and fed him for that purpose.'

Relations of this kind between prince and people impose the conclusion that there had grown up in the river cities a powerful merchant aristocracy. The city on certain occasions could take independent decisions—ignoring the prince or even opposing him. Such decisions were taken by the *Veche* or 'general assembly' of the town citizens. Actually the proceedings of the *Veche* were virtually formal and conventional. Decisions were secured before the meeting of the *Veche* by influential groups of citizens meeting together in a more intimate assembly, where were gathered the substantial men of the different quarters of the city. Theoretically the *Veche* was open to all, but in reality the voice of the crowd was seldom effective, and that body functioned under the leadership of a few outstanding citizens. These called the assembly together when they were certain that it would decide what they themselves wanted, or, more definitively, that it would 'approve' decisions which they had already taken. That the *Veche* was becoming the central power of a land is clear from the words of the chronicles: 'The Novgorodians from the very beginning as well as the Smolensk men and the Kievans and the Polotsk men and all those in power go to the *Veche* as though they were going to the council, but what the elder towns have in their minds the minor towns decide.'

Some Russian historians have yielded to the temptation of considering these *Veche* of Kiev and Novgorod as a strange and far-off echo of the citizens' meetings of the Athenian democracy. But it is not likely that even an obscure memory of the Hellenic Pontic cities lingered on in the south of Russia, after a thousand years of barbarism. The remote analogies between the fluvial city-states of the Russian Middle Ages and the Hellenic republics of the Pontic littoral derive from a similarity of material conditions which tended to produce a similarity in social organization—the merchant oligarchy based on a popular general assembly.

The trade of Kiev and Novgorod, which aimed at the opulent 'Tsargrad' market across two thousand miles of wild forest and steppe, required protection, and hence the Varangian Slav synthesis arose. But this peaceful trade could only for a time be alternated with the raiding tactics of the early Varangian 'konungs' in Kiev. It became increasingly difficult to combine trade with piracy against the Byzantine world—particularly in the tenth/eleventh century, when Byzantium was attaining a renewed strength under the Macedonian dynasty. Already by the middle of the tenth century a thriving Greek colony was established in Kiev. At the same period the first Christian church, of St Elias, was built, since there were already Christians among the merchants of Kiev and among the Varangian warriors of the prince. Princess Olga, herself, was a Christian, and in 957, accompanied by a great following, undertook a journey to Byzantium, where she was received by the Emperor. Vladimir gave expression to the natural tendency of the times. While he was making war against the Greeks under the walls of Chersonesus, he was already dreaming of an alliance with the imperial family. He became a Christian, and imposed the faith as the formal religion in Kievan territories. The other Russian states along the rivers were not slow to follow his example. From his Chersonesus campaign Vladimir brought back with him to Kiev Greek priests, Greek artisans and Greek church ornaments and books. He took also two bronze *quadrigae*—destined to decorate the Kiev of Vladimir, as the 'steeds of San Marco' were later to be carried to Venice after the Latin conquest of Byzantium.

The intentions of Vladimir were very definite; he aspired that Kiev should become a second Constantinople. He relinquished the 'viking' raids of his forbears, and set himself to consolidate, against the Pechenegs, the position of Kiev as a territorial power in order to ensure the security of the fluvial trade routes. He levied tribute from

the inhabitants of the forest and the dwellers in the steppes in order
to strengthen his resources. He was accustomed to repeat: 'A pity it
is that there are so few towns round Kiev.' New towns arose, and
those which already existed grew. 'Rus' of the eleventh century is
not only Kiev and Novgorod, Smolensk and Polotsk, all situated on
the great water road 'from the Varangians to the Greeks'. Rostov
had risen near the banks of the upper Volga; Murom on the Oka;
Chernigov on the Desna guarding 'the Khazar way'; Pereyaslavl on
the left bank of the Dniepr in the region of the budding agriculture
of the steppelands; Vladimir amid the forests of Volhynia. But Kiev
remained the leading city, the capital of the Great Prince, 'the mother
of all Russian towns'. The primacy of Kiev has become a part of
poetry and legend; but this primacy was real and primordial—in the
city life of the Russian rivers and in the transcontinental trade of the
Great Eurasian Plain.

Among his sons Vladimir distributed not lands but towns, in
order of their likeness to his incomparable dream city of 'Tsargrad'.
To his eldest son, Yaropolk, he designated Kiev; to the second,
Svyatopolk, Chernigov; to Vsevolod, Pereyaslavl; to Yaroslav,
Novgorod; to Boris, Rostov; to Gleb, Murom; and to the youngest,
Mstislav, distant Tmutarakan on the Azov Sea. Such is the hierarchy
of Russian towns at the beginning of the eleventh century (but from
this order must be excepted Smolensk and Polotsk, where princes
ruled who did not belong to the family of Vladimir).

Svyatopolk murdered three of his brothers, and the Russian towns
rose in revolt against him. He maintained himself in Kiev with the
aid of Boleslaw Chrobry, the first powerful Polish king, but Yaroslav came down from the north with his Novgorodians. It is note-
worthy that Yaroslav did not lead the Novgorodians so much as that
the Novgorodians carried him with them as a leader. Having
suffered defeat in his first campaign, Yaroslav lost heart and was
planning to escape on barges beyond the sea 'to the Varangians'.
But, according to the chronicler: 'His *posadnik* (lieutenant) Constantine the son of Dobrynya with the Novgorodians smashed his
barges and said—"We want to fight Svyatopolk and Boleslaw".'
The city of Novgorod raised money, hired men from the Varangians,
and levied an army in the region; nor did the Novgorodians desist
until they had defeated Svyatopolk, taken Kiev and made Yaroslav
Great Prince and ruler there. The story bears eloquent witness to the
unity of feeling and action of the fluvial city-states in eleventh-
century Russia. (7)

§ 6. THE GREAT DAYS OF KIEV

The flowering of the Kievan culture came with extraordinary rapidity under Yaroslav the Wise (1019–54). Western travellers of the eleventh century, Ditmar of Merseburg and Adam of Bremen, admired the hundreds of churches there and noted the eight great markets. Kiev had become the great metropolis between north and south—between the Greeks and the Balto-Scandinavian world. Trade also passed from west to east—between Germany and the new Slav kingdoms in Poland and Bohemia and the Volga and Caucasian states and the Muslim world. The Jewish and Polish quarters in Kiev and the existence in the city of colonies of Armenians and other Oriental foreigners indicate the importance of this east-west trade. The cultural connections between Kiev and the thriving Caucasian kingdoms of the Georgians and the Armenians are particularly interesting. In the swarming streets the sounds of the laborious toil of thousands of artisans mingled with the noise and bustle of the trading booths. Trade led to knowledge of the surrounding world, to the accumulation of riches and to the beginnings of a brilliant art. Adam of Bremen could write his eulogy of Kiev: *aemula sceptri Constantinopolitani et clarissimum decus Graeciae.*

Yaroslav was the typical king of an early medieval period of florescence. In the year 1037 Yaroslav began to build the church of St Sophia of Kiev. A few years later Greek masters and their Russian pupils were decorating this church (and many other churches and monasteries) with mosaics and frescoes. On the walls of St Sophia of Kiev can to this day be seen figures of the prince and his family. The walls of the annexes to the main edifice are adorned with wall paintings representing Yaroslav hunting and also festivals at the prince's court. On one of the walls is the portrait of the prince's consort, Ingigerd, a royal princess of Sweden; with her are her daughters Elizabeth, a future queen of Norway, wife of Harald Hardrada who became famous for his adventure in the East and who was destined to fall at Stamford Bridge in battle for the English crown with his equally unfortunate rival Harold Godwinsson; Anne, a future queen of France; and Anastasia, a future queen of Hungary. Yaroslav aspired to the alliance of all the contemporary courts of Europe: he married his eldest son to the sister of Casimir, the Polish king who had himself married a sister of Yaroslav. The Great Prince failed however to achieve the ambition of marrying one of his daughters to the Emperor Henry III.

Kiev was rich and alliances with Kiev were regarded with favour in the Western courts of the eleventh century. When, after Yaroslav's death, feuds broke out between his sons, and one of them, Izyaslav, fled and sought help from the German Emperor, he brought gifts with him which by their magnificence astonished the Germans. 'Never', wrote one of the German chroniclers, 'had German lands· seen so much gold, so much silver, and such profusion of costly cloth.'

During Yaroslav's life the court of Kiev itself received numerous exiles of high degree; the Norwegian King Olaf and his son were victims of the usurpations of Knut the Great, as also were the Princes Aethelred and Edward—the latter destined to be remembered with doubtful affection in English history as the Confessor. A pretender to the Hungarian throne also found refuge in Kiev—an event by which Yaroslav was quick to profit in marrying his daughter Anastasia to the fugitive.

The cosmopolitan court of Kiev read and enjoyed books and was familiar with foreign languages; the schools gave instruction to both youths and maidens—a novelty to contemporary Europe. The daughters of Yaroslav astonished everyone by their learning. In the monasteries, especially in the famous Pecherskaya Lavra, learned monks translated Greek and transcribed Bulgarian books: the Lives of the Saints; historical chronicles; the so-called *Izborniki* or 'Collections' which constituted the encyclopaedias of the time; the cosmography of Cosmas Indicopleustes; and Greek novels: the Romance of Alexander, the War of Troy, and the Tale of Barlaam and Josaphat (which has been interpreted by modern scholarship as a popularization of the life of Buddha derived from India by way of Iran and Georgia). At the same time were appearing sermons, messages and polemics by the hands of hierarchs of the Russian Church, which was then not a century old.

Under such auspices and into such a world was issued the first written code of Russian laws bearing the name of Yaroslav the Wise and called 'The Russian Right' (*Russkaya Pravda*). The originality of this code reflects the peculiar mode of life for which it was intended. In spite of the great influence of Byzantine legislation on the contemporary world, and in spite also of the close commercial and cultural relations between Byzantium and Kiev, the laws of Kievan Russia bear no similarity whatever to those of the Byzantine Empire, but reflect rather the Norse way of thought. It is not only that Russian law was more humane than the legislation of contemporary East European states: there was no death penalty, and it avoided the brutal forms of corporal punishment of the Byzantine and Oriental worlds. It was legislation adapted to the needs and mode of living of an advanced commercial community. The village, in *Russkaya*

Pravda, recedes into the shadow; it is of secondary importance. The primary place belongs to the inhabitants of the city; the laws are concerned with their interests and relations to each other. But the possessions of a man are valued higher than the man himself, than his well-being or personal security. Human personality is treated basically in relation to the possession or production of capital. '*Russkaya Pravda* is principally a legislation of capital' (Klyuchevski). Such a code could only develop so early in the history of a cultural organism where commerce had from the beginning been the basis of the social structure and where the interest of the dominant Viking trading oligarchy was paramount.

The Emperor Constantine Porphyrogenitus describes in great detail the Kievan trade in the tenth century. During the winter the Varangian princes busied themselves in collecting 'the tribute' in slaves and produce which was to make up their cargoes for the coming year. In the spring, along the Dniepr, below Kiev, great flotillas of boats were made ready. From the north, from Novgorod and Smolensk, other flotillas were collecting. All these flotillas floated down the Dniepr to the south as far as the rapids, where they unloaded for the portage, and loaded again beyond. They followed the Dniepr to the sea, and took the direction of the Bosporus, all the time hugging the shore in order to be able to take refuge if forced by inclement weather. Every boat was loaded with more than two tons of cargo, or thirty or forty traders, retainers and slaves.

In the eleventh century trade developed and its methods were perfected. Chersonesus in the Crimea and the settlements in the deltas of the Dniepr and the Danube became intermediary ports. Greek sailing ships, built for the open sea and not obliged to keep close to the coasts, came there to meet the Russian cargoes. It would have been difficult otherwise to maintain the supply of grain for Constantinople, which had now come to depend as much on the South Russian export as Athens had in a former age. Russia also exported immense numbers of slaves to Byzantium and the Levant countries; in an eleventh-century Greek legend of St Nicholas it is related that he who wants to buy a slave must 'go to the market where Russian traders sell rabble'. Thus the age-old slave trade of the Scythian steppe was continued by the Kievan Varangians as it was still to be continued in later centuries by the Kipchaks and the Mongols, using as intermediaries chiefly the Genoese, and the Turks. The slaves of the Kievan epoch were derived mostly from prisoners made from among the nomad peoples of the steppe and, in greater number, from the tributary forest tribes of Finns and Slavs.

Cattle, horses and furs, of which there was a great variety, were important items of traffic; also wax and honey, for which contemporary customs created a large demand. Thousands of barrels of honey filled the cellars of the Kievan merchant aristocracy.

Trade linked the towns of Kievan Russia from north to south, in a 'meridial' sense in accord with the direction of the principal commercial way. The unity between north and south was something greater than racial or geographical unity; it was vital. To analyse separately, in the eleventh century, the historical destinies of the south and the north of Russia would be to distort the evident truth. The unity between north and south could be disturbed by forces acting from west to east or from east to west—that is, in a latitudinal direction—but those forces were not yet of sufficient strength in the time of Yaroslav and his immediate successors. The great days of the nomad imperialism of the Magyars were past, and the power of Poland was not yet developed; it was the Russians, on the contrary, who were pushing west beyond the confines of Volhynia and the Polotsk land. The Pechenegs and the Ghuzz 'Torks' had been rendered comparatively harmless, and new waves of Altaian nomads like the Cuman Kipchaks (Russian Polovtsy) had not yet appeared.

The first threat to the unity of the Russia of Kiev and Novgorod arose from dissensions among the princes after the death of Yaroslav, and these feuds were the product of the peculiar order of succession from which even Yaroslav the Wise did not see fit to depart. Klyuchevski and other Russian historians have devoted much labour to the study of this strange rule of succession to which there was no system comparable in Western Europe. It was laid down by Yaroslav that his sons should reach the foremost position in the state by the process of mounting to the top of a 'ladder' one after the other. Kiev, the capital of the Great Prince, was allotted to the eldest living son. The other sons, according to their age, received towns in hierarchical order; Novgorod enjoyed the rule of the second; then came Chernigov, Pereyaslavl and the rest. On the death of the eldest brother, Kiev went, not to his son, but to the next eldest surviving brother. All the other brothers then moved automatically up the steps of the hierarchical 'ladder', each succeeding his elder in his superior town. This happened each time the Great Prince came to die in Kiev. The sons of each Great Prince started their careers at the very bottom of the 'ladder', and moved up its rungs in the wake of their uncles. The sons of the princes who did not succeed to the Kievan throne (i.e. of princes who predeceased their elder brothers) were altogether excluded from the succession and were regarded as 'outcasts'. It is easy to imagine the quarrels arising from such an unwonted rule of succession. The system had nevertheless a reason of its own. It was sought to establish a formula whereby no prince *possessed* a city or land of his own, but whereby he was established there as a sort of lieutenant of the Great Prince of Kiev with the temporary right to the enjoyment of revenues. The 'possessor' (conditionally) was the whole family of princes. Yaroslav established not so much the order of succession to a throne as a system for the filling of vacant posts in the different branches of a commercial firm. The best and most profitable post should go by right to the most competent, and in those days (when survival beyond early middle age was unusual) age was considered as a criterion for competence.

Circumstances, however, proved that age was not sufficient for those who could judge of their princes' competence from their own experience. The Kievans in the year 1068 decided to exile Izyaslav, who was Yaroslav's eldest son; and not only did they not address themselves to his second brother, but they chose Vseslav, who belonged to quite a different princely family ruling in Polotsk. Izyaslav returned to Kiev with the help of the Poles, but five years later he was driven out again by his more capable brother Svyatoslav II. Izyaslav turned for help to the German Emperor Henry IV and even to Pope Gregory VII. After the death of Svyatoslav Izyaslav succeeded in returning for a third time to Kiev, but only for two years. Izyaslav perished in his struggle with the sons of Svyatoslav, who, since their father had only reigned over Kiev in spite of the rule of succession, were considered to be 'outcasts'. During the years 1078–93 the Great Prince was Yaroslav's third son, Vsevolod I, who kept for himself not only Kiev but also Chernigov, Pereyaslavl, Smolensk and Suzdal.

Vsevolod's usurpation of power over the lesser towns in the hierarchy was undoubtedly justified by the necessity for a concentration of force to confront a renewal of the nomad menace from the east. The Polovtsy had already destroyed the remnants of the Khazar kingdom and were pressing their aggressions westwards. As early as the year 1058 the Russians had experienced a first defeat at the hands of the Polovtsy, and by the end of the century the lands of Chernigov and Pereyaslavl were exposed to the annual raids of the nomads.

The strange and forgotten world of Varangian Rus, of Byzantine Asia and of the Caucasian kingdoms was approaching its crisis. The drive of the Cuman Kipchaks (or Polovtsy) north of the Caspian and the Black Sea occurred simultaneously with the overrunning of the Caucasian lands and Asia Minor by the Seljuk Turks. The Altaian nomads from the deserts and grasslands of Central and North-Eastern Asia were again in movement. In 1054 the Kipchaks appeared on the borders of Rus; in 1070 they crossed the Carpathians, and in 1090 they were already on the Danube. In 1070 the imperial power of the East Roman Empire received its deathblow from the Seljuk Alp Arslan at Manzikert. Before three decades had passed the Crusaders were coming into the Levant. Turk and Norman Latin became the dominating alien forces in a Ponto-Anatolian world which had already lost its primacy. (8)

§7. THE BYZANTINISM OF VLADIMIR MONOMAKH

Vsevolod I was a cultivated monarch; he enjoyed the reputation of a competence in five languages and maintained numerous contacts with Byzantium and the Western world. He had married a daughter of the house of the Emperor Constantine Monomakh; his son Vladimir married a daughter of Harald Hardrada; and he had achieved a match for his daughter Eupraxia (Adelaide) with the German Emperor Henry IV (although this did not prove a happy union).

Vladimir, who received the second name of Monomakh in honour of his Greek descent, was educated in an atmosphere of Byzantine culture. Father and son shared the political conceptions of the imperial court and between them they elaborated the ideal of a new state which was to replace the old Varangian trading oligarchy of the princes who had grown to maturity during the tenth and eleventh centuries.

During the reign of Vladimir Monomakh, between the years 1100 and 1120, two learned Kievan monks, Nestor and Sylvester, compiled a chronicle which came down to posterity under the name of 'The Record of Passing Years'. The Record is a chronicle of events founded upon older annals as well as on legends which had been transmitted from earlier times by word of mouth. But all this material was systematically co-ordinated in a certain spirit and with certain tendencies. The learned authors had put to themselves the problem of explaining 'from whence came the Russian land'. They introduced into the Record the legend of the Apostle Andrew who had come to the hills of Kiev and predicted their destiny. Indicating the right bank of the Dniepr to his disciples, the Saint is reputed to have exclaimed: 'Look on these hills! On these hills will descend God's blessing.' The blessing of Heaven was in this wise, at the end of the eleventh century, officially attributed to the metropolis of the Kievan Great Princes. The whole account of 'the beginning of the Russian land' is constructed in such a way as to enhance the prestige of the house of Rurik as the only legitimate dynasty. The creation of Russia is their work. 'The Record of Passing Years' was the approved documentation of Kievan history. A strong aroma of the 'divinity' attributed to Byzantine Emperors hung about it and began to perfume the robes of the descendants of the piratical trading 'konungs' from the north. Shakhmatov, who more than anyone else has studied the Russian chronicles, wrote that 'the pen of the chronicler was guided by political passions and worldly interests'. Odinets is right when he calls the learned Kievan monks the predecessors of the official political thinkers of the Muscovite monarchy of the fifteenth and sixteenth centuries who found that Moscow was 'the third Rome' and that the lineage of the Moscow rulers could be derived from Caesar Augustus. (9)

Thus the political conceptions of the Kievan court at the beginning of the twelfth century were strongly influenced by Roman-Byzantine ideas of the monarchy based on divine right. To this new theory began to correspond new practice. Conferences of the Russian princes at the end of the eleventh century began formally to abandon the complicated 'ladder' rule of succession established by Yaroslav the Wise; different Russian territories were given into the complete ownership of the different princely families and a new order of succession was established, either from father to son or simply according to the will of the departing incumbent of a principality. Kiev passed into the full possession of Vladimir Monomakh, his sons and grandsons—the Monomakhovichi. (10)

At that time Vladimir Monomakh himself was still at the beginning of his career. As a 'travelling prince' under the system of Yaroslav, he had ruled the Suzdal lands, where he founded the town of Vladimir; he had sat in Chernigov and Pereyaslavl and had defended the lands of these towns against the Polovtsy. As Grand Prince in Kiev he showed by his example what was to be the hazardous destiny of the typical Russian prince during the epoch in which he lived. He went to war nineteen times against the Polovtsy and nineteen times he concluded peace with them. Vladimir defended not only Russian trade but also Russian agriculture. He went out into the steppes with a great armed force and harried the camps of the nomads, killing their chieftains, taking thousands of prisoners and driving their herds of cattle and horses before him. The dilettante of the formal and precious culture of Byzantium could beat the riders of the steppe. For a time he smashed the nomads and drove them back eastwards (battle of the Salnitsa, 1111). The same decades saw the Crusaders in Jerusalem; the reconquest of Western Asia Minor from the Seljuks; the repulse of the nomads from the Caucasian lands and the quick rise of the Georgian kingdom of David the Restorer.

Never before had the Altaians suffered such formidable checks over so wide a front.

Under Vladimir Monomakh the lands of Kiev, Chernigov and Pereyaslavl had respite from the Polovtsy; and he united them at the end of his life under his rule. His state resembled more a real military monarchy than had that of Yaroslav. (11)

In the fourth decade of the twelfth century, following the death of Mstislav, Vladimir's son, the feuds of rival princes revived and anarchy broke loose in the South Russian lands. A struggle for the possession of Kiev began not only between the Monomakhovichi and the Olgovichi (descendants of the adventurous Oleg of Chernigov, son of Svyatoslav II), but also between members of Monomakh's own family. The new order of succession to the throne had been established, but now the throne could be had also by force of arms. To take Kiev it was not now necessary to put forward legitimate or fantastic claims; it was only necessary to find 'allies' or mercenaries to attack it—Russians, Hungarians, Poles or Polovtsy.

The new order of succession had been established with the object of strengthening the unity of the Russian lands, but in practice it had brought about the weakening of that unity. Unity between Russian towns had been attained because that unity had been founded on trade and the use of common trading ways. But when the fluvial towns had acquired lands and these lands had become hereditary in certain princely families, unity gradually became an abstract idea which was frequently found to be in opposition to the practice of princely interests.

Towards the middle of the twelfth century, Novgorod, despairing of the establishment of a firm order in the south of Russia, becoming wary of the increasing uncertainties of 'the way to the Greeks' and doubtless well informed as to the perilous future of the Byzantine Empire, despite the magnificent Comnenian renascence, began to choose another direction for its trading activities. Bold and energetic pioneers, the Novgorodians, undertook explorations and settlements to the north and east—along the northern Dvina, the middle course of the Volga, the Kama and the Vyatka. They founded Nizhni-Novgorod, Vyatka, Perm—all these were originally Novgorodian colonies. In the west they developed intimate relations with the Hanseatic towns; they had lively intercourse with Lübeck, and succeeded in establishing their city as one of the *entrepôts* for German foreign trade of an importance equal to that of Bergen, Bruges and London.

By the second half of the twelfth century Novgorod surpassed Kiev in prosperity. During those decades no less than twenty fine churches were built and decorated with frescoes and icons—among them such a jewel of architecture as the cathedral of the Yuriev monastery. The famous little city of Pskov, called 'Novgorod's younger brother', was a product of this Western orientation. Both cities stubbornly adhered to 'the old order' and to southern tradition. Both cities answered the monarchical innovations of the Mono-makhovichi by frankly going over to the forms of state of merchant republics. 'The Lord Master City of Novgorod' limited the right of its prince, and he was not even allowed to dwell within the city walls. Without the sanction of the *Veche* the prince could not begin a war —'not to start wars without the sanction of Novgorod's word'; he could not independently appoint lieutenants (*posadniki*) in pro-vincial towns; he could not acquire lands either for himself or for his men; nor was he empowered to introduce any changes into the com-mercial agreements with the Germans. The Novgorod *Veche* in the year 1156 even refused to have bishops appointed by the Kievan Metropolitan—'the Metropolitan of all Russia'—but elected them itself. (12)

§ 8. THE END OF THE KIEVAN STATE

In the year 1169 the prince of the Vladimir-Suzdal territories, Andrew of Bogolyubovo, sent a big armed force to Kiev and took the town by storm and gave it over to his troops to plunder. The victors, ac-cording to the chronicler, 'did not show mercy to churches or women or children'. As a result of this victory Andrew of Bogolyubovo became Great Prince, but he did not choose Kiev as his residence. He returned to his beloved northern town of Vladimir.

Modern Ukrainian historians (Hrushevsky, Doroshenko and others) who wish to prove that differences existed between the south and the north of Russia at as early a date as possible and who oppose to 'Great-Russian Moscovia' the 'Ukrainian south of Russia' attach too great importance to this event. It really was an event of some importance, but not in the sense which Ukrainian historians attribute to it. 'This struggle showed the national antagonism existing be-tween Ukrainians and Great Russians,' writes Doroshenko. Accor-ding to Doroshenko, Andrew of Bogolyubovo from his youth 'did not want to live in the Ukraine because he hated the freedom-loving Ukrainian population'. Such interpretations of history can only be considered as strongly biased and founded on misunderstanding and as making no contribution to historical truth.

Russian historians have not been without responsibility for con-tributing to the Ukrainian view of the relation of Kiev to Vladimir-

Suzdal. For instance, in the opinion of Klyuchevski, Andrew of Bogolyubovo 'was a real northern prince, a true Suzdalian in his habits, notions and political education.... Andrew soon stood out among the crowd of contemporary southern princes in his character and in his political views.' In view of certain features of his activity and on account of some of his political views, it is possible to represent Andrew of Bogolyubovo as a sort of predecessor of the future Great Princes and Tsars of Moscow, but his characteristics can hardly be considered as typical 'northern' traits, nor is it anything but fantastic to speak of a 'Suzdal ideology' in contrast to a 'Kievan ideology'. Andrew, it is true, grew up in the north, but he was the son of Yuri Dolgoruki, one of the sons of Monomakh, and consequently was a real Monomakhovich. For a long time Yuri had been forced to govern the Suzdal lands (where by the way Vladimir Monomakh himself had sojourned) and under his rule those lands acquired a new importance. But all his life Yuri was striving to possess himself of Kiev, and he only became content when he attained the Kievan throne.

Before the time of Yuri population had been gradually migrating from the south to the north, and the civil war between Yuri and his nephew Izyaslav accelerated this tendency. Some of the migrating peasantry went along with the troops, and others left the Chernigov and Pereyaslavl territories on account of the feuds among the princes, always accompanied by Polovtsy raids fatal to the agricultural folk. An intensive colonization of Suzdal lands began; new towns were built, many of which received southern names (there were actually two new northern Pereyaslavls—the Pereyaslavl lands suffered most from Polovtsy raids and yielded the greatest number of migrants). On account of sentimental considerations southern names were given to northern rivers. It is curious that Ukrainian historians should wish to ignore the considerable proportions of this migration; but they appear to refuse to admit that among the inhabitants of the Russian north-east was a strong element from the Russian south.

When Yuri was fighting Izyaslav for the possession of Kiev he numbered among his allies certain southern princes, and troops recruited from southern lands shared in the sack of 'the mother of all Russian cities'. One of Yuri's allies was such a typical 'southern' prince as Vladimirko—the founder of the town of Halych and of the Halych (Galician) principality. Yuri married his daughter to the son of Vladimirko. Thus the Galician prince, Yaroslav Osmomysl, who played such a prominent part in his day in the politics of the extreme south-west, was married to Andrew of Bogolyubovo's own sister. Real friendship existed between these allied princely families, and

Andrew of Bogolyubovo, while he was sojourning in the south, during the life of his father, was a guest of the Galician court.

Notwithstanding their geographical orientations to north and to south, the Suzdal and Galician lands were united by similar conditions of development. Both the north-east and the south-west were being populated by labourers quitting the Chernigov and Pereyaslavl territories on account of the increasingly severe raids of the Polovtsy nomads. In the case of both principalities the importance of agriculture was growing; the possibilities of trade were declining owing to the fact that the centres of Slav power were being pushed away from the principal fluvial trade routes; the *Veche* was dying out, the commercial aristocracy was disappearing and a landed aristocracy was growing up in its stead.(13)

The Suzdal *boyars* killed Andrew of Bogolyubovo in the end (his body has recently been found with clear traces of their blows); and the Galician *boyars*, for their part, were responsible for many misfortunes which overtook the Halych principality. As for Andrew's political conceptions, they belonged neither to the north nor to the south; they were conceptions which sprang from his grandfather's family, who had not received by accident the name of Monomakh. They were Byzantine conceptions as understood in Kievan Russia following the disappearance of the Varangian way of life. Nor was it by accident that Andrew wanted the Metropolitan to reside in Vladimir on the Klyazma instead of in Kiev, for in accordance with Byzantine notions he required the presence and support of the highest hierarch.(14) Andrew fought against Kiev, not because Kiev was 'southern' but because it was a rebel city. Andrew also fought (very unsuccessfully) against the Novgorodian *Veche*, but it has not occurred to Ukrainian historians to include the Novgorodian territories among Ukrainian lands. Andrew of Bogolyubovo oppressed even the old trading towns of the Suzdal principality (Rostov, for instance) and preferred new towns to them—especially his own Vladimir.

During the reigns of Andrew and of his successors, the Vladimir-Suzdal towns were enriched by frescoes and icons and even sculptural bas-reliefs executed by the most talented Byzantine masters of the Comnenian renascence. But the intentions of this 'Byzantine on Russian soil' proved premature; he did not succeed in uniting the Russian lands; the processes of history did not depend upon his will. The ruinous Polovtsy raids were disintegrating the life of the south and, together with the feuds of the princes, led to a gradual desuetude of the great trade routes and to the downfall of Kiev. Under the pressure of the forces operating against it, the old Kiev-Novgorod 'meridial' connection was dying by the second half of the twelfth century. Those forces which operated in a 'latitudinal' direction were the wild force of the Polovtsy (the Altaian nomad pressure from the east), and the trading instinct of the Novgorodians which was turning away from the south towards the west and east. The more intelligent among the Russian princes were conscious of the tragic importance which the struggle with the Polovtsy had for the unity of the Russian lands. One of them put forward as an argument for a general campaign against the Polovtsy the consideration that 'now the pagans are getting hold even of our trading ways'.

It is significant also that the most celebrated epic of medieval Russia, 'The Tale of Igor's Host', is dedicated to an unfortunate campaign against the Polovtsy. It tells of the campaign undertaken by Igor, one of the princes of the Chernigov land, together with other princes in the year 1185. Written at the end of the twelfth century, it reflects the dominant conception of its epoch—the unity of Russian lands. This theme lends great pathos to the Tale. The unknown author urges all Russian princes to unite against the common enemy in the steppe—above all those who were most powerful at that time—Vsevolod of Vladimir-Suzdal, 'whose troops could drain the Volga with the splashes of their oars and make the Don run dry in their helmets', and Yaroslav Osmomysl, 'who with his iron troops can prop up the Ugor (Carpathian) Mountains' and 'who had closed the way to the Hungarian king and locked the gates of the Danube'. But 'Thou openest the gates of Kiev to the one whom thou art willing to let in there!'

In speaking of the duty of the Russian princes towards Russian lands, the author makes no distinction between the southern and northern princes. He knows the actual condition of affairs in Kiev. (Kiev was cruelly sacked a second time in the year 1203—on this occasion without the participation of 'northerners'.) But the Kievan idea, the all-Russian idea, remained strong at this period—twenty years before the disaster of the Mongol invasion.

A similar conception had not been alien to a Russian pilgrim of the middle of the twelfth century, the Igumen (Abbot) Daniel, who, having wandered from Chernigov to Jerusalem, petitioned King Baldwin that he might light a lamp at Our Lord's Sepulchre 'in the name of the whole Russian land, for all Russian princes and all Christians'.

'Everywhere talk of the Russian land and the Russian people mentioned nowhere,' comments Klyuchevski in considering the character of the ideal conception of the unity of the Russian land. Between the ninth and the twelfth centuries the Russian land had lived one common life in the measure prescribed by geographical and economic conditions. At the beginning of the thirteenth century these conditions ceased to operate in favour of this ideal unity based on the fluvial network and the 'meridial' link of 'the way from the Varangians to the Greeks'. And while the *internal* 'vital nerve', the line Novgorod–Kiev, was weakened, the *external* 'vital centre', which had always magnetized and tended to consolidate the life of fluvial Russia, was overwhelmed by disaster. In the year 1204 the Latins took and plundered Constantinople. The establishment of a Franco-Norman dynasty in Byzantium, ephemeral as it proved, marked a further stage in the disintegration of the East Christian world. Turks and Mongols, French, Catalans, Venetians, Genoese, fought for the spoils of a civilization which was stricken to death.

In the anarchic conditions of the Ponto-Anatolian area the principal export market for the trade of the Russian fluvial towns had disappeared. The Russian princes and the Russian Church had lost the support of 'the Second Rome'. The whole cultural basis of Orthodox Russia as a projection of the East Christian world had been removed. New orientations became inevitable.

The thirteenth century, the brilliant era of the medieval West, was for the Russians the time of their greatest historical catastrophe. About the year 1220 a new ·thrust of the Altaian nomads began. Under the leadership of Chingiz Khan, the Mongols destroyed the Turko-Iranian Empire of the Seljuks in Turkestan; ravaged Iran; overthrew in one battle the then powerful kingdom of Georgia; and, riding along the sandy foreshore of the Caspian, appeared in the steppe to the north of the Caucasus Mountains.

Spengler has emphasized the essential unity of the Byzantine and Irano-Islamic civilizations. The Seljuk Turks and the Norman Latins, in the eleventh and twelfth centuries, had disrupted the civil life of all the western half of the great cultural area which stretched from the Adriatic to the Indian Ocean. In that phase the Seljuks had struck the first blows, and then the Crusaders had come in from the Western Mediterranean and from over the Danube. In the second phase it had been the Norman Latins who had cast down Byzantium; the great ride of the Mongols into the West followed within three decades. Upon that strange civilization which had its roots in the most ancient lands of cultivated living the outer world swarmed in— 'the external proletariat' of Toynbee's brilliant thesis. Broadly, over a period of four centuries, it had been two groups of specialized destroyers who had blindly broken down this ancient civilization to make way for some new one; these two groups were the Vikings (specialized sea-raiders, whose successors, the Normans, acquired also a 'land' technique) and the Altaians (specialized land-raiding cavalry-men, who never managed to acquire an aptitude for sea-fighting). The stunted remnants of the great Byzantine-Islamic world are to be found to-day in the secondary 'folk states' of the Balkans and the Middle East.

The Russian half of the East Christian world succumbed as its counterpart, the Scytho-Pontic city-states, had succumbed with the collapse of the Hellenistic civilization.

When the Mongols appeared north of the Caucasus, the Polovtsy sent to seek aid of the Russian princes, and the forces of several allied princes were gathered to meet this new enemy. They went along the old trading way which led to the Azov Sea and linked Kiev with Tmutarakan. The horsemen rode along the banks of the Dniepr and the foot-soldiers followed down the river in boats. The Galician levies took the route of the Dniestr as far as the sea and then went up the Dniepr. The united Russian forces moved across the steppe, following the left affluents of the Dniepr, which brought them to the vicinity of the river Kalka, now called the Kalmius, which falls into the Azov Sea. In the battle which took place on the banks of that river the Russians suffered an awful defeat in the year 1223.

The significance of this event, however, was lost; the Mongols 'who had seemingly come from nowhere disappeared again in the same way into space'. The Mongols had, in fact, retired behind the Volga, and it was only some years after the death of Chingiz (in 1227) that they decided to renew their movement westward. In the year 1236 Batu plundered the lands of the Kama Bulgarians, and in the following year his hordes appeared in the Ryazan lands. Ryazan was taken and its population almost exterminated. The same fate befell all the north-eastern towns. Yuri, the Great Prince who at that time ruled in Vladimir, was defeated and himself killed in the battle on the river Sit. Owing to heavy snows and the overflow of rivers, Batu was unable to reach Novgorod and Pskov, Smolensk and Polotsk. He turned south and sacked Pereyaslavl, Chernigov and other towns. In the year 1240 came the turn of Kiev, which was at that time governed by a certain *boyar*, Dmitri, in the name of a Galician prince. Kiev was almost totally destroyed and for some time forsaken by the few of its inhabitants who had remained alive. The Mongols moved westward; they ravaged Volhynia, Galicia, Poland and Hungary. They were checked only in Silesia, at Liegnitz, by the prowess of German, Czech and Polish knights.

The Russian state which had been formed in the eleventh and twelfth centuries had ceased to exist. 'From that time onward the Russian land became a Tatar *ulus*' (Shmurlo). The Kipchak power, a combination of Mongol and earlier Polovtsy elements, was established behind the Volga and on the old ground of the Khazars.

The date of the destruction of Kiev by the Mongols can be considered as the date marking the end of the period when 'meridial' forces linked the north and south of Russia together. In the thirteenth century the pressure from the east had become incomparably greater than it had been during the eleventh and twelfth centuries; it had overwhelmed the Russia of the fluvial states. A reaction against the pressure from the east was coming and it came, naturally, from the west. But the western forces, as those from the east, acted in a 'latitudinal' direction and tended to be destructive of any renewal of 'meridial' development. (15)

BIBLIOGRAPHICAL NOTES TO CHAPTER I

(1) *On the Colonial Period in South Russia*

Minns, E. H. *Scythians and Greeks in South Russia*, Cambridge, 1913.
Ebert, M. *Südrussland in Altertum*, Bonn/Leipzig, 1924.
Rostovtsev, M. I. *Iranians and Greeks in South Russia*, Oxford, 1932.

(2) *On the Altaian Nomads*

Peisker, T. *Cambridge Medieval History (C.M.H.)*, vol. I, chap. XII, 'The Asiatic Background' (see also Bibliography).

(3) *On the Origin of the Eastern Slavs*

Peisker, T. *C.M.H.*, vol. II, chap. XIV, 'The Expansion of the Slavs' (see also Bibliography).
Shakhmatov, A. *Drevneyshiya Sudby Russkago Plemeni* (The Earlier Fates of the Russian People), Petrograd, 1919.
Niederle, L. *Manuel de l'Antiquité Slave*, Paris, 1923.
Vasmer, M. *Die Urheimat der Slaven*, Breslau, 1925.
Odinets, D. *Vozniknovenie Gosudarstvennago Stroya u Vostochnykh Slavyan* (The Rise of a State Structure among the Eastern Slavs), Paris, 1935.

(4) *On the Khazars*

Article 'Khazars' in *Encyclopaedia of Islam (E.I.)*.
C.M.H., vol. IV, chap. VII (A), Bibliography.
Grégoire, H. *Byzantion*, XII (1937), p. 225, 'Le "Glozel" Khazare'.

(5) *On the Varangians and on the Fluvial Trade Routes*

Mawer, A. *C.M.H.*, vol. III, chap. XIII, *The Vikings* (see also Bibliography).
Kendrick, T. D. *A History of the Vikings*, London, 1930 (see particularly chap. VII).
Arne, T. J. *La Suède et l'Orient*, Upsala, 1914.

Moshin, V. 'Nachalo Rusi: Normanny v Vostochnoy Evrope' (The Beginning of Russia: the Northmen in Eastern Europe), *Byzantino-Slavica*, Praha, 1931–2.
Smirnov, P. *Volzhski Put' v Starodavney Rusi* (The Volga Waterway in Ancient Russia), Kiev, 1928.

(6) On the term 'Rus' in Western sources

In the St Bertin Annals of the year 839 Bishop Prudentius writes about certain men who accompanied the envoys of the Emperor Theophilus on an embassy to the Emperor Louis the Pious: 'qui se, id est gentem suam, Rhos vocari dicebant, quos rex illorum, Chacanus vocabulo, ad se amicitiae, sicut asserebant, causa direxerat.' When the Emperor Louis began to ask who they were, he gathered from their answers that they were Swedes: 'comperit eos gentis esse Sueonum.' *M.G.H.* i, p. 434.

Luitprand of Cremona, about the year 970, writes: 'Rusios, quos alio nomine Nordmannos appellamus.'

In Arab sources

Numerous Arab writers mention 'Rus' or the 'King of Rus' or the Rus 'Kagan' (e.g. Ibn Rusta and Gardizi). The latter: 'Many men among the Slavs go over to the Rus and serve them in order to be under their protection.'

See A. Harkavy, *Skazaniya Musulmanskikh Pisateley o Rossii* (Statements of Moslem writers concerning Russia), Petersburg, 1870.
Minorsky, V. F. *Ḥudūd al-'Ālam*, London, 1937, pp. 427–438.
Cf. also S. Rapoport, 'Mohammedan Writers on the Slavs and Russians', in *Slavonic Review*, vol. viii, no. 22.

(7) On Kievan Russia

Courses of Russian history by V. Klyuchevski, Moscow, 1923; S. Platonov, Petersburg, 1917; M. Lyubavski, Moscow, 1913; E. Schmurlo, Praha, 1931; also M. Hrushevsky, *History of Ukraina*, Kiev, 1913 (Ukr.); D. Doroshenko, *Outline of the History of Ukraina*, Warsaw, 1932 (Ukr.).

(8) On the Nomads and Kiev

Golubovski, P. *Pechenegi, Torki, Polovtsy do Nashestviya Tatar* (Pechenegs, Turks and Polovtsy before the Tartar Invasion), Kiev, 1884.
Bruce-Boswell, A. 'The Kipchaks', in *Slavonic Review*, vol. vii, no. 16.
Macartney, C. A. 'The Petchenegs', in *ibid.* vol. viii, no. 23.

For an understanding of the role of the Altaian nomads in medieval Russia it is essential to read Boswell's brilliant study. 'The Arabs and the Georgians alone called the Kipchaks by their proper name. It appears in Western sources for the first time in Edrisi, who refers to the original Kipchak in Asia, after a detailed description of Comania. While the Greeks called the Kipchaks "Comans" the Saxons of Transylvania called them Valvi, or Falben, i.e. "sallow people". The Russians called them Pólovtsy, which some philologists derive from *polóvy* (*pálevy*), "sallow", but which is generally taken to mean "steppe folk" from *póle*, "field", i.e. it is a translation of the Turkish "Kipchak". (These Kipchaks should be distinguished from the Golden Horde, v, p. 42.)

'The main facts of Cuman history are quite clear, and their importance is undeniable. It is difficult to conceive of a successful Mongol penetration of Central Europe, if a great part of Eastern Europe had not been peopled by a Turkish folk not undisposed to welcome distinguished invaders with similar Turanian traditions of nomadic life, of rapacity and of unity under a despot.

'Kiev, Pereyaslavl and Chernigov lay near the southern frontier and were permanently exposed to the incursions of the crafty Turks. For their periodic migrations north and south they found the rich pastures of the Ozu, as they called the Dniepr, most congenial; and on the rich grasslands up the river, they found the Russians firmly established and beginning to practise agriculture. The eternal struggle of settled and pastoral folk was long and obstinate in this region, and the Kipchaks came to regard the capital of this coveted territory, Menkerman, "the great city" (as they called Kiev) as the centre of their world.'

After the victories of Vladimir Monomakh, according to Boswell, large numbers of the nomads left the steppe and transferred their allegiance to the Russian princes. They settled in parts of Chernigov and all over the lands of Pereyaslavl. 'In the usual Turkish fashion these petty tribes soon became merged in a new federation of Turks, who took the name of Karakalpaks or Blackcaps.'

'They even became an important factor in Russian political life; and we find the election of a prince carried out not only by Russians, but "by the Russian land and the Blackcaps". It is a matter for debate whether the exodus of Russian peasants to the north-east was not due to the peaceful penetration of these barbarians, as much as to the external pressure of the Kipchaks. In the bitter civil strife of the twelfth century, a Russian prince found these mobile horsemen more valuable subjects than the peaceful Russian peasants. The changed conditions on the frontier stand out sharply when we find a Blackcap Khan like Kuntuvdey invested with a Russian appanage on the River Ros. Finally at the time of the Mongol invasion we hear of a shadowy Izyaslav of Chernigov who is purely a Turkish chieftain. The process was inevitable, and no one can doubt that the weakening of the Russian element in the south was an accomplished fact before the Mongol conquest.... Apart from ancient cities like Tmutarakan, Oleshye, Cherson and Caffa, which were for a time Slav, and became Greek and then Genoese, we see the rise of a mixed population in the steppes, like the Cossacks of later times. The princes of Berlad and Bolkhov and the Brodniki of the Upper Don and of Moldavia represent semi-Slav communities with an admixture of Turk, Roumanian and other nationalities.'

The latest work is by D. A. Rasovski, *Seminarium Kondakovianum*, vols. VII–XI, 1935–40, 'Polovtsy'.

(9) On the Russian Chronicles

Shakhmatov, A. *Rozyskaniya o Drevneyshikh Russkikh Letopisnykh Svodakh* (Researches concerning the oldest Russian Corpuses of Chronicles). Also his critical edition of 'The Record of Passing Years', Petersburg, 1916.

Chronicles existed in Russia at a very early date. The most ancient Kievan Corpus dates from 1039, and the Novgorod Chronicle from 1017; the oldest Polish Chronicle from the end of the eleventh century, and the oldest Hungarian ones from the thirteenth century. The most ancient Russian Chronicles are only known in copies of a later period; the Lavrentiev copy of 1377, and the Ipatiev of the first quarter of the fifteenth century. In the Ipatiev copy the chronicle of events in South Russia is continued until 1292.

(10) On the Right of the Princes

Presnyakov, A. *Knyazhee Pravo v Drevney Rusi* (The Prince's Right in Ancient Russia), Petersburg, 1909.

The chief Prince, whether of Kiev or later of Moscow or Lithuania, is often called in the west 'Grand Duke', but 'Great Prince' best renders his title of *Veliki Knyaz'*, *Wielki Książę*.

(11) On Byzantium and the Kievan State

Schlumberger, G. *Nicéphore Phocas*, Paris, 1890; *L'Épopée Byzantine*, Paris, 1896–1905.

Vasiliev, A. *History of the Byzantine Empire*, vol. I, University of Wisconsin, 1928.

Leib. *Rome, Kiev et Byzance à la Fin du XI Siècle*, Paris, 1934.

(12) On Novgorod and Pskov

Kostomarov, M. *Severno-Russkiya Narodopravstva* (The North Russian Republics), Petersburg, 1886.

Nikitski, A. *Istoriya Khozyaystvennoy Zhizni Velikago Novgoroda* (History of the Economic Life of Great Novgorod), Warsaw, 1883.

(13) On the Rise of the Principality of Vladimir-Suzdal

In addition to the standard Russian histories mentioned above see:

Lyubavski, M. *Obrazovanie Osnovnoy Gosudarstvennoy Territorii Veliko-russkoy Narodnosti* (The Formation of the Original State Territory of the Great Russian People), Leningrad, 1929.

Presnyakov, *Obrazovanie Velikorusskago Gosudarstva* (Formation of the Great Russian State), Moscow, 1923.

(14) On the Relations between Church and State in Medieval Russia

Goetz, L. *Staat und Kirche in Altrussland (988–1240)*, Berlin, 1928.

(15) On the Mongol Invasion

The Mongol Invasion was described by a contemporary under the title of 'The Tale of the Ruin of the Russian Land'. Unfortunately only a small fragment has been preserved. It is in the spirit of 'The Tale of Igor's Host'.

For a recent summary, see H. T. Cheshire, 'The Great Tartar Invasion of Europe', in *Slavonic Review*, vol. v, no. 13.

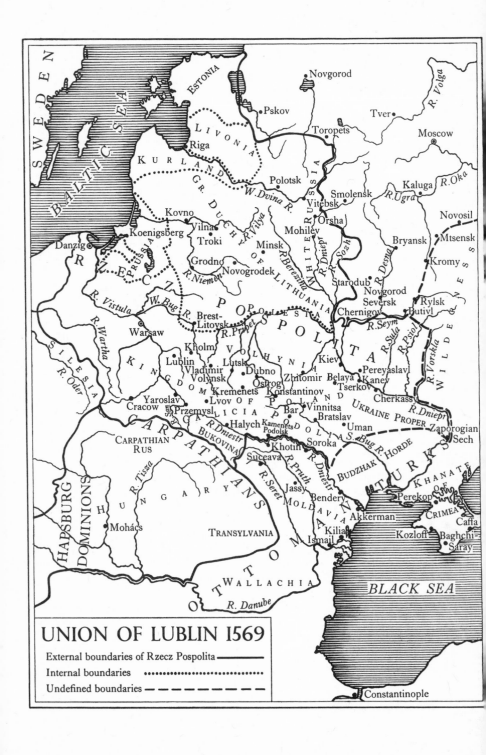

UNION OF LUBLIN 1569

External boundaries of Rzecz Pospolita ——————
Internal boundaries •••••••••••••••••
Undefined boundaries — — — — — —

THE RUSSO-LITHUANIAN STATE AND THE ORIGINS OF THE UKRAINIAN QUESTION (1240–1569)

§1. EASTERN EUROPE AFTER THE MONGOL INVASIONS

THE Mongol invasions of the thirteenth century produced a revolution in human affairs comparable to the changes occasioned by the rise of Islam and the expansion of the Arabs in the seventh century. But whereas the impact of the Arabs on the ancient civil life of Western Asia renewed the forces which sustained civilization in those lands and assured to those forces a continuing primacy in the affairs of the contemporary world, the Mongol *buran* razed all before it.

The beginnings of the supremacy of Western Europe in world history may be traced to the destruction wrought in Western Asia and in Eastern Europe by the last great ride of the Altaian nomads. In spite of the terror aroused in the West by the campaigns of Batu, the leaders of Christendom were conscious of the opportunities which lay before them when Islam had been stricken and the East Christian world disrupted.

Diplomatic embassies from the Western courts, co-operating with long-sighted Latin-Armenian rulers like Hayton, sought the alliance of the Mongols against the last stronghold of Islamic power in Egypt. The Venetians and the Genoese, always hungry rivals, quickly established a succession to the Greeks in the Black Sea countries conquered by the Mongols, and the ancient *entrepôts* of Russo-Byzantine trade at the mouths of the Dniestr, the Dniepr and the Don became the headquarters of the trading concerns of the Italian cities. The meridial 'way from the Varangians to the Greeks' had disappeared, but new explorations such as those of the Polos showed the way for a latitudinal economic development which by use of the excellent system of communications established by the Mongols was to let trade through from 'Cambalu' to the Bosporus.

The Papacy was not slow to supplement the commercial activities of the Italian trading cities. The effort to convert the Mongol ruling class to the Christian faith failed in the end, and in their decadence the heirs of Chingiz became the protectors of that Islam which they had broken down and patrons of a brilliant period of Muslim painting which suddenly blossomed like a flower in the ruins of a world.

But, as the executor of East Christendom, the Papacy enjoyed a greater degree of success. While the Bank of St George in Genoa set up an *Officium Ghazariae* (a 'Khazar Office' combining the functions of an East India Company and an India Office) to monopolize the Black Sea trade, the Pope created an archiepiscopal see of Caffa to comprise the whole area between Varna in Bulgaria and Saray on the Volga, and bishoprics in Sukhum (where an early incumbent was an Englishman) and Tiflis for the purpose of bringing the enfeebled Georgians within the Roman fold.

Over the vast expanse of country between the Baltic and the Black Sea the influence of the Latin West began to expand into the areas devastated by the Mongol invasions. In the plains and forests watered by the great streams of the Vistula and the Niemen, the Slav tribes had during the eleventh century been consolidated by the Piast, Boleslaw I, into the loose federation of principalities which made up the kingdom of Poland. In Poland, with her rivers flowing to the Baltic, as in the fluvial Kievan state, the Scandinavian warrior traders had played a certain role, while the Germanic-Latin influence in early Polish history is comparable to the Byzantine-East Christian influence in the development of Kiev.

But the German-Latin influence was much stronger. The Byzantine influence was commercial and cultural; it represented the percolation of a sophisticated and biologically sterile civilization. The German contact with the Slavs was that of frontiersmen; of a young and vigorous people, themselves only newly emergent from barbarism. It was the movement of a people bearing with them some culture; there was no Byzantine trickle of those refined and desiccated dogmas which were to influence Muscovite thought so strongly for centuries after Byzantium had fallen. The Germans sought land and settlement, and their intent was to build a German order. They were more dangerous than the Greeks, who essayed only to augment the wealth of their world city.

In the eleventh century Poland, like Southern Russia, was passing through one of those phases of anarchy which were typical of a certain stage of development in all medieval societies; the unity built by Boleslaw I had proved too new to continue. At the same time social unrest in Germany was fermenting and sending the peasantry eastward into new lands. Parallel with this popular migration, the crusading imperialism of rulers like Albert the Bear and Henry the Lion was carving the German Eastern Marks out of the Slav lands between the Elbe and the Vistula. The pagan Slavs and Balts resisted with an obstinacy and ferocity which was only equalled by the pertinacity and ruthlessness of the invading Germans. Out of those several centuries of obscure conflict was hammered that peculiar quality of hardness which characterizes the modern north German.

The Slavs of the Vistula had produced their reaction to German pressure in the foundation of the Polish state. At the beginning of the thirteenth century the more primitive Baltic tribes, harried and harassed by the Germans, reacted in a similar way. The wild Lithuanian tribes in the forests along the Niemen, the last and most determined pagans in Europe, founded a state which was to become a strange and indeed unique phenomenon in the history of Eastern Europe in the following three centuries. During the same period the German knightly orders, Teutonic and Livonian—modelled on the Western orders of chivalry—established themselves on the Baltic seaboard in order to pursue the pagans into their most remote fastnesses. Supported by Emperor and Pope, the rough knights were carrying the German power and Latin Christianity into the illimitable forests of the north Eurasian Plain.

It was at this juncture that the Mongols overthrew the Russian principalities and ravished the lands of Orthodox Christianity which had looked towards Byzantium—itself recently fallen into Latin hands. The Mongol devastations were continued into Poland, and the Polish kingdom, the last important organized Slav state, suffered a depopulation hardly less severe than that which had overtaken the Russian lands.

'The chief result of this wholesale depopulation was an enormous influx of Germans. It appeared as if the Poles would disappear between the grinding pressure of the Germans both in the west and in the north, and the sporadic but ruinous raids of the Lithuanians and the Asiatic nomads in the east' (Boswell, *Poland*).

The Poles were placed in somewhat the same relation to the Germans as were the surviving Russian principalities between the Oka and the upper Volga to the Mongol-Tartar Golden Horde established in the vast region of Kipchak stretching between the Dniepr, the Urals and the Caucasus. The marked differentiation between the Poles and the Eastern Slavs dates from this epoch. For the Poles not only survived the impact of the Germans but absorbed much of the Germanic-Latin culture of medieval Christendom with no small proportion of German blood, while the Muscovite state which rose with the decline of the Golden Horde was built by a people impregnated with Altaian blood and oppressed by Asiatic conceptions of life.

'The Germans did succeed in absorbing Lower Silesia, but in Poland itself they were gradually assimilated by the Poles. These German peasants introduced higher methods of agriculture, and made definite contracts with the landowners, who allowed them a measure of local autonomy. The Polish peasants profited by the scarcity of labour to imitate them, and a period of prosperity and liberty ensued for the peasants. The Germans also poured into the towns, where they received autonomy under Magdeburg law, which remained in force for centuries. They formed a middle class whose prosperity depended on the Eastern trade through Cracow.... The Germans, in fact, failed to colonize any part of Poland except Lower Silesia; but the Teutonic Order made great advances on the Baltic seaboard, and by 1283 the Prussians were practically exterminated by the Germans, who took their name and formed a state which cut Poland off from the sea' (Boswell, *Poland*).

The first decade of the fourteenth century saw the revival of the Polish kingdom under Vladislav* the Short (Łokietek); and his son, Casimir the Great, made Poland a power in Eastern Europe. 'The great historical events of the reign were the renunciation of all Polish claims to Pomerania and Silesia in 1335, and the annexation of Galicia in 1340. This is one of the turning-points in Polish history. She now definitely retreated before German aggression to an inner line, which the subsequent disorganization of the Empire enabled her to hold till the rise of Prussia in the eighteenth century; and she embarked on a policy which diverted Polish expansion to the south-east, brought under her sway the bulk of the Ruthenian or Little Russian people, and opened the way to contact with Moscow, Turkey and the Crimean Tartars' (Boswell, *Poland*).

Two centuries were to pass before the North Russian princes between the Oka and the upper Volga were to emerge as the successors of the Kipchak-Tartar power which had been established on the Volga as a result of the Mongol invasions. The significance of the Kipchak state of the Golden Horde in the thirteenth and fourteenth centuries has been strangely ignored by historians. Founded by Beréké, the son of Batu, it was the most northerly of the succession states which arose out of the Empire of Chingiz. It represented in fact a revival of the ancient Khazar kingdom, and its people, like the Khazars, were an amalgam of the races of the steppe—among which the Turkish Kipchak stock was the dominant factor. Already in 1261

* Vladislav: this name is now spelt in Polish Władysław, appears in Russian as Vladislav, Latin and German usually Ladislaus, French Ladislas, Hungarian László. Vladislav seems the convenient form. So Casimir for Polish Kazimierz.

Beréké was challenging the supremacy of the Western Mongols, whose state comprised the Iranian and Anatolian dominions of the Il-khans. The close relations of the Kipchaks with the Egyptian Mamluks, whose force was largely recruited by slaves from the Kipchak steppe and from the Circassian tribes of the western Caucasus (Sultan Baybars was a Kipchak), allowed the Khans of the Golden Horde to play an influential part in the politics of the Near and Middle East. A combination of the Golden Horde with the Mamluks always threatened the hegemony of the Il-khans in Western Asia, and while the feeble Crusading states in the Levant with the Armenian kingdom generally leaned for support against Egypt on the Iranian Mongols, the weakened Georgian kingdom, still controlling the Caucasian passes, began to recover place as her kings could play for favour between the Il-khans and the Horde.

Tamerlane was at once the last great Altaian conqueror and the destroyer of the supremacy of his own race in Eastern Europe and Western Asia. He revived the power of the Iranian Mongols and used it to struggle for mastery over the Osmanli Turks in Asia Minor and over the Golden Horde in the northern steppe. In the last decade of the fourteenth century his great campaigns against Tokhtamish effectively broke the nomad state north of the Black Sea. A century and a half later Ivan IV took Kazan, and the Altaian dominion on the Volga was at an end for ever. Tamerlane broke also the strength of the young Osmanli state in his famous victory over Bayazid at Ankara. It is a curious historical paradox that while the Eastern Slavs—first the Poles and later the Muscovites—became the beneficiaries of the ruin of the Golden Horde, the Hungarian and Slav kingdoms in South-Eastern Europe failed to profit from the catastrophe of Bayazid. The explanation is that the Osmanli state was itself partly Slav and partly Greek in its composition, and that the Osmanli, when Tamerlane attacked them, were building that earliest centralized Renaissance state which was to dominate the politics of South-Eastern Europe and the Mediterranean during the following century. The young state had within it the élan vital of its age, and it had the strength to survive the disaster at Ankara. But in the Golden Horde Tamerlane dissipated the final projection of a type of community which in essentials belonged to a remote Scythian and Khazar past.

Thus, while the Poles were to recover from the effects of the Mongol invasions a century before the Russian principalities and were to prove to have gained a decisive advantage in the race for control in the wide 'no man's lands' which stretched to the south of both, the Balkan Slavs were to remain for five hundred years in durance as the prisoners of that curious synthesis of Byzantine-Saracenic forms and Turkish nomad's force, Slavonic manpower and Levantine competence which was the Ottoman Empire.

§2. THE WEST RUSSIAN STATE IN GALICIA

Plano Carpini, emissary of Pope Innocent IV to the Great Khan at Karakorum, passed through the South Russian lands six years after the sack of Kiev by the Mongols. He saw everywhere traces of fire and mounds of human bones and skulls. In Kiev, in the shadow of the charred walls of St Sophia, he found only two hundred houses standing. Such had been the fate of one of the most populous cities of medieval Europe—at the beginning of the twelfth century Kiev had contained about 100,000 inhabitants. Chernigov, Pereyaslavl and Vladimir-Volynsk had been burned to the ground, and they never really recovered from the catastrophe which had overtaken them. Half the people of Pereyaslavl had been slaughtered and the other half had been led away into captivity. 'In Vladimir-Volynsk not a soul remained alive and the churches were filled with corpses' (Shmurlo). In fact the whole of the Russian population to the east of the Dniepr either had been butchered or had fled into the forests along the upper Desna and the Sozh. The inhabitants of the lands of Kiev and Volhynia had taken refuge in the forests along the affluents of the Pripet and in the swamps of Polesia.

To the end of the thirteenth century and even into the middle of the fourteenth these fertile lands of the south of Russia continued desert. The invasion of Batu was only the first and most devastating of many Tartar raids across the open lands between the rivers. The resistance which Daniel of Galicia opposed to the Golden Horde provoked ferocious Tartar incursions in the years 1259–61. In the year 1285 Telebuga Khan passed twice across the southern steppe in the course of his attack upon Poland, and, in the words of a contemporary chronicler, he 'swept clean the whole of the Vladimir-Volynsk lands'. In the second half of the thirteenth century there were no princes in Kiev—even as nominees of the Horde. Some stray folk began to settle in the city, but the recurrent Tartar raids forced the Kievan Metropolitan Maxim—still 'Metropolitan of all Russia' —to quit the south and establish himself with his retinue and belongings in the north at Vladimir on the Klyazma. According to the chronicler: 'Then the whole of Kiev ran away.'

Conditions in the south were more difficult than in the north. The favourite pasturages of the Horde were along the lower Volga and between the Volga and the Don. The nomads wandered along the shores of the Azov Sea and in the winter frequented the coasts of the Crimea. Lesser bands of nomads were scattered all over the steppe—the remainder of the Polovtsy, Torks and Karakalpaks who had been disturbed by the tempest of Batu's invasion. The way to the west, to the Dniestr and the Danube lands, lay open to these plunderers as to the horse of the Golden Horde. In the north, after the first onslaught, the Khans in Saray contented themselves with levying tribute on the settled populations. The long winters, the overflow of rivers in the spring, the forests and the swamps did not make the northern lands attractive to the nomads. For over a hundred years the northern princes did not attempt to contest the overlordship of the Horde, and the princes of Moscow by careful and subservient policy avoided Tartar incursions upon their lands during the nine decades between 1293 and 1381.

In the West Russian lands bordering on the old South, groups of nomads made attempts to effect permanent settlements throughout the latter part of the thirteenth century. The princes of Galicia sustained a struggle with the inhabitants of the so-called 'Bolkhov land' to the north-east of Volhynia; these were part uprooted labourers and part remnants of steppeland tribes mixed with Tartars. A similar half-nomad, half-settled population appeared in the 'new land' of Podolia, which till that time had been relatively thinly inhabited.(1)

The Galician Prince Daniel failed in the end in his struggle with the Tartars. With the decay of the Kievan state, Galicia, under the Princes Roman and Daniel, had gradually become the focus of South and West Russian life. A brief florescence of the Galician principality had been interrupted by the Mongol invasion, and Daniel had been forced to recognize the supremacy of the Golden Horde. The same necessity had overtaken Alexander Nevski in the north. Both princes found that they had to contend not only against nomad incursions from the east but also against continuous pressure from the west. Against the pressure from the west Alexander Nevski was victorious; he held Novgorod and Pskov against the Swedes and the Livonian Order. He had laid the foundations of a future Russian recovery towards the Baltic. But Daniel of Galicia had no possibility of consolidating the existing order of things. That is why, though both princes died about the same time, Daniel belongs to the past; he closed 'the pre-Mongol period' in the south, while with Alexander Nevski began a new epoch in the north.

The achievements of the Galician prince were quite ephemeral. After his death (1264), the Galician principality, that 'last remnant of South Russia', began to sustain the weight of the growing power of the Polish and Hungarian kingdoms. There was a brief period of prosperity under Daniel's son, Leo. The towns built and adorned by Daniel, Kholm and Lvov (i.e. 'the town of Lev or Leo'), with their large colonies of Jews and Armenians, attained a considerable prosperity, for they were on the trade route from Regensburg to Byzantium, and some of the traffic which had previously passed down the Dniepr to the Black Sea now went down the Dniestr. The revival of the Pontic trade by the Genoese and the Venetians during the period of Mongol hegemony gave an additional importance to the Galician towns which were placed on the line of the new latitudinal trade route from west to east.

But towards the middle of the fourteenth century the position of the Galician principality became critical. Poland was ruled by the most able of the Piasts, Casimir the Great; in Hungary the new Angevin dynasty was gaining strength; Gedymin was building the Lithuanian power. Conditions in the Galician principality made it easy for powerful neighbours to influence its fate. The Galician princes had never been successful in mastering their unruly *boyars*. Roman, the father of Daniel, had justified the execution of a number of them by the words: 'If one does not kill bees one will not be able to take honey.' But the bees were always swarming angrily round the heads of the Galician rulers. Different groups of *boyars* for varying reasons fell under the influence of neighbouring monarchs, and the foreign enemy found allies in the land itself. In the year 1323 the dynasty of Daniel became extinct, and rule passed to a Polish prince, Boleslaw of Mazovia, who proceeded to adopt the Orthodox faith and to change his name to Yuri. In his time the *boyars* became so powerful that he had to sign state documents not only in his own name, but in that of his entire baronage—*nos una cum dilectis et fidelibus nostris baronibus militibusque*. His amiability did not prevent the *boyars* from poisoning him in 1340. Nine years later Casimir annexed the Galician principality to the kingdom of Poland. At the same time Volhynia passed to the Great Prince of Lithuania.

The north-eastern Carpathians, which form the watershed between the affluents of the Dniestr and the Tisza and divide the South Russian steppe from the Hungarian plain, had been peopled by a steady influx of fugitives from the Kievan lands. Leo of Galicia had taken advantage of the disorders in Hungary which followed the death of Ladislas the Cuman and the extinction of the Árpád dynasty, to occupy this country of 'Carpathian Rus' which depended on the Hungarian county of Munkács. With the extinction of the principality of Galicia, the Russian inhabitants of the high Alpine valleys of Carpathian Rus became the subjects of the Hungarian kings. (2, 3, 4)

Thus the last centres of independent political life in South and

West Russia were extinguished by the middle of the fourteenth century. The Galician princes had proved incapable of establishing a new focus for the revival of Russian political life after the catastrophe of the Mongol invasions. The Altaian Kipchak state still dominated the middle and southern reaches of all the great South Russian rivers which flow to the Black Sea. The Polish kings were looking towards the south-east to find compensation for the steady Germanic advance in the west and north-west. The strange Lithuanian monarchy was looming as a new power in the West Russian lands. Only in the north the commercial oligarchies of Novgorod and Pskov survived, and the leaders in those cities, fearful like the Poles of the military power of the Germanic knights and of the Swedes, were attempting to find new sources of strength by expansion into the empty vastness of the north-east. And in the Moscow lands between the Oka and the upper Volga, a house of astute and patient princes, careful vassals of the Golden Horde, were laying their hands year by year on petty territories—and biding their time.

§3. THE RISE OF LITHUANIA

Already in the first decades of the thirteenth century, the Lithuanian tribes inhabiting the forests between the lower Vistula, the Niemen and the western Dvina, had formed a primitive military state. The German pressure, particularly on the kindred Prussians, caused the Lithuanians to move south-eastward. The Lithuanian Prince Mendovg began by conquering the outermost Russian lands, the so-called 'Black Russia', the borders of which extended to the banks of the upper Niemen. The towns of Black Russia, Grodno and Novogrodek, became the first civil centres of the Lithuanian principality. Mendovg then proceeded to take possession of the Polotsk lands, and tried, unsuccessfully, to possess himself of Smolensk.

Daniel of Galicia, uneasy at the new Lithuanian danger, concerted an alliance with the Poles and the Teutonic knights against Mendovg, but the latter showed himself to be possessed of that astute sense of diplomacy which was to characterize his successors. Like the Habsburgs, the Lithuanian house was to develop the matrimonial tactic in politics to the highest degree. Mendovg conciliated the coalition against him by a personal adoption of the Christian faith (which he forsook later for his native paganism); he married his daughter to a son of Daniel, and to another son granted the Black Russian districts.

Under the great Gedymin, the Lithuanian territory was further expanded by matrimonial alliances. The peaceful acquisition of

Volhynia was secured at the time of the disintegration of the Galician principality as the result of the marriage of one of Gedymin's sons with a Volhynian princess; by the same process the Vitebsk lands were brought within the Lithuanian realm. The Minsk and Pinsk territories also fell into Lithuanian hands through the diplomacy of Gedymin. When he died in 1341 the Lithuanian state was already of considerable dimensions; and of its population about two-thirds were of Russian stock.

The extension of Lithuanian territory to the south made a conflict between Gedymin's heir, Olgerd, and the Tartars inevitable. And the struggle with the Tartars caused a further rapid growth of Lithuanian power, for the prestige of Olgerd attracted to his allegiance wide areas where the Russian population had hitherto been hypnotized by the legend of the invincibility of the Altaian hordes. The terrible memories of the great Mongol invasion of the middle of the thirteenth century seem to have grown dim in the minds of the generation which was living a hundred years later. In spite of the terror of recurrent raids, the Tartars no longer seemed irresistible, and the idea of an armed struggle with them passed out of the domain of dreams into the realm of reality at about the same time in both the Eastern and Western Russian lands. The famous symbolic victory over the Tartars rewarded the arms of the Muscovite prince, Dmitri Donskoy, when he routed the horde of Khan Mamay on Kulikovo Field (1380). The great Olgerd was already dead at this time, but two of his sons and many Lithuanian nobles shared in the victory.

In his life the Lithuanian prince had played the same part against the Tartars in the West Russian lands which Dmitri Donskoy played in the East, and in fact the initiative in the struggle against the Tartars came from the Lithuanian ruler rather than from the princes of Moscow.

Leaving his celebrated brother Keystut to confront the Teutonic knights on the western marches, Olgerd extended his frontiers towards the south in a series of campaigns. Kiev and the lands of Chernigov and Novgorod Seversk passed into his hands, and his writ ran to the shores of the Black Sea. He proceeded to the organization of the 'new' fertile lands of Podolia, after expelling the Tartar khans who had been ruling there with the help of Russian *atamany*. 'New towns' rapidly arose—Smotrych, Kamenets-Podolsk, Bratslav, Vinnitsa and others—defended by castles and governed by royal Lithuanian princes. Hope and life revived in the old Russian lands along the Dniepr. On the shores of the Black Sea, near the mouth of the Dniestr, the port of Belgorod grew up, later the Turkish Akkerman (*ak kerman*, 'the white city'—a literal translation from the

Russian), and Russian villages appeared in the neighbourhood of the modern Odessa.

The Russo-Lithuanian state now extended, somewhat fantastically, in an irregular belt of country from the shores of the Baltic to those of the Black Sea. The greater part of the territory of the state was composed of purely Russian lands—Vitebsk, Polotsk, Kiev, Podolia and Volhynia—and nine-tenths of the population of Olgerd's dominions were of Russian blood. In Olgerd's capital of Vilna the majority of the inhabitants were Russians. Sixteen Russian princesses were married to Lithuanian princes, and fifteen Russian princes to Lithuanian princesses. Olgerd had remained a pagan until shortly before his death; but at that time fifty-six Lithuanian princes had already been received into the Orthodox faith. Orthodox churches were being built in Vilna, where, however, the pagan tolerance of the conqueror also allowed the erection of Roman Catholic churches. 'Gradually the Russian language became the official language of the administration and the law. Legislative acts, governmental edicts, were published in Russian. In the capital of Lithuania, at the court of the Lithuanian princes, Russian replaces the language of the dominating race' (Shmurlo). 'The historical process in Western Russia seemed to have found a new unifying centre after the downfall of the former centres, Kiev and Halych (Galicia). It could be hoped that the Lithuanian dynasty and the Lithuanian element would play a role similar to that of the Varangians in the tenth and eleventh centuries, in other words, that they would be capable of cementing the weakened Russian elements, and that later they would themselves become assimilated with Russians. It all turned out quite differently' (Doroshenko).

The Russo-Lithuanian state under Gedymin and Olgerd (1321–1377) grew and extended with such remarkable rapidity that it became impossible to create within it any form of uniform political structure. At the end it became a conglomeration of different principalities, lands and dominions, acquired by all sorts of means. All these territories recognized the supreme authority of Olgerd, but his power over them was in fact based on a community of interests which happened during that period to coincide. Olgerd made wars all his life, and those who recognized his rule did so in order to help him and so secure for themselves his powerful support. Military necessity was the only basis of the Russo-Lithuanian state. The politics of the Lithuanian princes served the interests of the defence and recovery of Russian lands. Therefore the Russo-Lithuanian state became a military federation comprising communities of varying origins and degrees of culture, and little attempt was made by the

Lithuanian princes to elaborate a coherent state order. In the principalities and lands which came under the authority of Olgerd, the old
order was maintained without any change. 'Military organization,
the building of the fortified towns, the governmental structure, the
economics of the princes, the administration—all was offered ready
to the Lithuanians and was easily accepted by them' (Shmurlo). In
one of the Lithuanian documents of the period it is stated: 'We do
not disturb the old order, and we do not introduce a new one.'

§4. THE UNION BETWEEN LITHUANIA
AND POLAND

'After the Mongol invasion and conquest, the Russian lands gathered
round two centres, Lithuania and Moscow, and it appeared at first
as if the chances of completing the process favoured the headship of
Lithuania rather than that of Moscow' (Lappo).

Russian and Ukrainian historians with perfect justice underline the
preponderance of the Russian element in Olgerd's Russo-Lithuanian
state, but they ignore the influences which tended to associate that
state with Poland. It is for this reason that an event which was to
have a decisive effect upon the future of Lithuania and the Russian
lands united with Lithuania comes as a surprise. This event was the
marriage of Olgerd's son Jagiello (Yageylo) with Jadwiga (Hedwig)
of Anjou and Hungary, heiress to the throne of Poland. The result
of the marriage was the 'union' between Lithuania and Poland. In
reality this 'union', which was regarded as an event of great political
importance throughout the contemporary world, was less surprising
than it seemed and was, in fact, the logical result of processes which
had been developing during the preceding half century.

Both Gedymin and Olgerd had made a practice of marrying
members of the Lithuanian royal house into Polish as well as into
Russian princely families. Himself a pagan married to the daughter
of the Orthodox Prince of Tver, Olgerd had some personal inclination towards the Greek Orthodox Church, but he had no antipathy
to Rome. As an ally of Tver, Olgerd had supported its prince in his
struggle for primacy over Moscow, and he showed himself sufficiently interested in ecclesiastical politics to complain that the
Muscovite Metropolitan Alexis was continuing to call himself
'Metropolitan of Kiev and All Russia'. In fact there was at that time
no political centre of the Orthodox Church throughout the West
Russian lands which were included within the Lithuanian state. On
the other hand, the increasing power of the Roman Catholic Church

in the Eastern Europe of the fourteenth century, operating through the twin but opposed agencies of the Polish monarchy and the Teutonic Order, could not but attract the small and half-barbarous dominant nation in the Russo–Lithuanian state.

At the same time the social order in the lands included within the dominions of Olgerd was gradually beginning to assume Western forms which tended to bring these lands within the Latinized Polish cultural sphere.

Already in the thirteenth century the social structure of the Galician principality had acquired a character quite different from that of old Kievan Rus. The importance of commercial towns had diminished, and agriculture had become the industry in which the roots of society were planted. A somewhat similar development could be observed in North-Eastern Russia; but there, although Andrew of Bogolyubovo had failed to subordinate his *boyars* to his 'byzantine' conceptions of state, the position of the prince was being continuously strengthened until it formed the basis of the early Muscovite monarchy of the fourteenth century.

In the Galician principality, in contrast to the Muscovite, the *boyars* had kept the upper hand, and had not only come into possession of vast territories but had assumed the right to distribute parts of these at their own will among their retainers. In the fourteenth century an important class of great magnates had emerged and upon them was dependent a larger class of agrarian petty 'nobles'. These phenomena bore more resemblance to the Polish order than to the Russian.

The status of the peasants in Galicia developed on lines similar to that of their Polish fellows. The peasants were ceasing to be 'free', in the sense that they were submitting to obligations not towards the state as represented by the monarchy but towards their local lords to whom they paid tribute and for whom they worked. Being without any obligations towards the state, they were deprived of even the most modest rights in the state. The similarity with Polish conditions had been completed in Galicia by the introduction into the town administrations of the Magdeburg Statute—carried into Poland through the influence of the German immigration after the Mongol invasion.

The processes of social development in Galicia were repeated in Volhynia, and in Podolia after Olgerd had driven out the Tartars; there appeared the same classes of territorial magnates, petty nobles (who borrowed even the Polish denomination of *szlachta*) and peasants without civil rights. In 1374 Kamenets-Podolsk received the Magdeburg Statute.(5)

Such was the social and political background against which took place the marriage of Jagiello and Jadwiga—a marriage which broke the heart of the princess, but which was pleasing at once to the Catholic Church and to the military chieftains in both Poland and Lithuania.

Jagiello had already in 1385 concluded the Treaty of Krevo with the Poles, whereby he agreed to incorporate 'for ever' the lands of the principality of Lithuania with their largely Russian population and culture within the kingdom of Poland, while he himself was recognized as King of Poland and Great Prince of Lithuania. The Krevo agreement was not a mere personal 'union' but something far more definite. The drastic form of the agreement was, of course, dictated by the Church, and its character was such as almost to wreck the political conceptions on which 'union' had been based.

There were still great numbers of Lithuanians who had remained pagan and who might be christened according to the Roman Catholic rite, but there were also, particularly among the nobility, many who had already embraced the Greek Orthodox faith. The attempt in the year 1387 to proclaim a law forbidding marriages between Orthodox and Roman Catholic provoked general indignation, and the Catholic clergy began to find that they were the authors of a growing antagonism between the two confessions which had not existed before. Vitovt (Polish Witold, Lithuanian Vitautas), the son of Olgerd's brother, the famous warrior Keystut, who had fled to Germany some years before on the poisoning of his father by the servants of Jagiello, took swift advantage of the situation. He was supported by the Orthodox princes and magnates of Lithuanian as well as of Russian extraction who feared to lose their rights and privileges on account of their faith. In 1392 Jagiello, under threat of a general rising, was forced to modify the clauses of the Krevo agreement. Vitovt was recognized as Great Prince of Lithuania for life, while Jagiello remained King of Poland; after Vitovt's death all his dominions were to pass to the Polish crown with the exception of certain lands which were reserved for his brother Sigismund (who also promised to serve the Polish crown).

Having become Great Prince of Lithuania and the ally of Poland, the bold and gifted Vitovt now conceived vast plans of dominion in the east. In the first year of his rule he took possession of Smolensk, demanded the submission of Novgorod and promised Pskov to the Teutonic knights. The minor princes inhabiting the lands on the borderland between Lithuania and Muscovy along the upper Oka and its affluents recognized the suzerainty of Vitovt. The Ryazan principality accepted his authority and Tver became his ally.

In the last decade of the fourteenth century the young Muscovite state was passing through the most critical phase of its existence. The victory of Dmitri Donskoy on Kulikovo Field had had no morrow; a renewed invasion by Mamay Khan had at once devastated the Moscow lands and proved that a latent power of aggression still rested in the Golden Horde. In 1382 a new usurping Khan, the celebrated Tokhtamish—a figure in Altaian history second only to his more famous master and rival Tamerlane—plundered Moscow and exacted from Dmitri a renewal of the tribute. Dmitri's son, who was to succeed him as Vasili I, was carried away to the Horde as a hostage for a time. When Vasili returned to Moscow it was to defend dominions which were threatened by two of the foremost soldiers of the day—by Vitovt, the Lithuanian conqueror on the west, and by Tokhtamish in the east. The Muscovite state was saved by a peculiar combination of events and by the intervention of a force more powerful than Vasili, Tokhtamish or Vitovt.

In the summer of 1395 Tamerlane marched north from the Caucasus to pursue his final and most destructive campaign against the Golden Horde. He defeated Tokhtamish on the Terek, and, advancing through the Kipchak country into Russia, reached Yelets. It appeared as though the weakened Muscovite principality was about to experience the fate of the lands of Kievan Russia a century and a half before. But Tamerlane turned to pursue the destruction of the Kipchak cities of Azak (Azov), Hajji-Tarkhan (Astrakhan) and Saray. At this juncture the Kipchak allies in the Caucasus, the chief of whom was the young Georgian king, George VI, who had already sustained two ruinous campaigns against the Mongols, rose in the rear of Tamerlane. The combined forces of the Georgian king and of the Mussulman dynasts of the Eastern Caucasus attacked Miran-Shah, a son of Tamerlane, who had been installed as governor of Azerbaijan. The Mongols were defeated before Alindjak, and in the spring of 1396 Tamerlane himself hastened south to Derbend to undertake the repression of the insurgent Lesghian tribes of Daghestan, while the terrified inhabitants of Moscow could attribute their salvation to the miraculous intervention of the holy icon of Our Lady of Vladimir.

The double threat from the east had vanished and now a further happy accident was to conjure the threat from the west. The fugitive Tokhtamish had sought refuge with Vitovt and now secured his help to restore him to his Khanate. Hoping to take advantage of the dissensions in the Horde, Vitovt, during the year 1399, led south a great army which contained the flower of the warlike chivalry of Lithuania with large levies from the Western and Southern Russian lands. One of Tamerlane's most able lieutenants, Khan Edighey (Idegü), met the Russo-Lithuanian host on the banks of the Vorskla, a left tributary of the Dniepr, and inflicted a crushing defeat. The Mongols failed to follow up their victory with an incursion into the lands of the Lithuanian principality, but Vitovt had lost his best troops and his fighting heart was broken. He abandoned his ambitious designs on Moscow and Novgorod, and subsequently gave his daughter in marriage to Vasili I.

The Moscow state was saved by these events. The defeat on the Vorskla had also, however, the effect of strengthening the ties which united the cousins ruling in Poland and Lithuania. The weakened Vitovt now came to regard the Poles as a protection against both the Tartar and the German dangers. And in the year 1410 the chivalry of Poland and Lithuania, reinforced by numerous Russian detachments, inflicted a decisive defeat on the Teutonic Order at Grünwald (Tannenberg). Tannenberg was the only mighty Slav victory over Germans, but it delayed for several centuries the progress of German conquest in Eastern Europe. The Teutonic Order henceforth ceased to constitute an important political and military force, and the prestige of the Polish monarchy was notably enhanced. (6, 7, 8)

In the first half of the fifteenth century the non-German races, Poles, Lithuanians and Hungarians, were ascendant in Eastern Europe under the leadership of the brilliant Jagiellons. The Hussite movement in Bohemia was another aspect of the Slav anti-German reaction which had received great impetus from Tannenberg. Both Jagiello and Vitovt played with the notion of supporting the Hussites (Ziska had fought with the Poles in the wars against the Teutonic knights) and Vitovt was offered the crown of Bohemia. But the Catholic hierarchy in Poland obstinately opposed the Hussite cause, and refused to confuse the national struggle against the Germans with a Slav crusade against Latinism. Vitovt, who had originally grasped power with the aid of the Orthodox Lithuanian and Russian magnates, had himself come under the influence of the cultural and political ideas which were represented by the Western Church.

In the year 1413, three years after Tannenberg, Vitovt made a new agreement with his cousin, known as the Union of Horodlo, whereby the conditions providing for the incorporation of the dominions of the Lithuanian Great Prince in the kingdom of Poland after Vitovt's death were abandoned. It was provided, however, that a successor to Vitovt would not be chosen without the consent of the King of Poland, while similarly a successor to the Polish throne would not be appointed without the agreement of the Great Prince of Lithuania.

It is evident that by the Union of Horodlo a situation was created whereby both the Polish and Lithuanian rulers were placed in a position of formal dependence on the magnates of the two realms.

The Roman Catholic hierarchy took advantage of the agreement to strengthen the position of the Church among the ruling classes in Lithuania. To the Russo-Lithuanian nobility who adhered to the Catholic faith were accorded all the privileges enjoyed by the nobility of the kingdom of Poland, including the right to a coat of arms—an attractive distinction to the bucolic magnates of the eastern principality. But these rights and honours were not granted to nobles of the Orthodox confession. In the same way the lesser Lithuanian gentry could only receive the same rights as their fellows, the Polish *szlachta*, on the condition of being received into the Church.

Vitovt began to surround himself with Catholic counsellors and to appoint members of the Catholic aristocracy as governors (*starosty* or *voyevodes*) even in the Orthodox Russian principalities. He pursued at the same time a policy of increasing centralization and suppressed the important regional principalities in the lands of Vitebsk, Polotsk, Smolensk, Kiev, and in Volhynia and Podolia. An administration modelled on Polish forms was established in Vilna, with Polish appellations for the different dignitaries of state. The Russian language, however, continued to be used for official purposes. Vitovt even attempted to sever the administration of the Greek Orthodox Church in the Great Principality from dependence on the Metropolitan in Moscow. In 1416 a Kievan Metropolitan was named, but the experiment did not prove successful, and when the Metropolitan died no successor was appointed.

In the northern provinces of Lithuania, where many of the Russian districts had been but newly detached from a Muscovite orientation and where the cultural influences of Novgorod and Pskov persisted, the Union of Horodlo provoked a certain degree of antagonism between the Russian and Lithuanian members of the nobility—since the latter more easily adhered to the Roman faith. In the south, however, in Volhynia and Podolia, many Russian aristocratic families became Catholic, although the lower classes, townsfolk and peasants, evinced great devotion to the Orthodox faith—the more so since the act of 1413 did not provide for them the advantages which attracted the gentry.

In the last years of his life Vitovt enjoyed the prestige of a great Catholic leader in Eastern Europe. Loyal by interest to his engagements to Jagiello, he at the same time aspired that Lithuania rather than Poland should be the leading partner in the association of the two realms. He desired also to be accorded a royal crown. There is little doubt that his ambitions were secretly supported by the Emperor Sigismund and the Grand Master of the Teutonic Order. 'At the famous Congress of Lutsk (in Volhynia) in 1429 Vitovt entertained a brilliant gathering of princes, ostensibly to discuss the question of defence against the Turks. Besides his son-in-law, the Grand Prince of Moscow, the chief guests were the Emperor Sigismund, Jagiello, the King of Denmark, the Grand Masters of both Orders, the Papal Legate, the ambassador of the Byzantine Emperor, the Khans of the Volga and Crimean Tartars, the Hospodar of Wallachia, Princes of Silesia, Pomerania and Mazovia together with all the nobility of the province of Volhynia. At this picturesque assembly, where the guests and their retinues, according to the chronicler, consumed daily 700 oxen, 1400 sheep, and 100 bisons and boars, and drank 700 barrels of mead besides wine and beer, the Turkish question was used as a pretext to cover the attempt of the Emperor to persuade Jagiello to consent to the coronation of Vitovt. This intrigue was frustrated by the determined opposition of the Polish magnates under Olesnicki, and the proposal was dropped on the death of Vitovt in 1430. The tortuous diplomacy in which his position involved him, his failure against the Tartars, and his soaring ambition cannot obscure his greatness as a man. He was the last brilliant soldier of the house of Gedymin, an able diplomatist, and a great influence for progress in a backward area of Europe. He ruled his vast principality with ideals that could never merit the approbation of Polish or Russian patriots, and while enhancing the prestige of Poland, his main work was devoted to his own principality and entitles him to be considered as one of the great men of his age' (Bruce-Boswell, *C.M.H.* viii, 576).

The death of Vitovt provoked a crisis between the Orthodox and Roman Catholic parties in Lithuania. The Russo-Lithuanian magnates refused to elect as Great Prince the aged Jagiello in whose favour the Poles were intriguing. The majority chose the Orthodox Svidrygiello, a brother of Jagiello and an old rebel in Lithuania against Vitovt. The Catholics favoured Vitovt's brother Sigismund. Civil war broke out, during which Jagiello's brother, as the nominee of the Orthodox party, was supported by the Catholic interests of the Emperor and the Livonian Order. 'The action of (the Emperor) Sigismund was particularly treacherous in that Polish troops were helping him in his Turkish campaigns.' The war continued until 1435, when the combined forces of the Orthodox magnates and the Livonian knights were signally defeated at Wilkomir.

Following the death of Sigismund of Lithuania, the Catholic

candidate, Casimir, younger son of Jagiello, and brother of the new Polish king, Vladislav III, was elected Grand Prince of Lithuania. With. the death of his brother in battle against the Turks on the famous crusade of Varna (1444), Casimir 'the Jagiellon' became also King of Poland. Casimir IV, whose long reign reached the last decade of the century, was to prove one of the ablest and most distinguished of Polish kings, and the architect in Eastern Europe of those *étatiste* conceptions in public policy which were to dominate the history of the sixteenth century.

With the passing of the two crowns to the person of Casimir IV the union of Poland and Lithuania had been practically effected, but the events of 1432–5, when the Germanic powers had attempted to exploit Russian Orthodoxy against the Catholic Polish state, were not without their influence on the astute mind of the new King. (9) He proceeded to reverse the policy imposed by the Roman Catholic hierarchy, and by an act of 1447 extended to the Orthodox magnates and gentry of Lithuania all rights and privileges enjoyed by their Catholic fellows. Further, the landlords, Orthodox as well as Catholic, received the right to exact from the peasants who had settled in the new lands tribute for themselves payable either in produce or in money. The peasant became the subject, as in Poland, not of the monarch but of his own landlord who now enjoyed the power of life and death over him. By such measures Casimir forestalled all danger of serious opposition from the Orthodox Russian magnates, but he at the same time strengthened their position to the ultimate cost of the crown. His political finesse was such that he even appointed the 'rebel' claimant to the Great Principality, Svidrygiello, as *voyevode* of Volhynia, and in Kiev he named another representative of the Orthodox party, Olelko, a grandson of Olgerd and a son of the Prince Vladimir who had governed Kiev as an 'ally' of his father following its recovery from the Tartars. Casimir then proceeded to found in Kiev a Metropolitan see whose first incumbent was Gregory, one of the sponsors in 1439 of the Florentine Union of the Eastern and Western Churches. This Union, having its origins in a desperate surrender of the Byzantine court in order to secure Papal and Western support against the impending Turkish assault on Constantinople, failed even in its immediate object. But the background of the Council of Florence, where the Metropolitan Isidore was the representative of both Muscovite and Lithuanian Orthodoxy, long continued to influence the religious politics of the Russian lands.

In Moscow the acceptance by Isidore (a Greek by birth) of the decisions of the Council of Florence had aroused a storm of indignation, and he had been forced to flee not so much the wrath of the

Great Prince as of the people. But in the Kiev lands, in Volhynia and in all the Russian lands of Lithuania, the appointment of a Uniate Metropolitan was quietly accepted. The South Russian magnates were becoming Catholic and allied by marriage to Catholic Polish and Lithuanian families, and they were adopting the customs and fashions of Polish aristocratic life. In Volhynia, at the beginning of the sixteenth century, the members of the princely houses of Ostrozhsky, Czartoryski, Vishnevetsky, Verenetsky and Chetvertinsky differed in little respect from their Polish contemporaries (v. p. xi). Only among the peasantry and the burghers of the small towns did devotion to the old Orthodox confession persist.

§ 5. THE UKRAINE BETWEEN POLAND-LITHUANIA AND MUSCOVY

A consolidation of a series of large centralized monarchies and a general tendency to expansion in a westerly direction were characteristics of the history of the sixteenth century. The establishment of the centralized monarchies was a social phenomenon which followed the final disintegration of the feudal system as the way of life in Western Europe—a phenomenon which found spiritual expression in the Renaissance. The bases of the social transformation were economic, arising from causes which had been accumulating during a long period.

The most typical example of the modernist possibilities of the bureaucratic Renaissance state was to be found not in Christendom but in the Ottoman Empire where Padishahs like Selim I and Suleiman the Magnificent applied all the resources of the new age to the building of a gigantic naval and military power round the eastern and southern shores of the Mediterranean in the area of Justinian's former 'world-state'. Even the exploratory initiative of the Age of Discovery infected the military bureaucrats newly established in Istanbul when they attempted to extend Ottoman naval power from the Red Sea to the Indian Ocean and planned canals to unite the Mediterranean with the Red Sea and the Black Sea with the Caspian by way of the Don and the Volga. The expansion of the Ottomans round the Eastern and Southern Mediterranean and into South-Western and Central Europe met with rather less opposition owing to the preoccupation of the recently constituted Austro-Spanish Empire with maritime politics in the Low Countries and with new dreams of world dominion in the Americas. World politics were taking a vast sweep into the illimitable west, and Hungary and Poland were left by the Germanic Powers to bear the brunt of the modern Turkish menace—a strange fusion in itself of the destructive Altaian and the imperial Byzantine traditions.

The pressure of the Turks in Eastern and Central Europe certainly weakened the capacity of the Poles and Lithuanians to maintain and extend their hegemony in the Western and Southern Russian lands. As the drive of Tamerlane had saved the Muscovite state of Vasili I, so, towards the end of the fifteenth century, the conquests of Muhammad II favoured the rapid growth of the Muscovite state of Vasili II and Ivan III.

The rise of the Muscovite state and its expansion into the north over the Novgorod and Permian lands, into the east over Siberia, into the south over the former dominions of the Golden Horde, and westward at the expense of the Polish-Lithuanian monarchy, was a phenomenon of the sixteenth century comparable to the building of the Mediterranean empire of the Ottomans and the European and trans-Atlantic world power of the Austro-Spanish Habsburgs.

The Ottoman Padishahs, in the latter part of the fifteenth and throughout the sixteenth century, pursued the ultimate potentialities of the traditions of the East Roman Empire at the height of its splendour. They maintained a steady pressure on the Danube which transformed the politics of Central Europe and destroyed in favour of the Germans the brilliant promise of its varied cultures—the Latin Slav florescence of the Jagiellonid Empire, the strange and fine synthesis of French and Magyar genius in Hungary, and, indirectly, the important intellectual and puritan leadership of the Czechs. In Syria, Egypt and North Africa the Ottomans combined the pretensions of the Byzantine Emperors and the Caliphs. On the Anatolian plateau and in the Armenian highlands they resumed against the Iranian Safavids the old Imperial feud against the Parthians and the Sassanids. In the Black Sea they entered into the ancient heritage of the Hellenic cities, of Rome and of Byzantium. Too late the Venetian Signory and the Papacy, having neglected to succour Byzantium, endeavoured to conjure the danger to the remains of Latin cultural and maritime interests beyond the Bosporus. The celebrated voyages to the east of Barbaro, Contarini and Zeno had as object the combination of the forces of the Georgian petty potentates, the powerful Ak-koyunlu Turkomans and the Persian Safavids with the Mediterranean sea powers in a grand alliance to check the Turk. But while Contarini was waiting for a ship to carry him from Georgia to Caffa, he heard that the great Pontic metropolis for the trade of the Italian cities with the East had already fallen to the Turks (1475).

Turkish sea power was to remain for more than four hundred years the dominant factor in Black Sea politics. Tana (Azak) at the mouth of the Don, *entrepôt* for the trade of the Italian cities with Muscovy and the Golden Horde; Cherson in the Crimea; Belgorod (Akkerman) serving the trade route from Central Europe which ran from Regensburg through Lvov (Lemberg) to the Dniestr; the Italo-Moldavian foundations at the mouths of the Danube—all these keys to the life of the great fluvial hinterland of the Black Sea were soon in Turkish hands.

The effect on the politics of the Polish-Lithuanian state was almost immediate. Following the Mongol invasions the Tartars had established themselves in the Crimea. In continuous contact with the Italian trading colonies in Caffa and Tana, and as useful intermediaries with the Golden Horde, they had become wealthy and during the first part of the fifteenth century a certain Khan Hajji Giray, after the weakening of the Horde by Tamerlane, had established a court at the beautiful little town of Baghchi-Saray. He maintained friendly relations with his imposing Lithuanian neighbour and with the Muscovite prince with whom he had common commercial interests. At the beginning of the reign of Ivan III the Crimean Khan, Mangly Giray, actually went to the help of the Muscovites when his suzerain Ahmet Khan of the Golden Horde threatened Moscow, and it was the ill-success of this last formidable attack of the Horde on the Muscovite lands which enabled Ivan III in 1480 to finally throw off 'the Tartar yoke'. But with the appearance of a Turkish fleet in the Black Sea and the establishment of a Turkish garrison in Caffa, Mangly Giray accepted the suzerainty of the Padishah, and the Tartars of the Crimea became the principal agents of Turkish hegemony round the shores of the Black Sea from the Roumanian principalities as far as Daghestan and the shores of the Caspian.

At the same time the Crimea became the centre of a portentous revival of the traffic in slaves. The slave trade had existed round the shores of the Black Sea since the most ancient times and had flourished under the Byzantines. It was, in fact, with serfdom, a normal social phenomenon of the medieval world—although condemned by the Churches. It was a factor in piecemeal migration and the basis of the supply of the industrial and domestic labour markets of the Mediterranean countries. It is generally forgotten that the traffic in human beings was regarded as a tolerable if disagreeable condition of economic life among Western communities into the last century. The modern 'liberal' capitalist system has abolished and condemned the theory of slavery but, under varying euphemisms, its practice is widely maintained in the best regulated modern communities.

Apart from exploiting the commercial, industrial and domestic possibilities of the slave trade, the Turks, with their genius for military organization, used it in war by the establishment of their famous Janissary corps. The conception of regiments of devoted and highly trained slave troops was borrowed from the Mamluk corps of Egypt, where male slaves recruited from the Caucasus and Kipchak had for two centuries constituted themselves the dominant military force in the Levant and had proved the first capable of decisively defeating the Mongols.

The population of the South Russian lands was to prove an inexhaustible reservoir for the supply of the camps, the harims and the labour market of the Ottoman Empire. As early as 1484 Mangly Giray undertook his first big raid into the Lithuanian dominions and sacked Kiev. In the following year he ravaged Podolia, which, under the rule of Olgerd and Vitovt, had become a populous and flourishing land. In the year 1490 the Tartars swept through Volhynia and rode north as far as Kholm. In the following years they continually pillaged along both banks of the Dniepr and the Desna and towards the north reached the Pripet.

In these decades hundreds of thousands of men, women and children were driven down to the Crimea and from there distributed to the markets of the Ottoman Empire. About the middle of the sixteenth century the Lithuanian envoy residing at the court of Baghchi-Saray could remark despairingly that 'it seemed that no population would be left in the South' (Doroshenko).

The Turkish pressure in the south, along the Danube, overcame the powerful Hungarian kingdom, which a century earlier under Lewis the Great of Anjou, the father of Jadwiga of Poland, had dominated the politics of Central and Eastern Europe. On the field of Mohács, in 1526, the Hungarians lost two-thirds of their territory, which was to remain for a century and a half under Turkish rule. Between the Danube and the Dniestr and the Dniepr the Turks imposed their suzerainty over the Roumanian principalities and gravely threatened the Polish-Lithuanian dominions. The Poles performed the great service to Germanic and Western Europe of withstanding the brunt of Turkish aggression during the heyday of the great Ottoman sultans, and it was a Polish king who finally broke the Turkish menace under the walls of Vienna in 1683. But the effect of the protracted Turkish wars was to stultify and derange the whole development of Polish political and cultural life and to prepare the way for the revival of a great Orthodox Slav state in the East and for the recrudescence in the West of the old Germanic imperialism of the Teutonic knights under the Prussia of Frederick the Great.

The period of the preoccupation of Casimir IV with the final phase of the great Northern War against the Teutonic Orders corresponds with the opening years of the expansion of the Muscovite state under Ivan III. Ivan became Great Prince in 1462, four years before the Treaty of Thorn crowned the victory of Casimir over the Orders and brought to an end the great medieval epic of German expansion into the East. In 1471 Ivan, following the battle of Shelon, secured ascendancy over the historic city of Novgorod and the whole of the Russian north-east. In the following year he married Zoë (Sophia) Palaeologu, whose father Thomas, ex-Despot of Morea, was a brother of the last Emperor of Byzantium and whose mother was a lady of the brilliant house of Montferrat. With the heiress to the lost glories of Byzantium in his bed, Ivan began to assume all those vague pretensions which were henceforth to constitute such an important item in the conceptions of Great-Russian statesmanship. Ivan assumed the titles of *Samoderzhets* (Autocrat) and *Tsar* (Caesar), and the learned needy flatterers who accompanied Sophia to Moscow discovered that her rugged husband was 'a descendant of Augustus' who was supposed to have 'divided the world among his brothers', of whom 'Pruss' had received the lands on the banks of the Niemen and from him 'descended in the fourteenth generation the great Prince Rurik'. With less reliance on genealogical fancy, Ivan might himself recall his descent from Vladimir Monomakh and remember that his ancestor had been Great Prince of Kiev and ruler of all the south. Ivan began to sign documents as 'Lord of all Russia', and his successor in 1503 was to apostrophize the Lithuanians in the words: 'Do I not mourn my ancestral lands, all those Russian lands taken by Lithuania, and Kiev and Smolensk and all those other towns?' (10, 11).

The differences between the Orthodox and Catholic nobles in Lithuania which Casimir had tried to temper in the Treaty of Horodlo naturally attracted the intrigues of the Muscovite ruler. Already in 1470 the uneasy Casimir had replaced the Orthodox Olelko by a Lithuanian and Catholic *voyevode* in Kiev. 'The son of the last Kievan Prince, Michael, together with other princes, started secret *pourparlers* with Moscow, promising all sorts of advantages in White Russia for her help against Lithuania. The conspiracy was discovered and Prince Michael had to pay for it with his life. That however did not stop the other princes and only the more clearly indicated to them the road to Moscow' (Doroshenko). Many lesser princes who owned territories along the upper Oka and who had previously been dependent upon the Lithuanian crown 'left' and offered their allegiance to Ivan III. Their example was followed by other lords of small principalities on the borderland between the Seversk and Chernigov lands. The boundaries of the Moscow state were suddenly enlarged in the direction of the Dniepr. Finally Chernigov submitted to Moscow.

In 1485 Tver, formerly the rival of Moscow on the upper Volga supported by the Lithuanian Great Princes, surrendered her independence without a struggle. Ryazan and Pskov fell to Ivan's successor, Vasili III.

In the first years of the sixteenth century, following the destructive Tartar and Turkish attacks in the southern provinces of the Lithuanian crown, Vasili conquered Smolensk, while his troops reached the banks of the Dniepr and made their appearance along the rivers Desna and Seym. The Muscovite borders were approaching Kiev; and in that city a West Russian noble, Prince Michael Glinski, raised an insurrection in favour of the restoration of the 'old Kievan monarchy'.

Turko-Tartar aggression had made it easy for the Muscovite rulers to encroach on the eastern frontiers of the Lithuanian state, and neither Ivan nor Vasili were slow in exploiting the sentiments of the Orthodox; at the same time the general reaction of the Russo-Lithuanian aristocracy, with their estates and the welfare of their provinces under the constant menace of the Tartar raids, was in favour of closer union with Poland.

In the year 1529 a law, known as the Lithuanian Statute, introduced throughout the lands of the Great Principality a social order similar in all respects to that existing in Poland. The magnates now acquired the right—which had since the end of the last century been merely a 'privilege'—of participating in the government through the *Rada* (Senate). Without the consent of the *Rada*, the Great Prince could no longer introduce any changes in the laws or government of the country. (12)

In 1566 a further Statute extended representative rights to the numerous class of gentry (*szlachta*) who, meeting together in local *Seyms* (Councils) elected their delegates to the *Seym* of the whole Russo-Lithuanian state.

The *Seym* was representative of the corporate opinions of the whole Russo-Lithuanian gentry, and it sat in general session with the *Rada*. The Great Prince had to swear an oath that he would safeguard the rights of 'the nobility of his nation'. According to the Polish view he had no duties whatever towards the rest of the population of the country. When, in 1592, Sigismund III Vasa was elected King of Poland, he was told that 'he was going to reign over nobles and not over peasants like his father John, King of Sweden'.

The Polish-Lithuanian sovereigns had, since the middle of the fifteenth century, been confronted with the problem of dealing with classes of great territorial magnates. Casimir IV and his successors had endeavoured to base the monarchy on the support of the gentry, but circumstances, including the elective character of the Polish monarchy, had been against them—with disastrous results, as it was to prove, to the future of the Polish nation.

The Polish kings, in their policies, were always, perhaps, over-shadowed by the elective character of the neighbouring 'Holy Roman Empire of the German Nation', and political thought in Poland was influenced by Western forms. The Muscovite Tsars had behind them the dim glamour of the Byzantine autocracy and the shadow of the Golden Horde. Vasili II the Blind was the last Muscovite ruler to be oppressed by the magnates of his realm, and the Church, which supported him, won the Moscow mob to his side. Ivan III intrigued with the leaders of the Novgorod mob be-fore he seized the city; and in the whole process of the acquisition of the smaller Russian princely cities, the people generally showed themselves to be on the side of the 'Autocrator' of Moscow. Some-thing of the flavour of plebeian politics was borrowed by the Muscovite Tsars, together with the dogma of autocracy, from the dead Emperors of Byzantium.

The internal reforms in Lithuania of 1529 and 1566 prepared the way for the Union of Lublin of 1569.

Ivan IV (Grozny), having taken Kazan (1552) and Astrakhan (1555) and established Muscovy as the successor to the Golden Horde on the Volga and the Caspian, turned his attention to the west. In 1558 he began a war against the Livonian Order. The Grand Master appealed for help to the Lithuanians. But the combined forces of the knights and the Lithuanian magnates were unsuccessful, and in 1563 Ivan took the important city of Polotsk.

Confronted now with a serious Muscovite menace, Sigismund Augustus, Grand Prince of Lithuania and King of Poland, succeeded in effecting the complete administrative union of the two states. In the last month of 1568 the Lithuanian Seym met at Lublin, and in the middle of the following year the Union of Lublin was declared.(13)

The Rzecz Pospolita (Res publica), the realm of Poland, which emerged out of the union of the Kingdom and the Great Principality, was a state of several nationalities in contrast to the old predominantly national Polish kingdom. The very conception of Rzecz Pospolita laid the state under the obligation to maintain equality between the different nationalities and confessions; but the bases of this strange construction with its elected monarch and generously enfranchised noble classes remained essentially Polish, and moreover traditionally Catholic and therefore alien in spirit to the very large population of Greek Orthodox confession included within its borders.(14)

BIBLIOGRAPHICAL NOTES AND ADDITIONS TO CHAPTER II

On the History of the Russo-Lithuanian State

Lyubavski, M. *Ocherk Istorii Litovsko-Russkago Gosudarstva* (Sketch of the History of the Russo-Lithuanian State), Moscow, 1915.

Kolankowski, J. *Dzieje Wielkiego Księstwa Litewskiego za Jagiellonów* (History of the Principality of Lithuania under the Jagiellons), tome I, 1377–1499, Warsaw, 1930.

Wolff, J. *Rod Gedymina* (The House of Gedymin), Cracow, 1886.

Vladimirski-Budanov, M. 'Naselenie Yugo-Zapadnoy Rossii ot poloviny XIII Stoletiya do Lublinskoy Unii' (The Population of South-Western Russia from the middle of the Thirteenth Century to the Union of Lublin), *Arkhiv Yugo-Zapadnoy Rossii*, vol. VII, Kiev.

Lappo, I. *Zapadnaya Rossiya i eya Soedinenie s Polshoy* (Western Russia and her Union with Poland), Praha, 1924.

For an appreciation of the relations of Lithuania, South Russia and Poland with neighbouring countries during the period under review the following chapters of the *Cambridge Mediaeval History* should also be consulted:

Vol. VI, Bruce-Boswell, A., 'Poland (1050–1303)'; vol. VII, *idem*, 'The Teutonic Order'; vol. VIII, *idem*, 'Poland and Lithuania in the Fourteenth and Fifteenth Centuries'.

The following general works. also contain excellent chapters on the historical role of Poland and Lithuania during the period under review:

Bruce-Boswell, A. *Poland and the Poles*, London, 1919.

Dyboski, R. *Outlines of Polish History*, London, 1925.

Halecki, O. *La Pologne de 963 à 1914; Essai de Synthèse Historique*, Paris, 1933.

For the history of the Black Sea during this period see W. Heyd, *Histoire du Commerce du Levant* (2 vols. Réimpression, Leipzig, 1923); W. E. D. Allen, *History of the Georgian People*, London, 1932; G. Bratianu, *Commerce de la Mer Noire*, Paris, 1932; and the periodical, *Baltic and Scandinavian Countries*, vol. III. no. 3 (5), M. Malowist, 'The Baltic and Black Sea in Mediaeval Trade'; vol. III, no. 3 (7), G. Vernadsky, 'The Baltic Commerce of the West Russian and Lithuanian Cities during the Middle Ages'.

(1) *On the Destruction of Kiev and the Devastation of Kievan lands by the Tartars*

Ukrainian historians (e.g. Doroshenko) endeavour to deny the complete devastation of Kiev and Kievan lands after the invasion of Batu in 1240. Here their views are in direct opposition to those of Polish and Russian historians. In 1857 M. Maksimovich went so far as to compose a work 'On the supposed devastation of Ukraina by Batu's invasion'. This tendency of Ukrainian historians is explained by the desire to establish that Ukraina was not re-peopled by newcomers from the west during the sixteenth century, and that the majority of the population of the land is descended from those who had survived the Mongol devastations. The view is not, however, really confirmed by Ukrainian historians themselves, in that they describe facts concerning the conditions in the Dniepr region during the fifteenth and sixteenth centuries which justify the 'immigration theory'.

(2) On the West Russian State in Galicia

Dashkevich, N. *Knyazhenie Daniila Galitskago po Russkim i Inostrannym Istochnikam* (The Reign of Daniel of Galicia according to Russian and Foreign Sources), Kiev, 1873.

Tomashivsky, S. *Ukrainska Istoria* (History of Ukraina), vol. I, Lvov, 1909.

Andryashev. *Ocherk Istorii Volynskoy Zemli do kontsa XIV stoletiya* (Sketch of the History of the Volhynian Land to the end of the fourteenth Century), Kiev, 1887.

Ivanov. *Istoricheskiya Sudby Volynskoy Zemli do kontsa XIV Stoletiya* (Historical Fate of the Volhynian Lands till the end of the Fourteenth Century), Odessa, 1895.

(3) On Daniel of Galicia

The personality of Daniel of Galicia appears to have been attractive, although he did not prove to be one of the great leaders of his difficult time. 'Courageous and fearless, generous and kind-hearted to the point of being naive, Daniel was a politician least of all' (Shmurlo). Tomashivsky calls Daniel 'an intelligent, chivalrous, cultured, humane and energetic prince'.

(4) On the Galician Chronicle

The principal source for the history of Galicia and Volhynia in the thirteenth century is the Galician-Volhynian Chronicle, an anonymous work which embraces the period from 1209 to 1292. The Chronicle is written in a vivid and rather flowery style. It contains many picturesque episodes, and is ornamented with poetical comparisons and allegories which indicate that the author was familiar with Classical and European medieval literature.

The chronicler writes with sympathy of Prince Daniel and refers thus to his relations with the *boyars*: 'The Galician *boyars* called Daniel their Prince but in reality they ruled the whole land themselves.'

(5) On the Annexation of Galicia to Poland

Doroshenko writes: 'In the fourteenth century Galicia was politically disorganized, and, though culturally on the same level as Poland, was much weaker than the latter. She lacked inner stability and suffered from the feuds of the *boyars* and the absence of a strong central power.'

Until 1434-5 the Poles allowed the old order of things to remain (*tempus juris Ruthenorum*). After 1430, however, Jagiello granted to the Galician nobility the same privileges as were enjoyed by the Polish nobility. At the same time the Polish King began to grant wide lands in Galicia to his Polish favourites, and the Galician *boyars* came under the influence of and were rapidly absorbed into the world of their Polish neighbours. 'A great part of them were swept away by the wave of Polish colonization and returned to their primary origin—the people' (Efimenko). In the sixteenth century, according to Hrushevsky, there remained no noble Galician families who retained their Russian or Ukrainian nationality. At the same time as the Polish gentry were overflowing the countryside, the towns were being populated by Germans and Jews. Under the Magdeburg Law municipal power was in the hands of the Catholics—Poles and Germans. The former Russian urban population was gradually eliminated from the towns and lost among the peasantry. (See A. Halban, *Zur Geschichte d. Deutschen Rechts in Podolien, Volhynien und Ukraina*, Berlin, 1896.)

(6) On the Rivalry between Muscovy and the Russo-Lithuanian State

The rivalry between Olgerd and Dmitri Donskoy did not prevent Russo-Lithuanian detachments—who were much better trained than the Muscovite militia of the day—from taking part against the Tartars on the famous field of Kulikovo. A decisive role was played in the battle by a certain 'Volhynian *Voyevode* Bobrok', who was the initiator of the manœuvre which decided the day in favour of the Russians.

An original view is taken of the relations between Lithuania and Muscovy by a group of Russian historians and publicists who call themselves 'Eurasians'. The ideology of the Eurasians is based on the affirmation that the Moscow State owed the whole of its interior structure and rapid external expansion to the example of 'the great Mongolian Empire'. Russia is considered only as a projection of the 'Eurasian State' created by the Mongols. In the opinion of the Eurasian school, the Mongols who defeated Vitovt in 1399 rendered Russia a great service because they undermined 'the pressure of Latinism in the East'. (See articles by Trubetskoy, Savitski, Vernadski and others, and for a summary of the Eurasian theory see article by Prince D. S. Mirsky in *Slavonic Review*, vol. VI, no. 17.)

(7) On Vitovt

Barbashev, A. *Vitovt i ego Politika do Grunvaldskoy Bitvy* (Vitovt and his Policy to the Battle of Grünwald), Petersburg, 1885.

Idem. Vitovt: Poslednie 20 let Knyazhenya (Vitovt: the Last Twenty Years of his Rule), Petersburg, 1891.

Piltzner, J. *Grossfürst Witold in Lithuanien als Staatsmann*, Brünn, 1930.

In *C.M.H.*, vol. VIII, Bruce-Boswell gives a good description of the campaign of Grünwald-Tannenberg. 'The complete army was of imposing size and unusual diversity. Alongside the Polish knights and the clan groups, each with its common arms and slogan, rode thousands of Tartars under Soldan, soon to be Khan of the Golden Horde. Martial Lithuanians marched side by side with sturdy Czech mercenaries who were destined to astonish the world. The model of Polish chivalry, Zawisza the Black, was in striking contrast to the turbulent Russian *boyars* or the rude skin-clad Samogitians.'

(8) On Tokhtamish and Tamerlane

Articles in *Encyclopaedia of Islam* under names Tokhtamish and Timur Leng by W. Barthold and L. Bouvat respectively. The latter erroneously states that Tamerlane 'occupied Moscow for over a year'.

For the influence of events in Georgia and the Caucasus on Tamerlane's movements in Kipchak, see W. E. D. Allen, *History of the Georgian People*, where the connection between Tamerlane's campaigns in Georgia and his policy in Kipchak and Turkey is not sufficiently emphasized, and V. F. Minorsky, 'Transcaucasica', in *Journal Asiatique*, 1930, Juillet–Sept. pp. 41–111.

Tokhtamish, originally a lieutenant of Tamerlane, appeared from behind the Volga with a part of the Kirghiz 'Blue Horde'. He completed the downfall of Mamay after the defeat of the latter at Kulikovo in 1380. In 1382 he sacked Moscow. According to contemporary sources he was a just and vigorous ruler; he is also said to have been a handsome man (Barthold). In the years following his usurpation of the Golden Horde and his defeat of Dmitri Donskoy, he came into conflict with Tamerlane in Central Asia (Khvarism) and in the eastern Caucasus. Tamerlane, in his campaign of 1395, reached the region of the upper Don; and he rendered a signal service to the Muscovites when he devastated the encampments of the Blue Horde and destroyed Saray on the Volga—the old capital of the Golden Horde. The Kirghiz Blue Horde did not rally after the blow, and retired first beyond the Volga, and later behind the Ural.

The empire of the Golden Horde which Béréké established had lasted for a little over a century. In the fifteenth century, following the attacks of Tamerlane, it became divided into three parts governed by three different Khans—The Golden Horde proper (Kazan), the Crimea, and Nogay (with a capital at Astrakhan).

(9) *Casimir the Jagiellon*

He showed tolerance towards the Greek Orthodox Church. In the chapel of the Holy Cross in the cathedral of Cracow—where his grave is—there are frescoes dating from the end of the fifteenth century painted by Russian masters in the Russo-Byzantine style. Similar frescoes can be seen in Lublin, Sandomierz and other Catholic churches in Poland of the fifteenth–sixteenth centuries.

(10) *On the Discovery of 'Moscovia'*

'The Discovery' of 'Moscovia' was first made by Ritter Poppel and other foreigners, mostly military men, during the reign of Ivan III (1462–1505). Until his visit there, Poppel regarded 'Moscovia' as a remote dependency of the Polish kings.

The most celebrated description of the period is that of Sigismund von Herberstein, who was sent on two missions (1517 and 1526) to the court of Vasili III. His book was published only in 1549.

The German powers soon became conscious of the possibilities of exploiting antagonism between Muscovy and Poland. In the first decade of the sixteenth century the Hohenzollern Grand Master of the Teutonic Order was sending arms and military organizers to Moscow; while, at the Congress of Vienna in 1515, the Poles were concerned to secure the withdrawal of Habsburg support from Vasili III. In the seventies of the sixteenth century the intrigues of the city of Danzig with Ivan IV forced the intervention of the Polish king Stephen Báthory, and in 1581, Ivan, after the victories of Báthory in Russia, sought the intervention of both the Emperor and the Pope.

(11) *On the Muscovite Tsars as 'Descendants of Augustus' and
on the Lithuanians as 'Italians'*

The Lithuanians shared with Ivan III a desire to seek ancestors in the Classical world. At Lutsk, in 1429, during Vitovt's entertainment of the Emperor Sigismund, the Lithuanian nobles declared to the Emperor that 'the Poles were not nobles before but just simple folk who had bought their coats of arms from the Czechs, while the Lithuanian nobility was the old Roman nobility, their ancestors having come from Italy'. The chronicler relates that the Emperor replied that 'we know ourselves that you are the descendants of the old Roman nobles'. (*Chronicle of Bykhovets*, cited by Lappo.)

(12) *On the Lithuanian Statute*

The first Lithuanian Statute was established in the year 1529. Considerable alterations were introduced into the second version published in the year 1566. It was only then that the political and social privileges of the Lithuanian gentry were definitely confirmed. After the Lublin Union other alterations in the Statute became necessary, and its last and final version was approved by Stephen Báthory and adopted in the year 1588. All three texts of the Lithuanian Statute were written in Russian.

(13) *On the Union of Lublin*

Maksimeyko, N. *Seymy Litovsko-Russkago Gosudarstva do Lublinskoy Unii* (The *Seyms* of the Russo-Lithuanian State to the Union of Lublin), Kharkov, 1902.

Halecki, O. *Dzieje Unii Jagiellońskiej* (History of the Jagellonian Union), Cracow, 1919–20.

Kutrzeba, S. *Unia Polska z Litvą* (The Union of Poland and Lithuania), Cracow, 1914.

The Minutes of the Lublin *Seym* were written in Russian.

(14) *On 'Rzecz Pospolita' (= Res publica)*

The Lublin Union of 1569 created out of the Kingdom of Poland and the Great Principality of Lithuania (and the Duchy of East Prussia) one common state 'Rzecz Pospolita'. The fusion of two different states and two different dominant nationalities was completed. A single ruler, the King of Poland, who was at the same time Great Prince of Lithuania, was elected in full session by the *Rada* (Senate), and the nobility of Poland and Lithuania. During his coronation at Cracow he confirmed the rights and privileges of both nations, the Poles and the Russo-Lithuanians, and swore to maintain those rights and privileges. But the Russo-Lithuanian state (with the exception of the Ukrainian provinces which were severed from it and incorporated in Poland) retained a separate administration, its own seal, its Lithuanian Statute, and its separate army and budget. 'One cannot but note the vital contradiction at the basis of which are two absolutely opposite ideas—of a unitary and of a federative state. This was the result of the contradictory tendencies and wishes brought to the Lublin *Seym* by the representatives of Poland and of the Russo-Lithuanian state' (Lappo).

CHAPTER III

RZECZ POSPOLITA AND THE COSSACK UKRAINE (1569–1654)

§1. THE UKRAINE AT THE TIME OF THE UNION OF LUBLIN: THE COSSACKS

BY the Union of Lublin the direct authority of the Polish crown was extended to the South Russian provinces which had hitherto formed part of the Great Principality of Lithuania. No less than four Russian lands were included within the territory of *Rzecz Pospolita*. But while Black Russia (region to the east of the Niemen including the ancient towns of Grodno and Novogrodek) and White Russia (lands of Minsk, Vitebsk, Polotsk and parts of Smolensk) remained a part of Lithuania, Red Russia (Galicia) and Little Russia (or Russia Minor, comprising the country between the Dniestr and the eastern affluents of the Dniepr) were now ruled directly from Warsaw, whither Sigismund III transferred the capital from Cracow.

The name Little Russia or Russia Minor first became current in the fourteenth century, and is used in the latter and more correct form in a document of Yuri II, the last Prince of Galicia. In a Greek text about 1370 Galicia and Volhynia are named Μικρὰ ʿΡωσσία. In this form the conception of 'older Russia' in contrast to 'greater' or expanded Russia was conveyed. The identical conception is to be found in the classical distinction between Asia Minor and Asia Major, and in the application of the name 'Magna Graecia' to the colonies of Greater Greece in Southern Italy and the Western Mediterranean. The form 'Russia Minor' continued to be used by Muscovite scribes writing in the Byzantine tradition, and *Malaya Rossiya* was the Russian translation; this appellation, through some strange misunderstanding, somewhat offends Ukrainian nationalist writers, although it in no way diminishes, but rather enhances, the historical dignity of the South Russian lands.

In relation to Poland the South Russian provinces occupied a special position: *Ukraïna* (more properly *Okraïna*) was the 'borderland' (*u* = 'in, at', or *o* = 'round', and *kray* = 'border') between the inner parts of the Polish realm and the steppes occupied by the Tartars of the Crimea. Here again the use of the name *Ukraïna* is of ancient origin. As early as the year 1187 a chronicler, in describing the death of a Pereyaslavl prince, states that 'the whole

Ukraina mourned him'. At that time the Pereyaslavl lands were the 'borderland' of the earliest Russian state; in the sixteenth and seventeenth centuries the term is used to describe the frontier lands of the Muscovite state—about Ryazan, the Tula lands, and the Don region. The term was used in the same sense to denote the borderland of the Russo-Lithuanian state in White Russia. It is hardly possible then to discuss the question of a distinctive 'Ukrainian' nationality and its origins, before a peculiar combination of historical factors operating between 1590 and 1700 produced a community on the borderland of the Polish realm which became united by common economic and political circumstances, the vast majority of whose members confessed the Orthodox Greek faith, and which made use of a form of Russian speech—itself continuously subject to modification and adaptation in accord with the circumstances of day-to-day social and economic life.

In the decades preceding the Union of Lublin the south-eastern confines of the Russo-Lithuanian state had remained very sparsely populated. The country along both banks of the Dniepr south of Kiev, and the southern part of Podolia, were subject to the intermittent raids of the Crimean Tartars. Muscovite garrisons occupied fortified posts along the Desna and the Seym in the Seversk lands annexed from Lithuania at the beginning of the century. Nominally, Lithuanian rule extended over the former Pereyaslavl lands along the left bank of the Dniepr, but in reality none knew what went on in that part of the world. To the south of the Seym, in the direction of the Donets and in the region of the left affluents of the Dniepr—the Sula, the Psiol and the Vorskla—stretched the so-called 'Wilderness'. Solitary 'bold men' wandered, or perhaps even settled there, whose main occupation was hunting, who lived at their own risk and peril, sheltered by the empty vastness of the steppe and free of obligation to any landlord or government. The Russo-Lithuanian administration paid little attention to the country lying to the east of the Dniepr, where its only 'bastion' was the small and ancient fortified town of Pereyaslavl surrounded by a wall and moat. To the west of the Dniepr the most populated parts were the northern Kiev lands, bordering on Volhynia and the forests of Polesia. 'Undertaking' landlords preferred to settle there within reach of the protection of the forests and marshes. The more fertile but open and dangerous lands of the southern grassland held no attraction for them.(1)

At the beginning of the sixteenth century rural economy had a character quite different from that which it acquired later. Feudal revenues were chiefly dependent on the proceeds of the trapping of beavers and other fur-bearing animals whose pelts found a ready sale in Central Europe. Fishing was more important than agriculture. Patches of forest were cleared, ploughed and sown, worked out and later abandoned for new clearings. 'Not the fertile black earth was valued, but the marshy and forest districts' (Antonovich).

By the year 1540 Kiev was beginning to become a city again; it numbered about 20,000 inhabitants and possessed six Orthodox churches. A stone castle commanded the upper part of the town; in the lower part along the bank of the Dniepr (the *Podol*) lived a mixed population of artisans and tradesmen, including Poles, Germans, Jews and Armenians. The Cracow canon Mathias a Michov, in his *De Sarmatia Asiana atque Europea*, describes 'the ancient Russian capital which once upon a time was a magnificent and regal city, which is proved by its ruins as well as by what is left standing among its ruins'.

Along the western bank of the Dniepr the small fortified town of Kanev had been built, and still further south was the similar small town of Cherkassy. To the south of Cherkassy stretched 'the Wilderness'; the populated belt of country took a turn to the west, and the southern border of the Kiev lands and the marches of Podolia were marked by the small towns of Belaya Tserkov, Bratslav, Vinnitsa and Bar. In the middle of the sixteenth century the whole of this south-eastern frontier region of the Russo-Lithuanian state did not contain more than 50,000 inhabitants. But from the sixth decade of the century the population began to increase rapidly. The Ukraine was beginning to come into existence.

Two reasons may be found for the spontaneous and natural increase of population in the Ukraine during the latter half of the sixteenth century.

First, a certain measure of over-population had overtaken the neighbouring provinces of the Russo-Lithuanian Great Principality which, up to the beginning of the sixteenth century, had attracted from the Dniepr plains and the land of Podolia great numbers of fugitives from the recurrent attacks of the Crimean Tartars and the invasions of the Turks. Volhynia, for those days, had become relatively densely populated; by the middle of the sixteenth century the province contained not less than 300,000 inhabitants—thus surpassing the density of population in contemporary Prussia and Pomerania.

In these thickly populated regions during the course of the fifteenth and sixteenth centuries the peasantry were gradually being transformed into landless workers. The policy of Casimir IV had been to enhance the power of the lesser gentry at the expense of the great magnates, and one of the results of the strengthening of the influence of the *szlachta* in Polish politics had been to worsen the statutory position of the peasants. In Galicia in the fifteenth century a peasant had still the right to leave his landlord and go over to another on payment of a fine in money and produce. The *szlachta* suffered under this system, since the big landlords, in need of tenantry to open up new lands, could offer attractions to the discontented. After 1435 the peasant was deprived of his right to transfer his services, except once a year—after Christmas. From 1505 even this right was abolished, and throughout Galicia and other parts of Poland a peasant could no longer leave his landlord without sanction. Legal migration from one place to another was at an end, and the peasant was bound to his cot from birth to death. An epidemic of secret flight of individual peasant families from Galicia to Volhynia soon began; and later from Volhynia the area of refuge was extended further eastward, since, although in Volhynia the peasant was not yet definitely bound to the land, the Russo-Lithuanian *szlachta* showed that it would not be slow to follow the example of its Polish fellows. The agrarian reforms of the year 1557 were based on the abolition of all independent peasant farming and on the absolute regulation of peasant labour. The peasant could 'go away' only if he found another to replace him—which was not always an easy matter.

But beyond Volhynia lay the Dniepr region where 'the old Russian order' still continued—admitting free agricultural labour and the free migration of peasants from one place to another. There was therefore a natural drift of the discontented into the Dniepr lands, where there was no authority to ask whether the newcomers were there 'legally' or 'illegally'. In these frontier settlements the peasant way of life was of course less assured, but with the turn of the sixteenth century the Tartar danger had become somewhat less, for protection was afforded by the growing strength of the Cossack communities.

The appearance of the Cossacks was the second reason for the ever-increasing repopulation of the banks of the Dniepr. This reason was the more vital because it had twofold action: the Ukrainian Cossacks more or less effectively protected the new settlers from Tartar and Turkish raids; at the same time they themselves acted as a magnet to the desperate and the adventurous—to all who were not afraid to try their luck in a new life. Men began to go to the Dniepr, not only 'to be with the Cossacks', but also to become Cossacks. Thus the number of the Cossacks grew rapidly. In a very short time —before the Lublin Union—they had already become a potentially significant force in the politics of the Black Sea river lands.

The rise of the Ukrainian Cossacks was the result of a gradual and scarcely noticeable process—scarcely noticeable because it was organic. Ukrainian Cossackdom rose out of necessity, 'by itself', from the submerged classes of the Russo-Lithuanian state, and without any special patronage or encouragement from the administration. This organic growth is the essential characteristic of Ukrainian Cossackdom.

§2. ORIGIN OF THE COSSACKS

The idea of Cossackdom was far from being novel in the sixteenth century, and the word 'Cossack' had a long and not a very lucid history behind it.

The West European form 'Cossack' is, according to Barthold, the result of the Little Russian and Polish pronunciation of the Turkish word *Kazak*, meaning 'robber', 'disturber of the peace', 'adventurer'. It is therefore an occupational rather than a racial designation; but the origins of many racial names are, of course, to be found in popular descriptive appellations, often occupational. 'The existence of the word in Turkish can be first shown in the fifteenth century. During the civil turmoils under the Timurids the pretenders, in contrast to the actual rulers, were called *kazak*: those who would not accept the verdict of fortune but led the life of an adventurer at the head of their men (cf., for example, the *kazak* years (*kazaklik*) of Sultan Husain, afterwards ruler of Khurasan). The name *kazak* is also applied to whole bodies of people who had separated from their princes and kinsmen; in the *Tárikh-i-Rashídi* the Uzbeg, who had abandoned their Khan, are called Özbeg-Kazak or simply *Kazak*; the latter name has been retained by their descendants as an ethnic to the present day. In Russia the word *kazak* first appears about the same time as in Central Asia (in the second half of the fifteenth century) and is probably borrowed from Turkish, although it appears in Russian in a large number of meanings; thus individuals without kinsmen or possessions are called *kazak* even although they did not lead a wandering or marauding life; the word therefore had not yet the exclusively military meaning which it had afterwards' (Barthold, *E.I.*).

Barthold concludes that 'no definite etymological explanation of the word *kazak* has yet been found'; but it is difficult to concur in his statement that 'the last suggestion by N. Marr (*Zhurnal Min. Nar. Prosv.*, 1913, June, p. 286), according to which the old Caucasian ethnic *Kasog* mentioned in the Russian annals under 6473 = 965 is preserved in *Kazak*, is a hypothesis which can hardly be accepted by the historian'. The Circassians (Turkish, *Cherkess*), after the Slavs and the Altaians, were the third—and the oldest—racial factor in Black Sea history. In the eighteenth and first part of the nineteenth century they inhabited the mountains of the Western Caucasus and the country watered by the affluents of the Kuban as far as the Sea of Azov. In the middle of the nineteenth century they were virtually exterminated by the Russians and their remnants scattered throughout the Turkish Empire. In the period between the fifteenth and eighteenth centuries they were an important element in the political and military life of Turkey; and in earlier times they had constituted the backbone of the Mamluk corps in Egypt.

The area occupied by the Circassians has continuously contracted with the expansion of the Muscovite Slavs, but in the fifteenth century the Circassians, with the Alans, certainly extended as far as the Manych and the Don, and both peoples were an element in the mixed population of the Crimea (see Markov, *Ocherki Kryma*).

The subject is obscure and merits exact research, but there can be no doubt that the Circassians were among the mixed racial elements which contributed to the formation of the Ukrainian Cossacks. The Circassians are themselves called *Kasah* in numerous sources, and Russian documents of the sixteenth and seventeenth centuries frequently use the Turkish name *Cherkass* in writing of the Ukrainian Cossacks. The town of Cherkassy was probably originally a purely Circassian settlement; and some Ukrainian names, like Psiol (Circassian, *psu*, 'water'), Khoper, Kremenchug, betray a Circassian derivation.

The root *kas*, *kaz* is very ancient in the Caucasus. It may possibly be connected with the word for 'horse' (*kaz*, plur. *kaz-ar*) in Svanian, one of the oldest of the languages of Georgia. The Georgian pluralization would be *kaz-eb-i* (Kazbi, Kaspi), the Aryan-Armenian, *kaz-kh*(*-i*) (Kazakh, Kasog, Kasah, (?) Gaska). It does not seem fantastic to suggest that from the Caucasian root *kaz*, *kas*, may be derived the names of a number of the horse-riding peoples of the ancient and medieval world. The Kassites who established themselves as an alien dynasty in Babylon in the eighteenth century B.C.; the Gaska of the Hittite world; the Caspii, the remnants of whom were living round the south shores of the Caspian in the time of Herodotus; all these were possibly horse-riding peoples whose names had an occupational origin.

If this derivation be acceptable, the name of the mountains of Caucasus can be explained as *Koh* (Persian, 'mountain') combined with the Svanic-Caucasian root *kaz*, i.e. 'the mountain of horses' or 'horsemen', or more probably of the Kaska; the name of the Caspian Sea, based on the same root, is undoubtedly derived from the ancient

Caspii people—as similarly the Arabs called the sea *Bahr-ul-Khazar*, 'the Sea of the Khazars'.

The borders of the Khazar kingdom ran along the Terek and the Kuban. The Khazars were in constant contact with the Russian principalities on the west and with the Circassian tribes, the Alans, the Georgian kingdom and the peoples of Daghestan on the south. The watch over the frontiers of this very mixed state was given over to mercenaries—Circassians (Kasah), Alans (remnants of the old Sarmatians and progenitors of the modern Os (Russian, *Ossetiny*, from whom is derived the name of the Sea of Azov—'Sea of the Az or As') and Russians. The Don Cossacks consider the Khazar frontiersmen to have been their remote ancestors who, irrespective of tribal origin, had adopted the Russian language and the Greek Orthodox faith. In their turn the Circassian element imported into the life of the Orthodox Russian-speaking Cossacks the typical Circassian dress and arms and many of the customs of the Caucasian mountaineers. When the Kipchak-Polovtsy appeared, the different nationalities who had constituted the population of the Khazar kingdom were driven to the Azov Sea (Tmutarakan) or towards the north. The Tartar invasion of the thirteenth century found their survivors living in the lonely forest region along the left affluents of the Don—the Khoper and the Medveditsa, which in their upper courses run close to and parallel with the Volga. These people, in whom the Don Cossacks see their nearer ancestors, became enrolled as frontier guards of the Golden Horde.

In the fourteenth century Cossacks of Russian and other origins were posted as sentries to guard the fords and convenient crossings along the Don, the Khoper and the Donets. They were considered skilful watermen and undertook the protection of Genoese merchants in the Azov Sea and along the Crimean coast. The Cossacks at that time formed part of the Mongol imperial organization.(2)

In the fifteenth century the Russians adopted the word *kazak* and the conception which it conveyed. In the reign of the Great Prince Vasili II, who had made long sojourns among the Tartars and who had friendly connexions with them, many Tartars of rank were invited with their men to settle on the borders of the Muscovite state and to keep guard against the raids of the wild Finnish tribes of the upper Kama—the Cheremises, Mordva and Meshchera. Thus the mixed Russo-Tartar region of Kasimov on the Oka, east of Ryazan, came into existence. The southern boundaries of the Ryazan lands were protected by settlements of 'Ryazan Cossacks'.(3, 4)

Under Ivan III frontier Cossacks became a regular institution of the Muscovite state. Beside the Ryazan Cossacks who were guarding the southern frontier, there appeared Cossacks on the Lithuanian border, for instance, near the town of Toropets south of Pskov, who undertook the same service. In the Seversk land, conquered by Vasili III in 1517, the Seversk Cossacks were organized to settle in the districts of Putivl, Rylsk, Novgorod-Seversk and Starodub. Thus the Tartar system of frontier organization was adopted and developed by the Muscovite state. The neighbouring Russo-Lithuanian Great Principality might have been expected to follow, but after the time of Vitovt the administration became increasingly weak and defective in military matters and the significance of the Cossack system was ignored.

A document of the year 1504 mentions, in the districts bordering on Muscovy, not only 'town Cossacks' but also 'village' and even 'country Cossacks'. In the end all people living along the Dniepr began to be called Cossacks without distinction—whether they were the remains of former populations or newcomers from the west who had arrived of their own free will and not been brought there by some adventurous 'undertaking' landlord.

At the end of the sixteenth century the Dniepr Cossacks formed the country population, owned land—leading a settled life under their *starosty* (elders)—and made up the armed contingents for guarding the border. They made their living by agriculture, fishing and trade. They hunted and tamed the wild horses of the steppe, and were skilled trappers of beavers and other fur-bearing animals. Bee-keeping was widely practised in the Bratslav and Vinnitsa districts. Beehives stretched for thirty versts around the town of Bratslav. The Ukrainian Cossacks also served as guides to the Genoese caravans trading between the Crimea and the interior and to Armenian and Jewish merchants out of Turkey. Relations with the government were maintained exclusively through the *starosty*, who invariably were members of the Russo-Lithuanian nobility. These *starosty* resided in Kanev, Pereyaslavl, Chigirin, Belaya Tserkov, Bratslav, Vinnitsa and Bar. It was in the capacity of *starosta*, at Bar, that Prince Ostrozhsky, celebrated for his victory over the Muscovites at Orsha, started his career. Eustace Dashkevich, who went over with Michael Glinski to the service of Vasili III and who later returned to Lithuania, had been *starosta* in Kanev and Cherkassy.

As *starosty* Ostrozhsky and Dashkevich were incessantly occupied with the struggle against the Crimean Tartars. In 1524 Dashkevich and his Cossacks repulsed a raid of the Crimean Khan who was trying to possess himself of the town of Cherkassy. Soon after this event Dashkevich made a proposal in the Lithuanian *Seym* that, following the example of Muscovy, a regular organization should be granted to the Dniepr Cossacks, but the government refused. Dashkevich was the first to change Ukrainian tactics in the struggle with the Tartars and from a purely defensive attitude to go over to the attack: he used to lead the Cossacks beyond the Dniepr and capture from the Tartars their herds of sheep and horses.

§ 3. THE ZAPOROGIAN *SECH;* LANDLORDISM IN THE UKRAINE

A decisive part in the history of the Ukrainian Cossacks was played by the Cherkassy *starosta* Dmitri Vishnevetsky. His exceedingly stormy life did not last long, but it was full of picturesque episodes. Vishnevetsky decided to create a base for those Cossacks who went in search of game and good fisheries in the region of the lower Dniepr beyond the cataracts, and in the year 1557 he secured from Sigismund II authority to build a fortress on the island of Khortytsa. Such was the beginning of the *Zaporózhskaya Sech* (in Ukrainian *Sich*), 'the Clearing beyond the Rapids'. All the bold and adventurous elements among the Cossacks had been dreaming of escaping *za porogi* (Ukrainian *porohy*), 'beyond the rapids', where the labyrinth of small islands in the Dniepr, covered with dense vegetation, was full of game, and where fabulous quantities of fish were to be harvested, but where, owing to the vicinity of the Tartars, life was dangerous. Soon it became the ambition of every Cossack to call himself a Zaporogian.

From his stronghold beyond the cataracts, Vishnevetsky, profiting by the campaigns of the Muscovite *voyevodes* Adashev and Rzhevski, undertook a series of successful attacks against the Tartars of the Crimea. He extended the sphere of his operations also to the neighbouring principality of Moldavia, and began that long epic of Cossack attacks on the Turkish power which was to prove often so embarrassing to the policies of the Polish kings.

In the year 1563, Vishnevetsky was taken prisoner and tortured to death in Istanbul. The memory of Vishnevetsky still lives among the Ukrainian peasantry; there is a famous song about 'Bayda' which is sung to this day.(5)

The activities of the Zaporogians disturbed both the Lithuanians and the Turks. In 1568, the year before the Lublin Union, Sigismund II, anxious lest the Turks should be provoked to war, gave an order for the destruction of the fortifications on the Dniepr islands and forbade the Cossacks to settle beyond the cataracts. The royal fiat was ignored by the Cossacks; the Zaporogian *Sech* continued to exist and soon its fame spread far and wide among the whole of the population of the Ukraine.

During the decade of the Union of Lublin, along the Dniepr round Kanev and Cherkassy, in southern Podolia and on the confines of the steppes, life ceased to be as full of danger and adventure as it had been fifty years before in the time of Ostrozhsky and Dashkevich. The feats of Vishnevetsky's Zaporogian Cossacks, the campaigns of the Muscovite *voyevodes*, and the attacks of the Don Cossacks—who, about the middle of the century, had settled on the lower Don—all these factors had tended to weaken the Tartars. The theatre of war between the Ottoman imperial power and the peoples of Eastern Europe was spreading from the Danube countries and the Carpathians to the whole of the northern shore of the Black Sea, and the initiative in the defensive against the Ottomans was passing from the stricken Hungarians and the embarrassed Poles to the new communities of frontiersmen on the Dniepr and the Don and to the Muscovy Tsars.

The Turks seem to have been conscious of this development when the Grand Vizier Mehmed Sökölli—himself a Herzogovinian Slav—in the years 1569–71 undertook a great counter-offensive against Muscovy, which was combined with the ambitious plan to build a canal from the Don to the Volga. But a Turkish army was defeated before Astrakhan (1569), and the great raid of the Crim Tartars on Moscow, disastrous as it proved to the Russians, was without any permanent effect. The naval defeat at Lepanto and the subsequent preoccupation of Sökölli in the war with Venice and Spain effectively deferred further operations against Muscovy and the Cossacks; when Sökölli again turned his attention to the Black Sea, in the last year of his life, it was in an effort to substitute Turkish for Iranian hegemony in Georgia and Daghestan (1578).(6)

The Ukraine enjoyed some years of comparative quiet, and this short time allowed the Dniepr lands and Podolia to blossom into prosperity. In these vast and fertile lands the old peasant order, which had long been forgotten in the other parts of the Russo-Lithuanian state, continued to subsist. The system of a landowning nobility did not extend far south of Kiev; in the region round Cherkassy, until the middle of the century, only three estates are known as having been the property of nobles.

Until the Lublin Union the Vilna government had been content to do no more than appoint its *starosty*, who represented the administration, while the people lived in communities which they themselves had freely organized; elected trusted men from among themselves as judges and officials; and protected themselves and the frontiers of the state by their own efforts and their own means.

So soon, however, as it was known that the Ukrainian provinces were to come under the direct administration of the Polish crown, the movement of migration from west to east which had hitherto had only an individual character assumed mass proportions. 'When the decision of the *Seym* was published, which bound the peasants to the land after an interval of ten years, the result was a wholesale flight. Peasants escaped without fulfilling the conditions of their contracts; there followed a general migration and pursuit. The further lay the region, the more welcome, since it was easier to hide there. From all parts of the Great Principality peasants were now flying to the steppes which offered them enormous advantages. The ratio of growth of population in the Ukraine during that period exceeded by far that of the growth of population in North America during the nineteenth century. There the population doubled in twenty-five years; here it grew in fifty years from 50,000 to 500,000' (Antonovich).

But the rapid growth of population was not due only to the migration of fugitives. There came also peasants who were transported to the east by 'undertaking' landlords. In this respect the Lublin Union had had the effect of drastically altering the earlier state of affairs, when the Russo-Lithuanian gentry unwillingly settled on estates in the dangerous steppeland zone and when the Polish gentry were prohibited from acquiring lands in the territory of the Great Principality. Under the Union the prohibition was ended, and Poles could now settle in the Ukraine.

The Union coincided also with a decisive change in the conditions of agriculture: uncultivated lands suddenly acquired an attraction for Polish landlords. There was a growing demand for wheat in Western Europe, and the eastern wheatlands were beginning to assume an importance in relation to the general economy of Europe. Trade in cereals by way of the Baltic developed with great rapidity. Danzig became the principal *entrepôt* for this trade, and in Danzig were founded numerous export houses by Dutch, German and Scotch merchants who received and shipped the cereal cargoes which were floated down the Vistula. 'The Polish gentry were now petitioning the government to grant them fertile lands for which there was a great demand in the last twenty-five years of the sixteenth century' (Doroshenko).

Already in the year of the Lublin Union a register had been made of unowned lands in Podolia and Volhynia. On his succession to the throne of the last Jagiellonian King, the Hungarian Stephen Báthory had realized that the first problem which presented itself to his government was the distribution of lands in the eastern border provinces and the foundation there of important estates. After the death of Báthory, during the election of Sigismund III Vasa, lands were lavishly distributed among those members of the *Seym* who had voted in his favour. On that occasion the two brothers Vishnevetsky received vast estates on the left bank of the Dniepr, where large settlements arose with incredible rapidity—Lubni, Romen, Piryatin, Pryluka and, at the beginning of the seventeenth century, Poltava. That part of the Ukraine situated to the west of the Dniepr numbered hundreds of villages by the end of the sixteenth century. Along the right bank, on the confines of the steppe, a commission of the *Seym* ordered the *starosta* of Vinnitsa, Kolanovsky, to make a report on the unpopulated region of Uman. Kolanovsky sent in a report to the effect that these lands were no good, and in the meantime himself took possession of the whole of the Uman region— comprising all the southern part of the later Government of Kiev. The Government prosecuted him for this ingenuous action.

The force of attraction which the Ukraine had for that generation of Polish landlords is well illustrated by a literary document of the year 1590. 'The Ukraine is the most precious possession of the Polish crown. Her meadows are as beautiful as the Elysian Fields. They either stretch along plains or are intersected by hills, forests and woods. The prospect is pleasant and suggests abundant harvests. In the Ukraine domestic and wild birds and animals are so plentiful that it makes one think that this is the birthplace of Ceres and Diana. Her beehives are so full of honey that one forgets about the Sicilian Gela and Attic Hymettus. The vine also grows there and wine might easily be made. Italian nuts are so plentiful there that it makes one think that the Ukraine was once upon a time Italian soil. It is impossible to make a list of all her lakes overflowing with fish. Oh, why waste words when one phrase expresses all! This is the Promised Land about which God spake to Israel! Rivers of milk and honey flow here! He who once has been to the Ukraine can never leave her because she attracts men as the magnet attracts iron' (quoted by Doroshenko).

It is easy to imagine how such enthusiastic descriptions appealed to the imagination of Polish landlords eking out their existence on thin sandy soil covered with straggling undergrown pinewoods somewhere to the west of the Vistula or on the borders of East Prussia. It is not surprising that as a result of the migration to the east of both Polish landlords and labourers, the poor and unprofitable lands of Mazovia and Malopolska soon became depopulated. Complaints on the subject were voiced in the *Seym*. In Volhynia, at the end of the sixteenth century, the population exceeded 600,000; and with the flow of migrants to Podolia, to the Dniepr, and beyond the Dniepr, the numbers of the inhabitants of the whole of the Ukraine (excluding Galicia) had, by the beginning of the seventeenth century, reached 1,500,000.

The Poles were confronted by the greatest opportunity in the history of their race. They were stumbling into the Promised Land at a moment when their enemies and neighbours were not capable of disputing it with them; for the Turks were entering into that first period of decline which has been so memorably delineated by Sir Thomas Roe; the Russians were about to fall into the Time of Troubles; and the Germanic powers, with Sweden, were approaching the decades of the Thirty Years' War. For the Poles it should not have been difficult to have effected a racial fusion with the heterogeneous and uncultured population of the Ukrainian new lands. The religious rivalry between Orthodox and Catholic was the principal obstacle; in a more devout century the astute Casimir IV had succeeded in going some way to reconcile the religious feud which was always latent between the Poles and the Russo-Lithuanians. Sigismund III Vasa, who ruled in Poland during the crucial decades, was not so bigoted as his detractors would hold, but he was sombre and uninspired, and the imperial politics of Central Europe interested his ordinary mind more than the original problems of the new southeast.

The problem was social even more than racial and religious, and the social structure of the Polish realm was such as to make it impossible for any but the autocrat, which Poland never had, to solve the unprecedented difficulties which confronted government in the Ukraine.

Stephen Báthory, the predecessor of Sigismund and the brilliant favourite of the Polish *szlachta*, had been no more suited than the pious Catholic King to curb the gentry and befriend the peasants. His early life as a Hungarian magnate predisposed him to mirror the prejudices of the feudal class and to regard free peasants as mutinous serfs. And on the incorrigible class instincts of the Polish gentry, the future of the Polish nation was wrecked. The Promised Land of the Ukraine became the graveyard of *Rzecz Pospolita*.

The Polish order and Polish law knew only three classes: the nobles (landowners); the burghers of the towns; and the peasants—who were entirely dependent on their landlords, and who had therefore to be governed through the lord who owned the land on which they were living. The Cossacks did not belong to any of these categories; but the whole of the rural population of the Ukraine called themselves Cossacks. The intelligent and energetic Stephen Báthory was confronted with the problem of how to deal with the Cossacks, and he attempted to solve it with characteristic directness. He declared as state property all lands which were not owned by nobles. Such lands could be given to a noble in recompense for services to the crown or leased to individuals for their lives. Many of these lands were, however, inhabited by people who stubbornly continued to call themselves Cossacks, and who maintained the right to a free social status which the Polish Government refused to recognize. The authorities pretended to regard these people as tenants of landlords to whom their lands had been nominally granted or of those who had taken up Government leases. It proved, however, impossible to impose this formula during the first decades of the seventeenth century; on the one hand, the Cossacks who had settled independently in different districts were so numerous that interference with them would have proved dangerous; on the other hand, there was still so much unoccupied land that newly arrived 'undertaking' landlords preferred to select districts where they might avoid conflicts. The majority of the Ukrainian population continued to live as of old 'on its own will', subject to little control, and, for the time being, not much troubled by anyone. They were aware that their right to their chosen form of social organization was formally denied, and remained ready to rebel against any attempt to introduce Polish law by force.

Meantime, Stephen Báthory had been attracted by the military possibilities of the Cossacks. Attempts had already been made under his predecessors to register those men who could really be called Cossacks—to enrol those capable of giving effective military service. Special Cossack detachments were created, and in the year 1578 the first Cossack regiments were formed. The number of men included in the lists of 'registered' Cossacks was about 6000; at least this is the figure upheld in the Cossack tradition of the following century. Cossack regiments on campaign formed part of the Polish army. The experiment was, however, developed on a very modest scale owing to the chronic lack of funds in the royal exchequer, and to the objection of the Polish *szlachta* to allowing the King to reward military service (as was usual among 'free' Poles serving with distinction in war) with the status of nobility.

Apart from the few thousands of 'registered' Cossacks, who gradually acquired a privileged position and came to be favoured and relied upon by the Polish administration, there remained the tens of thousands of 'unregistered' Cossacks who claimed the right to a free status which the Government did not recognize. It was in the Zaporogian *Sech*—in 'the Clearing beyond the Rapids'—that these 'unregistered' Cossacks, comprising the mass of the Ukrainian settlers, found the natural focus of their discontent and of their love of freedom.

It is very characteristic that the first Government document in which the Zaporogian *Sech* is mentioned is the order of Sigismund Augustus for its dissolution. The numbers of the Zaporogian Cossacks who were living out of reach of the authority of the Polish Government grew very rapidly in the years following the Union of Lublin. 'After the year 1570', as Kulish writes, 'beyond the cataracts, on the islands of the lower Dniepr, far from the Polish gentry, a Cossack brotherhood was founded where all were equal, where the chief who enjoyed the power of a dictator was dressed in the same way as the rest, where fine clothes were of no account unless a bold hand had taken them off some slain Turk or Tartar. This brotherhood, which adopted poverty because it wished to do so, founded the famed Zaporogian *Sech*, which kept large supplies of arms and gunpowder, where chivalry was instilled into young Cossacks and where no women were allowed under any pretext. The *Sech* was the refuge, the home of all Cossacks, and all Cossack troops, wherever they were, called themselves Zaporogians.'

Accounts of foreigners at the end of the sixteenth century give a vivid image of life and customs in the Zaporogian region.

The Italian Gambarini wrote about 1584: 'Some of the Cossacks are in the King's service and live on the islands under the rule of the Hetman to protect the frontiers against the Tartars. Others in the majority are labourers who earn their livelihood by plundering Turkish and Tartar lands and return home with their booty. If one tried one could assemble about 14,000 or 15,000 men who would make excellent troops out of these daring fellows. They are not so much in quest of loot as of glory and are ready to meet any kind of danger. Their armament consists of sabres and guns and they never miss a target. They are excellent both as infantry and as cavalry, and they are called Cossacks because they are as lithe as goats (Russian, *koza*, 'goat'). They live in huts covered with reeds and eat whatever is at hand. Their principal food consists of fish and what they can take from the Tartars. They never eat bread and they drink pure water. There are all sorts of nationalities among them: Poles, Germans, Frenchmen, Italians and Spaniards, who for some reason cannot go back to their own countries. They find a sure refuge here. No hand can reach them. Comradeship is strong among them. They live on small islands if they are few, and go over to larger islands as they become more numerous. Wood is plentiful and they build hurdles out of it, so that even in winter when the Dniepr is covered with ice they are not afraid of their enemies attacking them unawares. In summer the river cannot be forded because wide marshes stretch along its banks. No one can possess himself of these islands; not only possess himself of them, but not even find them if he does not know the right way to them. These Cossacks are also good sea-fighters; they have all sorts of craft in which they sail in order to plunder the Turkish coast.' Gambarini's account is based on the narrative of a Cossack who was made prisoner by the Turks and later escaped to Italy.

In 1594 the Hungarian Eric Lassota arrived at the Zaporogian *Sech* as the emissary of the Emperor Rudolf II to persuade the Cossacks to take part in war against the Turks. He met there the envoys of the Muscovite Tsar Theodore, who were concerned to direct the energies of the Cossacks against the Crim Tartars. It was indicative of the growing fame of the *Sech* that the Emperor should have chosen to enter into direct relations with the Cossacks, who were formally the subjects of the King of Poland. Lassota brought with him as gifts from the Emperor 8000 gold ducats, horns, tambourines and imperial standards. He was greeted by an artillery salute.

Lassota found about 6000 men suitable for a regular campaign. He saw great stores of arms on the islands; herds of horses; whole flotillas of varied craft. The *pourparlers* continued for long, for the Cossacks had a love of bargaining. When agreement was reached, horns were blown, guns thundered and fireworks were discharged during the night. Lassota received as a parting gift a hat and coat of black fox.(7)

§ 4. THE POLISH COUNTER-REFORMATION AND THE CRISIS OF THE ORTHODOX CHURCH

The first half of the seventeenth century was a period of convulsion and revolution throughout Europe. Emergence from the feudal relationships of the Middle Ages and the development of commercial capitalism was the occasion for a widespread (often subconscious) two-century long struggle for power between the forces of liberal oligarchy and of imperial autocracy. The struggle, like all struggles of principle, was never solved, and eventually was lost in the newer forms of antagonism which grew out of the history of the eighteenth and nineteenth centuries.

In France the Huguenot Wars, in Germany the Thirty Years' War, in England the Civil War, gave varying results which were to influence the history of the succeeding centuries.

The history of Eastern Europe during this same period had an important influence on affairs in the West. The first period of decline in the Ottoman Empire (death of Mehmed Sökölli, 1578 to majority of Murad IV, c. 1630) undoubtedly allowed time to the house of Habsburg to establish a short-lived hegemony in Germany and to impose the Counter-Reformation in several countries which would otherwise have remained or have become Protestant. In 1576, when Rudolf II succeeded to the Habsburg dominions, 'the whole of Austria and nearly the whole of Styria was mainly Lutheran; in Bohemia, Silesia and Moravia, various forms of Christian belief struggled for mastery; and Catholicism was almost confined to the mountains of Tirol' (Encyc. Brit. 11th ed.). Hungary preferred the Zapolyas (Turkish protegés) to the Habsburgs, and the Sultan was supporting the Translyvanian Protestants. By 1630, when Turkey was again becoming an aggressive imperial force under Murad IV (whose work during the middle decades of the century was to be continued by the Köprülü viziers), the obstinate and narrow personality of Ferdinand II had combined with the military genius of Wallenstein to impose the Counter-Reformation in Germany, and it seemed that Austria would establish its predominance throughout Germany and that the Baltic would become an Austrian lake' (Encyc. Brit. 11th ed.)

During this same time the Slav peoples of Eastern Europe were engaged in a titanic struggle which was to have results as far-reaching as those of the contemporary Thirty Years' War in Germany. This struggle endured for sixty-four years—from the appearance of the first False Dmitri as claimant for the Muscovite throne in 1603 to the Treaty of Andrusovo between a renascent Muscovy and an enfeebled Poland in 1667. It had many dramatic episodes, for it opened with murderous civil war in Muscovy and grew into an epic attempt to impose a Polish Tsar and a Polish hegemony in Moscow. It witnessed the popular revolts of the Ukrainian Cossacks culminating in 'the Deluge' of 1648. It ruined the brilliant culture of the Polish realm and carried the Muscovites to the threshold of world power, which they were destined to cross in the opening decades of the eighteenth century.

The influence of the Slav struggle on the Thirty Years' War may be briefly considered, if only because the Polish struggle for hegemony over the Orthodox Slavs was in many respects an easterly projection of the Counter-Reformation. The check administered to Sultan Osman II at Khotin in 1621 by the Poles and Cossacks had the indirect effect of relieving the position of Ferdinand II on his eastern frontiers at the beginning of the Thirty Years' War, and the

policy of Sigismund III, who at the same time adhered to the
Catholic reaction and pressed his own claims to the throne of
Sweden, greatly strengthened the imperialists during the first decade
of the war. But after the Truce of Stumdorf with the Swedes (1635)
the growing pressure of the Cossack revolts (1636 and 1638)
weakened the influence of the Poles in German and Baltic politics.
The terrible revolt of Khmelnytsky broke out in 1648 when the
Treaty of Westphalia was crowning the victory of the Protestant
powers in Germany. And the disappearance of Poland as a great
power after the Treaty of Andrusovo prepared the rise of first,
Sweden and later, Brandenburg-Prussia as the dominant Baltic
powers.

The struggle of the Poles with the Eastern Orthodox Slavs in the
seventeenth century had three main aspects.

First, the effort of the Polish kings to subordinate the Greek
Orthodox Church in the Ukraine to the influence of the Catholic
religion and culture had social and political implications, but it was
at the same time a manifestation of the Counter-Reformation in
Poland which had received its impulse from the Jesuits who had been
introduced into the kingdom by Stephen Báthory—with the original
object of assisting him in his educational reforms. It was Jesuit in-
spiration too which gave some ideal colour to the marauding attempts to establish a Polish nominee in the Kremlin.

Secondly, the struggle between Poles and Russians represented a
contest of two differentiated racial groups for control over the whole
area of geographical unity contained within the fluvial network between the Baltic and the Black Sea. That it was not impossible of
achievement by the Poles is sufficiently proved by the fact that it was
achieved by the less advanced Muscovites during the following
century. Two centuries before, Vitovt had come near to imposing
a Lithuanian hegemony over the whole of the fluvial area of geographical unity. Stephen Báthory, after Henri IV, the first soldier of
his age, had shown that the Muscovite military machine could easily
be broken by a commander of European experience. Vladislav IV,
the second Polish Vasa, was a man of real genius, with a wide popularity among the masses of the Ukrainian Cossacks, and he had been
prepared to abjure the Catholic faith in order to secure the Muscovite
crown.

The third aspect of the struggle was that of a conflict between two
systems of government. It is a paradox that the liberal or rather anti-
monarchical individualism of the Polish gentry should have been the
factor fatal to Poland when the view of life which they represented
was considered to be the modern and the winning force in the

Protestant West. But an addiction to extremes, an obsession with the ideal, is probably a fatality of the Slav character, the origins of which are to be sought in the whole of Slav history. The individualism of the Polish *szlachta* was a reduction to absurdity of all the principles of liberty on which an ordered social life can be based. Their infatuation with liberty disguised in fact a narrow exclusiveness which was intent to confine all its benefits to their own class. Few countries have produced such wise monarchs as the first two Sigismunds or such royal paladins as Stephen Báthory, Vladislav IV and John Sobieski, commanders so gallant as Chodkiewicz and Żółkiewski, or statesmen of the calibre of John Zamojski. That none of these could win permanent fruits in face of the inherent anarchy and factiousness of the Polish social system is sufficient condemnation not only of that system but of the class who upheld it and of the minds of the successive generations of men who composed that class. Against the anarchic liberalism of the Polish gentry the sombre and in many respects clumsy and primitive despotism of the Muscovite state could not lose; and it was only a ruthless autarchy which had the possibility to master those vast plains between the Urals and the Vistula and to tame the dark-minded millions of their inhabitants. So the pupils of Edighey were victorious over the heirs of Vitovt.

The Reformation—which indeed had its origin in Bohemia—attained a greater strength in Central and Eastern Europe than is generally remembered. In Austria, in Hungary and Transylvania, and in Poland, the forces of Protestantism gained and maintained varying degrees of influence for considerable periods of time. In Poland, in the Hussite times, the Jagiellonian princes had not regarded the early Reformation with disfavour; the extreme individualism of the Polish gentry usually imposed a degree of tolerance in religious affairs (the Jews, for instance, had been treated for centuries with marked consideration). The two Sigismunds, enlightened princes of the Renaissance, held a balance between the numerous Protestant sects and the less tolerant of the prelates of the Roman Catholic Church.

'The rising tide of the Reformation reached Poland from the West. The first distinguished poet in the Polish language, Rey, became a Calvinist in middle age; the first distinguished prose writer, Orzechowski, was a priest who married and quarrelled with his bishop. Parliament after Parliament demanded the Polish language in Church ritual, also civil jurisdiction and state taxation for the clergy, abolition of their celibacy, the Communion in both kinds, and the Convocation of a National Church Assembly. The King himself (Sigismund II) leaned to the reformed side, and quarrelled with the

Pope over a divorce, like Henry VIII. And yet the ideal of a Polish National Church, which might have given strength to the State, was wrecked on the shoals of unlimited Polish individualism. The Protestant movement at once split up on Polish soil into sheer sectarianism, and even the genius of one of the makers of the Reformation—the Pole, John Łaski, who had won fame in the history of Frisian and English Protestantism—did not succeed in bringing the wrangling factions of the dissenters to a common understanding. On the other hand, the conflicts with Orthodox Russia on one side, and Lutheran Prussia on the other, united the Roman Catholic Poles under the banner of their common faith. It was a symbol of the ultimate victory of Catholic Counter-Reformation over Protestant Reformation in Poland when the King accepted the Book of Decrees of the Council of Trent from the hands of the Papal Nuncio (1564). Soon afterwards the Jesuits, that vanguard of militant Catholicism, came to stay, and a ramshackle alliance of the Protestant sects—the Concord Act of Sandomir (1570)—was no wall against such a disciplined power' (Dyboski).

The Roman Catholic Church had never abandoned interest in the Eastern Slavs since the days of the Archbishopric of Gazaria and the Council of Florence. Ivan IV had even held out the prospect of the mass conversion of Muscovy when he sought to secure the mediation of the Pope after his defeats at the hand of Stephen Báthory.

Now stimulated by the rising force of the Counter-Reformation, and with a devout king upon the throne whom a countryman has with some exaggeration compared to Philip II of Spain, the Catholic hierarchy in Poland set themselves to compass the conversion of the mass of Orthodox people in the south-eastern provinces who had come under direct Polish control as the result of the Union of Lublin. They were the Church of the higher culture and the Church of the ruling race, and the bucolic *naïveté* and ignorance of the Orthodox priesthood was no match for the worldly wisdom and devoted discipline of the soldiers of Ignatius Loyola. But the Catholic Church was also the Church of the Polish landlords, and neither its subtle propaganda nor the real worth of its organization could overcome the suspicious tenacity of the wary Ukrainian peasants.

In the middle of the sixteenth century the Orthodox Church in the Russo-Lithuanian Great Principality had presented a spectacle of utter decadence. The Church had considerable wealth at its disposal, and some of the monasteries owned vast lands. Turbulent and licentious nobles acquired the bishoprics and the abbacies through family influences. Typical of these princely prelates was the Bishop

of Lutsk, Jonas Borzobohaty ('the very rich'), who took monasteries by storm with the aid of artillery, and who closed churches
until a fine was paid for reopening them. No better was his successor Cyril Terlecki, who was tried for murder, rape and brigand-
age. The Patriarch of Constantinople had to depose one of the
Kievan Metropolitans for bigamy. Many members of the higher
hierarchy, although they stopped short at crime, led lives of notorious
debauchery. The lower priesthood was entirely under the patronage
of local landlords, and their position was difficult where the latter
was a Catholic and their flock consisted only of the peasantry. In
many cases the landlord simply closed the church or monastery on
his land and confiscated its goods in his own favour. Under such
conditions the position of the rural clergy was becoming intolerable.
Only 'the last of the last', the hungry and ignorant, became Orthodox priests, and the saying was current at that time that one sooner
met an Orthodox priest in a tavern than in a church.

Greek Orthodoxy became the religion of 'menials', that is, of
peasants, and the nobility of Russian origin who had adopted Polish
ways of life and become Catholic were ashamed of the old religion.
Among the nobility the number of those who remained faithful to
Orthodoxy diminished every year. There were exceptions, but these
exceptions were few. The Lithuanian Hetman, Gregory Chodkiewicz,
remained Orthodox; so also did the widely celebrated Prince Constantine Ostrozhsky, who was one of the most prominent and active
members of the Orthodox Church and who founded the only
Orthodox college in Ostrog, where, in the year 1580, the Bible was
printed in Slavonic. But even in ancient families of the most distinguished lineage where Orthodoxy was a time-honoured tradition
—as, for instance, the powerful and wealthy Vishnevetskys—a turning of the younger generation to Catholicism could be observed at
the beginning of the seventeenth century. Jeremy Vishnevetsky became one of the most irreconcilable enemies of Orthodoxy; Constantine Ostrozhsky's daughter became a fervent Catholic and
destroyed all her father's work. The lay of Meleti Smotritski called
'The Wail of the Orthodox Church', written on the death of old
Prince Constantine, has the ring of one of the Irish laments of the
eighteenth century for the lost glories of the Catholic Anglo-Celtic
lords, although the influence of formal Oriental metaphors deprives
it of the same charm. 'Where is the mansion of the Princes Ostrozhsky, from which the old faith radiated? Where are the other jewels
of that crown, the priceless sapphires and precious diamonds and all
the glory of the great princely Russian houses?' Meleti then recites
the shameful list of the descendants of Russian princes who had

abjured the faith of their fathers—the princes Vishnevetsky, Slutsky, Sangushko, Czartoryski, Masalsky and many others.

The younger generation among the Russo-Lithuanian aristocracy and gentry were generally converted to the Catholic faith through the influence of the Jesuit schools, which had spread all over Lithuania, Galicia, Podolia, Volhynia and the West Russian lands since the time of Stephen Báthory. The unworthy mode of life of the higher Orthodox hierarchy, the ignorance and low morals of the priesthood, were contrasted in Jesuit propaganda with the spiritual resurrection and discipline of the Roman Church since the Counter-Reformation. The comparison was not in favour of Orthodoxy and had a strong influence on the more thoughtful members of the younger nobility. The propaganda, however, failed to affect the peasantry, the Cossacks and the town workmen, since it was made through schools and the written word.

It was with the object of bringing members of the higher Orthodox clergy under the influence of the Roman Church and of converting a part of the priesthood who could influence the town populations and the peasantry in the Orthodox provinces that the idea of a Union between the two Churches was promoted by certain leaders of the Catholic Church in Poland. The plan held promise of success, for many of the Orthodox hierarchy were attracted by the prospect of material gain, while others favoured union out of genuine concern for the decadence of their Church. The Union was planned in a moderate and mild form on the basis of the decisions of the Florentine Council of 1439; the Orthodox Church was to retain the Eastern Rite, and celibacy was not to be exacted from the priesthood. The Catholics were not so much interested in dogmatic differences as in the recognition of Papal authority by the Orthodox clergy and congregations. The bishops who recognized the Union were to receive the right to sit in the *Seym* like the Catholic bishops, and all Orthodox who accepted the Union were to be placed on a footing of equality with Catholics in the distribution of governmental posts.

Four Orthodox bishops elaborated a decree concerning the Union which in the year 1594 was laid for approval before King Sigismund III and the Papal Nuncio at Cracow. The Kievan Metropolitan, Michael Ragoza, who was not a strong character, was inclined towards the Union. In the following year Pope Clement VIII formally acknowledged 'the Newly United Church', and, to commemorate the event, medals were stamped with the inscription 'Rutenis receptis'.

The whole affair seemed to have been brought to a successful conclusion, but subsequent events proved that hopeful expectations were premature. With Prince Constantine Ostrozhsky at their head, the Orthodox gentry came forward with a series of protests; and signs of nervousness were shown among the townspeople of Lvov, Vilna and Kiev, where the Orthodox unions of merchants and artisans, the so-called brotherhoods (*bratstva*), had well-established craft organizations and considerable means at their disposal.

By the King's order the controversy was submitted to a Church Council which met at Brest at the end of the year 1596. There, instead of coming to agreement, the two sides to the dispute within the Orthodox Church came to a definite break. An armed conflict was narrowly avoided, since the noble supporters of the two interests had attended the Council with their levies and artillery. The Orthodox Church was henceforth divided, and a bitter struggle soon developed between 'the Uniates' and those who adhered to the old Orthodoxy. In the course of this struggle the Orthodox Church attained to a certain spiritual rejuvenation. The national consciousness of the Russian-speaking Orthodox masses was aroused, and Orthodox polemists and orators began to emerge who found a degree of material support among the remaining families of the Orthodox gentry and deep moral support in the sentiment of the townsfolk and the peasantry. Even the Uniate Church in the end 'became the very fortress of Ukrainian separatism against Poland' and 'this was largely due to the illiberal narrow-mindedness of Polish Church dignitaries, who grudged to the Uniate prelates the privileges of their rank and thereby stamped the Uniate faith as the Church of the lower people against Roman Catholicism as the religion of the governing class. The nobles who abandoned Eastern Christianity largely became Roman Catholics, and not Uniates, and thereby deepened the social and national gulf' (Dyboski). (8)

§5. EARLY COSSACK REVOLTS: CHRISTOPHER KOSIŃSKI AND SEVERIN NALIVAYKO

A formidable Cossack revolt against the Polish authorities occurred as early as the year 1590. An adventurer named Christopher Kosiński, a Pole by origin, persuaded a number of the Zaporogians to follow him, not for a campaign against the Tartars or Turks nor to go over into Moldavia as had been customary until then, but to plunder the estates and to burn down the manors of the nobility in Volhynia. A sinister feature of the movement was that a good number of peasants who were Cossacks only in name joined Kosiński in his fortified camp at Tripolye, while local agrarian risings broke out in many parts of Volhynia and Podolia and beyond the Dniepr.

Plundering and arson spread throughout the Ukrainian provinces during the whole of 1592. In the following year Kosiński again ravaged Volhynia, but now the frightened nobles, Orthodox as well as Catholic, appeared in arms, and near Zhitomir, old Prince Constantine Ostrozhsky and Alexander Vishnevetsky routed the Cossack forces, slaying 2000 men and taking twenty-five cannon. Kosiński himself surrendered, but was allowed to go free and perished soon afterwards, no one knew how.

The revolt of Kosiński did not assume sufficient proportions to attract the attention of the Polish court, particularly since 'registered' Cossacks took no part in it, and it had taken the form of disorders committed by an extraordinarily large gang of malefactors. The revolt indicated, however, that there existed elements in the Ukraine which were capable of undertaking an armed struggle against the régime of the Polish landlords.

In 1594 the outbreak of the Long War, in which the Austrians, the Turks, the Transylvanian Prince Sigismund Báthory and the Wallachian Hospodar Michael the Brave became involved in a desultory but murderous quadrilateral struggle, was the occasion for a further movement among the Cossacks which grew to proportions more substantial than the revolt of Kosiński.

The Cossacks found a new leader in Severin Nalivayko, a young officer in the service of Prince Ostrozhsky. He came of a well-to-do family, knew how to read and write and had the reputation of being a trained artillerist. The massacre by the Wallachian and Moldavian Hospodars, Michael the Brave and Aaron the Tyrant, of all Turkish garrisons and settlers in the two principalities, and the capture by the Transylvanian Prince Sigismund Báthory of Rustchuk, Silistria and other towns on the right bank of the Danube was a signal to the Cossacks to attack the Turkish garrisons in the towns along the lower Dniestr. Nalivayko sent a message to the Zaporogian *Sech* calling for men to join him in Moldavia in a Holy War against the Turks. His appeal was more successful than the elaborate negotiations of the Emperor's envoy Eric Lassota earlier in the same year, and not only from the *Sech* but from the whole region round Kiev several thousand Cossacks rallied under the Zaporogian Hetman, Gregory Loboda, to take part in the war on the Danube.

Campaigns in Moldavia had a special attraction for the Cossacks. They had a certain sympathy for the Orthodox Moldavians, and the frequent hostilities between rival candidates for the succession to the thrones of the two Roumanian principalities offered recurrent opportunities for plunder. In 1577 a Cossack, John Potcoava or Podkova, had actually become Hospodar of Moldavia. The Poles generally resented a Cossack intervention which embarrassed their own relations with the Porte, and Stephen Báthory had not hesitated to execute Podkova in order to satisfy the Sultan.

Now 12,000 Cossacks crossed the Pruth, defeated the Turks at Suceava and occupied Jassy; and their intervention was probably a decisive factor in Sigismund Báthory's great victory over the Turks at Mantin, and in Michael the Brave's defeat of Sinan Pasha at Bucarest. Sigismund III had been angered by the Emperor Rudolf's negotiations with the *Sech*, and by the probability that Austrian intrigues were promoting the opposition of the Orthodox nobility to the Union of the Churches which was then under discussion at Brest.

The gifted but half-insane Emperor was playing a fantastical game, for whilst he was pursuing a war against the Turks which was to end in the first definite check to their progress into Central Europe (Treaty of Zsitvatörök, 1606), he was attempting on the other hand to encourage the Orthodox nobility of the Little Russian provinces and the Cossacks against the Catholic Polish monarchy, and to use the brilliant but unstable force of Michael the Brave of Wallachia against the Báthorys in Protestant Transylvania. At the same time Michael, who for a few brief months made himself master of all the Roumanian-speaking lands, was hoping that the twin menace of Boris Godunov and the Ukrainian Cossacks would prevent the Poles from intervening in Moldavia, while the differences between the Habsburg and the Magyar magnates might give him Transylvania (where in 1599 his Cossack body-guard helped him to the victory of Schellenberg).

In the meantime the Poles had struck against the rising Cossack danger. During 1596 a peasant rising had broken out in the town and province of Bratslav. The bands of Nalivayko began to devastate Volhynia where they burnt Polish and Uniate estates, and completely ruined the lands of one of the principal sponsors of the Union of the Churches—the notorious evil-liver, Cyril Terlecki, Bishop of Lutsk. As the champion of Orthodoxy and the Russian-speaking peasantry, Nalivayko himself moved north, and took the towns of Slutsk, Bobruysk and Mohilev, devastating Polish estates and burning down Uniate churches on his line of march. At the same time, Loboda and his Cossacks were making themselves masters of eastern Volhynia and the Kiev region.

While landlords were in headlong flight from all their new lands in the south-east and panic was spreading throughout the country, a small Polish force under the celebrated commander Żółkiewski sought contact with the Cossacks. Nalivayko began to retreat towards the south in the direction of Uman, then turned north to join

Loboda at Belaya Tserkov. Here the Cossacks formed their usual camp of wagons covering a formidable park of artillery, and Żółkiewski, after some fighting, was forced to retreat in the direction of approaching reinforcements.

Nalivayko and Loboda, however, did not find the support among the local population which they had recently enjoyed in Podolia and Volhynia. The local Cossacks, who were mostly 'registered', refrained from joining the rebels against the Government.

Nalivayko and Loboda now crossed to the left bank of the Dniepr and entered the Pereyaslavl lands. Żółkiewski moved in pursuit of them. The peasant population, fearing Polish reprisals, accompanied the Cossacks in the direction of the steppe, hindering their march and destroying their military formation. About 12,000 people, including women and children, left their homes to which they were never to return.

Żółkiewski succeeded in overtaking the Cossacks on the river Solonitsa, near Lubni, and surrounded their camp where, owing to the number of superfluous mouths, hunger broke out. Disagreement arose between Nalivayko and Loboda, in the course of which Loboda was killed. The Zaporogians, wishing to avenge his death, consented to the conditions of surrender proposed by Żółkiewski, which provided for the delivery of Nalivayko and all his artillery, upon which the rest were to be allowed to depart as free men. However, when twenty guns and the Hetman's symbolic staff (*bulava*) had been handed over, the Polish troops killed a large number of those who had surrendered. About 4000 Cossacks perished, and a still greater number of the refugees who had followed them into the steppe, including many women and children. Only 1500 Cossacks succeeded in reaching the *Sech*. Nalivayko was taken to Warsaw and put to the torture. A Ukrainian legend says that he was roasted in a brass bull, and another that he was put astride a red-hot iron horse. Actually he was quartered during the sitting of the *Seym* of 1597. (9, 10)

§ 6. THE COSSACKS A POWER ON THE BLACK SEA: SAMUEL KISHKA AND PETER SAHAYDACHNY

The same *Seym* of 1597 which condemned Nalivayko decided to make an end once and for all of the Cossacks and solemnly declared them to be 'enemies of the country'—*hostes patriae*. Orders were given to the Lithuanian Hetman Żółkiewski to exterminate them. That experienced commander, however, refused to move, for he realized the dangers and difficulties inherent in a campaign against the *Sech*. He preferred instead to conciliate the 'registered' Cossacks, who were themselves anxious to prove their loyalty and to repudiate association with the leaders of the late rising. The 'registered' Cossacks were taking the lead in trying to eliminate the rebellious elements, and this conservative attitude justified Żółkiewski in refusing to interfere with them in spite of the fact that they had been legally dissolved. The flow of 'unregistered' Cossacks who had taken part in the rising to the regions beyond the cataracts only increased as a result of this policy, and new life came to the *Sech* when suddenly an old and popular leader, a Zaporogian named Samuel Kishka ('The Cat'), reappeared, after having made his escape from a long captivity in Turkey.

Hardly had the Polish *Seym* come to the drastic decision to exterminate the Cossacks, when difficulties abroad forced the King, Sigismund III Vasa, to seek Cossack military aid. In 1598 Sigismund, in an effort to establish his legitimate dynastic claim to the Swedish throne, was ignominiously driven out of Sweden by the Protestant party which supported his cousin, Charles, Duke of Sudermania. The possibility—based on the union of the crowns of Poland and Sweden on the head of Sigismund III as the heir both of the Jagiellons and the Vasas—of founding a dominant alliance of Sweden and Poland in Eastern Europe and the hope of carrying the Counter-Reformation into Scandinavia were lost, and Sweden and Poland became involved in a series of wars which were destined to prepare the way for the establishment of Muscovy as a Baltic and Black Sea power.

The dynastic feud between the Polish and the Swedish Vasas affected decisively the internal struggle in Russia, when the Time of Troubles opened in 1603. United under a single Vasa head the Poles and Swedes might have succeeded in annihilating the Muscovite monarchy, but as it was, the Swedish and Polish policies in the Russian civil war were opposed. While the Catholic Poles supported the False Dmitris and later Vladislav Vasa in an effort to fulfil the ancient dream of Vitovt and to establish a hegemony over the whole Eurasian Plain, the Protestant Swedes, temporarily masters of Novgorod, 'believed, for a moment, in the creation of a trans-Baltic dominion extending from Lake Ilmen northwards to Archangel and eastwards to Vologda', and maintained the pretensions of Vasili Shuyski.

In 1600, while Sigismund III was himself preoccupied with the Swedish war, his great chancellor John Zamojski, was pursuing a minor interest of his own in supporting the claims of his cousin Jeremy Movila to the Moldavian throne. The support of the Cossacks became a matter of importance both on the Baltic and in Moldavia, the more so since the Polish armed forces were largely maintained out of the privy purse of the King or out of the private fortunes of great military aristocrats like Zamojski, Żółkiewski and Chodkiewicz. The continual difficulty of extracting monies from the *Seym* to maintain the armed forces generally limited the army at the disposal of the crown, even in time of war, to twenty or thirty thousand men, and it was therefore convenient to resort to the Cossacks, who would fight 'for the love of fighting' and the remote hope of plunder.

When, in the year 1600, John Zamojski appealed to the *Sech* for help in Moldavia, Samuel Kishka persuaded the Cossacks not to go to the aid of those who had declared them 'outlaws'. A letter under the King's own hand failed to move Kishka unless 'all injustices towards the Cossacks ceased' and their former privileges were restored. The King gave all sorts of assurances and promised that at the next session of the *Seym* the measures instituted against the Cossacks should be formally repealed. Four thousand Cossacks then joined Zamojski in Moldavia, but it was only after the King's undertakings had been fulfilled at the session of the *Seym* of 1601, that the Cossacks rode north to join Chodkiewicz in Livonia where the strenuous—and victorious—campaign of 1601-2 awaited them. 'The Cat' himself was killed under the walls of Fellin. (11)

The occasion of the outbreak of civil war in Muscovite Russia in the year 1603 was the appearance of an individual who claimed to be Prince Dmitri, the younger son of Ivan IV, who had in fact probably been put to death as a boy in 1591 on the orders of Boris Godunov. The candidature of the False Dmitri became a private speculation of some of the great Russo-Lithuanian nobles like the Ostrozhskies, the Vishnevetskies, and the Sapiehas. But complicated historical issues were involved. Sigismund III himself was always an uneasy supporter of an adventure which was ultimately to prove disastrous to the Polish monarchy, but his son Vladislav dreamed dreams of empire and had a genius which might have attained their fulfilment, while the Jesuits aimed, both through Vladislav and through the gifted personality of the first False Dmitri, to secure a Latin-Polish hegemony in Muscovy and to attain the union of the Russian Orthodox Church with Rome. At the same time the Time of Troubles first unleashed the anarchic and terrifying strength of the Russian people which found expression, in the beginning in support of the first False Dmitri as a champion of the poor and an innovator and later in a popular revolution against the foreign invader.

It was natural that in the chaos of the Time of Troubles the turbulent and warlike population of the Polish Ukraine should take a blood-stained part. Many Polish, Russo-Lithuanian and Ukrainian nobles were seeking their fortune in the army of the first False Dmitri. With them went numbers of the 'registered' Cossacks, and a far greater number of adventurers and landless men calling themselves Cossacks swarmed into the ranks of the pretender's army. Twelve thousand 'Zaporogian' Cossacks, of whom the majority had never been anywhere near the *Sech*, participated in the defeat of Boris Godunov's forces at Novgorod-Seversk. The Don Cossacks fought for the False Dmitri at Kromy. They had come, 6000 strong, 'to put him on the throne'. During the following years the number of armed men going over from the Ukraine into Muscovy grew in proportion to the growth of anarchy. About 30,000 of them fought under the Polish banners before Smolensk, and at least an equal number were scattered about the country in small detachments, plundering the towns and the rich monasteries and devastating the estates of the *boyars*. Much wealth had been accumulated in Muscovy in the period extending between the reigns of Ivan III and Boris Godunov. During the Time of Troubles it was all plundered, and a considerable part of it was carried into the Ukraine as well as to the Don. To distinguish them from the Don Cossacks, the Ukrainian Cossacks were called by the Muscovites 'Zaporogian Cherkasses'—'the Cherkasses (or Circassians) from beyond the Rapids'.(12)

The processes of civil anarchy in Russia and the vast loot acquired tended both to recruit with great rapidity the numbers of the 'unregistered' Cossacks and to increase the military and political importance of the *Sech*. In the decade between 1606 and 1616 the Zaporogian Cossacks assumed the initiative against the Crim Tartars and the Turks in a number of bold attacks on the Crimean peninsula and the coasts of Asia Minor.

In the year 1606 a flotilla of Cossack craft appeared off Varna, sank nine Turkish galleys and took the town and looted it. A large number of slaves were set free—not only Ukrainians, but also Hungarians, Poles and Germans.

In the winter of 1608–9 the Zaporogians took Perekop, and penetrated into the Crimean peninsula. During the same winter they burnt down the Turkish towns in the delta of the Danube—Kilia and Ismail. In these maritime exploits the Cossacks showed extraordinary ingenuity and courage. They succeeded in their light craft in gliding unseen past the Turkish forts at the mouth of the Dniepr which had been built for the purpose of checking their sorties into the Black Sea. The most difficult part of an expedition was often the return laden with booty, but generally this was happily achieved.

The most fantastic in their recklessness were the raids of the

Zaporogians under their Hetman Peter Sahaydachny, who became one of the most celebrated figures in Cossack history.

In the year 1614 Sahaydachny appeared quite unexpectedly before the wealthy port of Sinope on the coast of Asia Minor. Sinope was looted, and the Turks could count their losses in millions of ducats. The Turkish fleet sent in pursuit of Sahaydachny did not succeed in overtaking him, and in the following year the light Cossack craft suddenly made their appearance in the Bosporus. Sultan Ahmet I suffered the humiliation of seeing with his own eyes smoke rising from the country-houses fired by the Cossacks in the immediate suburbs of Istanbul. On this occasion a Turkish squadron overtook the Cossack flotilla at the mouth of the Danube, but the Cossacks, taking advantage of a dark night, boarded the Turkish ships and captured their admiral. They then took the captured ships to the vicinity of the Turkish fortress of Ochakov, and maliciously burned them under the eyes of the garrison.

In the year 1616 Sahaydachny, in company with the Don Cossacks, undertook his famous expedition against the Crimean town of Caffa—the principal mart for the slaves captured by the Tartars on the Muscovite and Polish borders. About 14,000 Turks and Tartars perished, and thousands of Christian slaves recovered their liberty. In the same year Sahaydachny made a bold raid on Trebizond, and, before returning to the *Sech*, sailed along the coast of Asia Minor and again made his appearance in the vicinity of the Bosporus. (13, 14)

The fame of the Cossacks spread far and wide. They became the paladins of the Orthodox East, and their feats were bruited to Venice, Austria and Spain. It was with no exaggeration that Sahaydachny's friend whom he had made Metropolitan of Kiev, Job Boretsky, could write: 'When the Cossacks go to sea prayers are sent up to Heaven, for their first aim is to fight the Infidels in the name of the Christian Faith. Their second aim is to free captives. No one in the world showers such benefits on Christian captives as they do; not the Greeks with their ransoms, nor the King of Spain with his powerful fleet. How much have the Cossacks achieved owing to their courage and intentness of purpose? What with other nations ends only with fine words and high-flown speeches, the Cossacks put into action.' (15)

Peter Sahaydachny, with whose name are connected so many Cossack exploits, was from every point of view an extraordinary man. He was born at the town of Sambor in Galicia, and passed through Prince Constantine Ostrozhsky's Orthodox school at Ostrog before, owing to some unknown circumstances, he found his way to the Zaporogian *Sech*. Remarkable even among the Zaporogians for his courage and ingenuity, he differed from most of them in his learning. His spectacular services soon caused the *Sech* to elect him as Hetman, and circumstances were such that the Polish Government had to recognize him also as chief of the 'registered' Cossacks. In this wise, in the person of Sahaydachny, the Poles first gave formal recognition to the principle of the unity of all the Ukrainian Cossacks which, up till that time, it had always refused to do.

The different *Seyms* during the second decade of the seventeenth century were still occupied in trying to find a solution of the Cossack question, and in 1614 a special commission was set up with Stanislas Żółkiewski at its head. The commission finally recognized the existence of the Zaporogian *Sech*. The Zaporogians were henceforth to be regarded as Cossacks in the King's service, and were allotted a remuneration as a corps of 10,000 gold pieces a year with a supply of cloth for their wear. The right of the Cossacks to self-government and to their own courts was recognized. Zaporogian administration was not admitted for 'town' Cossacks living on 'royal' territory, who were, however, allowed their own *starosty*. Those who were living on the estates of nobles continued to be considered as peasants.

The recommendations of the commission really remained in the domain of theory, since, in the year 1614, Sahaydachny was virtually ruler of all the Ukrainian Cossacks of the *Sech* and of the Dniepr region from Chigirin to Kiev and beyond the river. The situation could hardly be otherwise, when involved in war on the Baltic, in Muscovy and in Transylvania, the Polish King was under the necessity of constantly appealing to Sahaydachny for military help. In 1616 Sahaydachny went to the rescue of Vladislav Vasa, who had become involved in difficulties in his last Russian campaign; five years later, after the defeat and death of Żółkiewski at the hands of the Turks, Sahaydachny marched with a force of 42,000 men and thirty-two cannon to the relief of Vladislav Vasa and old Chodkiewicz who were surrounded by a large Turkish army at Khotin, and it was this Cossack intervention which brought about the discomfiture and retreat of Sultan Osman II.

Sahaydachny was successful in avoiding sharp conflicts with the Polish Government, which indeed valued him for his worth. At the same time he was not too popular among his own people, since he did not disguise his desire to enforce severe discipline in the 'free' Cossack community. For a short time he was deposed by the Zaporogian *Rada*, but he was restored to the post of Hetman at a difficult moment of the Khotin campaign. Some historians speak of his inclination towards Moscow, but others hasten to deny this. The Muscovite state which Sahaydachny knew and against which he had waged war in 1613 and 1616 was not such as could attract a Ukrainian leader in the struggle against Polish rule. Sahaydachny, on the other hand, with his leaning towards the Orthodox Church, may have looked forward to an eventual alliance of Kiev and Moscow against Warsaw.

Sahaydachny was not only an outstanding military chieftain and the hero of legendary Cossack exploits. He led the struggle for the Orthodox Church with the same intelligence and boldness which he showed in his seafaring feats. It was on his initiative that the centre of Ukrainian Orthodoxy was removed from Lvov to Kiev so that it might be under the protection of 'Cossack sabres'. In Kiev was founded a strong 'Brotherhood' similar in character to that already existing in Lvov (1615), and an Orthodox school was established which soon became a college and later an academy. In the year 1617 the energetic *Igumen* of the Pecherskaya Lavra, Elisey Pleternetsky, set up a printing office where liturgical books, dictionaries and scientific and polemical books were published. A close friendship united Sahaydachny and the Rector of the Kiev College, Job Boretsky, and this remarkable son of the Orthodox Church was established by the Cossack Hetman as the 'secret' Metropolitan of Kiev.(16)

At this time the higher Orthodox hierarchs had been completely eclipsed by the Uniates. Out of ten Orthodox bishops only one had failed to recognize the Union, and the Metropolitan Photius was a Uniate. Sahaydachny decided to reinstate the higher Orthodox church administration. He took advantage of the passage through Kiev on his way from Moscow to Constantinople of the Patriarch Theophanes, and persuaded him to secretly ordain Job Boretsky as Kievan Metropolitan and to ordain also several Orthodox bishops. In order that the Patriarch might not be subsequently subjected to any offence from either Poles or Uniates, Sahaydachny ordered a whole regiment to escort him as far as the Moldavian frontier.

It was not the destiny of Sahaydachny to witness the further development of events when the Swedish and Muscovite wars came to an end for a short period and the Polish Government ceased to depend on the military collaboration of the Cossacks. Sahaydachny died from the consequences of a wound received at Khotin and was buried in the monastery of the 'Brotherhood' at Kiev. Ukrainians consider him with perfect justice to have been one of their most prominent men. Sahaydachny never came into conflict with the Polish Government; in his time the activities of the Cossacks were directed into other channels—either against the coasts of Turkey or against anarchic Muscovy in search of plunder, and the position of the Polish Government was such that, instead of struggling to check the ever increasing force of the Cossacks, it was obliged to appeal to them for aid. As for Sahaydachny's protection of Orthodoxy, in his lifetime the intervention of the Cossacks in Church affairs had not yet become open. This intervention became open a few years after Sahaydachny's death, and then also became apparent the differences existing between the conditions under which the Cossacks wished to live and the conditions which the Polish crown desired to prescribe for them.

§7. LAST DECADES OF POLISH HEGEMONY: MICHAEL DOROSHENKO, SULIMA, PAVLUK

The growth of a spirit of independence in the Ukraine during the three decades between the death of Peter Sahaydachny and the revolt of Bohdan Khmelnytsky must be considered in relation to the contemporary state of the surrounding world.

Round the whole of the basin of the Black Sea, from the middle Danube to the Caucasus, imperial power, after the florescence of the first century of the Renaissance, was in temporary abeyance. The Habsburgs were involved in the struggle for power within Germanic Europe; Poland was seriously weakened by long and unlucky interventions in the politics of Sweden and Muscovy; and Muscovy was slowly and with difficulty recovering from the Time of Troubles; in the Ottoman Empire, where the events of the brief majority of Murad IV presaged the capacity for recovery which the Turks were to show under the Köprülü viziers in the sixties and seventies of the century, the brief revival of the thirties was directed almost entirely to the recovery from Iran of the conquests made by Shah Abbas I.

Over the vast belt of territory watered by the affluents of the Black Sea, from the middle Danube and the Tisza even to the Don and the Caucasian Rion, old peoples stirred to revival; new peoples began to become conscious of their being. It was natural that the streams of thought which ran counter to the imperial Renaissance should infuse the movements which were taking form. An insurgent Protestantism inspired the Transylvanian gentry as Gabriel Bethlen (1613–29) and George I Rákóczy (1629–48) strove to rebuild the Magyar kingdom a century after Mohács. The trampled splendours of Byzantine Orthodoxy haunted the day-dreams of the Roumanian Hospodars, Matthew Bassarab of Wallachia (1632–54) and Basil the Wolf (Vasile Lupu) of Moldavia (1634–53).

The growing wealth of the Orthodox communities in the Ottoman Empire, the influence of the Phanar in the court life of Istanbul and in the policies of the Porte, were significant currents in the contemporary life of the Balkan-Black Sea regions. Corrupt and unstable as they were, the princely régimes in the Roumanian principalities were the centre of the political hopes of the Orthodox Balkan Christians, and the Orthodox culture which was favoured by the princes (the worst of them were often patrons of painting and literature and builders of churches) was the only civilizing influence which could be opposed to the Latin-Catholic ambitions of the Poles and Jesuits.

The relations between the Ukrainian Cossacks and the Moldavians had been intimate since the last quarter of the sixteenth century. One of the Movila princes sat as Metropolitan in Kiev; and there were two Cossack episodes in the chequered history of the succession to the Moldavian throne. The families of George Rákóczy, of Basil the Wolf and of the Hetman Khmelnytsky were allied by marriage. The astute Wolf, a typical 'character' of seventeenth-century Near Eastern history, who was regarded as 'Emperor' by the Orthodox population of Constantinople, was the leading diplomat of his day, and was always intervening—generally on behalf of the Porte—in the dynastic crises of the Girays in Baghchi-Saray and even in the affairs of the Don Cossacks (in 1642 he was sufficiently accommodating to send 3000 Moldavians to work on the rebuilding of the fortress of Azov for the Turks after its evacuation and destruction by the Don Cossacks).

Beyond the Dniestr, the Crim Tartars shared in the tendency to assert regional independence, and in 1624 one of the Girays, who subsequently expelled the Turkish garrison from Caffa, had sent a message to Istanbul that his house was more ancient than that of the Osmanli who ruled the 'womanish' Turks. Even in distant Georgia, ravaged by the invasions of Shah Abbas, the Imerian King, Alexander III, had begun to enjoy an unusually long reign and was astonishing Russian ambassadors and Capuchin friars by the wealth of his court in Kutais.

In the Ukraine and throughout the Russian Orthodox territories of *Rzecz Pospolita* the death of Peter Sahaydachny removed a wise and calculating head from the leadership of affairs. In the Polish *Seymy* which assembled in the years 1623 and 1625 very far-reaching demands were put forward by members of the Orthodox nobility. These demands, although they were never formulated in full, included (1) the abolition of the Union of the Churches, liberty of worship, and the recognition of Orthodox hierarchs ordained by the Patriarch of Constantinople, with the legalization of the 'brotherhoods' and schools founded by Sahaydachny; (2) special law courts for Cossacks and mixed courts in cases of disagreement between Cossacks and other classes of the population; (3) the regularization of the position of the 'registered' Cossacks, and the liberty for the people to settle where they chose—which implied the removal of the restrictions on the migration of peasants; and (4) the recognition of the right of the Cossacks to take service with foreign states, with the recall of Polish garrisons from the Ukraine and their replacement by Cossack units.

In opposition to these demands, which threatened at once the supremacy of the Catholic Church and the privileges of the land-owning class, Sigismund Augustus and his nobles for once found themselves in agreement; and the Orthodox leader, Laurence Drevinsky, went so far as to declare that while the King lived there was no hope for the Orthodox.

Conflicts between Orthodox and Uniate factions began in many parts of the Ukraine. In Kiev, attempts by the Polish soldiery to take possession of Orthodox churches and monasteries resulted in the killing of a Uniate priest and of a Polish official. The Metropolitan, Job Boretsky, and other bishops ordained by the Patriarch of Constantinople, were only safe under the protection of Cossack guards.

The Orthodox hierarchs made overt appeals to Moscow; Job Boretsky wrote to the young Tsar Michael Romanov that 'our only thought is to be taken under thy powerful hand. We have no one to turn to except thyself.' In 1625 delegates from the Ukrainian Cossacks made their first appearance as suppliants in the capital which little more than a decade before they had delighted to pillage.

Meanwhile, in 1624, Cossack detachments with the Nogay Tartars had helped a Giray pretender to evict the Sultan's nominee from Baghchi-Saray and to oust the Turkish garrison from the important slave port of Caffa. Another Cossack raid on the Bosporus further angered the Turks, and a Turkish squadron, after a hard-fought battle off Kara-Kerman on the Bessarabian coast, annihilated a Cossack raiding flotilla.

Embarrassed by Turkish complaints, Sigismund Augustus was moved to action; and the Crown Hetman Koniecpolski marched through the Ukraine with 8000 men. The Cossacks mustered a force of 30,000, and much confused fighting took place round the Kurukovo Lake (near the Dniepr opposite the modern town of Kremenchug). There were divisions between the prosperous element of 'registered' Cossacks and the ruck of the rebels, and finally, through the mediation of the former, peace was made with Koniecpolski.

The Kurukovo Agreement provided for an increase in the permitted number of 'registered' Cossacks to 5000, and lists of these men were to be handed to the Polish authorities within six weeks. The 'registered' Cossacks were confirmed in the right to choose their own Hetman, who was to undertake to prevent further raids against Turkey, to supervise the burning of all sea-going craft of the Zaporogians and to secure the surrender of their artillery. 'The illegally taken lands' were to be surrendered to the nobles, and all who wished to remain on them were to accept the obligations of serfs under Polish law.

The *Seym* of the year 1626 approved the Kurukovo Agreement, but neither the Polish Government nor the Hetman Michael Doroshenko proved able to carry it into effect.

In 1628 a Tartar raid into the Ukraine as far as Belaya Tserkov provoked Cossack reprisals. Michael Doroshenko crossed the Isthmus of Perekop and penetrated as far as Baghchi-Saray, where he was killed during the fighting. The Cossacks were able to pillage Caffa before they returned to the *Sech*.

The 'registered' Cossacks now elected a certain Chernoy as Hetman, but the Zaporogians found him too yielding to the Poles on Church matters; he was arrested and taken to the *Sech*, where he was tried and condemned to be quartered. The Zaporogians elected as Hetman an old warrior, Taras Fedorovich, and this event became the signal for a new rising.

The 'registered' Cossacks at first joined the Polish detachments near Korsun, but on the approach of the Zaporogians, whose numbers had been swollen by discontented townsfolk and many peasantry, they began to go over to the rebels.

The Polish Government now concerted measures with the Porte to check both the Cossacks and the Crim Tartars, who, in contrast to their alternate raids into the territories of the other, had already shown an alarming tendency to combine action as in the sack of Caffa in 1624. A treaty was formulated by Murtada Pasha, the new Vali of Ochakov, under which the Poles agreed to dissolve the *Sech* and to secure the return of all Muslim prisoners, while the Porte undertook to stop all raids into Polish territory. The Turks on their side drew off from the Crimea large numbers of Tartars for the war against Iran which had broken out in Georgia following the death of Shah Abbas. During the same year (1630) Koniecpolski again marched into the Ukraine, and after some indecisive fighting brought Taras Fedorovich to terms.

By the Pereyaslavl Agreement most of the terms of the Kurukovo Agreement were confirmed; but the numbers of the 'registered' Cossacks were increased to 8000.

The abortive character of the two risings of 1626 and 1628 had in many ways strengthened the position of the Polish Government. The increases in the numbers of the 'registered' Cossacks at least enabled the Government to reinforce the element most inclined to favour the established order, and it tended at the same time to accentuate the division of the Cossack mass into two groups whose interests were often opposed. Not all sections of Cossacks and peasants had participated in the risings; but some of the most prominent of the Orthodox clergy had played a provocative hand. Men like Peter Movila (or Mohila), the princely Moldavian Archimandrite of the Pecherskaya Lavra, and Job Boretsky, whose son was a Cossack officer, were suspect (Antonovich).

The lack of a leader of parts, the reluctance of the 'registered' Cossacks to risk their growing prosperity in civil conflict, the absence of foreign aid—all these factors produced a feeling of discouragement in the Cossacks. The bishops who had placed their hopes on Tsar Michael Romanov could not but acknowledge to themselves that Muscovy had by no means recovered from the Time of Troubles. Gustavus Adolphus entered into relations with the Cossacks, but his death in 1632 deprived them of all immediate prospect of Swedish support.

After the death of Sigismund Augustus, his son was elected King of Poland as Vladislav IV by the *Seym* of the year 1632. 'After his cousin Gustavus Adolphus, whom in many respects he strikingly resembled, he was indubitably the most aimable and brilliant of all the princes of the House of Vasa' (Nisbet Bain). A veteran of the Muscovite wars and of the Khotin campaign, Vladislav was a gifted commander who enjoyed the admiration and respect of the Cossacks. His genius had conceived the union of the two Slavonic crowns under the Vasas, and in his willingness to conciliate the Orthodox Church he had displayed a certain liquidity of spirit in doctrinal matters which recalled the flippant opportunism of Henri IV.

In face of the opposition to the election of Vladislav, Cossack contingents entered Volhynia and quartered themselves on the estates of Polish magnates under pretext that they had come to give protection against a supposed Tartar raid.

Immediately following the election of Vladislav, freedom of confession was granted to Orthodox believers, and the right was conceded to build churches, and to found schools, hospitals, printing establishments and 'Brotherhoods'. The cathedral of St Sophia and the Pecherskaya Lavra were surrendered to the Orthodox Metropolitan in Kiev. In the Ukraine and White Russia four dioceses went over to the Orthodox, four remaining in the hands of the Uniate bishops. Peter Movila, a son of a Moldavian Hospodar and a suspect of the rising of 1628, was allowed to become Metropolitan on the death of Job Boretsky. A man of talent, who had acquired the Phanariot culture of the Roumanian courts and had studied in Paris, he continued to enjoy the respect of the people while he remained a willing collaborator of King Vladislav. In the newly established Academy of Kiev, which owed the origins of its foundation to Peter Sahaydachny, studies were undertaken, after the contemporary usage of the West, in Latin and Greek.

The Cossacks participated loyally in the successful Swedish and Russian campaigns with which Vladislav began his reign. Twenty thousand Cossacks joined the 8000 troops of the Polish King before Smolensk and assured his resounding victory over the Russians; and the Cossacks came down the Niemen to aid in the blockade of Königsberg.

The years of Vladislav's Russian and Swedish victories saw the resurgence of Ottoman power under the vigorous and ferocious young epileptic Murad IV. In the autumn of 1633 the redoubtable Abkhasian Abaza Pasha crossed the Dniestr to try conclusions with Koniecpolski at the head of an army recruited from the Tartars of the Crimea and the Nogays who had been settled in the previous decades in the coastal districts of southern Bessarabia, called by the Turks, Budzhak. Abaza met his match in Koniecpolski and the fighting was indecisive; in the following spring, while Vladislav was collecting an army in Lvov, Murad moved out to his war capital in Adrianople. But the trial of strength between the royal paladins of the Christian and Islamic worlds did not come to pass. A magnificent Polish embassy was received in Istanbul and the Treaty of Murtada Pasha was renewed; Murad marched into Asia to the bloody conquest of Erivan and Tabriz.

The result of the Turko-Polish treaty was a renewed effort on the part of Koniecpolski to establish order in the borderland. He engaged the French engineer, Beauplan, author of *Description de l'Ukraine*, to construct the fort of Kudak which was planned to interrupt the communications of the *Sech* with the rest of the Ukraine.

This move was the occasion for a renewal of the Cossack revolts. The Zaporogian Hetman, Ivan Sulima, took Kudak by a surprise attack and destroyed its fortifications to the foundations. Sulima then marched against the Poles, capturing on his route the towns of Chigirin, Cherkassy and Korsun. Koniecpolski met him with an army which included a large number of 'registered' Cossacks who were veterans of the recent Swedish campaigns on the Baltic. These latter, desiring to avoid an issue with the Poles, took Sulima by ruse and delivered him who was considered as 'the flower of Cossack chivalry' to Koniecpolski. Sulima and other leading Zaporogians were taken to Warsaw, where the old Hetman was beheaded. Taking advantage of the moment which seemed propitious, Koniecpolski decided to consolidate the organization of the 'registered' Cossacks. Seven regiments were formed numbering a thousand men each, divided into *sotni* ('hundreds'); of these five were posted on the right bank of the Dniepr (the Belaya Tserkov, Kanev, Cherkassy, Korsun and Chigirin regiments) and two on the left bank (the Pereyaslavl and Mirgorod regiments).

The spirit of the Cossacks was not yet broken. In the Warsaw prison with Ivan Sulima had been incarcerated his 'adopted brother', the Zaporogian Pavluk, who managed to return to the *Sech* swearing to avenge old Sulima. Pavluk was elected Hetman and he immediately began to prepare a new rising. He called to his aid the Crim Tartars and the Don Cossacks. But the moment was unlucky. Both the Tartars and the Don Cossacks were engaged on opposing sides in the epic battles round Azov where, during the years 1637 to 1641, no less than three powerful Turkish expeditions were despatched to evict the Cossacks from the former Turkish stronghold which dominated the mouth of the Don. Four thousand Zaporogians, the best fighting men of the *Sech*, had gone to the Don to help their 'brothers'.

Pavluk moved into the Ukraine, taking the towns of Korsun and Cherkassy and capturing the artillery park of the 'registered' Cossacks, whose *starosty* he arrested and executed for 'treason'. A part of the 'registered' Cossacks went over to Pavluk, but others joined the Polish Crown Hetman Potocki.

Pavluk published a 'Universal' addressed to all Cossacks; many peasants joined him, while bands burned down Polish and Uniates' manors and slaughtered landlords and their families. Pavluk's army amounted to 23,000 men, but of these 17,000 were peasants armed only with scythes, pitchforks and sticks.

Potocki, with Polish troops and part of the 'registered' Cossacks, came in contact with the rebels near Kumeyki in the vicinity of Cherkassy. The Zaporogians and the peasants fought bravely, but the Polish cavalry penetrated their front, and over 6000 of the rebels were cut down. Pavluk and his lieutenant Gunya succeeded in retreating with their cannon to the village of Borovitsa near Chigirin, where they fortified their camp. But as in the retreat of Nalivayko and Loboda forty years before, the camp became crowded with the families of fleeing peasants and of the frightened townsfolk of Cherkassy. Further resistance became impossible. Potocki proposed surrender and promised quarter if the leaders were delivered up to him. Pavluk made a speech to the Zaporogians and himself asked to be surrendered to the Poles; while the 'registered' Cossacks on the Polish side guaranteed his life.

Potocki, however, behaved with a ruthlessness which had never been displayed by the veteran Koniecpolski, who had spent his whole life in fighting the Cossacks. Pavluk and other Zaporogians were executed immediately after the surrender. Potocki then crossed the Dniepr, where along the left bank in the Pereyaslavl and Poltava regions nearly the whole of the peasantry had risen in revolt, and he proceeded to decorate the roads with stakes on which, after the Turkish fashion, rebels were impaled.

Potocki now prepared for operations against the *Sech* itself. As successor to Pavluk, the Cossacks had elected Hetman Ostranitsa, a colonel of the 'registered' Cossacks. Ostranitsa won a first fight against Potocki at Goltva on the Psiol, but, when the Poles were re-inforced, he was badly defeated at Lubni. Ostranitsa, with a few comrades, left his camp and went eastward into the steppe—into that 'Slobodskaya or new Ukraine' (in the region of modern Kharkov) which was at that time being populated by fugitives from the Polish Ukraine and the Seversk lands.

Gunya, who had taken command after the flight of Ostranitsa, surrendered in the end and received an amnesty.

The rising of 1637–8 had both frightened the Polish Government and inspired in it a certain optimism. The Poles had been frightened by the adherence of the mass of the peasantry to the Zaporogians—particularly on the left bank of the Dniepr. The majority of the 'registered' Cossacks had, however, remained loyal to the Government, and had both helped Potocki to put down the rising and participated in his reprisals against the peasantry. It was decided therefore to allow the organization of the 'registered' Cossacks to continue, but to diminish their number to 6000 and to maintain only three Cossack regiments—those of Chigirin, Korsun and Cherkassy. The Cossack rights of election and self-administration were abolished; colonels were chosen by Potocki from among the local nobility, and the loyalty of junior officers was submitted to severe tests. The rest of the inhabitants of the Ukraine were to be treated as peasants, and in order that they should not be able to escape to the *Sech* the fort of Kudak was rebuilt and provided with a standing garrison and artillery. The *Sech* henceforth ceased to be a safe refuge from the authority of Polish officials. Fugitives had to follow the example of Ostranitsa and go eastward into the steppe. The position of the peasants became intolerable. The lands which had been confiscated from those of the 'registered' Cossacks who had

participated in the rising were given to Polish 'undertaking' landlords, who in their turn often leased them to Jews. There were many
cases where even Orthodox churches on the estates of Polish landlords were leased to Jews, who would charge the villagers a substantial fee before they would allow them to celebrate divine service
therein. (17, 18)

§ 8. 'THE DELUGE': VLADISLAV IV AND BOHDAN KHMELNYTSKY

The calamitous period remembered in Polish history as 'The
Deluge' opened with the great Cossack rising of 1648 and was con-
tinued by the invasions of the Swedes, the Transylvanians and the
Russians.

This period in Polish history is in many ways comparable to the
Time of Troubles in Russia. But whereas the Time of Troubles saw
the birth pangs of the Russian state, the Deluge foreshadowed the
imminent death of that strange anarchic oligarchy which was *Rzecz
Pospolita*.

The nineteen years of the Deluge between 1648 and 1667 may also
be characterized as the second period of crisis in the struggle between
Poles and Russians for hegemony over the fluvial network which
constitutes the geographical unity of the Great Eurasian Plain. In the
first period of crisis (1603–13) the Poles were making a national
effort to establish their dominance over Muscovy, and the Polish
Vasas were pursuing their dream of a union of the two Slavonic
crowns. In the second period of crisis, Tsar Alexey Mikhailovich,
with more prudence and more sense of the processes of history, was
content to consolidate the primacy of Muscovy and to reduce the
Polish realm to a condition of weakness which during the following
century became one of lingering decline. In each period of crisis
Sweden was at once the partner and the rival of the aggressive power.
But while Charles IX pursued the comparatively limited aims of
acquiring territory on the east Baltic littoral and of preventing the
stabilization of Polish hegemony in Moscow, Charles X, by joining
in the attack on Poland, cast down *Rzecz Pospolita* to the ultimate
profit of the Great Elector in East Prussia and of the Muscovites in
White Russia and the Ukraine.

The seventeenth century in Eastern Europe has already been described as a period of growing national consciousness among the
peoples, old and new, who found themselves on the peripheries of
the great Renaissance states—Turkey, Austria, Poland and Muscovy.
Influences of the Reformation, strong in Hungary, varied but sterile

in Poland, remote in Muscovy in the sect of Judaizers; the tenacious traditionalism of the Eastern Church, reborn with some brilliance in the Greek and Roumanian lands, sturdy and turbulent among the Ukrainian peasantry, dark and mystical among the Russian sectaries; the yearning for justice and freedom which found expression in the frequent *jacqueries* in the Ukraine and in Muscovy during the Time of Troubles—all these factors combined to make up the background of the political and military struggles of the epoch.

Above all, the gradual disruption of the Polish and Ottoman state structures was characterized by the development of groups and movements whose nature was purely anarchic. The Cossacks of the Dniepr and the Don with an economy based on piracy, the Budzhak and Crim Tartars with their land-raiding and slave-hunting economy, were manifestations of the social phenomenon which Professor Toynbee has described as 'the external proletariat'. Comparably, proletarian movements, internal in operation and contemporary with the great Ukrainian 'peasants' fury' of 1648–51, were the popular Anatolian risings of the two Abazas (1623–4 and 1656) and the celebrated revolt of Stenka Razin on the Volga (1670).

The history of the Deluge of 1648 possesses all the classic features of the disintegration of a state structure which had not been adapted to the social realities of the epoch and of the savage swarming of a submerged proletariat.

Vladislav IV, the brilliant hero of the Muscovite, Swedish and Turkish wars, had become in middle life a weary and sophisticated Machiavellian. He had conceived, not without reason, that the only hope of reforming the Polish state lay in a royalist reaction. In his Order of the Immaculate Conception he had formed a knighthood of seventy-two young Polish nobles who had sworn a special oath of allegiance to the crown and who were to form the core of a national movement hostile to the anarchic usurpations of the *Seym*. He further planned to make the Cossacks the instrument of his re-forms, and to use a Cossack army against the *Seym* much as ten years before Strafford had thought to use an Irish army to uphold the prerogatives of the crown against the oligarchs of the English Parliament.

Vladislav's plans were based upon the knowledge of his personal popularity with the Cossacks, and upon the secret collaboration of Koniecpolski, who knew the Cossacks better than any man alive. 'Vladislav proposed to provoke the Tartars to a rupture by repudi-ating the humiliating tribute with which the Republic had so long and so vainly endeavoured to buy off their incessant raids. In case of such rupture, he meant, at the head of 100,000 Cossacks, to fall upon the Crimea itself, the seat of their power, and to exterminate the Khanate. This he calculated would bring about a retaliatory invasion of Poland by the Turks, which would justify him in taking the field against them also with all the forces of the Republic. In case of success he would be able to impose the will of a victorious king upon the discredited *Seym*, and reform the constitution on an English or Swedish model. Events seemed at first to favour this audacious speculation. Almost simultaneously a civil war broke out in the Crimea and the Porte declared war against the Venetian Republic, with which Vladislav at once concluded an offensive and defensive alliance (1645). He then bade the Cossacks prepare their boats for a raid upon the Turkish galleys, and secured the co-operation of the Tsar in the Crimean expedition by a special treaty. Unfortunately, Venice insisted on the publication of Vladislav's anti-Turkish alliance; the Porte, well informed of the course of Polish affairs, remained strictly neutral despite the most outrageous provocations; and Vladislav, bound by his coronation oath not to undertake an offensive war, found himself at the mercy of the *Seym*, which, full of consternation and rage, assembled at Warsaw on 2 May 1647. The Venetian alliance was repudiated and the royal power still further reduced' (David Hannay, *Encyc. Brit.* 11th ed.).

Koniecpolski was already dead, after a last victory over the Tartars at Brody (1646). The King did not long survive discomfiture at the hands of the outraged *Seym*, for he died at his hunting lodge of Merecz on 20 May 1648. But he had conjured up a storm which it is doubtful whether even he could have controlled, and which three weeks before he died had already broken over the heads of those who had thwarted and defeated his designs.

Bohdan Khmelnytsky was the first leader of genius whom the Cossacks had found since Peter Sahaydachny. He was a strange contrast both to the good and sagacious Sahaydachny and to the dying scion of the Vasas and the Habsburgs. 'With all his native ability Khmelnytsky was but an eminent savage. He was the creature of every passing mood or whim, incapable of cool or steady judgment or the slightest self-control—an incalculable weather-cock, blindly obsequious to every blast of passion. He could destroy, but he could not create, and other people benefited by his exploits' (Nisbet Bain).

Bohdan Khmelnytsky came of a family of the lesser nobility of Volhynia; his father had been a 'registered' Cossack who had tried his fortune in the *Sech* and had been killed during Chodkiewicz's disastrous Cecora campaign. About the same time the younger Khmelnytsky had fallen into the hands of the Crim Tartars, from whom he had been later ransomed. He became a junior officer in the Chigirin regiment, and inherited the enjoyment of the small hereditary estate of Subbotovo. He attracted the notice of King Vladislav during the Russian war of the early thirties, and at the time of Pavluk's rising occupied the responsible administrative post of *pysar* or 'general secretary' of the Chigirin regiment. A man of some education, Khmelnytsky had passed through a school of one of the Orthodox 'brotherhoods' and had continued his studies at the Jesuits' school at Yaroslav in Galicia. His knowledge of the world was further expanded when he was appointed to command a Cossack contingent which King Vladislav had hired to the Government of Cardinal Richelieu, and he took part in the operations against the Spaniards in Flanders and in the siege of Dunkirk. Khmelnytsky was essentially a 'King's man' and a member of the small nobility, and even when he became leader of the Cossack revolutionary movement he retained the sentiments and prejudices of his caste.

That a man of Khmelnytsky's record and environment should have been converted into an inveterate enemy of the Polish state well illustrates the shortcomings of the Polish 'ascendancy' in the Ukraine, since the injustices inflicted on Khmelnytsky were only typical of hundreds of similar cases throughout the country during the first half of the seventeenth century. Khmelnytsky came into conflict with one Czapliński, the Polish *pod-starosta* of Chigirin. Some property was in question, and also the possession of Khmelnytsky's beautiful Cossack mistress whom he intended to marry after the death of his wife. Legal proceedings were dragging on, until, taking advantage of the absence of Khmelnytsky, Czapliński sent his men to Subbotovo, where they seized the land in dispute, ravaged the rest of the property, kidnapped the lady and thrashed to death a small son of the *pysar*. Even a man of Khmelnytsky's weight could obtain no redress, either in the local courts or before the Senate in Warsaw—where he was laughed at and told to forget about the estate and to find another beauty.

Khmelnytsky made a personal appeal to the King. Vladislav was already planning to use a Cossack army against the factious *szlachta*, and he is stated by some Polish historians to have reminded his outraged official that 'Cossacks have sabres' (Khmelnytsky had a sabre which the King had presented to him during the Smolensk campaign).

Khmelnytsky returned to the Ukraine, where he took part in Koniecpolski's operations against the Tartars in 1646—operations which were cut short by a decree of the *Seym* which refused to sanction the continuance of what was in fact a defensive campaign. As a 'King's man' and a Cossack, Khmelnytsky was doubly suspect, and in the autumn of 1646, after some conversations with the Cossack *starosty*, he was forced to go into hiding.

The exposure of the King's plans in the *Seym* of May 1647 made the position of Khmelnytsky even more desperate. Whether or not the King was privy to his movements, Khmelnytsky now appeared in the *Sech* with an alleged 'writing from King Vladislav'.

The Zaporogian *Sech* had been reduced to a state of complete decadence. Only three hundred Cossacks remained there in the pay of the Polish crown, and Polish guards were posted on the Island of Khortytsa. But the vigorous personality of the distinguished fugitive soon brought the Wilderness to life around the *Sech* and along both banks of the Dniepr. Men began to appear who had been in hiding among the countless islets of the great river; others came in from the steppe on the right bank—called *Velyky Luh* ('the Great Meadow'); and many swarmed in who had gone far to the east of the Dniepr. By the early spring of 1648 Khmelnytsky had gathered several thousand men round him; muskets and gunpowder appeared, and the Cossack cannon, buried in the sands of the river since the days of Pavluk and Ostranitsa, saw the light of day again. (19, 20)

During the month of March, the Polish *voyevode* in Bratslav, Adam Kysil, himself an Orthodox Ukrainian by birth, wrote contemptuously to warn Prince Dolgoruki, the Muscovite marcher *voyevode* in Putivl, that 'a certain number, a thousand or more, of self-willed Cossack Cherkasses have escaped to the *Sech* and their leader is a common menial, by name Khmelnytsky', and he requested the Russians, 'should Khmelnytsky escape from the Zaporogian *Sech* to the Don, not to receive him there, not to show him mercy, and not to allow him to go to sea'.

In April Kysil wrote again to inform Dolgoruki that 'should this menial of ours, the Cherkass traitor and his troop, not escape to the Crimea, he will have to pay with his head for his treason, as our army is marching in pursuit of him through the *Velyky Luh* to the Dniepr'.

Meanwhile, Khmelnytsky had proceeded with confidence and caution. While his men took possession of the fort of Kudak by a surprise attack, he himself went to the Crimea to seek the help of the Khan, Islam Giray III. While the Khan still hesitated, the Nogay *Mirza* Tugay Bey, the half-independent chieftain of the Budzhak Tartars, joined the insurgent Zaporogians with 4000 horsemen.

At the beginning of April, on his return to the *Sech*, Khmelnytsky called for war on the Poles, and was acclaimed Hetman.

At Korsun, the Crown Hetman, Stephen Potocki, had concentrated 30,000 men, and he was preparing to crush the rising in the

Sech before the rebels had time to raid into the populated parts of the Ukraine. Barabash, the official Hetman of the Cossacks, was descending the Dniepr with 6000 'registered' Cossacks in boats, to join the royal forces. In the third week of May Potocki sent forward a corps of 12,000 men into the *Velyky Luh* to meet Khmelnytsky. So certain was the Crown Hetman of an easy victory that he had confided the command to his son in order that he might distinguish himself. But while a Zaporogian band intercepted the 'registered' Cossacks on the river and persuaded them to join forces with the insurgents (the Hetman Barabash being thrown into the water), on May 19 Khmelnytsky attacked Stephen Potocki on the Zhovti (Zhëltÿa) Vody ('Yellow Waters'). The Polish force was taken in front by the Zaporogians and in rear by the Budzhak Tartars, and absolutely annihilated except for one man who escaped with the news to Korsun—where he was at first taken for a madman.

Reinforced by the 'registered' Cossacks, Khmelnytsky advanced on Korsun, while the whole countryside rose in the Crown Hetman's rear. Potocki, in this difficult situation, lost his head and began to retreat; but on 28 May he was overtaken by the Cossacks at Kruta Balka ('Steep Ravine') and suffered an overwhelming defeat. Seven thousand Poles were killed and 9000 taken prisoner; only 2000 cavalry made good their escape. Potocki himself was handed over as a gift to the Tartar Khan and sent in chains to the Crimea, where he was held against a fabulous ransom.

With the news of Khmelnytsky's victories, revolts broke out everywhere throughout the Ukraine. The whole of the region along the right bank of the Dniepr, and all the lands situated along the left bank from Pereyaslavl to Poltava, were swept clean of nobles and of the small detachments of regular Polish troops in an incredibly short space of time. Khmelnytsky showed himself as able a tactician in revolt as he had been in battle. While a great Cossack army was in course of formation at Belaya Tserkov, small detachments of Zaporogians were sent into those districts where Polish landlordism was comparatively firmly established in order to foment revolt among the peasantry. Famous Zaporogian 'colonels' like Bohun, Nechay, Ganza, Perebeynos ('Broken-Nose') and Morozenko penetrated into the Bratslav region and Podolia. Other bands moved into the districts of Nezhin, Chernigov and Novgorod Seversk where—after the re-annexation to Poland of the Seversk lands—Polish landlordism had had a rapid development under the protection of garrisons of regular troops. By July the whole of the Seversk lands from Nezhin to Starodub and Novgorod Seversk had been 'liberated'.

The slaughter, arson and terror of 'the serfs' fury' (*khlopskaya zloba*) spread throughout the country. Everywhere landlords, Catholic and Uniate priests and Jews were hunted down and blinded, burnt, decapitated or sawn between boards. The rebels took the castle of Bar by storm and put to the sword the thousands of Poles and Jews who had taken refuge there. In Volhynia Prince Jeremy Vishnevetsky was perpetrating reprisals against the peasants with an equal ruthlessness. Executions were carried out in his presence, and he was in the habit of shouting to the executioners—'Let them feel that they are being put to death!' The Zaporogian answer to Vishnevetsky was to slaughter all the nobles, priests and Jews who had fallen into their hands. Near Tulchin, Prince Janus Chetvertinsky was beheaded by his own miller and his wife was raped by the Zaporogian Ostap.

By the end of the summer a new Polish army, 40,000 strong with 100 guns, had been collected on the borders of Galicia and Volhynia to defend the home territories of the Republic against the advancing Cossack horde. The Polish army consisted almost entirely of the noble militia, and was tricked out with a splendour more befitting a bridal pageant than a battle array. For Khmelnytsky and his host these splendid cavaliers expressed the utmost contempt. 'This rabble must be chased with whips, not smitten with swords', they cried. The Polish chivalry were stiffened by a force of German mercenaries; but after a three days' battle near Pilyavtsy the last grand display of the glories of the feudal Republic was scattered to the winds. 'The steppe for miles around was strewn with corpses, and the Cossacks are said to have reaped 10,000,000 guldens worth of booty when the fight was over.'

With its army broken and in flight, the Republic now lay at the mercy of the Cossack Hetman. The Russian peasantry of Galicia rose in revolt, and Khmelnytsky entered Lvov, the ancient capital of the West Russian princes. Cossack bands scattered northwards into the countryside of White Russia and Lithuania, while Khmelnytsky himself laid siege to the fortress of Zamość. But the brilliant commander and astute revolutionary proved to be no statesman. Indeed, a strange spiritual struggle appears to have disturbed the mind of Khmelnytsky during the months before Zamość. The former 'King's man', the petty landowner and easy living gentleman of the days before the Czapliński episode, appears to have been, if not appalled at the enormity of the calamity which he had brought down upon his own world, at least desirous of checking the social implications of the Deluge. His environmental inhibitions corresponded with the direction of his personal ambition. There is a flavour of 'M'lord protests too much' in his rhetorical declaration to the Polish peace commissioners that he did not propose to betray the interests of the peasants.

While Khmelnytsky delayed before Zamość and the Zaporogians urged him to march to Warsaw, where in the Square of Stare Miasto so many Cossack heads had fallen in the dust—Podkova's, Nalivayko's, Pavluk's, Sulima's—the *Seym* was gathered for the election of a successor to Vladislav IV. To Khmelnytsky, who had spent all his life in the Polish service, the event was one of supreme importance, and he was greatly flattered when emissaries arrived to consult his wishes, since it was considered that the result of the election depended upon him. Khmelnytsky gave his support to John Casimir, Vladislav's younger brother, who had not appeared to have any chance of election since he had accepted a cardinal's hat. But the Pope absolved him from his vows and the last King of the house of Vasa ascended the throne with the support of the Cossack army (the new King immediately married Vladislav's widow, Marie Louise of Angoulême).

The Crim Tartars were dismissed to the Crimea loaded with booty, and the Cossack regiments, now excellently armed and under strict military discipline, began to march back through Volhynia to the Dniepr. In October, at the head of his own Chigirin regiment, mounted on a white charger and arrayed in cloth of gold, Bohdan Khmelnytsky entered Kiev—acclaimed as 'the father and the liberator of the country and the people'.(19,20,21)

§ 9. 'THE DELUGE': BOHDAN KHMELNYTSKY AND TSAR ALEXEY MIKHAILOVICH

Bohdan Khmelnytsky spent the turn of the year 1648–9 at Pereyaslavl celebrating his marriage with the beautiful mistress who had been the cause of his feud with Czapliński. He delighted to entertain at alternate feasts the peace commissioners sent by King John Casimir, with Adam Kysil at their head, the ambassadors of the Muscovite Tsar, and the envoys of the ambitious Transylvanian Prince George II Rákóczy.

The pallid and mediocre personality of John Casimir, though it was to rise to a certain heroism in the following years, lacked the vision and the capacity for sympathy of Vladislav IV. The atmosphere which had won him the support of Khmelnytsky in his candidature for the throne was conducive to a settlement which might have retained the connection between the Ukraine and the Polish state. Khmelnytsky was in relations with both Moscow and Istanbul, but the terms which he put forward showed that he had no ambition to sever the Ukraine from Poland and to exchange a master whom he had beaten in the field for a new and untried overlord.

Khmelnytsky demanded the abolition of the Union of the Churches in the Kiev region and on the left bank of the Dniepr; seats in the Polish *Seym* for the Metropolitan of Kiev and all the Orthodox bishops; the promise that Jeremy Vishnevetsky should resign the office of Crown Hetman; the formation, by Whitsuntide, of a commission which was to agree on the number of 'registered' Cossacks and allot to them definite territories; until then Polish troops were not to pass the line Kamenets-Podolsk-river Goryn-river Pripet.

Adam Kysil brought only from the King the *Bulava* or Hetman's Staff and proposals which amounted to an assumption of the restoration of the old order of things with the concession that the number of 'registered' Cossacks should be increased to 15,000.

Standing in a red cloak trimmed with sables, the Hetman received the Polish delegation with every sign of honour and respect, but when Adam Kysil somewhat tactlessly recalled that he himself was a Ukrainian and a member of the Orthodox Church, saying: 'I am flesh of your flesh and bone of your bone', Khmelnytsky gave vent to one of his bursts of ferocious anger. 'The bones are ours, perhaps', he shouted, 'but they are overgrown with Polish flesh.' He continued to declaim: 'I will do as I think best. At first I fought to avenge my personal insult, but now I fight for the Orthodox faith. The whole land from Lublin to Cracow will be subject to my will. I will no longer fight Tartars and Turks; enough for me of Volhynia and Podolia. I will take everything—Lvov and Halych. And on the Vistula I will proclaim to the Poles: "Stay where you are and keep your mouths shut." I will drive all the princes and dukes beyond the Vistula, and if they dare to stir, my will shall reach them wherever they are.'

Adam Kysil returned to Warsaw with the demands of the Hetman which, imperious as they were, were not so immoderate as to have failed to suggest a basis of negotiation to men of the experience and wisdom of Vladislav IV and Stanislas Koniecpolski. But the new King was weak and obstinate and the Crown Hetman, Jeremy Vishnevetsky, was a truculent hater. The demands to such characters provoked refusal, and not only war but the separation of the Ukraine from Poland became inevitable. (22)

John Casimir had levied by the spring of 1649 a formidable army which amounted to some 70,000 men; the Hetman, cautious and impulsive by turns, was uncertain of his position and was negotiating for foreign support. In Istanbul, the new Sultan, Muhammad IV, was only eight years old and his grandmother, the Sultana Validé Kosem, was struggling against Sipahi mutinies, street riots and palace plots. The long Cretan War with Venice was exhausting the resources of the Empire, and seven years were to pass before the first Köprülü Vizier was to initiate an aggressive policy on the European frontiers. With the returning Muscovite ambassadors Khmelnytsky despatched his confidant, the Cossack Colonel Theodore Vesnyak, with the gift of a fine horse and a Turkish bow for the young Tsar Alexey Mikhailovich. Vesnyak urged that the propitious moment had arrived for the recovery of Smolensk and the conquest of White Russia.

That a man of the gentleness and patience of Alexey Mikhailovich should have successfully ruled Russia during the turbulent decades of the mid-seventeenth century proves perhaps the practical effectiveness of the Christian ethic in human relations. The mild Tsar had a gift for choosing men; and a succession of capable and gifted ministers—the Patriarch Nikon, Ordyn-Nashchokin, Matveyev— were guiding Russia from the anarchy of the Time of Troubles into the imperial destiny of the eighteenth century. But in 1649 the Muscovite state was in no condition to undertake foreign adventure. Agrarian and religious disorders were rife throughout the country. In the preceding year the Tsar had only himself escaped the violence of the Moscow mob by surrendering some of his officials. There had been dangerous riots in Novgorod, Sol'vychegodsk— seat of the princely merchant house of Stroganov—and in Ustyug. In Pskov rebels had successfully withstood a three months' siege and exacted an amnesty from the Government. The Moscow court had little sympathy for the Cossacks whose excesses during the Time of Troubles were still bitterly remembered; in 1642 the Moscow *Zemski Sobor* had compelled Tsar Michael Romanov to repudiate the Don Cossacks when they had sought his aid to hold Azov against the Turks. And Tsar and *boyars* alike condemned movements against a crown; the execution of Charles I in England was fresh news in Moscow when Vesnyak rode in with the ambassadors from Pereyaslavl, and the Tsar had ordered the rupture of all commercial relations with the regicide Commonwealth.

With no ally but the Tartar Islam Khan Giray, Khmelnytsky moved into Poland in the month of March to measure his strength with John Casimir. The seventeenth century saw the growth of large armies first in the Great Eurasian Plain—owing to the relatively great numbers and restlessness of the indigenous populations; and the Hetman was at the head of a host of 320,000 men—composed of Crim and Budzhak Tartars, great herds of undisciplined peasants, and rather less than 100,000 Cossacks.

The Polish forces, numbering about 70,000 men, were divided into two armies—under the King and the Crown Hetman Jeremy Vishnevetsky—which occupied positions in two fortified camps at Zborov and Zbarazh. Vishnevetsky's bold sallies out of the camp of Zbarazh ended in failure, but he continued to hold his lines although his troops were suffering cruelly from hunger. John Casimir was blockaded in the Zborov camp, but Khmelnytsky only passively continued the siege, as though reluctant to force any decisive action which might place his King as a prisoner in his hands. At the same time secret *pourparlers* for a peace were being carried on. These *pourparlers* were advanced when Islam Giray, either weary of the inactive siege or bribed by the Poles, drew off his men. In the end the Zbarazh camp surrendered and the so-called Zborov Agreement was concluded between Khmelnytsky and the King.

'This agreement was made exclusively in the interests of the Cossacks. All the privileges they had ever possessed were recognized. The number of "registered" Cossacks was raised to 40,000. Three *voyevodstva*, Kiev, Chernigov and Bratslav, were cleared of Polish garrisons. The Orthodox dioceses were recognized and the Orthodox hierarchs were given the right to sit in the *Seym*. The administration continued to be Polish as before, but it was to be formed from the local inhabitants who were members of the Orthodox Church. Chigirin and its district became the appanage of the *Bulava* (the Hetman's ceremonial Staff of Office)—in other words was given to the Hetman as his own property. Not a word was said about the peasants, and the estates of the nobles were restored to them. In this fashion, Galicia, Volhynia and Podolia were given back into the hands of the Polish nobility. The Cossacks were limited in their number, which was not to be exceeded by anyone wishing to be put down on their lists' (Antonovich).

Ukrainian historians have condemned Khmelnytsky for the Zborov Agreement, but it is unscientific to judge the men and actions of the seventeenth century on the basis of the social philosophy and standards of the twentieth century. Khmelnytsky was a Cossack officer and a member of the lesser nobility living in a period when the rights of the submerged agrarian population of Europe were scarcely comprehended by the finest minds of the day. Khmelnytsky secured the interests of his own class, peace, and his own personal position; more sophisticated and more modern statesmen have often gone no further. But events, as ever, moved more rapidly than either ambitious men or fine minds.

'For the next eighteen months Khmelnytsky ruled the Ukraine like a sovereign prince. He made Chigirin, his native place, the Cossack capital, subdivided the country into sixteen provinces, and entered into direct relations with foreign powers.' But his position was a difficult one. He was unable to limit the numbers of the Cossacks to be registered to 40,000, when all the 300,000 Ukrainians who had been encamped before Zbarazh and Zborov considered that they had acquired the right to call themselves Cossacks. He essayed a compromise by allowing each 'registered' Cossack family to inscribe 'helpers', so that it became possible to include about 200,000 men in the lists. But the arrangement did not please the Polish Government. On the other hand the peasants bitterly resented the return of landlords to their estates, and Khmelnytsky found himself drifting into an increasingly false position.

In October 1650 the Muscovite agent Unkovski could write that 'The Hetman receives former retainers of Prince Vishnevetsky and of the Lubni *starosta* Nagorecki and also many other Poles—retainers of Potocki, of Adam Kysil, of Koniecpolski. They all bow down before the Hetman so as to obtain from him the necessary papers and orders that the peasants should now obey them.' But Adam Kysil, who had become *voyevode* in Kiev, complained to the King that 'it appears that the rabble use all sorts of means to avoid being the subjects of their lords. Some forsake their possessions and become the orderlies or servants of Cossacks. Others wander off beyond the Dniepr with all their possessions, and only a small minority bow down before their lords. God alone in His wisdom knows how it will all quieten down and be peaceful.'

Under the Zborov Agreement—which in fact was to prove no more than an armistice—Khmelnytsky had assumed the impossible position of a viceroy of the Polish King, administering a triple state in which existed side by side the two privileged but opposing castes of Polish landlords and Cossack military yeomen with around them a vast and restless peasant proletariat who understood darkly that they had been cheated and betrayed. It was only a matter of months before the frequent local conflicts grew into a renewal of general war.

Abroad Khmelnytsky was becoming a figure of European fame. The marriage of his son Timosh to the beautiful daughter of Basil the Wolf was the occasion for his obtrusion into Moldavian and Transylvanian politics. Admirers compared him to his contemporary Cromwell; he was regarded as the arch-enemy of the Roman faith in Eastern Europe and the Pope granted a plenary absolution to all who should take up arms against him. The Hetman, however, did not lack ecclesiastical approval. The Archbishop of Corinth girded him with a sword which had lain upon the Holy Sepulchre, and when he at last rode out to battle again against the Poles the Metropolitan of Kiev absolved him from all his sins without the usual preliminary of confession. (23)

In renewing the war against Poland, Khmelnytsky had relied upon the help of his old but always doubtful friend Islam Khan Giray, but the Tartar contingents which came to join him withdrew before the heavy fighting began. Nor were the Cossack Regiments supported either by the 'free' Zaporogians, who were angry at the Zborov Agreement, or by the mass of the peasantry, who remained disappointed and disillusioned. On 1 July 1651 Khmelnytsky was defeated by Stephen Czarniecki at Berestechko. Vishnevetsky was invading the Ukraine from the west, and from the north Prince Jan Radziwill, after putting down peasant risings in the region of the affluents of the Pripet, was advancing on Kiev. Khmelnytsky, who had retreated to Belaya Tserkov (in Ukrainian Bila Tserkva), was obliged to accept any conditions.

The Agreement of Belaya Tserkov replaced that of Zborov. The number of the 'registered' Cossacks was reduced to 20,000 men; the Bratslav and Chernigov *voyevodstva* ceased to be Cossack territories, only the Kiev *voyevodstvo* on both banks of the Dniepr being retained by them.

Khmelnytsky's power was by no means broken and he renewed preparations for a final struggle. *Rzecz Pospolita* had been gravely weakened by the chaotic civil war of the preceding three years. The surplus of grain which produced her means of exchange with Western Europe as well as providing for the extravagant expenditure of the bulk of the great aristocratic families of the realm was derived from the Ukraine. And the peasant labour, as well as the rich black earth, was an essential part of the capital which produced this surplus. Even in Galicia life had not resumed its normal course after the Cossack invasion. Volhynia had been badly devastated, and Podolia with all the country along the right bank of the Dniepr was rapidly becoming depopulated. The landlords who secured the return of their estates in these regions found no peasants to work the land for them. The peasants wished to become Cossacks and not to remain serfs any more, and they moved away beyond the Dniepr. By contrast to the right bank of the Dniepr, the region stretching from Poltava to the Donets and even as far as the Don was becoming thickly inhabited. Ukrainian Cossacks made their appearance in Chuguev, Izyum, Akhtyrka, and even round Ostrogozhsk (to the south of Voronezh), in territories which were outside the boundaries of the Polish realm and which were considered to come within the jurisdiction of the Tsar of Muscovy.

Khmelnytsky, after Belaya Tserkov, realized that his own position was perilous; at the same time he knew the exhaustion and the weakness of the Poles. Through the Roumanian princes and the Crimean Khan he had relations with the Turks; during the current period of anarchy in Istanbul he had actually assumed the high-sounding style and title of 'Guardian of the Ottoman Porte'. There was in his entourage a strong party in favour of an understanding with the Turks—which in the following two decades was to acquire a predominating importance. They held that the Turks respected courage; kept their word more often than Christian monarchs; and could be trusted to allow the Cossacks the same loose self-rule which was enjoyed by the Wallachians, the Moldavians, the Transylvanians and the Crim Tartars. The Turkish system, with all its faults, was suited to the taste of rough and simple men. The Hetman negotiated with the Turks and at the same time with the Muscovite Tsar. But the Porte, in the summer of 1653, was not in a position to engage in war. The gallant old Sultana Validé Kosem had recently been strangled with a curtain string during a mutiny of the Janissaries, and the Circassian Ibshir was preparing to grasp the Grand Vizierate.

With his Turkish alternative still in view, Khmelnytsky wrote to the Muscovite *voyevode* in Putivl—'If His Majesty does not take us under the protection of his mighty hand and shield us from our enemies, I the Hetman and the Regiments will have to think of something else.'

'Alexis was thus implored to succour a numerous people, Russian and Orthodox, oppressed by a Polish aristocracy. The Romanov dynasty had not courted this appeal, for the sense of its penury and weakness was always kept before it by constant signs of exhaustion in Russia....But a new dynasty in Russia could not be less careful than the old of that mission of reuniting the Russians which had been so vividly before the minds of the two Johns and the spokesmen of opinion of their time' (Pares).

In Poland, in the spring of 1653, the *Seym*, whose most prominent members were suffering in their own fortunes by the continuance of Ukrainian anarchy, for once took drastic action and voted subsidies of 17,000,000 gulden to provide an army of 60,000 men for the liquidation of Cossack independence.

In the meantime 'a great embassy', including Prince Repnin-Obolenski and the *boyar* Khitrovo, left Moscow. The pretext was the discussion of minor frontier incidents, but in reality the Muscovite ambassadors, who made their appearance in Lvov in the month of

July, had to transmit the Tsar's desire to make peace between the Cossacks and the King. The Muscovite ambassadors declared that during five years the Hetman and all the Cossacks had been making complaints to the Tsar about the oppression of their land, about the persecution and humiliation of the Orthodox Church; and that the Agreements of Zborov and Belaya Tserkov had not been kept. The King and the Polish Senate replied by accusing Khmelnytsky of treacherous dealings; of alliance with the Crim Tartars and negotiations with the Turks.

The Muscovite intervention was in fact ultimative in character. But the shrewd old Patriarch Nikon was playing for time. The Imperial *Prikaz* (Chancellery) was accurately informed of the preparations which Charles X of Sweden was making for war against Poland.

During the summer of 1653 confused fighting was taking place throughout the Ukraine. In August the Cossacks of Khmelnytsky came into contact with the army of John Casimir at Zhvanets, south of Kamenets-Podolsk. For a third time Islam Khan Giray deserted the Hetman on the field of battle. The Tartars drew off to scatter into bands which plundered indiscriminately Polish manors and Cossack villages. The Tartars, taking advantage of the absence of the Zaporogians, appeared on the Dniepr and, as in former days, carried away thousands of men and women into captivity. The Poles suffered similarly; according to contemporary accounts over five thousand women and girls of noble birth from towns and estates in Volhynia and along the affluents of the Pripet were carried off to the slave markets of the Crimea. In these conditions of general anarchy the opposing armies of the King and the Hetman gradually dispersed over their respective territories in abortive pursuit of the elusive Tartar bands.

After the return of the ambassadors from Lvov, on 1 October 1653, Tsar Alexey Mikhailovich assembled the *Zemski Sobor* in Moscow and secured the approval of the *boyars* and the clergy 'to include Hetman Bohdan Khmelnytsky, all his Zaporogian Cossacks, troops, towns and lands within the realm of Muscovy, not only out of respect for the same faith which is shared by Little Russia, but also on account of the danger threatening her from Poland and Lithuania as well as from Turkey and the Tartars'. (24)

On 9 October, the *boyar* Vasili Buturlin, the courtier Ivan Alferiev and the clerk Ilarion Lopukhin received the commission 'to go to the Hetman on the Monarch's most urgent business'. Delayed by the difficulties of travel arising from the Tartar depredations, the mission did not arrive in Pereyaslavl until New Year's Eve. The Hetman, who was still on the right bank of the Dniepr, was expected. He arrived on 6 January, accompanied by the Cossack General Secretary Vyhovsky and many colonels and *starosty*. On the following day Khmelnytsky visited the Muscovite envoys 'quite privately'. On the 8th all the colonels and *starosty* gathered at Khmelnytsky's quarters for a secret council, and later in the day the *Rada* met, when a great number of Cossacks of different ranks and callings were present. The Hetman made a speech at which he stated that a choice had to be made between the four monarchs—the King of Poland, the Sultan of Turkey, the Khan of the Crimea and the Tsar of Muscovy. The decision of the Hetman and the *starosty* was known already, and the *Rada* answered by acclamation: 'We want to go to the Tsar who belongs to the Eastern Orthodox Faith. God help us, God make us strong and united for all time!'

BIBLIOGRAPHICAL NOTES AND ADDITIONS TO CHAPTER III

On the History of the Ukraine from 1569 to 1654

Hrushevsky, M. *Istoriya Ukrayiny-Rusi* (History of Ukraina-Rus), vol. v, Lvov, 1905; vol. vi, Kiev, 1907; vol. vii, Kiev, 1909; vol. viii, part 1, Kiev-Lvov, 1913 (Ukr.).

Idem. *Istoriya Ukrainskago Kazachestva* (History of Ukrainian Cossackdom), Kiev, 1913 (Russ.).

Efimenko, O. *Istoriya Ukrainskago Naroda* (History of the Ukrainian People), vol. i, Petersburg, 1906.

Doroshenko, D. *Narys Istorii Ukrayiny* (Short History of Ukraina), Warszawa, 1932 (Ukr.).

Vasilenko, N. *Ocherki po Istorii Zapadnoy Rusi i Ukrainy* (Essays in the History of Western Russia and Ukraina), Kiev, 1916.

Antonovich, V. *Istoriya Yugo-Zapadnoy Rusi* (History of South-Western Russia), University Lectures, Kiev, 1879.

Evarnitski, D. *Istoriya Zaporozhskikh Kozakov* (History of the Zaporogian Cossacks), Petersburg, 1895.

Jabłonowski, A. *Historya Rusi Południowej do upadku Rzeczy Pospolitej Polskiej* (History of Southern Russia to the Fall of Rzecz Pospolita), Krakow, 1912 (Pol.).

Idem. *Zrodła Dziejewe*, XVIII, *Rus Czerwona*; XIX, *Wołyń, Podole*; XXII, *Ukraina* (Historical Sources; XVIII, Galicia; XIX, Volhynia-Podolia; XXII, Ukraina).

The following rather antiquated studies, which contain many errors and inexactitudes, still merit reference:

Bantysh-Kamenski. *Istoriya Maloy Rossii* (History of Russia Minor), 1-2, Moscow, 1830.

Markovich, N. *Istoriya Malorossii* (History of Russia Minor), Moscow, 1842.

(1) On the 'Wilderness' and its Population

Herberstein calls Putivl a frontier town 'from whence travellers sally forth on their journeys through the Wilderness to the Crimea, called Tauris in Latin'. Kursk, which had existed in the days of Kievan Russia, was re-founded and rebuilt towards the end of the fifteenth century. The place where it had formerly stood was covered with dense forest.

It is probable that at the end of the fifteenth and the beginning of the six-teenth centuries isolated settlements of Russians had been established along the upper courses of the Seym, the Psiol and the Vorskla—where they had intermixed with Turkish nomads. Doroshenko remarks on the Turkish type of the population in certain localities of the Poltava region.

(2) On the Origin of the Cossacks

One of the earliest authors who treated of the origin of the Ukrainian Cossacks proved to be nearest to the truth. This was Martin Bielski, a Protestant, the nephew of a Cossack *starosta*, and the author of *Kronika Polska*—written in the year 1597. In Bielski's view the Cossacks were formed from the lower classes of the original Ukrainian population. This idea was shared by the French military engineer Beauplan, author of *Description de l'Ukraine* (seventeenth century). Some fantastic theories on the subject of Cossack origins were adumbrated by writers of the seventeenth, eighteenth and even nineteenth centuries. Pyasetski and Kakhovsky derive the name Cossack from the fact that in battle 'they were as light and agile as wild goats' (Russian, *koza*). Hrabyanka, a Cossack writer of the eighteenth century, held that the Cossacks were the descendants of the Khazars, and another, Simonovsky, affirmed that they originated from the Caucasians on the ground that in the region of the Caucasus is Hyrcania and that *hircus* means 'goat' (*koza*).

The belief that the Cossacks were not of Slavonic origin was widespread in the nineteenth century. Russian historians like Karamzin, Miller and Soloviëv sought their origin in the Kara-Kalpaks; others from the Torks or from the Polovtsy. Bantysh-Kamenski regarded them as Circassians who had settled on the Dniepr (there was certainly a substantial Circassian ele-ment established as far west as the Crimea, see Markov, *Ocherki Kryma*, pp. 417 *et sqq.*). Recently Lyubavski expressed the view that the Cossacks were Russified Tartars.

In the second half of the nineteenth century Antonovich and Kulish elaborated the theory that the Cossacks did not owe their characteristic indi-viduality to any ethnic particularities but to certain special social conditions. This theory is accepted by most of the modern historians of the Ukraine.

Jablonowski, the Polish historian of the Ukraine, came to the following conclusion: 'At the end of the fifteenth century Lithuanian princes who had settled in Kiev attracted to the border regions Tartars who entered their service and who were joined by people who were descendants of "wan-derers" (*brodniki*), who had been scattered over the steppe since the twelfth century. Amongst these could have been Torks and Kara-Kalpaks. In the sixteenth century the Slav element begins to predominate decidedly, and

then was formed the special nationality of the Ukraine which colonized the steppe.'
Ukrainian Cossacks 'appear in history' at a comparatively late date—about 1500. The historians of the Don Cossacks, probably with some justice, attribute the origin of the Don Cossacks to the pre-Mongol period and affirm their service with the Golden Horde. They contend that the parishioners of the Orthodox Diocese, founded by Khan Beréké at Saray and called 'the Diocese of Saray and the Don', were mostly Cossacks who had settled along the rivers Don and Khoper. (See Bykadorov, *Istoriya Kazachestva* (History of Cossackdom), vol. I, Praha, 1930.)

(3) On the Ryazan Tartars and the Ryazan Cossacks

Among the Ryazan Cossacks who undertook sentry service along the borders of Muscovy were doubtless many Tartars. In the year 1452 Vasili II invited Tartars to settle along the Oka in the lands of the wild Finnic Meshchera. Along with these Tartars came their *mirzas* or princes, including Kasim, a member of the royal house of Kazan (and founder of the Kasimov principality, see bibliographical note under 'Kasimov' in *E.I.*). During the fifteenth and sixteenth centuries the Muscovite rulers accorded a willing welcome to Tartar nobles and made them grants of land. Between the fifteenth and the seventeenth centuries official documents mention about 120 noble families of Tartar descent, among whom are the Apraxins, Bakhmetievs, Bibikovs, Golovins, Muratovs, Naryshkins, Saburovs, Turgenevs, Uvarovs, Urusovs and Yusupovs. The prevalent notion in the West that the Tartar element is stronger in the north of Russia than in the south is incorrect. For polemical reasons Polish and Ukrainian propagandists have repeatedly described the Muscovites as 'rather Tartars than Slavs'. Actually in the peasant population of Northern and North-Eastern Russia there is a strong strain of Finnic blood, and in many localities the Finnish ethnic element predominates over the Slav. As for the Tartar strain, it is not so much Mongol as Turk (it is estimated that even in the horde of Chingiz the proportions were one-third Mongol and two-thirds Turk). The Tartar element is more noticeable in the southern than in the northern rural population.

(4) On the Southern Border of the Muscovite State in the Sixteenth Century

About the year 1550 the border ran in a north-east to south-west direction from Sviyazhsk on the Volga through Alatyr, Temnikov, Ryazhsk, Pronsk, Epiphan, Novosil, Mtsensk, Novgorod-Seversk, Rylsk, Putivl to Chernigov.

(5) On Dmitri Vishnevetsky ('Bayda')

The popular song about 'Bayda'—Prince Dmitri Vishnevetsky, who was the first Zaporogian Hetman—begins with the words: 'In Tsargrad, on the market-place, Bayda sits and drinks his vodka.' It goes on to relate that the Sultan tried to persuade Bayda to become 'his true and faithful knight', promising to reward him by giving him 'a little princess in marriage' and making him the lord of all 'little Ukraine'. Bayda, however, tells the

Sultan that both his faith and his little princess are unclean. The irate Sultan thereupon exclaims:.'Good people, take Bayda and hang him on a hook by the rib.' (Kashchenko, *Opovidannya pro slavne voysko Zaporozhske* (Tales of the Zaporogian *Sech*), Leipzig, 1923 (Ukr.)

(6) On the Turkish Volga Campaign of 1569 and the Raids of the Crim Tartars on Moscow in 1570–1

The Turks regarded the Tartar Khanates of Astrakhan and Kazan as their vassals, and Mehmed Sökölli appears to have fully recognized the significance of the expansion of Muscovite power down the Volga. Azov, situated at the mouth of the Don, became the base for a formidable Turkish military expedition to Astrakhan. The Turkish army advanced along the Don and the sparse settlements of the Don Cossacks were suppressed. Work on the canal which was to link the Don with the Volga was at the same time begun. The siege of Astrakhan, however, ended in disaster. The moment had been judiciously chosen; the Muscovites had been exhausted by the Livonian War and by the struggle of Ivan IV with the *Boyars*. In the following two years, 1570–1, the Crim Tartars made two raids on Moscow, during which they crossed the Oka and burnt the suburbs of the capital. Many thousands of men and women were carried off to slavery in the Crimea.

For the Turkish campaign on the Don and Volga see von Hammer, *Histoire de l'Empire Ottoman*, vol. VI; Jorga, *Geschichte des Osmanischen Reiches*, vol. III. For the effect on the internal situation in Muscovy of the Crimean raids of 1570–1, and for their influence on the external policy of Ivan IV, see Pares, *A History of Russia*, chap. VI. The Turkish naval defeat at Lepanto (1570) undoubtedly had a negative influence on Sökölli's Black Sea policy during the following years; but the invasion of Georgia and Daghestan in 1578 was probably in part designed to check further Russian expansion in the Caspio-Volga region.

(7) On Life in the Zaporogian Sech

Gogol, the greatest Ukrainian literary figure (who incidentally wrote in Russian), gives an attractive description of the Zaporogian *Sech* in his romance entitled *Taras Bulba*. The *Sech*, founded by Dmitri Vishnevetsky on the island of Khortytsa, was later transferred to other islands in the Dniepr (although for a time it again returned to Khortytsa). The *Sech* was a fortified camp surrounded by trenches and moats. The moats themselves were defended by stockades of tree-trunks (in Russian, *zaseki*, from which the name *Sech* was derived). Stiff hedges built of dried branches and clay constituted an inner line. Two gates gave entry. Within the hedge-wall were built long huts or *kurenyi* (with which it is interesting to compare the communal huts of the Circassians where the English travellers Longworth and Bell found lodging during their travels in Circassia during the second quarter of the nineteenth century). These *kurenyi* were covered with reeds. Here the Cossacks lived—a hundred or several hundred men in each. In normal times there were thirty-eight of these huts, which were named after different Ukrainian towns or after famous Zaporogians. Apart from the living quarters there were a 'chancellery', an arsenal and food magazines;

and in the seventeenth century the church of Our Lady's Protection was built. Beyond the gates of the *Sech* was a market-place with shops and taverns. There travellers were allowed to lodge—Russians, Armenians and Jews—and, in time of peace, Turks and Tartars. The outer market was a kind of trading centre where the booty won on campaigns could be sold. There was also a small river harbour which was visited by Turkish, Greek and Italian ships.

Once a year each of the *kurenyi* elected its *ataman*, and all the *kurenyi* together, in other words the *Rada*, elected the Hetman and also all men who had to fill posts in the administration. All important matters were decided by the *Rada*. At the end of the winter lots were drawn to decide who among the Cossacks were to prepare for campaign, who were to remain to defend the *Sech*, and who were to go off on hunting and fishing expeditions. Booty was divided into two equal parts. One part went to the treasury of the *Sech*, and the other, after withdrawing what was destined for the *Sech* Church and for certain monasteries which were supported by the Zaporogians, was divided equally between all the Cossacks—both those who had taken part in the campaign and those who had remained behind for defence and supplies.

Every Zaporogian was free to leave the *Sech* whenever he wanted to do so. He might also leave the *Sech* for a time and return later. Entry into the *Sech* was confined to the following simple question and answer: the Hetman would ask a candidate: 'Dost thou believe in God?' and if the man answered 'Yes', he would be told to cross himself, and if he crossed himself it was considered a sufficient proof that he was a Christian. After that no one asked him who he was, from where he was or why he had come to the *Sech*. The majority of Zaporogians were of Ukrainian origin; but there were many who had come out of Muscovy and White Russia and a certain proportion of all sorts of nationalities.

The *Hetman* was the "headman" of the free Cossacks, but also in Poland and Lithuania the C.I.C. was called Grand Crown Hetman.

Ataman, Ukr. *otaman*, seems to be the same word, but is applied to minor chiefs, e.g. of *kurenyi* or small gangs.

(8) On Church History and the Union of the Churches

Titov, T. *Russkaya Pravoslavnaya Tserkov v Polsko-Litovskom Gosudarstve* (The Russian Orthodox Church in the Polish-Lithuanian State), vols. I–III, Kiev, 1905.

Bodnov, V. *Pravoslavnaya Tserkov v Polshe i Litve* (The Orthodox Church in Poland and Lithuania), Ekaterinoslav, 1908.

Hrushevsky, M. *Kulturno-Natsionalny Rukh na Ukrayinyi v XVI-XVII vv.* (The Cultural and National Movement in Ukraina in the Sixteenth and Seventeenth Centuries), Wien, 1919 (Ukr.).

Polosz, J. *Geschichte der Union der Ruthenischen Kirche mit Rom*, vols. I–II, Wien, 1879–81.

Likowski, E. *Unia Brzeska* (The Union of Brest), Poznan, 1895 (Pol.).

Zhukovich, V. *Seymovaya Borba Pravoslavnago Zapadno-Russkago Dvoryanstva s Uniey* (The Struggle in the *Seym* of the West Russian Orthodox Gentry against the Union), Petersburg, 1901.

See also two articles in the *Slavonic Review*: K. Gorski, 'Some Aspects of the Polish Reformation', vol. IX, no. 27; J. Mirtshuk, 'The Ukrainian Uniat Church', vol. X, no. 29.

(9) *On the Early Cossack Insurrections*

Domanitsky, V. *Kozachchina na Perelomï XVI–XVII Stoletiy* (1591–1603) (Cossackdom at the turn of the Sixteenth–Seventeenth Centuries), Lvov, 1904 (Ukr.).

Nikolaychik, F. *Pervyya Kozatskyya Vozstaniya v Rechi Pospolitoy* (First Cossack Risings in Rzecz Pospolita), *Kievskaya Starina*, 1884.

Antoni, D. *Naliwajko: Opowiadanie Hystoryczne* (Nalyvayko: A Historical Narrative), Warszawa, 1882 (Pol.).

(10) *On Ivan Podkova*

In 1574 the Moldavian Hospodar Ion (John) III ('The Terrible' or 'The Armenian') appealed to King Stephen Báthory for help against the Turks. A Polish noble, another John, Swirgowski, with or without the knowledge of the Polish authorities, gathered a troop of Zaporogian Cossacks and entered Moldavia. The Cossacks were at first victorious, but were finally defeated by the Turks and their nominee Peter III the Lame; both Johns were killed. Three years later, the Moldavians called in the Cossacks to help in a revolt against Peter. Among the Zaporogians who rode into Moldavia was a certain Ivan Podkova who gave himself out to be a brother of the deceased Hospodar Ion III (the cognomen of Podkova ('horseshoe' in Russian) was given him on account of his great strength because he could break horseshoes with his hands). With 600 of the Zaporogians Podkova crossed the Dniestr and was proclaimed Hospodar in Jassy, where he established himself in great pomp. But Stephen Báthory, fearing war with the Turks, ordered Podkova to quit Moldavia; he was later arrested in Poland and beheaded in Lvov in the presence of the Turkish ambassador.

Cf. also Jorga, *Geschichte des Osmanischen Reiches*, vol. III, and *Histoire des Roumains et de leur Civilisation*, Bucharest, 1922.

A valuable biography of Stephen Báthory has recently been published as the joint work of the Polish and Hungarian Academies: *Étienne Bathory, Roi de Pologne, Prince de Transylvanie*, Cracow, 1935. See also, *Revue du Sud-Est Européen*, vol. VII, nos. 1–3, 'Moldavie et Pologne au commencement du XVIIme siècle', and other articles on Roumano-Polish relations.

(11) *Samuel Kishka: Popular Songs*

The Zaporogian Samuel Kishka ('the Cat') is the hero of the longest historical song of the Ukrainian people. It relates, with a great many details, how Samuel Kishka, after languishing for long years in captivity among the Turks, seized the galley in which he worked with other Ukrainian prisoners and brought it to the mouth of the Dniepr, where he met a band of Zaporogians about to set out on a sea raid. These songs were composed and sung by the *kobzars*—old men, often blind, who wandered round the Ukraine, going from one village to another, singing, or rather declaiming, about 'deeds done long ago', to the accompaniment of the plaintive notes of the *kobza*, a very primitive chord instrument. These *kobzars* continued to survive in the Ukraine until the Revolution. As a social phenomenon they may be compared to the Irish bards who flourished in the Gaelic-speaking villages and Jacobite country-houses of eighteenth-century Ireland and who survived even into the early decades of the nineteenth century (for the spirit of this late bardic world of the hedgerows, read Donn Byrne's 'Blind Raftery').

The Ukrainian laments for the bygone glories of the noble Russian Orthodox houses may be compared to the Irish laments for the passing of the Anglo-Irish Catholic families in the proscription which followed the surrender of Limerick.

George Fox's rendering in English of the Irish country poem 'The County of Limerick' is a fine example of a lament for the Jacobite emigration.

> On the deck of Patrick Lynch's boat I sit in woeful flight,
> Through my sighing all the livelong day and weeping all the night,
> Were it not that from my people full of sorrow forth I go,
> By the blessed sun! 't is royally I'd sing thy praise, Mayo!
>
> 'T is my grief that Patrick Laughlin is not Earl of Irrul still,
> And that Brian Duff no longer rules as lord upon the hill,
> And that Colonel Hugh MacGrady should be lying dead and low,
> And I sailing swiftly from the County of Mayo.

The numbers of blind among the Ukrainian *kobzars* of the seventeenth century is explained by the fact that the Crim Tartars severely punished Ukrainian captives after a first unsuccessful attempt at escape, but after a second attempt they put out their eyes and let them go free. When these men returned to their own districts they usually eked out a livelihood by singing. The recorded songs of the Ukrainian villages contain much valuable historical material. Cf. Dragomanov's *Politicheskiya Pesni Ukrainskago Naroda* (Political Songs of the Ukrainian People), vols. I–II, Geneva, 1883–5; Kashchenko, *Opovidannya pro slavne voysko Zaporozhske* (Tales of the Zaporogian *Sech*), Leipzig, 1923.

(12) *On 'The Time of Troubles': Ataman Zarutsky*

Among the Ukrainian Cossacks who participated in the chaotic events of the Troubled Times was the Zaporogian Ataman Zarutsky. He gained a certain prominence owing to the fact that Marina Mniszek, the Polish lady who had become successively the wife of the first False Dmitri and the second, fell into his hands. When the second Pretender, known to his enemies as 'the Thief of Tushino' (owing to the fact that he had made his camp at the village of Tushino near Moscow), quitted the field of action, Zarutsky carried off Marina Mniszek to Astrakhan together with her son by the second Dmitri—who became known as 'the Little Thief'. 'The Little Thief' continued to be a source of anxiety even after the election of Michael Romanov as Tsar in 1613. The following missive was sent to the Don Cossacks from the new Tsar: 'Write to your brothers the Volga, the Ural and the Terek Cossacks, that if they have the fear of God in them they must not lend their support to the Little Thief.' The *voyevodes* Princes Odoevski and Golovin descended the Volga in boats, supported by the Don Cossacks, against Zarutsky and the adherents of 'the Little Thief'. Zarutsky disappeared into the steppes beyond the Caspian and perished there.

(13) *On the Raids of the Zaporogian Cossacks in the Time of Sahaydachny*

Many legends and songs about the sea raids of the Zaporogians are re-membered to this day in the Ukraine. The Zaporogians acquired great fame through the raid on Caffa in 1617 during which large numbers of captives were liberated. Mansurov, the Muscovite ambassador in Stambul, and the clerk, Simonov, give a contemporary account of the raid when the Cossacks, whose ladders were too short to allow them to scale the walls, commandeered grazing camels on which they proceeded to mount the ladders.

For the Turkish accounts of the sea raids, see von Hammer, *Histoire de l'Empire Ottoman*, vol. IX.

(14) *On the Relations between the Zaporogian and the Don Cossacks*

Except on a few occasions when the Zaporogians found themselves in the Polish ranks and the Don Cossacks fought under the Muscovite banner, the two Cossack communities never came into serious conflict. Both the *Sech* and the Don were allies in their common struggle against the Turks and the Crim Tartars. The Don annals frequently record occasions during which the Zaporogians came to their aid. Many individuals and groups from the *Sech* fled to the Don to escape from the sphere of Polish authority. A Muscovite report of the seventeenth century states that: 'There are Zaporogian Cherkasses on the Don and many people do not know why these Cherkasses live on the Don. The *atamans* and the Cossacks are in contact with the Cherkasses. The *atamans* and the Cossacks visit them also beyond the cataracts, and the Cherkasses come to the Don' (Bykadorov, *Donskoe Voysko v Borbe za Vykhod v More* (The Don Cossacks in their Struggle for Issues to the Sea), Paris, 1937).

In the year 1621, 1500 Don Cossacks and 300 Zaporogians went off in company on a sea raid. In 1629 the Don Cossacks and the Zaporogians combined in an attack on the coasts of the Crimea. In 1639, 3000 Zaporogians went to the Don to take part in the operations round Azov, thus considerably weakening Pavluk in his rising against the Poles.

(15) *On the Liberation of Captives by the Cossacks*

The desire to liberate their captive compatriots gave a real spiritual background to the exploits of the Cossacks; and the miseries of the thousands of prisoners in Turkish hands form the motive of many Cossack legends and songs (the popular 'propaganda' of those days). For instance: 'There is a fire beyond the river where the Tartars are dividing their prisoners. Our hamlet has been burned and our goods plundered. The old mother has been killed and the wife carried off captive. The tambourines are heard from the valley. People are led to slaughter there, with nooses round their necks and chains that clatter on their feet. I am all done with my grief and despair, with only small children beside me. I will away into the forest along the tracks.'

Many songs were composed about Ukrainian girls who became the wives of Turks. A usual motive is: a Ukrainian girl is loved by a Turkish Pasha and lives a life of luxury, but her heart is wrung at the sight of the hard lot of her compatriots. A very popular song was one about a girl—'Marusya the priest's daughter from Bohuslav'. Marusya enjoyed the confidence of her Turkish lover, but she stole the key of the prison from him and set the captives free: 'from hard captivity, from the Muslim Faith, to the land of bright dawn where still rivers flow, to the happy land, to the Christian world'.

The Cossacks considered the liberation of captives to be their holy duty, although it imposed on them much onerous trouble, and the keep of the liberated prisoners often cost them much money. The Don Cossacks reminded the Muscovite Tsar of this fact when the pay due to them did not reach them in time. In 1614 we find the Don Cossacks writing: 'My Lord, this year we have sent off three hundred souls, male and female, to Your Majesty's Ukraine, and yet there did not come your high order to send craft and food for these captives. They are dying of hunger; they cannot live, as we live, on grass and water.' The Don Cossacks were accustomed to reproach Moscow, recalling that they served 'not for lucre or lands but only for grass and water' (Bykadorov).

(16) *Kiev as an Intellectual Centre*

Owing to the initiative and influence of Sahaydachny, Kiev became an intellectual centre for the Ukraine. In the time of the Metropolitan Peter Movila the young men who were educated in the Kievan schools and monasteries and in the newly founded Academy of Kiev differed little in the quality of their learning from those educated in the Polish Jesuit schools and colleges. The influences of the Orthodox revival in the Roumanian principalities and at Constantinople also spread to the Ukraine. After the incorporation of the Ukraine with Muscovy, the superior learning of the Kiev Academy and the influences from the Orthodox lands of the south-west were felt in Moscow. Graduates of the Kiev Academy played an important part in the reforms of the Patriarch Nikon during the sixties of the seventeenth century. The Ukrainian factor, with its Danubian and Italo-Greek connections, had a significant relation to the spread of Western influences in Russia half a century before the period of Peter the Great. Apart from commercial contacts with North-Western and Central Europe, these influences were exemplified in the Danubo-Aegean and Romance tendencies to be noted in the sacred literature, church painting and ecclesiastical architecture of the time.

Notwithstanding wars and internal dissensions during the second half of the seventeenth century, Kiev continued to be an intellectual centre. But the intellectual groups in Kiev who showed themselves particularly active in Church politics failed to exercise any important political influence on events because they became and remained alien to the mass of peasants and Cossacks. In this sense, a very characteristic example is the personality of Yuri Nemirich, who completed a very thorough education in Holland (Leyden), where he spent ten years of his life. When he returned to his native land he took part in Khmelnytsky's movement and in the subsequent political conflicts. But in spite of the best intentions, his activities were not successful. The Cossacks could never understand him and he perished.

(17) On the Risings between 1630 and 1638

Shevchenko, the Ukrainian national poet of the nineteenth century, dedicated one of his poems, 'Taras's Night', to the rising of Taras Fedorovich. There is a Ukrainian song about the Hetman Sulima very similar to that about Samuel Kishka. Pavluk, who sacrificed himself in order to save the others, has remained the hero of many legends. Ostranitsa appears to have been one of the most talented of the Cossack military leaders. Despairing of the struggle, he abandoned it in time and withdrew beyond the Donets. (Cf. P. Kulish, 'Ukrainian Cossacks and Polish landlords in the decades before Khmelnytsky's Rising', in The Russian Review, vols. I–V, 1895.)

(18) On the Ukraine after the Suppression of the First Cossack Risings

The Ukrainian lays picture the period between 1638 and 1648 as one of misery and humiliation. 'Nothing good ever happened in the King's land from the time of the Kumeyki battle till Khmelnytsky. The "undertakers" came down like a swarm of locusts. All the Cossack roads were leased and at intervals of every three miles a toll-house was opened. In dear old Ukraine even churches were leased to the Jews.'

The Sech was dead; sea raids and raids on the Crimea had ceased. 'The Dniepr asks the gentle Danube: "Why hast thou no more my own Cossacks on thy banks?" The gentle Danube murmurs: "Father Dniepr, I am myself wondering and guessing why thy Cossacks no longer come my way".'

In spite of the tendency of Polish historians to minimize the intolerable conditions which the Orthodox population endured, some who lived at dates not far removed from the period, as for instance the author of Three Kings of the House of Vasa, are not sparing of abuse of the landlords for their oppression of the peasants. Twardowski, a contemporary of Khmelnytsky, frankly admits that all which happened was the fault of the Poles, whose treatment of the peasantry provoked the rising. The French engineer Beauplan expressed the opinion that the condition of the Ukrainian peasantry was only comparable to that of French peasants serving sentences of forced labour. Modern Polish historians do not ignore the true significance of the peasant revolt under Khmelnytsky (cf. Halecki, La Pologne de 963 à 1914).

(19) On the Rising of Bohdan Khmelnytsky

A series of classical works by Russian historians has been dedicated to Bohdan Khmelnytsky's rising. Most important of these are the works of N. Kostomarov (1817–85) and P. Kulish (1819–97). The work of P. Kulish remains of considerable historical value (Istoriya Obedineniya Rossii (The History of the Unification of Russia), vols. I–III, Petersburg, 1874–7). Kulish was a contemporary of Kostomarov, but their outlook differs. It is curious that Kostomarov's work—though he was not a Ukrainian by birth —pleased the Ukrainian nationalists of his time; he idealized the 'love of liberty' of the Cossacks and sought to see social and revolutionary motives in the movement of 1648–54. Kulish, on the other hand, although he was a Ukrainian, considers that the union of the Ukraine with Muscovy was a matter of historical necessity, and that the Ukrainians, left to themselves, would have been unable to establish an ordered life in their country. At the time Kulish's conclusions called forth indignant protests from Ukrainian nationalists, but at present Ukrainian scholars consider the work of Kulish as more serious than the talented literary essays of Kostomarov.

The events of 1648–53 are described in great detail by Hrushevsky in his *History of Ukraine-Rus*, vol. VIII, part 3 (1648–50), Wien, 1922; and in vol. IX, part 1 (1650–3), Kiev, 1928. See also, D. Odinets, *Prisoedinenie Ukrainy k Moskovskomu Gosudarstvu* (The Union of the Ukraine with the Muscovite State), Paris, 1936; and especially the important work of Myakotin, *Ocherki Sotsialnoy Istorii Ukrainy v XVII–XVIII vv.* (Sketches in the Social History of the Ukraine in the Seventeenth and Eighteenth Centuries), vols. I–III, Praha, 1924–6.

(20) *On the Internal Policy of Vladislav IV*

For an interpretation of the relations of Vladislav IV with Bohdan Khmelnytsky, summarized in David Hannay's brilliant essay on Polish history in the 11th edition of the *Encyclopaedia Britannica*, see the Polish work by Szajnocha (which has not been accessible to the present writer), *Two Years of our History* (1646-1648), Lvov, 1865. See also the Polish works by Czermak: *The Plans of the Turkish Wars of Vladislav IV*, Cracow, 1895, and *Letters and Other Writings of Vladislav IV*, Cracow, 1845.

If, as is probable, the 'Royal Letter' of Vladislav IV to Khmelnytsky never existed, there is little doubt that the King had taken the Hetman into his confidence with regard to his political plans. These plans included an intention to undertake decisive action against the Turks (an action which would have anticipated the Ottoman revival and offensive of the third quarter of the century) in alliance not only with Vienna and Venice, but also, if possible with Moscow. In the event of war, the whole-hearted participation of the Cossacks would have been of the greatest value to Poland and—whether or not the King went so far as to conspire with the Hetman against the liberties of the Polish oligarchy—it is likely that he promised Khmelnytsky to restore all the ancient privileges of the Cossacks.

(21) *On the Polish Army in August 1648*

The Polish troops which were hastily raised after the defeat of the Crown Hetman Potocki at Zhovti Vody and near Korsun consisted of numerous detachments of feudal militia together with a force of trained German mercenaries. The Polish nobles could not agree upon one commander, and three of their number were appointed to lead the troops: Dominic Zasławski, Ostrorog, and the younger Koniecpolski. Khmelnytsky described the Polish command as 'a feather bed, a Latinist, and a babe'; for Zasławksi was known for his luxurious habits, while Ostrorog was renowned for his classical learning, and the son of the veteran friend of Vladislav IV was only eighteen years of age. Like the doomed army of Kara Mustafa, which three decades later was to be scattered by a Polish King before Vienna, the host which advanced against the Cossacks was over-burdened with all the appurtenances of a court upon the move. The camp at Pilyavtsy was so gay that people went to celebrate weddings and christening feasts there. The Poles came furnished with thousands of chains for the prospective prisoners, and no one doubted the utter defeat of 'the rabble'. A special prayer was even composed: 'Oh God, do not proffer Thy aid either to us or to the Cossacks, but just witness from above how we will deal with this rabble.'

(22) On Jeremy Vishnevetsky or Wiśniowiecki

The Vishnevetskys owned very extensive lands on the left bank of the Dniepr. Prince Jeremy was the only important man who did not lose his head on the outbreak of Khmelnytsky's rising. Having collected a small but well-disciplined troop of nobles, in the summer of 1648, he crossed to the right bank of the Dniepr, and began a counter-offensive against the Zaporogian bands on the borders of Podolia and Volhynia. He was victorious in a number of fights, but all round him the peasants were rising and burning estates.

After the defeat of the Poles at Pilyavtsy, Vishnevetsky began to prepare for a continuation of the struggle. In 1649 he was elected Crown Hetman, and he won fame by his heroic defence of the Zbarazh camp, where he held out for six weeks with 15,000 men against a horde of Cossacks, Tartars and peasants ten times as numerous.

Prince Jeremy was a remarkable man, extremely gifted, and with an iron will; he was very popular among the gentry, but was hated by the magnates and courtiers who surrounded King John Casimir. Though a devout Catholic and a man of culture, Vishnevetsky was brutally cruel towards the peasants. After a rising in his village of Pohrebishcha, he put to death all the men, and ordered all the women to be blinded, but so that there should be some left to lead these crowds of sightless wretches, he ordained that among every hundred women there should be one left who had had only one eye put out. Vishnevetsky was also a ruthless persecutor of the Orthodox Faith. There had never been any Catholics established in the region of Poltava, but during his rule there he organized the construction of Catholic churches and monasteries.

(23) On Timosh Khmelnytsky: policy in the Danubian Principalities

Bohdan Khmelnytsky's intervention in the politics of the Roumanian principalities is associated with the romantic story of the love of his son Timothy (Timosh) for Ruxandra, the second daughter of Basil the Wolf (Lupul) of Moldavia.

According to the Deacon Paul of Aleppo, who has left a contemporary account of his travels in Moldavia, Timosh 'really was the most courageous man in the world. The Beys and Pashas who were sent from Constantinople to try and make things go the way the Sultan wished, were astonished by his skill.' The less enthusiastic Moldavs found him pock-marked and uncouth. The lady, who had already enjoyed an affair with the son of a Venetian official and had subsequently been affianced to a brother of George II Rákóczy of Transylvania, was noted for her beauty.

In 1648, during the height of Bohdan Khmelnytsky's successes against the Poles, Basil the Wolf had applied for Cossack support against a pretender, George Stephen, who was a protégé of the Transylvanian prince. Timosh, who had been sent into Moldavia with a detachment of Cossacks, had then met the Princess Ruxandra. After the Zborov Agreement, Khmelnytsky extracted the consent of the Moldavian Hospodar to a marriage only on the threat that 'he would send 100,000 Cossacks to further his son's suit'.

During the course of the year 1650, Timosh Khmelnytsky, after defeating the Polish detachment of Kolinowski which attempted to bar his way, entered Moldavia, and his marriage with Ruxandra was celebrated with great pomp in Jassy.

After the defeat of Bohdan Khmelnytsky at Berestechko in the summer of 1651, the partisans of George Stephen drove the Wolf out of his capital, and he again applied to the Cossacks for aid. Timosh crossed the Dniestr and routed George Stephen, who had raised a mixed force of Wallachs, Magyars, Germans and Serbs. 'Young Khmelnytsky entered Jassy. The town was sacked by his troops. Turks and Jews were slaughtered after they had been questioned as to where they kept their treasures. The bells were ringing in the town. The Patriarch of Antioch offered a Te Deum for the weal of Basil, Bohdan, Timothy and his spouse. Basil came back and the Cossacks welcomed him with an artillery salute.'

The triumph of Timosh was short-lived. The Wallachian Hospodar, Matthew Bassarab, defeated the forces of the Wolf in spite of Cossack support; chased out of Jassy by George Stephen, the old man was forced to take refuge in Bohdan's capital of Chigirin. When Timosh collected a new force of Cossacks and again crossed the Dniestr, he was surrounded by George Stephen at Suceava. Wounded in the knee, he died after a few days. His body was brought back to Chigirin and buried on the family estate at Subbotovo. His wife, who meantime had given birth to twin boys in Chigirin, many years later fell into the hands of Polish troops and was beheaded.

For the complicated political combinations of these five years in which Bohdan Khmelnytsky, with the Transylvanian Prince Rákóczy and the two Roumanian Hospodars, became involved, see Jorga, *Geschichte des Osmanischen Reiches*, vol. III, cap. 4; cf. also his *Geschichte des Rumänischen Volkes*, vol. II, Absch. 6. The Turks, Bohdan Khmelnytsky and George Rákóczy, all from different angles, appear to have envisaged the stabilization of a block of states (including Translyvania, Wallachia, Moldavia, Ukraine and Crim Tartary) which would have constituted a buffer area between the Ottoman dominions and those of the Habsburgs, Poland and Muscovy, and the rulers of which would have been dependent on the Porte. The imperial policy of the Turks in Circassia, the Georgian kingdoms and Daghestan, over against Muscovy and the Iranian monarchy, was based on a similar conception. This policy was pursued during the following three decades by the Köprülüs, and even by Kara Mustafa, in their support of the Hungarian and Transylvanian rebels against the Habsburgs, and of Michael Doroshenko and Yuri

Khmelnytsky against Poland and Muscovy. This Turkish policy, which implied a wide local autonomy, and a certain toleration as between rival Christian creeds, and which suited the interests of an irresponsible local aristocracy, always found a substantial degree of acquiescence in the countries concerned.

(24) *Muscovy and the Support of Rebels*

For several decades after the Time of Troubles, the Muscovite Chancellery regarded the Ukrainian Cossacks (whom they called generally 'Zaporogian Cherkasses') with the greatest suspicion. The statesmen of the new Romanov monarchy were stern upholders of the monarchical tradition and of the amenities of relations between monarchs (*vide* the rupture of relations with the English Commonwealth after the judicial murder of King Charles I). The advisers of Tsar Alexey Mikhailovich hesitated to accept the advances of Khmelnytsky, whom they regarded as a rebel against his King. In view of the possibility, however, of his coming to an understanding either with the Turks or with the Swedes, they could not afford to ignore his proposals. During the year 1653 the Muscovite lawyers arrived at a compromise which might justify the Tsar's support of the Cossacks. A formula was evolved whereby while it was accepted that subjects were bound by oath to be loyal to their King, the King himself was obliged by oath to maintain the rights and privileges of his subjects. The Muscovite lawyers found that the King of Poland had forsworn his oath to the Cossacks, and that therefore 'the Zaporogian Cossacks with all their lands and towns' were free of their oath to the King.

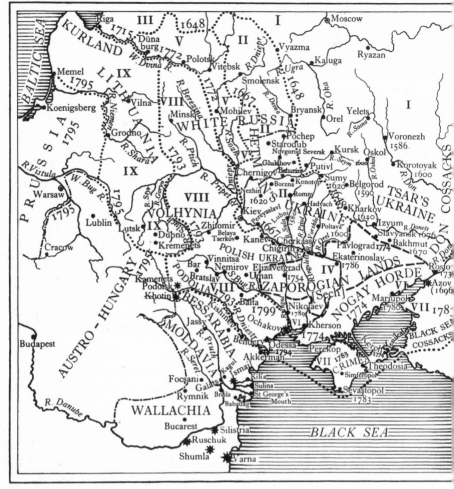

EXPANSION OF RUSSIA, 1648–1795

Roman figures denote the order in which the various regions came un[der] Muscovite rule.

Large Arabic figures—the dates when boundaries were constituted.

Small Arabic figures—the dates when towns were founded and th[e] environs settled.

•••••• Definite, —— — — Indefinite, boundaries.

I Muscovy, when the Hetman's Ukraine transferred its allegiance in 1648.

II Smolensk and left bank Ukraine, 1667.

III Duchy of Kurland, 1715.

IV Zaporogian Country, 1750–1775.

V Polotsk and East White Russia, 1[772.]

VI Coast from Bug to Don (N[ew] Russia), 1774.

VII Crimea and the Kuban, 1783.

VIII West White Russia to Podolia, 1[793.]

IX Lithuania and West Volhynia, 1[795.]

CHAPTER IV

THE UKRAINE OF THE HETMANS
(1654–1709)

§1. THE NEW ORDER IN THE UKRAINE

THE Pereyaslavl Agreement was an historical event of the first importance. Muscovy became Russia in the union of the two principal blocks of Eastern Slavs of the Orthodox Faith. The old meridial line smashed by the Mongol invasions of the thirteenth century was restored. Rus had been reborn—from Novgorod to Kiev, 'from the Varangians to the Greeks'. The integration of the Russian lands—of the Ukraine with Great Russia—had come about as a natural historical process rather than as the result of a determined imperial policy. The Muscovite state, still slowly recovering from the period of the Time of Troubles, weak from internal social and religious dissensions, had never resumed the stern expansive policy of the great Ivans. The careful advisers of Tsar Alexey had flinched from compromising the new Romanov monarchy in the turbulent politics of the Cossacks. On his side Bohdan Khmelnytsky—a bold reiver swimming in the tide of great events—had harboured in his simple flaunting mind no dream of Russian unity. He would have preferred to have played a role as a half-independent prince like the Roumanian Hospodars or the Crimean Girays or George Rákóczy. Never was a great event less planned and determined by men; geographical facts and the unconscious needs of nameless masses imposed an empire of vast possibility on men who at first quite failed to comprehend the significance of what was happening.

The potential of Russian power was enormously increased. The control of the principal rivers debouching to the northern shore of the Black Sea had been shifted from Poland—a state structure based on the Baltic-Vistula-Niemen-Dvina square—to Muscovy, which, until the middle of the seventeenth century, had remained a Volga power with an expansion—the significance of which was as yet not understood in Western Europe—north-eastward down the White Sea rivers and eastward across the Urals.

The prospect of coming Russian military and economic spread now had no limit within the area of the Great Eurasian Plain. Its exploitation was only a matter of time and men; and in a very short time Tsar Peter appeared as the first man to organize power 'out of the immeasurable regions' where 'the countless millions of Slavs' had been swarming 'so noiselessly'—'unnoticed by the annalists'.

But the problems presented to the advisers of Tsar Alexey were formidable. The incorporation of the Ukraine with Muscovy was a challenge to the Ottoman power on the Black Sea and to the very existence of the weakened Polish state. Immediate war with Poland was inevitable; the Russians could not fail to participate in the attempted partition of *Rzecz Pospolita* which was to engage all the predatory powers of Northern and Eastern Europe during the coming two decades, and Khmelnytsky was quick to urge on Moscow the occupation of Smolensk and White Russia. The Swedish King, Charles X, began to aim at balancing the Russian incorporation of the Ukraine by attaching Lithuania to the Swedish crown. The presence of the Muscovites on the lower Dniepr implied the doom of the bandit state of Crim Tartary and provoked the Khans, at the first opportunity, to renew their coursing of the Ukrainian plains with desperate ruthlessness. And when the Köprülü viziers came to power in Istanbul, a revived Ottoman power was to meet the Russian challenge on the Black Sea with a prolonged and determined attempt to substitute Turkish for Russian hegemony between the Dniestr and the Don.

The social problems which confronted the Muscovite Tsar were equally grave. For on the one hand the Cossack military leaders in the Ukraine soon showed that they were intending to establish themselves as a territorial aristocracy in succession to the Polish nobility whom they had slaughtered or expelled, while on the other hand the peasant masses were not only bitterly determined to oppose the growth of a new class of landlords, but their truculent and restless spirit was to spread beyond the Cossack lands into Great Russia and to inspire such movements as the *jacquerie* of Stenka Razin which swept the valley of the Volga in 1670.

Although before the conclusion of the Pereyaslavl Agreement the Tsar had sent an assurance to Khmelnytsky through his envoys that 'all the old rights and customs of the Cossacks would be maintained and confirmed by his signature', and Buturlin had promised that 'the Tsar would grant the Cossacks greater liberties, more riches and privileges than were ever granted to them by the Kings of Poland', no definite agreement as to the future status of the Cossack communities had been reached when the Pereyaslavl *Rada* acclaimed Alexey Mikhailovich on 8 January 1654.

Some doubts appear to have troubled the minds of Bohdan Khmelnytsky and the Cossack elders when, after the acclamation, Buturlin made a speech in which he stated that 'the Tsar was taking under the protection of his high and mighty hand the Hetman and all the Cossacks with their towns and lands'. In the cathedral church of Pereyaslavl, where the elders were assembled to swear allegiance, Khmelnytsky suddenly proposed to Buturlin that he should take an oath in the name of Tsar Alexey that 'he would not betray the Cossacks to the Polish King, that he would defend them and respect their liberties'. To this the imperial envoy made the sharp retort that: 'No one has ever taken an oath in the name of our liege lord and master and no one ever will. It is not even seemly for the Hetman to speak of such things.... That Polish Kings swear oaths to their subjects is no fitting precedent because those Kings are heretics and not Autocrats.... The Tsar's word is sufficient and cannot be altered.' It was an ill-chosen moment at which to attempt to decide a constitutional issue, and the Hetman and the elders proceeded to declare that 'they would rely in everything on the Tsar's mercy and humbly prostrate themselves before him imploring him to deign to look after their needs'. In this wise allegiance was sworn to the Tsar without his having accepted any preliminary conditions. Two months later the clauses of an agreement which had been elaborated between the Cossack leaders and the imperial representatives took the form of a petition to the highest authority in the land.

It is difficult to understand how this unconditional union of the Ukraine with Muscovy, confirmed by the *Rada* of 8 January 1654 and by the oath of allegiance sworn to the Tsar, could be explained by certain historians of the nineteenth century (Kostomarov, for instance) as 'an act of personal union' between Muscovy and the Ukraine. An examination of the different clauses of the draft agreement which was brought to Moscow in March 1654 by the Cossack judge Samuel Bohdanov and Colonel Teterya does not convey the impression that the Ukraine was then conceived by the representatives of the Hetman as a 'vassal' but independent country (the opinion of Hrushevsky and, in part, that of Myakotin). The statutory position of the Ukraine in relation to the Muscovite state was that of a region forming part of that state, but, by reason of the special character of the Ukrainian territory as a borderland, possessing a peculiar military organization, and, hence, certain privileges of a regional and social order.

The written agreement signed in March 1654 did not create a Ukrainian state and did not put the Hetman at the head of such a state. Nor did Khmelnytsky's preliminary draft for the agreement aim at either of these objects. The draft brought to Moscow by Bohdanov and Teterya contained twenty-three clauses, and only in one of them (15) was there any hint of a 'vassal' relationship between the Ukraine and Moscow. In Clause 15, which dealt with the receipt of revenues for the Tsar's Treasury, the authors of the draft proposed that the Tsar should receive a certain tribute from the Ukraine in the same way as the Sultan received tributes from the contemporary vassal states of the Ottoman Empire—Moldavia, Wallachia and Hungary. The advisers of Tsar Alexey did not accept this proposal, and it was dropped—the more easily since it dealt with a question of method and no political importance was attached to it. It was agreed instead that officials appointed locally should gather the taxes and that these should be handed over to *voyevodes* sent from Moscow for their receipt.

Some historians find another indication of the conception of the independence of the Ukraine in Clause 14, according to which the Hetman might receive foreign ambassadors—with the obligation to notify the Muscovite Chancellery of their arrival. But, as Odinets has observed, the right to maintain certain relations with foreign countries was not limited to the Hetman, nor was it regarded by Moscow as a sign of 'independence'. 'Purely technical conditions such as distance, the bad state of the roads, were the reasons why the *voyevodes* of border lands had the right to receive and dismiss the ambassadors of neighbouring states. Envoys sent on account of "unimportant affairs" were usually received and dismissed by the *voyevodes*, who later sent a report to the Tsar. The Novgorod *voyevode* had the right to conduct diplomatic relations with the ambassadors of a country as important as Sweden and in that respect was more privileged than the Hetman.' In fact, the Muscovite negotiators made important additions to Clause 14, stipulating that the Hetman should report to Moscow when foreign ambassadors came to him 'with good intentions', while if they should come 'with bad intentions' he was to detain them until he had received orders from the Tsar. The Hetman was also notified that 'he was to have no relations whatever with the Turkish Sultan and the King of Poland'.

The remaining clauses of the draft were accepted by the Moscow Government without objections and with scarcely any alterations. The most important feature of the agreement was the concession of a wide autonomy to the Cossacks. On the death of the Hetman, the Cossacks had the right to elect his successor and had only to report the result of the election to the Tsar 'so that their choice should not grieve His Majesty'. The estates of the Cossacks' elders became hereditary. The Cossack law courts were to be in the hands of their own men, and *boyars* and *voyevodes* sent from Moscow were to have no right to interfere with them. In the towns, the administrations, which were to be composed of local men, were to be responsible for justice and for the collection of revenues for the imperial Treasury. The Orthodox nobility were to retain their special privileges and to choose their officials from among themselves. All privileges and rights granted by the Polish Kings were to be maintained by the Tsar.

No clause in the agreement definitely recognized the Tsar as the liege-lord and master of the Ukrainian land, but the current conception of the position of the Tsar had been adequately indicated during the preliminary negotiations. 'The Hetman and the Cossack elders gave over to the Tsar the lands that had belonged to the Kings of Poland as well as the estates of the Polish landowners and those of the Catholic monasteries' (Myakotin). The Tsar could dispose of this enormous reserve of lands at his pleasure and could grant lands for services rendered. With the draft agreement Bohdanov and Teterya brought with them to Moscow numerous petitions for the imperial bounty, for the Cossack leaders did not disguise their anxiety to assure their positions as territorial magnates.

All serious investigation justifies the conclusion that the principal object of the agreement in the minds of its sponsors was to assure to the privileged Cossack classes the rights which they had enjoyed, or had thought themselves entitled to enjoy, under the Polish crown. Tsar Alexey Mikhailovich was in fact regarded as the heir of the Polish Kings, and he confirmed 'the rights and privileges which were granted by the Kings of Poland and the Great Princes of Lithuania'. Men of the type of Bohdan Khmelnytsky, who had grown up in the atmosphere of the libertarian hierarchy of *Rzecz Pospolita*, were incapable of evolving another conception; and the Muscovite statesmen—alien though this loose relationship was to their own system—could not afford to be doctrinaire in the environment of crisis in which the negotiations were transacted.

Special rescripts were granted to the Cossack communities, to the Orthodox nobility and to the clergy of Russia Minor, defining the rights of the respective groups. The Magdeburg Law and other rights and privileges granted by the Polish Kings to the towns were also confirmed.

The number of Cossacks to be registered was fixed at 60,000, and Khmelnytsky undertook, in the event of war, to furnish troops corresponding to that number. It was understood at the same time that if the Hetman could provide more the Government of the Tsar would make no objection; and this understanding could justify the Cossacks in increasing their numbers beyond the figure fixed, without interference, during peace time.

Khmelnytsky's conception of life in the Ukraine under the new dispensation was that of a stratified class hierarchy, sanctioned by the authority of the Tsar but based on Polish traditions, with a Cossack and Orthodox class of landed proprietors recruited from among the Cossack officers and substituted for the former Polish Catholic gentry. The Russian Government envisaged a state of affairs in which the Tsar was master of the whole land, and confirmed by rescripts the possessions of monasteries and churches, nobles and Cossacks, and also existing rights of property in the towns. The duty of the Cossack community was to furnish troops, and of the town popula-tions to provide revenues. Taxes were to be paid to the Exchequer also by those peasants who had settled on lands which were the property neither of the Orthodox nobility nor of the Cossacks nor of the Church—in other words by those who lived 'on the Tsar's land'. For the administration of the peasant lands and also of the towns *voyevodes* were to be sent from Moscow who would be re-sponsible for the appointment of officials from among the local in-habitants. The Cossacks remained divided into regiments based territorially on military districts. At the head of the regiment was a colonel, who not only commanded the regiment, but, in time of peace, was responsible for the government of the Cossack population living on the territory of the regiment. Regiments were divided into 'hundreds' (*sotni*), at the head of which, both in war and peace, was a captain.

The achievement of modern historians of the Ukraine (principally Myakotin) has been to show the extent to which the theoretical con-ceptions both of Khmelnytsky and of the Moscow Government differed from the realities of social relations which had already de-veloped in the Ukraine in the year 1654.

First, the Orthodox nobility, to whom a special status had been allocated, proved to be far from numerous (two or three hundred families). They were already indistinguishable from the commanding element among the Cossacks with whom they had intermingled and in whose ranks they had achieved influence owing generally to the superiority of their education.

But far more important was the absence of any clear line of di-vision between the Cossacks and the peasants. As Myakotin writes, 'the peasant masses, having liberated themselves from the authority of the landlords, had acquired personal freedom and civil rights'. In this connection it must not be forgotten that the agents of the Tsar and the propagandists of the Orthodox Church had for decades been responsible for encouraging a 'revolutionary' outlook in antagonism to the Polish crown and the Roman Catholic Church.

Immediately after the acclamation of the *Rada* on 8 January 1654,

Buturlin sent to all the towns and villages of the Ukraine Muscovite officials who were to receive the allegiance of the *whole* population, including, of course, townsfolk and peasants (Buturlin himself received the allegiance of the inhabitants of Kiev, Chernigov and Nezhin). The South Russian peasantry had never before participated in such an experience and they naturally regarded it as an imperial confirmation of the revolutionary change in their social status which resulted from the events of 1648–53.

Myakotin continues: 'During the whole period of the rising townsfolk and peasants freely joined the ranks of the Cossacks.... At Starodub, for instance, the Muscovite officials, sent to receive the allegiance of the inhabitants to the Tsar, found no townsfolk; all had registered themselves as Cossacks. However, if people joined the Cossack ranks with such ease they also quitted them with the same ease. Impoverished Cossacks, who no longer had the possibility of doing military service and of going off on campaign, again became townsfolk or peasants without any difficulty. The better elements among the population took upon themselves the obligation of military service, which entailed considerable expense but set them free from other liabilities; the poorer ones either remained peasants or became peasants and bore the burden of taxation from which the Cossacks were free.' There was thus a considerable degree of occupational fluidity among the masses of the population, and conceptions of social organization based on stratified classes were divorced from the realities of a vigorous and expanding life in a new and undeveloped country.

As Myakotin justly remarks: 'If such phenomena could exist, it proves that no special privileges were attached to being a Cossack in comparison to belonging to the peasantry. The peasantry had acquired at that time all civic rights, including particularly that of owning their own pieces of land. The right of owning property became general to such a degree that it spread even to those peasants who were officially dependent upon Orthodox landlords or Orthodox monasteries.' Myakotin gives examples of occasions when, even in the eighteenth century, the peasants sold 'their' pieces of land which theoretically formed parts of the estates of landowners, and were upheld by the law courts.

The conflict between the interests of the mass of the peasant and Cossack population and the leaders who were hungry to profit from the new order soon took form in opposition to the Tsar's grants of land to the more prominent of the Hetman's lieutenants. In March 1654 the envoys of the Hetman petitioned for a rescript of the Tsar confirming the possessions of leading Cossacks. To Khmelnytsky himself were granted the Chigirin regiment, the town of Hadyach and numerous estates scattered throughout the country. Bohdanov asked for the town of Imgleev and Teterya for the town of Smela—both, of course, with the adjoining lands. The General Secretary, Vyhovsky, Colonel Zolotarenko, and a flock of colonels and Cossack elders followed with similar requests. Petitions came streaming in for vast lands, whole groups of villages, mills and towns. Most of the petitioners received satisfaction from the imperial authorities. When, however, Teterya again arrived in Moscow in 1657 as envoy from the Hetman and amongst other business produced a petition from Vyhovsky for the grant of estates in White Russia (which land had recently been conquered from the Poles), some astonishment was expressed. Teterya explained that although the Tsar had showered bounties on the General Secretary, his father and his brothers, the Vyhovskys were afraid to claim their rights for fear of 'the Zaporogian troops'. The Muscovite officials promised to confirm through the *voyevodes* in Russia Minor the fact that the Tsar had actually made the grants in question to the Vyhovskys and others; upon this Teterya took fright and admitted that 'if only the Cossacks get to know that himself and others had been granted by the liege lord and master such vast properties they would be beaten...the Cossacks would say that all towns and lands were to be owned by His Majesty and that he (Teterya) and others were to have nothing but their pay'. Teterya confessed that in the Cossack lands they had not the right to own vast property and that even the document he had received granting the town of Smela 'had been buried in the soil'. He begged for a copy of it on parchment 'so that it should not spoil' and that 'nothing about it would be said to the Cossacks'.

While Khmelnytsky and his friends were finding themselves baulked in their desire to establish new dynasties of territorial magnates, the Moscow Government was discovering that its theoretical conception of the new order in the Ukraine did not correspond with the facts of the situation as it continued to develop. A numerous new class of officials was rapidly growing up in the towns and villages of the Ukraine; these officials were not all Cossacks, for many men came in from Poland and White Russia to share in the new opportunities. These included priests' sons and 'people of different callings' whose relative education gave them some standing in the Cossack lands. But the effective political and administrative power remained in the hands of Cossack officers, and no revenues found their way to the Tsar's Exchequer. 'These revenues were to have been collected by the local people on behalf of the Tsar's *voyevodes* sent to govern the town and country population (except of course the Cossacks who enjoyed the privilege of self-government). In practice it soon became apparent that the Muscovite *voyevodes* were altogether superfluous in the Ukraine. The peasantry during the rising and after the union with Muscovy continued to be ruled by the captains supervised by colonels—and in the jurisdiction of the Hetman. Cossack officials, even in towns which were governed under the Magdeburg Law, occupied in the sphere of legislation and local government more or less the position which had been designed for *voyevodes* from Moscow. As a result the administration passed into the hands of officials of local origin. The revenues were not delivered into the Tsar's Exchequer. After several unsuccessful attempts, the Moscow Government had to give up sending the Tsar's *voyevodes* to Ukrainian towns' (Odinets).

In this wise it soon became apparent that the actual state of affairs in the Ukraine did not correspond to the conceptions of the Agreement of March 1654. According to the Agreement the Ukraine was to form in reality a province of the Muscovite state, enjoying certain privileges and a wide autonomy on account of its situation as a frontier region and the necessarily military character of its local social structure. In fact, the Ukraine of the Hetman was in process of becoming a separate state united with Muscovy only by 'an eternal alliance', but in essence practically independent. The whole of the administration of the Ukraine was in the hands of the Cossacks at whose head stood the Hetman—freely elected by them. Into the Hetman's, and not into the Tsar's, Exchequer went the revenues from the towns and the taxes paid by those who preferred the life of a peasant free from military obligations to that of a Cossack. It was only after the death of the Hetman that the officials in Moscow came to realize quite definitely that Russia Minor was a country socially and politically quite different from anything which had been represented by Khmelnytsky. But the deliverer of the Ukraine from the Poles had never himself understood the character of the great revolt which he had led nor the implications of the social upheaval which that revolt had precipitated.(1, 2, 3)

§2. FIRST RUSSO-POLISH WAR: REVOLT OF VYHOVSKY

During the Pereyaslavl negotiations, Khmelnytsky, well aware that neither the Poles nor the Crim Tartars would accept the union of the Ukraine with Russia, had asked for a Muscovite diversion against Smolensk and White Russia.

War broke out during the spring of 1654. The Hetman himself took up a position with 30,000 Cossacks on the borders of Volhynia, while Buturlin with a Muscovite detachment was stationed at the point where the Vorskla falls into the Dniepr in order to arrest any Tartar incursion from the Crimea; in his support 3000 Zaporogians were sent to garrison the important fort of Kudak. Another force of 25,000 Cossacks under the Hetman's brother-in-law, Colonel Zolotarenko, joined the Muscovites under the walls of Smolensk, where Tsar Alexey himself was present.

The powerful fortress which Vladislav IV had retaken from the Romanovs, and the possession of which gave to one Slav monarchy the military initiative over the other, fell to the Muscovites on 10 September 1654; and the amiable Tsar—often more successful in war than his more military predecessors and successors—conferred upon all the barbaric captains of Zolotarenko's *sotni* titles of nobility.

After the capture of Smolensk, the troops of Prince Khovanski moved on Vitebsk and Polotsk, while the Cossacks of Zolotarenko, operating further to the south, entered Homel.

Meanwhile in the Ukraine events had taken an unexpected turn. The attention of the Poles had been concentrated on the White Russian campaign, and the Tartars had hesitated to begin hostilities. It was only after the death of Ibrahim Giray that his successor Muhammad Giray, having received generous presents from King John Casimir, suddenly moved against the Zaporogians and inflicted a crushing defeat on them. *Ataman* Tomilo and the Zaporogian hero Morozenko, about whose exploits the *kobzars* composed one of the finest of their songs, were both killed.

During the winter, the Tartars, avoiding Buturlin's Muscovite troops on the left bank of the Dniepr, rode towards Uman, while Polish detachments, coming through Moldavia, combined with them to drive the Cossacks under Colonel Bohun with heavy losses northwards towards Belaya Tserkov.

Khmelnytsky was forced to withdraw from the Volhynian border. The ranks of the Cossacks had thinned perceptibly, and the Hetman appealed for aid to the Muscovite *voyevodes*. The Tartars were devastating all the lands on the right bank of the Dniepr—Chigirin, Uman, Vinnitsa and Bratslav. More than 200,000 of the peasantry were rounded up and sent off into slavery to the Crimea and the Turkish ports between the Bug and the Danube.

But the warlike enthusiasm of the Tartars declined as their booty accumulated, and in the spring Muhammad Khan Giray withdrew beyond the Dniepr. The Swedish intervention in the Baltic provinces during the summer of 1655, which was made more dangerous by the defection to Charles X of such prominent Polish and Lithuanian magnates as John Sobieski and the Radziwill brothers, now made desperate the position of the Polish King. Prince Khovanski took and sacked Vilna; the wealthy Lithuanian capital was so devastated that, according to a Russian historian, 'a blow was dealt to Vilna which even the besiegers had not intended'. On 10 September Warsaw fell to the Swedes. The historic city of Lublin was stormed by the Hetman's Cossacks. The inhabitants of Lvov were withstanding a Cossack blockade; and detachments sent by the Hetman took part in the Swedish entry into Cracow, the ancient capital of the Polish Kings. John Casimir fled to Silesia. *Rzecz Pospolita* appeared to be in process of disintegration.

But the plight of their country roused the proud Poles, and a movement of resistance to the foreign armies, religious in its fervour, swept the country. The famous defence of the monastery of Częstochowa, marking as it did a combination of the heroism of the peasants with the devoted leadership of the Catholic Church, proved to be the beginning of a wave of national regeneration. John Casimir, elderly and inept but brave and kingly, returned from exile, and by the beginning of 1656 Charles X 'had discovered that it was easier to defeat the Poles than to conquer Poland.... For weeks he scoured the interminable snow-covered plains of Poland in purusit of the Polish guerillas, penetrating as far south as Yaroslav in Galicia, by which time he had lost two-thirds of his 15,000 men with no apparent result.'

The Austrian Emperor Ferdinand III regarded the extremity of the Catholic Vasas with alarm, and feared an alliance of the might of Sweden with George Rákóczy and the Protestant dissidents in Transylvania and Hungary and the Turks. He secured a diplomatic combination of the maritime powers in favour of the Poles, and in the following year the armed intervention of the Danes against Sweden in the Baltic was to have the effect almost of extricating Charles X from his Polish embarrassment.

Meanwhile the Russians had been contemplating with mistrust the extension of Swedish power over Poland and Lithuania. The possibility of an alliance of the Swedes with the Transylvanians and the Turks disturbed the advisers of Tsar Alexey no less than those of Ferdinand III. The issue was the more urgent for the Russians, since Khmelnytsky had come into close contact with Charles X during the Polish campaign of 1655, and he was known to have renewed his old relations with George Rákóczy, with the Roumanian Hospodars, with the Girays and the Turks. While the Austrian Emperor set on foot negotiations between John Casimir and Tsar Alexey on the ground that both should unite their efforts 'against the common enemy of the Christian Faith', Khmelnytsky received orders to withdraw the Cossack contingents which were co-operating with the Swedes. In May 1656 the Russians opened hostilities against the Swedes in Livonia, but the Cossacks were still with the Swedes when, in June, Charles X was compelled to evacuate Warsaw; and about the same time Khmelnytsky himself paid a visit to Muhammad Khan Giray at Baghchi-Saray, where he signed an armistice which relieved his territories of further Tartar incursions. There followed, probably with the approval of Mehmed Köprülü, who in September of this year became Grand Vizier, agreements between the Hetman and George Rákóczy and the Wallachian and Moldavian Hospodars. The diplomatic combinations of the Emperor were well countered by those of Charles X and the first of the Köprülü Viziers.

In the summer of 1657, while Charles X turned to confront the League which the Emperor had conjured against him in the west, Muscovite *boyars* arrived in Chigirin to bring Bohdan Khmelnytsky to account. The ageing Hetman of the Cossacks was now seriously ill, exhausted by the fatigues and anxieties of the three years of war. He was no longer able to leave his couch, and the *boyars* were received by his son Yuri and the General Secretary Vyhovsky.

At first relations were so strained that Buturlin and his suite refused to dine with the Hetman's wife, Yuri and Vyhovsky. At last a table was laid near the bed of the sick Hetman, who raised himself from his pillows to drain a goblet of Hungarian wine to the health of the Tsar and to utter a malediction on 'the cursed and infidel Turkish Sultan'. After a few days Khmelnytsky was somewhat better and was able to answer the reproaches of Buturlin. He defended his right to continue 'his old friendship with the Swedes', claiming that he had been in contact with them six years before his allegiance to the Tsar. Khmelnytsky could not understand the turn of Muscovite policy towards Poland; he also complained of the ruin of the Ukraine, and justified his armistice with Muhammad Khan Giray by the care which he took of the welfare of his Cossacks.

The great services rendered by the Cossacks during the recent war obliged the Muscovite envoys to adopt a lenient attitude towards the dying Hetman. His last day was now approaching, and he hastily summoned the colonels and Cossack elders. These, assembled at the bedside of their dying leader, named as his successor his son Yuri, who was neither a very competent nor a very pleasing youth. Ivan Vyhovsky and Colonel Martin Pushkar were chosen as advisers to the future Hetman, and Paul Teterya was to be his representative in Moscow.

On 15 August 1657 Bohdan Khmelnytsky breathed his last. His death was a great loss to the Ukraine because Bohdan Khmelnytsky was the only man who had real prestige among Cossacks of all ranks. The Muscovite Government respected and trusted him, and his military reputation stood high in Poland and Turkey, among the Tartars and among the Swedes. Khmelnytsky, who by a freak of fate had played a most important part in the history of his time, was no politician. He had the simple mind of a soldier and a country squire. There was a boyish naivety even in his ambition, and, in spite of his relations with all his neighbours, he was not by nature an intriguer. Khmelnytsky was certainly no statesman, and the fine political instinct which guided the more complicated Sahaydachny was completely lacking in him. It was not through any personal qualities in him but through the force of circumstances that he was the cause of the upheaval which changed the whole course of his life and altered the history of Eastern Europe of his time. He was not in fact capable of directing the destinies of his country into any definite channel, not even into that of agreement with Moscow, although this had been his work and he remained true to the principle until the end of his life.

Notwithstanding Khmelnytsky's foreign contacts, Moscow had had no serious reason for doubting his loyalty. Nevertheless the general position of affairs in the Ukraine at his death could not fail to arouse the most serious misgivings. Officials sent by the Tsar reported that instead of 60,000 Cossacks there were 300,000 of them; that everywhere the peasants were ruled by colonels and captains; and that there was no question of any revenues for the Exchequer. Neither the Hetman's conception of his right to maintain relations with foreign potentates nor the general interior structure of the Ukraine corresponded to the spirit of the agreement of March 1654. The Muscovite Chancellery, however, decided that it was better to observe and to appraise what was going on in the Ukraine before embarking on any definite measures. An order was given to the official Chirikov sent to Poltava 'to observe in secret, so that no one should know of it, what sums are collected in Poltava and other towns and whether they are given over to the Hetman, or to the colonels or to some others; if the money goes to the troops or somewhere else'. It was proposed to enquire 'how it was all done in the King's time, and what the people liked or disliked, and what are their customs, whether they keep to the old ones or whether the colonels have introduced new ones, and whether people are pleased or displeased and for what reason?'

From these instructions, which were also given to other men sent into the Ukraine, it will be seen that the Muscovite Government, no longer believing in the practicability of the clauses of the Agreement of 1654, was acting with great circumspection. Events, however, were progressing at such a rapid pace and soon took such an unexpected turn that these reasonable and serious methods, which needed time, had to be relinquished.

The first surprise awaiting the Muscovite Government was Vyhovsky's proclamation of himself as Hetman a few days after the perfectly 'legal' election of Yuri Khmelnytsky: the formal explanation for this was that Yuri Khmelnytsky was 'too young', and that he had still to complete another three years' studies in Kiev, and for these reasons Vyhovsky had undertaken to become Hetman 'for three years'.

The ex-General Secretary, Khmelnytsky's principal collaborator and the author of the text of the March Agreement, belonged by origin to the lesser Volhynian nobility. In the year 1648, as a registered Cossack, Ivan Vyhovsky had fought under Potocki at Zhovti Vody, had been taken prisoner, and, together with other prisoners, given over to the Tartars. Khmelnytsky, in need of educated men or of men who simply knew how to read and write, had exchanged him for a horse. While Khmelnytsky and he subsequently proved to be the principal leaders of the struggle against Poland, Vyhovsky had, even to a greater degree than Khmelnytsky, engrained within him the traditions and notions of the Polish class régime in which both had grown up and been educated. Vyhovsky nourished no strong enmity against the Poles and regarded the upheaval which had made him his career from a purely personal point of view. During the negotiations in Moscow he had shown great insistence in obtaining lands for himself, his father, his brothers and even his brother-in-law. But most of the Tsar's awards had proved to be worth no more than papers to be 'buried in the ground', because the Cossack masses were proving themselves to be drastically opposed to the creation of a new class of landed proprietors in succession to the expelled Polish magnates. Vyhovsky had then sought compensation in White Russia and had met with a refusal. His disappointment over the distribution of lands was evidently the main reason which prompted him to betray the Tsar and to seek an accommodation with the Polish King. His whole personal history indeed is of interest as indicating the social outlook and the class tendencies of the upper strata of the Cossacks.

Soon after his proclamation as Hetman, Vyhovsky despatched a colonel to Moscow to beg the Tsar to send his *voyevodes* to all important Ukrainian towns to make lists of the Cossacks so that their

number should not be allowed to exceed the stipulated 60,000—
'that the high and mighty Lord should send men of position and
power accompanied by troops so that the Cossacks would be
frightened and not revolt and that no one should dare incite them to
show insolence'.

The Moscow Government showed, however, no intention of
alienating the population of the Ukraine by satisfying the Hetman,
whose conduct already appeared suspicious. At the same time they
continued to ignore the report of Martin Pushkar to the effect that
Vyhovsky was negotiating with the Poles, and the subsequent
warnings of the *boyars* Khitrovo and Portomoin. The policy of
Moscow towards Poland was exceedingly conciliatory during the
years 1657–8; for the Poles had promised that Tsar Alexey should
become one of the 'Electors' for the throne of Poland, while the
probable abdication and in any case ultimate death of John Casimir
encouraged the ambition that within the next decade the crowns of
the two Slav monarchies might be united in the person of the
Romanov ruler. The Polish *Seym* of 1658 received in great solemnity
a pompous embassy sent by Alexey Mikhailovich with gorgeous
presents for the principal magnates of the kingdom; and the recognition by this *Seym* of Vyhovsky as Hetman of the Ukraine only
affirmed the gracious relations established between the King and the
Tsar.

But Vyhovsky soon abandoned all caution. In September of the
same year two Polish senators visited him, and in secret discussions
with his most faithful elders the so-called Hadyach Agreement was
concluded (16 September 1658). This Agreement provided for the
abolition of the Union of the Churches in the Ukraine; for the right
of the Metropolitan of Kiev and four Orthodox bishops to sit in the
Seym; for a full amnesty for all past activities; that Kiev should become the official residence of the Hetman; that Polish troops should
be sent into the Ukraine only at the request of the Hetman; and that
no taxes should be payable to the Polish crown either on the left or
on the right bank of the Dniepr. The Cossacks agreed no longer to
recognize the Muscovite Tsar as their liege-lord, but in case of war
between Muscovy and Poland they retained the right to observe
neutrality. 'Friendship' with the Crim Khan was to be permitted;
but not with the King of Sweden. Other clauses provided for the
right to found two academies and numerous schools and typo-
graphies for printing books—an indication of the influence on the
drafting of the Agreement of the unfortunate Yuri Nemirich, who
wished his compatriots to develop their Orthodox culture in the
tradition of the great Sahaydachny. The Hetman also received the

right to present a hundred Cossacks each year to the King for ennoblement. (4)

In the Hadyach Agreement Vyhovsky and his friends sought to secure the support of the Polish crown in establishing the Cossack officer ranks as a governing and landowning class in the Ukraine; they aimed in fact at a reproduction of the *szlachta* system of the Polish state, into which system they had been born and in which they found themselves at ease. Their quarrel with the Poles was that they had not been treated as the equals of the Polish ruling gentry; now they were to return to Poland 'as free men to free men, as equal to equal'. The dislike of the Cossack colonels for the newly established Muscovite administration was the dislike of a feudal oligarchy for an imperial bureaucracy which itself showed tendencies to seek the support of the masses as a balance to check the insubordination of a local ruling class. Vyhovsky knew also that 'the rabble' would support the Tsar, since through its allegiance to the Tsar it had stabilized itself in the possession of new rights which it had itself conquered through revolt.

The Muscovite Government remained to the last moment reluctant to credit the Hetman's treason, the more so since it realized that Vyhovsky had the support of all Khmelnytsky's principal collaborators—men like the Colonels Bohun, Teterya and Hulyanitsky—and of the higher Ukrainian clergy. It remained repugnant to the Moscow officials to lend support to the discontent among the lower ranks of the Cossacks and the peasantry which was voiced by the Poltava regiment and the Zaporogian *Sech*, since they would have been sustaining mutiny against 'the legal authority' of the Hetman. At the same time Alexey Mikhailovich somewhat peevishly withdrew his embassy from Warsaw, and 30,000 Muscovite troops entered the Ukraine—with the assurance to Vyhovsky that they were sent 'to help him to deal with rebels'.

The formidable revolt of Vyhovsky which now broke out was destined to weaken Russia at an important juncture of international politics, as the revolt of Khmelnytsky ten years before had exposed the Poles to disaster.

Aware that he could delay no longer, the Hetman, in September 1658, gathered a force of 15,000 trusted Cossacks, secured the aid of Tartar auxiliaries, and attacked and annihilated the detachment of the unfortunate loyalist Colonel Pushkar.

The Zaporogian *Sech* and some of the regiments on the left bank of the Dniepr rose in revolt against the Hetman, but the lack of a competent leader was a serious impediment to the development of this movement of the Ukrainian lower classes. The Muscovite detachments which were scattered about the country also lacked effective command. Vyhovsky's supporters, together with the Tartars, took a number of 'rebel' towns between Poltava and the Dniepr, but they failed in an attack on Kiev. Prince Romodanovski, with a Muscovite corps on the left bank of the Dniepr, compelled Vyhovsky to retire, and with the help of the Zaporogians and Cossack detachments he took Romen, Lubni and Piryatin. These towns were burnt and plundered. 'God will find the guilty ones', observed the prince, 'the troops, meantime, have to enjoy their fun and receive some reward for the hardships of the campaign.' But the Muscovites failed to bring the Hetman to a decisive action and throughout 1659 all left-bank Ukraine was devastated by civil war. In the summer of that year, Vyhovsky, having augmented his forces by 30,000 Cossacks, 15,000 Tartars and 3000 Poles, routed the army of the *voyevodes* Trubetskoy and Pozharski near Konotop. Seven Muscovite regiments were annihilated; Prince Pozharski was taken prisoner; and the Tartars began to raid the border districts of Muscovy proper. The Polish *Seym* of 1659 now solemnly confirmed the Hadyach Agreement, and Vyhovsky's brothers with Yuri Nemirich swore allegiance to John Casimir in the Hetman's name.

The Muscovite position in the Ukraine was saved, not by the efforts of the imperial commanders, but by a general rising of the lower classes of the population on both banks of the Dniepr. While they nourished no special liking for 'the Tsar's soldiers' the Cossacks harboured no enmity towards them, but deep hatred for Poles and Tartars filled the wild Zaporogians and the masses of the Orthodox peasantry. Sometimes circumstances had forced the Ukrainians to fight with the Poles against the Tartars, and sometimes they had gone with the Tartars against the Poles, but now their Hetman required them to combine with both Poles and Tartars against the Orthodox Muscovites. The naive simplicity of the peasantry was tempered by a rugged common sense and it was too much to ask of them. The Zaporogians had found a leader of quality in the popular *ataman* Sirko. Sirko appeared on the right bank of the Dniepr, where he was joined by colonels who had grievances against Vyhovsky. Young Yuri Khmelnytsky, whose interests were pressed by Ivan Bryukhovetsky, a simple Cossack but a faithful servant of the family, was proclaimed Hetman. Vyhovsky crossed to the right bank of the Dniepr, and this part of the country which had hitherto been spared became the scene of bloodthirsty partisan warfare. It soon became apparent that on the right bank the whole population was saturated with hatred of Polish domination and that Vyhovsky's game was lost even before he had fought a pitched battle; his troops dispersed; some of his principal adherents, including Yuri Nemirich, were killed; and the Hetman himself fled to Poland after having surrendered the ensigns of his office to Yuri Khmelnytsky.

Colonel Peter Doroshenko was sent to the Muscovites to inform the *voyevode* Prince Trubetskoy of these events; but the latter demanded that the election of Yuri Khmelnytsky should be officially confirmed by the *Rada*, which he proposed should be convened at Pereyaslavl. Before the new *Rada* assembled, attempts were made both by the Muscovite commissioners and the Cossack leaders to secure modifications of the Agreement of 1654. The Muscovites required that all the Seversk lands, including Novgorod-Seversk and Starodub, should pass out of Cossack jurisdiction and be included in the territory of Great Russia, since these territories had originally been detached by the Poles. This proposal met a firm refusal from the Cossacks; it was these very lands which were becoming the most prosperous in the Ukraine, for on the banks of the Seym and the Desna, far away from Polish and Tartar attacks, new towns and villages were arising almost every year. Peter Doroshenko and other colonels on their side formulated the demand that a Muscovite *voyevode* should reside in Kiev only; but the Muscovite commissioners insisted on appointments also for Pereyaslavl, Nezhin, Chernigov, Uman and Bratslav. Yuri Khmelnytsky undertook to provide Cossack regiments for the Tsar's service, and 'not to offer assistance to anyone' without an order from the Tsar. These negotiations were embodied, on 17 October 1659, in the Second Agreement of Pereyaslavl.

Neither side could afford delay, since another war with Poland was threatened, and the frightened population of the right bank of the Dniepr was fleeing in thousands to the left bank and beyond into 'new Ukraine', where already the towns of Akhtyrka, Sumy, Izyum and Kharkov were growing up.

§3. SECOND RUSSO-POLISH WAR: TREATY OF ANDRUSOVO

In February 1660 the unexpected death of Charles X and the desire of the Regency of the infant Charles XI to liquidate the international commitments of Sweden entirely transformed the situation in Northern and Eastern Europe. The Treaty of Oliva, negotiated through French mediation, at last ended the long feud between the Polish and Swedish Vasas (3 May); the Treaty of Copenhagen between Denmark and Sweden terminated the Baltic War (27 May); and in the following year the Treaty of Kardis which the Regency

made with the embarrassed Government of Tsar Alexey confirmed
the restoration to Sweden of the temporary Russian conquests in
Estonia and Ingria (2 July 1661).

In spite of the vicissitudes of the Polish campaigns, Sweden had
emerged from the war as a Great Power. 'All the islands in the
Baltic, except the Danish group, belonged to Sweden. The estuaries
of all the great German rivers (for the Niemen and the Vistula are
properly Polish rivers) debouched in Swedish territory, within
which lay two-thirds of Lake Ladoga and one-half of Lake Peipus.
Stockholm, the capital, lay in the very centre of the empire, whose
second greatest city was Riga, on the other side of the sea.' The confirmation of the sovereignty of Brandenburg over East Prussia and
the release of the Elector from the nominal suzerainty of the Polish
King marked the emergence of Brandenburg-Prussia as a power of
some importance.

As in the time of Casimir IV the Poles turned towards the south-
east to seek compensation for losses on the Baltic, and the rapid expansion of the market for grain after the end of the Thirty Years'
War excited the Polish magnates to restore their shaken fortunes
from the teeming produce of the Black Sea river lands. The remarkable capacity of the Poles for recovery was never more evident than
in the Russian campaigns of 1661–7; indolence and cynicism prevented the Polish aristocracy from rallying their tenantry for the
King's service in the hour of need; but this looseness of social and
military organization implied also resilience; defeats in the field
shook the Polish monarchy, but they no more than bruised the
flexible structure of Polish society, based as it was on the feudal
economy of the fortified mansions and monasteries of the magnates
and bishops rather than on the royal towns.

In Russia, on the other hand, the effort to establish a modern state
structure after the chaos of the Time of Troubles combined with the
exhaustion of the Polish, Ukrainian and Swedish campaigns had
overstrained the strength of the new monarchy. The confusions in
the Ukraine were contemporary with social and religious disorders
in Great Russia; the tumults of 1648 were renewed in those of 1661–2;
in the latter year Tsar Alexey was faced at Kolomenskoe with an
angry mob calling for vengeance on some of his officials, and 'he was
saved only by the ruthless action of his guard, by which some 7000
persons perished'.

In the summer of 1660, following the conclusion of the Treaty of
Oliva with the Swedes, the Poles resumed the war with Russia;
Sapieha and Czarniecki, the veteran of Berestechko, invaded Lithu-
ania and White Russia, and Prince Khovanski was defeated at

Polonka. The decisive influence of the Ukrainian Cossacks in Russo-Polish campaigns of the period immediately became evident; with Khmelnytsky on their side the Russians had carried all before them at Smolensk, Lublin and Lvov. Now, with the Cossacks divided, the Russian military strength proved incompetent to oppose the Poles.

In the Ukraine, the old Crown Hetman Stephen Potocki, whose defeat at Zhovti Vody twelve years before had precipitated 'the Deluge', was joined by 20,000 Crim Tartars, and moved against the Muscovite *voyevode* Sheremetiev on the borders of Volhynia. The newly elected Hetman, Yuri Khmelnytsky, rode to the help of the Muscovites. But rumours of Russian failures in the north revived the influence of the supporters of Vyhovsky; Peter Doroshenko opened relations with the Poles, and Yuri Khmelnytsky not only recognized the Hadyach Agreement but joined forces with Potocki. Sheremetiev found himself surrounded by the Poles, Tartars and dissident Cossacks, and decided to capitulate on condition that he should be allowed a free passage through the Ukraine with his troops. But no sooner had he surrendered than the Tartars started to massacre the helpless Muscovite soldiery, while Sheremetiev, and his *voyevodes* Princes Shcherbatov and Kozlovski, were carried off to the Crimea, where the unfortunate *boyars* remained in captivity for the next twenty years.

The treason of Yuri Khmelnytsky did not save the lands on the right bank of the Ukraine, for Potocki, ignoring the Hadyach Agreement, set his riders to take vengeance on the peasants for all the excesses committed on the Polish gentry during the preceding twelve years.

On the left bank of the Dniepr the Chernigov, Nezhin and Pereyaslavl regiments decided to depose Yuri Khmelnytsky and to elect as temporary Hetman the Pereyaslavl Colonel Samko. Tsar Alexey sent a recompense to Samko for his loyalty, but in view of the chaotic state of affairs in the Ukraine throughout the year 1662 the Muscovite Government was in no hurry to recognize any-one.

Civil war was flaring up alternately on the left and on the right banks of the Dniepr. Samko was not the only man who wished to be Hetman; there were a good many candidates for the title—the Nezhin Colonel Vasili Zolotarenko (a relation of the hero of the last war with Poland, who had been killed in 1665), Peter Doroshenko, Paul Teterya, and Ivan Bryukhovetsky, the former faithful servitor of the Khmelnytskys, who had now become the favourite of the Zaporogian *Sech*. Yuri Khmelnytsky was losing ground every day, and had been defeated in many affrays by the troops of Samko and of the Muscovite *voyevode* Romodanovski. Finally he lost heart and became a monk at Moshnin. The Poles now recognized as Hetman Khmelnytsky's adherent, Paul Teterya; Samko continued to maintain his election on the right bank, while in the *Sech* the Zaporogians acclaimed Bryukhovetsky. Moscow refused to recognize anyone, but two officials who had been sent to investigate, Prince Gagin and Cyril Khlopov, reported that Bryukhovetsky was one of those men who gather harvests where nothing was sown and that 'he is fit to be Hetman because, though ignorant, he is intelligent and as for thieving—none like him. Should he be appointed, we can all sleep soundly in Moscow'.

The Muscovite officials had decided that Bryukhovetsky, ambitious, unscrupulous and capable, who had risen from the lower classes, was the most convenient candidate for the imperial Government, exactly on account of his nearness to the lowest layers of the Ukrainian population. The upper ranks of the Cossacks, the men who had been Khmelnytsky's closest collaborators, like Vyhovsky or Paul Teterya or even his own son Yuri, had all proved traitors, not only to the Tsar, but also to their own people, who desired neither a restoration of Polish dominion nor a class régime.

A description of the *Rada* which assembled at Nezhin during the year 1663 for the election of a Hetman gives an impression of the chaos which reigned in the Ukraine at that time. 'On 18 July the sound of drums assembled the people to the envoys' tent where were Prince Gagin, Khlopov and others. Never had there been such a *Rada* in Ukraine. Bryukhovetsky, standing among the Zaporogians, was gibing at Samko and Zolotarenko. The Pereyaslavl regiment was yelling "We want Samko"; "Zolotarenko" screamed the Nezhin Cossacks. The yells of the Zaporogians, "Bryukhovetsky, Bryukhovetsky", drowned all other sounds. The Tsar's envoys tried to enforce silence; but the noise and confusion was growing, scuffles began, knives glistened; the different factions in the crowd were fighting each other, and it all ended in bloodshed. Samko fled through the tent of the Moscow representatives, but was nearly killed by blows. In the envoys' tent itself and around it many were beaten to death by the Zaporogians. Prince Gagin was nearly thrashed by the surging crowd. The Cossacks of Samko and Zolotarenko, seeing the impossibility of resisting the Zaporogians, joined them; Bryukhovetsky was put upon a table covered by a standard and proclaimed Hetman' (N. Markovich).

Bryukhovetsky was not satisfied with this; having been made Hetman, he arrested Samko, Zolotarenko and several other colonels, evidently fearing that the wheel of fortune might turn. In September of the year all the prisoners were executed without any adequate reason, since none of them had ever proved traitors to the Tsar. A contemporary describes the decapitation of Samko carried out by a Tartar executioner. 'Struck by the manly comeliness of Samko's face and his herculean body, the executioner was amazed. He hesitated for a long time to lift his axe, but was forced to do so, and the head of a gallant man rolled in the dust.'

The situation in the Ukraine during the autumn of 1663 seemed to take on a definite shape: on the one side were the Polish troops supported by such prominent Cossack colonels as Paul Teterya, Peter Doroshenko, Bohun and Hulyanitsky; on the other were the Muscovites with 'the rabble'—Bryukhovetsky, the darling of the people, and his Zaporogians.

The Polish successes in Lithuania (where Vilna had been taken from the Muscovites) and White Russia now allowed the ageing King John Casimir to turn his attention to the reconquest of the Ukraine. Forty thousand Polish troops were concentrated in Volhynia; the King himself took command, seconded by such celebrated commanders as old Stephen Czarniecki and John Sobieski. Bearing the title of 'Voyevode of Kiev' Vyhovsky made his appearance in the royal camp. John Casimir crossed the Dniepr, and neither Bryukhovetsky's Cossacks nor the scattered Muscovite detachments dared to meet him in the open field. They fled to the fortified towns, which then surrendered easily to the Cossack colonels with the Polish army. The Poles, with their Tartar auxiliaries, were ruthless, plundering the countryside and burning the villages, while the terrified peasantry trekked in their thousands towards 'the new Ukraine' in the north-east. Only Nezhin held out for the Tsar, and leaving it on their flank the Poles invaded the Seversk lands. But the King sat down before the fortress of Glukhov (Ukr. Hlukhiv) which, garrisoned by the regiments of Chernigov, Nezhin and Starodub, put up a stout resistance. With the approach of spring, bringing the overflow of rivers and increasing difficulties in supply in a devastated country, the Poles were threatened by the advancing army of Prince Romodanovski. John Casimir suddenly left the army (the political situation in Warsaw was becoming critical), and Czarniecki began to retire beyond the Dniepr. Bryukhovetsky followed the retreating Poles, while, on the right bank of the Dniepr, the news of Polish failure helped the Zaporogian *ataman* Sirko to incite the Cossacks and peasants to revolt. Sirko took Uman and Bratslav; but, still faithful to the King, Vyhovsky and Teterya continued to resist in Chigirin and Belaya Tserkov. Dissensions however arose, and

Vyhovsky, without any grounds whatever, was accused of 'treason to the King' and hastily shot.

Czarniecki himself proved a match for the Cossack leaders. This old enemy of the Ukrainian Cossacks dealt a series of severe blows to Hetman Bryukhovetsky and *ataman* Sirko. He was conducting a merciless war, destroying all towns and villages which were on the side of 'the rebels'. He ordered Subbotovo, the hereditary estate of the Khmelnytsky family, to be burnt. The bodies of Bohdan Khmelnytsky and of his eldest son Timosh were taken out of their graves and burned and their ashes scattered to the wind. Since the battle of Kumeyki in 1638, Czarniecki had spent all his life in incessant warfare. The campaign of 1664 proved to be his last; he died during the autumn at a very advanced age.

In the meantime while negotiations for a peace between Muscovy and Poland had opened at Durovichi—negotiations which should at that juncture have resulted in a settlement favourable to the Poles—the revolt of the new Grand Hetman Lubomirski had precipitated a dynastic crisis which the failing health of King John Casimir and his lack of a male heir made sooner or later inevitable.

The extinction of the Polish Vasas, like the extinction of the Jagiellons ninety years before, opened the field of Polish politics to all the ambitious dynasts of Europe. Alexey Mikhailovich, as Ivan IV had done, tendered his pretensions, and the project of a union of the Slav monarchies had always its attractions for a section of the Polish magnates; but the resumption of warfare promoted by the defection from Moscow of Vyhovsky and the Cossack leaders had prejudiced the prospects of the Romanovs. The Rákóczys, recalling the fame of Stephen Báthory, had had high hopes of a union of the Transylvanian, Polish and Moldo-Wallachian crowns; but in 1660 the reviving power of Turkey, which was soon to menace both the Habsburg and the Polish dominions, had crushed the sturdy and over-reaching independence of the Translyvanian princes. Since the Emperor Ferdinand III had intervened in favour of John Casimir in 1655, Austrian influences had been ascendant at the court of Warsaw, where the Gonzaga Queen, Maria Ludwika, had influenced the policy of her always hesitant and vacillating husband. So strong was the Austrian interest that 'schemes were entertained for adding the great Slav kingdom to the possessions of the house of Habsburg'. But about 1660 the Queen had been won to the French interest, when the wide conceptions of Cardinal Mazarin, reviving the French policy of the preceding century which had secured passing possession of the Polish crown for a Valois prince, planned to bring Poland again within the sphere of the French system. In 1663 the marriage of the favourite niece of the Polish Queen to the Duc d'Enghien, heir of the great Condé, introduced a scheme to persuade the Poles to elect either Enghien or his father during the lifetime of John Casimir. 'As soon as this should be done, John Casimir pledged himself to abdicate and to retire to a more congenial life in France, where rich benefices were allotted for his maintenance.'

The Habsburg Leopold I, 'the little Emperor in red stockings', whose election to the imperial dignity in 1658 had been seriously incommoded by the intrigues of Mazarin, was quick to counter any extension of French influence in Eastern Europe—particularly when that influence might combine again with the military power of Sweden. The help in French troops which enabled Leopold to repulse a Turkish invasion of his hereditary dominions at the battle of St Gotthard (1 August 1664) did not prevent him from sending his agents to stir up resentment in Poland against the project of allowing a reigning King to direct the choice of his successor. But the revolt of the new Grand Hetman Lubomirski against the French court party failed, and John Sobieski, whose wife Marie d'Arquien was a Frenchwoman, received the ensigns of Grand Hetman and identified himself with the project of a French succession.

On the eastern frontiers, the dynastic crisis had at the same time wrecked the Polish prospects in the Durovichi negotiations and betrayed the military position in the Ukraine. Muscovite detachments appeared in Kiev, and with the aid of Bryukhovetsky's Cossacks forced the Poles and their adherents to withdraw from the Ukraine.

Neither the Russians nor the Poles were now prepared, after years of exhausting warfare, to continue the struggle. Meanwhile, in the summer of 1665, Bryukhovetsky was received in Moscow, where he came in order 'to do humble homage to the Tsar on behalf of the Ukrainian towns'. The Hetman was received with many honours and, in spite of his lowly origin, was married to a daughter of the proud house of Sheremetiev. Some of the Cossack elders and colonels in the suite of the Hetman, which according to a contemporary writer 'formed a numerous cavalcade', also contracted alliances with the daughters of Muscovite officials. The whole of September 1665 was spent in rejoicings and marriage feasts. The results of all this junketing were additions to the Agreement of March 1654 which were published on 11 October 1665. According to the new clauses 'all the land belonged to the Tsar and not to the Hetman', and therefore all taxes paid by the townsfolk and the peasantry, were to go into the Tsar's Exchequer; also 'the taxes on taverns where spirits were drunk', the taxes on mills, 'the tribute of honey' and the duties paid by foreign merchants. The right of the Cossacks to self-government was confirmed, as also their right of election of their own Hetman and officials; but, in order that the taxes should be duly collected by the Tsar's Exchequer, Muscovite *voyevodes* were sent to many Ukrainian towns accompanied by flocks of officials and troops for permanent garrison duty.

In many respects the terms of the 'additions' merely clarified the Agreement of 1654 and carried into effect the original bases on which that Agreement had been concluded. But the Ukraine received the news of 'Bryukhovetsky's Agreement' as proof of his treason. Very few Cossacks indeed knew the contents of the Agreement of 1654, and those who had known them had forgotten them or wanted to forget them, the practice of recent years having been in absolute contradiction to the theoretical rights of the Muscovite Tsars. Furthermore, Moscow had made a dangerous enemy in the higher Ukrainian clergy, who had been angered by Bryukhovetsky's petition that the Metropolitan of Kiev should be appointed from Moscow.

During the first months of 1666 news spread through the Ukraine about the concessions extracted from Bryukhovetsky in Moscow. The worst rumours were confirmed by the arrival of *voyevodes*, not only in Kiev, Pereyaslavl, Chernigov and Nezhin, but also in many smaller towns where tax-collectors appeared who 'gathered taxes with such zeal that not even a copeck escaped their vigilant eye'. Precise schedules were drawn up of different properties and revenues. Non-payment of taxes was severely punished. As an old Ukrainian historian somewhat naively remarked: 'This innovation, perhaps usual in other lands, in ours seemed cruel, pernicious and unbearable.'

It was no easy task to attempt to establish order in the Ukraine. Bishop Methodi began to preach, calling on the people to rise against Bryukhovetsky and, hence, against Moscow. Doroshenko, who controlled much of the territory on the right bank of the Dniepr, crossed to the left bank, took Pereyaslavl, where a Muscovite official was murdered, and attacked Zolotonosha, where the *voyevode* Prince Shcherbatov and many Muscovites were put to death. The whole of the left bank now flamed into revolt; Nezhin and the towns of the Poltava region recognized Doroshenko. Everywhere Muscovite officials were either killed or driven away. Even the Zaporogian *Sech*, which until then had been friendly to Moscow, dismissed the 'auxiliary' Muscovite detachment stationed there; and the Zaporogians threw into the Dniepr the Muscovite ambassador, Lady-zhenski, on his way home from the Crimea.

The renewal of anarchy in the Ukraine finally decided the Muscovite Chancellery to conclude peace with the Poles on the basis of the partition of the country, the struggle for the mastery of which had imposed such a long and exhausting trial of strength on both combatants.

In January 1667, in the village of Andrusovo, near Smolensk, a treaty was signed between the representatives of Tsar Alexey and John Casimir. Muscovy retained all the lands in occupation of her troops as far as the line where the course of the Dniepr turns to the south. The right bank Ukraine was recognized as Polish territory; and it was agreed that Kiev should remain for two more years in the occupation of the Muscovites, after which it should be handed over to the Poles. As for the Zaporogian *Sech*, it was clearly stated in the Treaty that the Zaporogians should do military service for both the Tsar and the King. (In this connection it should be re-called that in 1655 Bohdan Khmelnytsky had given a special charter to the Zaporogians—which was always kept on the altar of the church of Our Lady's Protection in the *Sech*—whereby the pos-session of all lands on both the left and right banks of the Dniepr below the rapids was conceded to them.)

The Treaty of Andrusovo established not only amicable relations but a form of alliance between Muscovy and Poland. In this sense the division of the Ukraine between the two powers must be re-garded rather in the nature of a *condominium* than of a partition. Not only the exhaustion of the two Slav states, but also the sudden re-vival of the Ottoman power under the Köprülüs, must be taken to have formed the common ground on which the two states abandoned the feud which had kept them at war intermittently for more than half a century and entered into a common understanding for the defence of their mutual interests in the fluvial plains to the north of the Black Sea. The significance of the Treaty of Andrusovo is quite clear: to the Muscovites fell the duty of combating the Crim Tartars and to the Poles that of confronting the menacing power of the Ottomans on the Dniestr and in Transylvania. But Muscovy further undertook to support the Poles at any time with 20,000 troops and 5000 'of her own Cossacks'. And the two Governments agreed not to allow Peter Doroshenko to rule in any part of the Ukraine. The policy of Alexey Mikhailovich, developed at Andrusovo by the shrewd Ordyn-Nashchokin, was consecutive and long-sighted. Moscow established her frontier, for the time, along the Dniepr, with the prospect that with the aid of the Poles an issue to the sea in a southerly direction could be secured at the expense of the Crim Tartars, and in a northerly direction to the detriment of the Swedes, who in the recent wars had taken Livonia from Poland and deprived Muscovy of its reversion. Peter I was to continue the policy of his father which at Andrusovo, in 1667, had been clearly defined in a meridial direction—after the hopes, which had been inspired in 1655 by the capture of Smolensk, of a wide and rapid expansion towards the west had failed to mature.

§ 4. THE TURKS IN THE UKRAINE: PETER DOROSHENKO AND YURI KHMELNYTSKY

Peter Doroshenko, outlawed by the Treaty of Andrusovo, proved to be a formidable obstacle to the development of a combined Russo-Polish policy in the Ukraine. He belonged to a family well known among the Cossacks. His grandfather, Michael, had been elected *ataman* in the *Sech* in 1625 and three years later had fallen in battle against the Tartars; and the glamour of the dead hero gave Peter a certain prestige among the lower ranks of the people. Further, although he was a colonel, he did not share the enthusiasm of other Cossack elders for the Polish class régime, and he did not subscribe to the Polish orientation of the adherents of the Hadyach Agreement of 1658.

After the Treaty of Andrusovo Doroshenko became an irreconcileable opponent of the Polish and the Muscovite regimes in the two parts of the Ukraine. The natural consequence was that he reverted to the ideas of collaboration with the Turks which had once attracted Bohdan Khmelnytsky. His Turkish orientation actually gave him a certain moral prestige, since he was basing his plans on a definite political conception in contrast to Vyhovsky, Teterya, Bryukhovetsky and others who had appeared to the Cossacks to be mere adventurers seeking their own personal profit in the post of Hetman. The aim of Peter Doroshenko was that the Ukraine should become a vassal state of the Porte, like Transylvania, Wallachia and Moldavia, and like those countries should retain an independence subject to tribute, a territorial unity, an autocephalous church, and the right to maintain an army, an administration and a treasury under a 'hospodar'—the Hetman—who might enjoy the international position which the Rákóczys had held in Transylvania until they had over-reached themselves. The fact that Doroshenko's plan was based on the conception of the unity of the Ukraine inspired respect, and it found justification in 'the partition' of Andrusovo; Doroshenko could count on the sympathy of those varied elements who did not wish to see the Ukraine divided, and he had on his side the clergy and the representatives of the new and active intellectual life of the Kiev Academy.

In his way Peter Doroshenko was an honest man; nor was he particularly concerned to acquire the goods of this world. He was firm, patient, reserved and silent. The difficulties of his policy were manifold; for he was on the one hand helping the Turks and Tartars who since 1665 had begun to harass the Poles on the borders of Podolia, and on the other hand he had to hold the support of the Zaporogians who, in the same year, had deposed Bryukhovetsky and named him as Hetman and who, at the same time, under the celebrated Sirko, had resumed their raids against the Crimea and had taken Perekop and burned Baghchi-Saray and Caffa. But so strong was the position of Doroshenko that both the Poles and the Muscovites, before the ink was dry on the Treaty of Andrusovo, made attempts to conciliate him. The former, embarrassed by the dynastic crisis in Warsaw, went so far as to remove Teterya as Hetman of the right bank, and recognized Doroshenko. In Moscow, at the same time, it was decided to depose Bryukhovetsky, whose rapacity, as well as his acceptance of the modifications of the Agreement of 1654, was making him excessively unpopular. Before the deposition had been effected, however, Doroshenko had raised another revolt on the left bank. The Muscovite *voyevodes* were only able to maintain their authority in Kiev, Chernigov and Pereyaslavl; in twelve other towns the officials were either killed or arrested and sold to the Tartars. To save his own head, Bryukhovetsky was actually taking a hand in the slaughter of the Moscow men. The rising spread into the 'new Ukraine' as far as Kharkov. Doroshenko himself appeared on the left bank and his Cossacks seized Bryukhovetsky, who was brought to Doroshenko's camp where he was beaten to death 'with oak sticks'.

For a few weeks the right and left banks were again united. But having received news from Chigirin of some misconduct of his wife, the irate Hetman hurried to the right bank, leaving Colonel Mnohohrishny (Mnogogreshny) in command. Before the end of the year, Mnohohrishny himself made terms with the Moscow Government. In January 1669 Cossack deputies appeared in the capital, and two months later a *Rada* assembled at Glukhov elected him as Hetman. A 'pardon' was sent from the Tsar to the Ukrainian Cossacks, and the old agreements were once more confirmed, with the concession that the presence of Muscovite *voyevodes* should be restricted to Kiev (which under the Treaty of Andrusovo was soon to be delivered to the Poles), Pereyaslavl, Nezhin, Chernigov and Oster. The Hetman's capital was established at Baturin, and (since Moscow apparently feared the spread of the anarchic spirit of the Dniepr Cossacks to the Don) a strong military force under old

Prince Romodanovski was sent to the Seym and the Desna and permanently stationed in the neighbourhood of the new capital.

The Moscow Government was still trying to conciliate Doroshenko, but meanwhile the latter had definitely committed himself to the Turks. In December 1668 Colonel Portyanka and the judge Bilohrud had arrived in Istanbul as envoys of the Ruthenians and Cossacks, and an agreement was concluded with the Porte whereby Sultan Muhammad IV graciously accepted the petition of the Hetman to take the Ukraine under his protection; the complete autocephaly of the Orthodox Church in the Ukraine was recognized, and a yearly tribute was to be paid to the Sultan. A Hetman's staff and a standard were presented to the envoys, and the Porte undertook to send a force of 6000 men to uphold Doroshenko against his enemies. But the proposal that garrisons of Janissaries should be posted in the Doroshenko's capital of Chigirin and in the Zaporogian fort of Kudak disturbed the equanimity of the Cossack emissaries.

The intervention of the Turks in the affairs of the Ukraine was no accident arising from the personal policy of Doroshenko. The revival of Turkish power under Viziers of the Albanian family of Köprülü influenced the history of the last half of the seventeenth century in many ways as profoundly as did the contemporary expansion of France under Louis XIV. The popular interpretation of Turkish history as a continuous decline from the days of Suleiman the Magnificent reflects the superficial and erroneous studies of West European Liberal historians of the nineteenth century. As the historical and geographical heir of Byzantium, the Ottoman Porte remained throughout the sixteenth and seventeenth centuries a prime factor in European politics; the Empire was in many respects more efficiently administered than were any contemporary European states with the exceptions of France and Sweden; indeed Greeks, Hungarians and Ukrainians, who as contemporaries must be admitted to have been good judges, frequently showed that they preferred Ottoman to Venetian, Austrian or Polish rule.

The disorders which rent the Ottoman dominions during the first part of the seventeenth century were no more grave than the commotions of the time, in France during the Huguenot Wars and later during the Fronde, and in England during the Civil War; they were, moreover, far less sanguinary and less disastrous than the Thirty Years' War in Germany, the Time of Troubles in Russia and the period of 'the Deluge' in Poland. The Ottoman army, if it showed at St Gotthard that it no longer retained the ascendancy over European troops which it had enjoyed under Suleiman the Magnificent, at least remained superior in fighting quality to the forces which either

Poland, Muscovy or Venice could put into the field; though it was markedly inferior to those of Sweden and France, and inferior in command to those of Austria. The great campaigns of the Thirty Years' War had in fact vastly improved the military technique of Western armies, while those of Eastern Europe had not yet abandoned the fashions of the sixteenth century; but in this respect even, after the series of defeats which led up to the Treaty of Karlowitz, the Turks showed a remarkable capacity for adapting themselves to the military novelties of a new age. Indeed, in the first decades of the eighteenth century they were able to inflict defeats on the Russians (victors over Sweden) and on the Austrians (who had participated in the overthrow of the French hegemony).

The decline of the Ottoman Empire as a great power may be said to have arisen eventually, not from any inherent defects by contrast with neighbouring Austria and Poland, but from more profound causes—the shift of the centre of world politics from the inner seas to the oceans, from the 'peninsular' basis which was represented by the Mediterranean world to the 'continental' basis which came into being with the expansion of Russia and America into sub-continental powers at the end of the eighteenth century and the trans-oceanic extension of the Western maritime powers over Africa, the Americas and Southern Asia. The stage of history had been immeasurably widened, and the old actors found themselves dwarfed.

In 1661, the year in which Louis XIV assumed the reins of government in France, Ahmed, the son of old Mehmed Köprülü, was at the age of twenty-six called to the office of Grand Vizier. Ahmed Köprülü, in his private life a libertine and a drunkard who died from his excesses at the early age of forty, was at the same time a scholar and a man of taste whom contemporary European writers unite in praising for his infallible judgment and penetrating intellect. For fifteen years Ahmed Köprülü ruled the brilliant and fantastic court of Muhammad IV, giving his master who delighted in great hunts the credit for great victories. With his caustic tongue, his incisive wit, and his superb insolence, the Albanian Grand Vizier was, with Louis XIV, the arbiter of Europe. His policies directed the course of events in Russia, Austria and Poland, and the Government of Louis XIV waited upon rather than influenced their trends.

In 1669, a few months after Doroshenko's mission, Ahmed Köprülü completed the conquest of Crete from the Venetians. At the same time events in the Habsburg and the Polish dominions were engaging the attention of the Porte. In those parts of Hungary which were subject to the Habsburg crown, the Emperor Leopold was confronted by a widespread conspiracy of the Hungarian magnates to set up an independent kingdom with Turkish or French support. The position of the Roumanian principalities in vassalage to the Sultan—which later Liberal historians have found so degraded—attracted the Hungarian nobles no less than the Cossack colonels. Contemporary leaders in these border countries found freedom of confession and a real autonomy more easily in Istanbul than in Vienna; and the character and tragic career of Emeric Tököli, the Protestant chieftain of the Hungarian gentry, was strangely similar to that of Peter Doroshenko.

Meanwhile in Poland the pathetic old King John Casimir had finally summoned the courage to abdicate, and the *Seym*, in June 1669, harassed by the importunities of the rival Austrian and French candidates for the vacant thrones, had elected as King Michael Vishnevetsky (Wiśniowiecki), a descendant at once of the old royal Piast house and of the most ancient nobility of South Russia. He was, moreover, a son of the celebrated Prince Jeremy. That King Michael was a poor creature who had none of his father's spirit and wept tears on his election was no doubt almost a recommendation to his peers. The offence to Louis XIV in the neglect of Condé's claims was deepened in the following year by the new King's marriage to the Archduchess Maria Eleonora, a sister of the Emperor Leopold. But the Grand Hetman Sobieski, whose wife, Marie d'Arquien, was the principal agent of French intrigue in Poland, continued to make all government impossible, and in the following year he conspired with the Primate Prażmowski to dethrone the King.

In the Ukraine, towards the end of 1669, the news of Doroshenko's agreement with the Turks provoked a serious rising against him on the right bank. Colonel Khanenko was elected Hetman and appealed to the Poles and Muscovites for aid. Doroshenko defeated his rival and crossed to the left bank, where in his turn he was worsted by the detachments of Romodanovski and Mnohohrishny. The time had come for Kiev to be delivered to the Poles under the terms of the Treaty of Andrusovo, but the Moscow Government, insisting on the threat to Kiev from Doroshenko, persuaded the Poles to leave the city temporarily in their hands so that it should not fall into those of the Turks. At the same time the new King Michael recognized Khanenko as Hetman of the right bank.

Throughout 1670 and the summer of 1671 confused fighting continued. The Muscovite Government was confronted by the rising of Stenka Razin, which, beginning already as early as 1668, had in 1671 assumed the most formidable proportions. Turkish sources indicate that the Porte, both through its own agents and through Doroshenko, was fully informed on the internal situation in Poland and

Muscovy. In 1671 Ukrainian Cossacks, together with the loyal Cossacks of the Don, were sent to the Volga to fight the hordes of Razin, which themselves contained many lawless elements who had originally come from the Ukraine. While the Muscovites were still trying to conciliate Doroshenko, and envoys from the Tsar were urging the Hetman 'for the weal of the Ukraine to break with Turkey and to become a loyal subject of the King of Poland', Polish detachments, supporting Khanenko, drove Doroshenko's Cossacks out of Bratslav and Bar. At the same time another envoy, Vasili Loboyko, arrived in Istanbul to seek Turkish intervention on behalf of the Hetman. The interpreter of the Polish Embassy was informed by the Porte that the Polish attack on the Hetman had 'caused the Sultan to abandon the plan which he had formed to pass the winter in Asia Minor and not to quit Adrianople', and that unless the King ceased 'to torment Doroshenko' the Sultan would invade Poland in the coming spring. With social war on the Volga and dynastic conspiracies in Poland, the moment was well chosen for a powerful Turkish intervention in the Ukraine. Ahmed Köprülü prepared the ground for his Ukrainian conquest with the same astute competence which he was applying to his struggle for supremacy with the Habsburgs in Hungary. During the spring of 1672 a large army was concentrated on the line of the Dniestr; vast requisitions of provisions were extracted from the Roumanian principalities; and the Crim Khan, Adil Giray, accused of hostile actions against Doroshenko, was replaced by the more pliable Selim.

Meantime, on the left bank of the Dniepr, the Cossack elders had been plotting against the Tsar's Hetman, Mnohohrishny, with whom they were displeased owing to his appointment of near relatives to all important posts. The whole affair ended in a kind of palace revolution. One fine night the Hetman was seized, bound, and put into a peasant cart covered with skins and sent off to Moscow on the charge that 'through Doroshenko he was having secret relations with Turkey'. People in Moscow knew that Mnohohrishny was innocent, but thought it better not to send him back to the Ukraine. He was given a post in Siberia, where he proved himself to be a loyal man.

In July 1672 Ivan Samoylovich, who had been a judge until then, was elected Hetman. He was the son of a priest, astute and intelligent, and he tried to please both the Cossack colonels and the Muscovite *voyevodes*. He was the first Hetman who had not been a military man and he belonged to the class of officials which had grown up since the Agreement of 1654. It was easier for Moscow to have dealings with a man of this type than with some unruly son of the *Sech* or with some Cossack colonel who could not forget the class traditions of the Polish *szlachta*.

In August 1672 a powerful Turkish army made up of the veterans of the recent Cretan War crossed the Dniestr; Sultan Muhammad IV, with the Moldavian and Wallachian Hospodars and Selim Khan Giray in his suite, accompanied the troops. Under the walls of Kamenets-Podolsk they were joined by 12,000 of Doroshenko's Cossacks. The city fell after a twelve days' siege (31 August); and, although the principal churches were converted into mosques, the inhabitants were treated with consideration, for the Turks meant to stay.

The Grand Admiral Kaplan Mustafa Pasha—'a tiger on the land and a crocodile in the sea' as a contemporary describes him—who was one of the team of turbulent and grasping brothers-in-law with whom Ahmed Köprülü ruled the Empire, moved on Lvov, supported by Doroshenko and his Cossacks. While the ancient city purchased its immunity from a Turkish and Cossack occupation by the payment of a heavy ransom in gold, the Grand Hetman Sobieski, who had been skirmishing in Moldavia, chose the opportunity to renew his conspiracies against the King.

The unfortunate King Michael summoned a national armed assembly (*ruszenie pospolite*), but it failed to assemble in time; and in the middle of October, through the mediation of Selim Khan Giray, he hurriedly signed the shameful Peace of Buchach. Poland ceded to the Porte the whole of Podolia with the fortresses of Kamenets-Podolsk, Bar and Vinnitsa; and Doroshenko was recognized as Hetman of the right bank of the Dniepr and vassal of the Sultan. In addition to the ransom for Lvov, which had not all been paid, the King undertook to remit to the Porte an indemnity of 220,000 ducats.

Aroused by disasters for which he was by his rebellious conduct primarily responsible, Sobieski now prepared to resist the Peace of Buchach. When the *ruszenie pospolite* met at Golenba and ordered an enquiry into the conduct of the Grand Hetman and his accomplices, he frustrated the intentions of his peers by summoning a counter-confederation to meet at Szczebrzeszyn. Unable to oppose the rebels, both the King and the *Seym* submitted, and the rival groups composed their differences on the basis of a repudiation of the Treaty and the indemnity and a renewal of the war.

In the summer of 1673 a large Turkish army was again concentrated on the Dniestr, while the luxurious hunting camp which constituted the court of Muhammad IV took up its quarters on the coast of the Dobrogea. Sobieski, who had been joined by numerous

Roumanian *boyars*, had invaded northern Moldavia, but it was only at the beginning of November that the main armies met on the historic field of Khotin, where half a century before Vladislav IV, with Sahaydachny at his side, had beaten the army of Osman II. The battle began badly for the Poles when the Wallachian Hospodar, Gregory Ghica, who had rallied to the camp of Sobieski, deserted to the Turks; and the impetuous impact of the Cossack and Roumanian horse was broken by the ranks of the Janissaries. But the regiments of Russian dragoons and hussars, who had come to the help of the Poles under the clauses of the Treaty of Andrusovo, followed Sobieski in a charge which overwhelmed the Ottoman left flank, and the army of the Sultan scattered in headlong flight.

The Polish victory was complete. On 3 December their troops entered Jassy to set up as Hospodar Stephen Petriceicu, and in Bucarest the deserter Ghica was replaced by Constantine Bassarab; while in the Dobrogea, where the Turks maintained their winter quarters, the Zaporogian Sirko sacked Braila under the eyes of the Grand Vizier.

The position of Doroshenko now became perilous. At the beginning of 1674, Prince Romodanovski and the Hetman Samoylovich crossed to the right bank of the Dniepr. Doroshenko lost Cherkassy and Kanev. Later Korsun and Belaya Tserkov surrendered, and only Chigirin was left to the Sultan's vassal.

At this juncture Sobieski abandoned the war to return to the intricate game of dynastic politics in Warsaw. The unhappy King Michael had died on the very day of Khotin, and the triumphant Grand Hetman, at once the betrayer of his country's interests and the vindicator of his country's honour, was the obvious candidate for the succession. But, despite the parlous situation of the country, there was no lack of foreign candidates—among them James, Duke of York, who had just been deprived of office in England by his failure to comply with the conditions of the Test Act. Sobieski attended the *Seym* of 1674 at the head of 6000 veterans of Khotin and in the teeth of the opposition of the Lithuanian magnates secured election.

While the ambassadors of Austria and France and the great Polish lords trafficked in intrigue in the drawing-rooms of Warsaw, Ahmed Köprülü in his camp of Babadagh was preparing a new invasion. On 2 July the Sultan crossed the Danube; the agents of France, Austria and the United Provinces were in his train—the first in regular communication with Louis's ambassador in Warsaw, the Bishop of Marseilles. The campaign of 1674 was little more than a triumphal progress; the Roumanian strong places were retaken and the

Turkophil Hospodars, Ghica and Cantacuzene, restored in Bucarest and Jassy.

The principal Turkish military effort was now directed towards the restoration of their Hetman Doroshenko on the right bank of the Dniepr. Kara Mustafa Pasha, another of Ahmed Köprülü's brothers-in-law, destined soon to succeed him, took Ladyzhin and Uman. The bloodthirsty and arrogant Albanian wreaked cruelties which were in violent contrast to the moderate and far-sighted Turkish conduct of the campaign of 1672—cruelties which had the effect of prejudicing all Turkish prospects in the Ukraine. At Uman the Turks flayed the Cossack elders, and, stuffing their skins with straw, made scarecrows out of them. Thousands of girls and young boys were despatched to the Turkish slave markets. Doroshenko was horrified by the ruin wrought, by the closing of churches and the forcible conversions to Islam. He felt that his own downfall was near and appealed to the Tsar, promising to abandon his Turkish ally if he were recognized as Hetman by Moscow. The Tsar did not even deign to reply. When, in December, the numerous Turkish court with the bulk of the army retired to Adrianople to celebrate the somewhat insignificant victories of the year's campaign in fabulous feasts and mammoth hunting expeditions, the new Polish King, John III Sobieski, invaded the Ukraine and took back Bar, Vinnitsa, Bratslav and Nemirov with little resistance from the scattered Janissary garrisons.

In June 1675 the Turks undertook their fourth summer campaign against the Poles. They captured Zbarazh but were defeated under the walls of Bar, while a march against Lvov was repulsed by the King. Meanwhile John III had concluded a treaty of alliance with Louis XIV, and the weight of French diplomacy was directed towards the conclusion of a lasting peace between the Poles and the Turks which should prepare the way for Louis's designs against the Habsburgs.

'Sobieski was bound to France by early associations, by the influence of his wife, Marie d'Arquien, and by his identification during recent years with the French party in Poland. Louis naturally sought to make the most of what might prove invaluable assistance in the east. He sent the Marquis de Béthune, who had married an elder sister of the new Queen of Poland, to carry his congratulations to Sobieski; and on 11 June 1675 a treaty of alliance was concluded between France and Poland. The Polish King was to receive a subsidy of 200,000 crowns, and French assistance in the design of restoring Polish suzerainty over East Prussia. In return, he was to allow recruiting in his dominions for the French service and to give a helping hand to the Hungarian rebels. Thus Louis had it in his power to stir up formidable difficulties which would divert the forces of Austria and also those of the Elector of Brandenburg, who had rejoined the coalition against France.... Great efforts were made by France to bring about peace between Poland and Turkey. So long as the war lasted neither power could give effective assistance to Hungary; but its termination would enable France to bring either the Turks or the Poles into the field against the Emperor. The task was a difficult one because Köprülü refused to surrender any of the conquests of 1672, and Sobieski could only hope to make the Crown hereditary in his family by freeing Polish soil from the infidel' (Lodge, *Camb. Mod. Hist.* vol. v).

In the summer of 1676 a Turkish army under Ibrahim Pasha Shaitan ('the Devil') resumed the offensive on the Dniestr. In October, King John III with 30,000 men was surrounded at Żurawno; the Turks proved unable to storm the camp, but after a twenty days' blockade the Poles were beginning to suffer from shortage of provisions; and a treaty, known as that of Żurawno, was concluded. As Köprülü, a fine statesman but an indifferent soldier in the field, had gained the favourable Treaty of Vasvár after the defeat of St Gotthard, he now, after the disaster of Khotin, retained by the Treaty of Żurawno all Podolia with Kamenets-Podolsk. The right bank of the Dniepr was to remain independent both of the King and of the Sultan, but the Poles were obliged to recognize the Sultan's authority over the Zaporogian territories beyond the rapids. This last condition affirmed the consistent policy of the Porte, which aimed at maintaining direct control of the immediate littoral of the Black Sea (which they now had in a semicircle from the Dobrogea and Budzhak territories, through Zaporogia and the Crimea, to the Kuban and Circassia) and leaving the hinterland to be administered by autonomous vassal potentates (the two Roumanian Hospodars and the Hetman). Ahmed Köprülü, who was almost in the last week of his life, was so delighted with the Treaty that he ordered the courier who brought the news—a Moldavian captain—to be given a purse of 200 ducats.

The victory of the Turks in the five years' war did not save Doroshenko. During the summer of 1676 Romodanovski and Samoylovich had been besieging the Hetman in Chigirin, and in September, a month before the conclusion of the Treaty of Żurawno, he had surrendered and sworn allegiance to Tsar Alexey (who too was approaching the end of his life). The Moscow Government treated Doroshenko with remarkable consideration. After he had been brought to Moscow, he was appointed *voyevode* of Vyatka, and to him and his family was granted the estate of Yaropolets (which later became the property of the family of Nathalie Goncharova, the wife of the poet Pushkin). The tolerant attitude of the Moscow Government towards Doroshenko seems strange, for he had not only been the cause of the death of many thousands of Ukrainians but also of thousands of Muscovite soldiers and of hundreds of officials. The Chigirin Hetman had been a traitor to the Orthodox Church, and had become the ally and vassal of the Sultan. When the terrible fates of rebel Cossack chieftains in Poland are remembered, it is surprising that this honourable exile was all the penalty which Doroshenko suffered for his misdeeds. The new Tsar Theodore Alexeyevich was exceedingly tolerant and humane and was free from the fits of rage which later were to characterize his younger brother Peter I. There were deeper reasons, however, for the patient and lenient attitude which the Moscow Government adopted generally towards the refractory leaders of the Ukrainian Cossacks. Moscow men of the seventeenth century were on the whole less inclined towards sanguinary repressions than their Polish contemporaries. The savagery of the Polish reprisals against the rebel Ukrainian Cossacks and peasants was inspired by the feeling of class: fear is always the source of cruelty and the Polish gentry feared 'the rabble' which they were oppressing. Executions were carried out not only in the name of an implacable Nemesis for past excesses but as an example to others. Tortures and executions were also carried out in Moscow after the suppression of the rising of Stenka Razin and for the same reasons. As for Doroshenko, from an official point of view, he could not be treated as a traitor to the Tsar since, according to the Andrusovo Treaty, he was a subject of the King of Poland. In fact everyone knew that, although mistaken, Doroshenko had not been guided by personal motives nor ambitions. The Tsar's Government understood this and treated him accordingly. Peter Doroshenko was no political adventurer of the type of Vyhovsky, Yuri Khmelnytsky, Bryukhovetsky and Ivan Mazeppa. Together with Sahaydachny and Bohdan Khmelnytsky he may be considered as one of the outstanding figures of the history of the Ukraine in the seventeenth century—in spite of the fact that his activities proved unfortunate and brought disaster to his native land.

Ahmed Köprülü had died a few days after the conclusion of the Treaty of Żurawno, and the accession to the Grand Vizierate of his brother-in-law, Kara Mustafa Pasha, caused satisfaction at Versailles: 'In all his actions he displayed that hatred and haughty contempt for the Giaurs which had been handed down from the days of Turkish triumph'; it was known that the new Grand Vizier had long nursed the ambition to excel the achievement of Suleiman the Magnificent by becoming the conqueror of Vienna, and that before his accession he had persuaded the Sultan to express to the French Ambassador his willingness to make war upon the Emperor as soon as peace had been made with Poland. 'This momentous decision was formally approved by the French Council of State, and the conclusion of the Treaty of Żurawno was welcomed with enthusiasm at Versailles.'

But events in the Ukraine were to postpone for nearly seven years the great Turkish advance upon Vienna; and the diversion of Turkish power from the Danube undoubtedly modified the ambitious schemes of Louis, who in 1678 gave Europe a short respite in the Peace of Nymwegen.

Repin's famous picture depicts the refusal of the Zaporogians to submit to Turkish authority in accordance with the Treaty of Żurawno. Their humorous truculence found justification in the disaster which they had inflicted on a force of 10,000 Turks sent to subdue the *Sech* in the summer of 1675. Nearly the whole of the Turkish force had been slaughtered before the primitive fortifications of the Cossack camp. In the following year, while King John III. was lying beleagured in Żurawno, the almost legendary Sirko had led his men on foot across one of the shallow lagoons of the Azov Sea and fallen upon the rich towns of the Crimea; Akmechet (now Simferopol) and Baghchi-Saray were sacked, and Selim Khan Giray had only escaped capture by flight into the mountains.

After Żurawno and the defection of Doroshenko, the Turks produced as Hetman Yuri Khmelnytsky, who had found his way to Istanbul, where he had been living in obscurity as a monk. At the beginning of 1677 he was sent with some little pomp into the Ukraine, and in the summer he accompanied the army of the Seraskier Ibrahim which advanced on Chigirin. The siege of Chigirin was, however, interrupted by the converging forces of Romodanovski and Samoylovich and of Prince Vasili Golitsyn. The Turkish army retired in disorder beyond the Dniestr; and so great was the anger of the Sultan that the Seraskier's life was forfeit, while Selim Khan Giray fled to the Caucasus.

In the campaigning season of 1678, Kara Mustafa himself marched against Chigirin; the new Crim Khan Murad Giray and the Hospodars of Wallachia and Moldavia were with his army, which amounted to 100,000 men. On the Russian side troops nearly equal in numbers awaited the Turkish invasion—newly equipped Muscovite regiments trained on the Western model under the veteran Romodanovski; the Dniepr Cossacks of Samoylovich and Cossacks from the Don; Kalmucks from the plains of the Kuma and Circassian auxiliaries from the Kuban. After a series of confused and hard-fought battles fortune favoured the Ottoman arms, and the Russian commanders retired beyond the Dniepr. Kara Mustafa took Chigirin and razed the former capital of Bohdan Khmelnytsky to the ground. The issue of the campaign seemed to be in favour of Yuri Khmelnytsky, but his sour triumph was ephemeral. In the spring of 1679 the whole country rose against him and his Turkish garrisons; and when he tried to escape beyond the Dniestr he was overtaken and killed.(5) Throughout the summer of 1679 slaughter raked the Ukraine; flourishing towns like Cherkassy and Kanev were completely destroyed; hundreds of villages and estates were devastated and the whole of the population fled to the east of the Dniepr.

In 1680 another picturesque figure of the Ukrainian seventeenth century disappeared from the scene: old *ataman* Sirko died. His personality was so characteristic of his epoch and surroundings that its study may give some understanding of that amazing and contradictory medley of heroism and treason, of passionate patriotism and indifference, of cunning and naivety which made up the background of the Ukraine of the Hetmans. During the three decades 1650–80 Sirko was on fifteen different occasions elected chief *ataman* of the *Sech*. His victories over the Tartars are countless; he invaded the Crimea several times and twice took Baghchi-Saray, the capital of the Khans. When the Turks built the forts of Kizil Kerman and Aslan Kerman at the mouth of the Dniepr he took them; and once again, as in the days of Sahaydachny, the light Cossack craft attacked the coast of Asia Minor. Twice Sirko repulsed the attacks of Ottoman armies on the *Sech* (the second time was just a year before his death). All knew that Sirko was an honest man, disinterested, loved his country dearly and was a faithful son of the Orthodox Church; yet despite these qualities of character he was incapable of playing a constructive part in the events of the revolutionary times in which he lived. He was too credulous, too impressionable, too impulsive and too obstinate. It was easy to deceive him and to make a fool of him. Thus he, the bitterest enemy of the Tartars, found himself from time to time fighting in their ranks. In the critical months of 1677 he refused to go to the relief of Chigirin although the Sultan's troops were besieging it—and three years before he had been boasting about his insolent answer to the Sultan's emissary.(6)

No one was so skilled as he in waging war against the Turks and Tartars; the successive Ukrainian Hetmans, the Muscovite *voyevodes*, and John Sobieski were well aware of his military talent; and when at one moment the Russian authorities exiled him to Tobolsk, the

Polish leader quickly asked for his recall. During the whole period of these thirty years, among all the Hetmans and Cossack elders who played more or less important roles, Sirko only respected Bohdan Khmelnytsky and only loved Peter Doroshenko. Bryukhovetsky pleased him at first and he helped him to come to the fore, but later he turned against him. Samoylovich he could not stand at all on account of his cupidity. He could never pardon Vyhovsky for the Hadyach Agreement. In spite of all his regard for Doroshenko he highly disapproved of the Turkish orientation, and for this reason was alternately fighting and becoming reconciled with the luckless Hetman. He considered the union of the Ukraine with Muscovy to be the least of different evils, but he could never admit 'the partition' of the Ukraine under the Andrusovo Treaty. Moscow men considered him unreliable and therefore rather dangerous. Such was Ivan Sirko—a real Ukrainian national hero 'but a great muddler in the eyes of God'. Many of his compatriots were of the same mould and their versatility puzzled both cultured Polish diplomats and experienced Muscovite officials.

The inconclusive and exhausting character of the war in the Ukraine was, during the year 1680, inclining both the Russians and the Turks to peace. Kara Mustafa, after the barren triumph of Chigirin which had been fêted as a great victory in Istanbul, was concentrating on the greatest ambition of his exhalted brain—the conquest of Vienna. In Central Europe Sobieski, whose Queen had become alienated from the French court and who himself desired to maintain rather than to destroy the Habsburgs since he regarded their power as the main bulwark against Turkish aggression, had exchanged a French for an Austrian alliance (1677). Both the hopes of the Porte and of Versailles were centred on the dissident Hungarians, whose chief, Emeric Tökölyi, while maintaining constant embassies in Istanbul, had recognized Louis on his coins as 'Protector Hungariae'.

Russia, still at war with the Turks, was attracted to the Austro-Polish alliance; in June of 1679 ambassadors of the new Tsar Theodore had appeared in Vienna, and in August Polish ambassadors had gone to Moscow to discuss an alliance of the Emperor, the Tsar and the King of Poland against the Ottoman Empire. Large numbers of Muscovite troops were sent into the Ukraine, where the Scot Gordon was engaged in fortifying Kiev after the latest European designs and in building a pontoon bridge over the Dniepr—an innovation which had never before been seen in the Ukraine.

While the negotiations between Moscow and the Western courts were dragging on, Kara Mustafa decided to secure the neutrality of

Russia in the coming war by proposing an advantageous peace. Tsar Theodore Alexeyevich was not a man inclined to vast military undertakings and he needed peace at the beginning of a reign which was destined to be very short. In January 1681 the Treaty of Baghchi-Saray was concluded for a period of twenty years. It provided that the Crim Khan was to desist from his raids into the Ukraine and to exchange captives with Muscovy and the Ukraine; it was thus that *boyar* Sheremetiev returned from a captivity of twenty years. Muscovite authority over the region on the right bank of the Ukraine in the neighbourhood of Kiev was recognized; while neither Muscovites nor Turks were to send troops or officials into the remaining parts of right-bank Ukraine. After the sanguinary campaigns of 1677–9 all the country along the right bank of the lower Dniepr had been completely devastated and its population had fled to the left bank. The Baghchi-Saray Treaty condemned Zaporogia to remain a kind of wilderness which divided the parts of the Ukraine administered by Moscow from the territory of the Crim Tartars.

§ 5. HETMAN SAMOYLOVICH: THE RISE OF IVAN MAZEPPA

Ivan Samoylovich, who in 1672 had been elected Hetman by the favour of the Moscow Government, had chosen as secretary and tutor to his sons a certain Ivan Mazeppa, who had attracted the somewhat rough priest's son by his intelligence and knowledge of the world.

Ivan Mazeppa was apparently born about the year 1642 on the small estate of his Cossack parents near Belaya Tserkov. A candidate for the priesthood, the boy acquired an excellent education at an institution in Kiev, becoming competent in 'clerical Latin'—an advantage which was to stand him in good stead in later life. After the Hadyach Agreement in 1659 or 1660 a hundred young men were sent to Warsaw, probably as representatives of Ukrainian youth who were to be given a Polish introduction to the world and to receive subsequent ennoblement in accordance with the plan of Vyhovsky. Ivan Mazeppa was not only fortunate enough to be accepted, but like some others of his fellows he was made a page at the court of King John Casimir. It is doubtful whether under such circumstances he could have seriously continued his studies, but he learned Polish and a little German and a good deal of the ways of the world.

Mazeppa, heralded into the romantic literature and opera of the nineteenth century by two such distinguished sponsors as Voltaire and Byron, now began a life which recalls rather the adventures of the disreputable heroes of the French and English novels of his period. His contemporary Passek gives an amusing account of an attractive and unscrupulous young man whom he describes as 'a liar and a swindler', and whose career at the Polish court ended with his being flogged at the order of an outraged husband, and bound naked to a horse which was set loose 'into the grassy scented wilderness of the boundless steppe'.

The serious admirers of Mazeppa indignantly deny as an invention of 'the spiteful Passek' the truth of an episode which has become famous in European literature and the theatre. But whatever the truth of Mazeppa's Polish romance may have been—and the facts appear more unfortunate than discreditable—the next events in the hero's life were of a definitely unsavoury character.

Mazeppa appears to have returned to the Ukraine in the army of John Casimir in 1663. He is later heard of in the entourage of Peter Doroshenko, with whom he found favour owing to his education and knowledge of languages. He has to do the Hetman's correspondence and is sometimes entrusted with delicate missions. During this period of his life Mazeppa married 'a rich widow', but she soon disappeared from the scene. But even with Doroshenko the enterprising young Cossack was not very successful, and one of his delicate missions nearly cost him his life. During the course of Doroshenko's intercourse with the Turks, he decided to send Mazeppa first to Pereyaslavl for *pourparlers* with Romodanovski and Samoylovich, and afterwards with important papers to Istanbul. Instead of gifts for the Sultan, Mazeppa brought along with him some scores of Zaporogian prisoners—men who had shown insubordination to Doroshenko by attacking the Tartars or Turks. As misfortune would have it, during his journey through the steppe he fell in with a Zaporogian band and was taken to the *Sech* with his papers and the men whom he was to deliver into the hands of the Turks. Nothing, so it seemed, could save Doroshenko's envoy from a most painful death. He was sentenced to the Zaporogian execution 'of the stake', which was carried out in the following manner: the victim was tied to a stake, and a heavy stick, a jar filled with vodka, a cup and a piece of bread were put beside him. Every Zaporogian could have a drink and a bite if, before doing so, he gave a good blow with the stick to the man tied to the stake.

Mazeppa was saved by the chief *ataman* of the *Sech*—the famous Sirko. Mazeppa's admirers pretend that Sirko was struck by the unusual personality of the young man and understood that a great future was awaiting him. Considering what actually occurred, the truth would seem somewhat different. Sirko at that time was indignant against Doroshenko on account of his dependence on Turkey, and learned from Mazeppa all he wanted to know. Seeing what sort of a person he had before him, he decided to send this 'trusted secretary' of Doroshenko to Samoylovich in order to report to him the intimate details of the relations between his master and the Turks. It was at this stage that the versatile and erudite young man made his impression on Hetman Samoylovich.

At the end of 1680, during the Baghchi-Saray negotiations, Mazeppa, who had by this time obtained a considerable influence over the Hetman, was sent to represent the Cossack interest in Moscow. With the skill which was characteristic of him he soon unravelled all the intrigues of the Muscovite court. He understood that the ambitious Tsarevna Sophia, sister of the ailing Tsar Theodore, was destined to play a prominent part in the immediate future, and he won the good graces of her favourite, Prince Vasili Golitsyn. Mazeppa returned to Samoylovich a still more necessary man; after the death of Tsar Theodore, Sophia was proclaimed Regent for her infant brothers, and the ascendancy of Golitsyn procured for Mazeppa the post of War Secretary for the Ukraine.

The year 1683 saw the spectacular victory of John III Sobieski over Kara Mustafa under the walls of Vienna. Amongst the conqueror's troops had been a detachment of 4000 Cossacks who had left the desolate region of the right bank of the Dniepr and sought refuge in Poland. (They were commanded by Colonel Gogol.) During the summer of 1684 the Poles and Cossacks cleared Podolia of the Turks, but they were unable to recover the fortress of Kamenets-Podolsk.

The Holy League now formed between Austria, Poland and Venice aimed at the partition of the Ottoman dominions in Europe; John III, having failed to oust the Turks from Kamenets-Podolsk and avoiding the sterile task of recovering the devastated territories between the Dniestr and the Dniepr, reverted to the schemes of John Zamojski, which had comprehended the inclusion of Moldavia and Wallachia within *Rzecz Pospolita* and the extension of the Polish frontier to the Danube.

It was natural that the Western confederates should desire to extend the front against the Turks by including Russia in the League, while the ambitions and the necessities of the Tsarevna Sophia imposed an abandonment of the pacific policy of the late Tsar Theodore. In 1686 Moscow joined the Holy League, reverting thus to the Andrusovo policy of Ordin-Nashchokin, whereby the Poles were to fight the Turks in the Danubian principalities while the Russians confronted the Crim Tartars and the powerful Turkish fortresses which covered the approaches to the Black Sea littoral. Sobieski forewent all Polish claims on Kiev and Smolensk against an indemnity (which in reality was rather a subsidy) of half a million gulden, and it was agreed that the territories of the Zaporogian *Sech* lying along both banks of the lower Dniepr would in future be subject to the Tsar only, and not as under the terms of Andrusovo to the Tsar and the King of Poland in *condominium*.

Montecucculi, the greatest commander of his age in Eastern Europe, had once observed that the Emperor should never wage a long war against the Turks, as their power always remained unshaken by defeats in the field; and although the Turks were fighting on all fronts from the Adriatic to the Sea of Azov, neither the Poles nor the Russians in superior force achieved effective success during a series of campaigns which dragged on for a decade. In annual operations which were continued until 1694 the Polish King exhausted his dwindling resources in Moldavia, where Constantine Cantemir, a former Polish officer of Tartar extraction who had been nominated Hospodar by the Porte, proved a difficult antagonist.

Vasili Golitsyn, the elegant favourite of the Tsarevna Sophia who had many of the faults of a Buckingham, was no more successful in the Crimea, which was not destined to become Russian until a century later, when a more manly favourite was to deliver the sunlit peninsula to an even more imperious princess.

In the summer of 1687 an army which, including the Cossacks of Samoylovich, numbered nearly 200,000 men opened the campaign against the Crimea. The Russians moved forward with a huge baggage train in their wake and herds of cattle for the supply of the troops. The Tartar detachments, during the hot summer days, had recourse to their old tactic of setting fire to the steppe. Beyond their encampments the Russian soldiers saw nothing but scorched stretches of steppe; in the parched weather the rivulets were running dry, and men and beasts began to perish from thirst. There was murmuring in the ranks; and disputes broke out among the commanders.

The moment had arrived to provide a scapegoat, and Vasili Golitsyn, who did not wish that responsibility for the disaster should fall upon him, was delighted when the adroitness of Mazeppa supplied the need.

Mazeppa had always been aware of the unpopularity of Samoylovich among the upper ranks of the Cossacks, who envied and detested him. The rapid rise to power and wealth of this 'priest's son', his lordly ways, appeared ridiculous and hateful to the Cossack colonels. Further it was generally known that Samoylovich had been opposed to the campaign; he was ill, getting old, and had imprudently often spoken in Mazeppa's presence of 'this cursed war which Moscow has forced us to take part in'.

When lack of water and disease, which had begun to spread among the troops, forced Golitsyn to retreat into districts where the rivers had not dried up, Mazeppa decided to act. His wily plot was based on the consideration that by betraying Samoylovich he was saving Golitsyn's reputation and thereby rendering service to the Tsarevna Sophia who was Regent of the realm.

A rumour was spread among the Muscovite troops that it was not the Tartars but the Cossacks who had set fire to the steppe by order of the Hetman, who did not wish to invade the Crimea. At the end of June a group of colonels, Mazeppa's friends (Mazeppa himself had arranged to be absent), presented to Prince Golitsyn a list of twenty-five accusations against the Hetman Samoylovich. Some of these accusations were true, such as the charges of cupidity and other abuses and the statement that Samoylovich had always been opposed to the Polish alliance and the war with Turkey.

On 22 June, in the village of Kolomak to the east of Poltava, the Hetman and his two sons were arrested as they were coming out of church. Brought to judgment before the Cossack elders, the Hetman tried to protest his innocence, but was not allowed to speak; his judges threw themselves upon him, brandishing their sabres, and Golitsyn had to intervene to save his life.

Old Samoylovich was banished to Tobolsk; his son Jacob to Yeniseysk. All their estates, the whole property of the family, were confiscated. This, however, was not enough to satisfy the guilty malice of Mazeppa; the other two sons of the Hetman, Mazeppa's former pupils, Gregory and Simon, who had become colonels by this time, were also arrested and brought to Putivl, where they were tortured and not even allowed to see a priest before they were beheaded.(7)

The dream which Mazeppa had nourished certainly since he had gained the patronage of Samoylovich was realized at last. The *Rada* met at this same village of Kolomak for the election of a new Hetman. Mazeppa could rely on Golitsyn's support, but he had to make certain of the votes of the elders and had a large recourse to bribes. The election took place on 25 July 1687. According to contemporary stories it cost Mazeppa 11,000 roubles paid to Prince Golitsyn, besides smaller sums distributed among the elders.

Samoylovich, on whose misfortunes Mazeppa had built his triumph, had very few friends; neither does he find any friends among Russian and Ukrainian historians. All accuse him of boundless greed; of not having been very particular about the means whereby he acquired his wealth; of having a contempt for the law and of being addicted to favouritism; of a cringing attitude towards Moscow and at the same time of underhand intrigues against the Government. Samoylovich of course had not been a Hetman in the sense in which Bohdan Khmelnytsky had been or in which Peter Doroshenko had tried to be. He bore the title of Hetman, but in reality had been nothing more than a sort of viceroy of Moscow in the Ukraine. The constant presence during the time when he was Hetman of large numbers of Muscovite troops excluded all thought of independent action on his part. However, if such was the case it only goes to prove that the Ukraine of those days needed a man of that kind.

During the fifteen years when Samoylovich was Hetman, 1672–87, life at least on the left bank of the Dniepr had become peaceful again. The Ukraine, when Mazeppa became Hetman in 1687, was even geographically a different country from that which Khmelnytsky had left at his death. Except for Kiev and the surrounding district, life had migrated to the east of the Dniepr, and all the principal vital centres were now situated on the Desna and the Seym, on the Psiol, the Sula and the Vorskla. The Ukraine had spread to the north towards the river Sozh, and to the east far along the Donets and beyond that river. Baturin, not far from where the Seym falls into the Desna, had become the capital of the Hetmans, while only ruins far away to the south-west marked the place where once Bohdan Khmelnytsky had held court in Chigirin.

The growth of population on the left bank had been incessant since the time of Khmelnytsky's revolt, for the region to the east of the Dniepr was regarded as secure from Tartars and Poles. The process had rather slowed down in the sixties, when, owing to the conditions of civil war, Poles, Tartars and Muscovite regiments appeared even in that relatively peaceful quarter. Settlement in the 'new Ukraine' was again reinforced during the Turkish invasions of Podolia and the territories on the right bank of the Dniepr beginning with the year 1672. After 1680 the 'mesopotamian' belt between the Bug and the Dniepr was officially declared by the representatives of Moscow and the Porte at Baghchi-Saray to have become a desert, and a year or two before Doroshenko in a letter to Sirko, in which he referred to Samoylovich as 'a Sardanapalus', had expressed his horror at the utter devastation for which his own policy had been responsible: 'Where once stood towns and villages surrounded by gardens there only remain ruins of single walls and hungry dogs fight each other. The churches are all closed because there is no one to worship in them. All the fields are covered with weeds and our native land, formerly so gay and bright, has become a dreadful wilderness.'

'Sardanapalus Samoylovich', indifferent to the troubles of the right bank, was even ready to avail himself of these calamities when they tended to the advantage of 'his' left-bank Ukraine—especially when his own personal interests were also served. When he came to the relief of Chigirin he observed with satisfaction the crowds of peasants who were fleeing to the left bank. Some pretend that he even accelerated this movement by sending his Cossacks to drive away the inhabitants from their homesteads.

During the seven or eight years before 1680 hundreds of thousands of peasants migrated to the east of the Dniepr. These migrants were most welcome to the Hetman as well as to his fellows who were following his example. The Hetman himself, all his relations, all the dignitaries of the Baturin 'court', all elders and judges, all in a word who were able to do so owing to their privileged positions, were trying to possess themselves of the free lands, of which there were still plenty beyond the Desna or along the upper courses of the Sula, the Psiol and the Vorskla. These new landlords preferred a new element to the old settlers who had lived there since Khmelnytsky's time and looked upon their land as their own property. It was much more pleasant and profitable for the new landlords to be able to deal with immigrants who were ready to agree to any conditions so long as they could procure a roof to replace the ruined home which they had left behind them on the right bank. The desperate need of the hundreds of thousands of migrants from the right bank was the real reason why large estates began to flourish on the left bank during the last two decades of the seventeenth century. The social hegemony for which Khmelnytsky and Vyhovsky had struggled and intrigued without success was attained almost without effort by Samoylovich owing to the peculiar conditions of his time.

Mazeppa, who succeeded him, found himself not only at the head of the Cossack administration but also the leader of the relatively important group of landowners into which the Cossack elders had managed to transform themselves. This 'inheritance' was of greater importance than all the gold chervontsy and silver thalers which 'Sardanapalus Samoylovich' had accumulated in his coffers.

After the downfall of Samoylovich, Golitsyn's troops wintered in the Ukraine, and in the summer of 1688 the war against the Crimea was renewed. The Russians approached Perekop, but, according to the popular explanation of the abortive outcome of the campaign, 'the Tartars saved themselves by sending sacks full of gold coins half of which were faked'. In reality the accumulating difficulties of the Tsarevna Sophia imposed the return of her lover to Moscow.

In the capital the conflict between the factions of the Regent Sophia and of the young Tsar Peter came to a crisis during the following summer (August–September 1689). In the outcome the Tsarevna was incarcerated in a convent, while Golitsyn disappeared into the obscurity of Siberian exile. The reign of the great Peter had begun.

In the circumstances of Golitsyn's fall, Mazeppa might easily have lost all that he had achieved. His enthusiastic biographers ascribe his immunity to his having won the admiration of the young Tsar by his oratory and charm. It is perhaps nearer to the truth to suppose that the men surrounding Tsar Peter thought it wiser at that troubled moment not to make any changes in the Ukraine which might give the pretext for revolt in that tumultuous land. At any rate Mazeppa returned to Baturin at the end of September 1689—the zealous and most loyal and faithful servant of the Tsar.

Moscow needed the support of an artful viceroy. The war with the Turks and Tartars continued and held the country in a state of uncertainty, while the discontents of the praetorian *streltsy* regiments and of the religious dissidents, who found a wide support among the people, had infected the Zaporogian *Sech*.

On the right bank of the Dniepr the Poles had recovered many districts from the Turks, and peasants both from Galicia and Poland and from the left bank were beginning to trickle back into the regions of Korsun, Belaya Tserkov and Bratslav. Colonel Paley, a simple Cossack by origin, was becoming popular and the old Polish pretensions to suzerainty on the right bank were again becoming a reality. At the same time another Cossack, Petrik, appeared in the *Sech* and, taking advantage of the social and religious discontents, began to intrigue, on behalf of the Turks, in favour of a rising against Moscow. 'Moscow gives our people over into slavery to the landlords so as to turn Cossacks into peasants' proclaimed this new evangelist of a Turkish orientation. Tartar bands joined the adherents of Petrik in some dangerous raids, and it was only the political skill of Mazeppa which prevented his movement from becoming formidable during the first five years of Peter's reign.

In 1695 Peter's first Azov campaign brought a Muscovite force under Boris Sheremetiev to the mouth of the Dniepr, and Mazeppa's Cossacks took part in the storming of several Turkish forts along the littoral. Peter's failure before Azov in the summer of 1695 was redeemed next year by the capture of the fortress which both Turks and Russians regarded as the key to power on the Black Sea; Mazeppa, who had been covering the flank of the besieging army against the attacks of the Crim Tartars, was able to greet his sovereign with the gift of a fine Turkish sabre, the golden hilt of which was studded with precious gems.

In 1697, when Peter went off on his foreign travels, Mazeppa, reposing in the boundless confidence of his young master, was left as absolute lord of the Ukraine. And when, after the Tsar's return and the suppression of the revolt of the *streltsy* in Moscow, Peter commanded his faithful Hetman to meet him in Voronezh, the highest honours were showered upon him. Mazeppa was made the second knight on the roll of the Order of St Andrew, which had just been founded and on which the Tsar himself ranked only as sixth in precedence. Such was the recompense 'for many military labours, constant zeal and loyalty during thirteen years of gallant service to the Tsar marked by incessant victories'.

In 1700 Mazeppa was nearing his sixtieth year. He was very active and full of energy. He used to have amorous affairs one after the other, and sometimes several simultaneously. Around the Baturin 'palace' lived a whole seraglio of adoring women. The old Hetman was always accompanied on his travels by several ladies. Soon, however, his last love affair with Kochubey's daughter was destined to have a fatal influence on his life. The old Hetman led a luxurious life in the Baturin palace, which had been lavishly furnished: it was filled with many beautiful carpets, many costly mirrors, a great quantity of that heavy gilt furniture so characteristic of the epoch; also table silver, pictures, portraits and even books. Mazeppa liked reading and was proud of his knowledge of the Latin classics. For the Ukraine of those days his erudition was really remarkable: when he visited the Kiev Academy he answered the welcoming speech of the Rector in Latin. Those coming ornaments of the Orthodox Church of the time of Peter I, Theophanes Prokopovich and Stephen Yavorski, wrote panegyrics about the cultivated Hetman who at the same time remained a real pillar of Orthodoxy.

Owing perhaps to the remote memories of his youth, Mazeppa had a sincere liking for theological books and solemn church services. He liked architecture also, and built the wall round the Pecherskaya Lavra in Kiev and the church of St Nicholas in that city, and the cathedral in Pereyaslavl as well as churches in other Ukrainian towns—all in that Ukrainian baroque which is sometimes called the 'Mazeppa style'.

A special etiquette was elaborated by the Hetman for his receptions in the Baturin palace of the Tsar's envoys and of notable foreign guests. Samoylovich had already founded a sort of Hetman's Guard, the *Serdyuky*, who were constituted in paid regiments and wore gorgeous uniforms—scarlet jackets, white dolmans and wide blue trousers. Three of these Serdyuky regiments, each consisting of men of a different nationality, were paid out of the Hetman's personal revenues.

In his old age Mazeppa became incredibly rich. Part of the taxation in the Ukraine went not to the Hetman's Exchequer but to him personally—as for instance all the income from the Hadyach regimental territories. He left behind him, after his flight, millions of gold and silver rubles, scores of estates, hundreds of mills. The Tsar petted and spoiled his old Hetman and liked giving him costly presents—robes made of cloth of gold, sables, yards of satins and velvets, barrels of Rhine wine; he even sent him on occasion baskets filled with lemons—a great delicacy in those days.

There is no doubt that the young Tsar had a sincere affection for Mazeppa. He liked his shrewd intelligence and domineering character, his leaning towards reading and his 'European ways'. Peter was always more than condescending to the morals of those around him: adventurers, Russians and foreigners, surrounded the young Tsar, and he preferred that type to men of strict morals who were opposed to his policies. Mazeppa on his side showed great finesse in his understanding of Peter and realized that one of his leading traits was an insatiable curiosity. Knowing that the young Tsar took an interest in everything, Mazeppa never forgot to send him things which might interest him—sometimes strange Oriental arms and sometimes ancient 'Assyrian' coins found somewhere near Kiev. A man who could always tell Peter something new or which he did not know was ever welcome at his court.

§ 6. THE GREAT NORTHERN WAR: PETER THE GREAT AND MAZEPPA

The turn of the century saw dramatic changes in the distribution of power in Eastern Europe. Within the span of two decades the three historic empires between the Arctic and the Mediterranean succumbed in varying degrees to the new state structures which were to dominate Eastern Europe in modern times. The north-to-south belt of Sweden, Poland and the Ottoman Empire failed to sustain the pressure of the Germanic powers from the west and of the Muscovite state from the east.

As early as the middle of the fifteenth century both Vienna and Moscow had been conscious of the common interest of Germany and Muscovy against the states which occupied the vast area which intervened between their respective borders. And in no period was that common interest—which has now become a sinister factor in world politics—more clearly followed than in that phase which opened at the turn of the seventeenth century when the established empires of Turkey, Poland and Sweden were successively struck down. The Austro-Russian combinations against Turkey and the partitions of Poland which took place during the course of the eighteenth century merely served to complete the process which had already been decided by the long wars against Poland in the seventeenth century, by the signal weakening of the Ottoman imperial power after the defeat of Kara Mustafa before Vienna and by the waning of the Swedish Empire during the Great Northern War.

It is a paradox that the last Polish paladin, King John III Sobieski, should have brought about the Ottoman overthrow which definitely tilted the balance of power in Eastern Europe in favour of the Germanic and Muscovite states.

Three years before the Treaty of Karlowitz (1699) brought to an end the predominant influence of Turkey in South-Eastern Europe, the death of Sobieski had marked the abandonment by Poland of any pretension to place as a Great Power.

Louis XIV, whose system of checks on Germanic Central Europe was damaged by the weakening of Turkey, made serious efforts to sponsor first Condé and Conti princes and later Stanislas Leszczyński for the Polish throne; and a majority of the Polish magnates, conscious of the danger of their growing dependence on Muscovy, favoured the candidates of Versailles. But 'Tsar Peter even went so far as to threaten the Polish Senate with an invasion if they dared to choose a Frenchman'; and Augustus of Saxony (whose cognomen of 'the Strong' was derived from his remarkable proficiency in bed rather than from any qualities of character) imposed his own election with a Saxon army and Austrian support.

Poland was now ruled by a German dynasty dependent on Russian goodwill. Augustus had a certain restless brilliance, an itching need for money and a big dynastic appetite. He was a predestined tool for the ruthless politics of Tsar Peter and an appropriate victim for the cold violence of Charles XII of Sweden.

In the conflict of singular personalities which has always given an epic character to the Great Northern War, a Livonian noble, John Reinhold Patkul, played the fatal role of the over-intelligent intriguer—and it eventually brought him to the wheel. Patkul was a slighted Swedish subject who professed to represent the discontent of the Livonian nobility with Swedish rule, and he negotiated an alliance of the impressionable Augustus and the calculating Peter (in which the Danish King Frederick IV also took a hand), aimed at the partition of the Swedish dominions, which appeared an easy prey under the minority of the unknown boy, Charles XII.

In November 1700 the crushing defeat of the Russians at Narva revived the old Vasa dream of the extension of Swedish hegemony over Poland, and at the same time seriously threatened the position of Tsar Peter, whose reforms were exceedingly unpopular.

The news of Narva was received not without a certain spiteful satisfaction in Baturin, in the Zaporogian *Sech*, on the Don and beyond the Volga among the Old Believers—and even in Moscow, for the Tsar had many enemies everywhere. When Peter's Chancellor wrote to Mazeppa urging him not to believe the exaggerated and lying rumours about the battle at Narva, the old Hetman replied with a message of vague consolation. Mazeppa had spent his youth in Poland in the days of 'the Deluge' and he had a healthy respect for Swedish arms; at the same time he shared the poor opinion of most Cossacks as to the worth of Peter's 'new model' regiments.

In the summer of 1702 the capture of Warsaw and Cracow made Charles XII master of Poland, and the 'French party' of Stanislas Leszczyński rallied to the support of the Swedes.

Events in Poland necessarily reacted on the whole situation in the Ukraine, and the covetous interest of Ivan Mazeppa was at once attracted to those provinces on the right bank of the Dniepr which had reverted to the Polish crown as a result of the Treaties of Andrusovo and Karlowitz.

The Treaty of Karlowitz had restored to Poland Podolia with Kamenets-Podolsk, and the first care of the Polish *szlachta* had been to restore 'law and order' in right-bank Ukraine. A simple Cossack, Samus, had been appointed Hetman of the right bank, but a certain Colonel Paley, who enjoyed a greater influence among the Cossacks, constituted himself the leader of the peasants in their opposition to the return of the Polish landlords and continued to send messages to Baturin urging Mazeppa to take advantage of the unpopularity of Polish rule and of the weakness of the garrisons in the country. The subordination of Poland, however, to Peter's larger plans excluded any intervention in the dominions of King Augustus.

In 1699 the *Seym* proceeded to abolish all Cossack privileges in the Polish Ukraine, and even the 'loyalist' Samus joined Paley in open revolt. The Polish Cossacks declared themselves subjects of Tsar Peter and Mazeppa, and the Muscovite resident in Warsaw sent despatches to the Chancellor Golovin urging that it was of the greatest importance to persuade Mazeppa to refrain from giving aid to Paley.

At the beginning of 1703 the Tsar indited a stern letter to

Mazeppa ordering him to post patrols and not to allow any help to cross the Dniepr; he was to influence the rebels also 'to desist from their vile plans'. Peter also sent a special emissary to Paley and Samus urging them to help their King against the Swedes.

But the Tsar was far away on the Baltic shore and Mazeppa began to play an intricate game.

During the year 1703 Polish troops under the command of Adam Seniawski came into the Ukraine to put down the rising. Paley, who had established himself in Belaya Tserkov, offered a stubborn resistance. The situation was complicated by the fact that Paley was not only in contact with Mazeppa but also with the Crown Hetman Lubomirski, who was head of the faction supporting Stanislas Leszczyński against King Augustus, the ally of the Tsar. Mazeppa must have been well aware of the dangerous character of the chain of personalities which was beginning to connect him with the policies of Charles XII, for he had numerous agents in Poland—amongst them a mysterious 'Princess Dolski'. The muddle became further complicated by the intrigues of Seniawski's wife, who had connections with the Lubomirski faction; and by the appearance of Patkul, who arrived on an abortive mission to persuade Paley to make his peace with Augustus.

At this time, as a modern Ukrainian historian (M. Andrusyak) has justly pointed out, Mazeppa's relations with Paley do not afford any indication that the Hetman was already plotting against the Tsar; in fact Mazeppa, who may have seen in Paley a possible future rival for influence on both banks of the Dniepr, was not slow in reporting Paley's relations with Lubomirski to Moscow.

Early in 1704, when Lubomirski was putting himself forward as a candidate for the Polish throne, Mazeppa reminded the Tsar of Paley's close relations with the pretender, and he then received authority to put an end to the rebel, who was still holding Belaya Tserkov.

In April 1704 the old Hetman crossed the Dniepr, warily stalking his game. The Swedes were in Lvov and Augustus had taken refuge in Volhynia, where he was desperately awaiting aid from the Tsar or the Cossack chieftain. Mazeppa's aid was limited, however, to harrying and plundering the estates of any Polish nobles who could be said to be supporters of Leszczyński or of Lubomirski.

At the beginning of August Mazeppa induced Paley to visit him and arranged a feast to celebrate 'their fifteen years' old friendship'. During the night the drunken Paley was seized and taken first to Baturin and later to Moscow. Peter was very pleased at the clever trick of his old henchman. The Hetman had anticipated the imperial wish; Paley had bored the Tsar by 'his stupid obstinacy' and he was packed off to Siberia.

All right-bank Ukraine was now effectively in Mazeppa's hands. During the existing state of war it could scarcely be handed over to the representatives of the fugitive Augustus. As 'Hetman of all Ukraine', Mazeppa returned in triumph to Baturin in October 1704.

He now became involved in his 'old man's love' for Maria Kochubey; a passion which, like the better known affairs of Lassalle, Parnell and Boulanger, really seems to have influenced history—at least to a degree.

The daughter of the chief judge and wealthy landowner Kochubey, Maria appears from all accounts to have been a really lovely girl. The rascally old roué sued for her hand in marriage, but the parents refused their consent—apparently owing to the fact that their other daughter was already married to a nephew of Mazeppa. The romantic Maria, who was already the mistress of the Hetman, then left her paternal roof and took refuge in his palace. The scandal outraged the Orthodox population of the Cossack capital. The despair and shame of the parents that 'such disgrace and dishonour should befall them' knew no bounds; the father ordered the bells of the church to ring as for a funeral. The Hetman himself appears to have feared popular outcry, in particular the wrath of the clergy.

Finally Mazeppa took the contemptible course of turning the girl out of his palace—not without some difficulty. Maria's grief was pitiful. 'Whatever happens, our love can never cease. Let God punish me—and whether thou lovest me or not I will love thee until death.' To judge by the letters which Mazeppa wrote to Maria and which have come down to posterity, the old Hetman was genuinely grieved. His hard old heart ached for his beloved who was being regularly whipped at her father's house. The embarrassment of the Hetman was further increased by the necessity which official duty imposed on him of having to continue to visit the house of the grim and vindictive Kochubeys.

The Kochubey affair marked a turn in the luck of the fantastic old man. His Cossack elders were reported to be openly complaining at the continuance of the war, while Peter's generals—many of them foreigners—with their modern ideas were frequently expressing their contempt for the military qualities of the Cossacks. The rumoured conversion of some Cossack regiments into dragoons shocked and displeased the Hetman and all sections of the Cossack community.

At the beginning of 1706, after the Swedish victory at Fraustadt, the Tsar, who feared a Swedish drive through Volhynia against Kiev, arrived in the city to supervise its fortification. Peter's fear of a Swedish invasion undoubtedly created a strong impression on the Hetman, who shared the general view that the Tsar would never overcome the invincible Swedish King. The visit in no way improved the relations between master and vassal. About this time Mazeppa began to play upon the discontent of the Cossack elders by confirming their suspicions that the Tsar's entourage planned to abolish 'the old Cossack privileges'. He gave currency to rumours that his rival Menshikov, 'Fortune's nameless favourite', was plotting to be made Hetman, and that Peter was offering the whole of the Ukraine as a principality to Marlborough as a reward for securing English mediation with Charles XII.

Actually there was some justification for the Hetman's nervousness, for at the end of the year 1706 the Duke, who had been approached by Peter's Dutch agent Huyssens, promised to meet the Tsar's wishes if a principality in Russia were granted to him, and the Tsar replied by giving him the choice between Kiev, Vladimir and Siberia, besides promising him, in case a peace with Sweden was concluded by his efforts, 50,000 thalers a year, 'a rock ruby such as no European potentate possesses', and the Order of St Andrew in brilliants (*Camb. Mod. Hist.* v, 595).

But the curious intervention of Marlborough in the affairs of Peter took another turn, when in the summer of 1707 he visited Charles XII at the Saxon castle of Altranstädt in order 'to endeavour to penetrate the designs of the King of Sweden'. The great Duke, who was certainly the superior of both the King and the Tsar in diplomacy as in war, satisfied himself that Swedish arms were not about to be turned against Austria, and returned to the Low Countries while Charles made preparations for his fatal Russian campaign.

Peter, during the autumn of 1707, had to contend with a formidable Bashkir rising on the Volga and with the revolt of the Don Cossacks under Kondrati Bulavin 'against the innovations'.

From the beginning of 1707 the Zaporogians had also been showing signs of insubordination. Mazeppa, who had a great nose for his own popularity among the Cossacks, was attentively studying their opinions.

When the news arrived in January 1708 that the Swedish armies were invading Russia, Mazeppa began to utter open doubts concerning 'Moscow's strength'. He gave free rein to his defeatist views and did not refrain from expressing them in the house of his worst enemy Kochubey.

The mind of the old Hetman was so intricate that it is difficult to determine whether at this date he had already entered into treasonable relations with Charles XII or whether he was merely trying to trap Kochubey into denunciations which he would not be able to substantiate. Some of his biographers affirm that at the beginning of 1706 he had already entered into treasonable relations with Charles XII, who was then in Saxony, through the Jesuit Zieliński. This does not seem probable. But the agents of Charles XII were working in Turkey and had penetrated to the Crimea and the Zaporogian *Sech* and it is possible that one or more of them had been in Baturin.

Open to doubt also are the theories of those biographers who affirm that in September 1707 the Hetman was inviting the Swedish King to enter the Ukraine and undertaking at the same time to destroy all the Muscovite garrisons stationed there. During Easter 1770 Mazeppa had been present at Peter's great War Council at Żolkiew, while his favourite nephew Voynarovsky was with Menshikov at Lublin. During the summer and autumn Cossack regiments were with Peter's General Baur in observation on the Lithuanian frontier; 3000 Cossacks were sent to the Volga to put down the Bashkir rising; and at the moment when the Don rebellion was causing serious embarrassment to Peter, support for Bulavin was forthcoming neither from the Hetman nor from the *Sech*. None of these facts confirm the proposition that in September 1707 Mazeppa was in relations with the Swedish King and already plotting treason. (Nordberg, the spiritual adviser and biographer of Charles XII, is cited as authority for the treasonable correspondence of Mazeppa with the King at this time, but he is a biased apologist for the whole of the Ukrainian campaign, the wisdom of which was much criticized in contemporary Sweden.)

All the evidence goes to show that pique, panic, and, above all, the sequel to the ugly feud with Kochubey hustled the ageing Hetman into ill-considered and ill-prepared treason.

In the late autumn of 1707 Kochubey had already made an unsuccessful denunciation of Mazeppa, which was treated as ridiculous by the Tsar, who had in mind the enmity between the two old men on account of Maria Kochubey.

The unfortunate Kochubey, however, not satisfied with his first blunder, hurried to make a second and more fatal one. Spurred on by his wife, and after asking the advice of the Poltava Colonel Iskra, Kochubey decided to send another messenger to Moscow repeating his accusations against the Hetman. This messenger was a certain Poltava schoolmaster—a converted Jew named Yatsenko. When Yatsenko reached Moscow he obtained by some sort of means an interview with the Heir to the Throne. The Tsarevich Alexey told the informer to put down on paper all he had heard from Kochubey. The only part of Yatsenko's accusation which could be taken seriously were Mazeppa's interviews with King Stanislas Leszczyński's intermediary, the Jesuit Zieliński, who was always introduced into the Hetman's presence by his confidant and secretary, the Czech Orlik. The rest was but idle rumour. Yatsenko quoted Kochubey as saying that 'he would tell all when he would stand before the eyes of the Tsar'.

Yatsenko's denunciation was made in January 1708. In February the Cossack Osipov wrote to Prince Dmitri Golitsyn in Kiev that 'Kochubey and Iskra advise your Lordship to tell the Tsar to beware of Mazeppa, who might cause trouble to you and the good town of Kiev'. Kochubey and Iskra had told Osipov that Mazeppa intended passing the Dniepr and joining King Stanislas at Belaya Tserkov, from where he would begin to wage war against the Tsar. Kochubey and Iskra affirmed that 'all the colonels and elders know of the Hetman's intention but keep silent—some because they are devoted to him and others out of fear'.

Tsar Peter now got angry and ordered an investigation to be held by Golovkin and Shafirov. The Hetman himself, having heard of the accusations against him, was clamouring for this investigation which should establish 'his spotless life' and 'thirty-eight years of faithful and unblemished service'. Peter answered graciously, saying that there could be no question about an investigation into the conduct of the Hetman, who 'need have no sorrow or doubts on that score'.

Kochubey, Iskra, Osipov, Colonel Apostol and others who were involved were summoned to head-quarters at Vitebsk, where they duly arrived in April. The Tsar had already left for Petersburg.

During their trial neither Kochubey nor Iskra could produce any proofs. All was vague talk about 'criminal things' having been uttered by Mazeppa. Aware that the Tsar really wanted to find out who was the real author of the plot against 'his faithful Hetman', the investigators ordered first Iskra and then Kochubey to be put to the torture of the knout. Kochubey was weak and old and could not hold out for long; he owned that he knew of no disloyalty on the part of the Hetman and that his accusations had been made under the influence of his anger on account of his daughter. But Kochubey could not own to having had any 'relations with the enemy'—as suspected by Peter—because there had never been any. Torture and questionings continued for a whole month, until at last Golovkin and Shafirov understood that they could extort no further confessions. Kochubey and Iskra were sentenced to death; Yatsenko was set free; Osipov was rewarded and Apostol cleared of all suspicion.

Both Kochubey and Iskra were delivered to Mazeppa. The Hetman ordered their execution on 14 July 1708 in the neighbourhood of Belaya Tserkov; their estates were confiscated and their wives and children sentenced to imprisonment for life.

Thus ended the sad tale of the Kochubeys. Rumour accused Golovkin and Shafirov of having been bribed by Mazeppa. Peter's two satellites were by no means incorruptible and it is possible that the Hetman found a way to give them presents which would have been gratefully accepted. But at least the fearful investigation established that there was no solid evidence for denunciations which seem to have originally been stimulated by old Kochubey's unhappy wife. The usually perspicacious Peter suspected rather that the informers were being used as tools to secure the removal of the Hetman with a view to creating difficulties in the Ukraine at a critical moment of the war. Kochubey paid by a ghastly death for his accusations against the Hetman, but in his agony he avenged himself on his old enemy. Mazeppa now found himself involved in the intricacies woven by the deviousness of his own character. Having kept open too many roads, he could in the final crisis of his life find no road which offered safety. His courage faltered and his judgment failed. He had lost his flair for events as a man loses his sight, and he had lost his confidence in his own luck.

§7. MÁZEPPA AND CHARLES XII: POLTAVA

The legend of the invincibility of Russia derives from the disastrous invasions of Charles XII and of Napoleon. Poltava and Moscow are beacons in history which seem to proclaim the supreme folly of a military advance into the vast spaces of the Eurasian plain. Yet the Polish Kings Stephen Báthory and Vladislav IV, with the inadequate resources of a feudal state, each succeeded where two of the world's greatest commanders ended their careers in disaster; and in modern times, in the War of 1914–18, the Germans secured the effective mastery of great areas of European Russia during a period when they were simultaneously confronted with the combined forces of the Western Powers—and it was the victory of the Allies in the West and no military recovery in Russia which finally imposed the retirement of the German armies.

In the case of both Charles and Napoleon a late start involved the invaders in natural difficulties of transport and supply which could have been avoided if full advantage had been taken of the summer months. The over-confidence of the Swedes and the madly adventurous character of their monarch impelled an advance with wholly inadequate forces; on the other hand, Napoleon attempted to manœuvre unwieldy masses of men over great spaces deficient in communications.

Above all, lack of adequate political preparation characterized the Swedish and French invasions as compared with the sixteenth–seventeenth century Polish campaigns and the modern German. Napoleon's anxiety to conciliate Alexander induced in him always a very cautious policy towards the Poles, and he failed to exploit the Ukrainian possibilities and the Caucasian difficulties in the Russian Empire of that day. Forty years later in the Crimean War the Western Allies also neglected the chances of combining political with military action, although Palmerston showed himself conscious of the chances inherent in promoting Finnish, Polish and Georgian interests, and Omar Pasha—too late in the War—pressed for a strong intervention in Caucasia.

Charles XII was indifferently served by his political agents. His Frenchified Polish ally, King Stanislas Leszczyński, had no adherents of the quality of Jeremy Vishnevetsky or Stanislas Koniecpolski; he relied in his contacts with Mazeppa, with Hordienko (Gordêenko) the Zaporogian *ataman*, and with the Don leader Bulavin, on the correspondence of dubious women of the type of 'Princess Dolski' and on Jesuit and Orthodox Balkan priests.

Delays in Poland during the summer of 1707 deprived Charles of the advantages which might have been gained by attacking Peter during the Bashkir and Don Cossack risings. He had relations with the Ukrainian Hetman as his grandfather had had with Khmelnytsky, but his agents had failed both to estimate the worth of any aid which might be forthcoming from the discontented Cossack elements in the Ukraine and to make clear the issue which confronted the Hetman.

Charles XII crossed the Vistula on New Year's Day 1708 and on 28 January he entered Grodno. 'His plan was, apparently (for even now it is largely guess-work), first, after crossing the Dniepr, to unite with the army-corps of Löwenhaupt, which was advancing from Riga to join him, and then to winter in the fruitful and un-touched Ukraine, whose fortresses were to be held at his disposal by the Cossack Hetman Mazeppa. Simultaneously the Finnish army, under Lybecker, with the help of the fleet, was to take St Petersburg and recapture Ingria, while Stanislas, aided by a third Swedish army under Krassow, was to quell all disaffection in Poland. In the summer of 1709, the three Swedish armies, reinforced by the Poles, the Cossacks and the Crimean Tartars, were to attack Muscovy from the north, south and east simultaneously and crush Peter between them. The realization of such a scheme, which absolutely disregarded difficulties, and was to build upon nothing but the most fantastic hypotheses, lay far beyond the bounds of possibility' (Nisbet Bain, *Camb. Mod. Hist.* v, 697–8).

On 4 July 1708 Charles defeated the Russians at Holowczyn (Golovchino) and, marching through White Russia, reached the upper course of the Dniepr. The King stayed at Mohilev till 6 August, waiting for the arrival of Löwenhaupt. The Tsar's head-quarters were at Smolensk.

'The Swedes now began to suffer severely, bread and fodder running short, and the soldiers subsisting almost entirely on captured bullocks. The Russians, under Sheremetiev and Menshikov, would not risk another general engagement, but slowly retired before the invaders, destroying everything in their path, till at last the Swedes had nothing but a charred wilderness beneath their feet and a horizon of burning villages before their eyes.'

By the time the Muscovite frontier was reached at Michanovichi (1 October) 'it was plain to Charles that he could go no further eastward through the devastated land'. At Tatarsk he held his first council of war. His generals advised him to wait for the reinforce-ments and supplies which were expected with Löwenhaupt and then to retire to Livonia, where he might winter in his own lands. But Charles, relying on the legendary abundance of supplies in the Ukraine and the expected adherence of Mazeppa to his cause, took the fatal decision of marching south instead of north.

Meanwhile the executions of Kochubey and Iskra had not pro-cured any peace for the troubled soul of Mazeppa and on the Cossack elders they had produced an awful impression: all who disliked Mazeppa were indignant with the whole proceeding, and they understood well that the Hetman would not for a moment hesitate to sacrifice any of his old comrades in order to curry favour with the Tsar and to prove his loyalty to him.

Mazeppa himself was becoming increasingly uneasy at the dangerous game which he was playing. His agents were in the Swedish camp making facile promises of revolt, while his colonels still continued to consider him the Tsar's obedient servant. He was conscious of the thought that any day his ill-considered intrigues might be betrayed, and at the same time he could not convince him-self that the Swedes, on entering the Ukraine, might not be wel-comed by a spontaneous revolt which would sweep the unpopular Hetman away had he not already declared himself in favour of the invaders.

The defeat of Sheremetiev at Golovchino seems to have decided Mazeppa to show his hand. He began to compromise others and confided his intended treason to Colonels Apostol, Horlenko and Lomikovsky (who commanded the Cossack artillery). He knew these men to be opponents of Peter's régime and was aware that they had been slighted by the Tsar's generals during different campaigns. They all swore an oath to participate in the plot and to join the Swedish King.

Later Mazeppa's Czech secretary Orlik gave some details concerning the clauses of a secret agreement concluded between 'the King of the Swedes, Goths and Vandals' and the Hetman of the Ukraine. Orlik pretends that according to the terms of this agreement the Ukraine was to become an independent state with Ivan Mazeppa as its legitimate ruler. That such an agreement would have been signed by Charles XII before his arrival in the Ukraine and before Mazeppa had committed himself is unlikely. It is probable rather that Mazeppa and Orlik showed the draft of an agreement to the conspiratorial elders in order to convince them of the reality of their dreams.

At the beginning of September Charles XII appeared on the borders of the Ukraine. Each day was now precious to Mazeppa, since Peter expected him to take immediate action against the Swedes. The Hetman had promised to deliver the fortified town of Starodub, but this first treason did not succeed, for the Swedish General Lagerkron was late and Muscovite reinforcements arrived before the town had time to surrender.

On 29–30 September the army of Löwenhaupt, advancing to a junction with the King, was severely mauled in the sanguinary battle of Lesnaya. Löwenhaupt, however, managed to join the King, and in the first weeks of October the exhausted Swedes, emerging from the Severian forest, advanced into the northern districts of Ukraine, where they secured some provision for both horses and men.

But the promised Cossack rising was not forthcoming. At the same time Mazeppa was evading Peter's order to start on campaign with the excuse that he was ill.

In the middle of October Peter decided to go to the Ukraine to take over personal command of the army there. Protasiev was sent by the Tsar to Borzna to visit the ailing Hetman, whom he discovered to be 'seriously ill', in fact 'at death's door'; he had already asked the Kievan metropolitan to come to him in order to administer the Holy Sacrament.

Protasiev had not long departed before the sudden arrival of Voynarovsky, his favourite nephew, frightened the Hetman into taking an irrevocable step. The Muscovite cavalry under Menshikov had been reconnoitring in the region between Starodub and Chernigov, impatiently awaiting the arrival of the Hetman with his Cossacks. When instead Voynarovsky had come with the message that his uncle 'was dying' Menshikov had refused to believe it, and from conversations overheard among Menshikov's staff Voynarovsky understood that the Tsar's favourite was planning to march on Baturin and Borzna and force the Hetman's hand. Voynarovsky had had to take flight by night in order to warn his uncle.

'The dying Hetman' immediately ordered his horses and galloped off to Baturin. During the night the old man and his secretary packed all they could take away from the palace. (Mazeppa had already taken the precaution of transferring part of his money and valuables to Belaya Tserkov.)

At daybreak on 4 November the Hetman, at the head of his troops, rode off to join the Swedish King, leaving Colonel Chechel and the Serdyuky Guard to defend Baturin against the Russians. On the north bank of the Desna Mazeppa ordered his Cossacks to form a circle and made a speech. Until that moment the Cossack ranks had been under the impression that the Hetman was leading them to fight the Swedes. But Mazeppa now tried to persuade them that if they did not immediately join Charles XII the latter would, after his inevitable victory over the Tsar, deliver the whole of the Ukraine to the Polish King. The Hetman's words roused no enthusiasm among the ranks. About 5000 crossed the Desna with him, but less than half that number followed him further.

This trifling aid was a great disappointment to the Swedes. However, still hoping for better things in the future, Charles received the Hetman with all the honours due to his rank in the little Severian town of Horki on the Desna. The learned *Dux militum Zaporoviensium* addressed the King in his famous church Latin; and out of respect for his age the monarch bowed low before his visitor and offered him a seat while he himself remained standing.

When he heard from Menshikov of the Hetman's treason Peter wrote to Apraksin: 'Though it is quite against my principles to answer your good tidings with bad ones, necessity obliges me to tell you what the Judas Mazeppa has done. For twenty-one years he has been faithful to me and now on the brink of the grave he has turned traitor to me and his people.'

Exactly a week after Mazeppa had joined the Swedes Menshikov attacked Baturin and took it by storm. One of the Hetman's officers came to the Muscovites and showed them the easiest way into the town. The fall of the place was followed by a fearful slaughter of the Hetman's pampered Serdyuky Guard. Menshikov's soldiery did not even spare the peaceful inhabitants. Mazeppa's palace was plundered and burnt, and the unfortunate commandant Chechel was put to the wheel.

Such were the first not very pleasant consequences of the Hetman's fatal action. Peter now with his usual energy began to combat the repercussions which the treason of their chieftain might have amongst the Ukrainian population. The Hetman's unpopularity among the people made that object easy to attain. The Tsar, in a solemn proclamation, annulled all the taxes introduced by Mazeppa. 'The ex-Hetman in his low cunning laid heavy taxes on the people without our knowledge, pretending they went for the needs of the army, but in reality they only served to augment his riches.' The Tsar also tried to calm the fears of the Cossack elders which had been aroused by Mazeppa's excuse for his treachery—that the Moscow Government intended to abolish all the rights and privileges of the Ukraine.

It was still November when Peter assembled the *Rada* in Glukhov for the election of a new Hetman. The first candidate was Colonel Polubotok, an excellent soldier. Peter, however, declined his candidature, remarking not without humour: 'Oh, he is too witty for me; he might turn out a second Mazeppa.' The modest and loyal Starodub colonel, Skoropadsky, was elected. The ceremony was made the occasion for the reading of a message from the Tsar to the Cossacks in which he confirmed 'all liberties, rights and privileges granted by his august father which it was his holy duty to keep unchanged and indestructible'.

Peter's wise and vigorous policy brought the expected results; assurances of loyalty flowed in from all sides. Even the closest participators in Mazeppa's conspiracy, Colonels Apostol and Halahan, sued for pardon.

Mazeppa was left with about a score of elders and fifteen hundred Cossacks—many of whom were not even Ukrainians. His game seemed lost. He still rested hopes, however, on help from the Zaporogians and the Crimean Tartars; and it was these hopes which encouraged the Swedish army to move more to the south. In the beginning of 1709 Charles' troops occupied Romen, Hadyach, Priluka and Lubni in the region of Poltava.

Peter was concentrating important forces in the neighbourhood of Sumy and Kharkov. On the right bank of the Dniepr Golitsyn occupied Belaya Tserkov, so that all the treasure which Mazeppa had carefully transported there was lost.

The Great Frost of 1708-9, the most severe which Europe had known for a century, imposed terrible hardship upon the Swedes. Peter was waiting for the spring to finish with the invaders. In

February he spent some time in Voronezh and from there went to Azov.

The frost broke at the end of February, and the spring floods put an end to all active operations between the main armies for some months. But spring had unexpectedly brought with it new hopes for Mazeppa and the King.

Peter, after the election of the new Hetman, had concentrated his diplomacy on keeping the Zaporogian *Sech* in subordination. He had sent a message to the *ataman* Hordienko with a gift of 500 *chervontzy* for himself, 2000 for distribution among the elders and 1200 for the ranks. At the same time Mazeppa was pressing the *ataman*, an irreconcilable opponent of Muscovite *voyevodes*, to come over to the King.

About New Year's Day of 1709 Hordienko sent a sort of ultimatum to the Russian command demanding the evacuation and destruction of the Moscovites' forts in the *Sech* country, the banishment of all Russian and Ukrainian landlords, and the distribution of their lands 'among the people'. Aware of the intimate links between the Zaporogians and the peasant class throughout the Ukraine, Hordienko was playing for a peasant rising in which he might appear as the leader of the revolutionary mass and play for high stakes between the Tsar and the King. The social basis of his policy made him a far more formidable antagonist than the wealthy and disreputable old Hetman.

Hordienko's demands were of course ignored by the Russian authorities and he took the field with 6000 Zaporogians. Menshikov sent small detachments along the river Orel and along the line of the Vorskla. But Hordienko defeated the Tsar's dragoons at Tsvichanka and took Perevolochna on the Dniepr. The peasants began to rise in the neighbourhood of Poltava and Mirgorod. Fifteen thousand of them joined Hordienko, but the Zaporogians had no arms to distribute to them. In April Hordienko met Mazeppa's small detachment at Dikanka, the family seat of the Kochubeys. There followed the meeting with Charles XII at Budishchi, where the Zaporogian *ataman* was able to rival the Hetman in addressing the monarch in Latin.

In the beginning of May the King despatched the two Cossack leaders to open the investment of Poltava, which he proposed to capture and hold pending the arrival of the Swedish corps under Krassow which was with King Stanislas in Volhynia. The advance of a Russian detachment under General Renne threatened the Zaporogians, but a reinforcement of 3000 Swedish infantry under General Kruze enabled Hordienko to defeat Renne at Sokolno.

In the meantime Peter had decided upon the destruction of 'the accursed nest', as he called the *Sech*. During May Colonel Yakovlev was sent in ships down the Dniepr, while the 'pardoned' Chigirin Colonel Halahan followed along the right bank. Yakovlev retook Perevolochna, and with Halahan occupied the *Sech*, where only 1000 Zaporogians had been left in garrison. The historic stronghold which had played such a formidable role in the southerly expansion of the Eastern Slavs was destroyed to its very foundations; not only all the *kurenyi* but even the *Sech* Church of Our Lady's Protection were burned by the Tsar's soldiers (who, however, proved sufficiently pious to see to the prior removal of all the icons). The destruction of the *Sech* was a great blow to the followers of Hordienko.

With the beginning of June the contending armies concentrated in the region of Poltava and it became evident that a decisive action was imminent. Peter preferred to avoid pitched battle with 'the invincible Swede', but the extremity of the garrison of Poltava compelled him to take the initiative. The news that Charles had been wounded in the foot encouraged Peter to accept battle if it were offered. Such was the confidence of the Swedes, even after the incredible hardship of the preceding eighteen months, in their reputation and their leadership that, with a serious inferiority both in infantry and guns, they did not hesitate to attack the Russians in an entrenched position. The battle opened at dawn on 27 June 1709. By 9 a.m. all hope of victory for the Swedes had gone. Hordienko's Cossacks played no part in the bitter contest which the Swedes put up before they accepted defeat. The Zaporogians simply left the field and scattered all over the country. Mazeppa, Orlik, Voynarovsky, and the inevitable following of Ukrainian ladies, were among the foremost fugitives. The old Hetman succeeded only in rescuing two barrels of gold coin from the wreck of his magnificence.

The remains of the Swedish army capitulated at Perevolochna on the left bank of the Dniepr. A sad fate befell the Zaporogians, who were not included in the terms of Löwenhaupt's capitulation. Those who were not drowned in trying to swim the river were butchered at the order of the Tsar.

The wounded King and Mazeppa, with Hordienko in their suite, took refuge across the Bug in Turkish territory. At the beginning of August they reached the small Moldavian town of Tighin (Bendery) on the right bank of the Dniestr; here they were interned on orders from Istanbul.

Misfortune had greatly aged Mazeppa and Orlik had become the leader of the small band of Ukrainian refugees; their position was a dangerous one, for the Russian ambassador to the Porte was demanding their delivery, and to secure it Peter had written a letter in his own hand to the Grand Vizier which was accompanied by a substantial sum in gold. However, on Swedish intercession and also on instructions from Versailles, the French ambassador, the Marquis de Ferrioles, took up the defence of the wretched Hetman.

Soon the illness and death of Mazeppa delivered the Porte from further anxieties. He died on 2 October 1709 and was buried in the Orthodox Church of Tighin; but later the coffin with his remains was transported to the monastery of St George at Galatz.

A year earlier in Glukhov 'the state burial' of Ivan Mazeppa had taken place. With his love of macabre horseplay the Tsar himself was the author of this uncanny ceremony, which was called 'Mazeppa's speeding to Hell'. An effigy representing the dead traitor wearing full Hetman's dress and all the orders which he had received during his life was hung from a gallows. The hangman pulled down the effigy and dragged it into the cathedral, where Theophan Prokopovich, the former eulogist of Mazeppa's classical learning and taste in architecture, pronounced a curse. Menshikov and Golovkin then tore up all the Tsar's letters which had been addressed to the Hetman and ripped the decorations from the effigy. Clergy and choir, clad in black garments with black candles in their hands, intoned curses and spluttered black wax over it. Finally, Theophan Prokopovich hit the Hetman's effigy with his episcopal staff and pronounced 'anathema'. The effigy was then again hung on the gallows and afterwards burnt. 'Anathema' on Mazeppa, False Dmitri and Stenka Razin, all of whom had attempted to shake the foundations of the Muscovite state, continued to be proclaimed every year in all the churches of the Russian Empire. (8)

BIBLIOGRAPHICAL NOTES AND ADDITIONS
TO CHAPTER IV

Sources and General Bibliography for the Period of the Hetmans

A great mass of original documents concerning this period is preserved in the Russian Archives; notably the *Archives concerning Little Russia*. Originally Ukrainian affairs came under the control of the *Posolski Prikaz*—the Muscovite Foreign Office; later they were transferred to a special *Malorusski Prikaz* or Little Russian Office; and finally, at the beginning of the eighteenth century, the Little Russian Collegium was set up, and to the offices of this body were transferred all documents and archives concerning the Ukraine.

The most important papers were edited by D. Bantysh-Kamenski and were published in 1858 under the title of *Istochniki Malorossiyskoy Istorii* (Sources for the History of Little Russia). Valuable materials have also been published in *Arkhiv Yugo-Zapadnoy Rossii* (Archives of South-Western

Russia), a periodical edited in Kiev from 1860 onwards by the well-known Ukrainian historian and political leader, Professor Antonovich.

Ukrainian chronicles concerning events at the end of the seventeenth and the beginning of the eighteenth centuries contain much original material on the history of the country. Of these the most important is 'The Eye-Witness's Chronicle'; the author, Roman Rakushko, was a contemporary and participator in the events of the Khmelnytsky period. His Chronicle was edited in Kiev in 1878 under the title *Letopis Samovidtsa po novootkrytym spiskam* (Eye-Witness's Chronicle according to Recently Discovered Texts). Two other chroniclers, Velichko and Hrabyanka, wrote during the eighteenth century of the events of the epic period of Ukrainian history of which they themselves were not contemporary: S. Velichko, *Letopis Sobytiy* (Chronicle of Events), 3 vols. Kiev, 1855; *Letopis Grabyanki* (Hrabyanka's Chronicle), Kiev, 1854.

Based on these chronicles, an early history of Little Russia was written towards the end of the eighteenth century, but it only appeared in print in the middle of the nineteenth century. *Istoria Russov ili Maloy Rossii* (History of the Rus or of Little Russia), Moscow, 1846, was ascribed to Yuri Konisski, Archbishop of White Russia, but it is now generally attributed to Gregory Poletika, a Ukrainian political figure of the days of Catherine II. To the same category belongs General Riegelmann's *Letopisnoe Povestvovanie o Maloy Rossii i eya narode i kazakakh voobshche, sostavlennoe v 1786–1795* (Chronological History of Little Russia and her People and the Cossacks in general, composed in 1786–1795), 4 vols. Moscow, 1847.

In addition to the standard works mentioned in the Bibliography to Chapter III, the following biographical works are of value for the history of the Hetman period:

Antonovich, V. *Istoricheskie Deyateli Yugo-Zapadnoy Rossii* (Historical Figures of South-Western Russia).

Kostomarov, N. *Sobranie Sochineniy* (Collected Works): vol. II, *Getmanstvo Vigovskago* (*Vyhovsky Hetman*); vols. IX–XI, *Bogdan Khmelnitski*, Petersburg, 1903–4.

The following works should also be consulted:

Vovk Karachevski, V. *Borba Polshi s Kazachestvom vo vtoroy polovine XVII i nachale XVIII veka* (Poland's Struggle with the Cossacks in the second half of the seventeenth century and the beginning of the eighteenth century).

Doroshenko, D. *Narys Istoriyi Ukrayiny* (Outline of the History of the Ukraine), vol. II, Warsaw, 1933.

(1) *The Agreement of 1654 and the Actual Position in the Ukraine during Khmelnytsky's Lifetime*

One of the most valuable works on this subject is Baron Nolde's critical essay: *L'Ukraine sous le Protectorat Russe*, Paris, 1915 (a Ukrainian translation has been published in Lvov). See also D. Odinets, *Prisoedinenie Ukrainy k Moskovskomu Gosudarstvu* (The Union of Ukraine with the Muscovite State), Paris, 1938.

An old but authoritative analysis of the Agreement is to be found in G. Karpov's 'Peregovory o Prisoedinenii Malorossii k Velikoy Rossii' (Pourparlers on the Union of Little Russia with Great Russia), published in *Zhurnal Ministerstva Narodnago Prosveshcheniya* (Journal of the Ministry of Public Instruction), no. 11, 1871. According to Karpov, only a copy of the draft of the Agreement has been preserved in the Moscow Archives. When, in 1709, Peter I asked for the original, it could not be found.

For an appreciation of the actual social conditions existing in the Ukraine at the time of the Union, Myakotin's book is of great importance: V. Myakotin, *Ocherki Sotsialnoy Istorii Ukrainy v XVII–XVIII veke* (Essays on the Social History of the Ukraine in the Seventeenth and Eighteenth Centuries), 3 vols. Prague, 1924–6.

(2) *The Population of the Ukraine at the Time of the Union*

During the Cossack campaigns of 1648–53 Volhynia was terribly devastated. The Polish register of the year 1657 gives a detailed account. The town of Kremenets was entirely destroyed and not a soul was left alive in the scores of villages which lay in the surrounding countryside. The estates of the Vishnevetsky princes seem to have suffered most: in the borough of Monachin and twenty-two surrounding villages only six houses were left standing; in the town of Zbarazh and its thirty-five villages only nineteen houses remained, and in twenty-two other villages not even an empty house was left. In the town of Vladimir-Volynsk, 'rich and flourishing before', only two houses remained standing in 1657. In another formerly prosperous Volhynian town, Lutsk, only fourteen houses were left: 'the inhabitants had either fled or died of the plague'. The greatest part in this work of destruction was played by the Tartars, but the Cossacks and the Polish soldiery also ravaged wide stretches of country. The Jewish population was either slaughtered or fled to Galicia and Poland. The Tartars did not take the Jews prisoners but slew them on the spot. Only 10 per cent of the Jewish population of Volhynia, Podolia and the Ukraine survived. The Russian population suffered most in Podolia in the region of Bratslav; less in other parts of right-bank Ukraine.

As a result of these calamities there was a great increase of population on the left bank. In 1654 about 128,000 men were brought to swear allegiance to the Tsar's commissioners: this number represented apparently between one-third and one-half of the total grown male population. In the last years of Khmelnytsky's life the population of that part of the Ukraine which was under his rule numbered about a million and a half.

A curious feature of the Hetman's Ukraine was the unusual number of 'towns' for the period: in the district of the Bratslav regiment, 20; in that of the Nezhin regiment, 16; in that of the Poltava regiment, 15. There was one town to every three or four villages. But every strong place in which there was a fort surrounded by a wall and moat was called a 'town' (*gorod*). In the agitated period of the seventeenth century the inhabitants preferred these 'towns' to defenceless villages. In this wise and for similar reasons the old tradition of Kievan Rus was renewed in the Ukraine; in the twelfth century

the inhabitants of the Pereyaslavl, Chernigov and Kiev lands had had a distinct preference for living in towns.
See M. Vladimirski-Budanov, *Peredvizhenie Yuzhno-Russkago Naseleniya v epokhu Bogdana Khmelnitskago* (Migration of the South-Russian Population in the time of Bogdan Khmelnitsky), Kiev, 1888.

(3) *The Ambassadors of Tsar Alexey Mikhailovich in Warsaw in 1658*

The ambassadors sent to Warsaw, and at first very graciously entertained by King John Casimir, complain in curious terms about the Poles to Tsar Alexey Mikhailovich: 'In Warsaw the Poles often whisper in each others' ears; they also wink at us and make fun of us. When we are walking round the town or sitting in taverns, their soldiers make such a noise with their swords that we are often terrified. The whole countryside, they say, swarms with troops, and little Polish drunkards among each other speak of our Cossacks as belonging to them and they say that Smolensk will soon be theirs. As for our dignity as ambassadors no one gives it a thought, and they have also forgotten all about Thy Polish inheritance, My Lord. When we try and discourse with them about it, they answer us with grins and by clicking their heels together. And O My Lord, if truth be said, we are simply the Polish laughing stock.'

(4) *The Title of Hetman in the Hadyach Agreement*

'Russian Hetman and First Senator of the Voyevodes' Districts of Kiev, Bratslav, and Chernigov.'

(5) *The End of Yuri Khmelnytsky*

Colonel Samko defeated Yuri Khmelnytsky in July 1662. Among the latter's troops were Don Cossacks and a thousand German mercenaries. Yuri fled to his friend the Archimandrite Tukelsky and, after resigning the Hetmanship in favour of Colonel Teterya, became a monk. When King John Casimir embarked on his campaign on the Dniepr, Yuri went to him. The King proposed to make him Metropolitan, but Yuri wanted to be Hetman again. Tukelsky became Metropolitan instead of him. Together with Tukelsky Yuri was arrested by Czarniecki in 1664, and sent to the fortress of Marienburg. After two years' imprisonment, they were set at liberty through the intercession of Peter Doroshenko. During his residence in the Moshnin monastery Yuri received information about the relations existing between Doroshenko and the Turks. When the Poles again wanted to arrest Yuri and his friend Tukelsky, they took refuge with Doroshenko. At the end of the year 1667, the Muscovite envoy with Doroshenko, going to church, found that the officiating priest was none other than Yuri Khmelnytsky, who was now known as the Archimandrite Gideon. However, when Doroshenko's position became insecure, Yuri Khmelnytsky joined Khanenko. Khanenko was defeated by Sirko and some Tartar friends of Sirko's took Yuri to the Turkish fort at Akkerman. Doroshenko, who did not desire the return of Yuri to Ukraine, asked the Pasha to send him to Istanbul. This was done, and Archimandrite Gideon was incarcerated in the

castle of the Seven Towers, where he remained until 1677, when he was set
free and taken by sea to the Crimea.

(6) *Ataman Sirko*

Unreasoning and brave, Sirko was chaotic in all his actions throughout all
his life. He is the most fantastic of all the fantastic figures in the Zaporogian
Sech. Indifferent to booty, lucre and honours, Sirko was the very pattern
of the wild Zaporogian chivalry. However, owing to his childish imagination and trusting disposition he was quite incapable of understanding the
tortuous men and difficult circumstances of his time. There is an episode
which well illustrates the simplicity of the Zaporogian hero. One day a
young man appeared in the *Sech* who had been brought there by Don Cossacks. This young man gave himself out to be 'the Tsarevich Simeon', the
son of Tsar Alexey Mikhailovich, who, on account of some dark plot, had
been banished to the Solovetski monastery, whence he had managed to
escape. Sirko tried to persuade the impostor 'not to fool the Zaporogians'
but in the end believed his tale. In 1674 envoys came from Moscow to demand the delivery of 'the Tsarevich'. Sirko called the *Rada* together and
persuaded the Zaporogians not to surrender their guest. The Zaporogians
agreed and nearly drowned the Muscovite envoys. On second thoughts,
however, Sirko asked the Muscovites to procure him a 'writing' from the
Tsar himself to tell him whether Simeon was his son or not. Tsar Alexey had
the graciousness to send him such a writing. Simeon was then sent off to
Moscow, where he was executed.

There are many legends about *ataman* Sirko. In the spring of 1675, with
20,000 Zaporogians, he undertook his celebrated campaign to the Crimea.
Having defeated the Tartars and taken Baghchi-Saray and Ak-Mechet
(Simferopol), the Zaporogians were returning home with about 7000
liberated captives who had lived for years among the Muslims. Sirko
noticed that by no means all of them were delighted to return to the
Ukraine; many of them had married Tartar women and had really settled
down to the Muslim way of life. Sirko decided to give a lesson to those
'who go over so easily not only to the Moscow people and the Poles but
even to the enemies of the Christian Faith'. Having reached a place called
the Black Valley he ordered his men to halt and declared to the liberated
captives that he did not want to force anyone to go to the Ukraine and that
those who wished to do so could return to the Crimea. About 3000 of them
took him at his word and formed into a column to return to the south.
Sirko sent young Cossacks after them with the order to slaughter them all.
Later, looking round on all the heaps of corpses, he observed: 'Pardon me,
brothers, but it is better for you to sleep here until the Day of Judgment than
to settle in the Crimea and beget children and be damned to all eternity.'

Though the most bitter enemy of the Tartars, Sirko was respected by them
for his fairness. During periods of armistice, these children of the steppe often
asked him to act as an arbiter in their own quarrels. Hetman Samoylovich
rebuked him once for allowing the Tartar herds to graze over the Cossack
pastures. Sirko replied: 'Lord Hetman, if myself would help people in their
dire need, it is not well to look down on that. There is a saying that need

changes law. We and the Tartars are neighbours and help each other in a neighbourly way.' Legend ascribes to Sirko 'the answer to the Sultan's letter'. In his letter, according to the tradition, Sultan Muhammad IV called himself the Vice-Regent of God upon Earth, the King of Kings and so forth. Sirko is reputed to have begun his answer with the words: 'Thou art nought but the Turkish Shaitan, brother and comrade of the accursed Satan, Lucifer's own secretary.'

(7) The Disgrace of Hetman Samoylovich

All the property of the disgraced Hetman was confiscated to the Muscovite Exchequer. A touching love affair was taking place during the downfall of Samoylovich. His daughter was engaged to young Prince Chetvertinsky. 'For three years the young people hid in the village of Dunaytsy. A local tradition shows the deep wooded valley where they took shelter. Having fallen in love with a brilliant young woman, the Hetman's daughter, the fiancé did not desert her when events deprived her of rank, riches and even decent clothing. He was able to marry her only in 1690' (N. Markovich).

(8) Mazeppa

Hetman Ivan Mazeppa has not yet found a critical and unbiased biographer. Even in the nineteenth century Russian historians were inhibited from objective study by the fact that Mazeppa was considered as 'one of the greatest criminals against the State' and by the continuing anathema of the Church. This background influenced such works as, for instance, N. Kostomarov's Mazeppa i Mazeppintzy (Mazeppa and the Mazeppans), Petersburg, 1885.

On the other hand the idealization of Mazeppa by the Ukrainian nationalists as a hero who pursued a far-sighted policy against the Muscovite hegemony in the Ukraine is equally unscientific. As a sample of this school see E. Borshak and R. Martel, Vie de Mazeppa, Paris, 1931.

The Kiev professors of the latter half of the nineteenth century, as for instance Antonovich, formed a more objective view of Mazeppa as an adventurer in the grand manner who would stop at nothing to attain rank, pomp and wealth. The 'treason' of Mazeppa against Tsar Peter was almost accidental, and doubtless no great moral issue disturbed the mind of the old Hetman who, it must be remembered, had spent his youth at the Polish court where no sanctity surrounded the office of monarch, and where 'treason' was indistinguishable from faction. Like old Simon Lovat in the '45, Mazeppa at the end of his life was the victim of his own calculating brain, and his love of intrigue and combinations led him into a position from which he found it impossible to escape.

For Mazeppa's relations with Colonel Paley, see M. Andrusyak, Mazeppa i Pravoberezhye (Mazeppa and the Right Bank), Lvov, 1938.

The same author has written an essay in which he establishes that, until 1705, Mazeppa had never thought of going over to Charles XII. (See M. Andrusyak, 'Zavyazky Mazepy z Stanislavom Leshchinskim i Karlom XII', in Zapysky Naukovoho Tov. Shevchenki (The Relations of Mazeppa with Stanislas Leszczyński and Charles XII, in Proceedings of the Shevchenko

Scientific Society), vol. CLII, Lvov, 1933). See also for this period: J. Feldman, *Polska w Dobie Wielkiej Wojny Północnej* (Poland in the Great Northern War), Cracow, 1926; *Trudy Imp. Russkago Voenno-Istoricheskago Obshchestva*; *Pisma i Bumagi Petra Velikago*; *Dokumenty Velikoy Severnoy Voyny, Poltavski Period* (Works of the Imperial Russian Society for Military History, Papers and Letters of Peter the Great, Documents of the Great Northern War, Poltava Period), vols. III–VI, Petersburg, 1893–1907. See also Swedish biographies of Charles XII by Frixell and others and the series of memoirs in *Karolinska Krigares Dagböcker*, Lund.

Mazeppa has acquired a wide celebrity in international literature through Passek's Memoirs and Voltaire's *Histoire de Charles XII*. These works were the origin of Byron's poem and of Horace Vernet's well-known picture. Chaykovski also dedicated one of his operas to Mazeppa. The hero of the great Russian poet Pushkin, in his poem *Poltava*, is not Mazeppa but Peter the Great. Pushkin, in relating the tragic fate of Kochubey, represents Mazeppa as he really was: a man of violent passions who knew how to hide not so much his thoughts as his feelings. Pushkin rightly guessed the motive which led the old Hetman to his ruin: the fear, which tortured him, that, in remaining loyal to Tsar Peter, he might be supporting the losing side.

Some letters have been preserved which are considered to be Mazeppa's letters to Maria Kochubey. These letters are supposed to have been found in Kochubey's house after his arrest and to have been produced during the trial. It is related that Count Golovkin returned these letters to the Hetman with assurances that he had not shown them to anyone and that he had not had them copied: but he had in fact had copies taken. Even if these letters may be regarded as genuine they give no clue to the character of their author. Their theme is love, forced parting, the sufferings of lovers, and indignation against Maria's parents. The promises never to forget Maria are accompanied by explanations as to why the Hetman could not keep her in his house. Some of the later letters speak of 'the change in Maria's heart' and of the Hetman's grief on account of it. But it is possible that the melancholy lines of the old reprobate were only the considered epilogue to a love affair which was too perilous and which had lasted too long. Before Maria and after Maria, Ivan Mazeppa continued to be surrounded by 'Ukrainian ladies'.

For the comparative history of Eastern and South-Eastern Europe during the period of the Hetmans, the relevant volumes of von Hammer's and Jorga's great Histories of the Ottoman Empire have been consulted. The former, though over a century old, is based largely on original Turkish, Venetian, Dutch and Austrian sources, and contains a mass of material not otherwise available. The more modern and more critical work of Jorga is the best general history for South-Eastern Europe. Reference has also been made to the following excellent surveys in the *Cambridge Modern History*, vol. V: Prof. R. Lodge, chap. XII, 'Austria, Poland and Turkey'; chap. XVII, R. Nisbet Bain, 'Peter the Great and His Pupils'; chap. XIX, *idem*, 'Charles XII and the Great Northern War'.

The *Revue du Sud-Est Européen*, published in Bucarest by Professor Jorga, contains a number of papers covering this period, notably: vol. X, nos. 1–3, M. Kasterska-Sergescu, 'L'expédition de Sobieski en Moldavie en 1686';

vol. x, nos. 7–9, N. Jorga, 'Sobieski et les Roumains'; vol. xiii, nos. 7–9, O. Halecki, 'Relations Polono-Roumaines'.

A valuable article by the Ukrainian writer E. Borshak in the *Slavonic Review*, vol. x, no. 28, p. 138, surveys the 'Relations of England and the Ukraine' from the visit of Yuri Nemirich to the Universities of Oxford and Cambridge to the correspondence of Orlik and later Ukrainian leaders with English statesmen and private individuals. The writer gives numerous details about the mysterious Scotsman 'Krivonos' ('Broken-Nose') who was prominent in the immediate entourage of Khmelnytsky and who was believed by many to have been an agent of the Commonwealth Government.

CHAPTER V

THE UKRAINIAN LAND WITHIN THE
RUSSIAN EMPIRE (1709–1914)

§1. AFTERMATH OF POLTAVA:
HETMAN SKOROPADSKY

POLTAVA marked the end of the epic period of Ukrainian history. But like most great events it was the symbol of change rather than the cause of it.

The gallant and fantastic world of Eastern Europe in the seventeenth century was passing. The splendid Polish camps which had held the field against Cossacks, Tartars and Kalmucks; the half-Arabian, half-Byzantine panoply of the Turkish Sultans hunting and campaigning over all the lands between the Adriatic and the Caspian; the Zaporogian pirates; Transylvanian Princes, Crim Khans, Roumanian Hospodars and Georgian Kings were becoming spectres in the dim past with the Mongols, the Byzantines, the Pechenegs and the Kipchaks.

Even Charles XII, commander of the most efficient army in contemporary Europe, had in him some streak of the archaic; he pitted himself against realities which he did not comprehend and he went down. Peter the Great, Frederick the Great, were successful because they expressed the spirit of an age in which war was ceasing to be the finest blood sport and was manifesting itself the instrument of that blind automatism of natural forces which was to take form in the national state. The Age of Enlightenment as interpreted by the successors of Peter the Great cast its artificial and rather macabre glimmer on the century which saw modern forms of capitalist society burgeon over the steppes of Eastern Europe. While the tribes of Indian hunters withered before the prairie fire of new civilization in the Americas, mining camps and oil towns rose up in the Caucasian Mountains and industrial cities came to life in the swamps and creeks of the Zaporogians. The untamed savagery of the Eurasian soul which had pillaged with the Horde and slaughtered with Khmelnytsky and Razin was canalized in the gutters and alleys of a new synthetic life.

No roots of culture nor of hierarchic ways, no inhibitions of religion nor of settled ordered life tempered the raw nomad mass which was swept into the mechanism of the capitalistic epoch. The modern spiritual nomadism—the patternless mass psychology—of the population of the Communist state is the logical expression of this transformation of primitive humanity by the ruthless processes of economic determinism. So at the other end of the world, the Mexican *peon*—one of a mass uprooted from its primal culture—stumbles and grunts in the arc-light of modernity.

When the Polish *szlachta*, numerous and sturdy, and the imperious Hungarian magnates failed to resist the impact of the new states which were taking form in Europe, the inexperienced and parvenu class of Cossack colonels was doomed to extinction by the Moscow autocracy.

The absence of a governing class in the Ukraine, with traditions and usages hallowed by time and possessing also a certain culture of its own, was one of the reasons why the experiment of a more or less independent Ukraine could not succeed. V. Antonovich, the distinguished Kiev historian of the second half of the nineteenth century, though a sincere Ukrainian patriot, did not have any illusions as to the Hetman period, and his judgment of the situation after Khmelnytsky's death is worth recalling: 'The downtrodden peasant masses had shaken off the yoke but they did not know what to do with what had fallen into their hands.... When politically undeveloped masses become conscious of their power they put forward those who favour their instincts.' After Khmelnytsky, in the view of Antonovich, the Hetmans of the Ukraine were either shameless demagogues or clever adventurers; each type was guided by personal or venal interests.

Against the background of the naïve rascality and impetuous incompetent ambition of the local leaders it is easy to understand the preponderant part played by the Tsar's officials, particularly in a Ukraine which at the turn of the century had been exhausted by two decades of Turkish wars. The Muscovite official was the product of a bureaucratic system which was already old and tried and which dated back to the days of the first Ivans; something indeed of the Byzantine tradition had given it a hoary fibrous strength.

The Muscovite officials now came into the Ukraine as the intendants and organizers of a vast new royal domain, and while there was little of the haphazard enterprise of the nobles and Jewish middlemen of the Polish colonization there loomed behind the imperial administration the executants and profiteers of Peter's policy —the Menshikovs and Golovkins and Shafirovs greedy for lands and mills.

Mazeppa's successor, the Starodub Colonel Skoropadsky, had the reputation of being an honourable man but of no special account, entirely under the influence of his wife 'Nastya'. All the same he was

Hetman, and on the occasion of his election Tsar Peter had promised that it would be 'his holy duty to keep unchanged and unaltered all rights and privileges granted to Russia Minor'. However, at the Glukhov *Rada* (November 1708) the clauses of the Agreement of 1654 had not been read aloud as was customary on the election of a new Hetman. A few months later Skoropadsky had thought it his duty to remind the Tsar to confirm the clauses of the Agreement which from the time of Khmelnytsky had been looked upon as a sort of Ukrainian constitution. Golovkin had answered that His Imperial Majesty had already 'confirmed in general' the existing order in the Ukraine, and that as for the confirmation of the detailed Agreement of 1654, this 'would be given to the Hetman later when circumstances allowed'.

Soon after the Chancellor's ominous reply a confidential emissary of the Tsar, an official named Izmaylov, was attached to Skoropadsky with instructions to see that 'quiet and law and order should reign in Little Russia through the suppression of all agitators and rebels'. The Hetman was warned that he was not to dismiss Cossack elders without the Tsar's order and that their election must have the Tsar's approval. Peter continued to distrust the Ukrainians in the highest degree. Mazeppa's treason had made an indelible impression on his mind. And it was not only Mazeppa: the Hetmans Vyhovsky, Yuri Khmelnytsky and Bryukhovetsky had all proved traitors; and Mnohohrishny and Samoylovich had been removed from their posts on account of accusations of treason. 'Treason had become a sort of political tradition for Hetmans' (Nolde).

Throughout the winter of 1708–9, in the town of Lebedin, the commission investigating the affairs of Mazeppa and Hordienko continued its grizzly work. Trials, tortures and executions were the order of the day. According to local tradition about 900 persons are buried in the cemetery of Lebedin who were done to death on suspicion of having been connected with Mazeppa.

At the end of 1709 Mazeppa was no longer among the living, but Peter was extremely irritated by the presence in Turkey of the dead Hetman's secretary, the Czech Philip Orlik, and the Zaporogian *ataman* Hordienko. During May 1710 the rumour spread that the group of Ukrainian refugees in Tighin had elected Philip Orlik as their 'lawful Hetman'.

The remnants of the Zaporogians who had followed Hordienko were meantime seeking pardon through the intervention of Hetman Skoropadsky, but the news that thousands of Ukrainians were being transported to the north for work on the construction of the new capital of Petersburg or for the digging of the Ladoga Canal scared these doughty sons of freedom into migrating to the Crimea, where they became the subjects of the Khan. (1)

In March 1711 a war broke out between Russia and Turkey which had been promoted partly by the able intrigues of Charles XII in his internment at Tighin and which was inspired also by the desire of Peter to repeat on the shores of the Black Sea the triumphs which he had already gained on the Baltic.

On the outbreak of war the Crimean Tartars began to raid into the Ukraine. Hordienko put himself at the head of the Zaporogians who had settled in the Crimea and 'Hetman' Orlik also joined them.

At first the population of right-bank Ukraine received the invaders with sympathy and Uman and Korsun were captured. The Russian garrison of Belaya Tserkov, however, put up a stout resistance and the depredations of the Tartar bands soon cooled the enthusiasm of the malcontent peasantry.

The humiliating defeat of Peter on the Pruth in 1711 might have been the occasion for an attempt to revert to the days of Doroshenko had the Cossacks possessed a leader of mark or had sentiment adverse to the Muscovites retained any real strength.

As it was, the Peace of the Pruth reversed the results of Karlowitz as between Russia and Turkey: Azov was restored to the Porte and Peter's new fortress of Taganrog was dismantled, while Turkish suzerainty over the no-man's-land of the lower Dniepr was re-established. Peter's titanic effort to open the 'meridial' way 'from the Varangians to the Greeks', begun with such signal success in the north, had proved abortive. When in the following decade he diverted his enterprise from the Black Sea to the Caspian he met with little better luck: in fact, the Russian drive to the south-east was delayed for half a century by the disaster of the Pruth; the historical results were important, for when at the turn of the eighteenth and into the nineteenth century Russian armies began to appear on the Danube the new world-power of Britain (which first became concerned in Black Sea and East Mediterranean politics during the Napoleonic Wars) barred the way to the neo-Byzantine dreams of the Panslavists and to the rival (continental) capitalism which aspired to straddle the Varangian Way.

There is an element of pathos in the epilogue of the legendary Zaporogians—so long the scourge of Islam—now fallen to the condition of unwanted clients of the Crimean Khan. The Khan settled them at Aleshki at the mouth of the Dniepr opposite modern Kherson and they began to complain of all sorts of oppressions. The adherents of Hordienko were losing ground and there was a general desire 'to return to the Tsar'. The Russian Government would not have them; nor would it have been possible to accord them asylum without violating the terms of the recent Treaty of the Pruth. About 1500 Cossacks were leading a wretched life at Aleshki; the rest had gradually disappeared into the steppe.

In the meantime 'Hetman' Orlik, with Mazeppa's nephew Voynarovsky and several Ukrainian refugees were in Istanbul. Two of these refugees, Colonels Horlenko and Lomikovsky, who had been among the first to participate in Mazeppa's conspiracy, decided to return to the Ukraine. They received a pardon, although they were ordered to live under police surveillance in Moscow. Orlik, later, went to Sweden, where he continued to be treated as 'Hetman' and was accorded a pension. Voynarovsky was made a colonel in a regiment of Swedish Guards. However, his old friendship with Aurora Königsmarck, the favourite of Augustus the Strong and the mother of Maurice of Saxe, proved fatal to this able and bold adventurer. He met her in Hamburg in 1716 and gave credence to her promises of pardon made on Peter's behalf. Relying on Peter's magnanimity he went to Petersburg, where he was thrown into prison and subsequently exiled to Siberia. Orlik ended his days more agreeably; after the death of his patron, Charles XII, he settled down in France. (2)

In the Ukraine, after the Pruth campaign, Hetman Skoropadsky was trying to consolidate his position and to give no cause for displeasure to his formidable and exacting monarch. After Izmaylov another resident appeared in the person of Protasiev. Skoropadsky decided to win the good graces of these confidential agents of the Tsar by making them grants of Ukrainian lands, but he did not do so without the prior knowledge of his master. There were still enough free lands left in the Ukraine for this purpose; the properties which had been confiscated from Mazeppa and his adherents formed a large fund. At the time of the Hetman's election, Prince Dolgoruki, the Tsar's representative, received lands; and, a little later, Golovkin and Shafirov. The next year Field-Marshal Prince Sheremetiev also applied to Skoropadsky for lands. Following this distinguished example, a whole series of officials petitioned for lands, and some of these petitions, like for instance that of General von Weisbach, were accompanied by threats that in case of refusal application would be made direct to the Tsar.

In this sense a particular and insatiable greed was shown by Menshikov. Already in 1709 the Hetman had hastened to present him with Yampol near Nezhin and Pochep in the district of the Starodub regiment. In this latter estate alone 'his Serene Highness' came into possession of over one hundred and fifty villages. That did not suffice: by 1721 he had rounded off his properties in such a manner that he was lord of six thousand peasant farms. Menshikov availed himself in an original manner of the tracing of the new frontier with Poland—which passed in the vicinity of some of his domains. For the first time in their lives the village folk were shown an awful instrument called 'Astrolabia', and when the needle pointed straight at their lands this supernatural phenomenon awakened in them such awe that they no longer had the courage to raise complaints. Menshikov also wanted to be lord of Baturin, but here he met with the Tsar's refusal. 'The Duke of Izhora' had to wait for the reign of Catherine I before he got all he wanted; this however happened, as such things often do, just before his banishment to Berezov in the gloomy north of distant Siberia.

Under Skoropadsky private landowning developed rapidly. After the Muscovite officials appeared other more humble suppliants for free lands—Serbs and Wallachs who had been obliged to quit Turkey as a result of the failure of their insurrections at the time of the Pruth campaign. Cossack elders whom Skoropadsky thought useful and those individuals who, like Polubotok and Halahan, enjoyed the Tsar's favour, also profited. (Polubotok, by the way, was generously compensated for his failure to become Hetman.)

As the number of important landowners grew, the smaller landowners became progressively impoverished. Some of the poorer Cossacks were no longer able to appear fully equipped each with his horse for military service. They became peasants, and mostly no longer free peasants but dependent upon some newly established big landowner.

The Ukraine was passing through hard times. The years of war or military occupation, with the accompanying requisitions, whether Swedish or Muscovite, had depressed and discouraged the cultivator. New forms of service which began to weigh on them filled the people with resentment. Whole regiments were despatched to the Caucasus or to the shores of the Caspian, where they were decimated by fever. In 1725, 12,000 Cossacks with three colonels were simply sent to work on the Ladoga Canal. Only 10,000 returned to their native homesteads. But if Peter treated the privileged Cossacks so brusquely, the common peasantry were used with even less consideration. Owing to his manifold and varied activities the Tsar was always in need of workers: on the building of the capital and of the Ladoga Canal, on the abortive project of a Don-Volga Canal, and on the erection of fortified lines in Finland and the Northern Caucasus. According to the estimates of Ukrainian historians, between the years 1720 and 1725 over 20,000 men died while employed on these works.(1)

Tsar Peter continued to treat Skoropadsky graciously, and received him with all honours due to his rank when he visited Moscow in the years 1718 and 1722. At the same time he was planning a complete change in the system of government in the Ukraine. During the year 1722 the 'Little Russian Collegium' was set up, composed of Major-General Veliaminov and six other officers. The functions of the Collegium were to assist the Hetman in 'looking into procedure and investigating fairly all cases'; to control the collection of all taxes destined for the imperial Exchequer; and to supervise the activities of the Hetman's Chancellery. All Little Russian affairs were transferred from the Foreign Office to the Senate.

In July 1722 Skoropadsky died, and the Tsar, on the excuse that he was preoccupied with his Persian campaign, deferred the election of a new Hetman. In the following year Polubotok was rash enough to sponsor a petition for the election of a Hetman in accordance with the terms of the Agreement of 1654. He begged for the intercession of the Empress Catherine. Peter's answer put an end to illusions if anyone still had any. The Tsar wrote on 23 May 1723: 'Taking into consideration that except for the first Hetman Bogdan Khmelnytsky and the late Hetman Skoropadsky, all Hetmans were traitors and did great harm to our realm, especially to Little Russia where Mazeppa is still well remembered, and taking into consideration also that a perfectly reliable and honest man must be found to be elected Hetman and that a firm government is needed now so that affairs should not come to a standstill, I do not think it fit to trouble me any more with this question.'

Meanwhile, relations between Polubotok and the Cossack elders on the one side and the members of the Collegium on the other were rapidly deteriorating. Major-General Veliaminov was a rough man well known for his bad temper. During the sittings of the Collegium he used to shout at Polubotok: 'What are thy services compared to mine? Thou art simply a nobody compared to me!' He used to say to the Cossack elders: 'I will curb you so that you will feel it in your bones. The order is already given to change your old usages and to treat you quite in a new way!'

Having received notice of these dissensions, Peter made Polubotok and others of the Cossack elders come to Petersburg. They appealed there to the Emperor, to the Empress, to Chancellor Golovkin and to the Senate. It all ended for them in the fortress of Peter and Paul. Colonels Apostol and Miloradovich, who had formerly been respected by Peter, joined them there. After a year's incarceration some had died and Polubotok himself fell seriously ill. Peter in his way was fond of his old Cossack, and according to tradition he sent his own physician to the fortress. When Polubotok refused these offices, the Tsar went himself and promised to forget the past. Polubotok, knowing anyhow that his days were numbered, assured the Tsar that he bore him no ill-will. The old man exclaimed: 'Soon Peter and Paul will stand on the same board before the Almighty!' Paul Polubotok was not mistaken, for Tsar Peter only outlived him by a few months.

§2. UKRAINE IN THE MIDDLE OF THE EIGHTEENTH CENTURY: HETMAN RAZUMOVSKI

Catherine I, Peter's widow, once a Lettish peasant girl, and the all-powerful Menshikov, whose servant she had been when the Tsar's fancy fell upon her, now ruled Russia.

The Ukrainian prisoners in the fortress of Peter and Paul were set at liberty. It was their luck that 'the half-sovereign potentate' had his own account to settle with the Little Russian Collegium.

The Supreme Privy Council founded by Catherine I was inclining towards the restoration of the Hetmanship at the beginning of 1726. After Catherine's death and the downfall of Menshikov it was accomplished by an *Ukaz* of the boy Tsar Peter II in June 1727. On this occasion one of the highest officials of the Imperial Government, Naumov, was appointed 'Minister Resident with the Hetman', and Ukrainian affairs were transferred back from the Senate to the Foreign Office.

In October 1727 Naumov arrived in Glukhov. The *Rada* (including, in the words of Naumov, 'all those who wished to come') elected as Hetman the Mirgorod Colonel Daniel Apostol. Although the colonel, who was a greatly respected man nearly seventy years of age, appears to have been 'indicated to me by Your Majesty', his election found popular approval. His son Peter, a remarkably well-educated young man, received the Lubni regiment, and the son of the unfortunate Kochubey, married to a daughter of Apostol, the regiment of Poltava.

According to ancient custom 'the rights and privileges' of the Cossacks were confirmed during the ceremony of installation, although, as Baron Nolde points out, the significant phrase that 'His Majesty graciously permits a Hetman in Little Russia' was introduced.

It was probably the influence of the conservative Prince Ivan Dolgoruki which induced a return to the 'old order' in the Ukraine; but a change from the policy of Peter I had already been envisaged under Catherine I and Menshikov. The necessity of conciliating the Cossack leaders and maintaining peace in the Ukraine was imposed by the prospect of war with the Turks and new changes in Poland. Furthermore, the internal situation in Russia following the death of Peter the Great was exceedingly precarious. 'Three women, a boy of twelve, a babe of one and an idiot' were successively elevated to the imperial throne in the course of twenty years. Power was centred in 'the barrack capital of St Petersburg, situated outside Russian soil and cut off from the life of the Russian people'. Adventurous groups made up of foreign officers, aristocrats and officials, dependent on the uncertain tenure of the passing occupant of the throne and on their popularity with the Guards regiments, were in control of the machinery of government. In the first year of Catherine I even Menshikov discovered that the peasants' burdens were intolerable and that 'they were simply dying out'. Under the German favourites of the Empress Anne it was alleged that 'the people were treated like dogs'. 'In this reign great storms swept over Russia; vast famines, particularly that of 1733 when the peasants came in crowds to beg in the towns, were followed by widespread epidemics; great fires broke out. Meanwhile the country was traversed by punitive columns trying in vain to levy the enormous arrears of impossibly heavy taxes.... Peasant elders were knouted and peasant farmers were sold up wholesale' (Pares, *History*).

With the accession to the throne of Anne, Duchess of Kurland (the daughter of Peter I's sickly elder brother Ivan), in 1730 began the heyday of the German Balts who flocked to the un-Russian capital on the Neva. But with all their greed and ambition, favourites like Osterman and Münnich were not without great quality. Under the influence of Münnich, sense and foresight were shown in the organization of the frontiers of the Empire. In all those regions like the Ukraine, the northern Caucasus and the Orenburg Steppe where no natural boundaries existed the system of fortified lines and Cossack settlements was developed; and particularly on the Caucasian and Asiatic frontiers the value of the Cossack in mobile defence was realized.

The restoration of the Hetmanship in the person of Daniel Apostol had filled with joy the remnant of the Zaporogians who lingered on at Aleshki as clients of the Khan. When Hordienko, an old man now, appeared among the Zaporogians in order to persuade them to continue on their lands, they put him in chains; and setting fire to their settlement, they went back to their former homes on the islets of the Dniepr. Thus the so-called 'New Sech' came into existence.

In 1731 General von Weisbach took in hand the project of Peter I of building a fortified line between the rivers Dniepr and Donets (along the line of the affluents Samara and Orel). The Zaporogians received a friendly message from the General that 'their services would soon be needed', and in 1734 General Tarakanov arrived in the 'New Sech' with presents.

While the military favourites of the Empress Anne thus continued their leisurely preparations for a resumption of the struggle between Russia and the Ottoman Empire, events in Poland again provided the occasion.

After the defeat of Peter on the Pruth, the Turks had continued to control all the belt of territory along the Black Sea littoral, and with the retrocession of Azov the Russians had been deprived of their only access to southern waters. At the same time all right-bank Ukraine had remained under the feeble domination of the Polish King Augustus the Strong, and, as in the time of Mazeppa, it was not possible for the Russians to make encroachments in this direction without sacrificing the advantages which the friendship of Augustus afforded them in the north.

The policy of the Imperial Government in regard to the Ukrainian lands which remained under Poland had been confined to encouraging a migration from the right to the left bank of the Dniepr. But this policy met with scant success, for the fate of the Cossacks and peasants in Russian territory who had been sent off to labour on the shores of the Baltic and in the northern Caucasus had filled the population of the left bank with horror. Compared to forced labour the service of Polish landlords appeared preferable; and those who in preceding years had migrated to the east of the Dniepr began to seek means of 'going back to their native land'. A movement of the agrarian population from east to west set in and the previously deserted districts of Chigirin, Uman and Bratslav began to receive a numerous immigration. The Polish landowners, returning after the Great Northern War to the fertile lands situated between the Dniepr, the Bug and the Dniestr, were in need of workers and offered the peasants all sorts of inducements to come back. As they had to deal with illiterate people, the Poles put up boards with holes in them on their estates, the number of holes indicating the number of years during which peasants could settle and live on the estates without having any liability towards the landlord. This was done to impress the mind of the Ukrainian land labourer who had gone through so many changes and who had lost the habit of thinking of the future. When a privileged year passed a hole was filled up, and when all the holes were filled up the settler became the serf of the landowner. It might have been supposed that he could foresee this eventuality when he settled on the landowners' property, but he looked upon it as the greatest injustice to himself. After fifteen or twenty years of comparatively free and easy life in right-bank Ukraine many of these 'silent' agreements came to an end, and peasant discontent began to mount.

The so-called War of the Polish Succession which broke out on the death of Augustus the Strong when Stanislas Leszczyński, with French support, opposed the elevation, at the instance of Petersburg and Vienna, of another Saxon King to the Polish throne, was the occasion of widespread peasant risings throughout the lands to the west of the Dniepr.

In support of the new Saxon Augustus III, the Empress Anne sent troops into Poland under the command of the Irishman Lacy—one of those 'Wild Geese' who were so plentiful at her eccentric court. At the same time about 20,000 Cossacks, under the command of Colonels Lizohub and Halahan, rode through right-bank Ukraine and into Volhynia in order to give help to the adherents of 'the lawful King'.

The rival Polish factions distributed arms to their peasants, who proceeded to burn and plunder 'enemy' estates. The appearance of Russian troops accompanied by the Hetman's Cossacks and the Zaporogians was understood by the peasants to signify that 'the Tsaritsa has sent troops to rid us of lords and Jews'. The destruction of towns and manors was undertaken with a joyous hand, whether they happened to belong to the adherents of Stanislas Leszczyński or of Augustus III—the ally of the Empress.

Bands of armed peasants, *Haydamaky*, roamed about the country. The Polish gentry and the Jewish population of the towns fled in terror—especially in the neighbourhood of Bratslav and in the eastern parts of Podolia. Peasant risings spread further into Volhynia and Galicia. When at last Stanislas Leszczyński gave up the struggle and went abroad, Russian forces had to undertake the repression of the *Haydamaky*—many of whom fled for refuge to the 'New Sech'.(3)

The Crim Tartars had helped Leszczyński or had been expected to come to his assistance, and in 1735 the Russians had sent 'a punitive expedition' to the Crimea which had met with no success.

The conclusion of the War of the Polish Succession provided the ideal occasion for the attack on Turkey which the comprehensive military preparations in the Ukraine during the preceding years had foreseen. The close co-operation of Austria in Polish affairs was extended to South-Eastern Europe; while the recent victories which Nadir Kuli Khan had gained over the Turks in Armenia and Iraq seemed to indicate that their armies were in poor condition and that they would fall an easy prey to the combination of Germanic and Muscovite power.

It was natural that a strong régime in Petersburg should resume the struggle where Peter had failed—to re-establish the 'meridial line' from the Baltic to the Black Sea and the economic independence of the fluvial network of the Great Eurasian Plain.

The Turkish fortresses at the mouths of the Great Russian rivers and the Tartar stronghold in the Crimea stopped the main arteries of trade, and Turkish sea-power on the Black Sea was the arbiter of the economic life of South Russia. 'The Crimea at this time was very rich. The Steppes poured the inexhaustible wealth of their flocks and herds into it, and the trade between the peninsula and Turkey was enormous. Kozloff, the chief port on its western side, exported 200,000 head of cattle and an incalculable quantity of grain to Stambul every year, while the still more prosperous Caffa on the east coast was, perhaps, the largest slave-mart in the world.'

During the spring and summer of 1736 Marshal Münnich forced the lines of Perekop and took the Tartar capital of Baghchi-Saray, while Lacy, after a hard siege, compelled the surrender of Perekop. In the following year the Turkish fortress of Ochakov—the situation of which dominated the embouchures of both the Dniepr and the Bug—fell to the Scots General Keith; and in the campaign of 1738 the Russians invaded Moldavia.

But the terrible losses suffered by the Russians, more by disease than in battle, and the continued determination of the Turks, who had effectively repelled the Austrian invasion of the western Balkans, had wearied the Petersburg court of the war. French mediation secured the Peace of Constantinople, whereby Russia agreed to sacrifice all her conquests except Azov and the surrounding district, while the fortress of Azov itself was to be dismantled. 'On this occasion the Porte was induced to change the old title "Muscovy" into "Russia", but refused to concede the imperial title to the Russian Empress.' The recovery of the fortress on the stagnant Azov Sea which the Don Cossacks had offered to Alexey Mikhailovich a hundred years before was all that the Russians secured from this costly war—while the Turks still remained masters of the mouths of the South Russian rivers.

The ascendancy of Anne's German favourites had reversed the sympathetic policy towards the class of Cossack colonels which had been favoured by the Russian aristocrats, like the Dolgorukis and Golitsyns, who surrounded the boy Tsar, Peter II. The overbearing Münnich, at the height of his Crimean triumph, had actually solicited the Empress to make him 'Duke of Little Russia'. 'The Field-Marshal is far too modest,' the Empress had replied, 'I thought he would ask me for Moscow.' Even before the death of Apostol in the middle thirties, Prince Shakhovskoy had been sent to Glukhov 'to watch the conduct of the Little Russian people severely and incessantly'. These suspicions were already of a pathological order, since there were no signs of any sort of opposition to the imperial rule in Little Russia. The Cossack regiments were performing their military service with regularity and loyalty; the peasants were working on the Ukrainian Line without any of the murmurings which had accompanied their former transference to works outside their own land; and the colonels were only interested in enlarging their estates.

On the occasion of the death of Daniel Apostol, the Empress's advisers decided that it would be preferable not to appoint a successor 'under the circumstances', and the Little Russian Collegium was revived in the form of a Directory, to be known officially as 'The Hetman's Board of Government', consisting of three Little Russians and three Great Russians under the presidency of Prince Shakhovskoy. The Directory was placed under the authority of the Senate, thus again removing the affairs of the Ukraine from the sphere of the Foreign Office. At the same time Shakhovskoy was warned that he should act in such a way as 'not to awaken any suspicions among the people or give pretext for undesirable talk'. As it was, the 'temporary' absence of a Hetman passed more or less unnoticed, since the six members of the Board happened to be rather peacefully inclined people who desired to avoid all unpleasantness (they included General Keith, 1740–1).

In 1740 social relations in the Ukraine differed widely from those at the beginning of the eighteenth century. 'A general Survey' of Little Russian lands was carried out under the authority of Shakhovskoy in 1729–30. Documents concerning eight regimental districts out of ten on the left bank of the Dniepr have been preserved. The number of peasant farms amounted to about 56,000. Out of that number about 20,000 were in the full ownership of Cossack troopers or peasants. About 10,000 were situated on lands belonging to monasteries or towns. The remaining 26,000 formed part of lands belonging to landowners or temporarily allotted to colonels and judges by reason of their office. Thus, in 1730, only 35 per cent of small farms were the property of those who worked them; the rest belonged either to landlords, monasteries or towns. Seventy years before, after the rising of Bohdan Khmelnytsky, at least 90 per cent of Cossacks and peasants in the Ukraine had regarded themselves as absolute masters of their farms, and their most prominent chiefs had not dared accept grants from the Tsar which might intrude upon the ownership of the rank and file.

The fatal character of the tendencies which were dispossessing smallholders of their farms is seen when the figures of 1752 are compared with those of 1730. In 1752 the number of independent owners of farms had fallen from 20,000 to 3000; another 3000 Cossack troopers owned their own houses but not the adjoining farms. These figures date from ten years before the beginning of the reign of the Empress Catherine II, to whom popular tradition attributes the abolition of independent peasant proprietorship in the Ukraine. Catherine II merely legalized conditions which had been working during a whole century and which were due, not to the policy of the Imperial Government, but to the natural economic processes and human factors which tend to favour a landowning as opposed to a landworking class.

The military weight of the Cossack regiments was seriously affected. Myakotin estimates that, although regiments and companies continued to exist in the Ukraine as administrative Divisions, the number of Cossacks ready for military service in terms of the original obligations of free Cossacks had been reduced to about 15,000 by the year 1730. It is clear that Tsar Peter was aware of the ultimate effects on Cossack military strength of the changes which were taking place in the Ukraine. By an *Ukaz* of 16 April 1723 the Little Russian Collegium was instructed to give satisfaction to all petitions of 'Ukrainian inhabitants' who desired to resume the status of Cossack and who could prove that they or their fathers or grandfathers had served as Cossacks. The violent differences between the Hetman and Veliaminov undoubtedly had their origin in the efforts of the Major-General to frustrate the land greed of the Cossack notables. Polubotok succumbed in this struggle with Veliaminov, who had the support of the Tsar. However, 'neither the disappearance of Polubotok nor that of the prominent colonels who were with him nor the removal from office of numbers of elders and even captains ordered by Peter could weaken the stubborn opposition of Ukrainian landlords to the *Ukaz* of the 16th of April 1723' (Myakotin). The Cossack upper ranks proved faithful to the tradition of their class which they had inherited from Bohdan Khmelnytsky, Vyhovsky, Samoylovich and Mazeppa.

The weight of social tendencies combined with the fact that the development of the technique of war in the eighteenth century was diminishing the value of the Cossacks as a military instrument in European warfare, to weaken the interest of the Government in the maintenance of the Cossack system in the Ukraine. Where masses of ill-disciplined horsemen had served in the days of Romodanovski and Sobieski, Münnich employed armies trained on the German model and dressed in German uniforms even against the Crim Tartars and the Turks on the Dniestr. There was still a use for the Cossacks on the Caucasian Line against the Circassians and the Chechens or in the Orenburg Steppe against the Kirghiz. And bold spirits preferred to depart to the Asian outposts which continued to know no landlords. The Ukrainian Cossacks under the Empresses Elizabeth and Catherine II came to be looked upon as a picturesque element in the life of the South of Russia and, accordingly, they were given by the capricious Elizabeth 'a picturesque Hetman'.

The son of a simple Cossack of the Chernigov regiment, Alexey Razumovski began life as a shepherd; owing to his fine voice he was taken to sing in the church choir, and his good looks attracted the notice of Peter's daughter Elizabeth—the only real Russian among the Empresses of the eighteenth century. It all ended by Alexey Razumovski becoming a count and a field-marshal and the secret but lawful husband of Elizabeth Petrovna. His younger brother Cyril was sent to be educated abroad. The Cossack elders found all these circumstances extremely favourable to their aspirations and they took advantage of Elizabeth's sojourn in Kiev in 1743 to petition for the restoration of the Hetmanship. When Cyril Razumovski reached his twenty-second year in 1750 he was 'elected' Hetman of the Ukraine and held that post for fourteen years. The whole ceremonial of election was revived, and as part of the proceedings the clauses of the Agreement of 1654 were read aloud and confirmed. No one, of course, took this picturesque revival of old customs seriously. Cyril Razumovski was very young, fond of pleasures and court fêtes and had rapidly acquired expensive tastes. In Glukhov, his capital, he was bored to death and he did not miss an occasion when he could escape to Petersburg. He was of a kindly and extremely lazy disposition; affairs of state wearied him and soldiering did not interest him. The Empress presented him with vast estates: Hadyach with its surrounding lands; also Baturin and the district of Pochep which had once belonged to Menshikov. On the domains of the new Hetman were ten thousand peasant farms. However, in this respect he never competed with the records of Mazeppa and Skoropadsky, who had each accumulated between nineteen and twenty thousand peasant farms. Razumovski lavishly distributed lands; in the first place, of course, to his relatives and then to anyone who could gain admittance to him or to a certain Teplov who had been appointed to act as his 'tutor'.

The social processes already mentioned received a powerful impulse in Razumovski's time. All Cossack elders were able to acquire lands, not in temporary possession on account of the offices they filled, but in full proprietorship. A great many lands were also distributed among Russian officials and military men. In 1754, following a report of the Chancellor Bestuzhev, even the open-handed Empress expressed concern: 'The Hetman distributes whole towns and villages in full and hereditary property and the owners of these domains take away the lands of Cossacks who fill official posts. This is why the number of Cossacks diminishes compared with former times.' The Empress gave an order 'to stop such disorder', but no one paid any attention to it. When Catherine II ascended the throne there were scarcely any lands left to distribute in the Ukraine.

The Razumovski period was the happiest time in the Ukraine during the whole of the eighteenth century; it is comparable in many ways to the contemporary Golden Age of the Anglo-Irish gentry who were the beneficiaries of the huge redistributions of Irish lands which followed the Treaty of Limerick.

The landowners were rapidly becoming rich and civilized; they visited Petersburg and sent their children to be educated there. Many of them even sent their children to be educated abroad. When a certain Kulyabko, quartermaster of the Lubni regiment, asked the Hetman to grant him fifty farms, he put forward as a reason that he was sending three of his sons to foreign schools and that the other three were 'studying Latin and German in Kiev'.

In the middle of the eighteenth century the Ukrainian landowning class was acquiring Western ways more rapidly than were their contemporaries in Northern and Central Russia. The Ukraine took pride in the claim that it was the most advanced part of the Russian dominions in the cultivation of the arts. Levitski and Borovikovski, the most celebrated Russian portrait painters of the Age of Catherine, were Ukrainians by birth.

The landowners built country houses and churches. The Kiev cathedral of St Andrew is a remarkable monument of that period. When Razumovski resigned his post of Hetman he went to live in Baturin, where he built himself a *palazzo* in the Classical style to the plans of Catherine's favourite architect Cameron.

The general prosperity of the Razumovski period was not without benefit to the lower classes of the community. There were no wars on the frontiers of the Ukraine; and the Cossacks only took a modest part in the campaigns in Germany against Frederick the Great.

During this time the Zaporogians, not satisfied with their return to their old territory, spread over all the lands which they regarded as having been 'granted' to them by Bohdan Khmelnytsky. The *Sech* founded 'stockades' (*palanky*) on the Bug and the Ingulets to the west of the Dniepr and along the Samara and the Kalmius to the east. The 'possessions' of the Zaporogians stretched from the mouth of the Dniepr to the Azov Sea. Tartar raids had almost entirely ceased and men began to settle in the wild steppe to the north of the Crimea across which Münnich had marched 330 miles without finding human habitations. The Zaporogians, who still offered a refuge to miscellaneous fugitives and were thus increasing in numbers all the time, began to abandon their traditional pursuits of hunting and fishing and to take to stock-raising and even to agriculture. These Zaporogians 'of new formation', who included several scores of thousands of new-comers, began to take measures to protect the lands they claimed from passing into alien hands. Animated disputes with the Don Cossacks began concerning the lands along the river Donets around Lugansk and Bakhmut. In the west the arrival of several thousands of Serbian immigrants who had fled from Turkey was not welcomed. The Russian Government therefore allotted them lands round the fort of St Elizabeth, and these territories became known as New Serbia. The small town which later received the name of Elizavetgrad was destined to become the first centre of 'New Russia'.

§3. CATHERINE II: THE PASSING OF OLD UKRAINE

In 1762 Catherine II, a German princess, ascended the throne as the result of a *coup d'état*. Russia had already played a decisive role in the Seven Years' War and it was Catherine's aim to make her one of the leading powers of the Continent. 'The Empress was beautiful, witty and pleasure-loving; her views on matters of private morality were most free, but she kept unbroken control over her heart and reason, if not over her senses. It was thus easy for her to beguile men, to play them against each other, to lower them while she appeared to raise them to her own level, and to subjugate them by the very magnificence of the favours which she showered upon them' (Sorel). Like Frederick the Great she enjoyed the friendship of Voltaire, and the ideas of the French Encyclopaedists had no little influence upon her singular genius; but she understood the Russian people as perhaps it was only possible for a brilliant and impressionable foreign woman to understand them, and she enhanced a mystical matriarchy by a talent for romantic politics, intrigue and spectacular campaigns. 'It was with the Greek cross in her hand that she summoned her people to the two great enterprises which her predecessors had prepared, the achievement of which constituted in her eyes the historic mission of the Tsars—namely, the conquest of Poland which should open the road towards European civilization, and the conquest of the harbours of the Black Sea which should open the road to that Byzantine Empire whose greatness Holy Russia was summoned to renew, both by popular superstition and by political speculation' (Sorel).

The chief Zaporogian *ataman* Kalnyshevsky, who went to Petersburg to assist at Catherine's coronation, was graciously received by her. This was not the first occasion on which Kalnyshevsky had appeared in the capital. He had been to Petersburg to see Razumovski in 1755 and again in 1759, and each time it was to press those territorial claims of the Zaporogians which so greatly annoyed the Russian Government.

Catherine's attitude towards particularist interests within the Empire was soon made clear in the instructions under her own hand which she addressed to Prince Vyazemski, the General Attorney of the Senate.

'Little Russia, Livland and Finland are provinces possessing special privileges which were granted to them. It would not do to encroach on them or abolish them at once. On the other hand, to look on these provinces as foreign lands would not only be a mistake, but stupidity. They must be dealt with in the same way as Smolensk Province. They must gradually, by the most delicate means, be put into the position of Russian regions so that they cease to be like wolves yearning for the woods. It should not be difficult to achieve this object if only intelligent men are appointed to the head of these provinces. As for Little Russia, when there will be no more a Hetman there, it will be necessary to make her forget the very title of Hetman and the period of the Hetmans. That will be better than constantly observing the persons who fill this post.'

The first step taken in the direction indicated by Catherine was the summons to Petersburg of Cyril Razumovski. His arrival was heralded by that of his faithful Teplov, whose report on the existing state of affairs in the Ukraine did not fail to correspond with the views of the Empress. When Razumovski came to the palace Teplov threw himself into his master's arms; Gregory Orlov, present at the scene, quoted aloud the words of the Gospel—'he betrayed Him by a kiss'. Count Razumovski resigned his post of Hetman—'the last Hetman'. He was granted Hadyach in full ownership, part of the Menshikov estates and Baturin, where he continued to live until his death forty years later.

Little Russia was again transferred from the Foreign Office to the Senate, and governed by a Collegium composed of four local notables and four officials from the north delegated to assist the

Governor-General, whose residence was to be in Kiev. Count Rumyantsev was appointed to this post. He had the reputation of being a severe administrator and an excellent soldier.

The change did not evoke any protests. When in 1767 the Cossack elders and landowners were called upon to elect deputies to sit on a Commission which was to revise the legal code, only the mild complaint of a certain Gregory Poletika was recorded; he demurred at the danger of 'introducing into Little Russia an order which did not correspond to her rights and privileges and of violating thereby the sanctity of agreements' (Nolde). The Glukhov District instructed their deputies to 'ask the Empress to treat us like the rest of the Russian nobility so that we may take up service where we wish and enjoy the full possession of the estates which have been granted to us or which we have acquired.' The Commission was more or less forgotten in the course of the Russo-Turkish War of 1769–74, but after the conclusion of peace the Cossack elders and Little Russian nobles again petitioned Rumyantsev 'to bring their most pressing and vital needs' to the attention of the Empress. These needs were confined to questions of equality of rank and the confirmation of the title of landowners to their estates.

While the ancient 'rights and privileges' of the Ukraine were disappearing under the centralist policy of Catherine, the death of Augustus III, the last Saxon King of Poland, had precipitated the crisis which was to grow into the long agony and partition of the Catholic monarchy. Catherine imposed as King in Warsaw her former favourite, the pliable and rather liberal Stanislas Poniatowski. But in 1768 the exacerbated nobles formed the Confederation of Bar, which sought too late to redeem the country from the tutelage of the Russians.

The programme of the Confederates 'pro religione et libertate' sought amongst other reforms to the taste of the outraged gentry to reverse the concessions to Dissenters (Orthodox and Protestant) which the rulers of Russia and Prussia had lately extracted from the new King of Poland. A war, at once national, social and sectarian, flared up in Galicia, Volhynia and the Ukraine and all the horrors were renewed of the *Haydamak* risings of a quarter of a century before.

The agrarian revolts in the Polish Ukraine had never really ceased from the days of the *Haydamaky*, and recently the mutinous peasantry had found a leader of force and passion in the *Igumen* (Abbot) of the Chigirin Monastery, one Melchisidek Znachko-Yavorsky. In May 1768 a numerous detachment of *Haydamaky* gathered in a deep wooded valley in the neighbourhood of Chigirin, called Kholodny

Yar. Their chief was a Cossack, Maxim Zaliznyak, who had lived in the *Sech* and had spent some time in the monastery of the blood-thirsty Melchisidek. The latter looked upon Maxim as his disciple. In this wild spot the Abbot blessed the coming struggle and distributed to the *Haydamaky* a document 'written in gold letters'. After butchering all Poles and Jews in the region who had not time to escape into the towns and fortified mansions, Zaliznyak moved on Uman, where some 10,000 fugitives had gathered.

Uman was a wealthy town with a numerous population of Jews, Greeks and Armenians. The Basilian monks (Uniates) had a school there where four hundred pupils carried on their studies. The whole town was the property of Count Potocki, who had in his pay a detachment of a thousand Cossacks under the command of Captain Ivan Gonta. The hopes of the fugitives were centred on these Cossacks rather than on the regular Polish garrison, which consisted only of some sixty men with a few old cannon. Gonta actually marched out to meet Zaliznyak but only to join forces with him. The combined forces of the insurgent peasants and the Cossacks took the town by storm and there followed what is still remembered as 'the Uman slaughter'. According to tradition about 18,000 people, refugees and local inhabitants, were put to death. The greater part of the victims were Jews, but there were also members of the Polish nobility among them and all the pupils of the Basilian school.

After the Uman horrors, Zaliznyak was proclaimed 'Hetman' by the *Haydamaky* and Gonta was appointed 'Colonel'. The latter, however, felt that his achievement boded no good and was heard to say: 'We have brewed a strong beverage but I do not know how we are going to drink it.'

The Uman slaughter shocked the Empress Catherine and she did not approve of popular outbursts of emotion such as that represented by the movement of the *Haydamaky*. General Krechetnikov, who was then operating against the Bar Confederates, was ordered to turn his arms against the Orthodox crusaders, which he did in conjunction with the Polish detachments of Stanislas Poniatowski. The rabble, still sating themselves on the spoils of Uman, surrendered after scarcely any resistance and Gonta and others, as Polish subjects, were handed over to the Poles for execution. Zaliznyak escaped— no one knew where. Ukrainian legend holds him to have been a sorcerer who 'could put mist into the vision of the Muscovites'. Reprisals against the Orthodox peasantry, under the protection of the imperial troops, were carried out by the Poles in the region of Lisyanka and Chigirin. The *Haydamak* rising and its terrible end became the theme of many Ukrainian songs. Shevchenko, the great Ukrainian poet of the nineteenth century, wrote a poem about it.

The misdeeds of the *Haydamaky* reacted unfavourably on the Zaporogians, who were becoming increasingly unpopular with the Russian authorities owing to their violence against Russian and Serbian settlers in the territories which they claimed as theirs. The Zaporogian petition of 1767 'for the confirmation of their ancient liberties', for the return of lands occupied by Serbs, Russians and Don Cossacks, and for the transfer of Zaporogian affairs from the Senate to the Foreign Office, was regarded as an intolerable insolence by the Empress, who not unreasonably associated in her mind the peasant insurgents of the right bank of the Dniepr with the turbulent freemen of the Black Sea littoral. Only the outbreak of the Turkish War preserved for a few more years the anarchic liberties of the 'New Sech'.

There was an inevitable and profound connection between the Polish and Turkish Questions. The Germanic and Muscovite powers had a common interest in breaking up and undermining the two state systems which lay between their respective frontiers. Only at the beginning of the twentieth century when the Ottoman power had been finally destroyed by the wars of 1877–8 and 1912–13 did the two major beneficiaries of the process of decomposition come into conflict, and this was when the Slav power threatened the control of the Germanic power over minor Slav peoples. The result was fatal to both Germans and Muscovites.

Western Europe, represented in the eighteenth century by the Bourbon Monarchy, had pursued a policy of intervention—not generally successful—in favour of the states constituting the belt which separated the German powers from Muscovy. French diplomatic influence in Poland had been a tradition since the days of the Valois; in the eighteenth century the defeat of Sweden in the Great Northern War made French military intervention necessary if the 'belt states' were to be maintained. The French military rebuff at Danzig in 1734, when Russian troops under the command of the German Münnich first exchanged shots with the soldiers of a Western state, cast strange shadows before. To support their hazardous diplomacy in Poland the French made use of their political and commercial influence in Istanbul; and the Turks, in the war of 1736–9, on the Black Sea and in the Balkans administered an effective check to both the Austrians and the Muscovites.

Again, in the 'sixties, the French supported the Confederation of Bar and sent officers and munitions to the Poles. Again they used their important influence at Istanbul to exploit the latent conflict of interests between the Turks and the Russians in order to bring the former to the aid of the hard-pressed Poles.

The Russians on their side had been busily and not very effectively pursuing that policy of rousing the religious and social discontents of the Christian peoples of the Balkan peninsula which had first attracted the interest of the court of Alexey Mikhailovich and which had since been pursued without notable success by the advisers of Peter I and the Empress Anne. (The Turks were not behind in conducting a Pan-Islamic and anti-Russian propaganda among the Mussulman tribes of the northern Caucasus and the Tartars of the Volga—a by-road of history which has never been adequately studied.)

In view of the difficulties of the situation in Poland, however, the Russians were not planning for immediate war with Turkey, when, in the autumn of 1768, Sultan Mustafa, irritated by reports of Russian support of insurrection in Montenegro and Bosnia and encouraged by the French Ambassador, suddenly began hostilities—after a manifesto in which he declared that 'Russia had dared to destroy the liberty of Poland'. 'The rhetoric of the chanceries, which had made the Russians the defenders of liberty of conscience, now made the Turks the champions of political freedom' (Sorel).

The cynical Choiseul was of the opinion that 'the rottenness of the Turks in every department might make this trial of strength fatal to them; but that matters little to us provided the object of an immediate explosion be attained'. Frederick the Great in his Memoirs expressed the view that 'this war changed the entire political system of Europe'. 'There were', he felt, 'two alternatives, either to stop the course of Russia's gigantic conquests, or, which was the wiser plan, to endeavour by adroitness to profit by them.'

The Cossacks played only a modest part as auxiliaries of the regular Russian armies which took the field against the Turks; but their knowledge of steppe warfare was useful and made their part conspicuous. In the first year of the war (1769) the Zaporogians were engaged in bitter conflicts with the Crim Tartars who raided their *palanky*. In 1770 the Zaporogians fought gallantly before Ochakov and participated in Rumyantsev's crushing victories over the Turks in Bessarabia (Larga and Kagul).

At the beginning of 1771 a special *Ukaz* of the Empress thanked the Zaporogian troops 'for their gallant actions against the enemy'. The famous light craft, which had made Sahaydachny the scourge of the Black Sea a century and a half before, infested the mouths of the Danube in support of the Russian troops in Moldavia; while in the Azov Sea they were used to take the lines of Perekop in rear.

The soldiers and courtiers who returned to Petersburg from the theatre of war talked a lot about the Zaporogians—their courage, their strange customs and their picturesque apparel. The Zaporogians became the fashion in Petersburg society. Count Panin and Prince Prozorovski registered themselves as Zaporogians; and one of their greatest enthusiasts was Catherine's new favourite, Gregory Potëmkin, the future 'splendid Prince of Tauris'. He also had his name put down on the *Sech* register; was warmly welcomed there and received the nickname of 'Gritsko the Dishevelled'. Potëmkin wrote several times to the chief *ataman* asking for small favours, signed his letters with his Zaporogian nickname and addressed the *ataman* as 'father' (*batko*). All this, of course, was looked upon as a huge joke, but the Zaporogians took it seriously; they were counting very much on Potëmkin's support and were deeply hurt when Gritsko the Dishevelled turned out to be one of the chief agents in the abolition of the *Sech*.

Gregory Potëmkin was a remarkable statesman of outstanding intelligence and character; one of the foremost builders of the Russian Empire of the nineteenth century. He became the first Governor-General of New Russia. All the future of the South of Russia went the way which had been traced for it by Gregory Potëmkin. When, in 1774, the Treaty of Küchük Kainardji crowned the triumph of Catherine's arms, the Crimea, although nominally an independent state, passed virtually under Russian control together with the mastery of the fortresses of Kerch and Yenikale which gave free access from the Azov Sea and the Don basin: Ochakov remained in Turkish hands, but the cession of Kinburn assured the Russian exit from the mouth of the Dniepr. The life of the South of Russia immediately began to flower: new towns were planned; Ekaterinoslav ('Catherine's Glory') on the Dniepr, Kherson near its mouth, and Pavlograd on the land-way to the Crimea.

The Zaporogians considered the building of these towns to be encroachments on 'the *Sech* territory' which they claimed to have been allotted them by Bohdan Khmelnytsky. In 1774, at the close of the Turkish War, new dissensions arose between the Zaporogians and their Russian, Serbian and Don Cossack neighbours, and a Zaporogian deputation visited Petersburg to demand the confirmation of 'the ancient liberties' of the *Sech*. The dangerous Pugachëv rising on the Volga formed a sinister background to the insolence of the Zaporogians and Catherine abandoned all hesitations. In April 1775 she gave the order to Potëmkin to confiscate all the arms of the Zaporogians and to abolish the very existence of the *Sech*. It had in fact become quite impossible to admit the rights of an armed community inside the Empire which did not recognize Russian laws and chose to discuss when it should and should not obey the authority of the Government.

On 4 June 1775, without any warning, a strong force under General Tökölyi (a Hungarian by origin) surrounded the *Sech*. The chief *ataman* Kalnyshevsky was invited to attend upon the General. Later he proceeded to call the *Rada* together—'the last Zaporogian *Rada*'. There was a lot of noise and shouting during that last meeting. The *ataman* was trying to persuade the Zaporogians to offer no resistance, but at first none would listen to him. Some were already placing cannon on the mole and others were distributing muskets when Father Vladimir, the priest of the *Sech* church, made his appearance and began to adjure the Cossacks 'not to spill their brothers' blood and to surrender to the Will of God'. Shouts were heard among the crowd—'To the Danube', 'Back to the Turks'. A certain inclination for the Turks had never completely disappeared from the *Sech* since the days of Doroshenko: that night about three thousand die-hard souls made their way out of the *Sech* and scattered over the steppe, taking the direction of the Turkish frontier. The rest, about the same number, surrendered. General Tökölyi, for some unknown reason, arrested Kalnyshevsky, the judge Holovaty and the secretary Hloba. On the following day all arms were confiscated; all the archives of the *Sech* and all the standards and emblems of the Zaporogian troops. The funds and the whole of the property of the *Sech* were escheated to the imperial Exchequer. The Don Cossacks began to plunder the *Sech* church and to rip off the richly embossed silver frames of the icons. Old Zaporogians were silent witnesses of all this and tears ran down their weather-beaten cheeks. A garrison was left in the *Sech* and an order was given to the Zaporogians 'to disperse to the four corners of the world'. This sad episode was the end of the old order in the Ukraine. (4)

In a less spectacular way great changes took place six years later, in 1781, in what had been the Ukraine of the Hetmans. As a result of the new administrative division of the Empire introduced in 1775, the lands which had formerly been governed by the Hetmans were divided into three Governments: Kiev, Chernigov and Novgorod-Seversk. Two years later Little Russians found themselves called upon to pay taxes on the same basis as the rest of the inhabitants of the Empire: 1 ruble 50 copecks for townspeople and 70 copecks for peasants. The unification and centralization planned by Catherine when she ascended the throne was completely realized when, in 1793, the Second Partition of Poland united the Ukrainian lands on both banks of the Dniepr. These two parts of the Ukraine, which had been divided for more than a century, were united when every vestige of Ukrainian independence had disappeared and when even the word 'Ukraine' had lost its historical significance. Many decades were to pass before the name was used again in a quite different sense—in the sense in which it is used in the present period of history.

Catherine's second Turkish War, like the Second Polish Partition, was in fact an organic continuation of the first. The Crimea had been annexed in 1783, but the Turkish frontier still ran along the Bug and the redoubtable fortress of Ochakov could threaten the exit from the Dniepr lands.

Catherine, further, had not relinquished the ambitious schemes which, 'particularly after Potëmkin's rise to favour, became almost reckless in their scope. She dreamed of breaking up Turkey in order to form a new Greek Empire, which was destined for her second grandson, significantly named Constantine, while Moldavia, Wallachia and Bessarabia were to constitute a kingdom of Dacia, to be ruled by an Orthodox Prince—Potëmkin to wit'.

The German powers split on the issue of the partition of the Ottoman Empire, for, while Joseph II moved his armies in alliance with the Empress, Frederick, having abandoned the hope that differences would arise on the Danube which might promote a conflict between the Austrians and the Russians, entered into an alliance with Poland and Turkey (1790). Finally, in 1792, confronted with the prospect of a general war, Catherine accepted the Treaty of Jassy, which gave Ochakov with complete control of the embouchures of the Dniepr and Bug to Russia and fixed the Turkish frontier on the Dniestr.

On the eve of the war the Empress had made her famous voyage to the south in order to acquaint herself with her new dominions in Tauris and New Russia. The indomitable woman was approaching her sixtieth year as she made her gorgeous progress through the steppe. At Kanev on the Dniepr, the lover of her youth, her puppet King in Poland, Stanislas Poniatowski, came to pay his respects; and at Ekaterinoslav the Emperor Joseph II was her guest.

The ambassadors of the powers who accompanied Catherine on her progress sneered at 'the Potëmkin villages' which the Governor-General of New Russia had erected on the route, like theatrical scenery, in order to impress all eyes with the prosperity of the new dominion. But if Potëmkin did try to enliven the steppe scenery with decorative effects it was done, not to deceive his mistress, but to illustrate in picturesque manner the scope of his 'five year plans' and of his building projects. This fancy was quite natural in the eighteenth century when ephemeral architectural *ensembles* were erected and artificial scenery which pleased the taste of the period.

The colonization of New Russia was really a rapid and remarkable success and could certainly justify, in the view of the Empress and Potëmkin, the destruction of the *Sech*. In the decade after 1775 4,400,000 hectares of land were distributed. Enormous estates were granted to old Prince Vyazemski (about 200,000 hectares, including the islands on which both the old and the new *Sech* had stood). Potëmkin laid his hands on 150,000 hectares; Prince Prozorovski got the whole area round Ekaterinoslav; and even the former Hetman Cyril Razumovski was not forgotten with 35,000 *desyatins* of new land. A little later, a French emigré, Prince Polignac, received wide grants on the banks of the Bug. Fifteen hundred hectares could be had by any landlord who would undertake to settle thirteen peasant families and pay to the Exchequer 2½ copecks a year on each hectare. Potëmkin also encouraged the settlement of efficient small farmers—from the Baltic provinces and even from the Islands of Dago and Oesel. There was also a continuous and widespread immigration of Serbs, Moldavs, Czechs and Germans. In particular, every German settler received 65 hectares from the state in addition to a money grant and timber for building purposes.

Gritsko the Dishevelled even found a way to make his peace with the Zaporogians whom he had so cruelly offended in 1775 and at the same time to serve the interests of a wider colonization.

When, in 1783, a certain ferment occurred among the Crim Tartars, Potëmkin began to recruit the remnants of the Zaporogians who had scattered all over the steppe. A regiment of about 1000 men was formed with the former *Sech* elders Isidor Bily and Antony Holovaty in command. These Cossacks of Potëmkin met the Empress at Kremenchug on her journey to the south and performed aquatic feats to the admiration of the court. In view of the coming war, Potëmkin took advantage of the opportunity to secure an order to free all Zaporogians (the majority of whom had become serfs on the large estates following the dissolution of the *Sech*) for Cossack service. He set the example by freeing 247 former Zaporogians who were working on his own estates. In the vicinity of Ochakov on the lower Dniepr an organization resembling another 'New Sech' rapidly came into being—with Bily and Holovaty and Colonel Chapyga, as the official representative, at its head. The Empress stipulated only that the new Cossack formations should not have the name of Zaporogians. However, Suvorov, in 1788, granted to 'chief *ataman* Bily's gallant Zaporogian troops' their own standard—a blue cross on a white field. In May of the same year the traditional small

Zaporogian skiffs took part in the great sea battle off Ochakov. Bily was mortally wounded and Chapyga was elected *ataman* in his stead. Holovaty with his men captured the island of Berezan—one of the principal forts covering the fortress of Ochakov; and when that indomitable stronghold was finally taken by storm Potëmkin with his own hand pinned the Cross of St George on the breast of the Zaporogian leader.

As a result of their heroic services, the Empress issued a special Rescript granting the 'new Zaporogians' the name of 'Black Sea Cossacks' (*Chernomorskie Kazaki*), and Potëmkin himself assumed the style of their Hetman. Through his powerful intercession, the 'Chernomortsy' were granted all the lands conquered between the Bug and the Dniestr, to which was later added the newly conquered Taman region in the northern Caucasus.

The bloody assault of Izmail in December 1790 added to the battle laurels of the *Chernomortsy*; and in June of the following year they had their share in Repnin's great victory at Machin. Three months later, the genius who had presided over the creation of New Russia, the Hetman of the Black Sea Cossacks, the old Zaporogian Gritsko the Dishevelled, was lifted out of his carriage and laid on a rug to die in the steppe.

It seemed obvious, following Potëmkin's death, that the newly granted lands of the Black Sea Cossacks were destined to go the way of the lands of the Zaporogians. When Antony Holovaty went to Petersburg with a Cossack deputation he did not even mention the lands between the Bug and the Dniestr but turned all his efforts to securing the confirmation at least of the new lands in the northern Caucasus. As a result, the Empress, who loved and revered the memory of Potëmkin, granted, in July 1792, 'to the troops formed of loyal Cossacks of the Zaporogian *Sech* by the late Field-Marshal Prince Potëmkin of Tauris' vast lands between the Azov Sea, the Kerch Strait and the river Kuban. Such was the beginning of the Kuban Cossacks. By the following year the last Ukrainian Cossacks had left the South of Russia. A song tells how 'now the Cossacks received reward for their services from the Tsaritsa' and how in the Kuban 'they must serve loyally, the frontiers defend, fish catch and vodka drink'.

§ 4. POLISH INFLUENCES UNDER PAUL AND ALEXANDER: THE ROMANTIC REVIVAL

As a result of the Second Partition of Poland all those parts of the old Russo-Lithuanian state which had, since the Union of Lublin in 1569, formed part of Poland were incorporated in the Russian Empire. Of the West Russian lands only Galicia—which passed to the Habsburgs —remained outside the frontiers of the Tsar of All the Russias. But in the lands to the west of the Dniepr Polish institutions, the Polish and Catholic way of life, had taken strong root. At the same time, at the end of the eighteenth century, it had not become fashionable to regard the patois of a peasantry as the basis of claims to political authority. Thus, not only the Polish clergy and officials living in the territories ceded to the Russian crown, but also Russian officialdom, continued to ignore the Lithuanian, White Russian or Ukrainian character of the peasantry of different districts and to regard the 'territories annexed from Poland' as essentially Polish regions. Several decades passed before the Russian state and Russian society began to notice that the lower classes of these 'Polish Governments' consisted of Lithuanians, White Russians and Ukrainians and that there were very few Poles among them.

The Polish cultural ascendancy on the right bank of the Dniepr rapidly spread to the left-bank lands as the Polish nobility now subject to the Tsar began to influence both the Russian court and the upper ranks of Russian society.

In his Memoirs, which are such a valuable source for the history of Russian society in the earlier part of the nineteenth century, Wiegel relates how 'in my childhood I witnessed a great metamorphosis. The ancient capital of the Russian Great Princes, which even under Polish dominion had proved immune to Polish influences, suddenly became Polonized.' Thus he described Kiev in the last years of the eighteenth century during the short reign of the Emperor Paul I.

Paul I was inclined to encourage tendencies opposed to those of the Catherinian era and was in no way disposed to favour further measures of 'unification' and 'centralization'. He became the protector of the Roman Catholic Church in these Governments which had been annexed from Poland and he even re-established the local Seyms of the nobility which were nearly entirely Polish.

Catherine II had greatly strengthened the position of the nobility throughout Russia, and in those provinces where no real noble class had previously existed one had quickly grown up under her magnanimous auspices. In the Ukraine, the nobility, originating largely from the parvenu Cossack upper ranks, only came into legal existence in 1781 when the Little Russian Governments were definitely included in the social structure of the rest of the Empire. The Little Russian nobility then received the rights and privileges enjoyed by their fellows in other parts of the Empire and, when, after the Second Partition of Poland, right-bank Ukraine was incorporated in the

Empire, the same rights and privileges were extended to the Kievan, Volhynian and Podolian nobility which was either Polish or under the influence of Polish culture. The more ancient culture and infinitely more civilized way of life of the noble families who owned lands to the west of the Dniepr naturally exercised a strong influence on the new Ukrainian nobility to the east of the great river. Kiev was the place where the old Polish or Polonized nobility came into contact with the representatives of the Ukrainian upper class of recent formation, and the city therefore became the centre of a process of Polonization of the landed gentry of Little Russian origin. The Russian authorities of the end of the eighteenth century had no thought of checking this process. On the contrary, after the accession of Alexander I to the throne, the Government strongly supported Polish influences in the west and south of Russia.

A close friendship united the young Emperor to Prince Adam Czartoryski and the young Empress Elizabeth was romantically attracted to him. For some time Prince Adam Czartoryski directed the foreign policy of Russia, but the main work of his life was the creation of the Vilna educational district, at the head of which Prince Adam remained for twenty years (1803–23). The district was centred on Vilna University, an old centre of Polish culture founded at the end of the sixteenth century by King Stephen Báthory. The activities of the Vilna educational district extended not only to Lithuania and White Russia but also to Volhynia, Podolia and even to the Government of Kiev. In all the schools founded by Czartoryski's energetic collaborators lessons were given in Polish and according to Polish conceptions. In 1805 a gymnasium was opened at Kremenets in Volhynia, which became a sort of branch of Vilna University.

Later, in his Memoirs, Prince Czartoryski wrote: 'Vilna University was Polish in the full sense of the word and existed for the Polish provinces. A few years later all Poland was covered by a network of schools where Polish national feeling could develop freely.' The full significance of these words is evident when it is remembered that at this time Warsaw and nearly all the Polish-speaking provinces were incorporated in either Prussia or the Austrian dominions, and that in speaking of 'Poland' Czartoryski was referring to lands of which at least two-thirds of the population was Russian-speaking.

With the approval of Alexander, who remained under the influence of Czartoryski, another university, which was intended to become the educational centre of Little Russia, was opened in Kharkov. Count Severin Potocki was appointed Curator; he was a brother of the well-known Polish scholar, John Potocki, who was the first to study the question of the origin of the Ukrainian people.

In this wise, not only the capital of the right bank, Kiev, but also the new centre of the left bank, Kharkov, became the dispensaries of that peculiar Polish nationalism which had its source, not in the idea of a national state, but of a state which found its true and veritably 'catholic' expression in the *Rzecz Pospolita*. This somewhat strange form of nationalism sought support among various nationalities— Poles, Lithuanians, Russians, Ukrainians—all those peoples who were supposed to be united by a common historical tradition and by the Roman confession or its variant, the Uniate Church.

As a result of the activities of Prince Adam Czartoryski and his disciples a situation was created whereby 'the forces and means for the resurrection of Poland were being concentrated not in Poland itself nor even partially so, but in the lands of the ancient Russo-Lithuanian state, which had once so jealously insisted on its independence. These lands had now become the reservoir of Polish nationalism—a movement which denied the historical importance of the Russo-Lithuanian state and substituted for that idea the conception of a great and united Poland from sea to sea' (Lappo).

It is evident that the Polish interpretation of *Rzecz Pospolita* had an attraction for certain intellectual groups in Russian society. Alexander I himself came under its influence at the end of the period of his struggle with Napoleon. When, after his return from the West, he visited Warsaw for the opening of the *Seym*, he made no secret in conversation with members of his immediate entourage of his intention to re-establish Poland 'in her former boundaries'. The oscillations in policy of this exalted and impressionable mystic were a source of continual uneasiness to the Russian statesmen who represented the continuity of Muscovite policy. On this occasion the historian Karamzin did not hesitate to protest in an imperative tone. In a Memorandum which he addressed to the Emperor in 1819, he asked: 'Would it be compatible with Your sacred duties, Your love for Russia and with justice itself? Could you with a clear conscience take away from us old Rus, Lithuania, Volhynia and Podolia?' Taking advantage of the high esteem in which the Emperor held him, Karamzin did not mince his words: 'We should not only be deprived of excellent territories but of our love and reverence for our sovereign, and in our souls would be extinguished the flame of patriotism if we had to realize that our country was nothing but the plaything of autocratic caprice.' Confronted with opposition of such stern quality, Alexander abandoned plans which might have formed the basis of a dual Russo-Polish monarchy and which might have changed the whole history of Slavdom during the nineteenth and twentieth centuries.

Certain events had already gone to show that hopes for the restoration of *Rzecz Pospolita*, even with the support and approval of the Romanovs and under their patronage, were but the idle illusions of Polish romantics. In the years 1792–4, during the heroic struggle of Kościuszko and Dąbrowski against the armies of Prussia and Russia, it had become evident that, the moment the theatre of war was transferred to territories where the peasants were not of Polish origin, the sympathies of the population were not on the side of the defenders of Polish independence. For instance, in 1792, Prince Joseph Poniatowski, the future Marshal of France, wrote to the King that the Volhynian peasants were taking the part of the Russian troops and that 'the rabble was as usual on the side of Moscow'. In the month of June of the same year he wrote from his camp: 'The peasants, and sometimes their owners, were my enemies; my adversaries always knew my plans, receiving information about all that went on in my camp from spies of every kind and description, who were easy for them to find, while it was extremely difficult for me to do so.'

This undertone among the peasantry explains why the enthusiasm for 'Napoleon's epic' in the higher circles of Polish society could find no echo in those former territories of *Rzecz Pospolita* which had been annexed to Russia. Austria had been defeated in 1805; Prussia in 1806; Russia in 1807. The moment appeared to have arrived when Napoleon might re-establish *Rzecz Pospolita* in the frontiers which had been abolished by the three Partitions. Dąbrowski, who was serving with the French, sent an address to the populations of the lands severed from Poland calling upon them to rise. The appeal, however, evoked no response, and Napoleon himself took a practical view of the conditions existing to the east of the Vistula when, to the disappointment of the Poles, he concluded the Treaty of Tilsit. He thought it wiser to be content with 'the Grand Duchy of Warsaw', which had a purely Polish population, and to put at its head a member of the Saxon dynasty. Napoleon wanted to stabilize this new Polish state by granting rights and privileges to the middle classes and freedom to the serfs. But this latter measure met with such stubborn opposition on the part of the Polish aristocracy that it was never carried out.

After the Austrian defeat of 1809 the Grand Duchy of Warsaw received Cracow and Malopolska, but Galicia continued to form part of the truncated Empire of the Habsburgs. Napoleon seems to have well understood the complications which were implicit in the Polish claims to the Russian and Lithuanian lands of former *Rzecz Pospolita*. Even in 1812, when 100,000 Polish troops were serving in the ranks of the Grand Army which had occupied Polotsk, Mohilev and Smolensk, the Emperor maintained his prudent reserve in respect of Polish aspirations. In Warsaw the Grand Ducal *Seym* passed a resolution in favour of re-establishing Poland in her historical frontiers, but Napoleon withheld his approval from this decision— postponing it until he had obtained a clear idea of how it would be received in the territories which had at one time belonged to Poland and had been annexed to the Russian Empire. At the same time he never abandoned hope, until the eve of the evacuation of Moscow, of an accommodation with Alexander, and he seems to have hesitated to exacerbate the Russian court by promoting Polish—or, as he might have done, Turkish—claims.

The legend that Napoleon contemplated a campaign in the Ukraine has no foundation. His war with Russia was at no stage 'total', and his conceptions were quite different from those of Charles XII a hundred years before. The strong patriotic sentiment called forth in Great Russia by the French invasion was also shared in the Ukraine. When, at the beginning of the retreat from Moscow, the Grand Army took a south-westerly direction it was only to avoid the devastated belt along the Smolensk road. Kutuzov barred the way at Maloyaroslavets and, in spite of an ephemeral success, Napoleon did not dare to take the risk of forcing his way into the rich and fertile, but relatively isolated, regions of the south and west.

After the Congress of Vienna the Grand Duchy of Warsaw again became the Kingdom of Poland with the Emperor Alexander as King. The internal structure and 'Napoleonic' boundaries of the kingdom were preserved; and not only Russia but Austria and Prussia guaranteed 'Polish national particularities'. In the Poland of Alexander the whole administration remained Polish; the kingdom had a royal Polish army, and, with the aid of the senior establishments of Cracow and Vilna, a university was founded in Warsaw.

The period after 1815 was the heyday of Polish literature and science. But the intellectual movement of this period continued to be inspired by romantic notions of re-establishing a Polish state with the structure and boundaries of *Rzecz Pospolita*.

Forty years later, in 1867, the impractical idealism of Polish nationalist romanticism was vividly expressed in the address issued by the Polish emigration protesting against the Slavonic Congress in Moscow. The survivors of the risings of 1831, 1848 and 1863 proclaimed themselves 'the representatives of the one and indivisible great *Rzecz Pospolita* created by God and history'. 'In the ancient *Rzecz Pospolita*', they claimed, 'Rus and Poland, united to Lithuania by unbreakable ties of history and moral needs as independent states and equals, formed a union which alone could realize the happiness of the nations. We will always remain true to this principle of which our standard representing the Archangel Michael, the Eagle and the Chase (the arms respectively of Kiev, Poland and Lithuania) is the symbol.'

In 1867 this manifesto was an extremely antiquated expression of political romanticism which found no justification in the tragic events of the preceding four decades. In the years which led up to the armed struggle of 'the Congress Kingdom' with Romanov Russia, these notions concerning the Polish past and aspirations for the future had been prevalent among historians like Lelewel and Szajnocha and politicians of the school of Adam Czartoryski. Mickiewicz voiced all the pride and passion of the national yearning in his *Litania Pielgrzymska*. In Lithuania, White Russia and the Ukraine this Polish Messianism found many adherents among the lesser nobility who had received their education in Roman Catholic schools. Typical of their generation were the poets Goszczyński and Zaleski, both belonging to families of small Polish landowners. They were Polish poets, but they represented the so-called 'Ukrainian school' in Warsaw, and the two of them took an active part in the rising of 1830–1. From the Polish point of view of that period Goszczyński and Zaleski were looked on as 'Ukrainians', but in reality they were impoverished Polish nobles who had grown up in right-bank Ukraine and had received their education in the Polish school at Uman and later in Warsaw. Even in 1830–1 the revolutionary Polish Government failed to free the serfs in its own territories; and in the south the Polish detachments of Dwernicki and Romarino secured no support among the peasantry of Volhynia. For the representatives of the political romanticism of the time social questions were practically non-existent.

After 1830–1 the Polish emigration, which enjoyed a certain weight because it belonged to the aristocracy and gentry and therefore had many connections in the upper circles of European society, because also it was well-educated and sometimes gifted and had considerable financial resources and was supported by the Vatican, soon became extremely popular in Western Europe. The sympathies of European liberals were the stronger in that 'Poland's misfortunes' remained no longer the theme of poets and an unreal memory of days before the Napoleonic Wars but had become a grim reality of the present.

The Emperor Nicholas I was not a cruel man, but he was violent and unbending. Following 'the Polish mutiny' the Constitution was abolished; military courts were introduced; the administration of the country was completely changed; the Universities of Vilna and

Warsaw, the Gymnasium of Kremenets and all the schools founded by Adam Czartoryski were shut down. There were of course also executions and banishments, but these were not so systematic as after the rising of 1863. Europe rang with sympathy for Poland, but these sympathies did not go further than newspaper articles and rhetorical speeches. In the years between 1830 and 1848 the world was already seeking for ways and ideals other than those which had inspired the Italian Carbonari, the Decabrists and the Polish patriots. Social ideas had penetrated even the vague enthusiastic dreams of those who wept for their 'crucified country'; these ideas began to form a solid basis for new movements which were to take the form of a conscious or half-conscious struggle between the classes. (5)

Only fifteen years had elapsed after 1830–1 and the Polish political romantics seemed already 'prehistoric' in their beliefs and hopes. Europe in 1846 was on the verge of national revolutions in which the social factor was assuming a supreme importance; these new movements had infinitely deeper roots and wider possibilities than the risings of 1830, which had taken place generally through the initiative of officers' and students' 'secret societies', the members of which mainly belonged to the petty noble or middle classes.

In 1848 a conspiracy was formed in all the three parts of divided Poland, but unfortunately its gifted leader, Mieroslawski, happened to be a native of the Prussian provinces. Mieroslawski was arrested in Poznań, and Russian Poland did not respond to the movement. Only in Austria did the rebels succeed in taking control of Cracow, which at that time was a Free City. A 'Republic' was proclaimed there with a Directory at its head. The Republic was defended by a badly armed detachment which had been brought into the city by local landowners who were privy to the rising. The Habsburg administration, pressed throughout the Empire by dangerous national and revolutionary movements, had recourse to the stratagem of spreading rumours amongst the peasants to the effect that the Polish landowners were rebelling against the Government because it would not allow them to oppress their tenants and treat them as serfs. Peasant risings immediately flared up throughout all the countryside between Cracow and Lvov. A wholesale slaughter of the Polish gentry took place; about 800 families perished, of whom 180 were butchered in the vicinity of Tarnów alone.

As Russian and Prussian troops were marching into Cracow to dispose of the unfortunate Directory, Galician peasants were shouting across the small stream which divided the Austrian from the Russian provinces: 'We are killing off our Polish lords! When are you going to begin to kill yours?'

§ 5. THE BROTHERHOOD OF ST CYRIL AND ST METHO
DIUS: RISE OF UKRAINIAN LITERARY NATIONALISM

It was just prior to 1848, in 1845 or 1846, that the Brotherhood of
St Cyril and St Methodius was founded in Kiev. There were about
thirty members of this secret society, the originator of which was a
student named Hulak who had studied at Dorpat University, where
he had been initiated into the ways of some of the Polish secret
patriotic societies. (Many young Poles pursued their studies in
Dorpat after the closing of the University of Vilna.)

Among the members of the Brotherhood of St Cyril and St
Methodius were several personalities who afterwards became well
known: the historian Kostomarov (not a Ukrainian by birth), the
author Kulish, and the painter and poet Shevchenko. The members
of the Brotherhood were united by their common interest in the
history of the Ukraine. At this time the mind of the Ukrainian
people still had vital connection with the past of the seventeenth and
eighteenth centuries. The popular beliefs of the peasants, their songs
and legends and much of their common way of life continued to reflect the days that were not yet dead in the memories of old men.
It was this background which had inspired the genius of Gogol
(Hohol), a Ukrainian in his being but a Russian in his mastery of
Pushkin's language. A love of the past which was still so near united
the brilliant essayist Kostomarov, the profoundly erudite Kulish and
the poet Shevchenko who 'thought in verse'. There were also other
men in the Brotherhood who partook of those national revolutionary aspirations which were so characteristic of the time. They
doubtless had their connections with that Petersburg secret society
where, for the first time in Russia, Petrushevski was preaching
'Utopian Socialism' and young Dostoyevski was listening with rapt
attention to these idle speeches.

The police soon became aware of both the Petrushevski Society
and of the Kievan Brotherhood. Arrests followed: Kostomarov was
banished to Saratov, Kulish to Tula. Both, however, were able to
continue their historical studies. No criminal intentions could be
attributed to the majority of the members of the Brotherhood. At
the same time they were suspected of revolutionary tendencies. The
poems found among Shevchenko's papers left no doubts as to the
young poet's antagonism to the established order and, less fortunate
than his more learned fellows, he found himself despatched as a
private soldier to the fortress of Orsk in the Orenburg Steppe.

Shevchenko was a revolutionary in temperament rather than in
thought. The principal points in the indictment against him were

not so much the political programme of the Brotherhood (liberation of the serfs, a union of Slav Republics in which the Ukraine was to be included) as the terms which he used in speaking of 'crowned persons' and his generally inimical attitude towards the authority of the state. This attitude, and his great poetical gifts, account for the high importance attached to his personality by later generations of Ukrainian politicians, but it was his origin which made him a fashionable cult among the liberal intelligentsia of the Russia of his time. In the Decabrist decades poets and revolutionaries had generally been of noble origin, but Shevchenko was a son of the people.

Shevchenko was born in the year 1814 into a peasant family living on the right bank of the Dniepr in the Government of Kiev. His family were the serfs of a landowner called Engelhardt. Having become an orphan in early childhood, he was taken into the Engelhardt family as an under-servant; and in due course he accompanied his *barin* to Warsaw, to Vilna, and at last to Petersburg. Having noticed the boy's inclination towards drawing, good-natured Engelhardt, during his sojourn in Warsaw, sent him to study under the well-known portrait-painter Lampi the Younger. In Petersburg the painter Łosenko, a Ukrainian by birth, took a fancy to him. Łosenko showed Shevchenko's drawings to the celebrated Academician Karl Brüllow, who immediately became interested in them. A serf could not enter the Academy of Art, but Brüllow found a way out of the difficulty: he painted a portrait of the poet Zhukovski who was tutor to the heir to the throne. The portrait was bought by the imperial family for 2800 rubles, and this sum was paid in 1838 to Engelhardt as the price of Shevchenko's freedom.

Such wise and generous friends in the capital seemed to hold promise of a successful future for the young artist. Petersburg opened its doors hospitably to 'this son of the people'. Gogol had set a literary fashion for the Ukraine and the customs and legends of her country life. All was going well for the young man until Martos the sculptor found his first attempts at verse. In company with the writer Hrebenka, another Ukrainian, Martos began to occupy himself with this newly discovered talent of the student of the Academy of Art. After this Shevchenko very nearly gave up his painting. In 1840 he published his first collection of poems entitled *The Kobzar*, and the book had a great and merited success.

Shevchenko in his poems tried to keep to the Ukrainian dialect in which legends were related and songs were sung. This was by no means an attempt to create a special Ukrainian language in opposition to Russian. Russian readers could easily understand the Little Russian dialect and were charmed by its sincerity and brightness. The dialect transported the reader to the Ukraine more readily than Gogol's stories written in Russian. One of the attractive facets of Shevchenko's talent was his vivid recollection of all he had heard during his childhood in the land of his birth. One of his contemporary biographers writes: 'Folklore furnished an endless source of subjects and motives for the poet. Besides this fantastic world of folklore, Shevchenko was also haunted by the glorious and tragic memories of the past history of his native land.'

In the Russian literary circles of the time there circulated fragments of a history of the Ukraine entitled *History of Rus*, which was probably the work of the eighteenth-century Ukrainian political figure, Gregory Poletika, who had protested against the Catherinian reforms of 1767. The romantic and picturesque pages of this work were known to Pushkin and Gogol and also to Shevchenko. The latter dedicated his poems to the risings of Nalivayko and Taras Fedorovich and to the Zaporogian campaigns against the Turks. But the most popular of them all was '*The Haydamaks*' which is an epic description of the peasant rising of Zaliznyak and Gonta and of the taking of Uman. The Pole, Severin Goszczyński, born like Shevchenko in the region of Kiev, chose the same subject for a poem which was published about the same time as '*The Haydamaks*'. But in Goszczyński's work were described all the horrors of 'the Uman slaughter'. Thus the two different outlooks are mirrored: that of the Ukrainian peasant and of the Polish noble and rebel of 1831.

Of course neither Shevchenko nor his fellows of the Brotherhood of St Cyril and St Methodius ever gave a thought to the restoration of *Rzecz Pospolita*—particularly at a moment when the *Haydamaks* were again making their appearance in Galicia and killing off Polish landowners and plundering their estates.

When the young but already well-known author of *The Kobzar* returned to the Ukraine in 1843 he found many admirers among the landowners of the Kiev and Poltava Governments, who were cultivated and often very wealthy men. There were Ukrainians among them: Lizohub, Tarnovsky and General Kukharenko; but Shevchenko's most devoted friends were the family of the former Governor-General of Kiev, Prince Repnin, Count de Balmain and Countess Anastasia Tolstoy. During his exile in the Orenburg Steppe Shevchenko never ceased to correspond with Princess Barbara Repnin, who lived on her beautiful estate of Yagotin in the Poltava Government. Countess Anastasia Tolstoy also proved her friendship by procuring the poet an amnesty immediately after the death of Nicholas I. In 1857 Shevchenko returned to Petersburg, but he died four years later. His friends brought his body back to the

Ukraine and buried it on the high bank of the Dniepr near Kanev.

Shevchenko's success in Russian society of the forties is explained by the humanitarian movement of the period which considered the abolition of serfdom as its principal and immediate aim. People tried to like and be sorry for Shevchenko, not because he was a Ukrainian, but because he had been born a serf and had through his talent as a painter and a poet gained his liberty. There were many social motives in Shevchenko's verses, many eloquent and bitter words concerning the peasant doomed to be a serf and especially on the hopeless fate of the peasant woman. The life of the serf was not, of course, a particular Ukrainian theme, for many Russian writers of the period wrote about it, like Turgenev and Nekrasov, who knew even better than Shevchenko how to arouse indignation and compassion. But having come in contact with the Brotherhood of St Cyril and St Methodius the impressionable artistic nature of Shevchenko was influenced by the national and revolutionary tendencies of its members. Among his banned poems the best known is 'The Dream', where the poet, recalling the inscription on the monument of Peter the Great, exclaims: 'To Peter I from Catherine II—the First crucified our Ukraine and the Second finished off his victim.' In the poem 'Prometheus' Nicholas I is abused as 'the persecutor of liberty over the whole stretch of the Empire from Finland to Moldavia' and the state is denounced as 'only capable of building prisons and forging chains'. In 1847, if a man allowed himself the luxury of such flights of poetic fancy he was liable to wake up one fine day in some very distant region.

During Shevchenko's lifetime few people were familiar with his political pamphlets. But with the opening of the reign of Alexander II and the period of the great reforms the position of literary revolutionaries became far easier. In 1860 a group of Ukrainian historians and writers was formed round the journal *Osnova*. The group included Kulish, Kostomarov, Belozersky, Kistyakovsky, Antonovich and others. Shevchenko, after his arrival in Petersburg, joined them and published in *Osnova* fragments from his diary. The journal gave to the public a great deal of valuable historical material; as to its political background, it advocated, after the teaching of the Kiev 'Brotherhood', a federation of 'the Slav family of nations' in which the Ukrainian people were to be included on the same footing with the others.

The Emancipation of the Serfs in 1861 produced a revolution in social relations throughout the Empire and strongly influenced the Ukrainian movement, especially as it coincided with the Polish insurrection of 1863. The hopes of the Polish patriots had been stimulated by the Near Eastern War of 1854-5, and they were influenced also by the success of the Italian nationalist movement and by the general ferment of nationalities throughout Europe. Even in 1863 the Poles had not altogether given up hope of securing support among the populations of the former territories of *Rzecz Pospolita*, and they tried to make contact with the Ukrainian circles and with the Russian revolutionary groups in the capital of the Empire.

The rising of 1863, however, ended in complete failure. The Polish peasantry and a great part of the townsfolk regarded the movement with indifference and scepticism. This attempt, so obviously doomed to failure, was not even very enthusiastically supported by the strongly nationalistic class of Polish gentry. Technically badly organized, small detachments, after their first encounters with Russian troops, either scattered or crossed the Austrian frontier. Neither were the hopes of aid from England and France—encouraged by ill-advised friends among the publicists and politicians of London and Paris—nor from the Pope or Garibaldi, realized. The most serious result of the insurrection was the end of the Polish dream of a restoration of *Rzecz Pospolita*.

In the localities populated by Russian peasants who had just been liberated from serfdom by the Tsar the rising was represented as an attempt on the part of the Polish nobles 'to enslave again' the Russian Orthodox people. At the end of the rising the Government of Alexander II availed itself of the prevailing unpopularity of the Poles to limit as far as possible Polish landownership in White Russia, Lithuania, Volhynia and Podolia. The reprisals in Vilna carried out by Muraviëv were particularly severe. The executions and banishments ordered by him aroused the indignation of Europe and in Russian society he was called 'The Hangman'. The essential, however, in Muraviëv's activities was not in his brutalities but in his confiscations of Polish estates and the restrictions he imposed on the Roman Catholic Church. 'The Western Provinces', in his opinion, 'are part of ancient Russia, the majority of the population are Russian exceeding in numbers all other nationalities. Therefore every kind of Polish influence, whether national or religious, must be excluded.'

The Polish rising of 1863 finally removed all illusions which might have existed concerning the possibility of collaboration between the Ukrainian national groups and the enthusiasts of a Polish revival. In reality the Ukrainian intellectuals had nothing in common with the dreams of the romantic protagonists of *Rzecz Pospolita* of the epoch of Adam Czartoryski, Mickiewicz and Lelewel. With a few individual exceptions no Ukrainian joined the rising. There were many discussions in a certain *milieu* on the right bank of the Dniepr where Russian and Polish families had become related to each other or were united by long-standing friendships. The conflict of outlook which arose has been described by a Polish author, Sawiński, in his drama *Na Ukrainie*. In the end the tendencies of the principal group of Ukrainian nationalists triumphed. This group, originally centred round the periodical *Osnova* in Petersburg, had now gathered in the congenial atmosphere of Kiev University and founded a society called 'The Kiev *Hromada*'. When the appeal of the Polish rebels was received, Kostomarov, a member of the *Hromada*, proposed 'to send them all to the Devil'. Kostomarov, however, though an old friend of the Ukraine, was Russian, and a far more important part was played in defining the direction of Ukrainian nationalism by Antonovich, who was the most prominent figure in the Ukrainian movement during the years between 1860 and 1890.

Antonovich, while not a Pole, belonged to the local nobility, which had been Polonized for a long time; his father was a Catholic. After having passed through the University of Kiev, he began to study Ukrainian history with all the energy and persistence in his nature. He worked mostly in the Kiev Central Archives. Even during the early years of his researches he reached the conclusion that the Polish romantic interpretation of *Rzecz Pospolita* did not correspond with the ascertainable facts of history. The materials he found in the Archives enabled him to prove to his own satisfaction that social relations in *Rzecz Pospolita* were something quite different from what Polish historians of the first half of the nineteenth century, like Lelewel and Szajnocha, had represented them to be. On the eve of the rising of 1863 Antonovich wrote an ardent article under the title 'Confession' which was published in *Osnova*, in which he explained with absolute sincerity his reasons for opposing all Polish claims to territories inhabited by Russian peasants. He not only pointed out the mistakes made by Polish historians but accused them of deliberately falsifying historical facts. He ended his 'Confession' with a Ukrainian proverb: 'You can get to the end of the world with lies, but you will never be able to come back.'

The views of Antonovich were shared by other members of 'the Kiev *Hromada*' (Kistyakovsky, Zhitetsky, Hubinsky, Belozersky) and his example gave an impulse to the collection of historical materials concerning the Ukraine. The publication of *The Archives of South-Western Russia* was begun and continued during many years. During the period 1860–90 an enormous amount of historical research was carried out by the universities of the Ukraine. From the

year 1882 the periodical, *The Past of Kiev* (*Kievskaya Starina*), began
to appear in which, in addition to the historians already mentioned,
the collaborators included Levitsky, Shulgin, Lazarevsky, Efimovsky,
Skalkovsky, Dushevich, Golubovsky, Bahalia (Bagalêy), Storo-
zhenko and Vladimirsky-Budanov.

Basing their theories on these historical researches, Ukrainian
political leaders of the latter part of the nineteenth century elaborated
an ideology of a clearly defined 'democratic' character which was
in general accord with the tendencies of Russian educated society of
the period. Going back into the past of their country, they came to
the conclusion that from the fifteenth to the eighteenth century
nationality had been exclusively represented by the Ukrainian lower
classes, while the upper classes had either been Polish or absolutely
polonized until, in the seventeenth century, they had come under
'Muscovite' and later under 'Russian imperial' influences.

Research into the fate of the Ukrainian people inevitably led historians into becoming 'democrats', but in a specific sense of that
word. Antonovich and Lazarevsky opposed 'Ukrainian democracy'
to 'Polish aristocracy', or rather to the rule of the nobles in Poland.
To this kind of ideology the Ukrainian Cossacks were the expression
of 'the Ukrainian social idea', which was contrasted sharply with the
Polish one. The former *Radas*—the tumultuous assemblies where
more often than not unpopular leaders were done to death—were
idealized as the freely elected assemblies of a rural population consisting of small farmers and knowing no distinctions of class; and
these *Radas* were held by the more fanciful of enthusiasts to have
been a continuation of the ancient Kievan *Veche*.

Having adopted these conceptions, Antonovich and his adepts saw
the expression of 'the Ukrainian national idea' in the half-conscious
efforts of the lower layers of the Cossacks and the peasants during
the course of the seventeenth and eighteenth centuries, and they
strongly disapproved of the anti-social ambitions of the Cossack
elders of the Hetman period.

In all these affirmations of the Ukrainian 'national democrats'
there was much that was mistaken—particularly their idealization
of the Zaporogian *Sech*, which in their view was struggling for the
attainment of political freedom and social justice. It is unscientific
to explain the actions and men of a distant past from the point of
view of the emotions and aims of political groups of the present day.
Kulish, an old Ukrainian historian and politician and a veteran of the
Brotherhood of St Cyril and St Methodius, who had been the first
to try to give a literary character to the Ukrainian dialect and to
Ukrainian peasant songs, considered it his duty to refute these

exaggerations. He demonstrated the chaotic and destructive part played by the Cossacks and even went so far as to acknowledge that the Polish nobles had been the bearers of culture into the steppe regions on both banks of the Dniepr. Kulish also held that the union of the Ukraine with Muscovy had been an act of historical necessity which was confirmed by the whole history of the Hetman period when the Ukrainians proved themselves incapable of organizing a stable system of life in their country at a period when it was half independent. A storm of vituperative criticism was raised against the old scholar who proposed these ideas to political agitators who merely regarded history as material for propaganda, and many years passed before his serious and conscientious historical work received the appreciation which was its due (see Doroshenko, *P. Kulish*, Berlin, 1922).

The Slav Congress which was held in Moscow in 1867 proved to have had an important influence on the development of Ukrainian nationalism. At this Congress gathered representatives of all the Slav peoples of Central and South-Eastern Europe—Kashubians from Prussia and Lusatians from Saxony, Galicians, Czechs, Slovaks, Slovenes and Croats from the Habsburg dominions, Serbs and Bulgars from the Balkans. Only the Poles were absent, because they considered 'this demonstration of Slav solidarity under Russian protection to be a historical lie'.

The Austrian and Hungarian press denounced the Congress as a 'conspiracy' against the Habsburg Empire; and, although it had no immediate practical results, the Congress may be held to have influenced the direction of Russian foreign policy over the period between 1867 and 1914. Taking leave of the Slav visitors, Lamanski, one of the initiators of the Congress, announced that 'the Slav Question has been transferred now from books and private studies to the street, to public squares, to churches and to theatres'. Subsequent events were to prove that it had been transferred also to the battlefields of 1877–8, 1912–13 and 1914–18.

§6. AUSTRIA AND RUSSIA AND THE GROWTH OF UKRAINIAN NATIONALISM

The Slav Congress in Moscow had indicated to the Habsburg court that the Tsar's protection of the Western Slavs might not always be confined to the Balkan Peninsula. The Congress in fact had given an impetus to the dangerous Pan-Slav movement within the Russian Empire. Official circles in Petersburg, in encouraging this movement, without doubt intended to canalize all the social passions of the period into an emotional stream which should overflow to the greater glory of Holy Russia. Within ten years, however, the Pan-Slavists succeeded in compromising the whole of Russian foreign policy and in forcing the Government into the war of 1877-8. Though the war was successful, the burdens it entailed made worse the discontent and consequent repressions which brought the imperial system nearer to its end.

The House of Austria, weakened by the events of 1848 and by losses in Italy, and finally deprived at Sadowa of all pretensions to any further leadership in the Germanic world, was driven to an ultimate dependence on the rising power of Prussia (from which the friendship of either Russia or France might have saved it). The Habsburgs had their revenge on Louis Napoleon by leaving him to the mercy of the Prussians in 1870. In the east they prepared to face the Pan-Slavism of Petersburg by pursuing an independently predatory policy in relation to the Ottoman Empire (by contrast with the agreed policy which they had accepted in the Partitions of Poland); and along their common frontier with Russia they countered the Tsarist support of the Habsburg Slavs by undertaking a long-sighted exploitation of the differences in culture and psychology which were to be found among the Russian Slavs.

At the Slav Congress a small group of grey-haired men, who had dedicated their lives since 1830 to the task of awakening the Russian-speaking peasantry of Galicia to a consciousness of their nationality, shed tears as they listened to that part of Prince Cherkassky's speech which dwelt on the position of their compatriots under Austrian rule.

The new Constitution of Austria-Hungary, which was promulgated about that time, granted, however, a wide autonomy to the different regions which formed part of the Empire. Galicia was reckoned among these regions, and there the supremacy of the Polish element was recognized. At the same time the Central Government in Vienna, which adhered to an ingenious policy of upholding the lesser nationalities of a region against the dominant element, did not neglect to acknowledge the existence of the Russians, to whom was accorded the official denomination of 'Ruthenians' (a term generally used in old Vatican documents when referring to the Russians subject to *Rzecz Pospolita*, and in some cases to the inhabitants of 'Moscovia').

As a result of this new situation, as early as the following year (1868), a cultural society was formed in Lvov which was called *Prosvita* (Ukr. 'Enlightenment'). Four years later Lvov rejoiced in the Shevchenko Society for which Elizabeth Miloradovich (*née*

Skoropadskaya) furnished the funds from Russia. In this wise a link was formed between the Ukrainian political intellectuals grouped round the Universities of Kiev and Kharkov and the new Ukrainian centre of Lvov outside Russia.

The extremely unfortunate policy of the Tsarist Government soon created a situation in which Lvov came to play the leading role in the life of the Ukrainian national movement; and the Austro-Hungarian Government was not slow to avail itself of the opportunity of encouraging the Ukrainian movement to develop on lines agreeable to the policy of Vienna.

The Ministers of Alexander II who had recently passed through the anxious times of the Polish rising of 1863 conceived a profound distrust of the Ukrainian national renascence, and they failed to understand that the rising had been the occasion for a real break between Ukrainians and Poles.

The Secretary of State for Public Instruction, Valuev, thought it necessary to issue a circular in which it was stated that 'no Little Russian language exists nor has it ever existed' and that 'it is but bad Russian spoilt by Polish influences'.

It was further forbidden to print anything in Ukrainian except verses, stories and plays. This order did not trouble Ukrainian historians who had published their works in Russian. However, it evoked a certain irritation among Ukrainians who considered themselves loyal subjects of the Empire and saw no reason for this attempt at 'russification' on the part of the authorities.

This blunder of the Government of Alexander II had serious consequences. Until that time all attempts at creating a Ukrainian literary language had been confined to the Russian provinces. Kotlyarevsky in his jocular *Travesty of the Aeneid*, Kvitka in his stories, Shevchenko in his *Kobzar*, and Kulish in his articles, all availed themselves of the Poltava and Kiev dialect and, in order to make it sound more literary, borrowed words and expressions from pure Russian. Valuev's circular stopped all this sort of work, and in 1876 the Imperial Government issued measures which were still more severe. A law was promulgated which forbade the printing of any books, pamphlets or even plays in Ukrainian.

Very soon in Lvov the production of books and periodicals in the Ukrainian language was largely increased. Naturally the language elaborated in Galicia was based on the local dialect which differed from that spoken on the banks of the Dniepr. Furthermore, owing to local cultural conditions, many Polish and German ways of speech were introduced into this new language. Later, when this Galician Ukrainian reached the Russian provinces, it sounded much more foreign in relation to Russian than the Ukrainian which had been originated in the homeland of Gogol and Shevchenko.

The law of 1876 was among the restrictions which the Government of Alexander II considered necessary for the preservation of existing conditions in the South of Russia. At the same time the South-Western Section of the Imperial Geographical Society was closed because it was considered to be a centre of Ukrainian national propaganda. Yet no special Ukrainian national activities which could be regarded as subversive or separatist existed in the South of Russia in the seventies.

During this period there was developing in the Ukraine, as well as in Central and Northern Russia, a revolutionary movement among the youth and intelligentsia based on 'agrarian Socialism'. This agrarian Socialism was supposed to be a purely Russian conception of revolutionary Socialism entirely different from Socialist movements in Western Europe. The idealization of the peasant, which was a characteristic feature of this movement, naturally found adepts among the members of the Kiev *Hromada* who, owing to their cultural and historical studies, had conceived an almost religious admiration for the toiler. The spectacle of the sedentary intellectual 'fetishizing' the manual worker is a peculiar phenomenon of urban life which is undoubtedly pathological in its origins. Amongst many of the Ukrainian intellectuals their appreciation of the qualities of the peasant took the form of their modelling their own mode of life on peasant conditions, and they made a practice also of marrying peasant women.

In these fluctuating conditions of clumsy governmental repression and fluttering intellectual reactions it fell to a young Kiev professor, Michael Dragomanov, to be the first to start real political activity. Dragomanov proclaimed his sympathy not only with Russian agrarian Socialism but also with Socialism at it was understood in the West.

In the summer of 1875 Dragomanov decided to go abroad in order to have the opportunity of openly pursuing his propaganda against the Imperial Government. One of the first stages on his travels was Lvov, where he made friends among the local politicians. Dragomanov took up his abode in Geneva, where he began publishing the Ukrainian periodical *Hromada*, just as ten years previously Alexander Herzen had founded *Kolokol* ('The Bell') in the same city.

Michael Dragomanov's ideas soon began to penetrate to Russia. They also greatly influenced the Ukrainian movement which, in the last decades of the nineteenth century, had become definitely centred in Lvov.

In his political views Dragomanov was a Socialist of mild tendency and a Republican. The literary activities of Antonovich, Lazarevsky, and other Kievans, always seemed to him to be mistaken. In his opinion none had so 'misrepresented' Ukrainian history as the 'demophils' (the historians who painted in such dark colours those whom he regarded as the true champions of Ukrainian political freedom) Vyhovsky, Mazeppa, Polubotok, and yet were silent concerning such oppressors of liberty as Peter I and Catherine II. In his writings Dragomanov declared himself drastically opposed to Russian absolutism and he had no sympathy for any sovereign of the Romanov dynasty.

The strong views of Dragomanov left their imprint in the eighties on the Ukrainian politicians of Galicia. At the same time relations were strained between Petersburg and Vienna, and the Austrian administration was prepared to condone an Ukrainian revolutionary propaganda which had acquired an extreme anti-Russian character.

In 1890 the Austro-Hungarian Government decided to give active support to the Ukrainian political movement so as to direct it in accordance with its own aims. The direction favoured by Vienna was quite contrary to the teaching of the founder of Ukrainian nationalism. Dragomanov (who died in 1895) had never been a separatist. 'The Moscow state has done us much harm,' he once wrote, 'but bad weather is better than no weather at all.' And, again, he wrote in 1882: 'There are no grounds whatever and never will be for political separatism. Little Russians and Russians have the same historical traditions, the same creed and, concerning many things, the same notions. Our languages are extremely similar; we have no natural boundaries, and after all we are united by common economic interests. All talk of separatism is simply to be laughed at.' Dragomanov favoured the creation of a federation of autonomous national Slav republics; Galicia and Russian Ukraine being united, while the Slav countries under the domination of Austria-Hungary and in the Balkans would also form part of the federation. In his opinion 'this federation would have to decide the question of Constantinople and the Straits'.

Such an outlook could scarcely be approved in the Empire of the Habsburgs; but after 1890 Ukrainian political activity in Lvov completely departed from the teaching of the original prophet and acquired a totally different aspect which was not out of accord with the views of Vienna. The principal instrument of this change was Michael Hrushevsky, a man who lacked the depth and vision of Dragomanov, but who was superior to his elder in persistence and in political skill.

Hrushevsky's father was an important official in the Ministry of Public Instruction; he received his early education at the Tiflis Gymnasium and subsequently attended Kiev University. At the University young Hrushevsky became one of the most brilliant pupils of the historian Antonovich. When, after 1890, the Austro-Hungarian Government instituted a Chair for the History of South-Eastern Europe at the University of Lvov, Hrushevsky, on the recommendation of his master, was invited to fill it. In 1898 he published the first volume of his extensive *History of Ukraine-Rus*. The Shevchenko Society was, during the whole period between 1892 and 1914, extremely active, publishing 120 volumes of *Mémoires* besides a number of other works. The presiding genius was Hrushevsky and his numerous pupils became his fervent adepts.

Michael Hrushevsky, a man of serious and unquestioned erudition, understood the possibilities of furthering political work in Galicia through the instrument of historical research in such a way as to ensure the continued support of the Austro-Hungarian authorities. His magnificent *History* was to build a sound foundation for Ukrainian separatism. He succeeded in representing 'Ukraine-Rus' as something entirely different from 'Moscovia'. According to his thesis Kievan Russia was the cradle of 'Ukraine-Rus', but the Russian state which was later constituted round Novgorod and Vladimir-Suzdal and subsequently spread from its new centre round Moscow, was in no way the true successor of Kiev.

It was the easier for Hrushevsky to preach his original theories because the field of his activity happened to be Galicia which really was, since the thirteenth century, a fragment of Kievan Rus. Annexed to Poland in the fourteenth century, Galicia had been severed from the historical life of other Russian regions, but had retained her Russian population, Russian customs and Russian language.

Hrushevsky's versatile and insistent genius contributed also to the creation, out of the peasant dialect of Galicia, of a real Ukrainian literary language which others, under more favourable circumstances, had failed to create on the banks of the Dniepr.

All this work of Hrushevsky, both historical and linguistic, formed the basis for the activities of the Lvov politicians who, from the end of the nineteenth century, had declared themselves adherents of 'political separatism'. In this wise, only fifty years after the first attempt to create a Ukrainian national movement had found its expression in the Brotherhood of St Cyril and St Methodius, something entirely different took form—outside the boundaries of Russia. This movement had abandoned the comparatively moderate and really logical line propounded by Dragomanov and had become an extremely anti-Russian brand of separatism.

At the turn of the century the conception of Ukrainian separatism which was being propagated from Galicia had roused little interest among the people of Russian Ukraine. Like the Kievan movement of the second half of the nineteenth century, the Lvov movement was confined to a relatively small band of intelligentsia. The rural masses were hardly aware of the existence of a 'Ukrainian movement'— with a few exceptions who might have accidentally come in contact with members of the town intelligentsia. Neither of these movements had had the least influence on the vast changes which had been taking place in the Ukraine, particularly during the latter half of the nineteenth century.

In the time of Bohdan Khmelnytsky there were not more than two and a half million people over the whole of the area of the modern Ukraine including Podolia. In 1897 there were three and a half million inhabitants in the Government of Kiev alone; in the three Little Russian Governments (Kiev, Chernigov, Poltava) and the three New Russian Governments (Kherson, Ekaterinoslav, Tauris), together with Volhynia and Podolia, the population in the last years of the nineteenth century amounted to about twenty-five millions. At the end of the eighteenth century the density of population in the southern steppes was reckoned at about 1 to the square kilometre; a hundred years later it had risen to between 40 and 50 to the square kilometre. The process of colonization of the rich lands of New Russia had assumed truly 'American' proportions. According to the Census of 1897 the population of the three New Russian Governments was made up: 50 per cent of Ukrainians, 20 per cent of Great Russians, with the remaining 30 per cent composed of German colonists, Jews, Tartars, Moldavians, Bulgarians, Serbians and Greeks.

By the last two decades of the nineteenth century there were already signs of over-population in relation to the productive capacity of the country under the existing economic system. Between 1890 and 1914 about 1,700,000 peasants migrated from overcrowded districts to new lands beyond the Volga, to Siberia and the Far Eastern provinces; very large numbers, also, crossed the ocean to Canada and the United States.

Between 1860 and 1870 the beet-sugar industry had been developed in the densely populated countryside of Podolia. It soon expanded into the Governments of Kiev, Chernigov and Kharkov. The intensive development of the coal industry in the Donets Basin began in the eighties. Ten years later the exploitation of the rich deposits of iron ore in the Krivoy Rog (to the west of the lower Dniepr) was undertaken.

By the beginning of the twentieth century the steppes of New Russia had come to be regarded as one of the most important industrial regions of the Empire.

With the growth, particularly, of the mining and metallurgical industries of the Donets and the Krivoy Rog, both the social composition and distribution of the population began to change with great rapidity. The incoming labourers from the north became more numerous in the industrial regions than the Ukrainian natives. Old ·towns grew and new towns rose until, at the beginning of the twentieth century, the urban population represented 20 per cent of the whole. In Kharkov and other industrial centres and in the great ports of the Black Sea Ukrainians were in a minority. In Volhynia and Podolia and in the Kiev and Chernigov Governments Jews formed 40 per cent of the town population. All these important changes in the social and economic structure of the Ukraine tended to weaken particularist tendencies and to strengthen the ties with the rest of the Empire.(6)

The raw new industrial population of the Ukrainian cities was naturally infected by the revolutionary movement which culminated in the outbreak of 1905. But the national colour which was given to the social outbreaks in Finland, the Baltic Provinces, Poland and the Caucasus was not evident in the Ukrainian Governments. Revolutionary manifestations in the Ukraine were extremely violent, both in the industrial centres and in the country districts, where attacks on landowners were frequent. But there was no national motive in the fury of the people and, except among some small university groups, nothing was heard of Ukrainian national aspirations. In the subsequent trials staged during the reprisals of the imperial authorities against the revolutionaries accusations of separatist or autonomist tendencies were lacking.(7)

But the reforms which followed the period of repression after the revolutionary crisis gave new opportunities for the peaceful development of a cultural nationalism such as had not existed before. The Constitution of 1905 permitted the printing of books and periodicals in the Ukrainian language. Michael Hrushevsky immediately availed himself of the situation and transferred the scene of his activities from Galicia to Kiev. Here he continued the publication of volumes of his *History*, while the Ukrainian Scientific Society with the enterprising Professor at its head began the publication of the fourteen volumes of *Mémoires* which appeared within the next seven years.

An Indian summer of liberalism was illuminating the last decade of the autocracy. In 1906 the Imperial Academy of Sciences initiated a discussion on the subject of whether Ukrainian was to be considered as one of the Russian dialects or as a separate language, and by a majority of one the learned members approved the linguistic independence of the Ukraine. This decision opened wide possibilities for the Galician version of the Ukrainian idiom which had been so ably nurtured by Hrushevsky. A spate of print now began to appear in the newly recognized language. In Kiev appeared the daily paper *Rada*, which soon achieved a fairly wide circulation. Ekaterinoslav and Poltava also had their Ukrainian dailies. A special bookshop for Ukrainian editions was opened in Kiev, and in Kiev and Lvov the simultaneous publication was arranged of a periodical entitled *The Literary-Scientific News*. At the same time there appeared (in Russian) another periodical called *Ukrainian Life* on which Simon Petlyura and Vinnichenko (destined subsequently to become famous on a more lurid field) were collaborators.

Such a liberation of the Ukrainian movement could not help influencing its growth. The movement began to find many recruits, principally amongst the city intelligentsia and also amongst the so-called 'half-intelligentsia'—country schoolmasters and small officials of the local administration (*Zemstvo*). At the same time, not only did the separatist ideas which had been introduced from Galicia have little success, but the tension in the international situation and the intensification of the antagonism between the Russian and Austro-Hungarian Governments had the effect of impelling the Galician Ukrainians to take part with the other Slav groups of the Habsburg Empire against the Germanic enemies of Slavdom. The anti-Russian separatist Ukrainian movement sponsored by the Austro-Hungarian authorities in Lvov rapidly lost ground in face of a new local movement which aimed at the union of Galicia with Russia. Sympathy for Russia was particularly strong in Carpathian Rus, where the majority of the people considered themselves Russian and refused to hear anything in favour of the 'Ukrainian ideology' of Hrushevsky or of the 'Ukrainian language' elaborated in Lvov. In this remote and backward region of the Carpathians a revival of national consciousness had begun about the middle of the nineteenth century and it had been stimulated by the Russian occupation of Hungary during the Revolution of 1848. On the eve of the war of 1914–18 the Hungarian Government staged a state trial at Marmaros-Sziget where a number of inhabitants from Carpathian Rus were accused of secret relations with Russia and of high treason.

Professor Milyukov summed up the state of the Ukrainian Question when he spoke in the Duma on the occasion of a debate (spring of 1914) during which Russian members of conservative and nationalist tendencies were opposing the holding of festivals in Kiev on the occasion of the hundredth anniversary of the birth of Shevchenko. 'A Ukrainian movement exists', he affirmed, 'and it cannot be stopped.' He went on to declare that: 'As yet there is no separatist movement in the Ukraine. Even if it exists in an embryonic state it is very weak. But it can be brought to life—and that is what Russian Nationalists are doing.'

As it was, when in the summer of 1914 the crisis of the Slav world approached catastrophe, the Ukrainians showed themselves prepared to submerge their own national individuality in the cause of All the Russias.

BIBLIOGRAPHICAL NOTES AND ADDITIONS TO CHAPTER V

General Bibliography for the Period of the Later Hetmans

See works already mentioned in Notes to Chapter IV by Nolde, Myakotin, Doroshenko. *The Ukrainian Encyclopaedia* is also useful for the history of the Ukraine in the eighteenth and nineteenth centuries.

For the history of the Zaporogian *Sech* in the eighteenth century, see:
Skalkovski. *Istoriya Novoy Sechi* (History of the New *Sech*), Odessa, 1845.
Evarnitski. *Istoriya Zaporozhskikh Kazakov* (History of the Zaporogian Cossacks), vols. I–III, Petersburg, 1852–97.

For Hetman Cyril Razumovsky, see:
Vasilichkov. *Semeystvo Razumovskikh* (The Razumovski Family), Petersburg, 1880.
Cf. also *Camb. Mod. Hist.* vol. VI, chap. VII, R. Nisbet Bain, 'Poland under the Saxon Kings'; chap. X, *idem.* 'Russia under Anne and Elizabeth'.

For the period of Catherine II in general, see:
Bilbasov, V. *Istoriya Ekateriny II* (History of Catherine II), Eng. ed. London, 1895.
Kostomarov, N. *Poslednie Gody Rechi Pospolitoy* (The Last Years of *Rzecz Pospolita*), 1905.
Chechulin, N. *Vneshnyaya Politika Rossii v Nachale Tsarstvovaniya Ekateriny II*, 1762–1774 (Foreign Policy of Russia at the Beginning of the Reign of Catherine II), Petersburg, 1895.
Sorel, A. *The Eastern Question in the Eighteenth Century*, London, 1898.
Camb. Mod. Hist. vol. VI, chap. XIX, Prof. O. Hötzsch, 'Catharine II'.
Bagaley, D. *Istoriya Slobodskoy Ukrainy* (History of the Eastern or New Ukraine), Kharkov, 1918.

(1) *Ukrainians on Forced Works During the Reign of Peter I*

Many folk songs recall the memory of these forced works:

'Oh! They gave the boys large spades,
And they sent a young lad to dig ditches.
Oh! And a raven flew from the foreign land,
He flew and crowed
That the lad is sitting by the ditch,
Sitting and crying bitterly:
"I am only a lad so young,
And Oh! So strange am I here!
Oh father! Sell the black steed,
Pay ransom for me,
Then back to dear freedom again."'

Kashchenko's *Opovidannya.*

(2) *The Fate of Orlik and Voynarovsky*

Until the death of Charles XII and the end of the Great Northern War, Philip Orlik continued to entertain hopes that his services might prove of profit to one or other of the Great Powers. The Swedes had recognized him as the lawful Hetman of the Ukraine, and the Turks continued to allow him to remain in Istanbul in case they found themselves in need of his help in the Ukraine. The English even took some interest in him, since the Government of George I was irritated by Peter's passing patronage of the Jacobite cause (see Borshak, *Slavonic Review*, vol. x, no. 28, p. 138).

In 1722, however, Orlik found it necessary to leave Istanbul, and he wandered about Europe for some time. In Hamburg he was successful in marrying off his daughter to a French nobleman; and he ended his days peacefully at the Château de Dinteville near Chaumont.

Hamburg turned out to be a more tragic halting place for Mazeppa's favourite nephew, Andrew Voynarovsky. The old Hetman appears to have had a genuine and fatherly affection for his sister's son. Good-looking, gifted, courageous and adventurous, Andrew Voynarovsky appeared to the Hetman to have all the qualities which he may have imagined himself as possessing as a young man.

Voynarovsky had been sent to study abroad in Dresden where, owing to his uncle's friendship with Augustus the Strong, he was received into the most initmate circle of the court and became acquainted with the celebrated Aurora Königsmarck.

During his sojourn in Tighin and Istanbul, Voynarovsky found himself involved in quarrels with Philip Orlik in respect of the considerable sums of treasure which remained in the hands of the fugitives after Mazeppa's death. In 1715 Voynarovsky took up his abode in Vienna and from there removed to Sweden, since included in his inheritance was the enormous debt amounting to about a million *kröner* from Charles XII for monies borrowed after Poltava. In Stockholm he found difficulty in securing settlement from the hard-pressed King, but otherwise he was treated with consideration.

From Sweden Voynarovsky found occasion to visit Hamburg, where he again met Aurora Königsmarck, at that time living in the Free City which in those days was a centre for the fashionable international world, since it had a reputation for political intrigue, high play and agreeable life. In the salon of his old friend he met an English diplomat named Mattison, whom he tried to interest in 'the freedom-loving Ukrainian people': it was not an unfavourable moment, since the British Government were unquiet at the possible disturbance of the balance of power in the Baltic and the Black Sea as a result of the Russian successes in the Northern War. But Voynarovsky's advances, like Orlik's, had no result; and Mazeppa's nephew, possibly as a result of his failure in this direction, began to play with the idea of a reconciliation with the Russian authorities through the mediation of Aurora Königsmarck.

Peter I, however, being informed of Voynarovsky's presence in Hamburg, ordered his Resident there, Frederick Bettichger, to kidnap him, and to forward a demand at the same time to the Senate of the Free City for the delivery of 'the criminal'. Several Russian officers were sent to Hamburg to help Bettichger in these plans. At that time Russian troops were quartered in Mecklenburg under the command of Rumyantsev, who later was to have a hand in 'bringing back' the Tsarevich Alexey Petrovich from Naples. An ambush was arranged and Voynarovsky was kidnapped in the street and taken to Bettichger's house, where he could be held a prisoner owing to the extra-territorial status of the Resident. The Hamburg Magistrates protested and the Swedish envoy demanded the release of Voynarovsky on the ground that he was a 'Colonel in the Swedish Royal Guard'. It is difficult to say how this affair would have ended if Aurora Königsmarck had not intervened. She persuaded Voynarovsky to avail himself of the visit of the Russian court to Altona to go there on 5 December, the name-day of the Empress Catherine, and throw himself on the Tsar's mercy. The Swedish envoy, for some unknown reason, also advised him to do so. Voynarovsky imprudently yielded and was immediately sent off to Petersburg 'in order that the case might be investigated'. There he was incarcerated in the fortress of Peter and Paul, where he remained until 1723, when he was sent to Yakutsk in the far northeast of Siberia. He died there in 1740. The traveller Miller saw him in Yakutsk—a complete moral and physical wreck. This meeting became the theme of the poem 'Voynarovsky' composed by a Russian author at the beginning of the nineteenth century. This poet was himself involved in the Decabrist movement—so many of the participators in which ended their days in Siberia. (See Ilya Borshak, *Voynarovsky*, Lvov, 1938.)

(3) *The Haydamaky*

The *Haydamak* movement, beginning in the thirties of the eighteenth century, acquired ferocious and anarchical proportions during the sixties when Gonta and Zaliznyak took Uman. The movement has been idealized by Ukrainian nationalists—even by such eminent historians as Professor Antonovich (*Izsledovanie o Gaydamachestve po Aktam* 1700–1768 (Researches on the Haydamaks based on Documents 1700–1768), Kiev, 1876). Kulish, however, protested against this idealization, on the ground that the movement was the most vivid expression of the anarchic elements in the character of the Ukrainian people: in his view the movement demonstrated all those instincts of destruction and criminality which were exposed again in the Pugachev revolt. The author of a study of the eighteenth-century Polish Ukraine, Fr. R. Gawroński, found that 'the *Haydamak* idea was a consequence of the Tartar-Turkish, altogether Turanian, education received by the Russian people'. He proceeds to emphasize the idea propagated by Polish politicians in the nineteenth century when he adds that 'humanitarian and cultural elements among the Slavs only begin to predominate where they come in contact with the Catholic Church'. However that may be, the persistence of a wildly savage strain in the population of South Russia was again emphasized in the different environment of our epoch during the Civil War and the operations of Makhno and the *atamany* (v. p. 314).

(4) *The Zaporogians after the Destruction of the Sech*

After the destruction of the New *Sech* on the orders of Catherine II, the Chief Ataman Kalnishevsky, together with Paul Holovaty and Hloba, were arrested and taken to Moscow. Although there was really nothing against Kalnishevsky, he met with severe treatment: he was exiled to the Solovetskī monastery, where he was held until 1801. Alexander I offered him his freedom, but he refused to leave the quiet haven of the monastery and died there at the age of 112.

A typical Ukrainian song describes the destruction of the *Sech*:

'The world is so wide and the land is so vast
And yet it seems there is nowhere to go!
This is why they want to send the brave Zaporogian troops to their doom.
The Tsaritsa has thought it and Gritsko has done it.
They want to drive the Zaporogians far far away,
Far away where the Danube flows.'

After the destruction of the *Sech* the more turbulent among the Zaporogians decided 'to go off to the Danube'. During the year 1775 about 5000 left for Turkey, of whom only about half were genuine Zaporogians, the rest being outcasts who were in fear of falling into the hands of the Russian Government. All the Cossacks who had decided to become Turkish subjects gathered at Akkerman, from where they sent a deputation to the Sultan. The Porte decided to take them into service, and the Island of St George situated in the Sulina channel of the Danube delta was allotted to them, so that they might be able to organize a new *Sech* there. In the meantime they received orders to do frontier guard along the river Bug, which at that time was the limit of the Ottoman dominions.

These Cossacks who had gone over to Turkey received a standard, on one side of which was a golden cross on a white background, and on the other a silver crescent on a black background. Many peasant fugitives from over the Russian border joined them during the following years and their number increased to between 8000 and 10,000.

Potemkin, having decided to form the Black Sea Cossacks out of the remnants of the old Zaporogians, sent emissaries to persuade them to come back. This attempt was partly successful, since the Zaporogians had had a difficult time in their settlement in the delta of the Danube, where they had come into conflict with other Russian fugitives who had already settled and appropriated the best sites and the best fisheries. These Russians were Don Cossacks, named after their first chief, 'Nekrasov's men'. 'Nekrasov's men' had left the Don after the failure of the revolt of Bulavin during the reign of Peter I. Numerous quarrels started between the new-comers and the old settlers which soon grew into skirmishes and, later, pitched battles for the possession of meadows, lakes and creeks.

At this time, then, a few of the Zaporogians returned to Russia, but a much greater number accepted the invitation of the Austrian Government to migrate and settle along the banks of the river Tisza. The flow of peasants escaping from the Ukraine was, however, so great that the number of 'the Sultan's Cossacks' did not diminish. 'Going off to the Danube' became an every-day occurrence in the Ukrainian countryside. Many songs still recall this migration:

'There across the Danube,
    Yea, the peaceful blue Danube,
    A boy is feasting and drinking and calling:
    "Hey! A boat and row me across
    For another look at my native land,
    For a last look at my own Ukraine!"'

A curious situation arose during Catherine's Second Turkish War, when the old Zaporogians recruited by Potëmkin fought in the Russian Army, while those who had gone beyond the Danube had to fight in the Turkish ranks. Both sides had recourse to all sorts of subterfuges so that 'brother should not fight against brother', but they were not always successful, particularly when, in 1790–1, the delta of the Danube became the main theatre of the war. In the end Chapyga, the *ataman* of Potemkin's newly formed Black Sea Cossacks, had to give the order that 'the Sultan's Cossacks' were not to be looked upon as Christians but were to be treated as Turks.

After Potëmkin's death, when orders came from Petersburg that the Black Sea Cossacks were to be transferred to the Kuban, about 8000 of them obeyed, and the rest, about 4000, elected to join 'the Sultan's Cossacks' across the Danube. During the Russo-Turkish War of 1806–11 a considerable number of these late-comers deserted to the Russians. At the end of the war Bessarabia was annexed to Russia and the Turkish frontier withdrawn to the line of the Pruth and the Danube delta.

The former Zaporogians who remained in Turkish territory now had to fight a war of extermination against 'Nekrasov's men' for the control of the fisheries. The Turks were at first rather astonished at this civil war between the two groups of Cossacks, but the Turkish authorities did not interfere and used to say to the contending sides: 'If you are strong enough kill and drive away your enemies!' Finally the Ukrainian Cossacks got the better of 'Nekrasov's men' and the Turks transferred the remnant of these to Asia Minor. In the twenties of the present century one or two villages of the descendants of these Don Cossacks from the delta of the Danube were to be found in the neighbourhood of the Asiatic shore of the Sea of Marmara; the villagers retained the old style of dress and many of the customs of their ancestors.

In the nineteenth century the former Zaporogians gradually died out, and the Danube delta became a refuge simply for peasants escaping from over the Russian frontier; about 1820 these fugitives had become rather numerous; there were about 15,000 to 20,000 of them. The Russo-Turkish War of 1828–9 put an end to this situation. When the Russian Army crossed the Danube the last *ataman* of the Danube Cossacks, Hladky, went to the Emperor Nicholas I at Izmail to implore his pardon and mercy. Hladky was given the rank of colonel and later that of general. The Danube Cossacks went back to Russia; the majority of them joined the descendants of the Zaporogians on the Kuban.

For some interesting details on Polish military refugees in the Ottoman Empire, particularly during the nineteenth century, see Thadée Gosztowt, *La Pologne et l'Islam*, Paris, 1907.

(5) Decabrists in the Ukraine

The Decabrists had numerous supporters among the young officers in garrison in the Ukraine. The movement found scarcely any support among the people, but many landowners in the Ukraine, Polish, Ukrainian and Russian, favoured the aims of a constitutional monarchy in Russia, a liberal régime and the abolition of serfdom. Colonel Pestel, probably the most determined and gifted of the Decabrist leaders, was stationed in the Ukraine, and at the time of the attempted coup in Petersburg, a mutiny of officers took place at the small town of Tulchin in Podolia. (See Bagaley, *Povstania Dekabristov na Ukraine*, Kharkov, 1926.)

(6) The Development of New Russia during the Nineteenth Century

The fashionable intelligentsia who liked to sneer at 'the Potëmkin villages' at the beginning of the nineteenth century were fond of repeating the phrase: 'One can hear the steppe winds howl where Catherine's favourite built his ephemeral towns.' As a matter of fact, of the four towns founded by Potëmkin, Kherson, Ekaterinoslav, Sevastopol, Nikolaev, each already had a population of 100,000 or over within a century of his death. Potemkin did not live to supervise the building of Odessa, but the site was chosen by him. Odessa was built by French *émigrés*—de Ribas, Langeron and the Duc de Richelieu. During the reign of Alexander I it had already become a flourishing commercial town with a busy port and broad boulevards and buildings in the French 'Empire' style. The *Lycée* founded by Richelieu was transformed later into the New Russian University. Pushkin, who visited Odessa in the twenties of the nineteenth century, describes the gay and busy life of this cosmopolitan city which had arisen on the site of a forlorn Turkish hamlet. It had become a great centre for merchants and tradesmen of different nationalities—Greeks, Jews, Armenians, Italians, Moldavians, Germans and Poles—who streamed there from all parts.

After the Vienna Congress which marked the end of the period of wars, the South Russian grain trade began to develop on a prodigious scale and Odessa became the main port of export. The cultivation of the virgin soil of New Russia gave fabulous results; but there was a great lack of labour, which was not adequately supplied by the migrant population of fugitive peasants which was always on the move on the peripheries of the old settled Govern-ments. In the thirties and forties of the nineteenth century the peopling of South Russia assumed more regular forms when Ukrainian and Russian landowners who had acquired estates there began transferring a proportion of their serfs to the new regions.

The land fever and the speculation which accompanied this process have been described by Gogol in his novel *Dead Souls*. He relates how a small landowner named Chichikov made the round of his fellows in the remoter parts of Central Russia and for a few copecks bought 'dead souls', that is, serfs who were dead but who had not been struck off the rolls on account of carelessness or for some other reason. Acts of sale were registered, and on the strength of these the enterprising Chichikov became the owner of a number of 'souls', thus becoming entitled to acquire lands in New Russia on favour-able conditions—lands which he could sell later at a good profit. Gogol was not particularly interested in this land swindle, but used it as a vehicle for describing in a most vivid and entertaining manner the different types of provincial Russia of that period, their customs and their lives. However, not all purchasers of serfs were swindlers, and many did really buy living serfs from landowners in order to transport them to the South. The efforts of these 'pioneers', in pursuing their own private interests, proved more effective in a short space of time than a systematic colonization of the South under the auspices of the Government might have proved.

This epic has, unfortunately, produced no Gogol to describe it. Dani-levski, the author of three novels which depict the life of the settlers in New Russia, was a writer of no particular talent. Yet his works abound in pic-turesque and curious pages describing this 'Russian America' of the fifties of the nineteenth century. Like Gogol, Danilevski was a Ukrainian, the descendant of a Cossack captain who had taken up his abode in the neigh-bourhood of Izyum at the end of the seventeenth century. In 1849, in his student days in Petersburg, Danilevski was arrested together with Dosto-yevski on account of the affair concerning the secret society founded by Petrushevski. He was, however, found not guilty and was set free after two months' imprisonment. His later service in the Ministry of Public Instruction gave him plenty of opportunity for travel in the South of Russia, where he was engaged on the collection of historical and archaeological material. In 1860 he wrote *Fugitives in New Russia* and later two other novels in which the scene is laid in the South Russian steppe. One of Danilevski's characters puts the question: 'But who and what are these fugitives?' Another answers: 'It is here that Russian serfs have found a refuge. Here is their Kentucky and Massachusetts. If there had not been fugitives there would have been nothing —neither the Don, nor the Black Sea region, nor the good and fertile lands beyond the Rapids. All is the work of the fugitives: Rostov, Taganrog, Mariupol. All these prosperous tradespeople and wealthy exporters are the descendants of fugitives—serfs owned either by private landowners or by the Government.' Another character praises the fugitives: 'They are peaceful hard-working people, they don't drink, they are just like Liverpool Puritans.' Comparisons with the emigrants to America frequently occur in Danilevski's novels. Full of energy and not over particular about infringing the law, 'the pioneers' built their fortunes in the New Russian steppe.

(7) *Jews in the South of Russia*

The Jewish Question, which became so acute in Russia at the turn of the nineteenth century, originated in the Ukraine. Before the union with Little Russia, there were very few Jews living within the territory of the Moscow state.

All the rebellions of Cossacks and peasants during the seventeenth century were always directed, not only against Polish landlords but also against the Jewish population which was regarded as the instrument through which the Polish *szlachta* oppressed the Ukrainian peasantry. According to Ukrainian historians, after the stormy years of the middle of the seventeenth century, not a Jew was left on the left bank of the Dniepr, and on the right bank and in Volhynia only one-hundredth part of the former Jewish population remained.

Nevertheless, as soon as relatively peaceful conditions returned to the Ukraine the Jews swarmed back into the country; nothing seemed to check the process, neither 'the Uman slaughter' nor the sanguinary feats of the *Haydamaky*. The development of big estates in left-bank Ukraine was accompanied by the appearance of Jews in the numerous towns and villages of the Governments of Chernigov and Poltava. Just as in Poland, a large Jewish urban population seemed to be a phenomenon which characterized a rural economy based on serf-worked *latifundia*. In both cases and for the same reasons the result was similar. Important estates implied trade on a large scale in country produce—grain, cattle, leather, timber. Neither in Poland nor in the Ukraine had any strong native commercial class had the opportunity to develop—as had been the case in Novgorod and even in Moscow. The Polish and Ukrainian aristocracy needed middlemen for the profitable transaction of their affairs, and the Jews were ideally suited to fulfil the functions of middlemen. At the same time both in Poland and in the Ukraine the increasing wealth of the landowning class created a market for artisans, for these lands lacked the exclusive class of skilled craftsmen which had come into existence at an early date in the North Russian capitals. Furthermore, the increasing rigour of the legislation which bound the Polish and Ukrainian peasantry to the soil prevented enterprising young men from coming into the towns to learn crafts and trades. These conditions became more acute as the development of 'the new lands' in the Ukraine and New Russia during the eighteenth century accentuated the shortage of available labour.

After the First Partition of Poland a mass migration of Jews set in from White Russia, itself a poor land, into the rich and fertile provinces on both banks of the Dniepr. These new immigrants found plenty of opportunities for proving their peculiar commercial talents. After the Second and Third Partitions of Poland there followed a real 'transplantation' of the Jewish population of Galicia and Poland to Volhynia, to Podolia, to the Dniepr and to the towns of New Russia. Odessa proved a particular focus of attraction to these needy and capable Irsaelites. While the process of populating New Russia was going on, the institution of serfdom still subsisted in all its rigour and the peasants themselves had no chance of leaving their villages and founding a middle class of their own in 'the new lands'. The Government had for a long time been aware of this Jewish movement from west to east, but in view of their desire to encourage the colonization of the South of Russia, they regarded this flow of Jews as rather a useful phenomenon which favoured the development of 'crafts and trade'. Indeed, in view of the pressing need for agricultural labour, the Government made an effort to utilize the overflow of the Jewish population of the towns for purposes of land development. As early as the reign of Paul I, the senator and poet, Gabriel Derzhavin, had been sent on a mission to White Russia in order to investigate the famine which was ravaging that region. As a result of his tour, Derzhavin had made a proposal to found Jewish agricultural colonies in New Russia. The Law of 1804 granted Jews the right to acquire or lease land in the South, and in 1806 seven Jewish colonies were founded in the Government of Kherson. The Russian authorities continued to approve Jewish agricultural colonization during the whole of the first half of the nineteenth century. The Emperor Nicholas I hoped to accelerate the assimilation of Jews to the local population by inducing Jews to do military service, after a preliminary training beginning at the age of twelve in special schools. The Emperor patronized, at the same time, Jewish traders and artisans and encouraged his Governor-Generals, Prince Paskevich in Warsaw and Count Vorontsov in New Russia, to continue the experiment of the Jewish agricultural colonies.

The experiment was destined to end in complete failure. The Jewish inhabitants of these colonies were drawn by an irresistible attraction towards the towns. In the reign of Alexander II, when Jewish agricultural colonization ceased, it was found that in thirty-seven Jewish colonies in the South of Russia there were only 40,000 people. Such was the miserable result of an experiment which had been supported by the Government for forty years. Trotsky, who was brought up in one of these colonies which still existed during his childhood, describes it in the following way: 'On both banks of a small river were situated two colonies; one was Jewish and the other German. On the German side well cared for houses stood with tiled and thatched roofs. The horses were big, the cows well fed. On the Jewish side dilapidated houses, leaking roofs, cattle in a pitiable state.'

The end of Jewish agricultural colonization in 1865 was a result not only of its entire failure to that date but also of the abolition of serfdom. The new structure of peasant life required that large land reserves should be available. New land was needed for allotment to the liberated serfs overcrowded on the landlords' estates in the old settled lands of Russia; there was certainly no longer any sense in giving land into the hands of very poor farmers, as the Jews had proved themselves to be.

Twenty years after the liberation of the peasants there were already many signs of over-population in the South of Russia under the economic conditions of that period. The development of the phenomenon of over-population corresponded with the first wave of *pogroms* in South and South-Western Russia. The reason for these pogroms was purely social: an overflow of the liberated peasantry into the towns was increasing all the time, and in the towns the peasants found that many of the most profitable occupations were monopolized by Jews. During the years 1876–89 Jewish pogroms took place in Elizavetgrad, Kiev, Pereyaslavl, Balta, Ekaterinoslav, and many of the smaller towns of Podolia and Volhynia and the Chernigov and

Poltava Governments. These pogroms represented a purely instinctive movement among the Ukrainian peasantry which had nothing new in it; in the towns of Poland pogroms had occurred from time to time for centuries past. These riots were seldom accompanied by any actual slaughter of Jews, and in the majority of cases the Jews were not even beaten; only their property was plundered and destroyed. It was not the prosperous Jews who were chosen as victims but generally the poorer classes—artisans and small shopkeepers: the wealthy quarters of a town would be better guarded by the police.

It was as unjust to abuse the Imperial Government as the accomplice and instigator of the mob as it would have been to blame the British Government for the sectarian riots of the same period in the North of Ireland. No doubt some of the police who were recruited from the local population sympathized with the mob; but the movement itself emanated from the masses. The illegal Social Revolutionary paper wrote as follows on 6 October 1881: 'Pogroms are a revolutionary movement of the masses which, owing to local conditions, is tinged with Anti-Semitism. Landowners are considered an antiquated institution and this is why the people now have no enmity towards them and regard them even with a certain benevolence. The Jews are looked upon as the chief enemy.'

The international relations of Russia both with Germany and Austria and also with Great Britain were not cordial during that period, and the pogroms served as a pretext for violent attacks in the Press of Western Europe and America. At the same time the emigration of Russian Jews to America was accelerated, and influential Jewish groups were formed in New York and other American cities. A pogrom in Kishinev in which forty-seven persons were killed aroused a storm of indignation in America. When the Imperial Government had disappeared and the Ukrainian masses were, under the leadership of their *atamany*, giving vent to their natural instinct for savagery, the figure of forty-seven killed was destined to appear a very modest one.

Another consequence of the period of the pogroms was the tendency which they seem to have encouraged in the Jewish youth to turn to the more extreme revolutionary parties. At the same time the obligatory settlement of the Jewish population in the South-Western Governments of Russia tended to overcrowd the Ukraine and New Russia with Jews. Their number attained 2,000,000 by the end of the nineteenth century. According to the Census of 1897 the Jewish population amounted to 41 per cent in the towns of Volhynia and Podolia and in the Governments of Kiev, Poltava and Chernigov. In the big centres like Kiev, Kharkov, Odessa and Ekaterinoslav, a real Jewish proletariat took form and proved extremely accessible to revolutionary propaganda. On the other hand, the educated Jews who belonged to the free professions filled the ranks of the revolutionary intelligentsia.

Jews took a most active part in the revolutionary events of the years 1900–6; as a result, during the counter-revolutionary phase which followed in 1905–6 pogroms took a far more violent form than those of the eighties. During this period there is no doubt that the authorities sometimes supported the counter-revolutionary organizations which were the instigators of these pogroms. At the outbreak of war in 1914 Jewry remained a dangerous explosive element in the life of South Russia.

CHAPTER VI

NATIONALITY AND COMMUNISM IN THE UKRAINE (1914–1939)

§ 1. THE AUSTRIANS AND RUSSIANS IN GALICIA (1914–17)

THE Great War of 1914–18, having its immediate origins in the complications arising out of the dissolution of the Ottoman Empire in the Balkans, was a consequence of the history of the two preceding centuries in Eastern Europe.

So long as intervening states separated the frontiers of the Teutonic and Muscovite powers, those powers had a common interest. In Poland, at the end of the eighteenth century, Prussia, Austria and Russia had compromised on a division of territories, and their common concern to perpetuate the dismemberment of Poland had been a factor in averting mutual antagonisms and in maintaining a balance which found its most emphatic expression in the *Dreikaiserbund*.

But in the partition of the European territories of the Ottoman Empire, which was the inevitable sequel to the dismemberment of *Rzecz Pospolita*, the parties failed to agree. In the 'grand alliances' of the eighteenth century against Turkey, Austria had once failed (1736–9), and had later faltered (the Wars of Catherine), while Frederick of Prussia had in the end shown his inclination to oppose indefinite Russian expansion at the expense of the Ottoman Empire.

When for a brief period Napoleon formed a great continental power in Western Europe and became, in a way, the heir and executor of Central European policy in the Slavonic East, at Tilsit, anxious as he was to conciliate Alexander, he proved unwilling to satisfy Russian ambitions. His famous 'Constantinople! Never! That means the Empire of the World' expressed in a phrase the reasons why the Central European and Muscovite powers, who could agree to partition the Baltic coasts and the plains of Poland, could neither of them forego the mastery of the Straits which divide Europe and Asia.

In the seventeenth and eighteenth centuries France had not succeeded in upholding the Polish barrier in the east against the Germanic power.

In the nineteenth century the three Western powers whose interests or ambitions were maritime and colonial combined in the Crimean War to check a Slav hegemony in the Balkans. The Sardinian kingdom aspired to revive the Genoese and Venetian traditions of earlier centuries, while France had historic memories of Latin-Norman rule in the Levant. England, which had rivalled, and was during the rest of the century to continue to rival, France in the Eastern Mediterranean, recognized a communion of interest and declared for the first time a continuing challenge to the control of the Straits and the Aegean by a great land power. In the Crimean War the Germanic powers adopted a neutrality rather hostile to Russia and in 1854-6, as in 1877-8, waited to take their profits from the action of the maritime powers.

As events accumulated to the catastrophe of 1914, it was obvious that the ultimate policies of the Germanic and Russian powers, which in Poland had had a common basis, were mutually exclusive in the Balkans and the Near East. A Russian advance to the Straits and hegemony in the Balkans must block for ever German plans of dominion in the Near and Middle East; while if Germanic power were to straddle the Straits Russia would be confined within the landlocked Black Sea, and both her political structure and her economy would become more and more subordinate to the master of a belt which might stretch from the Kattegat to the Persian Gulf.

Weakened by the Japanese War and dependent for financial support upon the capitalist groups of the West, Russia was the natural ally, in the impending conflict, of the maritime powers which were in need of the alliance of great land armies capable of exhausting the man-power of Germany.

In the event both the Russian and Germanic power-machines succumbed to the strain of world conflict, and the maritime powers, passing masters of the Straits, by the restoration of Poland and the exploitation of East European nationalist tendencies, re-established in a new form the old belt of states from the Baltic to the Black Sea which had until the end of the eighteenth century separated the Germanic world and Muscovy. The new states were weak and their policies were divergent; it was inevitable therefore that the old Muscovite-Germanic pressure on the intervening belt should revive. It was inevitable at the same time, in a world where the space factor had really disappeared and where processes of thought and emotion were accelerated, that the community of interests which was to attract Germany and Russia together should be criss-crossed by the old German desire (expressed through the centuries in the activities of the Teutonic knights and the Baltic barons) to dominate Russia and by the Russian Messianism which had transmuted Panslavism into Communism.

On the outbreak of war in 1914, the Ukrainian Question occupied a relatively minor place in the minds of political and military chiefs .in Berlin and Vienna. At the same time both Berlin and Vienna contemplated an ultimate solution favourable to their respective views—views which differed in important essentials.

The course of events during the war obliged the Habsburg Monarchy to abandon all ambitious plans and to concentrate on the preservation of existing territory. The Germans, on the other hand, as the war developed, began to take the greatest interest in the Ukraine, especially after 1916 when German troops made their appearance in Podolia and Volhynia and when a year later, the Russian Revolution opened the way wide to the Dniepr and even to the Don. If at the beginning of the war the Ukraine was of interest primarily to Vienna, by the end it had been transferred into Berlin's field of vision.

Despite the drift towards Russia which had been noticeable among both Galician and Russian Ukrainian intellectuals after the Liberal reforms following the Revolution of 1905, Vienna had been encouraged by the weakness of Russia to supplement a more active policy in the Balkans by a more intense interest in the Ukrainians. The Slavs who remained 'loyal to the Habsburg Monarchy' and who were considered to have a historic aversion to Moscow—Poles and Ukrainians—assumed a certain importance.

A special periodical was founded in Vienna, *Ukrainische Rundschau*, and the Austro-Hungarian Government gave unofficial support to the so-called 'Union for the Liberation of the Ukraine' which openly proclaimed the struggle against Russia and promised in case of war to contribute to Russia's defeat 'by internal upheavals'. The leaders of this Union were certain Ukrainians of some ability—Skoropis-Zholtukovsky, Zhuk, Doroshenko and Zaliznyak. The organization conducted a propaganda on a considerable scale and could dispose of adequate funds which were provided by the Austro-Hungarian Government and supplemented by contributions from prosperous Ukrainians in America. It was proposed that, in the case of war with Russia and the invasion of Russia by the Austrian armies, representatives of the Union, with the help of their supporters in the Russian Ukraine, should organize a form of government which would be acceptable to Vienna. Some hotheads were even talking of a 'Ukrainian kingdom', and named as candidate for the 'Ukrainian throne' Archduke Wilhelm of Habsburg 'Vasili Vishevaniy'.

German political circles took a more prosaic view of the Ukrainian problem. The lightning rapidity of the economic development of the South of Russia, which even the revolutionary events of 1905 could not stop, attracted the attention of German specialists.

Two years before the war a commission of German economists and technicians under the presidency of Professor Auhagen visited Southern Russia and made a report to the German Government. The members of the commission were particularly impressed by the progress of the metallurgical and beet-sugar industries. The large investments of French and Belgian capital in the coal and metallurgical industries did not escape their notice, and they anticipated a flow of British capital following the Anglo-Russian Agreement. Professor Auhagen came to the gloomy conclusion that 'if some untoward event does not stop this rapid Russian development, Germany will soon be faced by a neighbour more powerful than herself'.

This economic development attracted the attention of the promotors of German *Weltpolitik* to the possibilities of Ukrainian separatism. Very exaggerated hopes of revolutionary and separatist movements in Russia inflated the mind of the Emperor William, who was encouraged in his miscalculations by the German Ambassador in Petersburg, Count Pourtalès.

In his memoirs (*Aus meiner Dienstzeit*, IV, 197 *et sqq.*), Field-Marshal Conrad recalls a meeting at which the Emperor William refused to listen to the objections of the Austrian Chancellor, Count Stürgkh, and insisted on 'revolutionizing' the populations of Russian Poland and the Ukraine. The Emperor proposed 'to use all means for this purpose and to send there tracts, emissaries and large funds'. The Emperor's amateurish excursion into the technical problems of organizing separatist diversions formed the basis of the so-called 'Pontus Expedition' (which was to include within its scope the raising of an insurrection among the Kuban Cossacks and the formation of a 'Georgian Legion' for action in the Caucasus). The Emperor urged that the Austro-Hungarian fleet should join the *Goeben* and *Breslau* in the Black Sea where, after panic had been spread among the population of the South Russian coasts, agents should be landed 'in lonely places', well supplied with money and revolutionary literature, with the object of organizing riots in the Ukraine in the rear of the Russian armies. The objections of Field-Marshal Conrad and of the Austrian Admiral Haus prevented this fantastic 'embryon' of the future 'manœuvre' of sending Lenin and Trotsky into Russia from being carried into effect (see also the memoirs of the Austro-Hungarian military attaché in Istanbul, General Pomiankowski, *Der Zusammenbruch des Ottomanischen Reiches*, pp. 80 *et sqq.*).

The outbreak of war dispersed alike the Emperor William's hopes of internal troubles in Russia during mobilization and the plans of 'The Union for the Liberation of the Ukraine'. Austrian cavalry raids on Kamenets-Podolsk and Vladimir-Volynsk proved abortive, and two strong Russian armies invaded Galicia.

The 3rd and 8th Armies of Generals Ruski and Brusilov, with the Reserve Divisions attached to them, were recruited almost entirely from the Ukraine; they proved their loyalty to the Tsar and their moral ascendancy over the enemy by defeating the Austro-Hungarians, first on the Zlota-Lipa, and later on the Gnila-Lipa.

Ruski marched on Lvov and Brusilov on Halych. The former town was reputed to be strongly fortified, but these fortifications proved to exist only on paper. While the Russians were preparing to bombard the Lvov 'forts', an Orthodox priest arrived at the headquarters of General Sherbachev, commanding the 9th Army Corps, with the information that the Galician capital had been evacuated and the unfinished fortifications abandoned. The occupation of Lvov on 3 September, exactly a month after the beginning of the war, was not only a spectacular triumph for the Russians but a serious blow to the prestige of the Habsburg Monarchy.

During the following two weeks the Russian armies (the 9th, Lechitski; the 4th, Evert; the 5th, Plehve; and the 3rd, Ruski) administered a crushing defeat at Rava Russka and south of Lublin to the main Austro-Hungarian forces (the 1st Army of Dankl; the 4th, Auffenberg; and the 3rd, Boroevich). At the same time Brusilov at Gorodok was beating back the desperate attacks of the 2nd Austro-Hungarian Army under Böhm-Ermolli. In the last week of September, the Russians crossed the San and, masking the great fortress of Przemysl, pressed back the demoralized Austro-Hungarian troops to the forts of Cracow, while simultaneously they occupied the most important passes of the Carpathians.

Russian Cossack units and regular cavalry spread over the Carpathians into the valley of the upper Tisza and the forests of Carpathian Rus and along the edges of the Great Hungarian Plain. By the end of November 1914 the whole of Galicia was effectively in the hands of the Russians. Difficult problems faced not only the military but also the civil authorities.

The population of Galicia (including the region of Cracow) numbered seven and a half million inhabitants; of these, apart from half a million Jews, four millions were Poles and about three millions were of Russian origin—of the same blood and language as the inhabitants of the Ukraine. In Eastern Galicia the Russo-Ukrainians equalled the Poles in numbers, but in the western districts the Poles predominated. The elections of 1907 had sent sixty-nine Polish deputies to the local *Seym*, and thirty-two Ukrainians. The results of the elections had been regarded as unjust by the Ukrainian political activists, and the struggle against the local Polish hegemony had been intensified; terrorist outrages had culminated finally in the assassination of the Viceroy of Galicia, Count Potocki. Finally, following the intervention of the Central Government in Vienna, the Ukrainians had secured an agreement whereby 27 per cent of the seats in the *Seym* were guaranteed to them in the future. The position was further complicated by the fact that a third of the Ukrainian deputies were stigmatized by their colleagues as 'pro-Russians' (*Promoskovity*).

The five years preceding the war were marked by an acute and growing antagonism, not only between Poles and Ukrainians, but also between the two sections within the local Ukrainian movement. Supported by the Vienna Government, and having at their disposal ten chairs in the University of Lvov, several gymnasiums, the Shevchenko Scientific Society, the educational organization of *Prosvita*, libraries, museums, publishers and several daily papers, the anti-Muscovite 'separatists' were always the stronger; but now the movement which had been created by Hrushevsky and his followers was only defending its former positions. The *Promoskovity*, in spite of difficulties, were gaining ground; they had founded their own scientific institute, formed their own academic group, established their own daily papers and their own political 'Russian Organization'. In their struggle with the *Promoskovity* the separatists appealed to the Austro-Hungarian authorities, and in 1912 elaborate lists were prepared of persons suspected of sympathies for Russia.

The events of the war changed in a most decisive manner all the relationships which had been established in Galicia. Simultaneously with mobilization began arrests of 'pro-Russians'. A few weeks later the defeats of the Austrian armies were attributed to 'the treacherous behaviour' of the Galician population. When complete units of Galician Landsturm surrendered without resistance to the enemy, repressions followed throughout the whole province: mass arrests and transportations, and executions—with or without the formality of military courts. All persons of any local importance who were considered 'pro-Russian' were sent to concentration camps—deputies of the *Seym*, priests, schoolmasters, business men and prosperous peasants. The Lvov prisons were filled with hundreds of prisoners who did not know why they had been arrested; and at the notorious camp of Telerhof 7500 unfortunates were interned.

The commander of the 8th Russian Army, General Brusilov,

wrote in his memoirs (subsequently published in Soviet Russia):
'I must say that, not only in Eastern Galicia, where the majority of
the population is Russian and has been well disposed towards us for
a long time, but also in Western Galicia where the population is
Polish, not only peasants, but even the clergy of the Catholic Church,
showed signs of sympathy and in many cases helped us as much as
they could. As for the Jewish population, numerous in both parts of
Galicia, it played an important part under Austrian rule: there were
many Jewish landowners and they were disliked by both Poles and
Russians. Nearly all wealthy Jews took flight and only the poor remained. On the whole the sympathies of the Jews were on the side
of the Austrians for very comprehensible reasons.'

Immediately after the Russian occupation the desire of the *Promoskovity* to avenge themselves on their neighbours found expression
in a flood of denunications. The Russian Governor-General, Count
Yuri Bobrinskoy, proved incapable of confronting the difficulties of
the situation. A humane and cultivated man, he failed to master all
the intricacies of intrigue in the Galician capital. The *Promoskovity*,
avenging themselves for former oppressions, influenced the Russian
authorities to close down not only the separatist political organizations, but also all newspapers, clubs, educational societies, bookshops
and certain schools. Ukrainian separatist politicians who had not had
time to leave were sent off to Russia. Professor Hrushevsky was
ordered to take up his abode in Nizhni-Novgorod, although later he
was allowed to visit the capital 'to work in the libraries'.

Such measures could be explained by the war, but the moment
was really ill-chosen for beginning a struggle against the Uniate
Church. Count Bobrinskoy, with the help of several Orthodox
bishops, began without delay the thankless task of bringing back the
Galician peasantry into the fold of pure Orthodoxy, and he completely ignored the fact that, although the Union had originally been
imposed in Galicia and was in its origin an artificial institution, it had
centuries behind it.

In a great many cases the people had become attached to their
Uniate churches and Uniate priests. The drive against the Uniate
Church vitiated the relations between the population and the
authorities of the military occupation and produced the strangely
paradoxical situation that in Western Galicia the Russian administration experienced fewer difficulties with the Poles and Catholics than
in Eastern Galicia, where the population was of Russian origin and
'half Orthodox'. The Russians finally succeeded in alienating a man
who stood above all his compatriots in moral stature. The Uniate
Metropolitan Count Szepticki had never belonged to any of the

Galician political factions, but his authority was great among the peasantry of Galicia and that authority might have been used to support the Russian administration had it shown more tolerance in Church affairs. But the Metropolitan was treated with more severity than the known separatist Hrushevsky; he was banished to Russia, where he had to live under provincial police supervision.

In Lvov, at the head of '.The Russian Committee', was a rather anaemic personality, a certain Dudkevich. Owing to the blunders of the Russian administration 'pro-Russian' tendencies did not make any progress during the period of the occupation. As for the Ukrainian separatist movement it was annihilated as a result of the war. 'The Union for the Liberation of the Ukraine' collapsed, and Doroshenko and Zaliznyak abandoned it. The attempt to form a Ukrainian Legion on the pattern of Piłsudski's Polish Legion had no success. Although the military importance of the Polish Legion was insignificant, the legionaries fought well and it served to form a nucleus for a future political organization. But no one ever heard anything about the military feats of the Ukrainian Legion of Austrian formation. Certain members of 'The Union for the Liberation of the Ukraine' found, however, new means to induce the Germans to take an interest in them.

When in 1915 the Germans captured enormous numbers of Russian prisoners an attempt was made to 'sort' them according to their national origins. Those who called themselves Ukrainians were sent to a special camp at Rastatt where lectures were read to them on Ukrainian subjects by a certain 'Professor' Bezpalko. At the beginning of 1917 about 15,000 Russian soldiers, who had qualified in German eyes as Ukrainians, were assembled in the camp at Rastatt and went through a sort of school of propaganda. A regiment even was formed, called the Taras Shevchenko regiment, numbering about 2000 men, but it did not have time to prove its valour on the German side before the Revolution broke out. When it is remembered that by the beginning of 1917 the number of Russian prisoners in the hands of the Germans was about 3,000,000, of whom between 700,000 and 800,000 were of Ukrainian origin, the success attained by the Germans in exploiting Ukrainian nationalism in the concentration camps does not appear very brilliant.

In the spring of 1915 the Emperor Nicholas II, after the surrender of Przemysl, visited Galicia and made a speech at Lvov in which he spoke of 'an indivisible Russia' reaching as far as the Carpathian Mountains. There were already signs, however, that the Russian dominion in Galicia would not last long. In the early summer a heavy German concentration pierced the Russian front at

Gorlice, and the Russian armies, after heavy fighting and enormous losses, began to retreat from Galicia into the Ukraine.

By the beginning of autumn the front had been established on a new line; the Russians continued to hold only a strip of Eastern Galicia and had been compelled to abandon to the enemy part of Volhynia with the towns of Kovel, Lutsk and Vladimir-Volynsk.

Anxiety was very great at that time and even Kiev seemed to be threatened. Podolia, Eastern Volhynia, right-bank Ukraine, had become regions in the immediate neighbourhood of the front. The evacuation of Galicia had been a difficult and painful proceeding. The Russian armies had been accompanied in their retreat by thousands of Galician peasants evidently in fear of the reprisals awaiting them at the hands of the Austro-Hungarian troops. They went on foot, and some in carts with their households, driving their cattle before them. Over a hundred thousand of such fugitives crossed the Russian frontier. Numbers of Jews followed the retreat in order to escape from the scene of war; and the Russian military authorities deported with them also all people who were considered 'suspicious' from the political point of view and such Ukrainians, Poles and Jews as were supposed to harbour 'criminal intentions'.

For the latter elements prisons were hastily improvised in Kiev, but no one knew what to do about them nor why they had been brought there. Charitable institutions had to feed and clothe them as though they were the most peaceful citizens. There were days when at the Kiev Central Station as many as 60,000 meals had to be provided for these swarms of unwanted 'guests'.

The Russian Committee from Lvov, with its chief, Dudkevich, also came to Kiev. Such an agglomeration of demoralized peasants and Jewish crowds in the rear of the South-Western Front was dangerous in every respect, and to begin with from a sanitary point of view. Beginning with the end of 1915 and all through 1916 the clearance of these 'new-comers' from Kiev went on. Dudkevich's Committee and other organizations were sent to Rostov-on-Don and later to Turkestan—whither was directed the main flow of fugitive peasants. Jews were allowed to go beyond the Dniepr into the Governments of the interior and the limits permitted them for settlement were temporarily abolished. Many of them remained in left-bank Ukraine and the towns of New Russia; and this migrant Jewish element, combined with the 'suspicious characters' who gained their liberty after the outbreak of the Revolution, constituted an unsettled and disintegrating factor during the period of social dissolution.

During 1916 life in the Ukraine approached normal conditions again, after the offensive of General Brusilov had broken the Austro-Hungarian Front at several points. Part of Volhynia was cleared of the enemy and the Russians again invaded Galicia, occupying Stanislavov and also Czernowitz and the whole of the Bukovina. The Front was again removed from the region of Kiev.

Under the influence of the Russian victories the Roumanians entered the war, but they proved to be unprepared for serious conflict. A Russian army was sent to check the German invasion in Moldavia, and a new 'Roumanian Front' was created, so that the battle-line now ran from the Baltic to the Black Sea. During the winter of 1916–17 the South-Western Front was stabilized. Headquarters were planning a new offensive in the spring against Lvov and believed in its ultimate success. Peace and quiet reigned in Kiev and in the neighbourhood of the Front.(1)

§2. HRUSHEVSKY AND VINNICHENKO: THE UKRAINIANS AT BREST-LITOVSK

When the news of the February Revolution (February according to the Old Style, March according to the New) in Petrograd reached Kiev neither the authorities nor the populace would at first credit the truth of it. However, it was not long before the events which had taken place in the northern capital were repeated in Kiev and the cities of the Ukraine.

The process of decomposition which was destroying the armies of the North-Western and Western Fronts infected somewhat later the forces on the South-Western and Roumanian Fronts. As for the Ukrainian national movement, no one thought about it during those first days of revolution. With the exception of Finland, where the revolutionary movement was accompanied by a wave of feeling in favour of national independence, in no part of the Russian Empire were nationalist aspirations the motive of the Revolution. The first impulse of the masses, irrespective of their nationality, was to look upon the Revolution as a means of ending the war which had lasted too long. The other motives which soon made themselves apparent were everywhere of a social nature.

The state of mind of the masses found expression in the institution of 'Councils (*Soviety*) of Soldiers', Workmen's and Peasants' Delegates', in the creation of which all the leading socialist groups and parties took a hand. People of all nationalities participated in these Soviets; Georgian politicians, who for a generation had played a leading role in Russian radical movements, made themselves particularly prominent (Chkheidze, Tsereteli and Chenkeli really dominated the first Petrograd Soviet).

At this early period the great majority of the Ukrainian population were really more indifferent to 'the Ukrainian movement' than they had been before the war. The soldiers in the trenches were only interested in two things: in an immediate return to their homes and in their participation in the land distribution which was to be a feature of the agrarian reforms in the new Russia. If in a comparatively short time 'the Ukrainian movement' became a factor of importance in revolutionary Russia, it was only owing to the exceptional energy and insistence of the small group of men who were leading the Ukrainian nationalists.

Already in March Professor Hrushevsky had made his appearance in Kiev; he was joined by one of the activists of 1905, Vinnichenko, who during that earlier phase had called himself a 'Ukrainian Social Democrat'. The journalist Simon Petlyura, who was destined to become the most picturesque of the Ukrainian leaders, also turned up in Kiev.(2) At the beginning of 1917 Petlyura had found himself in the modest post of accountant in one of the branches of the 'Union of the Towns' which, together with the 'Union of Zemstvos', had been largely concerned with the supply problems of the war. These two Unions became the stronghold of the Ukrainian nationalists; in Kiev alone there were 6000 people employed on the 'Union of Zemstvos' and 2000 on the 'Union of the Towns'. Branches of the two Unions existed in all the towns of the Ukraine and the staffs consisted for the greater part of 'intelligentsia' and 'half-intelligentsia'—just the social strata where, before the war, the Ukrainian nationalists had been gaining recruits.

Without losing any time, Hrushevsky and Vinnichenko gathered round themselves in Kiev an active group who shared their ideas, and they began to organize a 'Ukrainian Conference'. The sponsors of the Conference sent 'invitations' to 'elect delegates' from the nine Governments which they considered as constituting the territory of the Ukraine (three Governments on the right and three on the left bank of the Dniepr and the three Governments of New Russia). The elections were held 'according to the Revolutionary ways': in other words, delegates arrived in Kiev on the authority of some small 'circle' or club or of a 'Ukrainian Revolutionary Committee' which might have consisted of five or six people. There appeared also 'self-appointed delegates'—deserters from the Front and 'new-comers' from Galicia.

No one was particularly astonished at this strange assembly, since 'revolutionary enthusiasm' reigned supreme throughout the whole country. The Soviets and all sorts of other similar organizations which were supposed to voice the aspirations of 'great masses' had been organized in the same way. Hrushevsky and Vinnichenko, however, attained their first object, since 'the Ukrainian Conference' elected from its midst members of 'the Ukrainian *Rada*' which was to constitute a sort of Parliament for the Ukraine. These events caused considerable displeasure to the Provisional Government in Petrograd and it was not long before a struggle developed between the Provisional Government and the Ukrainian *Rada*.

'Self-determination of nationalities' had always formed part of the moral and political stock-in-trade of the various brands of 'liberals', 'democrats' and 'socialists' who composed the Provisional Government. But the realities of the situation in which they found themselves imposed on these ideologues a certain moderation in the application of their super-liberal principles. Harassed on all sides by self-constituted revolutionary and nationalist groups and factions, and themselves clinging nervously to the forms of an authority which was being rapidly dispersed by the cold winds of rising anarchy, the Provisional Government had recourse to their usual method of 'persuasion' and they asked the *Rada* to await the end of the war and the decisions of an All-Russian Constituent Assembly.

'Persuasion', however, was hopeless with opponents so skilled in political struggles and intrigue as Hrushevsky and Vinnichenko. Aware of the weakness of the Petrograd Government, the politicians of the *Rada* based their tactics on manœuvring for a gradual enlargement of the powers which they had attributed to themselves, while they avoided provoking the cabinet of Prince Lvov by premature demands of too drastic a nature. The *Rada* secured, for instance, the consent of the Provisional Government to the formation of Ukrainian national troops. In this case they could appeal to the precedent which had been created by the formation of Lettish, Georgian and Armenian national detachments.

Professor Paul Milyukov, a prominent member of the Provisional Government, describes the relations of Petrograd with the *Rada* in the following words: 'The Provisional Government was still continuing to plead with the Ukrainians not to detach themselves from the Motherland, not to go the fatal way of dividing liberated Russia, and not to introduce dissensions into the Army at a moment of great national danger. Weak and devoid of backbone, having itself laid down its arms, the Government could not but register *post factum* the triumphs attained by the Ukrainians. Hrushevsky's tactics consisted in proving that "nothing decisive" was taking place. The fiction that the Government was sanctioning the *Rada's* doings was kept up to the end. Summing up all the *pourparlers* one sees how false they were at the core: an enforced fiction on one side and deliberate deception on the other.'

Hrushevsky, according to his own words, put forward only a moderate programme: wide national and territorial autonomy within the Russian Federative Republic; but it was not long before he was shifting his ground and declaring that 'the adherents of an independent Ukraine consent to remain on a common platform with Russians' but that 'the colours of an independent Ukraine would be folded only for a time'.

With the resignations of Milyukov and Guchkov, who were regarded as the firm adversaries of Ukrainian separatism, 'the colours of an independent Ukraine' were duly unfolded. The *Rada* chose from among its members a 'General Secretariat' which was to function as a sort of Ukrainian cabinet. Always in pursuance of their tactics, Hrushevsky and Vinnichenko declared that the authority of both the *Rada* and the Secretariat was of a 'purely moral order' and that the organs set up in Kiev were purely 'national organizations'.

Soon, however, Vinnichenko, who had taken upon himself the role of 'Ukrainian Prime Minister', judged that the moment had arrived to proclaim that 'the limits between moral and public legal authority had been effaced' and that 'our moral authority has grown to such an extent as a logical result of events that painlessly, without a struggle, it has transformed itself into the legal rule of a national republic'.

All these manœuvres culminated in the publication of the first 'Universal' of the 'Central *Rada*' on 23 June 1917, according to which the 'Autonomous Ukrainian Republic' came into being, and the 'Central *Rada*' arrogated to itself the right to formulate legislation which would require the sanction of the All-Russian Constituent Assembly only as 'a matter of form'. In this way two authorities came into being claiming sovereign rights in the territory of the Ukraine: the 'moral' authority transformed into the 'legal rule' of the *Rada* on the one side, and on the other the former legitimate authority of the Provisional Government—which was losing ground every day, but which had not completely disappeared.

Under these circumstances several members of the reconstructed cabinet of the Provisional Government hastened to Kiev—Kerenski, Tereshchenko, Nekrasov and Tsereteli. At the time Kerenski was preoccupied with the South-Western Front, where a renewed Russian offensive was to prove to the Allies that the Provisional Government remained faithful to the idea of 'war to a successful end', and it is probable that the *Rada* had chosen this conjunction of circumstances to extract the maximum concessions from the harassed liberal leaders who could not risk a political crisis in the rear of the South-Western Army.

When the offensive ended in catastrophe with a loss of over 100,000 casualties and 47,000 prisoners, the complete demoralization of the Front and the appearance of thousands of fugitives in Kiev, the ministers of the Provisional Government had no alternative but to capitulate to the *Rada*. On 17 July, in the presence of Hrushevsky and Vinnichenko, the existence of 'the General Secretariat' was proclaimed and legalized.

The disaster at the Front was followed during July by the outbreak of riots and disorders in the interior of Russia. The Soviets openly declared themselves against the Provisional Government, while the Bolshevik faction, after the arrival of Lenin, began to gain strength and made their first attempt to gain power by armed insurrection.

The *Rada* began to concentrate what Ukrainian military elements it was able to attract round Kiev; two regiments, named respectively 'Bohdan Khmelnytsky' and 'Polubotok', were in process of formation. Both regiments consisted of undisciplined and disorderly deserters and mutineers. An attempt by the Russian Command to send the 'Ukrainian Regiments' to the Front provoked a real mutiny in the ranks of the 'Bohdan Khmelnytsky Regiment', who considered their presence in Kiev 'for the protection of the *Rada*' more necessary than in the firing line. After an encounter at the Central Railway Station at Kiev with a squadron of the Cuirassiers of the Guard, the Ukrainian troops surrendered and were deprived of their weapons.

Petrograd in the meantime was rejoicing over the suppression of the Bolshevik rising; Lenin had fled to Finland.

This success of the Provisional Government tended to calm both troubled and conspiratorial minds and, under the influence of the German offensive which had begun and which threatened both Kiev and Petrograd, the ministers of the Kerenski Government adopted a firmer attitude in their discussions with the representatives of the *Rada*, who had come to Petrograd to discuss the terms of the Statute which was to regulate the position of the Ukraine. Instead of the Statute only new 'instructions' to the General Secretariat were conceded. The territory of the Ukraine was to consist now of only five Governments: three on the right and two on the left bank of the Dniepr. The Government of Kharkov and the three New Russian Governments were excluded, although the delegates had tried to insist that, in addition to the nine Governments already claimed, Bessarabia and the greater parts of the Governments of Kursk and Voronezh should also form part of the Ukraine.

When the delegates returned to Kiev there was a regular storm of indignation in the *Rada*. Hrushevsky, however, was receding into the background, and most of the decisions of the *Rada* were now inspired by Vinnichenko. It was he who insisted on acquiescence in the 'instructions' of the Provisional Government. 'The right to possess something', he explained to his disgruntled followers, 'is not given on bits of paper; it is the result of the balance of the forces in conflict, which balance can always change in different circumstances. Let us take what is given to us and let us go on. After all, this is not a peace but an armistice.'(3)

'The different circumstances' which instilled caution into Vinnichenko developed with alarming rapidity. In August, Kerenski, quailing before the spectre of 'counter-revolution', applied to the Bolsheviks for help in order 'to safeguard the conquests of the Revolution'. Taking advantage of this fatal move, the Bolsheviks immediately intensified their propaganda throughout the country in favour of the immediate cessation of the war, and they spread the demand that all power should be transferred to the Soviets of Soldiers, Workers and Peasants as the only true defenders of the Revolution. The Bolshevik agitation, fed upon a progressive disintegration of the social order, ran through the cities of the Ukraine, and Vinnichenko could not help realizing that the ephemeral tactical victories of the *Rada* were nothing compared to the devastating victories of the Bolsheviks and of the extreme left wing of the Social Revolutionaries. After bitter experience, he wrote in his daily paper, *Novaya Rada*, that 'national questions at that time did not have the overwhelming importance which the Central *Rada* wished to ascribe to them'. He even went so far as to avow that the *Rada* and its members were hated and laughed at by the population. 'Everything Ukrainian was laughed at: songs, schools, papers, books. The son was cynically and resentfully making fun of his mother.' The former head of the General Secretariat continued: 'We did not have a strong proletariat conscious of its nationality because, in most cases, it had been denationalized and russified in most of the big towns.' As for the peasantry, according to Vinnichenko: 'We found our principal support among the peasants, not among the poor ones, but among the wealthier ones.' This fact, recognized by Vinnichenko, deserves to be noted.

Notwithstanding the blatant defects of the self-appointed 'organ of moral authority' in Kiev, there were some decent elements upholding the Central *Rada*. Among its six hundred members were men who hoped to build something even on the shaky foundations of Ukrainian autonomy. True, as Vinnichenko himself owns: 'We spoke of our success at the elections, but let us be honest amongst ourselves and to others: we availed ourselves of the ignorance of the oppressed masses. It was not they who elected us, but we who imposed ourselves on them.' But among these 'self-elected' were men who were acting in the hope of creating a dam against the raging revolutionary sea. Certain elements of sanity and order were to be found in the *Rada*: men who despaired of finding salvation in the weak and passive Provisional Government, and who hoped to achieve something themselves under the Ukrainian flag.

The candid Vinnichenko goes on to mention that the Central *Rada* 'had dreamed of founding its authority on the support of foreign bourgeois states and on the existing social order'. But if there was no real force on the side of the Provisional Government, there was also none on the side of the *Rada*. 'Our Ukrainian soldiers were not content with the gold-and-blue standard and with new red caps. When they saw that the *Rada* was on the side of the propertied classes, they naturally turned to those who offered them more tangible goods—the Bolsheviks. Not Russian but Ukrainian regiments took Kiev later for the Bolsheviks.'

In August and September 1917, under the growing pressure of Bolshevism, those political tendencies in the *Rada* which were represented by Hrushevsky and his group lost ground seriously. Hrushevsky and his followers had remained true to their 'Austrian orientation' which by 1917 had become an 'Austro-German orientation'. These defeatists in relation to Russia had been counting on Austro-German support because they were aware that the Ukrainian separatist movement could facilitate the attainment of the objectives of the Austro-German Command. But even in defeatism the *Rada* could not compete with the Bolsheviks, for the modest defeatism of the separatists was of little value to the Germans compared with the really gigantic defeatism of the Soviets, which were now entirely in the hands of Lenin and his adherents. The Bolsheviks had worked so successfully for the disintegration of the Front that Riga had now fallen to the Germans and the way lay open to Petrograd. The Germans were already within reach of their objective of a separate peace with Russia, and while the Soviets could answer for the whole of the Russian Front the romantics of the *Rada*—who could not even control the mutinous mobs in the Ukrainian cities— must continue to fail to inspire the interest of the German General Staff.

In September, as the fatal autumn of 1917 approached, Kiev was preoccupied with almost academic activities. Surrounded by a certain amount of pomp, a Congress representing all the nationalities of the Russian Empire was holding its sessions. About a hundred delegates representing thirteen nationalities and twelve Cossack lands were in attendance, and another six nationalities which had not sent delegates declared their 'adherence to the decisions of the Congress' without taking part in it. The decisions consisted of a plan for converting the structure of the Empire into a federation of autonomous states which were to have common internal and foreign policies. Apparently the Ukrainians were not entirely pleased with the moderate claims of the Congress, and delegates of the *Rada* proceeded to Petrograd to demand that all authority in the Ukraine should be exercised exclusively by the *Rada* and its General Secretariat. They also required the recognition of the right of all nationalities within the Empire to dispose of their own destinies and called for the meeting of a 'Sovereign National Constituent Assembly'. While still waiting in Petrograd for the satisfaction of their demands, the delegates had the exciting experience of being present at the taking of the Winter Palace by the Bolsheviks.

The October Revolution (November by the New Style) did not produce an armed struggle in Kiev as in Petrograd and Moscow. In Kiev Bolshevik elements were neither numerous nor strong: there were no important industrial plants in the ancient city by the Dniepr, and the few thousand proletarians were scattered round the arsenal and the railway workshops. The *Rada* could also rely on a certain number of obedient troops. The downfall of the Provisional Government did not result in the transfer in the Ukraine of its somewhat shadowy authority to the Soviets; such authority as there was remained in the hands of the *Rada*. This fact was underlined in the third 'Universal' published by the *Rada*. It was affirmed that the *Rada* would continue as the organ of power until the convocation of 'the Ukrainian National Constituent Assembly', freely elected, which would form a Government for the whole territory of the Ukrainian Republic. The *Rada* also confirmed its readiness 'to help Russia to become a Federative State of Free and Equal Nations'.

This 'Universal', published on 7–20 November, was regarded as a declaration of war by the newly established Soviet power. There was little chance for the Central *Rada* to emerge victorious from any armed conflict. In November 1917 the authority of the *Rada* only covered the agricultural districts adjacent to Kiev on both banks of the Dniepr. At the Front soldiers' Soviets ruled supreme, and in Kharkov and the big industrial towns of New Russia the Bolsheviks were gaining ground. Scarcely a month had elapsed before the authority of the *Rada* was overthrown in Kharkov, where on 27 December the Bolsheviks proclaimed a 'Provisional Ukrainian

Soviet Government'. A few days later Red troops took possession of Ekaterinoslav; by the first half of January Mariupol, Odessa and Nikolaev were in Bolshevik hands, and Red detachments were marching from Kharkov through Poltava on Kiev. Foreign intervention remained the only chance for the Government of the Central *Rada*.

Although the third 'Universal' had not definitely proclaimed the Ukraine to be an independent republic, the Kiev Government informed the Austro-Hungarian and German authorities of their wish to participate in the Brest-Litovsk negotiations as an independent state.

At Brest-Litovsk all parties were in a hurry. Lenin was anxious to conclude a peace at any price and as rapidly as possible in order to fulfil the promises he had made to the Soviets of Soldiers', Workers' and Peasants' Delegates; the Germans were concerned to accelerate the liquidation of the Russian Front in order to be able to transfer greater numbers of troops to the Western Front; and they, and more urgently the Austrians, were in desperate need of the supplies which they considered the conclusion of peace would make available to them in Russia. Now the Ukrainians appeared upon the scene in no less haste to secure the salvation of the Kiev Government before it should have been liquidated by the forces of the Russian Revolution.

Representatives of the new Soviet power had crossed the German lines on 27 November, but an armistice had not been signed until 16 December; two days later the Armistice of Focşanĭ had concluded the fighting on the Roumanian Front immediately adjacent to the Ukrainian lands. During the negotiations for an armistice the *Rada* Government had been virtually ignored, for the Bolshevik delegates had been at pains to persuade the Germans that the Ukrainian Republic was nothing more than a fiction which would be swept away by 'the workers and peasants'. But when the news reached Kiev and it became known that negotiations for the signature of a general peace would immediately begin, the *Rada* hastened to declare its wish to participate and, as a reinforcement to its request made by wire, sent emissaries to Vienna in order to take advantage of the old and long-standing connections between the Austrian Government and the Ukrainian separatists.

Peace negotiations started on 8 January 1918 in Brest-Litovsk; Trotsky was at the head of the Soviet Delegation; von Kühlmann and General Hoffmann were the German representatives; and Count Czernin was in charge of Austro-Hungarian interests. Ottoman and Bulgarian Delegations also attended.

Without any special invitation, three young men soon put in their appearance—'the three students' they were nicknamed by the representatives of the Russian Revolution and of the two Germanic Empires. Levitsky, Lubinsky and Sevryuk, who declared their wish to take part in the proceedings as the representatives of the 'Ukrainian Popular Republic', were three of old Hrushevsky's pupils who had hardly had time to finish their schooling.

The aspect of the delegates with whom the representatives of the two great Empires had to treat had ceased to astonish anyone in Brest-Litovsk. Compared to the 'Delegates of the Sailors, Soldiers, Workers and Peasants' with whom General Hoffmann and Prince Leopold of Bavaria had been obliged to sit at the same table during the discussions about the armistice, these 'three students' seemed quite ordinary decent young men. They were invited to lunch and dine with the Delegations of 'the bourgeois states'—an amenity which Trotsky forbade to his Soviet comrades.

Count Czernin, although a little 'shocked' by the youth of the Ukrainian delegates, was obliged by the force of circumstances to enter into friendly relations with them. As for the German delegates, they were frankly pleased with the presence of the representatives of the *Rada*, considering that it might make Trotsky more amenable.

Trotsky continued to deny the existence of the 'Ukrainian Popular Republic'. Levitsky and his colleagues produced documents which showed that during the last elections in the Ukraine (November 1917) the *Rada* had polled 75 per cent of the votes and the Bolsheviks only 10 per cent. It was difficult to realize in Brest-Litovsk that those were the elections about which Vinnichenko wrote 'it was not they who elected us, but we who imposed ourselves on them'.

Owing to the importance of the negotiations, there also arrived in the wake of 'the three students', the new Prime Minister of the Ukraine, Vsevolod Holubovich, also quite a young man (thirty-four years of age), a sincere enthusiast of the 'Ukrainian national cause'. During the session of 10 January the presence of the Ukrainians at the Conference was officially recognized and Trotsky, 'with a sore heart', had to give his consent to their participation in the discussions.

The Ukrainian delegates soon began to astonish Hoffmann and Czernin by their immoderate demands. They had instructions to exact the annexation to the 'Popular Republic' not only of the Kholm district, which had been allocated to the proposed new Polish state, but also of Galicia and Bukovina which formed parts of the Austro-Hungarian Empire. Hoffmann almost yelled at Lubinsky and Sevryuk, who were not much abashed and declared that they would ask for new instructions from Kiev: they felt a certain amount of strength to be on their side. A few days later Count Czernin wrote in his diary: 'The Ukrainians no longer lead the negotiations: they dictate their conditions.'

The situation in the Austro-Hungarian Empire had become critical about 15 January. 'The people are suffering from hunger', pleaded the Archbishop of Cracow; 'bread rations have been cut down by half', wired the Governor of Trieste; 'there is flour in Vienna only till next Monday', came from the Burgomaster of the capital. On the 17th the Emperor Charles wired to Czernin: 'The fate of the monarchy and of the dynasty depends on how soon you will be able to conclude peace in Brest-Litovsk....If peace is not concluded a revolution will break out here.'

It was Czernin's good fortune that at this juncture the Ukrainian delegation received news which obliged it to adopt a less extravagant attitude. The 'Popular Republic' had lost in the first weeks of January all New Russia and nearly all left-bank Ukraine. Trotsky smiled sarcastically when he met 'the three students' and Radek wrote in the Soviet press: 'Let those who want bread scream death to the *Rada*!' Radek's aimable outburst against the Kiev *Rada* indicated that Ukrainian supplies were as badly needed in the Soviet capitals as they were in Vienna. This aspect of affairs was duly appreciated by the Germans, and Hoffmann suddenly became more interested in making peace with the *Rada*. When the Kiev *Rada*, under pressure of a Soviet threat to Kiev, relinquished their claims to Galicia and Bukovina, Hoffmann persuaded Czernin to accept the other conditions, including the demand for Kholm.

On 18 January the negotiations were temporarily interrupted. The Delegations left in quest of fresh instructions from their respective Governments. When after a few days they returned to Brest-Litovsk, Trotsky brought along with him new visitors: the representatives of the 'Ukrainian Soviet Republic' which had chosen Kharkov for its capital. Trotsky warned von Kühlmann and Czernin that the 'Ukrainian Soviet Republic' 'did not recognize any agreements which might be entered into by the *Rada*'.

The German and Austro-Hungarian Delegations came to the decision not to pay any attention to Trotsky's manœuvre. Hoffmann calmly noted in his diary: 'At any time we could support the Ukrainian Government and establish it again.'

On 1 February dissensions were renewed in Brest-Litovsk in a somewhat chaotic atmosphere. The Germans and Austrians had to carry on discussions with three Delegations at the same time: those of the Soviet Government, of the Ukrainian *Rada* and of the Ukrainian Soviet Government. The *Rada* Delegation produced the fourth 'Universal' from Kiev, according to which on 22 January the existence of 'a free and sovereign Ukraine' had been proclaimed. The Government of this new independent state had instructed its delegates to conclude peace 'without paying attention to any obstacles which might arise from other parts of the former Russian Empire'.

In the meantime, on 30 January, 'Red bands' commanded by Muraviëv had approached Kiev and had begun to bombard the city from the left bank of the Dniepr. During the session of 1 February Trotsky could not resist the pleasure of reading out a telegram which announced that some of the Ukrainian regiments of the *Rada* had gone over to the Bolsheviks, and which claimed that the days of the *Rada* were numbered. The Ukrainian delegates, Sevryuk and Lubinsky, responded with sharp denunciations of the Bolsheviks. 'Lubinsky retorted with an hour-long speech which for pure vitriolic opprobrium far exceeded anything that had been heard at this strangest of peace conferences' (Wheeler-Bennett, *Brest-Litovsk*, p. 210).

But Trotsky's triumph partook only of the theatre, for at the end of this same sitting Count Czernin announced the recognition by the Allied Empires of the Ukrainian 'Popular Republic' 'as an independent free and sovereign state'.

After this there remained only the technical side of the agreement with the Ukrainians. If Czernin and Kühlmann waited a few days longer it was only in the hope that the threat of a separate peace with the *Rada* might oblige Trotsky to come to his senses. On 8 February the principal clauses of a treaty were established. The basic condition was an obligation on the Ukraine to furnish not less than a million tons of supplies to the Allied Empires. To ensure the fulfilment of this condition an Austro-German Commission was to proceed to Kiev. But it had not been quite in vain that Trotsky had gloomily affirmed during these days that Czernin and Kühlmann were making an agreement with 'legally non-existent persons'. The battle for Kiev was taking place now in Kiev itself. After having signed peace with the Ukraine, Count Czernin wrote in his diary: 'I wonder if the *Rada* is still sitting in Kiev!'

On 10 February Trotsky made his famous declaration, 'Neither peace nor war', which caused Hoffmann to exclaim 'Unerhört!' The Soviet Delegation left Brest-Litovsk the same day. The only tangible result of all the negotiations had been the peace signed with the Ukrainian 'Popular Republic'. But Kiev had now been occupied by the Red Army; the *Rada* had fled to Zhitomir and was getting ready to flee farther west. The small detachments which had remained true to the *Rada* and which had been organized by Simon

Petlyura (who had constituted himself a specialist in military affairs) were resisting fairly well in northern Podolia, but were certainly unable to secure the return of the *Rada* to Kiev. Trotsky's dramatic gesture had, however, simplified the problem. On 17 February the German Government denounced the armistice and ordered the armies of the Eastern Front to begin their advance. It was the only way of breaking the stubbornness of the Bolsheviks and of saving the *Rada* and the peace which it had signed with the promise of a million tons of supplies. (4, 5)

§ 3. THE GERMANS IN THE UKRAINE: HETMAN SKOROPADSKY

On 18 February, the German troops, without meeting any resistance, occupied Dvinsk on the road to Petrograd and Lutsk on the road to Kiev.

But it was no easy matter for the Austrians to resume the offensive. The Austro-Hungarian armies had been broken during the first two years of the war in the great battles with the Russians; in 1917 it had only been with German aid that they had succeeded in throwing back the Italians. No danger from without threatened the Habsburg Monarchy, but within the Empire dangers were growing with each day that passed. Hence on 17 February the Vienna Government had informed Berlin that Austro-Hungarian troops would take no part in the renewal of the war on the Eastern Front.

In the meantime, the Poles and Bohemians were in a state of agitation on account of the cession of the Kholm region to the Ukrainians. When the twenty-nine year old 'student' Sevryuk, who had signed the Treaty of Brest-Litovsk with Czernin and Kühlmann, made his appearance during a session of the Reichsrath on 19 February, Polish and Bohemian deputies met him with hoots and shouts of 'Clear out of here!' The Austro-Hungarian Government was compelled to put forward 'new conditions' in respect of Kholm.

The German troops continued their march through Volhynia in the direction of Kiev, and the Emperor Charles, fearful that the Austrians might fail to secure their share of the promised Ukrainian supplies, changed his mind. On 24 February the Austro-Hungarian divisions on the Eastern Front received the order to advance into the Ukraine. The Austrian decision had, however, already come too late, for on 1 March Kiev was occupied by the Germans and they alone reinstated the *Rada*.

By 3 March the rapid attainment by the Germans of the line Narva-Pskov and their seizure of the districts of Vitebsk, Mohilev and Homel, enabled Lenin to impose what he cynically described as his 'shameful peace' on his colleagues of the Soviets. Clause 6 of the Treaty obliged the Soviet Government 'to conclude peace at once with the Ukrainian People's Republic and to recognize the Treaty of Peace between that State and the Powers of the Quadruple Alliance'.

The occupation of the Ukraine was organized on the basis of a special agreement between Germany and Austria-Hungary. The Germans left about 500,000 men on the whole of the Eastern Front. Of these, apart from the troops which were stationed in Poland and Lithuania to protect lines of communication, there were about 12 Infantry and 2 Cavalry Divisions occupying the Front against Soviet Russia from Narva to Homel (the 8th and 10th Armies). The remaining 15–16 Infantry and 4 Cavalry Divisions were quartered in the Ukraine (with the exception of a few battalions which were sent to Poti for the protection of the new Georgian Republic from Germany's ally Turkey). The troops in the Ukraine constituted the *Heeresgruppe Kiev* and consisted of the 1st and 20th Army Corps, the 27th (Saxon) and the 22nd and 41st Reserve Corps, together with several independent divisions and detachments. These troops had little in common with the magnificent German armies which had invaded Russia in the first years of the war. The *Heeresgruppe Kiev* contained a veritable mosaic of different battalions—the majority of which consisted of elderly men belonging to Landwehr and Landsturm formations. During the whole period of the German occupation of the Ukraine there was a continuous process of transfer of single battalions and even of small detachments to the Western Front —and this became more noticeable after 8 August, the day which may be said to have marked the turning-point in France. Only the Cavalry Divisions and Artillery approached the standards of the German armies which had formerly been held on the Russian Front. Thus the legend that the military occupation of the Ukraine was 'a mistake', in the sense that important forces were engaged there which might have been decisively employed on the Western Front, seems to be without foundation. Out of all the *Heeresgruppe Kiev* it would have been difficult to select three or four fighting infantry divisions, and less could have been found among the miscellaneous collection of elderly and invalid troops which constituted the so-called 8th and 10th Armies.

The Austro-Hungarian forces in the Ukraine amounted nominally to 250,000 men; but their total in reality was far below this and the number of deserters grew every day.

The Germans from the first began to play the leading role in Kiev.

All authority was vested in the hands of the Commander of *Heeresgruppe Kiev*, Field-Marshal Eichhorn. To Kiev was sent also General Groener, who had a great reputation for his organizing capacity (amongst his collaborators was 'enigmatic' Meissner, who later was to play a certain role in the entourages of President Hindenburg and of the Führer Hitler). The representative of the German Foreign Office was Baron Mumm. Vienna sent as minister Count Forgacs, who, as minister in Belgrad in 1914, had his share of responsibility for the events which immediately preceded the outbreak of war.

Dissensions began between the Allies from the very first moment. Hoffmann, who was in Kovno, kept himself well-informed about what was going on in Kiev. He wrote in his diary: 'Endless troubles with the Austrians in Ukraine. They are behaving with their usual meanness when the knife is not at their throat. It is a pity that the Italians do not attack.' Quarrels broke out on account of the delimitation of the respective German and Austrian zones. The role of the Austrians in the advance into the Ukraine had been modest enough, since they arrived too late to take part in any operations with the exception of 'the capture' of Odessa. Nevertheless, their zone of occupation spread over all the south. At the end of March an agreement was at last reached. On the Black Sea the Austrians retained Odessa and Kherson; the Germans Nikolaev and Sevastopol. Three Governments, Ekaterinoslav, Kherson, Podolia and the southern strip in Volhynia, were reserved as the Austrian zone. In this wise, the Crimea, which shortly passed into German hands, was separated by the Austrian zone from the rest of the territories in German occupation.

The gradual advance eastward of the *Heeresgruppe Kiev* continued. The 22nd Reserve Corps remained in Volhynia: the 27th Reserve (Saxon) Corps was in Kiev: the 41st Reserve Corps, after crossing the Dniepr, occupied the Government of Chernigov, the 20th Army Corps that of Poltava: the 1st Army Corps marched into Kharkov on 20 April. General Groener, who was concerned to collect coal supplies, gave the order in May for the 215th Infantry Division and the 2nd Cavalry Division to march into the south-east into the Donets coal basin as far as the boundaries of the Don Cossack region, where an independent Government had been set up. At the same time the 212th Infantry Division occupied Melitopol and the northern part of the Government of Tauris, while the 15th Landwehr Division was sent to the Crimea and Sevastopol. By the middle of May the occupation had been accomplished.

The Government of the *Rada* had returned to Kiev with the German troops. An interesting light is thrown on the characters of the principal persons in this Government by the correspondence which passed between the Austrian and German authorities and their Governments—a part of which subsequently fell into the hands of the Bolsheviks and has been published by them (*The Crash of the German Occupation in Ukraine*, 1936, inf. p. 335). In his reports to Vienna the Austrian Chief of Staff, General Waldstetter, found Vsevolod Holubovich, the President of the Council of Ministers, 'eloquent, imaginative—a man of theories with no character at all; put there by the Germans'. Lubinsky, the Minister for Foreign Affairs, was 'a beardless young man extremely well read in Socialist and revolutionary literature; entirely in the hands of the Germans'. Zhukovski, the Minister for War, 'seems to me pro-Russian; he is an ex-Colonel of the General Staff and tries hard to appear before his colleagues as an untainted Socialist and revolutionary from head to foot; in reality a German puppet'. The same source gives a curious characterization of Hrushevsky. 'Hrushevsky—President of the *Rada*, a frightened old man all of a tremble; his old bones are supposed to give the *Rada* a noble patina worthy of so august an assembly. Holds on for all he is worth to the German Command and shows no sympathy at all towards Austria.' Hrushevsky had certainly changed with the times.

The *Rada* was composed of several hundred deputies, belonging to different Ukrainian parties; amongst them were National Democrats, Social Revolutionaries, Social Democrats and Social Federalists. Separatist tendencies prevailed, but among the more definitely Socialist groups it was possible to observe a more or less veiled distrust of and hostility towards the Austro-German authorities and the obedient cabinet which they had installed in Kiev. The more prominent representatives of these sentiments included Vinnichenko and Petlyura.

After its return to Kiev the *Rada* embarked on the purely academic task of elaborating a constitution for the Ukraine. The Occupation authorities were not much interested in this 'august assembly' and had 'no illusions about its importance'. General Hoffmann wrote at the time: 'The difficulty in the Ukraine is that the Central *Rada* has only our rifles behind it. The moment we withdraw our troops their authority will collapse at once' (Hoffmann, p. 207). The historian of the Brest-Litovsk peace, who has studied the documents of the period with great thoroughness, comes to the conclusion that: 'The separatist movement had no roots in the country and the people as a whole were completely indifferent to national self-determination; this had been thrust upon them by a group of political dreamers whose power was derived from the presence of German bayonets.'

But if the Occupation authorities were not much interested in the *Rada*, they could not help being interested in the Government which depended upon the *Rada* and which had undertaken, under the terms of the Peace Treaty, to procure supplies and raw materials for Germany and Austria. In order to comply with the formalities of diplomatic etiquette, the all-important clause of the Treaty had been worded in a somewhat vague and delicate way. Clause 7 ran as follows: 'The contracting parties mutually undertake to enter into economic relations without delay and to organize the exchange of goods on the basis of the following stipulations: until 31 July of the current year a reciprocal exchange of the surplus of their most important agricultural and industrial products for the purpose of meeting current requirements.' It proceeds to lay down that 'the quantities and classes of products shall be decided in the future by a special mixed commission'. It had only been in private conversations between the respective Delegations that the million tons had been mentioned.

The energetic and experienced Groener was entrusted with the realization of Clause 7, and for this purpose he established in Kiev the *Deutsche Ukrainische Kaufmännische Wirtschaftstelle*. This institution elaborated a detailed and rational mode of action. The Mixed Commission set up under the Peace Treaty sat for a long time before it could assess the classes and quantities of goods to be extracted from the Ukraine. At last, on 8 April, a Protocol was signed which formed a special Appendix to the Peace Treaty, and according to which the Government of the Ukrainian 'Popular Republic' undertook to send to Germany and Austria-Hungary a million tons of grain, 400 million eggs, cattle to the weight of about 46,000 tons, a great number of horses, a considerable quantity of coal, manganese, fodder, sugar, lard, etc. After the Protocol was signed it was not long before it became apparent that the theoretical calculations of General Groener would not be easy to realize in practice.

Field-Marshal Eichhorn himself gave vent to his scepticism when he grumbled that 'the whole trouble is that we have to treat this Ukraine as a friendly country'. But Baron Mumm hastened to retort: 'In my opinion it is absolutely necessary to keep up the fiction that the Ukraine is a friendly and independent country; otherwise we shall completely destroy the already shaky authority of the *Rada*.' General Hoffmann had no great confidence in all the methodical plans of General Groener and expressed the view that it would have been much better to have entrusted the whole business to Jewish intermediaries. By March, instead of the promised 300 train-loads of grain, only one train had arrived for Vienna and one for Buda-

Pest. In April the situation somewhat improved, but it was evident that there was no hope of receiving by the end of July any substantial proportion of the goods which had been stipulated under the Peace Treaty. It became clear that the enthusiastic delegates of the 'Popular Republic' had greatly exaggerated the agricultural wealth of their country. They had had in view 'potential possibilities', but they had quite failed to take into account the actual state of affairs in the spring of 1918. During the whole of the preceding year agrarian disorders had been taking place. The peasants had appropriated lands, and the countryside had been swarming with ex-soldiers who had completely lost their morale and who, although they had quitted the front, had no wish whatever to return to peaceful occupations. Under such conditions the harvest of 1917 had not been gathered as it would have been in normal times; and, furthermore, no one knew to whom what had actually been gathered really belonged. The cattle of the landowners had been in great part slaughtered or driven off when the Red Guards made their appearance in the Ukraine during the winter of 1917; the sugar factories were standing idle. At the same time, the well-to-do peasants had quickly learned to hide their grain and other produce, and they were no more willing to deliver to the Germans than they had been to the Bolsheviks.

As a result of all this, during the whole period of the Occupation, the Germans only succeeded in exporting 9293 wagon-loads of grain; 23,195 wagon-loads of fodder, sugar, cattle, eggs and other products; and 4567 wagon-loads of minerals (coal, manganese)—as a whole 37,000 wagons under the auspices of the *Wirtschaftstelle* and 5000 through 'private initiative'. This tonnage amounted to scarcely a fifth part of what had been expected before 31 July 1918. And even the quantities which Germany succeeded in securing were delivered after the Government of the *Rada* had given place to that of Hetman Skoropadsky, and for the most part during the first three months of the latter régime.

The failure of the *Rada* in 'the economic collaboration' with the Germans was the reason for its downfall. When the Germans came into the Ukraine their inspection of stocks of supplies not only revealed the relative scarcity of these stocks but also the chaotic state of Ukrainian economy at that moment. The estates of the landowners had almost completely disappeared, and the peasants had appropriated the land. This action of the agrarian proletariat had, however, received no legal sanction, and the *Rada* had not yet elaborated any land laws. To the Command of the *Heeresgruppe Kiev* the practical and not the legal state of affairs was important. Field-Marshal Eichhorn therefore issued an 'Order to the Ukrainian population', calling on them to resume agricultural production 'to the maximum extent'. The harvest was to belong to him who would plough and sow, whether he was the legal owner of the land or the peasant who had taken possession of it. If the peasant proved unable to sow, the landowner was to do it, and the peasant was to put no obstacle in his way. Persons guilty of disobedience to this Order were to be brought to trial and punished, not by the Ukrainian civil courts but by the military tribunals of the Occupation.

Not only was this Order issued without the knowledge of the *Rada*, but the *Rada* heard of it only two weeks later. The German authorities were well aware that Eichhorn's Order would arouse opposition among the peasants and also among numerous groups in the *Rada* itself. Such opposition, however, would afford a suitable pretext to put an end to a Government which had proved its incapacity for 'economic collaboration'.

A month's experience of the country had been enough to indicate to the Occupation authorities the only section of the population which was likely to help them to fulfil General Groener's plan with efficiency and rapidity. It did not require much perspicacity to observe that the stocks of sugar, vegetable oil and spirit on large estates where the landlord had owned the factories were greatly in excess of those accumulated by the peasantry. Furthermore, it always proved much more difficult to extract grain from peasants, who were guiltily conscious of having recently pillaged neighbouring granaries. The liberal Government of the *Rada* had not refused to sanction the formation of a landowners' union when the latter proposed to organize to defend their interests. Of course this union, in accord with the spirit of the times, had to be called a Union of Cornraisers (*Khliboroby*); but it was recruited not only from prosperous peasants who owned 20–30 hectares of land, but also from many middle-class and even aristocratic landowners. The Union maintained an aspect sufficiently 'democratic' to avoid provoking the radical majority of the *Rada*, but it had close connections with Russian conservative circles whose influence was beginning to make itself felt in Kiev.

The terms of the Soviet-Ukrainian 'peace' were still under negotiation, but the armistice imposed by the Germans continued in force, and the situation provided favourable opportunities for the higher classes of Russian society to leave Petrograd and Moscow and make their way to the Ukraine. Furthermore, after the chaotic demobilization of the army, thousands of Russian officers had gathered in Kiev. These officers were certainly in no hurry to go back 'into the hands of the Soviets'. Kiev presented a very strange picture in

April 1918. The capital of the Ukrainian 'Popular Republic' had all the appearance of a big Russian town living an animated and even boisterous life owing to the presence of large numbers of Russian and foreign 'guests'. Except for the names of certain shops which were written up in Ukrainian and the picturesque uniforms of the *Rada* regiments, there was no indication of 'the beginning of a new life'. Ukrainian was only spoken in Government offices and during the sittings of the *Rada*. This official language imported from Galicia was not always easily understood by the inhabitants of Russian Ukraine.

In the environment of the Union of *Khliboroby* and of the fashionable fugitives from the north the Command of the *Heeresgruppe Kiev* easily found a convenient person who could be the head of the administration which was to replace the Government of the *Rada*.

General Paul Skoropadsky had the advantage of being a descendant of that amiable and pliable Hetman who had been chosen by Peter the Great to succeed Mazeppa. An officer of the Chevaliers Gardes Regiment, he had distinguished himself during the war, first in command of a Guards Brigade and later of a Guards Division. Of Ukrainian origin and property, he belonged to a wealthy and distinguished family. Furthermore, General Skoropadsky was endowed with the necessary ambition, and had no objection to undertaking an important political role even if it should be a difficult one. He had many connections with the Union of Cornraisers and had established excellent relations with the German Command, which now designated him as their chosen 'Head of the State' when the propitious moment for his elevation should arise.

That moment arrived when at last the *Rada* learned about the Order issued by Field-Marshal Eichhorn, and peasant riots—provoked by the Order—broke out in the southern parts of the Governments of Kiev and Poltava. The members of the *Rada* were in a state of agitation; not only Petlyura and the extremists were urging opposition to the German measures, but also some of the cabinet ministers —including Lubinsky, that incorrigibly eloquent 'student' of the Congress of Brest-Litovsk. The German Command was well aware of the movement of opinion in the *Rada* and on 24 April they signed a formal agreement with Skoropadsky. Lüdendorff approved the choice of 'a man with whom one can work well' (Lüdendorff, *War Memoirs*, p. 624). On the same day the *Rada* declared the Order of Field-Marshal Eichhorn to be illegal and non-existent. Two days later, during a sitting of the *Rada*, a detachment of German soldiers entered the hall under the command of an officer who gave the abrupt order, 'Hands up!' The outraged deputies were searched for arms, after which they were allowed to go home with the exception of a few of their number, including several cabinet ministers, who were arrested on the spot. On the following day, during a meeting of the Union of Cornraisers, Paul Skoropadsky was proclaimed 'Hetman of the Ukraine'.

Skoropadsky remained Hetman for about seven-and-a-half months and resigned when the Germans were evacuating the Ukraine. Those seven months can be divided into two distinct periods: the first until the middle of August and the second until the end of November.

During the first period the Germans found that their manœuvre had been crowned with comparative success. In July, particularly, supplies of grain and coal were delivered at a regular and rapid tempo. The Germans, again, succeeded in securing thousands of horses of which they were badly in need, not so much for the cavalry as for the artillery and transport services. In Berlin and Vienna bread reappeared and meat and sugar was to be had in considerable quantities. Skoropadsky's Government turned out to be much more capable than that of the *Rada*, perhaps for the reason that the Hetman did not bother about any ideology whatever. The Foreign Minister, Doroshenko, was not over-burdened with work, but the energetic Minister of the Interior, Igor Kistyakovsky, and the Minister of Commerce, Gutnik, had plenty to do. Berlin and Vienna placed at the disposal of the Government the quantity of Marks necessary to cover the issue of 400,000,000 *karbóvantsi* (about 300,000,000 Marks) issued by the Hetman; and for this reason the *karbóvantsi* enjoyed a greater credit with the people than had the 'paper' of the *Rada*. In the meantime 'a real General', General Ragoza, formerly commanding the 4th Russian Army, undertook the task of organizing the Hetman's army. Not only officers of Ukrainian origin, but officers from all over Russia freely enlisted in it.

The historian of Brest-Litovsk justly remarks that in June 1918 'the Ukraine became for a short time a bourgeois Mecca and thither flocked thousands of refugees from Soviet Russia' (Wheeler-Bennett, p. 323). Kiev rapidly lost even that 'shade of Ukrainism' which it had worn in the *Rada* days. Baron Mumm, the German Minister Resident, was depressed by this aspect of affairs when he wrote to Groener: 'I tried to insist with the President of the Council of Ministers Lizohub that the German Government desires his cabinet to have more of *couleur locale*.' Mumm altogether was not particularly pleased with the *coup d'état*, since the military men had not asked his opinion about it and had not even troubled to let him know before it was accomplished. In another report Mumm suspects the Hetman's Government of being 'pro-Russian', but adds that 'this should not be taken too tragically as the Hetman's Government is under my control and that of the German Staff'. The Austrian Command, which did not like the Hetman on account of his 'independent tone in relation to Vienna', accused Skoropadsky himself of being 'pro-Russian'. Compromising documents were produced from somewhere according to which the Hetman had, in July 1914, denied the existence of a Ukrainian nation, while in July 1917 he was supposed to have spoken of Kiev as a centre of Russian and not of Ukrainian culture. He had also been guilty of advocating the union of all Russian lands in a federal state. The position of the Hetman, however, was then very firm, because he had the sympathy of the military Command who had no interest in the ideological side of the Ukrainian Question.

Baron Mumm and the Austrians were of course very near the truth in their views on Skoropadsky's Government. The Hetman and his cabinet, even if they were Ukrainians by origin, were of less than moderate tendencies in relation to separatism. They only 'tolerated' the separation of Ukraine from Russia while Russia remained in the hands of Lenin and Trotsky. At this time Kiev not only looked forward to the early downfall of the Bolsheviks, but was certain that the excellent relations existing between the Hetman and the German Command was the prelude to German support for the restoration of the Russian Monarchy.

At this time the Ukrainian and Russian conservatives in Kiev were not the only elements who were anticipating a German march on Moscow. The success of the German offensive in France in the spring of 1918 had convinced the Russian factions of the invincibility of the German power. Even Paul Milyukov, the protagonist of the Triple Entente, got into touch with the German Command in Kiev through the Ukrainian Premier Lizohub, who had been a member of the Cadet Party. But the Germans continued to stand where they were, and even the murder of the German Ambassador in Moscow, Count Mirbach, did not induce them to expel from Berlin the Soviet representative Joffe, whose staff was at this time propagating Communism in Germany with relative immunity.

Meantime a curious situation had been created on the Don, where the Germans had recognized the Don Cossack *ataman* General Krasnov as head of a separate state. In the north the *ataman* was fighting the Bolsheviks, while on the south he was collaborating with the Volunteer Army in process of formation by General Denikin, who was the favoured protégé of the Entente Powers as the allies of Imperial Russia. Skoropadsky, notwithstanding his dependence on the Germans and the German anxiety to conciliate the Soviet

Government, managed, with the connivance of German officers, to send some support in men and supplies to Krasnov and, through him, to Denikin.

As the summer advanced a serious deterioration took place in conditions in the Ukraine. The German and Austrian troops, weary of the war and in continuous contact with the anarchic and revolutionary incidents of the countryside, were becoming demoralized. After the German disasters on the Western Front at the beginning of August, their mood became mutinous, although it was not until October that open disorders broke out among the German troops in Kharkov, when certain battalions refused transfer to the Western Front.

The German official source (*Die Rückführung des Ostheeres*), published in 1936 with a Preface by Generals Blomberg and von Beck, describes the gradual demoralization of the Occupation troops in the Ukraine. The police functions which fell to the lot of the German troops undermined their morale in the existing situation. Too great temptations existed for soldiers employed in the collection of supplies. 'Illegal commerce and speculation flourished, and it was exceedingly difficult for the military authorities to prevent this on account of the troops being scattered over a vast territory and on account of the necessity of maintaining innumerable small posts. The conduct of isolated German detachments destroyed the prestige of the Occupation troops in the eyes of the local population. Even the authorized trading, the object of which was the despatch of parcels of food to their homes, brought the soldiers into undesirable contact with the population—especially with Jews who had most of this commerce in their hands. Jews were frequently the transmitters of Bolshevik propaganda' (*Rückführung*, pp. 5–6).

The same source gives a gloomy description of the Hetman's Government: 'Unfortunately Hetman Skoropadsky ruled in the Ukraine only with the support of German bayonets. His Government had neither the required authority nor the energy to take drastic measures for restoring law and order in the country. The majority of the population distrusted him on account of his monarchical and pro-Russian tendencies and on account of his support of important landowners. That population stood either for a Republic and friendship with the Entente or simply for the Bolsheviks. The peasants were clamouring most of all for a solution of the agrarian problem, the decision of which the Hetman's Government could not take upon itself. To judge by the beginning made, it was scarcely possible to form a Hetman's army. There were too many officers and too few soldiers—especially too few of those soldiers who later turned out trustworthy' (*ibid.* pp. 8–9).

Already in the month of April, before the *Rada* fell, peasant risings had flared up in the Governments of Kiev and Poltava in answer to German expeditions in search of supplies. Under Skoropadsky the execution of Eichhorn's Order was carried through in a firmer fashion—with the aid of German detachments; but it was accompanied with extremely dangerous moral consequences, not only for the Occupation troops but also for the Ukrainian Government. In many cases landowners applied to the Hetman for the re-establishment of their rights of property or for the restoration of order in their localities, but the Hetman, who had no trusty police force nor army of his own, had to ask the Occupation authorities for the aid of their troops. This was not refused, since the interest of the landowners coincided with that of the German Command. Among the peasants were many ex-soldiers who had left the Front, but who had taken their rifles with them. Shots were fired sometimes, and hasty reprisals followed on the spot, or at least arrests and military tribunals. There is nothing more perilous for any Government than 'to enforce order' with the aid of foreign soldiers. After two or three months the rural population, including the more prosperous peasants, were unanimous in their hatred of the Hetman and the Germans. Attacks on small German posts guarding railway stations, bridges and depots became more frequent. German soldiers disappeared through shots fired round a corner or the sudden thrust of a knife. These incidents caused fear and anger among the German soldiers—not so much against the local inhabitants as against their own commanders. The Hetman's Government contributed to the 'revolutionizing' of the Ukraine and, indirectly, to that of the Army of Occupation.(6)

Eichhorn and Skoropadsky were criticized in some Austro-German circles. The Austrians were displeased in part that a Russian general and not an Austrian Archduke should have been put at the head of the Ukrainian realm. They were also suspicious of ultimate German designs on the Ukraine, since they considered that this territory should properly be regarded as within the sphere of Habsburg policy. On 13 June General Waldstetter wrote in a secret report to Vienna that 'Germany pursues in the Ukraine definite economic and political objectives. She wants to keep for ever a safe way open to Mesopotamia and Arabia through Baku and Persia. The way to the East goes through Kiev, Ekaterinoslav and Sevastopol and from there by sea to Batum and Trebizond.' Somewhat later the Commander-in-Chief of the Austro-Hungarian Occupation troops, General Kraus, reported to his Government: 'On the one hand the German Command is consciously upholding the Monarchical movement, and on the other hand the German Minister Resident Mumm is doing all he can to democratize the Ukraine. On the whole they want to isolate from us both the conservative and left elements and enforce their own influence.' In his turn Mumm complained of the Austrians to Berlin: 'They are trying to secure the complete independence from the Kiev Government of that part of the Ukraine which is occupied by Austro-Hungarian troops.'

It is difficult to ascertain what in reality were the German plans for the future of the Ukraine during the summer of 1918. The High Command did not look very far ahead and believed with justice that the future of the Ukraine was being decided on the battlefields of France. When, in August, Lüdendorff ceased to believe in ultimate victory, he lost all interest in the Ukraine. Of course in those circles whose function it was to study the political and economic problems of the war (typical of which was the noted economist Dr Rohrbach who had been in Kiev) were discussed those theories which linked the destinies of the Ukraine 'for ever' with Germany. The Emperor William, in his missive to the *ataman* of the Don Cossacks, General Krasnov, expressed his own views on the future of Russia, which was to be divided into four independent states—'the Ukraine', 'the South-Eastern Union', 'Central Russia' and 'Siberia'. These views, by the way, were very far from what the patriotic advocates of a 'Russia one and indivisible' were at that time hoping for from the German Emperor.

In September the Emperor received the Hetman at his Headquarters in Spa with all the honours due to 'the head of an independent state'. The visit, however, did not contribute to raise the prestige of Skoropadsky.

Eichhorn, Skoropadsky and Mumm were also criticized by General Hoffmann and Dr Rohrbach. In their opinion, the policy of Eichhorn, supported by Lüdendorff, was pushing the Ukraine back into the arms of Russia. These critics, however, failed to take notice of the more evident danger of the presence in Kiev of a Soviet delegation, with Rakovski or Manuilsky at its head, which had appeared on the pretext of concluding the peace negotiations between the Soviets and the Hetman's Government. Professor Mohilansky writes in his memoirs (*Archives of the Russian Revolution*, vol. XI) that the Ukrainian Ministry of the Interior 'possessed numerous documents which testified with absolute certainty that the Bolshevik delegation in Kiev was spreading Bolshevik propaganda in the Ukraine and spent millions in organizing railway strikes and armed revolts. At the beginning of September the Minister of the Interior made a report to the Council of Ministers to the effect that the Germans put obstacles in his way when the question came to arresting Bolsheviks well known for their activities and even demanded that he should set at liberty those who were under arrest.'

The assassination of Field-Marshal Eichhorn by a Ukrainian terrorist on 30 July failed to sting the Germans into modifying the cautious and even conciliatory policy which they had adopted towards the Soviets. At the same time the Field-Marshal's successor, General Kirchbach, lacked his personal influence and had not the prestige necessary to counter the doubtful intrigues of Baron Mumm. The latter continued to have relations (directly or through the German Consulate) with the representatives of the *Rada*. He insisted that the Hetman's Government should set at liberty Simon Petlyura and other politicians who had been arrested. (7)

Intently watching and stimulating the growing unpopularity of the Hetman among the peasantry, the representatives of the Ukrainian Socialist parties organized themselves in the 'National Union', to the head of which Vinnichenko was elected. When this had been done, the Union, acting through the German authorities, began to try to secure the admission of some of their members to participation in the Government. Baron Mumm evidently very much doubted the solidity of Skoropadsky's position. At last the German Foreign Office, convinced by his reports, sent Mumm, on 10 October, categorical instructions to support 'the National Ukrainian Movement' and to 'ukrainize' the Government.

In October, however, it was plainly evident that the Austro-German Occupation could not endure for many weeks. In that month tempestuous national risings broke out in different parts of the Habsburg Monarchy and the ancient Danubian Empire appeared to be on the verge of dissolution. When the news reached the Austro-Hungarian troops in the Ukraine an irresistible movement swept the ranks for immediate return to their own country. The official German source describes how at the beginning of November disorderly crowds of Austrian soldiers in trains and on foot were going west selling their arms and munitions to the local population. 'A regiment consisting of Italians arrested the Commander and Staff of its Army Corps and declared them to be prisoners of war.' The Germans hastily sent the 7th Landwehr (Württemberg) Division to Odessa in order to clear the town of mutinous Austrian soldiers.

But the officers of the German Army of Occupation did not have to wait long to drain their own cup of bitterness. On 9 November came the news by radio that the Emperor William had abdicated; on the next day that Ebert had formed a Government and that the soldiers were electing Soviets; and on the 11th that an armistice had been signed on the Western Front.

The question of the evacuation of the German troops immediately arose and it was clear that this would present enormous difficulties. Lvov was seized by Galician Ukrainians; Lublin and Warsaw by the Poles: neither were willing to let troop trains through. From Kiev only one line of railway remained: Kovel-Brest-Litovsk-Belostok.

The news of the crash of the German Front in the West and of the impending evacuation of the Ukraine by the Germans was naturally the signal for a Ukrainian movement directed against the Hetman's Government. On 20 November, during street riots in Kiev, twenty people were killed. A whole Ukrainian Division declared itself against the Hetman and began to march from Konotop on Kiev; it was stopped by German troops. Large bands of 'Reds' appeared near Kharkov. New Russia was swarming with brigands who had armed themselves with what the Austrians had left behind. This was only the beginning.

The principal politicians of the 'National Union' were also on the alert and each of them acted according to his disposition. Vinnichenko formed a 'Directoria' of five members from the different Ukrainian Socialist parties, while Petlyura hastened to Belaya Tserkov, where he easily raised a mutiny against the Hetman in the crack regiment which had been christened with the romantic name of 'The Zaporogian Sech Rifles' and which had been recruited largely out of the Russian war prisoners from Rastatt who had been given the 'special education in the Ukrainian spirit'.

§ 4. DIE RÜCKFÜHRUNG DES OSTHEERES

Between Petlyura and Vinnichenko dissensions immediately arose not only on questions of principle: they were personal enemies. Vinnichenko wanted the Ukraine to be proclaimed a 'State of Workers and Peasants', but not subject to Moscow. Petlyura turned out to be a politician of a more practical turn of mind: he understood well enough that it would not be long before the Moscow Soviets would swallow up Vinnichenko's Ukraine. He also understood that it was necessary for the 'Directoria' to conciliate the sympathy and interest of the Entente powers if the Ukrainian nationalists were to gain sufficient time to establish any sort of stable régime. Petlyura was not a bad organizer and his firmness made him popular with the soldiers. Therefore he was the master of the situation.

Partly in consequence of Petlyura's 'Universal' and partly in response to Vinnichenko's proclamations which were plastered all over the Ukraine—even in the streets of the Hetman's capital, but most of all because of the peasants' overwhelming desire 'to get rid of the Germans', armed groups and detachments appeared everywhere. These bodies paid no particular heed to the self-appropriated authority of the 'Directoria' but obeyed their improvised *atamans* and 'colonels'.

Skoropadsky could not help realizing that his position had suddenly become desperate. His cabinet was powerless in every respect, and the last hope that remained was to get into touch with the victors in the war through the leaders of the 'White' Volunteer Army to which they were according their support. General Denikin had already issued an Order to the Volunteer Army in which he proclaimed that he assumed command 'of all the forces in the South of Russia'. This Order of course was intended to apply to 'the armed forces' in the Crimea and the Ukraine, and it was inferred that the thousands of Russian officers in Kiev and Odessa were now under the command of General Denikin's unofficial representative in Kiev, General Lomnovski. A 'South Russian Centre' consisting of several conservative professors and fugitive politicians who were all hoping and working for a united Russia was set up in Kiev. The trouble was, however, that neither the officers nor the politicians were able to protect the Hetman against the rising anger of the armed peasantry. The Volunteer Army was far away in Rostov-on-Don and the northern Caucasus and the Allied forces in Roumania were no nearer to the scared remnants of Skoropadsky's class régime in Kiev. In Odessa, it is true, the French Consul Hainnot soon made his appearance as the representative of the victorious Entente. He came in touch with Prince Dolgoruki, the Commander-in-Chief of the Hetman's troops, and promised him the speedy intervention of French forces in the Ukraine. At the same time Hainnot warned the German Command in Kiev that any leniency on their part towards the mutinous Ukrainian elements, 'especially any sort of agreement with them, would not be tolerated'. Hainnot went on to threaten the Germans with reprisals 'should any arms or munitions be given to the Ukrainians or if Kiev were surrendered to them' (*Rückführung*, p. 40). The French Consul, however, had no force at his disposal, and his promises and threats were made on his own initiative and on the advice of his Russian friends rather than as the result of instructions from his Government.

Skoropadsky and all the Russians in Kiev found themselves, as before, defended only by German bayonets. To make the situation still more paradoxical these German bayonets were now as a matter of fact at the disposal of the German 'Soviet of Soldiers' Deputies' which had been set up in Kiev and which openly sympathized with the Bolsheviks. Finally, on 28 November 1918, Skoropadsky, gambling on Hainnot's promises and on the understanding between the Entente and the Volunteer Army, issued a proclamation in which he declared the Ukraine to be a part of 'the great Russian realm'. He was too late to save either himself or the conservative interest in Kiev.

Ukrainian detachments were approaching Kiev from all sides. As early as 15–20 November all sorts of *atamans* and 'colonels' had occupied Kharkov and Poltava and even Rovno to the west of Kiev. On 19 November remnants of the army which remained loyal to the Hetman were defeated at Vasilkov by the 'Petlyurians'. Kiev would have been taken if the Germans had not been ready to defend it.

Notwithstanding the almost complete collapse of discipline among the troops of the German Occupation, some grounds for collaboration had been found between the Soldiers' Soviets and the Command. 'Only one impulse reigned among the troops, every soldier had only one thought: "Home! Home! Home!—at any price!"' (*Rückführung*, p. 40). The winter had set in, snow had fallen and the horrors of Napoleon's retreat haunted the minds of the Germans. The officers had little difficulty in persuading the men that it was necessary to hold Kiev for the time being as a centre from which the evacuation could be organized.

But the defence of Kiev and other large towns and important railway junctions by the Germans was interpreted by the population as a continued support of the Hetman. By spreading its propaganda against Skoropadsky the 'Directoria' was exciting the people against the Germans; in fact the association and exploitation of the two hatreds secured the maximum number of adherents for Petlyura. The peasants had many accounts to settle with the Germans, while considerations of a material order were eloquent enough. The rumour circulated that the Germans who were leaving the Ukraine were taking away with them a lot of money and great quantities of goods. There was an overwhelming desire not to allow them to do this and to take away from them all that they had appropriated. A logical development of this train of thought was the decision to deprive the Germans of their weapons and munitions: their artillery and machine-guns, rifles, lorries, carts, horses—and finally even their warm clothing and their money.

Attacks on railway stations began in many districts with the object of preventing the evacuation of the German troops. The German Command soon realized that under such conditions it had become an utter impossibility to organize the evacuation even along the lines which were still available after the events in Poland: Kiev-Kovel-Brest-Litovsk (for the 20th Army Corps and the 22nd and 27th Reserve Corps); and Bakhmach-Pinsk-Brest-Litovsk (for the 1st Army Corps and the 41st Reserve Corps). It became an absolute necessity to come to an agreement with Petlyura, and such an agreement was concluded on 2 December in Kiev. An 'armistice' was arranged during the duration of which the 'Directoria' undertook to make itself responsible for the organization of transport facilities. But with all the goodwill in the world Petlyura and the members of the 'Directoria' were able to give little real assistance in that direction —and that little only in the immediate neighbourhood of Kiev. In other parts of the Ukraine the struggle against the retreating Germans continued to assume more and more violent forms. In Kharkov *ataman* Barbashev and his staff had to be arrested before the Germans could board the promised train. At the important junctions of Bakhmach and Kasatin, the gangs in control continued to refuse to allow trains to pass through *en route* for Kovel and Homel. 'It was simply by a miracle that, up to 12 December, we succeeded in despatching 126 trains' (*Rückführung*). By this time skirmishes between German detachments and the local population had spread all over the Ukraine.

The numerous Ukrainian bands in Volhynia became a real danger to the Germans. Fighting took place 'with changing luck' in Berdichev, where a Bavarian Brigade beat back successive attacks by strong 'Petlyurian' forces. At the station of Zhmerinka the 'Petlyurians' defeated two Landwehr cavalry regiments with a loss of more than 200 killed and wounded. The disorganized Germans were disarmed and driven away from the railway line in the direction of the Galician frontier. On 7-8 December hot encounters took place for the stations of Sarny, Iskorost and Birzula. The Germans took several thousands of prisoners, but it was difficult to know what to do with them for, if set free, they would join new bands and reappear in a few days.

On 6 December *pourparlers* with Petlyura were renewed, and on the 11th, at the station of Kasatin, a definite agreement was concluded. Petlyura insisted with some reason that if his troops were to obey him it was necessary for the 'Directoria' to return to its capital —Kiev. A peaceful continuation of the German evacuation could only be procured by the immediate surrender of Kiev to the Ukrainians.

The first consequence of the Kasatin Agreement was the resignation of the Hetman and his Government. On 14 December, after a short affair with the remaining troops of the Hetman, the ragged bands of the 'Directoria' under the command of Colonel Konovalets entered Kiev. In their wake, on the 19th, arrived the 'Directoria' with Petlyura and Vinnichenko at its head.

During the Kasatin *pourparlers* the German Command had considered it a question of honour to stipulate that the Russian officers and men who were serving the Hetman should be allowed to go free after surrendering their arms. This condition was only partly kept. Some officers, among them General Count Keller, who had tried to organize resistance in the town itself, were shot on the spot. Another five hundred officers were arrested and kept prisoners in the Kiev Museum. Later they were divided into groups and distributed among different prisons; a number of them, under pretext that they had tried to escape, faced firing squads; after 29 December those who remained alive were sent off to Germany (*Rückführung*, p. 52).

The surrender of Kiev resulted in a change for the better in the conditions of the German evacuation. The Germans had to accept certain limitations on the disposal of military stores: the troops were allowed to take with them only machine-guns for one company in every regiment; guns for three batteries in every artillery regiment, etc. The balance had to be 'delivered to the Ukrainian Army'.

By the end of December the Command of the former *Heeresgruppe Kiev* had migrated first to Kovel and then to Brest-Litovsk. The evacuation was proceeding almost normally, although in some localities the troop trains were attacked and disarmed, and often the Germans could only secure uninterrupted passage by the payment of large sums of money. By the middle of January the bulk of the Army of Occupation had quitted the territory of the Ukraine, and was concentrated in the railway triangle: Brest-Litovsk-Pinsk-Kovel. But troops in left-bank Ukraine were still having a difficult time because the Bolsheviks had appeared there as rivals to the 'Directoria'.

On 9 November, when the first news arrived of the German Revolution, Lenin had denounced the Treaty of Brest-Litovsk. As a result, both the Ukraine of the Hetman and the Ukraine of the 'Directoria' found themselves in a state of war with the Soviets. The Bolsheviks had adherents enough in left-bank Ukraine and the industrial centres of New Russia: already in November they tried to take Poltava; at Ekaterinoslav, after the Austrians left, the Red Republic was proclaimed; and Soviets were set up in the mining towns of the Donets upon the departure of the Germans. At Kharkov the Staff of the 1st Army Corps and a certain number of German troops remained, but these could not protect the officials of the 'Directoria' when, on 3 January 1919, 8000 armed 'Reds' entered the city. The Germans in Kharkov found themselves in a parlous position, since they could no longer move westward owing to the state of war between the Soviets and the Ukrainians which existed all along the railway lines. There was talk about taking a south-easterly direction and going to the Don Cossacks. At last the Soviets gave permission for the Germans to go by a round-about way passing through Kursk, Orel, Polotsk. The Soviet authorities and the population of the 'Red' towns through which the Germans passed inundated the homing soldiers with propaganda and plagued them with organized 'fraternizing'. The morale of these men suffered far more than had that of their fellows from the anarchic attacks of the 'Petlyurians', and the dissolution of discipline and general demoralization reached a pitch unknown among the troops who had had to fight their way out through hundreds of miles of hostile country.

§5. ANARCHY IN THE UKRAINE: SIMON PETLYURA AND 'BATKO' MAKHNO

Having entered Kiev on 19 December, the 'Directoria' did not enjoy its triumph for long. Just as a year before in the anxious but not unprofitable days of Brest-Litovsk, 'Red' forces were moving on the Ukrainian capital. They were converging from three directions: through Konotop, through Poltava, and along the right bank of the Dniepr. At the same time the Poles—the most ancient enemies of Ukrainian nationality—with their own independence scarcely two months old were threatening all the western provinces.

Early in December an armed conflict had broken out between the Galician Ukrainians who wished to exercise the widely proclaimed right of self-determination and the Poles who looked upon Galicia as 'historically a Polish province'. The Poles had possessed themselves of the district of Kholm, promised once upon a time at Brest-Litovsk to the Ukrainians, and they were taking advantage of the opportunity of broadening its boundaries by infringing on the territory of the former Russian Government of Volhynia. Polish detachments had encounters, towards the middle of January, in the neighbourhood of Lutsk and Vladimir-Volynsk with 'Petlyurian' bands who until then had been more agreeably employed in holding up returning German troop-trains.

During the same weeks the 'Western Ukrainian Republic', proclaimed two months earlier in Lvov, got into a very critical position. The relatively weak Polish forces, collected in former Russian Poland after the Armistice, had now been reinforced by the highly trained and excellently disciplined army of General Haller formed in France out of prisoners of war who had been captured or who had deserted from the German and Austrian Armies. The armed forces at the disposal of the Polish Government now amounted to some 80,000 men. The whole of Galicia was occupied without much resistance, and after some street fighting the 'Western Ukrainian Republic' was driven out of Lvov.

The fugitive Government of this 'Republic' sought the aid of the Ukrainian 'Popular Republic', and on 23 January the 'Directoria' proclaimed in solemn session 'the union' of the 'Western Ukrainian Republic' with the Ukraine. But on the evening of the same day the first mounted patrols of Antonov-Ovseenko entered Kiev. The 'Directoria' surrendered its capital without a struggle and fled to Vinnitsa. This body, on which so much eloquence had been expended and which had shown always such little capacity, now went completely to pieces. When it left Vinnitsa and established itself in Rovno until the arrival of the Bolsheviks there in April, Vinnichenko used to say jokingly: 'The Directoria is a railway carriage and under that carriage is all its territory!' Petlyura, however, went to Kamenets-Podolsk, and at this point on the former Russian frontier the remnants of the Galician troops of the 'Western Ukrainian Republic' concentrated after their expulsion from Lvov.

The commanders of the Bolshevik forces did not take much interest in them, since at that time they were occupied in trying to gain possession of the ports along the Black Sea coast.

An extraordinary medley of events had been taking place in Odessa. The 7th German Landwehr Division, sent there in November to take over from the absconding Austrians, was duly cut off from Kiev and found that it could not fight its way through the swarms of 'Petlyurians' who were occupying the station of Birzula. Marching was out of the question owing to the snow-storms and the horrible state of the roads. British and French warships appeared in the harbour rather later in the month, but without disembarking any troops. Encouraged by their presence, the numerous Russian and Polish ex-officers in the city formed national detachments; but on 11 December important Ukrainian forces appeared in the suburbs. The Russian and Polish detachments took refuge in the port under the protection of the Allied naval guns. A week later transports arrived and landed a corps of French troops under General Borius. Hot street fighting began, and the French, with the Russians and Poles, drove the 'Petlyurians' out of the city.

Meantime the Germans were trying to remain strictly neutral. During the previous week the bulk of the Landwehr Division had succeeded in getting away, but there still remained in Odessa about 1600 German troops and a battery of field artillery. The 15th Landwehr Division in Nikolaev was in the same position: it too was cut off from communication with the German Command in Kiev.

French troops were now quartered in Odessa as well as all sorts of national volunteer formations—Russian, Polish and even Roumanian. Greek troops had disembarked at Kherson. The command was vested in the French General d'Anselm, who proceeded to entrust the 15th German Landwehr Division with the maintenance of law and order in Nikolaev.

'Petlyurian' troops and all sorts of *atamans*' detachments and brigand bands had cut off the cities of the coast from the rest of the Ukraine. After the flight of the 'Directoria' from Kiev, the 'Petlyurian' Colonel Grigoriev, who had gone over to the Bolsheviks, became for a time the dominant figure in that strange hinterland of anarchy. In the second half of February all the attempts of the French and the Volunteers to drive away Grigoriev's men from the immediate vicinity of Odessa and to enlarge the zone of occupation ended in failure. During the fighting at Berezovka the French soldiers of the 156th Division showed very little taste for a conflict which they did not understand. Seven tanks which had got stuck in the New Russian mud were left on the battlefield.

This event lent courage to Grigoriev's Bolsheviks, who on 3–5 March made an attempt to attack Nikolaev and Kherson, but were beaten back by a German armoured train. On 9 March Kherson was again attacked by 'Red' forces; the Greek troops in occupation hastened to evacuate the town and embark in their ships and Kherson fell to the Soviets. On 10 March began the evacuation by sea of the 7th Landwehr Division from Odessa and of the 15th Landwehr Division from Nikolaev. In the latter city the bands of Grigoriev entered the burning suburbs while the Germans were still embarking. No one knew what fate would befall Odessa, but on 2 April General d'Anselm received orders from Paris to evacuate. *Ataman* Grigoriev then 'took Odessa'. His troops did not amount to more than 2000 men. An enormous booty of military stores fell into the hands of the Bolsheviks.

These easy triumphs in the ports of the Black Sea did not consolidate the position of the Soviets, which was becoming really critical during the months of May and June 1919. It is true that beyond the Volga the imprudent advance during the spring of Admiral Kolchak's Siberian troops had ended in the defeat of the 'White' forces; at the same time, however, the Volunteer Army of General Denikin had occupied the Donets coalfields and was nearing Ekaterinoslav and Kharkov, while General Wrangel was advancing into the Volga basin from the northern Caucasus and on 30 June entered Tsaritsyn.

The Poles were taking advantage of the Russian Civil War by advancing into White Russia and Volhynia where, since April, they had been fighting with Bolshevik detachments which had been sent into the western Governments after the capture of Kiev from the 'Petlyurians'. Petlyura, also, had not exhausted his resources: his retreat into Podolia only served to renew his potentialities. At Kamenets-Podolsk, Petrushevich, 'the Dictator of Eastern Galicia', under pressure from the Poles, gave over the command of his own forces to Petlyura, and the latter now found himself at the head of about 40,000 men, of which some half were ex-soldiers of the old Austrian Army who had either come from Galicia or who were returning there from captivity in Russia. Among these former soldiers of Austria was a considerable number of officers, who were an important factor, since Petlyura's own men consisted only of armed peasants. Owing to the complete ruin of these lands and the impossibility of finding peaceful employment, service even in Petlyura's army had become a profession which at least procured food from day to day. Petlyura's troops were well armed out of the military stores which the Germans had abandoned or of which they had been deprived.

Some fighting with the Bolsheviks took place along the railway line Zhmerinka-Birzula, but what made the 'Petlyurian' campaign for ever memorable in Podolia was the extent and cruelty of their pogroms against the Jewish population. Pogroms began in January during the retreat of the 'Petlyurians' from the Kiev region when a particularly brutal slaughter took place at Belaya Tserkov. They continued in Podolia throughout the months of February, March and April, and what was probably the greatest pogrom of all time was enacted in the frontier town of Proskurov. The killings somewhat abated when the more disciplined Galician ex-soldiers became numerous in Petlyura's ranks.

All the combatants in the Civil War of 1919 took part in Jewish pogroms—the bands of the 'free' *atamans*, the 'Petlyurians', the 'White' Volunteers, the Bolsheviks and the Poles, but the 'Petlyurians' undoubtedly distinguished themselves most in this direction. According to official Jewish sources (*Ostjüdische Archiven*, Berlin) the 'Petlyurians' killed off 17,000 persons; the 'free' *atamans* 8000; the Volunteer Armies are accused of having 5000 to their score; the Soviet troops 1000; and the Polish Army several hundreds (Autumn

1917—April 1921). The 'Petlyurians' also occupy first place for the number of organized pogroms—493, or together with the 'free' *atamans*—852; the Volunteers follow with 233; the Soviets with 106; and the Poles with 32. How far Petlyura himself was guilty in the organization of these pogroms it is difficult to say. Arnold Margolin, himself a Jew, relates that Petlyura was extremely depressed by pogroms, and 'with tears in his eyes implored his men not to commit them'. But to persuade these 'last of the *Haydamaky*' to any moderation was no easy task.

Petlyura can scarcely be accused of having seriously favoured pogroms as part of a considered policy, since both he and the 'Directoria' were making every effort to attract the favourable attention of the representatives of the victorious Entente powers. Immediately after the Armistice a report had been addressed to Consul Hainnot, which was subsequently forwarded to General d'Anselm in Odessa and to General Berthelot, who was at that time in Jassy. This report was intended to establish the fact that the Ukrainian 'Popular Republic' was a quite normal, strictly democratic, and independent state. Although the French did not hesitate to drive away the detachments of the 'Directoria' by force of arms from the vicinity of Odessa, in January 1919 they went so far as to send a representative to Kiev in the person of General Tabouis. The British, at the same time, contented themselves with the despatch to Kiev of a member of the Consular Service. Altogether the impression gained ground in Kiev that the Ukraine had been reserved as a zone of French interest, while the British were more concerned with the Caucasian area and with the Volunteer Army.

The 'Directoria' viewed the question of its representation at the Paris Peace Conference as a matter of particular importance. A Delegation was hastily formed which included the 'Western Ukrainians' of Galicia with the engineer Sidorenko at their head; the 'Directoria' was represented by their 'Foreign Minister', A. Shulgin; and the numerous Jewish population of the Ukraine had a spokesman in Arnold Margolin. This Delegation, together with others of Governments which had been formed or which had tried to form themselves out of different parts of the Russian Empire, had not been invited to Paris by anyone and was recognized by no one. The Secretary of the Ukrainian Delegation, I. Borshak, summarizing the results of the work done between January and March 1919, reported to the 'Directoria': 'All asked us for information about the Ukrainian Question, but none gave any positive answer. No one promised to recognize our independence. The usual answer was: "Wait till the Conference discusses the Russian

Question!" There was talk on general topics—the territory, the numbers of the population, our relation with the Bolsheviks and General Denikin. Official French circles were against the Ukraine. Other states, the U.S.A., England and Japan, were on their guard and were only interested in the means at our disposal for struggling against the Bolsheviks' (I. Borshak, *Ukraine at the Peace Conference*).

The French were mainly concerned for the interest of Poland and the 'Directoria' undoubtedly made a serious tactical mistake when they involved the fate of Galicia with that of the Russian Ukraine. Furthermore, so soon after the recent hard struggle with Germany, the representatives of the Allies were not inclined to regard with favour envoys from the *de facto* succession states of the Russian Empire the Governments of which had owed their origin to German diplomacy and German bayonets.

Another member of the Ukrainian Delegation, Arnold Margolin, complains of 'the influence of Russians' who, from the monarchist groups to radical leaders like Kerenski, Avksentiev and Chaykovski, were all united in the belief that Russia 'one and indivisible' would be resuscitated. Margolin proposed that all 'the oppressed nationalities of the former Empire—not only Ukrainians, but also Georgians, Armenians, Azerbaijanians, the Cossacks of the Don and the Kuban, the Mountaineers of the Northern Caucasus and the White Russians adjoining the Polish provinces—should be invited to the Conference'. But when Margolin obtained an interview with Lansing, the latter told him frankly that 'he knew only one Russia which might perhaps become a federative state after she had got rid of the Bolsheviks'. Margolin betook himself to England, but there he found that people were only interested in the successes of the 'White' Armies of Denikin and Kolchak and believed in their ultimate victory. After having failed to raise interest in the fate of the 'oppressed nationalities' of the Russian Empire, Margolin broached the question of the fate of the Jews, but here too he found that people were not interested. In 1919 it was well remembered that the Jewish population of Poland and the Ukraine had been on the side of the Germans and that German Jews had taken upon themselves the role of intermediaries between the German High Command and the Bolsheviks.

The only practical result of the 'diplomatic relations' between France and the 'Directoria' was a categorical demand on the part of the French that Vinnichenko and another minister, Shakhovsky, should retire—because they were suspected of 'Bolshevism'.

The representatives of the Entente powers appear to have made every effort to unite all the forces which were struggling against

the Soviets, but they had no easy task. The Volunteer Army regarded the 'Petlyurians' with scarcely less distaste than it did the
Bolsheviks, while the 'Directoria' considered the 'White' movement
to be monarchical and reactionary, and the Ukrainian nationalists
aimed at separation rather than at federalism. The relation between
the Volunteer Army and the Poles was outwardly correct, but each
grudged the other success in their 'common struggle' against the
Soviets. The Russians were nervous about the Polish campaign in
White Russia and Volhynia; the Poles feared the resurrection of a
great Russia. The Poles went so far as to hold their advance against
the Red Army when this advance could have dealt a decisive blow
to the Soviets at the moment of Denikin's greatest success. These
dissensions, which were natural enough, in the end allowed the
Bolsheviks to extricate themselves from a position which, as
Trotsky relates in his memoirs, Lenin at that time regarded as
hopeless.

In July the Volunteer Army occupied Ekaterinoslav; then
Kherson, Nikolaev and Odessa; and on the 3rd Kharkov had been
taken after some fighting. Regardless of General Wrangel's proposal
to halt on the line Tsaritsyn-Ekaterinoslav and to put some order
into the disorganized rear, Denikin pressed the advance in a northerly
direction towards Moscow and westward on Kiev. As a result his
none too numerous forces were widely scattered over an enormous
territory.

At the same time Petlyura had begun his advance on Kiev from
the west, and this circumstance was one of the reasons for the false
manœuvre undertaken by the Volunteer Army. In the end the
Volunteers and the 'Petlyurians' came up to Kiev at the same time,
and the ancient city was taken on 1 September, from the east by the
'Whites' and from the south by the Ukrainians. No good could be
expected to result from this simultaneous but separate occupation of
Kiev by the rival armies. *Pourparlers* did not result in an agreement.
It only became clear that the Galicians were ready to come to an
understanding with the 'Whites', but the 'Directoria' was jealous,
and stubborn. Petlyura demanded complete independence and vast
territories. In his blind hate of 'the Russian monarchists and reaction-
aries' he secretly appealed for help to the Poles. When in the
second half of September armed conflicts between the Volunteers
and the 'Petlyurians' broke out and the latter were driven out of
Kiev towards the west, rumours of Petlyura's negotiations with the
Poles set the Galician regiments against him. On 7 November the
Galicians, tired of the lack of discipline and inefficiency rife among
the 'Petlyurians', decided to desert their leader and to go over to the

Volunteers in order to continue a joint struggle against the Bolsheviks and, if need be, against the Poles.

The remnants of the 'Petlyurians' went off into Podolia, where they renewed their brutal pogroms against the Jews. During the latter part of November and December they were decimated by a serious epidemic of black typhus which overtook them in the neighbourhood of Zhmerinka.

Having lost his army and almost alone, Petlyura betook himself to the Polish lines, where on 2 December he put his hand to a secret agreement, in the name of the 'Directoria', whereby he abandoned all claims on Galicia and 'recognized' Polish rule over Kholm, Polesia and Western Podolia—regions which were already in occupation of the Polish Army. On 24 December the 'Directoria' ceased to exist and gave over its phantom authority to a 'cabinet' formed by one Isaac Mazeppa, an ex-employee of the Union of Zemstvos.

In the meantime catastrophe had overtaken the Volunteer Army. Having occupied Kiev and Chernigov during September, the 'Whites' had reached Kursk and even Orel by the end of October. Their line was now dangerously extended and the advance succumbed to a sudden flanking attack delivered to the north of Kharkov. A serious defeat at Kromy to the south-west of Orel forced them out of the whole area between Kursk and Kharkov. Their collapse was now even more rapid than their progress had been. Kiev was evacuated, and within a few weeks all the Ukraine, in circumstances which grew more perilous every day.

The Volunteer Army had never been popular among the peasantry. During the preceding three years the peasants had lived through an evil nightmare of change and upheaval. They distrusted 'the officers' army' and suspected it, not without reason, of being the instrument whereby 'the former order' would be restored. In many cases the officials hastily appointed by General Denikin had contributed to this distrust by an ill-considered restoration of the rights of property in districts which they had been sent to administer. Though the peasant had never found any benefit from 'the new order' he was stubbornly opposed to a return to 'the old ways'. This frame of mind was the principal cause of the chaos which reigned in the rear of the White Army and it was more conducive to the catastrophe of the autumn of 1919 than either the unfortunate strategy of General Denikin or the superior abilities of the Red Army chiefs.

'The struggle which in 1919 drenched the Ukraine in blood recalled by its cruelties the Cossack risings of the seventeenth century. Thousands of peaceful citizens, principally landowners, Jews and German colonists, were ruthlessly put to death by "Petlyurians" and *atamans*. In their turn the Soviet authorities revenged themselves in the towns and villages on the hostages taken by the Bolsheviks and ordered mass executions of the bourgeoisie, intelligentsia and priests. The "Whites", too, had introduced the custom of hanging Communists' (Brégy and Obolensky, *L'Ukraine—Terre Russe*, p. 211).

The ultimate expression of rural anarchy during this grim period were the bands of armed peasants which roamed the country, slaughtering, looting and burning. Some of these bands called themselves 'Petlyurians', but most of them were acting on their own risk and peril. The *ataman* or *batko* ('father') was the head of a band consisting of several scores or several hundreds or even several thousands of armed men. The *batky* ruthlessly warred against any kind of authority, and their operations harmed the White Army most. The presence of this evil alone ought to have restrained the Volunteers from advancing too rapidly north, for as the area of occupation expanded and as little attempt was made to provide for adequate administration and policing, the number of the bands grew. Scores of important gangs were engaged in committing every kind of atrocity wherever they went. Zeleny devastated the Governments of Kiev and Poltava; Angel, Poltava and Chernigov; Grigoriev chose the lower course of the Dniepr; Tyutyunnyk, the region of Cherkassy; Struk and Sokolovsky, southern Polesia; and the famous Makhno became the terror of the whole of New Russia. Some of these fellows pretended to some kind of ideology: they were adherents of 'Communism without Jews' or, like Makhno, 'Anarchists'. These 'brigands with a social background' had some remote likeness to the *Haydamaky* of the eighteenth century, but then the *Haydamaky* in their own peculiar way had faith; they put religion before everything, and 'sought justice', not only social justice but also national justice, because they were believers and fought 'for the Ukrainian people oppressed by Polish landlords'.

In the course of the year 1919 *batko* Makhno rendered great services to the Soviets by seriously embarrassing the White Armies during the height of their advance on Moscow. Makhno belonged to what was called the 'half-intelligentsia' of peasant origin and was born in the big village of Gulyay-Pole to the north of Melitopol in New Russia. In 1907 he was exiled to Siberia, where he had to do hard labour for the murder of a policeman. Returning in 1917, owing to the wide amnesty at that time granted to numerous categories of common criminals, he had been cunning enough to assume a deep red coloration. Makhno returned to Gulyay-Pole, not as an ex-convict but as an 'anarchist'. The times were not for discussing anarchist theories but rather for applying anarchist practice. Soon the fame of the Gulyay-Pole *ataman* and his feats spread over the steppes between Melitopol and Taganrog. After the Bolshevik *coup d'état* Makhno alternately waged war or made peace with the local Soviets. In the spring of 1919 the Bolsheviks, retreating under the pressure of Denikin's army, had the brilliant idea of providing the *batko* with arms in order that he might harass the advance of the Volunteers.

During the advance on Kharkov the rear of the White Army became a promising field for Makhno's operations. It soon became an urgent necessity to put an end to him. This was done on 5–7 June, when the Caucasian Cossack Division of General Shkuro defeated at Gulyay-Pole great bands of 'Makhnovians'. They scattered but gradually gathered again in August in the neighbourhood of Elizavetgrad. Makhno reappeared as their chief; provided arms which he had secured from Petlyura; gained new recruits, and between 26 September and 7 October undertook his astonishing raid. He moved a distance of 600 kilometres in eleven days, twice defeating detachments of 'Whites' and plundering all the villages and towns which lay on his way. He turned up once more in the vicinity of Gulyay-Pole and thousands of uprooted peasants, deserters and brigands flocked to his standard. He was soon able to take Melitopol, Berdyansk and Mariupol, to make three raids on Ekaterinoslav and even to threaten the Headquarters of General Denikin in Taganrog. Two Army Corps of the Volunteers had to be detached to contain Makhno. The 'Whites', however, did not succeed in putting an end to the 'anarchist *batko*', who proved to possess great talents as a cavalry leader and who even invented 'new steppe-war tactics' (he put all his infantry in peasant carts and transported his machine-guns in wheel-barrows).

The Red Army finally liquidated Makhno's bands in 1920 at the same time as their last campaign against Wrangel in the Crimea. Nestor Makhno himself did not perish, but turned up in Paris, where he learned to earn his livelihood in the peaceful occupation of a cinema studio *figurant*; he died a few years later.

On 20 December 1919 Kiev was evacuated by the Volunteers, and the unfortunate city, about New Year's Day, fell for a third time into the hands of the Soviets. At the end of January the Red Army occupied Nikolaev and Kherson, and on 7 February Odessa fell. A large part of the 'White' forces crossed the border into Roumania and Poland, where they were disarmed.

Meanwhile Petlyura had not exhausted his resources. He had the skill to persuade Piłsudski that the situation in the Ukraine offered great possibilities for the re-establishment under new conditions of the ancient structure of *Rzecz Pospolita*, which should now spread to the Dniepr and the Black Sea. Petlyura for the moment refrained from raising the issue of left-bank Ukraine, but he persuaded the Polish leader that should he appear at the head of Ukrainian troops in right-bank Ukraine the whole country would rise against the Soviets. To strengthen his influence with the Poles, Petlyura succeeded in forming one Ukrainian Division under the command of Colonel Bezruchko, which was stationed on the confines of Volhynia with the Polish troops who were destined for the campaign.

In the middle of April 1920, when the Red Army was engaged against the Volunteers in the Crimea, Piłsudski concentrated between 50,000 and 60,000 men on the Volhynian border and struck suddenly at Kiev. On 7 May the Poles entered the hapless city on the Dniepr. Petlyura was following in their wake and he fixed his headquarters at Zhitomir from where, with the aid of numerous agents and a flood of proclamations, he hoped 'to mobilize all Ukrainian forces'.

Petlyura's effort was a failure. Not more than 2000 or 3000 needy vagabonds answered the call to arms. The people were utterly weary and exhausted after the events of the last three years, and they fled in terror from any kind of mobilization—'Petlyurian' or Bolshevik. Further, they were not inspired by the appeal to come forward to the aid of the Polish military authorities so suddenly established in their capital.

Piłsudski's adventure in any event had been undertaken six months too late. The Volunteers in the South of Russia were only holding the Crimea, while in the far north General Miller's front had collapsed, and General Yudenich had failed to drive home his attack from Estonia, even though it had reached the suburbs of Petrograd. At the beginning of June the Bolsheviks concentrated considerable forces to the south of Kiev while the new 'Red Mounted Army' numbering 16,000 sabres threatened the long and thinly held line of Polish communications.

On 11 June the Polish retreat began. After some hard fighting in the region of the river Teterev, Colonel Smygly-Rydz succeeded in extricating his army and retreated through Volhynia with heavy losses in men and material. 'The last of the Petlyurians' also left the territory of the Ukraine with numbers greatly reduced—not so much on account of losses in battle as of desertions.

The 'Red Mounted Army' of General Budenny invaded Galicia;

occupied Lvov, and advanced on Warsaw through Zamość by the same route which the Cossack hordes of Khmelnytsky had followed nearly three centuries before. But the Russians were checked at the gates of Warsaw (15 August), and their subsequent retreat was almost as rapid as their advance and the preceding Polish advance and retreat had been. On 12 October an armistice was signed, and in the following year the Peace of Riga was to stabilize conditions on the Russian borderlands for nearly twenty years. Poland retained most of the Ukrainian territory of which she had been in occupation prior to the attack on Kiev—large parts of Volhynia and Polesia as well as about half the area of White Russia. The much disputed Kholm district and all Galicia also remained in Polish hands, although the temporary occupation of these territories had only been authorized by the Paris Conference 'pending the solution of the Russian Question'. As a result of the activities of the tenacious Petlyura and the visionary politicians of the 'Directoria' the Poles received, therefore, about 150,000 square kilometres of Ukrainian territory and about 5,000,000 Ukrainian-speaking subjects.

Simon Petlyura, like so many of the picturesque figures of the Russian Revolution, retired to Paris where, some years later, he was killed by a revolver shot in the Boulevard St Michel. The shot was fired by a young Jew named Schwartzbrod, who stated at his trial that he was taking vengeance on Petlyura for the pogroms committed by the 'Petlyurians'. (8, 9, 10)

§ 6. THE SOVIETS AND THE GROWTH OF UKRAINIAN NATIONALISM

'The Ukrainian Soviet Republic' had been declared on 18 December 1918 in a proclamation of 'the Military and Revolutionary Committee of the Red Southern Army' signed by Stalin and Rakovski; the proclamation conferred all authority in 'the liberated territory' on 'the Ukrainian workers and the Ukrainian peasants'. On 3 January 1919, the day on which the Red Army entered Kharkov, then still occupied by part of the 1st German Army Corps, a proclamation of 'the All-Ukrainian Revolutionary Committee' announced that all authority in the Ukraine was vested in this Committee which had 'the confidence of the working and peasant masses'. This document was signed by the President of the Committee, Manuilsky, and by the following members: Rakovski, Grinko, Zatonsky and Skrypnik. Rakovski was a professional revolutionary, a Bulgarian or Roumanian Jew by origin, who had always lived in the *Quartier Latin* in Paris; Zatonsky and Skrypnik were the first Ukrainian politicians to go over to the Bolsheviks.

This same Committee, on 14 February, two or three weeks after the occupation of Kiev, announced the federation of the Ukrainian Soviet Republic with 'the All-Russian Republic of Workers and Peasants'. Subsequently, on 9 March, 'according to the Revolutionary order' 'the First Ukrainian Congress of Soldiers', Peasants' and Workers' Delegates' was called together. This body received for approval 'the Constitution of the Ukrainian Soviet Republic'. Seven months had not elapsed before nine-tenths of the territory of this first Ukrainian Soviet Republic had fallen into the hands of the Volunteer Army.

In spite of the ephemeral character of the first Ukrainian Soviet Republic it is worth considering the theoretical basis on which this state was founded, since its structure illustrates Lenin's conceptions as to the treatment of nationalities within the Communist State.

Following the November *coup d'état* two documents were published in Russia which had an 'ideological' importance in relation to the formation of national republics. The first was a 'Declaration of the Rights and Privileges of the Nations Forming Part of Russia'; it concluded as follows:

'According to the Will of the Congress of Soviets, the Council of People's Commissars has decided to adopt as a foundation for its activities in the question of nationalities the following principles:

(1) The equality and sovereign rights of all the nationalities of Russia;

(2) The right of self-determination of all these nationalities, including the right to form independent states;

(3) The abolition of all national and religious privileges and limitations;

(4) The free development of national minorities and ethnographic groups inhabiting the territory of Russia.'

The document bears the signature of Dzhugashvili-Stalin, Commissar for Nationalities, and of Ulianov-Lenin, President of the Council of People's Commissars.

The second document is a 'Declaration of the Rights of Oppressed Nationalities', dated 24 January 1918 and approved by the 3rd Congress of All-Russian Soviets. The setting up by this Congress of the Russian Soviet Federative Socialist Republic (R.S.F.S.R.) was based on the following principles: 'Russia is proclaimed the Republic of the Soviets of Workers', Soldiers' and Peasants' Delegates. The Soviet Republic is constituted on the basis of a free union of free nationalities as a Federation of Soviet National Republics. Striving to create the really free and voluntary union of the working classes of all the nationalities of Russia, the 3rd Congress of Soviets will limit itself to the establishment of the principles only on which the Federation of the Soviet Republics in Russia will be built, allowing the workers and peasants of every nationality to take independent decisions in their own Soviet Congresses as to whether and on what conditions they wish to take part in the Federal Government and other Federal institutions.'

The Federation, having been accepted by the All-Ukrainian Revolutionary Committee in February 1919, was approved by the 1st Ukrainian Congress of Soviets in the following month. It is clear that this declaration remained in force when, after the collapse of the Volunteer movement and the failure of the 'Petlyurians', the Soviets were restored in the Ukraine. And it is a notable fact that, notwithstanding the considerable changes in the constitution of U.S.S.R. which were introduced between the years 1920 and 1936, the Ukrainians together with the other 'minority nationalities' retained the right, in theory, to opt out of the Union. Only at the 8th Extraordinary Congress of Soviets, summoned to discuss 'the Stalin Constitution' of 1936, were certain limitations (not included in the published texts of the Constitution) introduced by Stalin himself. 'So that the right [of a Republic] to leave the Union shall not be an ephemeral right it is necessary:

(*a*) that the Republic should not be surrounded on all sides by territories of the Soviet Union, but should lie on its boundaries, because in the opposite case it would be impossible for her to leave the Union;

(*b*) that the population of the Republic should not be less than a certain minimum, because in the opposite case she would not be able to defend herself against the attacks of Imperialist beasts of prey;

(*c*) that in the population one nationality should form a compact majority.'

During the years 1921–2 the Ukrainian Soviets were otherwise engaged than in studying constitutional questions. The liquidation of the Volunteer Army in the Crimea and the suppression of the numerous bands of the *atamans* prolonged the period of warfare and the Red Armies terrorized the exhausted countryside. Many towns were becoming deserted, and vast stretches of land were left fallow by a peasantry which had neither the courage nor the security to sow or to reap. Black typhus decimated the destitute population, and in the winter of 1920–21 a serious famine developed which became worse during the spring and summer months. Although the conditions for peaceful labour had somewhat improved, since the war had come to an end and only reprisals and 'the settling of accounts' were going on, the weather contributed to make the new harvest catastrophically poor. The absence of any sort of organization but that of the police and the army, and the general exhaustion of the economic structure of Russia, produced conditions which were unparalleled in modern history. European charitable organizations, with all the goodwill in the world, proved inadequate to cope with the calamity. In the Ukraine it is estimated that not less than three million people died from hunger or from diseases resulting from it. Incredible horrors formed a background to this human tragedy; there were, for instance, numerous cases of cannibalism authenticated.

The ruin of the famine; the naval mutiny in Kronstadt with all its formidable implications; the stubborn armed struggle of the peasantry against the Soviet régime in the Tambov and adjoining Governments—all these factors induced Lenin, himself in 1922 a very sick man, to embark upon the New Economic Policy. It was a compromise between 'the Communism of the war period' and 'small bourgeois elements'—a compromise imposed by the dire necessity of the moment.

The same causes which imposed the New Economic Policy inclined the Soviet leaders towards a policy of conciliation in regard to 'the minority nationalities'. In the Caucasus it had been necessary to concentrate three Army Corps to suppress the insurrection of the Mussulman mountaineers of Daghestan during the winter of 1921–2; the Georgian Social Democratic Republic had recently been overthrown as the result of a six weeks' campaign in which four Army Corps were engaged, and the Armenian mountaineers of Karabagh were waging a guerilla war which was only terminated by an amnesty at the end of 1922; in Turkestan the savage Basmachi movement continued to devastate the country until 1926.

The Declaration of 30 December 1922 preceded the formation of 'the Union of Soviet Socialist Republics' (U.S.S.R.), the Constitution of which was published on 6 June 1923. This declaration confirmed in a different form the decision of the 3rd Congress of Soviets of 24 January 1918. It affirmed that the U.S.S.R. had been 'constituted by the free and voluntary union of free and equal Socialist Republics'. 'Representation of the different nationalities' in the central organ of government was provided in a kind of 'second chamber' which consisted of 114 members.

In the Ukraine the Bolsheviks were more successful than in Caucasia in recruiting to their ranks many of the former separatists who had been associated with the *Rada* and the 'Directoria'. Both parties had their reasons for conciliation. So far as the Soviet authorities were concerned the appearance of prominent non-Bolsheviks in the administration enabled them to improve their relations with the peasantry and to convince them that Lenin's New Economic Policy was indeed, in his own words, 'in earnest and for long'. It does not follow that the peasants had ever been particularly enthusiastic for the nationalist ideology of the *Rada* and the 'Directoria'; but the Ukrainian nationalist leaders, owing to their social origins, were nearer to the peasantry than the men at the head of the various Committees of the Communist Party and the Soviet administration. The latter were either 'new-comers' from the north or representatives of the local Jewish 'intelligentsia' or men drawn from the 'proletariat' of industrial centres. They owed their rise generally to their revolutionary services in the streets of the great cities. The former collaborators of Vinnichenko and Petlyura, on the other hand, were either peasants by origin or they belonged to the typically Ukrainian 'half-intelligentsia' of the countryside.

In encouraging these men to work with the Communist Party, the Soviet authorities did not contemplate allowing them to play a part in the political life of the country, and in this respect they kept them under the strictest control. On the other hand, they were allowed wide scope in the field of 'cultural work', because the Bolsheviks understood that these people would interpret 'cultural work' in the form of hasty 'ukrainization' which in its tendency to supplant the remnants of 'the imperial culture' in the Ukraine would serve purposes which the Bolsheviks themselves had in view. 'Ukrainization' was, in the view of the Bolsheviks, a harmless occupation for the active intellectual element in the Ukraine during a difficult period of transition—an occupation which at the same time would tend to tone down past bitterness and to divert renewing energies into a comparatively harmless channel. In Caucasia, where the Bolsheviks had to do with tougher men among whom the national idea had deeper roots, they were to find that within ten years the same policy was to produce formidable difficulties.

The first to set the example of going over to the Soviets was none other than the patriarch of the Ukrainian movement himself, Professor Hrushevsky, who was rewarded with the Presidency of the newly founded Ukrainian Academy in Kiev. Hrushevsky was followed by the former President of the Council of Ministers of the *Rada* Government, Holubovich, by the General Secretary to the *Rada*, Khrystyuk, and a number of other prominent radicals and separatists.

Ukrainian schools were again started; a number of Communist newspapers began to appear in the Ukrainian language; and generally the usual 'Galician technique' of opening Ukrainian publishing centres, museums, libraries, theatres and so forth was followed (incidentally many Galicians made their appearance in Soviet Ukraine during this period). The official 'state ideology' of Marxism was of course made obligatory for everyone, and the new volumes of Hrushevsky's fundamental history of the Ukraine which were now published in Kiev revealed that in his old age the distinguished professor had come to appreciate the truth of the doctrine of historical materialism.

The population remained as indifferent to measures of 'ukrainization' as it had in the *Rada* days, although now there were more numerous manifestations of it than in the past. Although Ukrainian had become a kind of official language, few appeared to have any taste for its use, either in the administration or in private life. One of the authors of *L'Ukraine—Terre Russe*, who occupied an administrative post in one of the Soviet institutions in the Ukraine between the years 1921 and 1924, confesses that he never once wrote a line in Ukrainian during the whole course of his employment.

In 1925 Kaganovich made his appearance in the Ukraine in the role of leader of the Ukrainian Communist Party. Stalin's future brother-in-law was also one of his most intimate friends, and at that time Stalin had already secured almost absolute power in the Soviet Union. Kaganovich's mission was to make a thorough inspection of the personnel of the Party in the Ukraine and to eliminate the 'unreliable and opportunist elements'.

At the same time Kaganovich had an opportunity of coming to the conclusion that Communism in the Ukraine was not at that date an overwhelming success. According to statistics published some time later by the Central Committee of the Party, out of every 10,000 inhabitants of the Ukraine the ratio of Communists was as follows: Jews, 155; Great Russians and 'new-comers', 88; Ukrainians, 39. About 15 per cent of women had joined Communist organisations—a far lower proportion than in the north. The proportion of Ukrainian students in the high schools which had been opened to form 'responsible Ukrainian workers and specialists' was disappointingly low in comparison to the number of their Jewish fellows: in the Social-Economic Faculty there were 1500 Ukrainians to 1000 Jews; in the Industrial-Technical Faculty, 2600 Ukrainians to 2200 Jews; in the Medical Faculty only 2000 Ukrainians to 2200 Jews; whereas the proportion of Ukrainians to Jews in the whole population was 10 to 1.

The predominance of the non-Ukrainian elements in the organs of administration and in educational institutions is of course explained by the fact that the Ukrainian people remained overwhelmingly peasant, and there had been in the nineteenth century, and even earlier, a large and heterogeneous alien element in the towns. Nevertheless Kaganovich, in his speech to the Ukrainian Congress of Soviets in 1927, was at pains to demonstrate the success of 'ukrainization'. 'Among us', he said with that graceful Jewish facility for identifying himself with the people among whom he had come, 'our Ukrainian culture has developed on a grand scale. Ukrainian culture has made such progress in all branches in these last years that even the most eager Ukrainian nationalists never dreamed of such rapid development. In primary schools Ukrainians are taught by Ukrainians in the Ukrainian language. The high schools are gradually becoming completely "ukrainized"; Ukrainian books and press are at present developing to an extent unknown in all the history of the Ukraine. In our Council of People's Commissars, which is the supreme administrative organ of our government, 13 out of 20 members are Ukrainian. In our Party's Executive Committee, 66 per cent are Ukrainians, 25 per cent are Russians, 14 per cent are Jews.'

Kaganovich's emphasis on the predominance of Ukrainians on the Central Committee of the Ukrainian Communist Party is, of course, meaningless, since in the Soviet hierarchy all power is vested in the Secretaries of the various regional and local Committees of the Communist Party, who are themselves responsible not to the members of the Committees but to the Secretary of the Central Executive Committee. Stalin filled this latter position, and Kaganovich himself was his nominee sent from Moscow with complete power over the regional and local Committees in the Ukraine. Kaganovich's successor, 'the dictator' Postyshev, who only occupied the position of 2nd Secretary of the Ukrainian Communist Party, was another importation from Moscow—as is Khrushchov, who is at present (1939) governing the Ukraine.

While Kaganovich was praising 'the achievements of "ukrainization"' he was already considering means of putting some limit on these achievements. In this same year when he made his genial speech before the Ukrainian Congress of Soviets, the Central Committee of the Ukrainian Communist Party under his influence issued a decree making Russian the second official language in the Ukraine. The First Five Year Plan was then beginning, and one of the most important features of this Plan was the wide development of industry in the Ukraine. The coal and metallurgical industries were to be modernized, and the construction of the great power station of Dnieprostroy was in view. Thousands of engineers, technicians and specialized workers were being sent into the Ukraine and these people not only had no knowledge of the Ukrainian dialect but they found that dialect most inappropriate for correspondence between different Government departments on complicated technical questions. The intensified industrialization of the Ukraine was obviously destined to strengthen greatly all connections with the north and linguistic differences gave promise of frequent and annoying difficulties. Very soon the Ukrainian language came only to be used in the sphere of 'cultural relations'.

Meanwhile Kaganovich, in surveying the various aspects of 'ukrainization', began gradually to investigate the part played in different branches of the administration by 'Ukrainian nationalists' or those suspected of being such. .

§ 7. 'THE REVOLUTION AGAINST THE PEASANTS': REPRESSION OF UKRAINIAN NATIONALISM

In 1929 the Communist Revolution was approaching its second and decisive stage: Marxist principles which had conquered the life of the cities were to be imposed on the countryside. But the process of 'collectivizing' agriculture was to prove even more difficult in the Ukraine than it was in the provinces of Great Russia. Individual property in land had always been traditional in the Ukraine, and the background of the social history of the country had been the unending struggle of the peasantry to maintain their right to own the land they worked—against Polish landlords and Cossack and, later, Great Russian landlords. The strength of the Ukrainian peasantry had always been their stubborn determination that each should own his plot of land, and their weakness had been a love of individual freedom degenerating often enough into libertarian anarchy.

The outlook of the Ukrainian peasant differed widely from that of the Great Russian. The *obshchina*—the old Russian form of possessing (but not of working) land collectively—was unknown in the regions of Chernigov and Poltava and in all right-bank Ukraine. The creation of *kolkhozy* (collective farms) was from the beginning opposed, generally passively and sometimes actively, by the peasantry. And Kaganovich hastened, so soon as peasant opposition developed, to deprive the Ukrainians of the weapon which the national idea might provide. (In Caucasia and Turkestan, during the same period, opposition to collectivization was combined with a renascence and strengthening of local nationalist movements directed against the Great Russian hegemony.) The Ukrainian enthusiasts of 'cultural acheivements' so recently lauded by Kaganovich himself were now accused of 'maintaining relations with nationalist political organizations in Galicia'. And it was not difficult to prove their connections with open or secret organizations 'suffering under the yoke of Poland'. The existence of such connections had been tolerated and even favoured by the Soviet administration to the extent which they furthered Communist propagandist activities in Poland, but there could be no difficulty, if necessary, in treating them as treason.

In 1930 the first Ukrainian political trial took place in Kharkov. A group of individuals were accused of having relations with 'the Union for the Liberation of the Ukraine'—the same organization which had been created before the war under the protection of the Austro-Hungarian Government and which was now supposed to be functioning in Galicia. In the following year, as a result of the growing resistance of the peasants to collectivization, action against Ukrainian 'suspects' became more violent. The peasants were bitterly opposed to the *kolkhozy*, but certainly not on 'national' grounds. Faced with the imminent danger of a peasant revolt, the Soviet administration decided to eliminate all persons who through their origins could be considered to be connected with the peasantry and who might organize this revolt and become its leaders. Regardless of their loyalty to the Soviet régime during the preceding years, there now began a systematic destruction of Ukrainians belonging to the 'intelligentsia' and 'half-intelligentsia'.

In 1931 the Bolsheviks professed to have 'discovered' a Ukrainian organization called 'the National Centre'. Holubovich (former head of the *Rada* Government and participator in the Brest-Litovsk negotiations), Shershel, Mazurenko and other 'ex-politicians' were accused of being the leaders of this secret organization. They were shot. Thousands of arrests followed, the victims of which suffered execution or exile to labour camps which were themselves living cemeteries. Two years later, in 1933, the political police (G.P.U.) declared that they had discovered a real military conspiracy on the part of 'a secret military organization'. After a theatrical trial, Kotsubinsky (Vice-President of the Ukrainian Council of People's Commissars), Kovnar (Commissar for Agriculture), and scores of other persons who had all occupied important posts in the army or the administration were shot. One of the most prominent figures in Ukrainian political life, who from the beginning had associated himself with the Communist Revolution and who had for a long time been an influential member of the Council of People's Commissars, Skrypnik, committed suicide in July 1933 in order to avoid arrest.

In that same year Postyshev replaced Kaganovich as 'dictator' in the Ukraine (he only occupied the position of 2nd Secretary of the Central Committee of the Ukrainian Communist Party). He arrived with orders 'to make an end of the counter-revolution that had woven itself a nest in the Ukraine'. The speech which Postyshev delivered at the 12th Congress of the Ukrainian Communist Party, soon after entering on his office, indicated the new line of Soviet policy.

'In Ukraine our leading Party members and Comrade Stalin himself are specially hated. The class enemy has been to a good school in this country and has learned how to struggle against Soviet rule. In Ukraine have settled the remnants of many counter-revolutionary parties and organizations. Kharkov has gradually become the centre of attraction for all sorts of nationalistic and other counter-revolutionary organizations. They have all been drawn to this centre and they have spread their webs all over the Ukraine, making use of our Party system for their own ends. You remember, Comrades, when twenty Secretaries of Party Regional Committees dared to declare that it was impossible to fulfil the Harvest Plan' (nos. 15–21 of the *Proletarian*, Kharkov, 1934). At the same Congress the chief of the Ukrainian G.P.U., Beletsky, read a report in which he declared that 'Imperialists, through agents and through the remnants of the inimical classes which we have not destroyed and to which belong all the *kulak* and 'Petlyurian' elements of the Ukrainian villages, will yet prepare in the country criminal activities and diversions against the principal objects of our Ukrainian Economic Plan' (*ibid.*). Beletsky then proceeded to read aloud a proclamation which was supposed to have been seized by the G.P.U. and according to which Ukrainian counter-revolutionaries were 'dreaming about the denationalization of the whole of Ukrainian industry and the re-establishment of large landowner-ship'.

Accusations of this type were of course inventions of the G.P.U., but the speeches of the head of this grim organization and of his political chief Postyshev indicate that the new policy of the Soviets was directed to the destruction both of the institution of private property among the Ukrainian peasants and of their national characteristics of stubborn individualism and love of freedom.

Postyshev had been given two problems to tackle: the first was to root out 'the counter-revolution' alleged to be lurking in the Soviet administration and in the Communist Party in the Ukraine;

the second was to crush the will of the peasantry. In the first he succeeded as best he could and added to the sensational trials of 1931–3 the discovery of 'a secret Ukrainian organization' which was accused of being in direct touch with the Ukrainian separatists who were working abroad under the leadership of Colonel Konovalets. It was, however, beyond the strength of Postyshev to cope with the chaos which reigned in rural Ukraine during the years 1932–4 as a result of the policy of forced collectivization. Despite the fact that Postyshev 'eliminated' from the Ukrainian Communist Party over a quarter of its total strength, and in spite of thousands of arrests and hundreds of executions, the Party Secretary was accused of 'weakness and lack of energy' and was replaced by a certain Kossior. The late 'dictator' was, after a lapse of time, himself arrested and probably shot together with many of his closest collaborators.

But all the cruel personal dramas which took place under the Secretaryships of Postyshev and Kossior were as nothing compared to the terrible miseries which overtook the Ukrainian countryside during the five years 1930–35 as a result of the introduction of the *kolkhozy*. In their very essence *kolkhozy* were organically opposed to all the traditions and ways of life of the Ukrainian peasantry. Collective farming on a large scale was carried through at the cost of ruining small and 'average' peasant farms through the instrument of the ruthless pressure of the administration. The very rapid development of 'the *kolkhoz* movement' so much admired by Communists all the world over was the result, not of the peasants voluntarily joining the collective farms, but of their being driven on to them often by the use of military force—a fact which Stalin himself acknowledged in his article 'Head-turning from Success' (*Pravda*, 2 March 1930). The immediate consequence of the *kolkhoz* policy was seen in the lowering of agricultural production throughout the whole country which quickly led to the increasing misery of the peasantry, famine and terrible mortality. One of the principal reasons of all this was the *mania grandiosa* which always characterizes the policy of extreme ideologues; having become convinced of the low productive capacity of the smaller *kolkhozy* already set up, the enthusiasts of the Communist Party, in 1930, demanded their enlargement on a 'gigantic' scale. According to the reliable testimony of a member of the Communist Party (the Ukrainian agronomist Mirkevich, the initiator of tractor stations) 'this measure, in a series of regions, was realized in an exceptionally bureaucratic and senseless manner. *Kolkhozy* of 55–100 hectares were suddenly transformed, without any adequate technical preparation, into *kolkhozy* covering some tens of thousands of hectares; as, for instance, the *Kolkhoz* of "Chervony Perekop" in the Government of Kherson which was set up to comprise 50,000 hectares. In some cases, "to simplify matters", a whole region containing hundreds of villages was declared to constitute one *kolkhoz*. All the boundaries between village lands were abolished; then the whole expanse of land arbitrarily included in the *kolkhoz* was divided into farms of several thousand hectares each—without any regard as to where the villages actually lay. Cattle and agricultural machinery were scattered about over scores of kilometres' (*Pravda*, 3 April 1930).

Nevertheless Stalin declared that: 'The time has come to finish with every kind of camouflage: we must destroy the *kulaks* and deprive them of the possibility to work on the land.' At that moment anyone who owned three cows or the equivalent in sheep, pigs, or even chickens, was considered to be a *kulak*. As a result of this policy it was not long before all the larger and more prosperous peasant farms were destroyed. These farms, since the disappearance of the large private estates, had been the principal producers of the agricultural surplus, since it was only the better-off farmers who had a surplus in excess of their needs for disposal in the towns.

As early as 1930 the policy of forced collectivization provoked open resistance in the Ukraine, and attempts were made at armed revolt; but geographical conditions did not favour the type of guerilla warfare which was undertaken with considerable determination and success by the peasants in Georgia, and particularly in the Armenian district of Karabagh and by the Tartars of the Daghestan foothills. These agrarian risings in the Ukraine were suppressed with the greatest cruelty and were followed by mass executions and by the transportation of tens of thousands of peasants. The Soviets applied methods which were then almost new in their struggle with the Ukrainian peasantry; they put them into concentration camps where they had to do forced labour. In the region of Odessa, near Tiraspol, a large and prosperous colony of 'Old Believers' completely disappeared. All the men, with the exception of a few youngsters who managed to cross the Dniestr into Bessarabia, were transported, and the women and children simply scattered over the steppe. The construction of the White Sea Canal, so much advertised by the admirers of Soviet methods in Western Europe, cost the lives of many tens of thousands of peasants, as the vast cemeteries along the banks of the northern lakes and rivers bear witness.

Very often the prospect of transportation to the far north or to Siberia caused the peasants, as in old time, to abandon everything and to wander off into the steppe 'where the eyes look'. Until the Bolsheviks erected barbed wire all along the frontier, the Volhynian peasants used to cross the Polish border in large bodies with their women and children and cattle—sometimes a thousand strong and more—with the merciless detachments of the G.P.U. hot in pursuit, held off by an armed rear-guard. According to reports appearing in the Polish Press in 1932 great numbers of these fugitive peasants were held in quarantine camps in Poland. At the same time gangs of fugitives from Central Russia and the Ukraine made their way into Transcaucasia under the leadership of ex-soldiers; conditions here, where a struggle against forced collectivization was also in progress, were little better than in the Ukraine, and large numbers, Russians and Tartars and Tats from the Talish region, forced their way across the Araks frontier into the northern provinces of Iran.

The abolition of small and 'average' farming, the disorganization in the newly formed *kolkhozy*, the passive resistance of the peasants, and the bestial brutality of the methods which accompanied the enforcement of the new system, brought about the famine of 1932–3. The first news of famine in the Ukraine came from the Polish frontier in the autumn of 1932. It became known that domestic animals were perishing wholesale and that the mortality among the population was enormous. Already, even in the summer, there was no more bread in the Ukraine. Millions of human beings were set in motion. Part of these great crowds infested the towns in the hope of being able to survive until the next harvest. But the main flow of movement was directed towards the northern Caucasus, the regions beyond the Volga, Siberia and Turkestan. In many districts only the old people remained where they were in the hope of somehow surviving on potatoes. There were wide districts which were almost completely abandoned by the population. Whole villages went to ruin, and the once prosperous gardens and fields were abandoned to weeds.

Early in 1933, before the time of spring sowing, orders were issued to drive back the migrant hordes by force to their villages. Great numbers of peasants who were arrested and coralled in camps died because they were not fed. Those who returned to their lands, sick and hungry, found that they had to set to work with spades and staves because only about a fifth part of the horses remained and most of these were too weak to work. A particular foreign correspondent who obtained permission to travel in the regions of Kiev, Chernigov, Kharkov and Poltava in the autumn of 1933, affirms that, according to statements which were made to him in the offices of the local administrations, about 10 per cent of the population of

South-Eastern Russia died of hunger in the first months of 1933. As in 1921-2 numerous cases of cannibalism were recorded.

In spite of this vast tragedy, self-satisfied and triumphant speeches were a feature of the Ukrainian Congress of Soviets which met at Kharkov in 1935. 'For glorious Ukraine the last years have been, as in the rest of our country, a period of brilliant unheard of achievements. The rapacious rural *kulak* class has been completely destroyed, annihilated. Never will the heroism of those days be forgotten! Never will the loathing against the oppressors disappear! Those were not idle words which Lenin wrote when he affirmed that the principal enemy of our Bolshevism is the peasant! Thousands of the best sons of our country have lost their lives in the great and ruthless struggle.' 'Against this enemy', in the words of *Pravda*, 'the economic structure which carries along with it joyous culture and a happy life to millions of Ukrainians suffering for centuries from privations has at last triumphed in the country.' Stalin's revolutionary Communist régime proved, as ever, logical. If 'thousands of the best sons of our country' had really lost their lives in 'the great and ruthless struggle' against the peasantry, the peasants had to count their losses in millions.

But notwithstanding the brilliant victory proclaimed on the internal front in 1935 the Soviet Government had new reasons for anxiety in the radical change which had taken place in the European situation as a result of the attainment of power by the Nazi Party in Germany. The official doctrine of the Nazi Government was based on 'the right of the German people to an adequate living space', and the Third Reich of Adolf Hitler, in search of a better and happier future, was taking a dangerous interest in the east and south-east of Europe. It was now nearly twenty years since *Die Rückführung des Ostheeres*; and the glib attribution of the military catastrophe of Germany in the last war to the evils of Marxism had had the result of reviving in a new generation of Germans all those vague aspirations after world dominion which recur from time to time to compensate that unfortunate people for the frustration which has been their historical lot.

In glowing passages in *Mein Kampf* Adolf Hitler had waxed lyrical on the subject of the Ukraine and the Urals, and the Führer seemed prepared to abandon the oceanic and colonial dreams of William II in favour of a continental imperialism which might carry the Germans into Asia in the first great movement in history of a people from west to east. In 1934 the ten years' Non-Aggression Pact concluded between Germany and Poland appeared to Soviet statesmen to be the first step towards a collaboration in the east at the expense of the Soviet Union in which the dream of a revived *Rzecz Pospolita* (never absent from the mind of the ageing Piłsudski) might be combined with a German *Drang nach Osten* which could give to the Third Reich effective predominance over a great economic land empire stretching beyond the Don and the Caucasus to Turkestan and the Altai. At the same time the German understanding with Japan threatened the Far Eastern dominions of the Soviet Union.

'The Ukrainian Question' began to be discussed in the German Press, and from 1934 'the foreign danger' ceased to be only a conventional formula at Soviet political trials. The uneasy masters of the Kremlin began to believe in its reality. The memoirs of the ex-Chekist Krivitski have made it clear that from an early date after Hitler's accession to power Stalin was planning to create a situation in which he might be able to arrive at a compromise with his adversary in Berlin—an event which was eventually consummated between the two parties in August 1939.

A direct collaboration with the Russians, as an alternative to joint aggression with Poland, had always attracted influential circles in Germany—circles which included the majority of those soldiers, technicians and business men who, during the Rapallo period, when many Germans were employed as specialists in Russia, had had excellent opportunities for forming a clear appreciation of realities in the Soviet Union. Many connections, direct and indirect, existed between these men and high officials in the Soviet armed forces, administration and industry.

The unsurpassed genius of Stalin for political manœuvre was never better illustrated than when he succeeded in annihilating all those elements most likely to be in—or in the future to enter into—relations with the Germans. Thus, at the same time, he was able to deprive the Germans of their potential collaborators, and was himself able to assume the position which his victims had intended to occupy vis-à-vis the Germans. From Stalin's point of view the execution of the 'Red' generals in 1935 was a preventive rather than a punitive measure, as were the subsequent widespread 'purges' in the armed forces and among the Communist officials in the national republics in the Ukraine, Caucasia and Central Asia. It was not by accident that the first to be eliminated were those who owed their revolutionary careers to their capacity for enterprise and daring action: the Marshals Tukhachevski, Uborevich and Yakir.

A Jew by origin, Yakir had distinguished himself in Budenny's 'Red Mounted Army' during the Bolshevik invasion of Poland in the summer of 1920, and later during the liquidation of the *atamans'* bands in the Ukraine. At the time of the 'purge' he occupied the highest military post in the Ukraine: that of Officer Commanding the Kiev Military District. The drama in the Ukraine did not end with the execution of Yakir; during the years 1935–7 several thousands of persons occupying important posts in the Red Army and in the Soviet administration were arrested and shot or exiled to concentration camps in Siberia and the North of Russia. This whirlwind of arrests and executions even carried away with it Postyshev and Kossior, the former instruments of 'the Revolution against the peasants'.

In the meantime the last remnants of the national Ukrainian Army, which had flourished in the years 1923–9, disappeared. Units of the Ukrainian Army, based on the system of 'territorial Divisions' in the Red Army, had been quartered in the Ukraine alongside the troops 'of the Union'. The struggle with the peasantry had made it desirable to abolish the territorial system in the Ukraine as well as in other parts of the Union. The Ukrainian units were broken up and distributed to other parts of the country and their place was taken by regiments recruited in Great Russia. After the execution of the staff of the Kiev Command and the senior personnel of many of the Ukrainian regiments, nothing remained of the Ukrainian Army except the names of certain 'Red' regiments which were retained for the sake of form; but the Ukrainian language continued to be used in units where the rank and file were predominantly of Ukrainian origin.

Stalin's Constitution of 1936—which evoked such enthusiasm among European Communists and which was even hailed in the capitalist Press of Western countries as a laudable 'return to democratic institutions' in contrast to the dictatorships of Central Europe —was a cynical accompaniment to the slaughter of so many thousands of Party members which was going on at that time within 'the Soviet Paradise'. Stalin's Constitution marked the final abandonment of the theory that the minority nationalities ranked as equal partners with Great Russia within the Soviet Union. The 'union of different states' was now transformed into one integral state (Paragraph 13: 'The Union of Soviet Socialist Republics is a unified state'). According to Paragraph 14 all authority on questions relating to international affairs, the declaration of war and the conclusion of peace, the organization of defence and the command of the armed forces, foreign trade, the safety of the state, the management of all banks, all forms of transport, the principles of land distribution, the basis of public instruction, hygiene, and criminal and civil laws, was reposed in the Central Government.

Section (c) of the same Paragraph reserved all questions of finance, including the local budgets of the constituent republics, to the discretion of the Central Government. Paragraph 60 provided that the Parliaments of the Republics could make changes in their respective constitutions, but that these changes must correspond to the spirit of the Constitution of the Union. Under Paragraph 69 the Central Government retained the right to veto any decisions taken by the governments of the local republics. As has already been stated, Stalin did not consider it necessary to deprive the national republics of the illusory right of opting out of the Union. At the same time he not only retained the conception of the Constitution of 1923 which provided for a special representation of the minority nationalities in the central legislature, but his pleasing sense of the ridiculous in regard to the automatic reactions of his admirers in foreign countries induced him to give orders for the members of this body to be elected. In this Chamber of Nationalities the Ukrainians have rather less than 200 representatives out of 574—a figure which corresponds probably to the relative numerical importance of their population in relation to the other nationalities in the Union. Any advantage which might theoretically accrue from this representation is lost at the joint sittings of 'the two Chambers of the Superior Council', when the delegates of the nationalities find themselves in a minority among 1143 of their colleagues.

Stalin would have been but a poor Marxist if he had forgotten that the laws regulating the political existence of the Soviet Ukraine would only correspond to the actual state of things if they expressed 'economic realities'. Though strengthened by the new Constitution of the Union, the link between the Ukraine and Great Russia would still remain only theoretical, in the Marxist view, if the Soviet Government had not succeeded in absorbing the economic life of the Ukraine into that of the rest of the Union and welding out of the two an indestructible whole. (11, 12)

BIBLIOGRAPHICAL NOTES AND ADDITIONS
TO CHAPTER VI

(1) *The Austrians and Russians in Galicia*

A full documentation of the Austrian repression of the *Promoskovity* in Galicia is to be found in the Telerhof Almanack published in several series by the Galicians after the war (*Telerhofsky Almanakh*, 1-4, Lvov, 1926-9).

Telerhof was the largest concentration camp for 'pro-Russians'; at times their number reached 10,000, and about 2000 died during the typhus epidemic. The Austrian authorities later acknowledged that 'among the people arrested in the war zone were many who were arrested by mistake or upon false denunciations'. (See also D. Yavorsky, *Dumy o Rodine* (Thoughts about my Native Land), Lvov, 1923.)

For the relations between the Russian troops and the population, see General A. A. Brusilov, *A Soldier's Note Book*, London, 1930; also Bernard Pares, *My Russian Memories*, London, 1925.

Russian blunders have been described with many exaggerations in Ukrainian 'separatist' literature. For a more balanced view see D. Doroshenko, 'Voyna i Revolutsia na Ukraine', in the periodical *Istorik i Sovremennik* ('War and Revolution in the Ukraine,' in *The Historian and Contemporary*), vols. I–V, Berlin, 1923.

(2) *Biographical Note on Vinnichenko and Petlyura*

Mark Vinnichenko belonged to the Ukrainian intelligentsia. He failed to complete his studies on account of revolutionary activities which he started when a boy at a Gymnasium and on account of which he had to leave the University of Kiev after his first year.

During the period 1906–14 Vinnichenko wrote novels (in Russian) which were quite widely read. The themes were not political but rather romantic, and the author delighted in the delineation of psychological conflicts which were intended for the imagination of readers who were not too exacting. Vinnichenko had tuberculosis and he seems to have been consumed by an 'inner fever' which can often be observed in persons who are suffering from that malady.

People who knew Vinnichenko do not deny that he possessed a certain honesty of purpose which was generally not one of the distinctive traits of his colleagues in the Rada.

Simon Petlyura was quite a different type. He was the son of a simple cabman, but received his education in the Poltava Gymnasium. Later he became a book-keeper in a commercial undertaking in Moscow, and collaborated in a periodical which appeared before the war called *Ukrainian Life* (in Russian). Petlyura belonged to a milieu which produced many capable and energetic men in the years preceding the war. It was such men, for instance, who had created the widespread co-operative movement in Russia. Many representatives of this class worked successfully during the war in the Unions of Towns and the Unions of Zemstvos. In contrast to Vinnichenko, Petlyura was eloquent neither in his speech nor with his pen. He was a man of action and practical capacity rather than a propagandist of ideals. However, unlike many of his more vocal and emotional collaborators, he maintained an irreconcilable attitude towards the Bolsheviks to the end; his assassin, Schwartzbrod, may well have been a (possibly unconscious) agent of the G.P.U.

(3) *The Conflict Between the Rada and the Provisional Government*

See Paul Milyukov, *Istoriya Vtoroy Russkoy Revolutsii* (History of the Second Russian Revolution), vols. I–III, Sofia, 1921; Bernard Pares, *The Downfall of the Russian Monarchy*, London, 1939; and other works dealing with the period March–November 1917. A series of interesting articles on the subject from the pen of Milyukov has been published recently in the Parisian Russian daily newspaper *Posledniya Novosti* (The Latest News), 19 March–1 April 1939. For the Ukrainian point of view see D. Doroshenko, *Istoriya Ukrainy* (1917–23), Uzhhorod, 1935; Vinnichenko, *Vozrozhdenie Natsii* (The Resurrection of a Nation), vols. 1–III, Vienna, 1925.

(4) *The Ukrainians at Brest-Litovsk*

A vivid description of the course of the Brest-Litovsk negotiations and of the part played by the delegates of the *Rada* is given in the scholarly work of J. W. Wheeler-Bennett, *Brest-Litovsk: The Forgotten Peace*, London, 1938. An Appendix gives the text of the Peace Treaty with the Ukraine, and a valuable Bibliography is included.

The reminiscences of the leading personalities at Brest-Litovsk have been published in English translations: Hoffmann, *War Diaries and Other Papers*, London, 1929; Czernin, *In the World War*, London, 1919; Trotsky, *History of the Russian Revolution to Brest-Litovsk*, London, 1919; *My Life*, London, 1935.

(5) *The First 'Siege' of Kiev by the Bolsheviks*

This 'siege' continued for about ten days—from 30 January to 8 February 1918. The first Bolshevik detachments approached the city from the left bank of the Dniepr. The city is situated on the high right bank and presented a perfect target for the Red artillery. Most of the damage was done by an armoured train mounting naval guns, which destroyed, among other architectural features, the block of flats built by Professor Hrushevsky when he decided to settle in the city. When other Bolshevik detachments and the 'Ukrainian regiments' which had gone over to them appeared on the right bank, further resistance became impossible. The brunt of the defence was borne, not by the supporters of Holubovich and Vinnichenko, but by volunteer detachments consisting of officers, students and even schoolboys; many young lives were lost.

(6) *The Austro-German Occupation of the Ukraine and the Régime of Skoropadsky*

Most interesting material is revealed in the documents published by the Soviets in an anonymous book entitled *Krakh Nemetskoy Okkupatsii na Ukraine: Sbornik Dokumentov izdannykh Gosizdatom* (The Crash of the German Occupation in the Ukraine: Collection of Documents published by the State Publishing Organization), Moscow, 1936. There is no reason to doubt the authenticity of these documents which fell into the hands of the Bolsheviks after they occupied Kiev (some of the documents are reproduced in facsimile). It will be difficult, however, for the reader to agree with the deductions made by the Soviet editor. He affirms, for instance, that the Occupation troops were unable to deal with the resistance of 'the great popular masses', and that whole German divisions were employed in putting down workmen's strikes and peasant risings. These assertions are not confirmed by any document. In the documents reference is only made to the assassination of isolated landowners and to the sending of punitive detachments to certain districts.

The principal reason for the downfall of the German occupation of the Ukraine was, of course, the defeat of the German Armies on the Western Front. The 8th of August is the date which marks a break in the frame of mind of the German Command in Kiev. This can be noted in the documents published in Germany: *Die Rückführung des Ostheeres*, Berlin, 1936.

Wheeler-Bennett describes the situation in the Ukraine in these terms: 'The early months of the Skoropadsky regime were marked by a substantial economic revival; the landowners, industrialists and bourgeois being anxious to co-operate with the new government and the agencies of the Germans and Austro-Hungarians.... Passive resistance in certain districts was coupled with acts of sabotage in others. In Odessa an aeroplane factory was set on fire, numerous munition dumps were exploded and trains wrecked.'

See also on the same subject: Pierre Brégy and Prince Serge Obolensky, *L'Ukraine—Terre Russe*, Paris, 1939, pp. 207–8. (Eng. translation, London, 1940.)

(7) Activities of the Bolshevik 'Peace Delegation' in Kiev

The German authorities were well informed of the subversive activities of the Soviet 'Peace Delegation' in Kiev, but they ignored them—as they ignored the assassination of their Ambassador, Count Mirbach in Moscow, and of their Commander-in-Chief, Field-Marshal Eichhorn in Kiev, in order to avoid the precipitation of a further conflict with the Soviet Government at the moment of crisis on the Western Front. In order to produce incontrovertible proof of the Soviet activities, the Hetman's Minister of the Interior, Igor Kistyanovsky, had recourse to a very original mode of action. With the aid of the Ukrainian police, he arranged 'a brigands' attack on the train in which Rakovski and Manuilsky were returning to Moscow. In order to give reality to the attack 'the brigands' confiscated all the valuables and personal possessions of the two delegates, together with the mass of compromising documents which Kistyanovsky desired to lay hands on and which he afterwards presented to Baron Mumm for perusal. The revelations failed, however, to change the German attitude.

(8) Revolution and Civil War in the Ukraine, 1919–20

Ukrainian historians of the Revolution and Civil War are often exceedingly biased in their accounts of military operations; see, for instance, Doroshenko, *Istoriya Ukrainy*, quoted above. General Denikin, also, cannot set aside his prejudices in writing of the 'Petlyurians' who not infrequently fought on his side against the Soviet forces; see General A. Denikin, *Ocherki Russkoy Smuty* (Sketches of the Russian Trouble), vols. I–V, Berlin, 1925–9.

Much interesting material concerning the Volunteer Army is to be found in the almanack published in Berlin: *Beloe Delo* (The White Cause), vols. I–VI, 1924–7. In the Soviet periodical, *Voyna i Revolutsia* (War and Revolution), 1932–5, many episodes of the fighting against the 'Whites', the 'Petlyurians' and the Poles are described.

For the Anglo-French intervention see James Bunyan, *Intervention, Civil War and Communism in Russia*, 1918, Baltimore, 1936.

Not devoid of interest are the reminiscences of 'Batko' Makhno which were published after his flight to Paris, evidently with the help of someone: Nestor Makhno, *Russkaya Revolutsia na Ukraine* (The Russian Revolution in the Ukraine), vols. I–II, published by the Anarcho-Communist Group of North America and Canada.

(9) Jewish Pogroms in the Ukraine, 1918–20

Jewish organizations in Western Europe have thoroughly studied this question and a series of works has been published which give a good deal of information: Schechtman, *The Pogroms of the Ukraine and the Ukrainian Government, 1917–21*, London, 1927; by the same author, *Pogromy Dobrovolcheskoy Armii na Ukraine* (Pogroms of the Volunteer Army in the Ukraine), Berlin, 1922; I. Cherikower, *Antisemitizm i Pogromy na Ukraine*, Berlin, 1923.

(10) The Ukrainian Delegation at the Peace Conference

The disappointment of the Ukrainian delegates on account of the reception which they met with in Paris from the representatives of the Great Powers is minutely described in I. Borshak's *Ukraintsy na Mirnoy Konferentsii* (The Ukrainians at the Peace Conference), Lvov, 1928; interesting also is Arnold Margolin's book: *Ukraina i Politika Antanty* (The Ukraine and the Policy of the Entente), Berlin, 1922.

(11) The Soviet Régime in the Ukraine, 1920–39

Owing to the control exercised by the authorities over all publications, particularly of a political character, in U.S.S.R., Soviet sources concerning the Ukraine are of a strictly official nature. Therefore, if these sources have a considerable importance for assessing economic conditions or cultural phenomena (science, art, even past history), they always describe Ukrainian conditions from a very definite point of view. For the first period of the Soviet régime in the Ukraine, the sources are the official newspapers, *Izvestiya* and *Pravda* (1918–20), *Konstitutsia Sovetskih Respublik* (The Constitution of the Soviet Republics), the daily *Visty* (in Ukrainian), Kiev, 1919, another daily *Kharkovski Rabochi* (in Russian), Kharkov, 1920. A publication of the Communist Academy should also be consulted: *Natsionalnaya Politika Vserossiyskoy Kommunisticheskoy Partii* (National Policy of the All-Russian Communist Party), Moscow, 1930. Information on political trials can be culled from a perusal of the files of the daily *Proletari*, Kharkov, 1934, in which the speeches pronounced at the Twelfth Congress of the Ukrainian Communist Party are reproduced. Stalin's Constitution was published in Moscow in 1937.

The works of Russian and Ukrainian refugees, some of whom occupied official positions under the Soviet régime, offer a second important source of information. See, for instance, Isaac Mazeppa (an associate of Petlyura), *Ukrayina pod Chervonoy Moskvoy* (Ukraina under Red Moscow), Lvov, 1935; M. Slavinski, *Natsionalno-Gosudarstvennaya Problema S.S.S.R.* (The National Problem as a State Problem in U.S.S.R.), Paris, 1938; V. Sadovski, *Natsionalnaya Politika Sovetov na Ukraine* (The National Policy of the Soviets in the Ukraine), Warsaw, 1937; Pierre Brégy and Prince Serge Obolensky, *L'Ukraine—Terre Russe*, Paris, 1939.

A third group of sources is to be found in the accounts of foreign travellers who have visited the Ukraine during the last two decades. Although few of these would claim to have had a proper opportunity of forming a true impression of the political and social struggle which has been going on in the Ukraine, there are some foreign newspaper correspondents whose knowledge and contacts gave them certain facilities for securing information which no passing tourist (however enthusiastic) could acquire. The most distinguished of these correspondents (up to 1934) was Paul Scheffer of the *Berliner Tageblatt* and Dr Basseches of the *Neue Freie Presse*.

The writer of an article in the *Fortnightly Review* of October 1934 gave an important account of the famine in the regions of Kiev, Chernigov, Poltava and Kharkov. He confirmed the fact that cases of cannibalism had occurred. One of these cases later became known from Soviet sources, in consequence of a trial which took place in the town of Izyum in the region of Kharkov. A female shopkeeper named Kovaleva was sentenced to twenty-five years imprisonment for selling human flesh. She confessed that she had also done so during the famine of 1920–21.

(12) The Diplomatic Representation abroad of the Ukrainian S.S.R.

A curious evolution in the views of the Soviet Government concerning the degree of independence to be enjoyed by the Ukrainian S.S.R. can be traced in the history of the diplomatic representation of the Republic abroad. After the first Constitution of the Ukrainian S.S.R. had been legalized in March 1920, a Commissariat of Foreign Affairs was established in Kharkov—which city had been made the capital of the Ukraine. The first Commissar for Foreign Affairs was Kovalev, who within a month was replaced by Rakovski —at that time also President of the Ukrainian Council of People's Commissars. In April 1920, Rakovski appointed his first diplomatic representative abroad in the person of M. Levitsky, who was sent to Prague, although the new Czech Republic had not yet recognized either the Soviet Union or the Ukrainian S.S.R. A little later a certain Aussem arrived as Ukrainian Ambassador in Berlin. In the autumn of 1921 a third Ukrainian diplomat appeared in Warsaw in the person of Shumsky. Not one apparently of the unfortunates who decorated the Ukrainian Foreign Office is alive to-day; all, including Rakovski, were 'eliminated' later—either with or without trial.

In 1920–21 Ukrainian representatives abroad were officially independent of Moscow, but they were under the orders of Rakovski. There existed, however, a secret decision of the Politbureau, according to which the Foreign Office of the U.S.S.R. had the right to send instructions to the Foreign Office of the Ukrainian S.S.R., and could interfere in the activities of the Ukrainian diplomats in the Central European capitals.

This situation continued until the new Constitution of the Union, proclaimed on 6 July 1923. The Ukrainian Commissariat for Foreign Affairs was then abolished. The Ukrainian representation abroad was fused with that of U.S.S.R.; but it was agreed that an Ukrainian Communist should be appointed as First Counsellor in the four capitals (Vienna was included) where the Ukrainians had had independent representation. This arrangement continued until 1925, when such appointments began to be considered only as 'desirable'. Ukrainian Communists soon vanished from important positions in the Soviet embassies and legations, and for the last thirteen years the Ukrainian S.S.R. has had not even the shadow of formal representation abroad.

(13) The Ukrainians in Poland

The Paris Conference, in 1919, only recognized the Polish occupation of Eastern Galicia pending a solution of 'the Russian Question'. The Polish position in Galicia was finally affirmed by the Council of the League of Nations (15 March 1923), but the Polish Government undertook to establish a 'gradual' autonomy for the Ukrainian population of Eastern Galicia.

The Ukrainians claimed that not less than three and a half millions of the population of Eastern Galicia were of Ukrainian stock, and they reckoned another three millions in Western Galicia, the Kholm region, and the Polish districts of Polesia and Volhynia.

The Polish census of 1939 admitted only 1,600,000 Ukrainians in Eastern Galicia, while the population of Russian origin in other regions of Poland was not allowed to be even in part Ukrainian. This great disparity in estimates can be explained by the fact that the Poles described as 'Russians' all those elements, formerly 'pro-Muscovite', who were lukewarm in their support of the separatist version of the Ukrainian national movement.

The Polish Government had some success in detaching from the Ukrainian nationalists a section of the rural population who were flattered by the discovery that they were in fact 'russified Polish szlachta'. It was affirmed that during the preceding two centuries many families of the lesser Polish nobility had become so impoverished that they had disappeared into the mass of the peasantry and had become the victims of systematic methods of russification. The movement of the so-called 'Szlachta Zagrodowa' (Smallholder Gentry) had great success, and the journal of the association, Pobudki, claimed recently that the number of 'russified szlachta' who were expected 'to return to the bosom of their mother Poland' amounted to 700,000 persons. Thus, if those who desired to remain Russian and those who desired to become Poles (together with real Poles, Jews, Armenians, and Germans) are deducted from the Ukrainian estimate, it will be found that the total number of conscious Ukrainians in all Galicia did not exceed two millions.

These two millions remain, however, an important factor in the Galician borderland where Polish, German, Russian, Roumanian and Hungarian interests are in dangerous conflict, and the energetic activities of Ukrainian groups and political parties continued to exercise a disturbing influence on the life of the Polish State during the whole period 1919–39.

The most important Ukrainian party is U.N.D.O. (The Ukrainian National Democratic Union (Obyedinenie)), which rose to importance about 1925 under the leadership of Dmitro Levitsky. The party could claim a membership of over one million, and it published a series of papers of which Dilo (Action) in Lvov was the most important. The ultimate aim of

U.N.D.O. was a united and independent Ukraine; but working within the structure of the Polish State the party refrained from advocating 'separatism at home' and claimed independence only for 'enslaved' Soviet Ukraine. The Soviet Government regarded U.N.D.O. as the most dangerous, because the most serious, of all Ukrainian political groups.

Relations between the Polish Government and U.N.D.O. were far from cordial during the years 1925–30. Both sides, however, were seeking compromise and the U.N.D.O. leaders, though they failed to acquire legalized autonomy, appeared temporarily satisfied with the position of *de facto* autonomy which they had attained through their social, educational and co-operative organizations (*Selsky Hospodar* (The Country Farmer), *Dnistr*, *Maslosoyuz* (Butter League), etc.). The policy of 'peace with Poland' was supported by the Ukrainian Catholic and Uniate organizations under the leadership of the Uniate Metropolitan, Count Szepticki with the periodicals, *Meta* (Aim), *Nedilya* (Week). On the other hand, certain fractions of U.N.D.O. maintained a hostile attitude towards the Polish Government, voiced in the papers *Nash Prapor* (Our Standard), *Nash Klych* (Our Warcry). Communist influences were noticeable in the propaganda of these fractions.

Abroad the U.N.D.O. was on the best of terms with the Government of the Czechoslovak Republic. Antagonism to Poland had become a tradition in Prague since 1920, when the passage of arms to Poland during the war with the Soviets had been refused. Ukrainian refugees, from both Soviet Ukraine and Galicia, were sure of a kindly reception in the Czech capital, which between the years 1925–35 became, if not the Ukrainian political centre, at least the cultural and educational focus where the idea of a Greater Ukraine, independent and sovereign, was openly preached in the high schools (in many of which special Ukrainian courses were available for students).

The intense interest shown by the leaders of the Third Reich in the Ukrainian problem—an interest which provoked the series of trials, banishments and executions in Soviet Ukraine—aroused the anxiety of the Polish Government. By no means confident of the loyalty of the population of Eastern Galicia, Kholm, and Volhynia, the Poles decided to accelerate the 'polonization' of these regions. This 'polonizing' process took unfortunate and sometimes arbitrary and violent forms: prohibition in some districts of the use of the Ukrainian or Russian languages, and the revival of the old struggle against the Orthodox and even against the Uniate Churches. A great number of Orthodox and Uniate churches were closed or 'turned back' into Catholic ones.

It would have been difficult to discover methods more likely to revive the age-old historic struggle 'for land and faith' between Poles and Ukrainians. A hatred of 'the Polish orientation' was quickly roused among the Ukrainian peasantry, and the moderate sections of U.N.D.O. with their policy of compromise began to lose ground. The U.N.D.O. party organization was forced to denounce the basis of conciliation reached in 1930 and confirmed in 1935. At the moment of the German attack on Poland, U.N.D.O. announced its loyalty to the Polish state, but the foundations of this loyalty had been sapped by the mistakes of the Polish politicians. It was Stalin, not Hitler, who reaped the benefit.

From time to time the struggle between Poles and Ukrainians in Galicia took an acute form and was accompanied by industrial strikes, peasant riots and acts of terrorism against the administration. These methods, violent and illegal, were not approved by U.N.D.O., but they were stimulated both by secret Communist organizations and by the unofficial Ukrainian Party which called itself the Ukrainian National Union (U.N.U.). U.N.U. repudiated all compromise with Poland, and proclaimed an armed struggle against her. Comparable in its organization and tactics to the I.R.A. (on which it was probably modelled to carry on a struggle in geographical and social conditions in some ways similar to those of Ireland), the U.N.U. organized a network of secret militarized groups all over Galicia. Galicia was looked on as a territory where the 'Army Corps' of U.N.U. was 'quartered': the territory was divided into four districts corresponding to 'Divisions', which were further divided into 'Regiments', 'Battalions' and 'Companies'. Some scores of thousands of men, young for the most part, and fanatically devoted to 'the cause', joined U.N.U.

At the head of the movement stood the bold and adventurous figure of Colonel Konovalets. A former officer of the Austrian Army, Konovalets had led the troops of the 'Directoria' which drove Skoropadsky from Kiev in December 1918. Later he had quarrelled with Petlyura on account of the latter's 'Polish orientation'.

Already in the twenties Konovalets had sought favour and aid in Germany. He was not the only one: about 1924 a certain Poltavets-Ostranitsa, who called himself 'Hetman', appeared in Munich with the same object. Konovalets, however, was much more successful than his rivals, and, towards 1930, he established firm relations with German political and military circles, and at the same time made really effective the secret organization of U.N.U. in Galicia. A newspaper of U.N.U., *Ukrainske Slovo* (Ukrainian Word) was published in Paris; other publications appeared in Germany.

The keen interest with which the Nazi leaders regarded the Ukrainian problem lent a serious meaning to the conspiratorial activities of Colonel Konovalets, who was not ashamed to express openly his 'German orientation'. In 1933 negotiations were set on foot between U.N.U. and representatives of the Nazi Party concerning 'preparatory measures' which were to be taken for the creation of a future 'Ukrainian, White Russian and Lithuanian State'. The German negotiators were principally interested in the organization of a potential 'Ukrainian Government'. The lack of suitable candidates for political office among his own supporters led Konovalets to make contact with the remnants of Petlyura's followers, among whom several 'ex-cabinet ministers' were to be found. There was a project to open relations with Ukrainian nationalists who had remained in Soviet Ukraine, and Konovalets was also in touch with the former Hetman Skoropadsky, who was living at Wannsee near Berlin. Konovalets obviously aimed at organizing a 'united Ukrainian front', and the Ukrainians undoubtedly lost one who might have proved a resolute national leader, when the colonel was killed in a café in Rotterdam by the explosion of a bomb in the form of a cigarette-box which was handed to him by a man presumed to have been a Soviet agent.

For U.N.U. the death of Konovalets was an even greater blow than it first appeared. Deprived of leadership, the organization began to go to pieces. The Polish police succeeded in arresting numbers of leaders of the regional organizations, and the movement's German supporters began to lose confidence in the conspiratorial method.

Both the moderate and the extremist Ukrainian political parties in Poland, the U.N.D.O. and the U.N.U., were born in Galicia in the atmosphere of the local political struggle. Distinct from these parties were the representatives of the erstwhile Ukrainian Popular Republic who had settled in Poland. This group continued to consider itself as the 'legal government' of Russian Ukraine with Andrew Levitsky as 'president' and several 'cabinet ministers' and 'diplomatic representatives' in different countries (Mazeppa, Prokopovich, A. Shulgin, General Salsky and others). Part of these 'Petlyurians' lived in Poland, others in Prague and Paris, where they published their periodical *Trizub* (Trident, the emblem on Vladimir's coins). Contrasting in this respect with the Galician political parties, which did not put their social programme in the first place, these former adherents of the 'Ukrainian Popular Republic', faithful to the traditions of the *Rada* and *Directoria*, had retained their socialist tendencies but in a very moderate form.

It is a curious fact that this group of 'the Ukrainian Popular Republic' enjoyed until recently not only the support of the Czech Government, with whose ideology it had much in common, but also that of the Polish Government, which at the same time was incapable of establishing normal durable relations with the Galician Ukrainians. The politicians of the U.P.R. kept themselves apart not only from the extremists of the U.N.U. but also from the moderates of the U.N.D.O. They did not of course preach separatism in regard to Poland, and as the years passed they became much more tolerant on the subject of the exact status of the Ukraine in the event of the downfall of the Soviet régime and the revival of a Russian state. Konovalets had tried to enlist them for 'the United Ukrainian front' patronized by the Third Reich, but such an orientation could scarcely attract the 'Petlyurians', penetrated by democratic and even socialist tendencies. Some of them remained faithful to the 'Polish orientation' of Petlyura himself, others struck up friendship with the Parisian group of *La Revue de Prométhée*—a periodical published by the representatives of different nationalities which had formed part of the Russian Empire and are now under Soviet dominion. *Les Prométhéens* are drastically opposed to the Soviet régime, denounce the absence of real autonomy in the Soviet Union and stand ultimately for a 'federal state of nationalities'. The Ukrainians who participate in this movement therefore abandon the idea of 'integral separatism' and profess opinions in the spirit of those expressed once upon a time by Michael Dragomanov.

Former 'Petlyurians' are at present less opposed to the ideas of which Hetman Skoropadsky was the symbol than they were at the time when they began their armed struggle against him. The ex-Hetman has retained a certain influence on Ukrainians and admirers of his title can be met in many parts of the world—in Paris and London, in Canada and the United States. His son Danylo is considered by them as 'the lawful successor' of the now ageing Paul.

Outside Poland, Ukrainians are to be found in many European and American countries. Political and academic circles of Ukrainian intelligentsia are grouped round periodicals of varying views, but these circles consist of scores, perhaps, of persons out of the hundreds of thousands of Ukrainian land labourers who have migrated from over-populated Galicia. After the war and revolution thousands of fugitives from the South of Russia and Volhynia joined them. In the Ukrainian press from time to time appear statements that the number of Ukrainians in Western Europe reaches 500,000, in Canada over a million, in the United States about 700,000 and in South America 200,000. These figures are undoubtedly exaggerated. In France the number of refugees from the South of Russia who can be considered 'Ukrainians' did not exceed a few scores of thousands, and the same must be said about Czechoslovakia and Balkan countries. However, among the Polish agricultural workers and miners in France (900,000) a third came from Eastern Galicia and Volhynia. And there is no doubt that hundreds of thousands have migrated from Galicia to the United States and especially to Canada where, owing to hard work and a certain capacity for organization, brought over from their native land, many have attained prosperity. America is the land where emigrants from Europe keep together according to their nationality more than anywhere else. The Ukrainian emigration in Canada and the United States has retained a vivid interest in everything pertaining to Ukrainian nationality. It has its own press, publishes its books, teaches its language and history in its schools. The Ukrainians in America consider it their duty to respond to the appeals of the different Ukrainian parties and groups which have remained in Europe. Therefore echoes of all the different tendencies of Ukrainian political life can be found in Canada and the United States: 'pro-Russians' who do not wish to be called 'Ukrainians', adherents of U.N.D.O., followers of Colonel Konovalets, partisans of Petlyura and the 'Petlyurians', admirers of 'the young Hetman' Danylo Skoropadsky. However, purely ideological discussions are not so acute there as among the different 'fractions' in Europe. 'The united Ukrainian front' would have a better chance in emigration, because its basis would not be so much political activity, as a common historical tradition and a common love of the Ukrainian land.

(14) *Literature on the Ukrainian Question*

Numerous papers, mostly by well-known Ukrainian writers and political leaders, have appeared in the *Slavonic and East European Review*. These papers have made available to English readers information on various aspects of the Ukrainian Question. The following should be noted:

Vol. v, No. 13, p. 169, Kolessa, A., 'Bibliography of the Ukrainian Language'.

IX, No. 27, p. 367, Paneyko, B., 'Galicia and the Polish–Ukrainian Problem'.

Ibid. p. 88, Skorowski, S., 'The Ukrainian Problem in Poland'.

x, No. 28, p. 116, Łoś, S., 'Ukrainian Question in Poland'.

Ibid. p. 138, Borshak, E., 'Relations of England and Ukraine.'

XII, No. 35, p. 323, Mazepa, I., 'Ukrainia under Bolshevist Rule' (valuable, based on careful study of the Ukrainian Soviet press).

Ibid. No. 36, p. 622, Doroshenko, D., 'The Uniat Church in Galicia'.

XIII, No. 37, p. 139, Kirkconnell, W., 'Ukrainian Poetry in Canada'.
Ibid. No. 38, p. 350, Shulgin, A., 'Ukraine and Its Political Aspirations'.
Ibid. Nos. 38, 39, pp. 363, 611, Krofta, K., 'Ruthenes, Czechs and Slovaks' (the official Czech view of the position of the Carpathian Ukrainians by the distinguished Czechoslovak politician).
Ibid. No. 38, p. 372, Voloshin, A., 'Carpathian Ruthenia' (the view of the luckless leader of the Carpathian Ukrainians).
XIV, Nos. 40–41, pp. 163, 372, Andrusiak, N., 'The Ukrainian Movement in Galicia'.
XVI, No. 48, p. 654, Doroshenko, D., 'Mykhailo Dragomanov and the Ukrainian National Movement' (a study of permanent value).

La Revue de Prométhée published in Paris and East Europe published in London have contained a number of topical articles on the Ukraine, many of which are of a polemical character. The former review is the organ of the Promethean League which professes to represent all the 'minority nationalities' of the former Russian Empire (i.e. Azerbaijan, Georgia, the Don and Kuban Cossacks, North Caucasia, Turkestan, Idel-Ural, the Ukraine, the Crimea, Ingria, Karelia, and the Komi (Zyryan) Region; the Armenians are, or were, not included). The League, which numbers among its members many notable political emigrants and writers of talent, held a 'First Promethean League Linguistic Congress' in Warsaw in the spring of 1936 (see *Baltic and Scandinavian Countries*, vol. III, no. 1 (5)).

The principal source for the contemporary history of the Ukrainian movement in Galicia is the work of the leader of U.N.D.O.—Dr Kost Levitsky: *Historiya Politichnoy Dumky Halytskykh Ukraintsev, 1848–1914*; *na Podstavi Spomynov* (History of the Political Thought of the Galician Ukrainians; on the basis of (the author's) Reminiscences), Lvov, 1926. See also A. Shulgin, *L'Ukraine contre Moscou*, Paris, 1935; A. Martel, *La Langue Ruthène*, Paris, 1938.

The period between 1914–18 and 1939 can be studied in the Ukrainian periodical press: *Dilo, Zhive Slovo* (Lvov), *Nash Klych* (Peremyshl). See also the newspapers published in Russian in Podkarpatska Rus: *Russki Golos, Russki Vestnik* (Uzhhorod).

The different political orientations of Ukrainian groups in emigration are illustrated in the pages of *Svit* (America), *Trizub* (Petlyurian), *Ukrainske Slovo* (the organ of U.N.U.), and *Ukraina*, also in *La Revue de Prométhée* (all published in Paris).

For the views of Russian polemists on the subject see: Shchegolev, S., *Ukrainskoe Dvizhenie kak Sovremenny Etap Yuzhno-Russkago Separatizma* (The Ukrainian Movement as the Modern Stage of South Russian Separatism), Kiev, 1912; Volkonski, Prince A., *Istoricheskaya Pravda i Ukraino-filskaya Propaganda* (Historical Truth and Ukrainophil Propaganda), Turin, 1920 (also in an Italian translation); Tsarinny, A., *Ukrainskoe Dvizhenie* (The Ukrainian Movement), Berlin, 1922.

CHAPTER VII

THE ECONOMIC HISTORY OF THE UKRAINE

§1. AGRICULTURAL HISTORY OF THE UKRAINE

IN the political mythology of the twentieth century the legend about 'the vast riches of the Ukraine' has played, and is destined to play, a certain part. In history the Ukraine will take place with the Route to the Indies, the North-West Passage, Golconda, the Empire of Prester John, and other phantasmagorias of the human mind which in their time have inspired the nations to the drama of effort and the tragedy of conflict.

In the modern world where generalization has displaced religion and where the generation made literate by popular education has thrown up 'Leaders' who are adepts in the exploitation of generalized ideas, it was inevitable that movements based on facile and false scientific, geographical and ethnical conceptions should become fashionable. 'The wheat-fields of the Ukraine' form a roseate hinterland to the Nordic Race and the Classless State in the dreamworld of the masses of Central Europe. Apart, therefore, from the intrinsic interest of the subject, it becomes a matter of current importance to analyse the extent of the real resources of the Ukraine and their actual and potential relation to the economic problem of Europe.

There exists a widespread idea that the Ukraine was 'the granary of the Russian Empire', but in reality it would be difficult to indicate the period to which this idea could be applicable. Certainly, during the eighteenth century, as the Tartars and Turks were driven from the mouths of the Ukrainian rivers, a period of progressive prosperity set in. But under Alexander I, during the Napoleonic Wars, the bulk of the grain supply of the Empire was drawn from the southern regions of Central Russia—from the Governments of Orel, Kursk, Voronezh and Tambov. This source of supply was adequate in view of the numbers of the population at that period, and the state of the roads between the Black Sea provinces and Central Russia put a prohibitive cost on transportation from the south.

During the reigns of Alexander I and Nicholas I export abroad developed through Odessa and the Azov ports—Taganrog and

Mariupol. The supply came from the big New Russian estates and from the German, Moldavian and Serb colonies founded in the eighteenth century. Towards the middle of the century the agricultural production of the Ukraine and the New Russian Governments began to form an important proportion of the general production of the Empire, but still these regions could not be called 'the granary of Russia' on account of the continuing lack of proper means of communication with the central provinces. The upper Dniepr and the upper course of the western Dvina were too shallow to serve adequately the needs of modern transport, and as late as the Crimean War the Russian railway system had not been extended south of Moscow.

The first important imperial trunk lines were constructed during the sixties and seventies: Moscow-Kursk-Kharkov-Rostov-on-the-Don (with branch lines from Kursk to Kiev and from Kharkov to the Crimea); Moscow-Voronezh-Rostov-on-the-Don (with extensions to the northern Caucasus); Petersburg-Vilna-Rovno-Kiev-Odessa; Kharkov-Kremenchug (on the Dniepr)-Nikolaev. Railway construction had taken the 'meridial' direction: the economic axis of the Empire during the three decades 1860–90 ran from 'the industrial north' to 'the agricultural south'.

The new railway system improved the conditions for the export of Ukrainian and New Russian grain through the Black Sea ports. At the same time access to the north was provided by the railway 'diagonal' connecting Orel (on the Moscow-Kursk line) with Riga: this 'diagonal' continued to the south-east through the northern part of the Don region to Tsaritsyn on the lower Volga. Further, a special 'grain line' linked the Ukraine with the Baltic: starting from Kremenchug on the Dniepr, it passed through the Governments of Poltava and Chernigov, White Russia and Lithuania to the new ice-free port of Libava (Libau).

It thus began to appear that the Ukrainian and New Russian provinces were indeed to become the granary of the Russian Empire. But the colossal economic potentialities of the outlying quarters of the Empire, which began to come into development during the second half of the nineteenth century, very soon overwhelmed this comparatively modest conception. In the seventies the first 'latitudinal' railway threw a bridge across the Volga at Samara and was continued as far as the southern Urals. The steppes beyond the Volga offered immense new space for agricultural exploitation. In the meantime the conquest of the Caucasus had been completed, and the rapid expansion of the economic life of the Kuban and Terek regions had begun. Soil conditions in the northern

Caucasus were not inferior to those of New Russia and climatic conditions were much more favourable: rainfall, owing to the proximity of the great Caucasian ranges, was more regular. The Kuban region did actually become a granary. Rostov-on-the-Don grew and flourished in true 'American style'. A new grain port, Novorossiysk, was built and soon became a rival to Odessa.

Further railway development accompanied the exploitation of the Donets coal-mines and the growth of a metallurgical industry centred on the Krivoy Rog iron-ore deposits located to the west of the Dniepr. Two parallel lines were constructed to pass through Ekaterinoslav and the old district of the Zaporogian *Sech*, connecting the Donets basin with Krivoy Rog. Thus, simultaneously with the industrial development in the south and the flowering of the North Caucasian region, a new 'granary' and new regions of great mineral potential began at the turn of the century to impose a 'latitudinal' direction on railway construction: the opening of the great Siberian railway gave almost a priority to the possibilities of agricultural production in western and southern Siberia, and connected Chelyabinsk, through Ekaterinenburg, Vyatka and Vologda, with the Baltic ports. At the same time 'diagonal' development was proceeding far to the south-east through Turkestan to the frontiers of Afghanistan and the Chinese Empire.

The importance of the natural riches of Asiatic Russia came to be realized with an ever-growing force during the reign of Nicholas II (1896–1917). The principal economic axis of the Empire was evidently changing direction from the 'meridial' to the 'latitudinal'. The political policy of the Empire during the same period, with its emphasis on the Balkan Slavs and on the 'Byzantine' dreams of the epoch of Catherine II, was certainly archaistic in tendency and bore no relation to the fundamental realities of Eurasian geography.

The War of 1914–18 brought down in destruction that peculiarly hybrid cultural synthesis which was Romanov Russia; it obliterated at the same time the neo-Byzantine plans of the Pan-Slavists and weakened the whole position of Russia as a European power. The loss of a wide belt of territories (the whole inheritance of two hundred years of Romanov autocracy) between the Arctic and the Black Sea imposed on the new Soviet state the sheer necessity of a 'latitudinal' rather than a 'meridial' development. During the last two decades new efforts have been made to open up the agricultural and mineral wealth of the steppes beyond the Volga and the Ural in western and southern Siberia and of the valleys of the Altai and the Tien-Shan; and, while historic Russian ambitions in the Balkans and the Middle East have been left in suspense, a territory the size of Europe and new routes into the heart of China and ultimately to the Pacific have been brought under Soviet control. Under these circumstances 'the wheat-fields of the Ukraine' receded again into the background and became of only local importance: the more so since, in the two Soviet 'Economic Plans', interest in South-Eastern Russia has been concentrated on the industrial development of the New Russian region. These conditions are illustrated by the growth of industrial centres like Kharkov, Ekaterinoslav, Lugansk, Zaporozhie, and the decline of the great grain port of Odessa.

The agricultural wealth of the Ukraine has never in fact justified the enthusiasm which it has inspired from the time of the seventeenth-century Polish poet quoted in an earlier context to the more recent period of Herr Hitler and his apostles of *Lebensraum*. The natural conditions of the Ukraine are such that they really generously reward agricultural labour, but they exact always patient, strenuous and systematic toil.

Natural conditions differ greatly over the expanse of the country which Michael Dragomanov considered to constitute 'Greater Ukraine'. The agricultural 'age' of these territories differs in the extreme. In New Russia agriculture is only a century old, while Galicia has supported a numerous population of husbandmen for nearly a thousand years.

Galicia is one of the oldest agricultural lands of all Europe and conditions there have hardly altered since the days of Daniel and his *boyars*. The Galician earth, black in the eastern part, is tired old soil, impoverished by incessant labour, itself prompted and intensified by the ever-growing care of an ever-growing population to acquire its daily bread. Owing to the density of the population (110, and in some regions 132, inhabitants to the square kilometre) the area of holdings had been reduced to a minimum: 46 per cent of the farms comprise 2 hectares of land and sometimes less; 37 per cent comprise from 2 to 5 hectares. In a countryside where urban life has remained relatively stagnant live 75 per cent of the total population; while all commerce and crafts remain in the hands of the Jews in the large towns and in many of the villages, there is a 50 per cent surplus of hands among agricultural labourers. The peasants, Poles and Ukrainians alike, used to migrate to Germany and France as casual labour; before the last war they emigrated also in large numbers to Canada and the United States.

These arduous conditions of peasant life gradually developed a capacity for organization. Driven by necessity, the Galician peasantry set up a network of co-operatives for production and distribution. These co-operatives formed the basis of a certain national unity which found expression in the political field.

Volhynia, partitioned after the war of 1920 between the Poles and the Soviets, is nearly as old an agricultural country as Galicia. Here the strips of rich black earth alternate with sandy and wooded country. Although density of population is not so great as in Galicia, poverty is perhaps even greater, owing to a lack of that capacity for organization which helps the Galician labourers to survive. The large estates of the Polish nobility have long disappeared; after the last war the Polish Government divided up the land. Numerous strips were allotted to Polish soldiers on the expiration of their service—with the intention of strengthening the Polish ethnic and cultural element in the region. The disappearance of the large estates, as in Transylvania and Roumania, had a deleterious effect on agricultural production and on the proper exploitation of the forests. The majority of the people lead a half-starved existence, and the young men dream of emigration to South America. In 1937, 25 per cent of the population of Polish Volhynia had neither bread nor wood.

Podolia has been a land of cultivation since the Middle Ages, although the soil was broken up two or three hundred years later than in Galicia and Volhynia. Now, as before the period of war and revolution (1914–20), Podolia remains in a close economic relationship to the other parts of the Ukraine. The black earth of this favoured province is really fruitful and well watered by numerous small rivers; climatic conditions are better than anywhere throughout the Ukraine—rain is plentiful and regular and the winters are short. It was probably the fields and pastures, the hillocks and woods of Podolia which the Polish poet had in mind when he wrote lyrically of 'the birthplace of Ceres and Diana'. Horticulture and apiculture have long flourished there.

In the past social conditions varied with the political situation according to whether the small landowners (Ukrainian Cossacks) or the Polish landlords were in the ascendant. During the eighteenth century Polish elements had the upper hand and for some time Podolia remained the last refuge of the Polish aristocracy. Polish social influences survived the Three Partitions, and it was only after the Polish Insurrection of 1830 that conditions began to change in favour of the Russian majority in the population.

Towards the middle of the nineteenth century this rich land with its soft climate had become very densely populated. By the end of the century Podolia ranked second in density of population of all the regions of the Russian Empire. The Government of Moscow took first place, but in its population was included the million inhabitants of the second capital of the Empire, while in Podolia there was no single town which numbered more than fifty thousand inhabitants. Density of population in Podolia reached the figure of 100 to the square kilometre, but the province was saved from the problems of over-population by the development of the large estates on capitalist lines. This process began about 1830 and developed on a large scale after 1870. The beet-sugar industry with its subsidiary alcoholic distilleries, flour mills and horticulture provided a variety of livelihood for a population which by 1897 had attained to nearly four and a half millions. Between the years 1896 and 1933 more than a million and a half peasants migrated from other districts of the Ukraine to Siberia and the steppes beyond the Volga, but in Podolia emigration was scarcely perceptible.

The southern part of the Government of Kiev along the right bank of the Dniepr enjoyed conditions somewhat similar to those in Podolia, while the northern districts resembled rather Volhynia. In the south a rich black earth supported a number of large estates where the beet-sugar industry, distilleries and mills flourished. In these southern districts were many well-to-do peasant farms covering up to 20 and 30 hectares apiece. Wheat was grown in sufficient quantities to satisfy local needs and to supply the six hundred thousand inhabitants of the city of Kiev. At the beginning of the century the population of the Government of Kiev amounted to over four and a half millions. At that time the three Governments of right-bank Ukraine (Kiev, Podolia, Volhynia) contained fourteen million inhabitants with an average density of 70–80 people per square kilometre. Such numbers were quite 'European' in their proportions and should have tended to discourage those Western dreamers who were even then casting envious eyes on the 'vacant lands' of the Ukraine.

It was almost equally difficult to discover 'vacant lands' in the Governments of *left-bank Ukraine*. In Poltava, Chernigov and Kharkov the density of population amounted to 60–70 people per square kilometre. The uninterrupted belt of black earth in the Governments of Poltava and Chernigov had been under the plough only since the seventeenth century—and many parts of it not before the eighteenth century. This was the land of which Alexey Tolstoy wrote: 'Know ye the land where all breathes plenty and content, where rivers flow as silver clear.' There were scarcely any towns of importance in this rural elysium. The characteristics of the Government of Kharkov, on the other hand, were quite distinct from those of the two adjoining left-bank provinces: in the north-west,

Kharkov, in its scenery and social conditions, resembles rather the neighbouring districts of the Government of Kursk, while in the south-east it is already really part of New Russia.

Climatic conditions on the left bank are rather less favourable than on the right bank of the Dniepr: there is a lighter rainfall which is not so evenly distributed; the winters are more severe and the region of Kharkov endures a distinctly 'continental' climate. Prince Shcherbatov, a former minister of the Imperial Government, writes that: 'One of the most important factors in agriculture is rainfall, which does not always occur under favourable conditions in the Ukraine. Most of the rain comes in summer and often takes the form of downpours which impede work in the fields and harvesting; and in the spring there is often not enough rain. Rainfall is better distributed on the right bank of the Dniepr than in other parts. The difficult climatic conditions in the Ukraine liken the average black earth harvests to average harvests in Central Europe on an average soil.'

During the nineteenth century conditions in left-bank Ukraine tended to favour the growth of a prosperous class of small farmers who supplanted the big landowners of the period of Peter I and Catherine II. These conditions derived from the shortage of labour on big estates which followed the opening up of the New Russian territories and from the wave of speculation which induced landowners to sell out their properties on the left bank of the Dniepr in order to participate in 'the rush' for the new lands. Left-bank Ukraine became a country of large peasant farms covering 10, 20, 30 and as much as 50 hectares, while a number of smaller 'working' landowners retained estates up to 100, 150 and 200 hectares. Land was worth in these parts 500 rubles (about £50 sterling on the pre-war exchange) a hectare.

At the same time the growth of these large farms in the Governments of left-bank Ukraine combined with a natural increase in the population to create a serious problem of 'over-crowding'. In the eighteenth century a numerous class of peasantry had existed who did not own any land of their own at all, but who merely possessed cottages and vegetable gardens and the right to graze their stock on common pasture lands. Following the Emancipation of the Serfs in 1861, the number of landless peasants showed a rapid increase. The small parcels of land allotted to the liberated serfs were soon redistributed between the thrifty and the shiftless; and the division of large estates did not contribute to the establishment of agricultural industries which might have provided a living for the less fortunate. Already in the eighties symptoms of over-population were noticeable in the Governments of Poltava and Chernigov. The peasants continued to move on into New Russia, but by this time that region was itself becoming fairly thickly populated. Migrants pursued their way to the newer lands in the northern Caucasus and beyond the Volga. From 1890 onwards the Government took a hand in the organization of this migratory movement. According to the Emigration Department, set up at this period, the greatest number of migrants over the whole Empire came from the 'rich black earth regions' of Poltava, Chernigov, Kursk and Kharkov. However, between the years 1907 and 1913, the Poltava and Chernigov Governments, from being first and second in this respect, ranked only third and fifth. This fact is explained by the initiative of important landowners and industrialists like Kharitonenko, Teresh-chenko and others who built up the sugar-beet industry on a large scale. Notwithstanding this factor, between 1906 and 1914, according to the statistics of the *Ukrainian Encyclopaedia*, 1,610,000 peasants migrated from the Ukrainian Governments, while migration was also taking place from different districts of New Russia. The Ukrainians mostly went to settle the steppe area in western Siberia and the region of Orenburg; others reached the Amur and the shores of the Pacific Ocean, where the Ukrainian settlements came to be known as the Green Wedge (*Zelëny Klin*) and where the names of the wealthy villages of Novo-Kievskoe, Poltavskoe and Cherni-govskoe piously recalled the origin of those who had come from the banks of the Dniepr and the Seym.

At the beginning of the twentieth century the classical 'three-field system', already prescribed as a law in the Lithuanian Statute of the sixteenth century, prevailed in left-bank Ukraine. This system answered the requirements of the small landowner or well-to-do peasant who farmed 20 to 100 hectares. Few troubled to produce more than a small surplus, the sale of which might cover their current wants. Horticulture, apiculture and some stock-raising served to supplement income. On the larger estates all the energies of the owners were directed to the lucrative exploitation of the sugar-beet industry. Stretches of land were bought or leased from peasants or small landowners in order to increase the acreage under beet. The rapid development and excellent management of the sugar-beet industry impressed and disturbed the German Commission of Professor Auhagen in 1912. By this time the industry had assumed a certain international importance. In 1914 there were over 190 sugar factories in the Ukraine out of 226 for the whole Empire (the bulk of the balance was produced in Poland). As against 2 million hectares under wheat in the Ukraine (excluding the New Russian Governments) there were over 1 million hectares under beetroot. Just before the last war the annual production of beet in the Ukraine reached 150 million quintals: i.e. 18 per cent of world production. The production of Ukrainian beet sugar ranked fourth—after that of America, Germany and France. In 1913 the Ukraine produced 11 million quintals of crystallized sugar. This output, together with that of the Polish factories, covered all the needs of the internal market (which during the preceding twenty-five years had augmented fourfold) and provided substantial surplus for export to the Baltic and the Middle East.

In addition to the beet processing plants, about 60 per cent of the alcohol refineries (corn, potatoes) of the Empire were located in the Ukraine. The production of vegetable oil (particularly from sunflower seed) was also important.

It has been estimated by the Soviet paper *Pravda* that approximately 1 milliard of rubles a year was paid for services on the semi-industrialized estates of landowners throughout Russia: of this sum a considerable proportion was paid for the hire of horse transport (since landowners did not maintain a large number of draught horses but hired from the villages). Of this milliard, about 300,000,000 were paid out in the Ukraine. As the peasant population of the Ukraine numbered about fifteen millions, some 20 rubles a year per head of the population was earned on 'supplementary' work on the large estates. 'Only owing to the sugar and other agricultural industries could the dense population of the Ukraine exist in such comparatively well-to-do circumstances.'

Thus the agricultural economy of Podolia, Volhynia, Kiev, Chernigov and Poltava was based only partly on the production of cereals. With a population which reached nearly twenty millions, only about 2 million hectares were under wheat, while in New Russia, with a population about half that of the Ukrainian Governments, there were 4 million hectares under wheat. The Ukraine exported only small quantities of wheat to Poland and White Russia, which provinces drew the bulk of their supplies from New Russia. The real 'granaries' of Russia which supplied the whole Empire and exported a surplus abroad were the regions of the northern Caucasus and Trans-Volga with western Siberia and New Russia (including the Governments of Kherson and Ekaterinoslav with the northern part of Tauris and the southern part of Kharkov). In those regions the black earth really had a virgin quality during the first half of the nineteenth century; and its richness remains exceptional even now.

As a rule, the climatic conditions in the *New Russian Governments* are much less favourable than in left-bank and especially right-bank Ukraine. They become worse going from west to east: the region of Odessa has the most equable climate and the shores of the Azov Sea the worst of all. In the east rainfall is insufficient, attaining in good years 50–40 cm. and in bad years not exceeding 20 cm., while in central and southern Ukraine it is 80 cm. and 40 cm. respectively. There is, furthermore, in the New Russian Governments an un-balanced distribution of rainfall: the country suffers from a shortage of rain in the spring when it is most needed, and from violent downpours in the summer. The climate of New Russia clearly inclines to aridity. In the old days the Black Sea steppes were covered for a short time in spring by a luxurious growth of high grass and wild flowers which disappeared in the following months. The steppe dries up completely during a period when the tempera-ture reaches from 30° to 40° Centigrade and even the rain-storms of July and August cannot give new life to the parched ground. Under such conditions field labour calls for special methods. The soil has to be ploughed deep, and great layers of earth have to be lifted—'the black fallow' which has not been dried out. The weak peasants' horses of the northern Ukraine are useless for such work. Ploughing in New Russia requires either two pairs of strong oxen or, better, mechanical traction. Before the last war, only wealthy landowners or agricultural colonies working on a co-operative basis could afford the latter method, which was introduced into New Russia as early as the end of the nineteenth century.

By force of circumstances farming in New Russia acquired quite a different character from that which had evolved in the historic countryside of old Ukraine: it even created a different landscape. 'Fruit-trees, especially cherry-trees, lend a charm to the Ukrainian landscape in the neighbourhood of Kiev and Poltava which recalls the rural landscapes of France. In New Russia, on the contrary, the lack of trees, the dryness of the climate, clouds of dust driven by the wind, lonely hamlets—all this goes to create an austere landscape which recalls rather the high plains of northern Castile. Only the endless cornfields with their undulating golden sea of wheat lend a lyric note to these flat unwooded spaces. Villages there are not picturesque and in agricultural colonies practical considerations take precedence over the desire to beautify the environment. The houses, however, are more modern, more spacious and better built. Thatched roofs have given place to tiles or sheet-iron' (Brégy and Obolensky).

Wheat forms the basis of the agricultural wealth of New Russia. Before the last war, wheat covered 25 per cent of all the farmed land in the Ukraine and New Russia: of 25 million hectares of arable, 6½ million were under wheat, and of these 4½ million were in New Russia. Ukrainian and New Russian production attained 90 million quintals a year, of which 70 million came from the New Russian Governments. (In addition, the Ukraine produced for internal consumption about 30 million quintals of rye—in the northern districts—nearly as much barley, and about 20 million quintals of oats.) The wheat crop of the Ukraine and New Russia represented 8 per cent of the total world, and 18 per cent of European, production. With an average production of 70 million quintals a year, the New Russian Governments could throw an important surplus on to the world market. Before the Revolution about 76 per cent of the crop was retained in the villages for food, storage and seed (on the larger mechanized estates and co-operative colonies the average was round 70 per cent). The balance, about 20 million quintals, went on the market: of it about one-quarter was absorbed by the towns and industrial centres of New Russia. Under these conditions the three New Russian Governments had available for export abroad 15 million quintals of wheat, i.e. about 1½ million tons. The crop of New Russia and the northern Caucasus was exported to the Ottoman Empire, Greece and particularly to Italy, where the 'hard' types of grain were appreciated as an ingredient of macaroni and other *paste*. Even after the last war and all the ruin of agriculture resulting from the Revolution, the Soviet Press, in 1929, could boast that about 1½ million tons of wheat had been exported through the New Russian and North Caucasian ports (Professor Brutskus holds that this export—the relation of which to total production greatly exceeded pre-War proportions—was one of the factors in preparing the way for the terrible famine of 1932).

'From remote times the Ukraine and New Russia were famous for their draught oxen. Further, many landowners possessed herds of foreign cattle, principally Swiss breeds. All the German colonies bred good milkers' (Shcherbatov). In 1914 there were estimated to be over 9 million head of cattle, 6 million sheep (numbers of them of valuable breed) and 5 to 6 million pigs in the Ukrainian and New Russian Governments (the pigs predominated in northern and western Ukraine and sheep in the New Russian steppes). South Russia, an ideal horseman's country, possessed also a vast number of horses. Before the last war there were reckoned to be 5½ million horses in the Ukraine and New Russia (1 horse to every 5–6 people, and one-sixth of all the horses in the Empire). Government studs, and those of private landowners and of certain *zemstva*, maintained a high standard of breeding—particularly of draught horses. The Army Remount Department fulfilled a third of its requirements in the south, and there was a considerable export abroad. As a result of the Revolution, breeding suffered probably more than any other branch of rural production. Statistics for 1922 illustrate the disastrous effect of the Revolution on livestock throughout the whole Empire. In 1916 the total head of cattle was about 60 million: in 1922, 23 million. The number of horses in 1916 was estimated at 35 million: in 1922 at 20 million. Sheep numbered 120 million in 1916: 46 million in 1922. In view of the fact that South Russia was the principal field of the Civil War, it is probable that about 50 per cent of the horses and cattle destroyed were lost in this region. It is reckoned that in the Ukraine and New Russia only one-third of the pigs remained and one-quarter of the sheep. Losses in domestic animals are much more difficult to recover than losses in other branches of domestic industry; further, the special conditions of field labour in New Russia required a large proportion of draught oxen and horses.

One of the principal reasons which compelled Lenin to formulate the New Economic Policy was the necessity of restoring the food production of the Soviet Union.

'"War Communism" and attempts to introduce "integral socialism" into the countryside ended in 1922. At that date began the period of "liberalism" in Communist policy in relation to the villages. The peasantry were allowed freedom in the choice of land labour and almost complete freedom in other economic activities. The years between 1922 and 1929 produced excellent results: the lost sowing area was recovered and breeding was resumed. The food question in the country was improving' (Prof. Markov, *Socialist Economy in U.S.S.R.*, Part 2, *Agriculture*, Paris, 1937). By 1929 agricultural production approached pre-war standards (150–160 million quintals of cereals compared with 200 millions average for the years 1909–13). In spite of the fact that, following the break-up of large estates, the peasants had expanded the sown area at the expense of pasture (and according to the *Ukrainian Encyclopaedia* were showing a diminishing average on arable of 15–20 per cent as a result of more primitive methods of farming), the breeding of cattle and horses was nearing pre-war figures and the production of pigs was improving.

§2. SOVIET AGRICULTURAL POLICY

The late Alexander Guchkov used to say that 'the social revolution begun by Lenin in 1917 was carried through during the following twelve years in the towns and industrial centres only. It did not profoundly affect the countryside until 1929.' Just for this reason Stalin in that ominous year undertook what was to amount to a second and more fundamental revolution in the life of the peoples of Russia.

The condition of the peasantry had so far improved during the years 1922–29 that the Communist régime was able to realize that the peasant was fast becoming the principal and most formidable adversary of the Marxist Revolution. An implacable struggle was therefore initiated against that enemy who had succeeded in recuperating in the social and economic sense, but who was not yet ready to enter the field as an organized political force contending for mastery with a Communist Party which derived its power from the support of the industrial proletariat.

The economic Five Year Plans elaborated by the Soviet régime were dictated by the necessity of reconstructing the social and economic structure of the country in a way which should correspond with the bases of state which the continuance of the political dictatorship of the Communist Party required.

'The main idea of the Soviet Five Year Plans was the accelerated industrialization of U.S.S.R. and, parallel with it in accordance with the political needs of the régime, a rapid collectivization of agriculture. It was always for political rather than for economic reasons that the New Economic Policy, which the Communists had been obliged to put into practice since 1922, was abolished in 1929. The Communist Party, under the leadership of Stalin, proceeded to a new experiment in collectivism in the countryside, using in this case unusually brutal and inhuman methods which completely ruined all more or less prosperous farmers. The peasantry were unable to offer any effective resistance to the authorities, since their risings were only scattered and isolated in character. The peasants chose instinctively the easier way of passive resistance which found expression in the contraction of production and in the careless and unsatisfactory operation of the first collective farms (*Kolkhozy*). As a result of the policy of the Communist Party and of the natural reaction of the peasantry, the country had again to endure a frightful famine which bore its worst aspect in those regions where the percentage of collectivized farms was greatest' (Markov).

The Party had finally triumphed over the peasantry by the end of

1934, and in January of the following year it proclaimed its political and social victory. Reference has been made in the preceding chapter to the social upheaval, the great losses in human life and the redistribution of population incurred during the 'Revolution against the Peasants'. Losses in natural wealth were also formidable: during the five years, 1929–34, horses declined by 50 per cent; cattle by 40 per cent; only about half the total number of pigs survived and one-quarter of the sheep.

The first efforts of the Soviet administration had been directed to the organization of *Sovkhozy*—the large Government farms which in effect replaced the 'capitalist' private estates of the pre-Revolutionary period. Grain, beet sugar and stock-raising *Sovkhozy* were set up. In 1934 there were already 10,500 of them, of which 1665 were situated in the Ukraine and New Russia. In 1935 the sown area of the *Sovkhozy* attained 15 million hectares as against 2 million in 1929 (i.e. 10 per cent as against 2 per cent of the whole sown area of the Union). Livestock confiscated from the peasantry stocked these 'model' farms, which soon began to evoke the admiration of urban tourists from the West. The *Sovkhozy* were well supplied with the most modern agricultural machinery: in spite or because of this fact they failed to absorb any large proportion of the rural labour which had been deprived of normal occupation by the new measures. In 1931 only 1½ million people throughout the whole stretch of the Union were employed on *Sovkhozy*: in 1934 nearly 3 million were employed (of which 1½ million were in Ukraine and New Russia).

The *Kolkhozy* proved to be a far more important factor in the new agricultural economy. Between 1929 and 1934 all means—including the most ruthless—were employed to force the peasants on to the collective farms. The number of *Kolkhozy* grew rapidly: in July 1930 only 23 per cent of all farms had been converted into *Kolkhozy*; by the beginning of 1932 the figure was already 60 per cent; by the beginning of 1934 it had reached 72 per cent; and in 1936, 90 per cent. During the last three years individual farmers in U.S.S.R. have almost completely disappeared: the sown area occupied by private farmers amounted to 34 per cent in 1934 and to only 4 per cent in 1936.

As a result of the widespread famine conditions and the really serious insurrections which had troubled the authorities in the Northern Caucasus and Trans-Caucasia during the period 1930–32, and as a result also of the deterioration in the international situation which followed the Nazi rise to power in Germany in 1934, the Soviet Government, in spite of its proclaimed 'victory', found itself forced to modify the principles on which rural collectivization had been based. '"Liberal" tendencies began already in 1932 in the sense that *kolkhozniki* (individual members of the *Kolkhozy*) were allowed to keep their own cattle (Decree of 4 February 1932). Subsequently, in 1935, *kolkhozniki* were accorded the right to farm their own private allotments within the boundaries of the *Kolkhozy*.

These modifications in policy soon gave positive results. It is difficult to say whether the *Kolkhozy* have come to be accepted by the peasantry as the permanent basis of rural life. At the same time there can be no doubt that the grant of certain rights of private farming to the *kolkhozniki*, combined with a relatively free market, has tended to a notable improvement in the conditions of peasant life. In consequence food production throughout the whole country has again increased.

There are now four forms of farming in existence side by side in the Soviet countryside:

(a) *Sovkhozy* (State farms);
(b) Individual farms;
(c) *Kolkhozy* (Collective farms);
(d) Allotments belonging to the *kolkhozniki* within the area of the *Kolkhozy*.

The relative importance of these different types of farm can be judged from the areas allotted to each in the 'sowing plan' of 1936: *Sovkhozy* covered 16 million hectares; individual farms, 5 million; *Kolkhozy*, 108 million; *kolkhozniki* holdings, 8 million.

Obviously, the *Kolkhozy* constitute the most important source of agricultural production. On an estimated yield of 8·3 quintals per hectare, the *Kolkhoz* pays 1·7 quintals to the state in taxes; 3·3 to the governmental 'machine stations' which provide and maintain plant; the balance goes to the *kolkhozniki*. The *Kolkhozy*, with a sowing area of rather over 100 million hectares and a yield of 7 quintals per hectare, supply the state organizations with about 150 million quintals (approximately 15 million tons) surplus over the consumption of the rural population. This reckoning is, of course, purely theoretical, but, in 1934, when bread rations existed for the town population, the administration did distribute about 10 million tons of bread.

The importance of the *kolkhozniki* (who are allowed to cultivate from ¼ hectare to 1 hectare each) lies in the production of vegetables and fruit and, to a certain extent, of livestock. The Plan for 1937 estimated that individual farmers and *kolkhozniki* possessed 29 million head of cattle as compared with 4½ million owned by the *Kolkhozy* over their vastly greater acreage. The private farmers and *kolkhozniki* were reckoned to be even richer in pigs, of which they counted 15 million against 5 million on the *Kolkhozy* and an even lesser number on the *Sovkhozy*. The tiny bits of land which belong to the *kolkhozniki* personally, as well as their domestic animals, have become a school of individual farming which has grown up in the middle of 'the Socialist experiment' as a compromise with the dictates of economics and human nature. In twenty-eight towns in 1938, 82 per cent rye flour, 74 per cent wheat flour, 86 per cent beef, 93 per cent milk, 97 per cent eggs, 87 per cent potatoes, and 72 per cent cabbages, were brought to market by *kolkhozniki* and individual farmers, and only the balance came from the state and collective farms. True the official statisticians could find comfort in the fact that as against the general balance of state commerce which amounted to 100 milliards of roubles the free market only absorbed 16 milliards: but the free market shows a definite tendency to grow and in four years has doubled its transactions.

The successful private initiative of the *kolkhozniki* has already begun to weigh upon the minds of the protagonists of the integral Revolution. In the spring of 1938 a Government Decree proclaimed that 'abuses are observed on those allotments of land which are given over to *kolkhozniki* for the personal cultivation of kitchen-gardens or other domestic needs. These abuses consist in the fact that the allotments are sometimes not situated next to the habitations of the *kolkhozniki*, but lie in the middle of *Kolkhoz* lands and exceed the size allowed by the law. The worst part of it all is that these allotments have become the principal care of *kolkhozniki*, and that they show negligence in the accomplishment of their duties in collective farming. It has also been affirmed that these allotments are sometimes cultivated by people who are not members of *Kolkhozy*. A stop has to be put to this state of things as it leads to the development of bourgeois tendencies. The dangerous influence of *kulaki*, who have succeeded in escaping, is suspected.' As a result of this situation, Stalin, by a Decree of 15 August 1939, ordered a 'verification' of all allotments taken over by *kolkhozniki* for personal cultivation: he took the opportunity to recall the law which provided that such allotments were not to exceed ¼ or ½ a hectare. It was also declared that all allotments in isolated situations in the middle of *Kolkhoz* land were illegal and should be abolished: special attention was directed to *Kolkhozy* lying in the Ukraine and Western Russia. *Kolkhozniki*, whose individual allotments were to be abolished, were themselves to be expelled from their *Kolkhozy* and united in new *Kolkhozy* in regions where 'new land' could be found. For this purpose attention was directed to the lands beyond the Volga, in western Siberia, the Altai and the Far East. The execution of Stalin's commands is to be completed by September 1940. It is not to be anticipated that the acute conditions of 1929–34 will be repeated as a result of this new drive against the human nature of the Russian rural masses: the Communist machine has broken the strength of peasant society. At the same time, there is little doubt that the harvest of 1939–40 will not be as abundant as those of 1936–8.

The influence of the Revolution and of the Soviet régime on forestry in the South of Russia has been no less baleful than on other branches of rural industry. At the end of the nineteenth century woods covered 20 per cent of the whole area of the Ukraine; in 1928, according to the most optimistic estimates of Soviet statisticians, they did not occupy more than 7 per cent. Even in such a 'half-steppe' region as Poltava, owing to the care of the Imperial Government and of large landowners, woods had covered 10 per cent of the total area. 'Destruction of forests is one of the greatest evils because it is followed by the formation of deep ravines which drain the district of underground waters. The consequence of the formation of such ravines is that streams carry away valuable soil to the rivers and the sea. Every year thousands of hectares of good black earth are lost to the labourer and only serve to make the Dniepr and its affluents more shallow. The destruction of forests, the formation of ravines, the drying up of underground waters, threaten the future of the Ukraine with the gravest consequences.'

The Soviet Government is well aware of the dark side of its 'achievement' in the agricultural life of the South of Russia. But, as is well known, the Soviet leaders intend to effect a radical change in the balance of productive forces within the Union. Their reasons for this intention are both political and ideological: political because they realize that their dictatorship rests upon the industrial proletariat and has always aroused the antagonism of the peasants; ideological because they are the apostles of the mechanistic conception of life and, hypnotized by the material achievements of the capitalist world, they ape it in their attempt to transform it and can seek nothing more profound than the realization of Stalin's dream 'to catch up and surpass America'.

In 1913 the relation of agricultural to industrial production in Russia was 59·4 to 40·6. Under the original Five Year Plan formulated in 1928 the Soviets aimed at the attainment of a balance which should allocate 80·2 to industry and only 19·8 to agriculture. This fantastic áim was based obviously on the possibilities of bringing into exploitation the vast mineral resources which were known to lie under the soil of the Soviet Union. And all the political ruthlessness and ideological fanaticism which are so characteristic of Communist psychology—itself a manifestation of a certain state of spiritual sterility—were brought to bear to achieve ultimate objects, which on the American continent during the preceding century had been attained by more balanced, hardly less heroic, and certainly less catastrophic methods.

§ 3. INDUSTRIAL HISTORY OF THE UKRAINE

The industrial development of the Ukraine has been based on the exploitation of the coal deposits of the Donets basin and of the iron-ore and manganese fields situated west of the Dniepr. Abundant layers of coal are found along both banks of the Donets. The eastern part of the carboniferous region lies within the territory of the Don with its Cossack population. The western part, which constitutes about two-thirds of the whole region, is situated within the boundaries of Soviet Ukraine.

Whether the Donets region properly belongs to the Ukraine is a question which has never been definitely settled. Historically, the lands along the right bank of the river Donets in its northern part belonged to that 'New Ukraine' which began to be populated in the second half of the seventeenth century by settlers from Muscovy and by fugitives from Hetman's Ukraine—at that time devastated by the Turkish invasions of Ahmed Köprülü and Kara Mustafa. Subsequently, these lands were incorporated in the Government of Kharkov. The lands along the southern course of the Donets formed part of the extreme eastern angle of New Russia where settled life only really began in the eighteenth century after the Tartar Nogay Horde, which roamed over this region, had retired beyond the Volga.

In 1917 the Provisional Government, in admitting five Ukrainian Governments as the legitimate area for the exercise of 'the national and cultural influence of the Kiev Rada', excluded the Government of Kharkov for the reason that the Donets coal area lay within it. The Ukrainian language is not commonly spoken in the coal-fields, and even if the large numbers of temporary labourers who come in from the north are ignored, not more than half the population of Donbass (the Donets coal area) can boast of their Ukrainian origin. In general, this region has nothing which unites its mixed industrial population to the essentially Ukrainian rural population of adjoining regions to the west. The only real link which connects the Donets coal-fields with the industrial districts along the Dniepr and the manganese and iron-ore regions is a purely economic one.

According to both German and Soviet geological calculations, the reserves of coal in the Donets area amount to about 55 milliard tons. The deposits are largely anthracite—inferior in quality to Welsh.

Donets coal was the basis of the early industrial development of the South of Russia. Exploitation was begun in the middle of the nineteenth century; the construction of railway lines speeded up development during the seventies, and in the eighties Donets coal was already in use in the industries of the Moscow and Petersburg regions. After the discovery, about 1890, of abundant iron-ore deposits to the west of the lower Dniepr, the Donets coal industry acquired a rapidly growing importance. Between 1900 and 1913 output was increased at the rate of 17 per cent per annum. In 1913 the Ukrainian part of the coal-field delivered 23 million tons: in 1916, 29 million. During this period the Donets fields supplied all the southern industries with coal, and its contribution to northern industries became important with the construction of a new line direct from the mine area to Moscow. More than half the coal industry, before the Revolution, was financed by French capital.

For some time after the Revolution the output of the mines was relatively insignificant: during 1919 the area was the scene of desperate battles between 'Whites' and 'Reds', and later it was devastated by the raids of Makhno and other anarchic *atamany*. The famine of 1921-2 accentuated the terrible conditions. During the period of the New Economic Policy, output of coal gradually revived, and in 1929 fell little short of that of 1913. The First Five Year Plan prescribed the accelerated industrialization of the Ukrainian mineral-bearing areas. The social struggle which formed part of the 'Revolution against Peasantry' did not particularly affect the Donets, but the famine of 1932–3 had its influence there. Nevertheless, if Soviet statistics are to be credited, the Government succeeded in coping with the difficulties, and in 1934 a production of 68 million tons of coal and anthracite was claimed—representing an output in excess of that of France. Ukrainian production occupied fourth place—after U.S., Great Britain and Germany. For 1938, Soviet statistics gave a production of 74 million tons out of a total of 104½ million tons for the whole of the Soviet Union. The average annual increase in production for the last five years, 1934–9, is substantially less than that for the preceding five years, 1929–34. One of the reasons for this is stated to be the difficulty of retaining labour which was available during the period of social conflict in the countryside, but which has drifted back to the farms following improvement in the conditions in the *Kolkhozy*. Labour is very fluid in Donbass; an annual turnover of 40–50 per cent is estimated.

Soviet official information concerning the iron-ore industry of Krivoy Rog is probably more reliable than that concerning Donbass. The reserves of iron ore of high quality (40 per cent iron) are reckoned at 1100 million tons; some Ukrainian economists put these in excess of 3000 million tons. Mining in the Krivoy Rog (south-west of Ekaterinoslav and south-east of Elizavetgrad) began in the nineties and attained considerable proportions by the beginning of the present century. For the years 1913–16 average output was about 5 million tons per annum. According to Soviet statistics, output for 1938 was round 18 million tons.

Conditions for the development of metallurgical industry are extraordinarily favourable in New Russia: on one side of the Dniepr coal, and on the other iron. This is not all: along the banks of the Dniepr itself, round Nikopol and Khvochevatka, to the south of the old ground of the Zaporogian *Sech*, are rich mines of manganese, the quality of which is little inferior to that of the Georgian deposits at Chiaturi. According to the estimates of Ukrainian economists, reserves on the Dniepr amount to about 400 million tons: even if these estimates are exaggerated, there can be no doubt that the deposit is one of the most valuable in the world.

The production of the Dniepr manganese mines has risen from 260,000 tons in 1916 to over 1,000,000 tons in 1938. If the U.S.S.R. is the principal world producer, the Ukraine alone ranks before British India and South Africa (from which two latter countries it is worth recalling that Germany imported 585,000 tons in 1937).

The deposits of coal in Donbass, of iron at Krivoy Rog and of manganese round Nikopol are connected by railway lines which function probably more efficiently than any others in U.S.S.R. The juxtaposition of the mineral deposits and the metallurgical plants ensures full loads both ways. Only 18 per cent of Donets coal is exported outside the Ukraine, and only 5 per cent of the iron ore; the balance is consumed by the South Russian industries. Manganese, on the other hand, is exported abroad in large quantities.

Important metallurgical plants (70 per cent of the capital of which had been found by French and Belgian houses) existed in the South of Russia prior to the Revolution. In the 'Eastern' (Donets-Azov) group were included the following works: 'The New Russian' (station, Yuzovka, recalling the name of the Welshman Hughes); 'The Russo-Belgian' (Enakievo); 'The Kramatorsky' (Kramatorskaya); 'The Konstantinovsky' (Konstantinovskaya); 'The Donets-Yuriev' (Alchevskaya); 'The Nikopol-Mariupol'

(Mariupol); 'The Russian Providence' (near Mariupol); 'The Kerch' (near Kerch). In the 'Western' (Dniepr) group the principal works were: 'The Gdantsev' (Krivoy Rog); 'The Dniepr' (near Ekaterinoslav); 'The Alexandrovsky' (near Alexandrovsk). Almost all these works have continued to function under the Soviets; during the course of the last twenty years some have been considerably enlarged and others modernized. Some have been re-named: e.g. 'Alexandrovsky', now 'Zaporogian Steel'; 'Gdantsev', 'Krivoy Rog'; 'Russian Providence', 'Azov Steel'. These three, particularly, have become very important plants.

The Ukrainian and New Russian metallurgical industry comprises 45 blast furnaces and 118 open-hearth furnaces. In the twenty-five years between 1913 and 1938 the output of pig iron has been expanded from 3 million to nearly 8 million tons; rolled iron from 1 million to 3 million; steel from 2 to 5 million tons. Thus, the metallurgical industry of Ukraine and New Russia (excluding the rest of U.S.S.R.) ranks fourth in world production of pig iron (after U.S., Germany and Great Britain) and fifth in the production of steel and rolled iron (after U.S., Germany, Britain and France). In 1938 the Ukrainian and New Russian industries produced 55 per cent of all Russian pig iron, 35 per cent of all steel and 25 per cent of all rolled iron. Concentrated within a comparatively limited region the heavy industry of New Russia and the Ukraine constitutes the most highly developed industrial area of the Soviet Union.

The Revolutionary régime was fortunate in inheriting a wide area of industrialization which, in the immediate pre-Revolutionary period, had been expensively equipped with modern plants by West European capitalist groups. The régime cannot be considered to have achieved anything remarkable in further development, and had the capitalist system of promotion been allowed to survive it is probable that progress would have been more rapid.

The most spectacular (and widely advertised) achievement of the Soviet régime in the Ukraine has been the construction of the grandiose hydro-electric plant in the neighbourhood of the rapids of the Dniepr (Dnieprostroy). A new source of energy (about 600,000 kilowatts), equivalent to a third of the electric energy produced in the Ukraine, has been made available for industry. Dnieprostroy may, however, be considered as a somewhat redundant reinforcement of the power sources of the country which could only have been undertaken by a régime which was not hampered by considerations of productive yield on capital investment. In view of the vast deposits of coal and anthracite to hand and of the as yet unexplored reserves of lignite, the development of a new source of energy was not of urgent importance. Dnieprostroy supplies neighbouring towns and industrial plants with light and power (including the new 'Dniepr Electrical-Metallurgical Works' and the 'Dniepr Aluminium Works'), but the electrification of the railways of Soviet Ukraine has not yet been undertaken, nor does this appear necessary in view of the cheap supplies of fuel locally available.

As for machine and other mechanical works, there were in existence before 1916: 'Hartmann's Locomotive Works' at Lugansk; the more modern 'Kharkov Locomotive Works' and 'The Electro-Mechanical Works', also at Kharkov; and a series of smaller machine works (particularly for the manufacture of agricultural machinery) at Sumy, Alexandrovsk, Berdyansk, Odessa and Kiev. The Soviet Government considerably enlarged the 'Lugansk Locomotive Works', and recently machine and locomotive works have been in process of construction and subsequent enlargement at Kramatorskaya (in the Donets region). New 'Tractors' Construction Works' have been built in Kharkov. Machinery plants have been founded in Berdyansk and Cherkassy; the old Kiev and Alexandrovsk works have been enlarged; and new agricultural machinery works have been built in Elizavetgrad, Melitopol and Kherson. The shipbuilding works in Nikolaev continue to supply the Black Sea fleet as before the Revolution. There, during the last war, ships were in construction for the Imperial Navy; armour-plate being manufactured in the 'Nikopol-Mariupol Works'.

Some progress has been made in the development of a chemical industry based on the abundant supplies of coal in Donbass. There are chemical processing plants at Slavyansk and Lisichansk, and near the railway stations of Gorlovka and Konstantinovka. The industry is still in the experimental stage, but Soviet 'Plans' envisage the supply of 30 per cent of the needs of the home market.

The Soviet emphasis on the development of Ukrainian heavy industry and a parallel neglect of the possible expansion of light industries has produced a badly balanced economy in Soviet Ukraine and the country remains dependent on other and often distant parts of the Union for the satisfaction of many of the needs of the people. Political considerations which aim at establishing the complete interdependence of the various parts of the Union are at the basis of the particular direction of the Five Year Plans in the Ukraine. The emigré Ukrainian economist, V. Sadovsky, writes: 'In 1934, 69·4 per cent of industry went to the production of materials and of the tools of production, and only 34·6 per cent for general needs. In this sense the relations existing in 1913 were different: 51 per cent and 49 per cent.' It is necessary to add that Sadovsky includes in production intended 'for general use' in both periods the output of agricultural industry: i.e. sugar, spirits, flour and sunflower oil. If these figures for rural industry are excluded, those for so-called 'light industry' remain practically negligible. For example, only 3 per cent of the textiles manufactured in U.S.S.R. are derived from the Ukraine; and there is no manufacture of cloth or leather goods.

As Sadovsky justly remarks, the policy of exclusively encouraging heavy industry has resulted in the neglect of the economic interests of the western and central Ukraine. In effect, with the policy of industrializing eastern and south-eastern Ukraine, the Soviets have shown a tendency to de-industrialize the wide and rich western provinces. Here the basis of their policy is probably strategic as well as political. 'In a series of towns of right-bank Ukraine such as Zhitomir, Berdichev, Zhmerinka, Mohilev-Podolsk, Uman, Smela, signs of decadence can be observed during the period of the Five Year Plans.'

The 'Economic Plans' of the Soviet Government are subordinated to a general political policy which, as has been explained in the preceding chapter, aims at the complete fusion of the Soviet Ukraine with the rest of U.S.S.R.; and according to Communist theory political unity can only be based on economic fusion. In forcing the pace of the development of heavy industry in the south and south-east to the detriment of the light and agricultural industries of the rest of the country, the Moscow Government pursues two objectives. First, the importance of the Ukrainian national element in the Ukraine is reduced. 'The Ukrainian people are an old people of agricultural civilization and have never shown any inclination for industrial work and life in big towns. The Ukrainian prefers the country if he can earn his living there, and if it is necessary he finds work in the different branches of rural industry' (Brégy and Obolensky). According to official Soviet statistics on the nationality of workers in the Ukraine, the coal industry employs 75 per cent Russians and 25 per cent Ukrainians; the metallurgical, 73 per cent and 22 per cent respectively; the building trades 56 per cent and 37 per cent (*The National Policy of the Russian Communist Party Expressed in Figures*, p. 177). About 50 per cent only of the people in the Donets region are Ukrainians, and among the urban population of the whole of Soviet Ukraine 70 per cent are not Ukrainians. In two big towns like Odessa and Kharkov only 25 per cent of the inhabitants are Ukrainians. The same phenomenon can be observed in centres like Mariupol and Lugansk. In this wise the development of industrial centres in the Ukraine and New Russia leads to a preponderance of 'new-comers'—in fact, of that social element on whose support the Soviets could rely in a political struggle with the forces of Ukrainian nationalism.

The second political objective which the Soviet Government has pursued is the strengthening of the economic dependence of the Ukraine on the rest of the Union. 'The Soviet Government systematically and intentionally binds Southern industry with strong bonds to the industries of other parts of the Union. This conclusion is imposed by a study of the categories of goods which are transported by the Soviet railways in a "meridial" direction. A considerable part of rail transport in Soviet Ukraine is engaged on the carriage of the half-finished products of industrial works by the most complicated and lengthy routes, e.g. from the banks of the Dniepr to the Urals or from the Moscow district to the Donets region and back. If a comparison is made of goods transported from south to north and from north to south, it will be seen that the machine works of the Ukraine do not "finish" their products, but that these are sent for the final processes to different and sometimes distant parts of the U.S.S.R. The motor industry, in particular, strongly binds the Central Russian region, South Russia, the Volga region and the Urals. Tractors and different agricultural machines can only be "finished" in Ukraine after being sent to receive certain parts from the north or north-east. The Soviet Government evidently is ready to make heavy sacrifices in finance and efficiency in order to attain its political ends which are to bind with strong economic ties all the different parts of the Union' (V. Levitsky).

Under such conditions, therefore, it is not possible to speak of 'Ukrainian economy' as an independent whole. Partly through natural causes and partly as a result of the political policy of the Soviet Government, the interdependence of the Ukraine and Great Russia has become even more definite than it was twenty years ago. The development of heavy industry, which has far exceeded the needs of the Ukrainian land itself, and the decline of agriculture has led to a strengthening of the 'meridial' tie (while at the same time Moscow, by somewhat similar measures, is strengthening the 'latitudinal' tie with the Urals, Siberia and Central Asia and is even extending it in this last direction into the outlying provinces of the former Chinese Empire).

The possibility of a wholly independent 'Greater Ukraine' (including present Soviet Ukraine with the additions of eastern Galicia (now incorporated in Soviet Ukraine), Bukovina and Carpathian Rus, may certainly be considered (as Ukrainians sometimes do) from the angle of the 'economic potentialities' of the country regarded as a unit separate from Great Russia. Neither over-populated Galicia nor the poverty-stricken Carpathian valleys could contribute to increase the sum of the wealth of a 'Greater Ukraine'. (The oil-fields of Kolomiya and Stanislavov, with their modest production of 500,000 tons a year, are not an important factor.) But the addition to the population of Soviet Ukraine (34 millions) of the 10 million poor peasants of the outlying provinces should not strain the resources of the Dniepr lands, and the new human material should, in fact, provide increased wealth.

The most remarkable feature of Ukrainian 'economic potentialities' is the fortunate balance between agricultural and industrial riches. Such a fortunate balance cannot be found in any country in Europe except France. The population of 'Greater Ukraine' rather exceeds that of France, as does the total area (588,000 sq. km. in Ukraine against 563,000 sq. km. in France). The average density of population (70.6 inhabitants per sq. km.) is also about the same as in France. 'Economic potentialities' are curiously comparable. The capacity of the Ukrainian harvest is about 200 million quintals (although this is not attained under the Soviet system of agriculture), double that of France which is not quite self-sufficient, but the French output of coal is about 55–60 million tons; the Ukrainian about 70 million. France produces 7–10 million tons of pig iron and from 8–10 million tons of steel. The corresponding figures for the Ukraine are 8 million tons of pig iron and 5 million tons of steel.

Ukrainian patriots who dream of a wholly independent 'Greater Ukraine' claim that the 'economic potentialities' of their country prove that this conception is not utopian. And in that sense, of course, they are right. 'Economic potentialities', in relation to the general complex of conditions which are required by the independent life of a country, are, however, to borrow an expression from mathematics, 'necessary' but not 'sufficient'. These 'economic potentialities' may promise a happy balance between agriculture and industry, but it is only in theory that the harmonious development of economic life remains possible, in practice it can encounter different obstacles in the political, social and cultural conditions which are determined by the course of history.

Ukrainian nationalists claim, for instance, that, should an independent 'Greater Ukraine' become established, life would arrange itself in the natural course of things and that light industries and crafts would arise to satisfy all the immediate needs of the population. Here, however, lies a far more difficult problem than would appear at first sight. Neither the Soviet nor the Imperial Governments can be held to have been primarily responsible for the backwardness of craftsmanship in the Ukraine nor of those 'light industries' which may be said to have taken the place of the crafts in the modern world. Crafts are created as a result of a long historical process which marches with the cultural development of a country. In the Ukraine a modern capitalist heavy industry was superimposed upon the structure of a rather backward rural economy in the latter half of the nineteenth century. By contrast France is the living embodiment of cultural processes which have produced a harmonious economic life where agriculture and both 'heavy' and 'light' industries are blended in such happy combination and where the work of craftsmen has reached perfection. But then France has a long independent historical past behind her, the political and social experiences of a nation of genius and great achievements in all the domains which challenge the human mind and human activities.

In this wise even 'the economic problem' of 'Greater Ukraine' is not limited by simple figures concerning her 'economic potentialities'. Therefore 'the political problem' which the present and future of the Ukraine represents becomes even more complex. With all the assets of her 'economic potentialities', with all the positive features which can be observed in her economic life even under present conditions, the Ukraine is still very far, as regards herself and other countries concerned, from a satisfactory solution of 'the political problem' of her form in the present and the future. The 'Ukrainian problem' is, perhaps, one of the chief reasons for the absence of balance in continental Europe.

BIBLIOGRAPHICAL NOTES AND ADDITIONS
TO CHAPTER VII

Sources for the Economic History of S.S.R. Ukraine

Any attempt to acquire an objective view of the course of economic life in the Soviet Union calls for an attentive, prudent and critical survey of the vast material published on the subject in Soviet periodicals during the past two decades. A work of this kind is beyond the resources of a single student and requires the corporate study of whole institutions, as for instance: the International Agricultural Institute in Rome; the East European Institute in Breslau (under the direction of Professor Auhagen); the Ukrainian Academy of Podebrady (Czechoslovakia); the Economic Cabinet of Professor Prokopovich in Prague; the Society for the Study of Modern Russia in Paris; the Bureau for Researches on Russia in Birmingham.

Particularly valuable is the material collated during recent years by Professor Prokopovich's Cabinet (unfortunately closed in 1938) and by the Birmingham Bureau of Professor Konovalov (which terminated its activities in 1935). The Paris Society has published the very instructive and impartial works of Professor Markov: *Krisis Selskago Khozyaystva v S.S.S.R.* (The Crisis in Agriculture in U.S.S.R.), Paris, 1933; *Sotsialisticheskoe Khozyaystvo v S.S.S.R.*; 1, *Promyshlennost*, 2, *Selskoe Khozyaystvo* (Socialist Economics in U.S.S.R.; 1, Industry, 2, Agriculture), Paris, 1937-8.

The principal Soviet publications on which the researches of the above institutions are based are:

Mirovoe Khozyaystvo i Mirovaya Politika (World Economy and World Policy).

Sotsialisticheskaya Rekonstruktsia Selskago Khozyaystva (Socialist Reconstruction of Rural Economy).

Sotsialisticheskoe Zemledelie (Socialist Agriculture).

Za Industrializatsiu (Towards Industrialization).

Ekonomicheskaya Zhisn (Economic Life).

Plan (The Plan).

Sotsialisticheskoe Stroitelstvo (Socialist Building-up, Yearbook).

Planovoe Khozyaystvo (Planned Economy).

Khozyaystvenniya Problemy (Economic Problems).

Sotsialisticheski Transport (Socialist Transport).

Significant information may be extracted from the files of the leading daily papers in U.S.S.R.: *Izvestia* and *Pravda*. The provincial dailies published in the Ukraine contain many items of interest for the study of conditions in that Republic: *Sovetskaya Ukraina*; *Visty* (News); *Proletariy* (Proletarian); and others.

The Ukrainian emigration in Poland and Czechoslovakia has been responsible for the publication of a number of valuable works:

Ukrayinska Zahalna Entsiklopedia (Ukrainian General Encyclopaedia), vols. I-III, Lvov, 1935.

Atlas Ukrayiny (with statistical material), Lvov, 1938.

Glovinsky-Matsievich-Sadovsky, *Suchasni Problemy Ekonomyky Ukrayiny* (Present Problems of the Economics of the Ukraine), Lvov, 1930.

Ukrayinsky Statistychny Yezhehodnyk (Ukrainian Statistical Yearbook), Warsaw, 1936-7.

The following books, published recently, are also important:

Hoover, Calvin B. *La Vie Économique de la Russie Soviétique*, Paris, 1934.

Brutzkus, Prof. Boris. *U.R.S.S.—Terrain d'Expériences Économiques*, Paris, 1937.

Basily, N. de. *Russia under Soviet Rule*, London, 1938.

Brégy, P. and Obolensky, S. Prince. *L'Ukraine—Terre Russe*, Paris, 1939.

Mikhailov, N. *La Nouvelle Géographie de l'U.R.S.S.*, Paris, 1937.

Mercier, Ernest. *U.R.S.S. Reflexions*, Paris, 1936.

Haudan. *Das Motorisierungs-potenzial der Soviet Union*, Hamburg, 1937.

The following Soviet books, in addition to the periodical publications, may also be consulted:

Mikhailov, I. *Evolutsia Russkago Transporta* (The Evolution of Russian Transport), Leningrad, 1925.

Ekonomicheskoe Polozhenie Sovetskago Soyuza (The Economic Situation of the Soviet Union), published by the Moscow Institute for Economics, Moscow, 1926.

Pyatiletni Plan razvitiya Narodnago Khozyaystva v S.S.S.R. (1928). Five Year Plan for developing the National Economy, I, II, Moscow, 1930.

Resultaty Vypolneniya pervago pyatiletnyago Plana (Results of the Execution of the First Five Year Plan), Moscow, 1933.

S.S.S.R. v Tsifrakh (The U.S.S.R. in Figures), Moscow, 1935.

Ekonomicheskaya Geografiya S.S.S.R. (The Economic Geography of the U.S.S.R.), published by the Communist Academy, Moscow, 1935.

U.S.S.R. Handbook, London, 1936.

Plan Narodnago Khozyaystva na 1936 god (Plan of National Economy for 1936), Moscow, 1936.

For economic conditions in Galicia see 'Galicia' in *Bolshaya Sovetskaya Entsiklopedia* (The Great Soviet Encyclopaedia); *L'Annuaire Statistique de la Pologne*, Warsaw, 1935 and after.

Soviet Statistics

No less a person than the President of the Central Executive Committee of the Communist·Party, Orzhonikidze, during the Moscow Regional Congress of the Party in 1929, said: 'It would seem that no one should be more trustworthy than persons employed in statistical work, conscientiously adding up their figures—and that is all. But no! These people with us have become a political factor and are well aware of it.' Orzhonikidze further affirmed that: 'The Statistical Bureau makes a terrible muddle of all its materials.' In 1930 Syrtsov, who was then President of the Council of Peoples' Commissars, found that: 'The pace of production in Soviet statistics is ordered beforehand and is not a result of calculation' (*Ekonomicheskaya Zhisn*, 2/18 December, 1930).

Dr Albrecht Kaysenbrecht is of opinion that: 'Among the staff of the statistical workers are very experienced and scientifically well-qualified persons. The whole misfortune consists in the fact that Soviet statistics are the slave of the Government and are dominated by purely political considerations' (*Die Entwicklung der Agrärfrage in Soviet Russland*, Schmöllers Jahrbuch, 1926). In 1927 Trotsky expressed the opinion that intentionally faked statistics had begun to alter the whole outlook on the actual situation. 'The figures of Soviet statistics are very doubtful' is the view of Professor Auhagen (*Ost-Europa*, Breslau, June, 1931).

As for agriculture, there is no doubt that the reports which come in every five days during the spring sowing season 'according to law' are frequently faked. 'The sowing area is often reckoned according to the quantity of seed which has been given out for this purpose without any assurance as to whether it has been properly used. For instance, one of the Ukrainian *Kolkhozy* reported that it had accomplished 50 per cent of the Sowing Plan when in reality it had only accomplished 2 per cent of it' (*Pravda*, 14 June, 1932). The harvest is continually assessed 'by the look of it in the fields' before it has been gathered in. Over a series of years the harvest has been between 20 and 30 per cent less than reports showed it to be.

The comparisons between Soviet actuality and pre-Revolutionary conditions are often unconvincing because Soviet statistics do not take quality into consideration. For instance, according to Soviet statistics, the output of peat has risen by 30 per cent. In reality, only the percentage of moisture retained in the peat accepted for delivery has risen.

In the *Times* article on 'The Plight of the Plan' (29 January, 1938) this question of quantity being the chief concern, irrespective of quality, in all the most important branches of industry in Soviet Ukraine, is discussed: 'The coal-mines show impressive figures but quantity is the chief concern. This has risen threefold or fourfold in the last decades, but recent disclosures indicate that the calorific value of the coal leaving Soviet mines is less even than that of the output in old Russia. The production of iron ore has gone up at a similar rate, but the final result is similar.' Cf. Makcheef, Th. (Maksheev), 'Heavy Industry in the Soviet Union,' *Contemporary Russia*, II, 2, London, 1938.

The Territory of Soviet Ukraine

Out of the 588,000 sq. km. claimed for 'Greater Ukraine', Soviet Ukraine occupied (before the incorporation of Eastern Galicia in September 1939) 452,000. This area represents 2·1 per cent of the whole extent of the U.S.S.R. Soviet Ukraine occupies the territory of eight former Governments of the Empire: Kharkov, Chernigov (less five northern districts), Poltava, Ekaterinoslav (now renamed Dniepropetrovsk), Kherson, Podolia, Volhynia (excluding, until September 1939, the western districts annexed to Poland in 1921), Kiev. Three northern districts of the former Government of Tauris (Berdyansk, Melitopol, Dnieprovsk) are also included. The Putivl district of the former Kursk Government as well as some villages of the former Orel Government are also deemed to form part of the Ukraine.

In 1924 an 'Autonomous Moldavian Soviet Socialist Republic' was formed out of the Podolian districts of Balta and Tulchin along the Dniestr in order to give a semblance of self-government to the Roumanian-speaking villages of that region. The area of A.S.S.R. Moldavia is 8288 sq. km. and the population 572,000. The capital is located at Tiraspol.

The capital of the Ukrainian S.S.R. until 1934 was Kharkov; it is now Kiev.

In 1925 the administrative divisions of the area occupied by the Republic were reorganized into 40 Districts, 662 Regions, and 10,733 village and town Soviets. In 1929 the Districts were abolished out of economy and 7 *Oblasti* (Provinces) were established, roughly equivalent in size to the former Governments. These are: Vinnitsa (formerly Podolia), Kiev, Dniepropetrovsk, Odessa, Kharkov, Chernigov and Donets. Seven 'National Minority' Regions have been set up, and also 366 'National Minority' village Soviets in localities where non-Ukrainian elements predominate—Great Russians, White Russians, Greeks, Germans, Moldavians, Jews. The largest towns of Soviet Ukraine are Kiev (625,000), Kharkov (650,000), Odessa (550,000), Dniepropetrovsk (former Ekaterinoslav, 325,000). Lvov, in 'Greater Ukraine', recently annexed to Soviet Ukraine, has 375,000 inhabitants. It is characteristic of current economic trends that the population has grown in Kharkov and decreased in Odessa (700,000 in 1916). Industrial centres have grown rapidly: Lugansk, Mariupol, Zaporozhie (formerly Alexandrovsk) have each of them over 100,000 inhabitants; Nikolaev and Kherson have each about 100,000. There are no large towns in Central and Western Ukraine: the most important of them, Vinnitsa and Poltava, have not more than 80,000 inhabitants each. Now we have Czernowitz (Chernovtsy), Kishinev and Jassy, each about 120,000.

The Population of the Ukrainian Soviet Republic

The Census of 1 January 1933 gave the population of the Ukrainian S.S.R. as 31,901,000 persons. The figures for the more recent Census of 1937 are not sufficiently clear. (It is well known that the Government was displeased at the incompetent way in which this latter Census was carried out, and Stalin himself has expressed his dissatisfaction.) At any rate it is not denied that the increase of population in the Ukraine during the five years 1933–7 was at a rate lower than that for the whole Union calculated (with obvious exaggeration) at 16 per cent. The rate of increase in the Ukraine was considerably lower than in many of the eastern parts of the Union, notably Turkestan and the Kirghiz steppe—for which the obviously fantastic figures of 30 per cent and even 40 per cent were given. For the Ukraine the official increase was 6·6 per cent. On the basis of the figures for 1933, therefore, the population, allowing for increase, amounts to about 34,000,000 for 1938–9.

On the same territory about 30,000,000 people lived in 1917. In view of the fact that the normal increase in Russia before the Revolution was reckoned at 1·5 per cent p.a. and in some localities at 2 per cent p.a., the population of the Ukraine, under the social and political conditions existing under the Imperial régime, should have reached about 40,000,000 by the present day, even had there been a continuance of the movement of migration to Asiatic Russia which marked the turn of the century.

The history of the growth of population in the Ukraine during the last twenty years is of course far more complex than the bare figures would indicate. There was a terrible mortality, owing first to the Revolution and Civil War, and secondly to the two periods of famine and to the general deterioration in social and sanitary conditions. Again, parallel to a considerable migration of the peasantry, particularly during the famine periods, there was a constant flow of industrial workers from the north as a result of the Economic Plans. It is difficult therefore to avoid the following conclusions: that the growth of population during the two decades since the Revolution has been abnormally slow, but at the same time the change in the composition of the population has been rapid. The Ukrainians were continually disappearing or leaving their homeland while new elements were replacing them, mostly 'new-comers' from Central and Northern Russia.

It is important to ascertain the number of Ukrainians who remain in the territory of S.S.R. Ukraine. According to Soviet statistics the urban population, amounting to 8,000,000, numbers only 30 per cent of Ukrainians. Among the rural population Ukrainians are in a majority, though they are not everywhere equally distributed: in some regions there are over 80 per cent; in others (like Odessa) 60 per cent; in the Donets rural areas a little over 50 per cent. In 1926, during the period of 'ukrainization' encouraged by the Government, 24,000,000 out of 30,000,000 registered as Ukrainians, but even 15 per cent of these 'native' Ukrainians gave their mother tongue as Russian. Since that date catastrophes have befallen the rural folk of the Ukraine: about 3,000,000 are reckoned to have perished during the famine of the early thirties, and another 2,000,000 certainly have migrated as a result of conditions which they found intolerable. These losses have not been wholly replaced by natural increase, and there is every reason to think that the number of 'native' Ukrainians in the rural population of the Republic has decreased since 1930 by at least 4,000,000. If at that time the number of persons speaking Ukrainian and considering themselves to be Ukrainians amounted to 20,000,000, there can scarcely be more than 16,000,000 peasants left now. If to these are added the number of Ukrainians living in the towns, the total probably amounts to about 18,000,000. In other words, the Ukrainian population of Soviet Ukraine (before the incorporation of Eastern Galicia) amounted to little more than half of the total population.

This figure is eloquent: the Soviet Government has gone a long way to achieve the result towards which its policy was directed, and in the Ukrainian S.S.R. Ukrainians can no longer be considered to be in a great majority. It follows therefore that nearly half the population (16,000,000 to 17,000,000) are not Ukrainians. Among these alien elements a little less than 2,000,000 are Jews; about 1,000,000 are Moldavians; another million belong to different nationalities—White Russians, Poles, Greeks, Germans. The remaining 12,000,000 to 13,000,000 consist either of people born in the Ukraine who do not wish to consider themselves Ukrainians or of 'new-comers' from other parts of the Union. The number of these 'new-comers' must amount to 8,000,000 to 9,000,000.

It is notable that in the last years (since 1930) the Government has used every means to encourage the settlement of these 'new-comers' not only in the industrial areas but also in the purely rural districts. It is obvious that Moscow does not desire vast rural areas with an entirely homogeneous Ukrainian population. The Government prefers groups of *Kolkhozy* on Ukrainian territory to be constituted on the mosaic principle. Each year, from all the Military Districts of the Soviet Union, soldiers who have finished their military service and who have sent in petitions that on account of lack of land they do not wish to return to their original homes are drafted to the new Red Army *Kolkhozy*. These *Kolkhozy*, recruited from the variety of nationalities throughout the Union, are being scattered over some of the best land of the Ukrainian countryside. In some regions there are as many as ten of these military collectivized farms. Reference has already been made to the measures taken by the Government against the bourgeois *kolkhozniki* during the summer of 1939. A new 'movement' of the population is in view in

U.S.S.R., and there is no doubt that one of the results will be a further weakening of Ukrainian elements where the Government considers them to be still too strong

Secondary Branches of Ukrainian Agriculture

In addition to wheat, *rye*, *barley*, *oat* and *maize* crops are important. *Millet* is also grown and forms the base of the broth (*psheno*) which is a favourite dish in the South of Russia (in the North this broth or porridge is made from buck-wheat).

Clover and *lucerne* are comparatively little cultivated, and almost exclusively in right-bank Ukraine and Galicia.

About a million hectares are under *potatoes* in right-bank Ukraine; the bulk of the crop goes to the alcohol distilleries.

Sunflower-seed is important in the production of oil; *hemp* and small quantities of *linseed* and *mustard-seed* are produced for the same purpose.

The cultivation of *hops* was always traditional in Volhynia; in pre-Revolutionary days half of the hop production of the Empire came from Volhynia and right-bank Ukraine. In late years production has greatly declined.

Tobacco, the cultivation of which was introduced by Greek immigrants in the eighteenth century, is a speciality of the districts of Nezhin and Romen. The quality is not good and the cultivation of tobacco has no future in the Ukraine.

Particularly in Podolia and the region of Uman, *kolkhozniki* take great interest in horticulture; about 200,000 hectares are under orchards. On many *Kolkhozy* the *kolkhozniki* occupy themselves on the private cultivation of *tomatoes*, and the Government has set up canning plants in order to encourage this branch of production.

The *vine* grows well on the banks of the Dniepr and the southern Bug, in the neighbourhood of Berdyansk and Odessa, and along the Dniestr. But wine production has not been developed on the scale which it has attained in Bessarabia and the Crimea.

The Soviet Government favours agricultural experiments, and some *Kolkhozy* in the South have tried to cultivate *rice*—so far with little success.

An experiment on a large scale was made in the cultivation of *cotton*. 190,000 hectares between the mouth of the Dniepr and Perekop were reserved, but it is not likely that cotton cultivation in the Ukraine will prove the success which it has in the more suitable climates of Azerbaijan and Turkestan.

Secondary Mineral Resources in the Ukraine

Reserves of different qualities of *lignite* are distributed over many parts of the Ukraine. In view of the abundance of other resources of calorific power, exploitation has not been greatly developed, but output of lignite in the region of Elizavetgrad attains 300,000 tons a year.

A million tons of *peat* is cut annually in Ukraine—about 10 per cent of the output of U.S.S.R.

Bauxites in the Dniepr region are utilized for the Aluminium Works near Dnieprostroy.

Mercury is mined near Nikitovka Junction in Donbass.

Graphite deposits in the vicinity of Uman have recently been prospected.

There are important deposits of *salt* in north-east Donbass.

Search has been made for *copper, tin* and *petroleum*. Indications of petroleum deposits have been discovered in the region of Poltava and on the shores of the Azov Sea. In different places deposits of high quality *clay (kaolin)* are found.

'The Mystery' of Soviet Production

A Russian mining engineer has contributed this note: 'It is quite impossible to ascertain where and how the enormous quantities of calorifics and metals which figure in Soviet statistics disappear, when one takes into consideration the absence of these products in the every-day life of the population. It is quite a usual occurrence that the simplest tools, common nails, sheet iron, are found to be unobtainable in U.S.S.R. Sometimes old roofs are torn off houses in order to cover new buildings....Further, the greatest consumer of iron, railway construction, so active before the Revolution, is practically non-existent in these days. During the Five Year Plan only 5000 km. of railway lines were laid; and in general, under the Soviet régime, railway lines begun before and during the war have been left uncompleted.

'Soviet officials have never been able to give a satisfactory explanation of what happens to the metals produced in U.S.S.R. In conversations with foreigners they speak of "military needs", but these do not explain in full the destination of the vast alleged production, nor does the consumption in tractor and motor factories, nor the building which has been proceeding in expanding industrial towns like Lugansk, Zaporozhie and Kharkov. There has also been great construction work undertaken in the Moscow area, but no exact statistics for the consumption of metals in the building trades have been forthcoming which can adequately explain the use made of the vast output alleged to have been mined.'

Th. Makcheeff (*op. cit.*) thinks that in the Soviet statistics of output in heavy industry is included a large proportion of "shoddy" products. The 1913 figures excluded goods not up to standard; for the metallurgical factories were private concerns and not consumers as well: shoddy products were accordingly not taken into account. The Soviet Government being at once consumer and producer puts all its shoddy products into circulation, and these, according to the Soviet press, amount to 90°/₀ and are referred to as "Second Quality Products."

CHAPTER VIII

POSTSCRIPT: UKRAINE AND EUROPE, 1939–40

A STUDY of the history of the Ukraine has, it is hoped, made clear the importance of this area in relation to the history of that half of Europe which lies between the Vistula and the Urals. At the same time the relation of the history of all Eastern Europe to the West—to Atlantic and Mediterranean Europe—has been examined; and the conclusion has been emphasized that West European history can only really be understood when considered against the background of the Great Eurasian Plain.

European civilization was originally Mediterranean and not Continental: it was based on the islands and peninsulas of the Middle Sea and expanded with difficulty to its natural desert marches in Africa, to the Euphrates in Asia and in the north to its fluvial frontiers along the Rhine and the Danube. We may hope that once again the armies of Britain and a resurgent France will re-establish these lines as did the Roman Legions after the disasters that befell the arms of Crassus and of Varus.

There have been contractions and expansions and shifts of the centres of power within the world of Mediterranean civilization. The failure of the Italo-Roman stock to sustain the imperial leadership during the third and fourth centuries A.D. was followed by the phenomenon of an Arabo-Mediterranean Empire which stretched from the Atlantic to the Indian Ocean and from the Red Sea to the Caspian: Mediterranean civilization thus expanded from a basis on the Middle Sea over an oceanic background, and the Franco-British dominion of the twentieth century was anticipated by a thousand years. The neo-Roman Empire reconstituted by Justinian, drawing its strength from the highland zone between the Danube and the Euphrates, failed to keep the hegemony of the Mediterranean world from passing to the Arabs. The emphasis shifted westward, where Charlemagne, a German ruling Gallo-Romans, designed at once to revive empire in Italy and the Mediterranean and to conquer the European hinterland. The great Rhineland king—the barbarian champion of young Christendom—began where the Romans had halted and carried the Sword of Christ to the Elbe and the Baltic. The Carolingian Empire was essentially Mediterranean and West European as was the Holy Roman Empire of the German Nation which followed: it thrust down the barbarian hordes of the Hunnic and Avaric nomad empires and beat Slav and Finn and Turkic tribes into German-speaking Christians. The epic period of the Crusades was born of the Carolingian dawn: to the South and East the Mediterranean world was half won back from the Arabs—who were of the old civilization so infinitely more "Mediterranean" than Latin-Norman Christendom: to the North and East the Teutonic Crusaders pressed on into the wastes of the Great Eurasian Plain.

The counter-stroke from the steppes between the eleventh and thirteenth centuries was much more formidable than the earlier Hunnic and Avaric invasions had been. The Turks who beat down Arabian Islam and overran the eastern kingdoms of the Mediterranean had acquired the military and administrative talents of their victims: in the same way the Mongols who came later had been apt pupils of the Chinese. The Mongol and later Ottoman states were the most advanced of their day.

The capture of Constantinople and the conquest of Syria and Egypt by the Ottoman Turks—which events virtually closed the Black and Red Seas to the trading peoples of the Western Mediterranean—occurred during the very decades when the discovery of the American and African sea roads was giving a new oceanic background to the life of Western Europe. With the occupation of large regions of Africa and the Americas during the course of the sixteenth century, "Mediterranean" civilization became definitely West European and "Atlantic" in character. At the same time with the closing of the Black Sea by the Turks and the final repulse of the German Orders from the shores of the Eastern Baltic, the Great Eurasian Plain became more isolated from the influences of 'Mediterranean' and 'Western' civilization, while the influences of 'East Christian' or Byzantine civilization had been almost entirely eliminated.

From the middle of the fifteenth century Muscovy began to emerge as the latest and greatest expression of steppeland ('Eurasian') power. In the Muscovite state and in the political genius of the Muscovites were combined the imperial traditions of the old Byzantine civilization with the military qualities (and, as important, *lack* of cultural weaknesses) of the Asiatic nomads. In the way of Muscovite expansion lay the feudal oligarchy of Poland (representing a transplanting of the already outmoded institutions of medieval Christendom on to Slav soil) and the Protestant militarism of Sweden (which held promise of a new Varangian hegemony over the Slavs of the Great Eurasian Plain). To the South, controlling the mouths of the great Pontic rivers, was the neo-Byzantine

Ottoman Empire. The Balto-Swedish Empire, *Rzecz Pospolita* and the Ottoman Empire formed a belt of states which separated the Germanic and Muscovite power centres. From the times at least of Ivan IV and Rudolf II there was a broad community of interest between the Muscovite and Germano-Habsburg powers. French statesmen of the Valois period appreciated the ultimate dangers, and in the days when France was coming to represent the principal focus of power in Western civilization the considered policy of French statesmen was to support Sweden, Poland and Turkey in Eastern Europe.

The great period of French power in the seventeenth century, the florescence of the Swedish and Polish Vasas and the revival of Ottoman power under the Köprülü viziers—all these phenomena had their origin in the check to Muscovite and Germanic expansion due to the Time of Troubles and the Thirty Years' War.

In the following century the consolidation of Germanic power under Frederick the Great and of Russian power under Catherine brought about the fall of *Rzecz Pospolita* and foreshadowed the end of the Ottoman Empire. The elimination of the states of the meridial belt—Sweden, Poland, Turkey—made inevitable also an ultimate struggle between the Germanic and Muscovite powers for mastery over all the lands between the Baltic and the Bosporus.

Prussia in the eighteenth century was a new phenomenon—a national state within the Holy Roman Empire with peculiar pretensions to modernity. With its submerged population of Finnic and Slavic serfs east of the Elbe, and its materialistic bias in current state philosophy, it had little of the old Germany about it. It was a new reality, ruthless and not a little sinister—born of all the stony sterility of the frigid Baltic wastelands. The historical function of the Prussian state was to force Western civilization, Catholic, oecumenical, Gallo-Italic and old Germanic, back across the Rhine and the Alps and to impose a new Balto-Prussian *ethos* over the plains between the Rhine and the Vistula.

Russia, again, as it arose before the uneasy eyes of our forefathers in the eighteenth century, had little of the European character of the medieval Varangian states of the Great Eurasian Plain. Novgorod and Pskov were mercantile oligarchies which might have evolved into something between the Hansa city-states and the Scandinavian kingdoms. Kiev had the potentialities of a more civilized Poland or Hungary—with a Byzantine instead of a Latin over-culture. But Muscovite Russia was in many respects a projection into the eighteenth century and into Eastern Europe of the nomad Turko-Mongolic Empires of an earlier epoch.

The *Grand Monarque* conceptions of the contemporary West gave a semblance of modernity to a structure which was essentially Asiatic. To the 'Phanariote' and 'Janissary' elements corresponded the Balt and Jacobite and other foreign adventurers who flocked to the service of the Romanov monarchs; and the two great waves of conquest under Peter I and Catherine II at once subjected large European populations to Muscovite rule and introduced the peruked favourites of German-born Empresses into the councils of Europe. The parallel may be taken further between the Muscovite and Ottoman societies. The Liberal elements in Russia during the nineteenth century were no more successful against the 'asiatism' of the Muscovite bureaucracy than were their Turkish prototypes in the Ottoman Empire. Both state-structures, the Muscovite and the Ottoman, were used by the rival capitalisms of Western Europe, first in the phase of Britain *versus* France, later in the phase of the two Western Powers *versus* the Germanic Powers. Both state-structures became involved in the World War, and while Pan-slavism served the purposes of London and Paris, Pan-Islamism and Pan-Turanism were hitched to the policies of Berlin and Vienna.

The Prussian national state founded by Frederick the Great and expanded into a Germanic national state under his successors down to Adolf Hitler must be contrasted with the 'state of nationalities' which was the Russian Empire. The Prussian state was a late copy of the French national state of the Louis. But in the nineteenth century, the French national state, as the result of the acquisition of vast transmarine possessions, and of the interplay of liberal and non-national influences in French politics, was becoming transformed into an oecumenical empire. At its best, too, French political culture stood for something extra-national, if not inter-national. No gross pretensions to racial divinity sullied the grace and enlightenment of a culture which was free for all the world to take. The French political culture, like the British with which it ran more and more parallel during the period following the Four Years' War of 1914–18 (probably because the two derive from the oldest traditions of the Roman Mediterranean and the 'Atlantic' West), had qualities which have adapted it to the needs of the world. Both the British and French political cultures, with all their faults and differences, give expression to the spirit and feeling of the modern West—as the Greek and Roman synthesis declared the genius of the varied populations of the Mediterranean world. The German conception of the national state, already a belated conception in the history of ideas, is irreconcilable with the spiritual and material needs of modern Europe.

As contrasted with the German national state, the Russian 'state of nationalities' represented also an antiquated conception comparable to the contemporary Habsburg and Ottoman 'states of nationalities'. All the European national movements of the nineteenth-twentieth centuries were mutinies against the conception of the 'state of nationalities'. The consolidation, with Soviet Moscow as a power centre, of the bulk of the territories which formerly comprised the Romanov Empire, was only achieved after a grim struggle with the many national groups who were finally coerced into remaining within the Soviet Union. But Lenin, like Napoleon before him, like the Entente war-statesmen contemporary with him, and like Hitler after him, was quick to harness the forces of nationalism in the interest of his particular brand of power politics. The right of self-determination of the national minorities within the former Russian Empire was cynically enough proclaimed at a moment when the Red armies were everywhere engaged in the bloody repression of national movements. At Baku, in 1922, a Congress of the Peoples of the East was convened. Social Revolution and Nationalism were combined in China, in India and the East Indies to further the policies of the new group of Asiatic conquerors who had established themselves in the centre of the Great Eurasian Plain and who called themselves alternately the Russian Government and the Communist International (giving expression thus to a typical Asiatic manifestation of the combination of the kingly and the priestly functions). With Caucasian and Jewish adventurers substituted for the Baltic German bureaucrats and Europeanized noblemen of the Petersburg Court, the Soviet Union emerged rather clearly as the successor of earlier Eurasian steppeland powers. The wig of a Potemkin could no longer conceal the skull of a Lenin. And the all-conquering and all-destroying nomadism of the Eurasian soul began to dream new dreams of world dominion in the decades which followed the Revolution 'against Europe'. Indeed the fire that had burned in Attila and Chingiz lit the devoted evangelism of Lenin and the doomed Caesarism of Tukhachevski.

It is a tragic fact in human affairs that political thought is generally half a century or more behind events, and that active political thought is directed almost always by interpretations of history which are themselves already outmoded. Thus while conceptions derived from the Ludovican national state influenced German statesmanship right down to the Four Years' War, the leaders of the nations at Versailles were themselves under the influence of those 'liberal' conceptions of revolutionary nationalism which reached their maximum expression in 1848.

Few Polish historians will deny that 'the Ukrainian problem' proved fatal to the old Polish state. Yet the Polish politicians at Versailles were infatuated by the tradition of the Polish revolutionaries of the preceding century who had been the prophets always of a resurrection of *Rzecz Pospolita*. After the Russian War of 1920, the frontiers originally conceded to Poland by the Great Powers were extended to include territories inhabited by nearly fifteen million Russians and Ukrainians. The historic frontiers of the old *Rzecz Pospolita* were by no means restored, but the Poles found themselves in possession of wide lands which were barren and over-populated, and in which they were confronted with the necessity of imposing the Polish conception of the national state by force. The Polish nationalists had in fact constructed another 'state of nationalities', and the ageing Marshal Pilsudski, far from content, did not abandon ideas which envisaged the inclusion of Lithuania and at least right-bank Ukraine within reborn *Rzecz Pospolita*. An effective federal association of the Baltic states with Poland, and a close alliance between such an association and the succession states in the Danube valley could alone have stabilized the congeries of independencies whose territories intervened between Germany and the Soviet Union. But the infatuation of the Poles with the conception of a revived *Rzecz Pospolita* was only equalled, to the south of the Carpathians, by the sterile dogmatism of the Liberal leaders of the Czech state—another 'national state' which had become a 'state of nationalities'—who proved ideologically incapable of coming to a compromise with the Catholic and Conservative elements in Austria and in Hungary. It was obvious, since no Slav power showed the capacity to constitute a focus in Eastern Europe for the consolidation and ultimate federation of the smaller states, that in time a renascent Germany would appear either as a dominant power or as a rival to Russia for the old hegemony between the Baltic and the Black Sea.

After Versailles Germany had not only lost weight as a national state within the European comity, but the Germans had lost also all possibility of filling an imperial role as the protector of the Austro-Hungarian 'state of nationalities'. Those different groups in Germany who, even before the rise of Adolf Hitler, had been looking for the revival of an imperial policy in Eastern and South-Eastern Europe, were fully conscious that since Austria-Hungary had ceased to exist, it had become necessary to seek some new power which might act as the 'auxiliary' of the German *Drang nach Osten*. No one expressed these notions more clearly than Adolf Hitler in *Mein Kampf*. Like the revolutionaries of 1848, and their successor Bismarck,

Hitler looked on the German state as a national and even 'racial' state and excluded the possibility of transforming the Reich into an Empire or 'state of nationalities'. At the same time it was necessary for the German national state to discover on its eastern and south-eastern frontiers a 'state of nationalities', agricultural in the economic sense, militarily weak, and destined politically to depend on the Reich. Another Austria-Hungary, in fact, must be brought into existence; but with the new conditions in Europe it was not possible to select a state in which a sufficiently strong German element was available to act as the directing and organizing force. The choice of Adolf Hitler therefore fell on Poland, and as early as the composition of *Mein Kampf* he speaks of the Poles as the only Slav nationality capable of organizing a state. An alliance with Poland would open the way to the Ukraine, the Black Sea, and those routes to the East which the Austrian General Waldstetter had divined when he wrote that 'Germany wants to assure for ever the safety of the ways leading to Mesopotamia and Arabia through Baku and Persia: the ways to the East lead through Kiev, Ekaterinoslav, Sevastopol, from where starts the way by sea to Batum and Trebizond'.

The conception that Poland might be substituted for Austria-Hungary as the vehicle of a new German *Drang nach Osten* was the motive which directed Adolf Hitler's 'pro-Polish policy' during the first years of his dictatorship. A Ten Years' Pact of Non-Aggression was signed, and solemn assurances were given to Poland that no questions existed between the two countries which could not be settled in a peaceful manner. The Germans began to take an interest in the condition of the Polish armed forces and of the roads leading to the Soviet frontier. The death of Pilsudski, however, removed the last Polish leader who seriously cherished the idea of a revived *Rzecz Pospolita*. At the same time the group of men who succeeded him displayed no wish whatever to undertake a campaign in the East. They were sceptical of the widely canvassed hopes of risings in U.S.S.R., and they were more inclined to fear Communist move-ments in Galicia and Volhynia. Furthermore, the Warsaw Govern-ment looked with extreme distrust on the relations which existed between the Nazis and the Ukrainian terrorist organization of Colonel Konovalets.* The principal factor which influenced the development of events was, however, the view of the Polish Govern-ment that any solution of the Ukrainian question profitable to Germany would prove extremely dangerous, if not fatal, to Poland. From 1936 onward, while the Poles maintained their 'friendship' with Germany, they made every effort to renew and improve their

* *V. supra*, p. 341.

former connection with France and even to establish an amelioration in their relations with the Soviet Union.

In the spring of 1938 the success of the bloodless coup in Austria greatly strengthened the position of Germany as against both Poland and Russia. At this time a book by a certain Sanders—a Georgian by origin—had a considerable vogue in Nazi official circles. In *Um die Gestaltung Europas* a pseudo-scientific historical background was given to German plans for expansion round the Black Sea. In the view of Sanders, neither the Mediterranean area (which was reserved for Italian hegemony), nor France, nor 'the island' Britain entered into the structure of 'continental Europe'. European space, for Sanders, is limited by the two 'perpendicular' great European rivers—the Rhine and the Danube. But the boundaries of this 'true Europe' are not clearly defined in the East—the result of 'the disorder of history'. The European river system is continued, in the view of the Nazi publicist, beyond the Black Sea to the Rion and the Kura and the Caspian Sea. With an ingenuity which is only equalled by his ingenuousness, Sanders constructs a cultural area, based on a community of trading ways, historical relations and art influences, uniting the northern seas through the great Russian rivers with the fabled streams of Caucasus. He even finds in the Scandinavian saga of Snorre Sturleson evidence for locating the first abode of Odin in the highlands between the upper waters of the Kuban and Terek. It is interesting to observe that the Ukraine is only a country of transit and not a final objective in the view of Sanders, and he recalls the prognostications of Waldstetter when he finds that 'the line Tiflis-Kiev-Warsaw-Berlin would serve as the new economic axis'.

Munich had a double significance for Adolf Hitler and his advisers. It not only marked the end of the real independence of the Czechoslovak Republic and of the system of Anglo-French checks and balances in the Danube-Carpathian area: but in his judgment untrained in history and in international politics, the compromise accepted by the Western Powers appeared to concede him a free hand in Eastern Europe as far as the Black Sea and, by implication, beyond to the east.

The Germans were impatient to exploit the fruits of a victory which might have been theirs for the waiting. In January 1939, when Field-Marshal Goering met Colonel Beck at the hunting-box of Białowice, the Poles were confronted for the last time with the offer of collaboration with Germany against the Soviets in the Ukraine. Colonel Beck still maintains silence on the details of discussions which do not appear to have attracted the Polish Government. Within a month or two of that ill-omened house-party, the campaign against Poland had begun on the diplomatic field. On the Baltic the Danzig question had become 'actual', and in the Carpathians the dissolution of the Czechoslovak Republic had brought German regiments to the southern frontiers of Poland.

The establishment of a separate Slovak Republic gave the Germans control of Bratislava (Pressburg), the first important Danube port, but the attempt to set up a 'Ukrainian Piedmont' in Carpathian Rus was finally abandoned in view of the opening of secret discussions with the Kremlin.

The majority of the population of the area of *Podkarpatska Rus* as constituted within the Czechoslovak Republic had in fact adhered to the 'pro-Muscovite' persuasion which had been so widespread in Galicia before and during the Four Years' War of 1914–18: in the Czechoslovak elections of 1937, the Rural Russian Union had received 120,000 votes as against the 4000 polled by the Ukrainian fractions. After Munich, the President of the R.R.U., Brody, had been entrusted by the Czechs with the formation of a Government at Užhorod; but two Ukrainians had been included in the 'cabinet' on instructions from Berlin. During October, however, Brody was replaced by the adventurous Roman Catholic Father Voloshin who declared. Carpathian Rus to be henceforth 'Carpathian Ukraine'. The new state immediately became the focus of Ukrainian politicians and adventurers of all kinds: the U.N.U. established its headquarters there,* and the organization of 'an Ukrainian army' was undertaken with the formation of such detachments as the romantically named 'Zaporogian Sech Sharpshooters'.

'The Carpathian intrigue' of the Nazis seriously disturbed the Poles—as was intended—and it must have contributed to the tension and mental discomfort of the Białowice house-party. But with the occupation of Prague and the final partition of Czechoslovakia, the Hungarians were allowed to establish themselves (after a short but gallant resistance on the part of the 'Sech Sharpshooters') in the mountain cantons which they now renamed Ugro-Rus, and while Mussolini had the satisfaction of procuring, for a few short months, a common frontier between Hungary and Poland, the abandonment of the Ukrainians proved for Ribbentrop a graceful prelude to the conversations which were already being undertaken between the representatives of the Third Reich and the Soviet Union.

These conversations had already been begun, through the intermediary of confidential individuals, as early as February–March 1939. 'The incredible *volte-face* of Adolf Hitler' was less incredible than it at first appeared. German army leaders had not excluded the possi-

* *V. supra*, p. 341.

bility of an understanding with the Moscow Soviet even during the period of the German occupation of the Ukraine; and the Rapallo *rapprochement* between the Weimar Republic and the Soviets in 1923 had had the approval of influential conservative circles in Germany. Historically, as has been shown, there has been a traditional community of interest between the Germanic and Muscovite powers as against the nations of the intervening 'meridial belt'. Ideologically, there was nothing in the cynical practice of power politics in the Wilhelmstrasse and the Kremlin which could exclude an understanding if such were convenient and profitable to both parties. And fear, as well as the prospect of advantage, impelled both parties to an expeditious transaction: the fear of the Nazis that they might be attacked from west and east as in 1914; the fear of the Soviets that the Western Democracies might be satisfied to see 'the new German dynamism' engaged in an exhausting, even if victorious, attack on Russia.

The first result of Adolf Hitler's understanding with Stalin was the fall of the Polish Republic, and the occupation of the Polish districts of White Russia and Galicia by the Red Army. The Soviet occupation of Galicia was a severe blow to the Ukrainian nationalist movement. Too late did the leaders of U.N.D.O. and U.N.U. come to appreciate the relative tolerance of the Polish system of government. At the same time both the Polish and Ukrainian questions have been potentially simplified. A revived Polish state will be a national state in federal relation to its neighbours rather than an outmoded 'state of nationalities'. The fate of the Ukrainians becomes altogether a part of the obscure destiny of the nationalities at present under the rule of the Communist Government in Moscow. And the destiny of all these peoples must be a Russian destiny in the sense that the fluvial network of the Great Eurasian Plain is one geographical and economic whole out of which it is impracticable and would be unreal to attempt to carve separate and politically independent national units.

In the present moment of history the old oecumenical civilization of the Mediterranean and of the West—a civilization of variegated peoples broad based on the oceans and spread over all the southern hemisphere—confronts the old menace. The tests of strength remain the same: they are moral and spiritual—a problem of the self-consciousness of civilization; they are also material—a problem of organization. There is too the strategic problem which remains classical—based on the great rivers and the Alps. But the bases of the strategic problem have been vastly extended. Sea-power is a relatively modern form of war power: it was only used by the

Romans for their lines of interior communication across the Mediterranean. If the Romans had been a great sea-faring people they would have mastered the Baltic and imposed civilization on the Germans from the north: and the whole history of the world would have been different; there would have been an easier, quicker flowering of the civil life of a united Europe.

NOTES TO 'POSTSCRIPT' CHAPTER

(1) *Father Voloshin and the Fate of Carpathian Rus*

See Scrimali, A., *La Ruthènie Subcarpathique et l'État Tchécoslovaque*, Paris, 1938.

An interesting account of an interview between Father Voloshin and the Croat leader Dr Maček was published in the Yugoslav Press.

The ex-head of the Government of 'Carpathian Ukraine' thus retails his misadventures:

'When I understood that the Czechoslovak Federation, which had been created under the Munich Agreement, was doomed to disappear, I communicated to Berlin an interesting proposal made to me by Hungary. Budapest proposed to include Carpathian Ukraine within the Realm of St Stephen and to grant us autonomy similar to that enjoyed by Croatia and Slovenia under the former Austro-Hungarian Empire. I was in favour of accepting this advantageous proposal, but could not do so without the permission of Berlin. This happened in the first half of March. Berlin forbade an answer to the Hungarian proposal on the grounds that it was not in the spirit of the Vienna Arbitration. Germany would not admit the existence of a common Polish-Hungarian frontier. Consequently, on the 14th of March, I proclaimed the independence of Carpathian Ukraine. I was again informed that we were indispensable to the Reich for the creation of a Greater Ukraine, the formation of which would begin by the annexation of the Polish Ukrainian provinces to be followed by that of the whole of the Russian Ukraine. In view of such a state of things, nothing was left for me but to defend the new independent Ukrainian state from Hungarian claims....This is why, when the Magyars crossed our border, I gave the order to resist, not doubting for a moment that I was acting according to the wishes of the leaders of the Reich and that the German Army was hastening to our aid. Otherwise, counting only on our own forces, I would never have taken such a decision. Finding that the German troops were not hastening to our aid, I again applied to Berlin asking for the necessary assistance to be despatched for our defence. But the German reply was diametrically different from what I had heard only a few days before. I could no longer contain my indignation when I was casually told: "All is changed! Surrender! Make the sacrifice!" What could I do then but flee? Those who but yesterday had been my protectors had left me to manage in the best way I could, without even bothering about explanations.'

As for the subsequent fate of Carpathian Rus, when it ceased to be 'the Ukrainian Piedmont' and was reincorporated in Hungary, the Budapest Government, owing to the dangers of the international situation, was obliged to act with a certain caution. The inhabitants of the annexed cantons—renamed Ugro-Rus—did not participate in the elections for the Hungarian Parliament in May 1939; nor has the promised autonomy so far been granted. Nevertheless, the 'Zaporogian Sech Sharpshooters', who had opposed the advance of the Hungarian troops, were amnestied, and Ukrainian nationalists who reappeared in Užhorod were allowed to publish a daily paper there. The former opponent of the Ukrainization of Podkarpatska Rus and the leader of the Rural Russian Union, A. Brody, has now appeared as the protagonist of the *fait accompli*. 'Ugro-Rus must have ten deputies in Budapest', he informed a correspondent of *Posledniya Novosti*, Paris, 24 August 1939. 'The Ukrainian cultural movement will not be persecuted, but all political activities will be forbidden to Ukrainians....The representatives of Ukrainian organizations in Hungary and abroad have recently made a declaration of loyalty to the Hungarian State. If behind this declaration there still lurks a hope of beginning their intrigues again, that hope is quite vain. It is not at all true that Russian autonomist tendencies have been set aside by Budapest. Only technical reasons and the international situation have prevented a decision concerning the legal rights of Ugro-Rus from being taken. There is no reason whatever to doubt that autonomy will be granted to the land in due course, as Regent Horthy and Count Teleki have promised.'

It remains to be seen what influence the appearance of the Red Army on the frontier of Ugro-Rus (September 1939) will have on the sentiments of the peasants who inhabit the mountain cantons which give access from Galicia into the Great Alföld.

(2) 'The Italian Orientation' among Ukrainians

The last, in point of time, of different Ukrainian political 'orientations' has proved to be an Italian one. This phenomenon arises out of the changes which occurred in Eastern Europe following the war of 1914–18. In many respects 'New Italy', particularly Fascist Italy, has come to assume certain pretensions to the succession to the role of the former Austro-Hungarian Empire in the Balkans and Eastern Europe. Italian Fascism gave expression to an 'anti-Slav ideology' during the early years of the dictatorship, and this ideology was manifested in a sharp antagonism to Yugoslavia. The 'Austrian role' of Italy seemed to be more clearly emphasized during the 'thirties when Italy became the junior partner in the Nazi-Fascist Axis. At the same time the position of Italy as a maritime rather than a continental power made Rome fundamentally less dependent on Berlin than the Habsburgs had been. So far as the Balkans were concerned, ultimate German and Italian imperial ambitions were irreconcilable. The independence of Italian policy was expressed, first in the unsuccessful support of the Dollfuss and Schuschnigg régimes against Berlin, and contemporaneously and later in the more fortunate support of Hungary and Yugoslavia against the formidable weight of German pressure. The anti-Slav tendencies of the

Fascist Government during the 'twenties gave place to other views which admitted the desirability of collaboration with the Balkan Slavs in face of the common dangers of Pan-Germanism and Bolshevism.

So far as the Ukrainians are concerned, the improvement in relations between the Roman Government and the Vatican facilitated contacts between the Italians and Ukrainian Catholic and Uniate groups in Galicia. Until recently, representatives of the Ukrainian movement have been scarce in Italy; but during the last year Italian interest in the Ukrainians, as in the Caucasian national groups, has become marked. Ukrainians have met with an amiable reception in Rome, and a special press office has been placed at their disposal—*Ufficio Stampa Ukraina.*

In all these circumstances, it would not be surprising if 'the Italian orientation' assumed a certain importance among Ukrainian political groups.

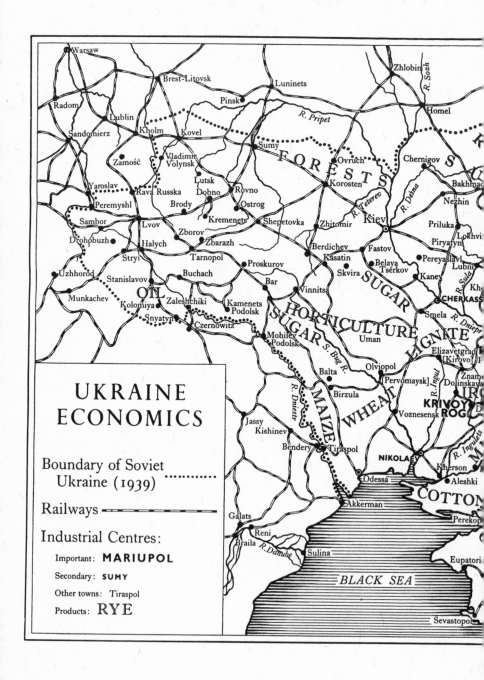

UKRAINE ECONOMICS

Boundary of Soviet
Ukraine (1939) ············

Railways ——————

Industrial Centres:

Important: **MARIUPOL**

Secondary: SUMY

Other towns: Tiraspol

Products: RYE

Warsaw

Brest-Litovsk

Luninets

Radom

Pinsk

Dublin

Kholm

Kovel

R. Pripet

Homel

Zhlobin

R. Sozh

Sandomierz

Sumy

FORESTS

Ovruch

Chernigov

Zamość

Vladimir
Volynsk

Korosten

Yaroslav

Lutsk

Rovno

Rava Russka

Dobno

Kiev

Bakhma

Peremyshl

Brody

Ostrog

R. Teterev

R. Desna

Nezhin

Sambor

Lvov

Kremenets

Shepetovka

Zhitomir

Priluka

Drohobuzh

Zborov

Berdichev

Fastov

Piryatyn

Lokhvi

Halych

Zbarazh

Kasatin

Lubni

Stryi

Tarnopol

Proskurov

Belaya
Tserkov

Pereyaslavl

Uzhhorod

Buchach

Skvira

Kaney

Kh

Stanislavov

Bar

Vinnitsa

SUGAR

CHERKASS

Munkachev

Kolomiya

Zaleshchiki

Kamenets
Podolsk

HORTICULTURE

Smela

R. Dniepr

OIL

Snyatyn

Czernowitz

Uman

LIGNITE

Elizavetgrad
[Kirovo]

SUGAR

Mohilev
Podolsk

S. Bug R.

Olviopol

Znam

Balta

[Pervomaysk]

R. Ingul

Dolinskaya

R. Dniestr

Birzula

MAIZE

WHEAT

Voznesensk

KRIVOY
ROG

IR

Jassy
Kishinev

Bendery

Tiraspol

NIKOLA

R. Ingulets

M

Kherson

Galats

Odessa

Aleshki

Reni

Braila

R. Danube

Akkerman

COTTON

Sulina

Perekop

BLACK SEA

Eupatori

Sevastopol

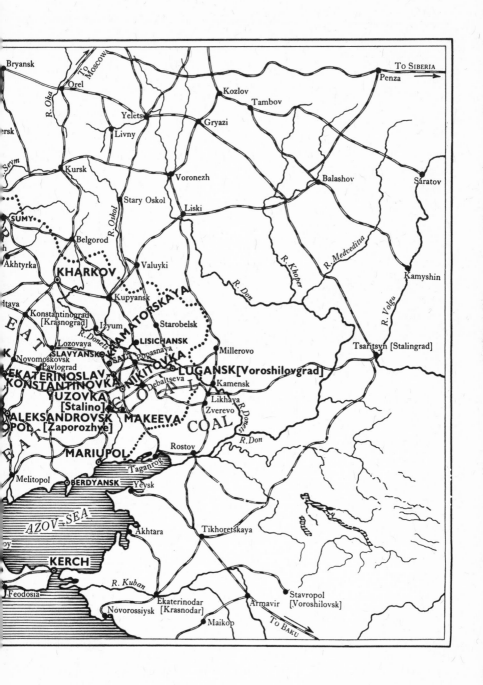

INDEX

Emperors, Kings and Princes will be found under their respective countries